SPSS® 11.0 Syntax Reference Guide

Volume I

SPSS

For more information about SPSS® software products, please visit our Web site at *http://www.spss.com* or contact

SPSS Inc.
233 South Wacker Drive, 11th Floor
Chicago, IL 60606-6412
Tel: (312) 651-3000
Fax: (312) 651-3668

SPSS® 11.0 Syntax Reference Guide, Volume I

Printed in the United States of America.

1 2 3 4 5 6 7 8 9 0   05 04 03 02 01

ISBN 0-13-034839-2

Preface

The *SPSS Syntax Reference Guide* is a reference to the command syntax for the SPSS Base system and the Regression Models and Advanced Models options. This manual does *not* provide an overview of SPSS, teach you how to create jobs and interpret results, or show you how to run SPSS on your computer and operating system. This information is supplied in a separate *SPSS Base User's Guide*.

Manuals for SPSS Release 11.0. Documentation for SPSS Release 11.0 consists of:

- The *SPSS Base User's Guide* provides detailed information on how to run SPSS on your computer's operating system, including complete documentation of the user interface provided for your system. It also explains many of the statistical concepts involved, how to use the statistical procedures correctly, and how to interpret the results.
- *SPSS Regression Models* provides techniques for analyzing data that do not fit traditional linear statistical models. It includes procedures for probit analysis, logistic regression, weight estimation, two-stage least-squares regression, and general nonlinear regression.
- *SPSS Advanced Models* focuses on techniques often used in sophisticated experimental and biomedical research. It includes procedures for general linear models (GLM), linear mixed models, variance components analysis, loglinear analysis, ordinal regression, actuarial life tables, Kaplan-Meier survival analysis, and basic and extended Cox Regression.
- The *SPSS Syntax Reference Guide* documents and provides examples of the command syntax. On some computer operating systems, the user interface makes it possible to obtain most of the features of SPSS without ever looking at command syntax. There are, however, some features that can be obtained only by entering and running SPSS commands.

Contacting SPSS

If you would like to be on our mailing list, contact one of our offices, listed on page iv, or visit our Web site at *http://www.spss.com*. We will send you a copy of our newsletter and let you know about SPSS Inc. activities in your area.

SPSS Inc.
Chicago, Illinois, U.S.A.
Tel: 1.312.651.3000
www.spss.com/corpinfo
Customer Service:
1.800.521.1337
Sales:
1.800.543.2185
sales@spss.com
Training:
1.800.543.6607
Technical Support:
1.312.651.3410
support@spss.com

SPSS Federal Systems
Tel: 1.703.527.6777
www.spss.com

SPSS Argentina srl
Tel: +5411.4814.5030
www.spss.com

SPSS Asia Pacific Pte. Ltd.
Tel: +65.245.9110
www.spss.com

SPSS Australasia Pty. Ltd.
Tel: +61.2.9954.5660
www.spss.com

SPSS Belgium
Tel: +32.163.170.70
www.spss.com

SPSS Benelux BV
Tel: +31.183.651777
www.spss.com

SPSS Brasil Ltda
Tel: +55.11.5505.3644
www.spss.com

SPSS Czech Republic
Tel: +420.2.24813839
www.spss.cz

SPSS Denmark A/S
Tel: +45.45.46.02.00
www.spss.com

SPSS Finland Oy
Tel: +358.9.524.801
www.spss.com

SPSS France SARL
Tel: +01.55.35.27.00 x03
www.spss.com

SPSS Germany
Tel: +49.89.4890740
www.spss.com

SPSS Hellas SA
Tel: +30.1.72.51.925/72.51.950
www.spss.com

SPSS Hispanoportuguesa S.L.
Tel: +34.91.447.37.00
www.spss.com

SPSS Hong Kong Ltd.
Tel: +852.2.811.9662
www.spss.com

SPSS India
Tel: +91.80.225.0260
www.spss.com

SPSS Ireland
Tel: +353.1.496.9007
www.spss.com

SPSS Israel Ltd.
Tel: +972.3.5795230
www.spss.com

SPSS Italia srl
Tel: +39.51.252573
www.spss.it

SPSS Japan Inc.
Tel: +81.3.5466.5511
www.spss.com

SPSS Kenya Limited
Tel: +254.2.577.262/3
www.spss.com

SPSS Korea KIC Co., Ltd.
Tel: +82.2.3446.7651
www.spss.co.kr

SPSS Latin America
Tel: +1.312.651.3539
www.spss.com

SPSS Malaysia Sdn Bhd
Tel: +603.7873.6477
www.spss.com

SPSS Mexico SA de CV
Tel: +52.5.682.87.68
www.spss.com

SPSS Norway
Tel: +47.22.99.25.50
www.spss.com

SPSS Polska
Tel: +48.12.6369680
www.spss.pl

SPSS Russia
Tel: +7.095.125.0069
www.spss.com

SPSS Schweiz AG
Tel: +41.1.266.90.30
www.spss.com

SPSS Sweden AB
Tel: +46.8.506.105.68
www.spss.com

SPSS BI (Singapore) Pte. Ltd.
Tel: +65.346.2061
www.spss.com

SPSS South Africa
Tel: +27.11.807.3189
www.spss.com

SPSS Taiwan Corp.
Taipei, Republic of China
Tel: +886.2.25771100
www.sinter.com.tw/spss/

SPSS (Thailand) Co., Ltd.
Tel: +66.2.260.7070, +66.2.260.7080
www.spss.com

SPSS UK Ltd.
Tel: +44.1483.719200
www.spss.com

Contents

Universals

This part of the *SPSS Syntax Reference Guide* discusses general topics pertinent to using command syntax. The topics are divided into five sections:

- *Commands* explains command syntax, including command specification, command order, and running commands in different modes. In this section, you will learn how to read syntax charts, which summarize command syntax in diagrams and provide an easy reference. Discussions of individual commands are found in an alphabetical reference in the next part of this manual.
- *Files* discusses different types of files used by the program. Terms frequently mentioned in this manual are defined. This section provides an overview of how files are handled.
- *Variables* contains important information on general rules and conventions concerning variables and variable definition. In this section, you will find detailed information on variable formats.
- *Transformation Expressions* describes expressions that can be used in data transformation. Functions and operators are defined and illustrated. In this section, you will find a complete list of available functions and how to use them.
- *Date and Time* deals with functions and formats used with date and time expressions. In this section, you will find ways to read and convert date and time, use them in analysis, and display them in output.

Commands

Commands are the instructions that you give the program to initiate an action. For the program to interpret your commands correctly, you must follow certain rules.

Syntax Diagrams

Each command described in this manual includes a syntax diagram that shows all the subcommands, keywords, and specifications allowed for that command. By recognizing symbols and different type fonts, you can use the syntax diagram as a quick reference for any command. Figure 1 is an example.

- Lines of text in italics indicate limitation or operation mode of the command.
- Elements shown in upper case are keywords defined by SPSS to identify commands, subcommands, functions, operators, and other specifications. In Figure 1, T-TEST is the command and GROUPS is a subcommand.
- Elements in lower case describe specifications you supply. For example, varlist indicates that you need to supply a list of variables.
- Elements in bold are defaults. SPSS supports two types of defaults. When the default is followed by **, as ANALYSIS** is in Figure 1, the default (ANALYSIS) is in effect if the

subcommand (MISSING) is not specified. If a default is not followed by **, it is in effect when the subcommand (or keyword) is specified by itself.

Figure 1 Syntax diagram

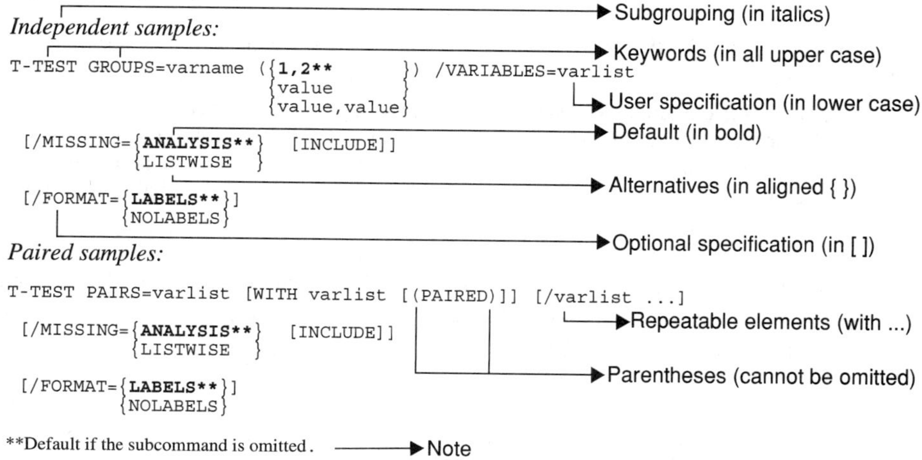

- Parentheses, apostrophes, and quotation marks are required where indicated.
- Elements enclosed in square brackets ([ ]) are optional. Wherever brackets would confuse the format, they are omitted. The command description explains which specifications are required and which are optional.
- Braces ({ }) indicate a choice between elements. You can specify any one of the elements enclosed within the aligned braces.
- Ellipses indicate that you can repeat an element in the specification. The specification

  T-TEST PAIRS=varlist [WITH varlist [(PAIRED)]] [/varlist ...]

  means that you can specify multiple variable lists with optional WITH variables and the keyword PAIRED in parentheses.
- Most abbreviations are obvious; for example, varname stands for variable name and varlist stands for a variable list.
- The command terminator is not shown in the syntax diagram.

Command Specification

The following rules apply to all commands:

- Commands begin with a keyword that is the name of the command and often have additional specifications, such as subcommands and user specifications. Refer to the discussion of each command to see which subcommands and additional specifications are required.
- Commands and any command specifications can be entered in upper and lower case. Commands, subcommands, keywords, and variable names are translated to upper case

before processing. All user specifications, including labels and data values, preserve upper and lower case.

- Spaces can be added between specifications at any point where a single blank is allowed. In addition, lines can be broken at any point where a single blank is allowed. There are two exceptions: the END DATA command can have only one space between words, and string specifications on commands such as TITLE, SUBTITLE, VARIABLE LABELS, and VALUE LABELS can be broken across two lines only by specifying a + between string segments (see "String Values in Command Specifications" on p. 5).
- The first word of a command can be abbreviated to a minimum of three letters provided no duplicates result. For example, AGGREGATE can be abbreviated to AGG, but COMPUTE can only be abbreviated to COMP to avoid confusion with COMMENT. A very small number of commands can duplicate an internal command when abbreviated to three characters (for example, LIST) and at least four characters should be used. For internal command structure, DATA LIST cannot be abbreviated.
- If the first word of a multiple-word command has a duplicate (for example, FILE LABEL and FILE TYPE), the first word cannot be abbreviated.
- All keywords after the first command word can be abbreviated to three characters. For example, ADD VAL LAB is a valid abbreviation for ADD VALUE LABELS, and EXA VAR=varlist is valid for EXAMINE VARIABLES=varlist. END DATA is an exception. You must spell both command keywords in full; END DAT is *not* a valid abbreviation for END DATA.
- Three-character truncation does not apply to INFO command specifications. Spell out all keywords in full. For procedure names specified on INFO, spell out the first word in full and subsequent words through at least the first three characters.

Running Commands

You can run commands in either batch (production) or interactive mode. In batch mode, commands are read and acted upon as a batch, so the system knows that a command is complete when it encounters a new command. In interactive mode, commands are executed immediately, and you must use a command terminator to tell SPSS when a command is complete.

Interactive Mode

The following rules apply to command specifications in interactive mode:

- Each command ends with a command terminator. The default command terminator is a period. It is best to omit the terminator on BEGIN DATA, however, so that inline data is treated as one continuous specification.
- The command terminator must be the last nonblank character in a command.
- Commands can begin in any column of a command line and continue for as many lines as needed. The exception is the END DATA command, which must begin in the first column of the first line after the end of data.
- The maximum length of any command line is 80 characters, including the prompt and the command terminator.

You should observe interactive rules when you:

- Submit commands from a syntax window or with an SPSS Manager, either one command at a time or as a group.
- Enter commands at a command prompt on those systems that run prompted sessions.

See the *SPSS Base User's Guide* for your version of SPSS for more information.

Batch (Production) Mode

The following rules apply to command specifications in batch or production mode:

- All commands in the command file must begin in column 1. You can use plus (+) or minus (–) signs in the first column if you want to indent the command specification to make the command file more readable.
- If multiple lines are used for a command, column 1 of each continuation line must be blank.
- Command terminators are optional.
- An asterisk (*) in the first column indicates a comment line (see the COMMENT command).

You should observe batch rules when you:

- Construct a command file for use with the Production Facility.
- Construct a command file that will be submitted to your operating system for execution.
- Construct a command file that will be included using the INCLUDE command. You can include a command file when you are working in interactive mode. The included command file, however, must follow batch rules.

The way you submit a command file for execution varies from operating system to operating system. Command files do not necessarily need to be submitted to a batch queue, although they can be on operating systems that have a batch queue. In batch mode, the commands in the file are executed one after the other, and output is displayed when all commands are executed.

The following is a sample command file:

```
GET FILE=BANK.SAV /KEEP ID TIME SEX JOBCAT SALBEG SALNOW
        /RENAME SALNOW = SAL90.

DO IF TIME LT 82.
+   COMPUTE RATE=0.05.
ELSE.
+   COMPUTE RATE=0.04.
END IF.

COMPUTE SALNOW=(1+RATE)*SAL90.

EXAMINE VARIABLES=SALNOW BY SEX /PLOT=NONE.
```

Subcommands

Many commands include additional specifications called *subcommands* for locating data, handling data, and formatting the output.

- Subcommands begin with a keyword that is the name of the subcommand. Some subcommands include additional specifications.
- A subcommand keyword is separated from its specifications, if any, by an equals sign. The equals sign is usually optional but is required where ambiguity is possible in the specification. To avoid ambiguity, it is best to use the equals signs as shown in the syntax diagrams in this manual.
- Most subcommands can be named in any order. However, some commands require a specific subcommand order. The description of each command includes a section on subcommand order.
- Subcommands are separated from each other by a slash. To avoid ambiguity, it is best to use the slashes as shown in the syntax diagrams in this manual.

Keywords

Keywords identify commands, subcommands, functions, operators, and other specifications in SPSS.

- Keywords, including commands and subcommands, can often be truncated to the first three characters of each word. An exception is the keyword WITH, which must be spelled in full. See "Command Specification" on p. 2 for additional rules for three-character truncation of commands.
- Keywords identifying logical operators (AND, OR, and NOT), relational operators (EQ, GE, GT, LE, LT, and NE), and ALL, BY, TO, and WITH are reserved words and cannot be used as variable names.

Values in Command Specifications

The following rules apply to values specified in commands:

- A single lowercase character in the syntax diagram, such as *n*, *w*, or *d*, indicates a user-specified value.
- The value can be an integer or a real number within a restricted range, as required by the specific command or subcommand. For exact restrictions, read the individual command description.
- A number specified as an argument to a subcommand can be entered with or without leading zeros.

String Values in Command Specifications

- Each string specified in a command should be enclosed in a set of apostrophes or quotation marks.
- To specify an apostrophe within a string, either use quotation marks to enclose the string or specify double apostrophes. Both of the following specifications are valid:

```
'Client''s Satisfaction'

"Client's Satisfaction"
```

- To specify quotation marks within a string, use apostrophes to enclose the string:

```
'Categories Labeled "UNSTANDARD" in the Report'
```

- String specifications can be broken across command lines by specifying each string segment within apostrophes or quotation marks and using a + sign to join segments. For example,

```
'One, Two'
```

  can be specified as

```
'One,'
+ ' Two'
```

  The plus sign can be specified on either the first or the second line of the broken string. Any blanks separating the two segments must be enclosed within one or the other string segment.

- Blanks within apostrophes or quotation marks are significant.

Delimiters

Delimiters are used to separate data values, keywords, arguments, and specifications.

- A blank is usually used to separate one specification from another, except when another delimiter serves the same purpose or when a comma is required.
- Commas are required to separate arguments to functions. Otherwise, blanks are generally valid substitutes for commas.
- Arithmetic operators (+, –, *, and /) serve as delimiters in expressions.
- Blanks can be used before and after operators or equals signs to improve readability, but commas cannot.
- Special delimiters include parentheses, apostrophes, quotation marks, the slash, and the equals sign. Blanks before and after special delimiters are optional.
- The slash is used primarily to separate subcommands and lists of variables. Although slashes are sometimes optional, it is best to enter them as shown in the syntax diagrams.
- The equals sign is used between a subcommand and its specifications, as in STATISTICS= MEAN, and to show equivalence, as in COMPUTE target variable=expression. Equals signs following subcommands are frequently optional, but it is best to enter them for clarity.

Command Order

Command order is more often than not a matter of common sense and follows this logical sequence: variable definition, data transformation, and statistical analysis. For example, you cannot label, transform, analyze, or use a variable in any way before it exists. The following general rules apply:

- Commands that define variables for a session (DATA LIST, GET, MATRIX DATA, etc.) must precede commands that assign labels or missing values to those variables; they must also precede transformation and procedure commands that use those variables.

- Transformation commands (IF, COUNT, COMPUTE, etc.) that are used to create and modify variables must precede commands that assign labels or missing values to those variables, and they must also precede the procedures that use those variables.
- Generally, the logical outcome of command processing determines command order. For example, a procedure that creates new variables in the working data file must precede a procedure that uses those new variables.
- Some commands, such as REREAD and END CASE, can appear only in an *input program* where the cases are created. Other commands, such as SELECT IF, can appear only in a *transformation program* after cases have been created. Still other commands, such as COMPUTE, can appear in an input or transformation program. For a discussion of these program states and command order, see Appendix A.

In addition to observing the rules above, it is often important to distinguish between commands that cause the data to be read and those that do not, particularly for large data sources such as databases. Commands that cause the data to be read include all statistical and graphing commands, all commands that result in creation of new files, AUTORECODE, EXECUTE, and SORT.

Transformation commands that alter the dictionary of the working data file, such as MISSING VALUES, and commands that do not affect the working data, such as SET, SHOW, and DISPLAY, take effect as soon as they are encountered in the command sequence regardless of conditional statements that precede them. Table 1 lists all transformation commands that take effect immediately.

Table 1 Transformation commands that take effect immediately

ADD VALUE LABELS	PRINT FORMATS
DOCUMENT	SPLIT FILE
DROP DOCUMENTS	STRING
FORMATS	VALUE LABELS
LEAVE	VARIABLE LABELS
MISSING VALUES	VECTOR
N OF CASES	WEIGHT
NUMERIC	WRITE FORMATS

Since these transformations take effect regardless of the conditional statements that precede them, they cannot be applied selectively to individual cases, as shown in the following example:

```
DO IF AGE>69.
MISSING VALUES INCOME EXPENSES (0).
ELSE.
COMPUTE PROFIT=INCOME-EXPENSES.
END IF.
LIST.
```

The MISSING VALUES command is in effect when COMPUTE is executed, even if the condition defined on DO IF is false. To treat 0 income and expenses as missing only for those older than 69, use RECODE in the DO IF—END IF structure to selectively recode 0 to a negative number and declare the negative number as missing:

```
MISSING VALUES INCOME EXPENSES (-1).
DO IF (AGE>69).
RECODE INCOME EXPENSES (0=-1).
END IF.
COMPUTE PROFILE=INCOME-EXPENSES.
LIST.
```

In addition, the order of transformations that take effect immediately in the command sequence can be misleading. Consider the following:

```
COMPUTE PROFIT=INCOME-EXPENSES.
MISSING VALUES INCOME EXPENSES (0).
LIST.
```

- COMPUTE precedes MISSING VALUES and is processed first; however, execution is delayed until the data are being read.
- MISSING VALUES takes effect as soon as it is encountered.
- LIST causes the data to be read; thus, SPSS executes both COMPUTE and LIST during the same data pass. Because MISSING VALUES is already in effect by this time, all cases with the value 0 for either *INCOME* or *EXPENSES* return a missing value for *PROFIT*.

To prevent the MISSING VALUES command from taking effect before COMPUTE is executed, you must position MISSING VALUES after the LIST command. Alternatively, place an EXECUTE command between COMPUTE and MISSING VALUES.

Files

SPSS reads, creates, and writes different types of files. This section provides an overview of the types of files used in SPSS and discusses concepts and rules that apply to all files. Conventions for naming, printing, deleting, or permanently saving files, and for submitting command files for processing, differ from one computer and operating system to another. For specific information, consult the *SPSS Base User's Guide* for your version of SPSS.

Command File

Command files contain commands, sometimes with inline data. They can be created by a text editor. Wherever SPSS allows you to paste commands, either in a syntax window or with an SPSS manager, the resulting file is a command file. You can also edit a journal file to produce a command file (see "Journal File" below). The following is an example of a simple command file that contains both commands and inline data:

```
DATA LIST /ID 1-3 SEX 4 (A) AGE 5-6 OPINION1 TO OPINION5 7-11.
BEGIN DATA
001F2621221
002M5611122
003F3422212
329M2121212
END DATA.
LIST.
```

- Case does not matter for commands but is significant for inline data. If you specified *f* for female and *m* for male in column 4 of the data line, the value of *SEX* would be *f* or *m*, instead of *F* or *M* as it is now.
- Commands can be in upper or lower case. Uppercase characters are used for all commands throughout this manual only to distinguish them from other text.

Journal File

SPSS keeps a journal file to record all commands either entered in the syntax window or generated from a dialog box during a session. You can retrieve this file with any text editor and review it to learn how the session went. You can also edit the file to build a new command file and use it in another run. An edited and tested journal file can be saved and used later for repeated tasks. The journal file also records any error or warning messages generated by commands. You can rerun these commands after making corrections and removing the messages.

The default name for the journal file is *SPSS.JNL* on most operating systems. You can turn off the journal or assign a different name to it (see SET). SPSS erases an existing journal file with the default name when it starts a new session. If you want to save a journal file for future use, rename it before you start another session. On some operating systems, SPSS allows you to overwrite or append to journals from a previous session. Consult the *SPSS Base User's Guide* for your version of SPSS for specific information. Figure 2 is a journal file for a short session with a warning message.

Figure 2 Records from a journal file

```
DATA LIST /ID 1-3 SEX 4 (A) AGE 5-6 OPINION1 TO OPINION5 7-11.
BEGIN DATA
001F2621221
002M5611122
003F3422212
004F45112L2
>Warning # 1102
>An invalid numeric field has been found.  The result has been set to the
>system-missing value.
END DATA.
LIST.
```

- The warning message, marked by the > symbol, tells you that an invalid numeric field has been found. Checking the last data line, you will notice that column 10 is *L*, which is probably a typographic error. You can correct the typo (for example, by changing the *L* to 1), delete the warning message, and submit the file again.

Data Files

SPSS is capable of reading and writing a wide variety of data file formats, including raw data files created by a data entry device or a text editor, formatted data files produced by a data management program, data files generated by other software packages, and SPSS-format data files.

Raw Data File

Raw data files contain only data, either generated by a programming language, such as COBOL, FORTRAN, and Assembler, or entered with a data entry device or a text editor. SPSS can read raw data arranged in almost any format, including raw matrix materials and nonprintable codes. User-entered data can be embedded within a command file as inline data or saved on tape or disk as an external file. Nonprintable machine codes are usually stored in an external file.

Raw data must be defined before they can be used by procedures. Data definition commands such as DATA LIST, KEYED DATA LIST, and MATRIX DATA can be used to read in raw data. Appropriate input formats must be specified on these commands (see "Variable Formats" on p. 21). If for some reason you need to write a raw data file, use the WRITE command or specify WRITE on a procedure with that subcommand. On most operating systems, the default extension of a raw data file produced by SPSS is *.DAT*.

Files from Other Software Applications

You can read files from a variety of other software applications, including dBASE, Lotus, SYLK, and Excel. You can also read simple tab-delimited spreadsheet files. Use GET TRANSLATE with different TYPE specifications to read files from common spreadsheet and database programs. To produce data files for these programs, use SAVE TRANSLATE.

Consult the *SPSS Base User's Guide* for your version of SPSS for the types of files (if any) that your system can read and write.

SPSS-Format Data File

An SPSS-format data file is a file specifically formatted for use by SPSS, containing both data and the dictionary that defines the data. The **dictionary** contains names for the variables, formats for reading and displaying values, and optional variable and value labels and missing-value specifications. SPSS-format data files are created by using a SAVE or XSAVE command during a session. On most operating systems, the default extension of a saved SPSS-format data file is *.SAV*. An SPSS-format data file can also be a matrix file created with the MATRIX=OUT subcommand on procedures that write matrices.

To retrieve an SPSS-format data file, use GET. SPSS-format data files speed processing and are required as input for combining files during a session. For a discussion of the structure of SPSS-format data files, see "SPSS Data File Structure" below.

SPSS Portable File

A portable file contains all of the data and dictionary information stored in the working data file but is specially formatted for transporting files between installations with different versions of SPSS (such as the PRIME, VAX, or HONEYWELL GCOS computers) or for transporting files between SPSS, SPSS/PC+, and other software using the same portable file format. Use IMPORT to read a portable file and EXPORT to save the working data file as a portable file. On most operating systems, the default extension of a saved portable file is *.POR*. Since a portable file needs conversion, it is always simpler to transport a file as an SPSS-format data file whenever possible.

Working Data File

The working data file is the data file you build to use in the current session. You can retrieve an SPSS-format data file using GET, which in effect makes a working copy of the specified file. You can also build a new file with DATA LIST or other data definition commands.

The working data file is not created until SPSS encounters a command (usually a procedure) that causes it to read the data (see Table 1). At that point, SPSS executes all of the preceding data definition and transformation commands and the command that causes the data to be read. The working data file is then available for further transformations and procedures, and it remains available until replaced by a new working data file or until the end of the session.

Some procedures can add variables to the working data file. Others, such as AGGREGATE and procedures that write matrix materials, can replace the working data file.

Any transformations and statistical analyses that you request during a session are performed on the working data file. Transformations performed during a session apply to the working data file only. Changes to the file are lost if the working data file is erased or replaced before you have saved it. See SAVE and XSAVE.

SPSS Data File Structure

An SPSS-format data file is a self-documented file containing data and descriptive information. The descriptive information is called the **dictionary**. It contains variable names and locations, variable and value labels, print and write formats, and missing-value indicators. To use an SPSS-format data file, you must retrieve it with GET, which creates a working data file from the SPSS-format data file. Only a few commands can use an SPSS-format data file directly without first specifying GET; they include MATCH FILES, ADD FILES, and procedures that can read SPSS matrix data files.

To view the contents of an SPSS-format data file, retrieve it with GET and then use LIST to display the variables in the working data file. Figure 3 shows a partial listing of a working file. The values are displayed using their print format, which is different from the way they are internally stored.

Figure 3 Part of a listed working data file

ID	SALBEG	SEX	TIME	AGE	SALNOW	EDLEVEL	WORK	JOBCAT	MINORITY	SEXRACE
628	8400	0	81	28.50	16080	16	.25	4	0	1.00
630	24000	0	73	40.33	41400	16	12.50	5	0	1.00
632	10200	0	83	31.08	21960	15	4.08	5	0	1.00
633	8700	0	93	31.17	19200	16	1.83	4	0	1.00
635	17400	0	83	41.92	28350	19	13.00	5	0	1.00
637	12996	0	80	29.50	27250	18	2.42	4	0	1.00
641	6900	0	79	28.00	16080	15	3.17	1	0	1.00
649	5400	0	67	28.75	14100	15	.50	1	0	1.00
650	5040	0	96	27.42	12420	15	1.17	1	0	1.00
652	6300	0	77	52.92	12300	12	26.42	3	0	1.00
653	6300	0	84	33.50	15720	15	6.00	1	0	1.00
656	6000	0	88	54.33	8880	12	27.00	1	0	1.00
657	10500	0	93	32.33	22000	17	2.67	4	0	1.00
658	10800	0	98	41.17	22800	15	12.00	5	0	1.00

The dictionary is created when an SPSS-format data file is built. You can display or modify the dictionary of a working file. Use DISPLAY DICTIONARY to view the dictionary, and use commands such as VARIABLE LABELS, VALUE LABELS, and MISSING VALUES to modify specific information contained in the dictionary. Figure 4 shows part of the displayed dictionary information of the working data file displayed in Figure 3.

Figure 4 Displayed dictionary information

```
            List of variables on the active file

Name                                                          Position

ID          Employee Code                                            1
            Print Format: F4
            Write Format: F4

SALBEG      Beginning Salary                                         2
            Print Format: F5
            Write Format: F5
            Missing Values: 0

SEX         Sex of Employee                                          3
            Print Format: F1
            Write Format: F1
            Missing Values: 9

            Value    Label

                0    Males
                1    Females
TIME        Job Seniority                                            4
            Print Format: F2
            Write Format: F2
            Missing Values: 0
```

SPSS Matrix Data Files

An SPSS matrix data file is similar to any SPSS-format data file. It is a self-documented file containing data and descriptive information. The descriptive information, stored in the file dictionary, includes variable names, variable print and write formats, and optional variable and value labels. You can assign or change the names, labels, and formats of the variables in a matrix data file, just as you can in any SPSS-format data file. Many procedures can read raw matrix data and write a representative matrix of the data values to an SPSS matrix data file, which can be used as input for subsequent analysis.

Table 2 shows the types of matrix materials written by SPSS procedures. The *ROWTYPE_* values (discussed below) of each matrix are also included so that you can see which procedure matrices are readable by other procedures. If a procedure produces more than one type of matrix, the subcommands required for each type of matrix are listed.

Table 2 Types of matrices and their contents

Command	Subcommands/Notes	ROWTYPE_ values
ALSCAL		PROX
CLUSTER		PROX
CORRELATIONS		MEAN STDDEV N CORR
DISCRIMINANT	/CLASSIFY=POOLED	N (1 per cell) COUNT (1 per cell) MEAN (1 per cell) STDDEV (pooled) CORR (pooled)
	/CLASSIFY=SEPARATE, /STATISTICS=BOXM, or /STATISTICS=GCOV	N (1 per cell) COUNT (1 per cell) MEAN (1 per cell) STDDEV (1 per cell) CORR (1 per cell)
FACTOR	/MATRIX=OUT(CORR=file) /MATRIX=IN(CORR=file)	CORR
	/MATRIX=OUT(FAC=file) /MATRIX=IN(FAC=file)	FACTOR
MANOVA		N (cell and pooled) MEAN (1 per cell) STDDEV (pooled) CORR (pooled)
NONPAR CORR	/PRINT=SPEARMAN	N RHO
	/PRINT=KENDALL	N TAUB

Table 2 Types of matrices and their contents (Continued)

Command	Subcommands/Notes	ROWTYPE_ values
ONEWAY	Separate variance Can be input and output	MEAN (1 per cell) STDDEV (1 per cell) N (1 per cell)
	Pooled variance Can be input only	MEAN (1 per cell) N (1 per cell) MSE (pooled) DFE (pooled)
PARTIAL CORR		N CORR
PROXIMITIES		PROX
REGRESSION		MEAN STDDEV N CORR
RELIABILITY		N MEAN STDDEV CORR

- All SPSS procedures that handle matrix materials use the MATRIX subcommand. The MATRIX subcommand specifies the file from which the input matrix is read and/or the file to which the output matrix is written.
- Matrix materials can be read from an external file as long as a working data file has been created. The working file does not have to be the matrix data file.
- The procedures that read matrix materials cannot read every type of SPSS matrix data file. For example, REGRESSION cannot read a matrix data file written by NONPAR CORR.

Figure 5 lists the structure of a matrix file and Figure 6 shows the dictionary information for the same file.

Variable Order. The following variable order is standard for all SPSS matrix data files:

1. Split variables, if any. In Figure 5, the split variable is *SEX*.
2. *ROWTYPE_* variable. The values of the *ROWTYPE_* variable describe the contents of the matrix data file, such as *MEAN*, *STDDEV*, *N*, and *CORR*.
3. Factor or grouping variables, if any.
4. *VARNAME_* variable (or *FACTOR_* variable for factor-loading matrices). The values of the *VARNAME_* variable are the names of the variable used to form the matrix.
5. Continuous variables used to form the matrix.

Figure 5 A matrix data file (LIST output)

```
FILE:      MATRIX FILE
SEX:   1   FEMALE

SEX ROWTYPE_ VARNAME_        FOOD       RENT   PUBTRANS    TEACHER       COOK   ENGINEER

  1 MEAN               73.3750000 134.500000 53.5000000 46.8000000 72.4375000 59.8125000
  1 STDDEV             15.4483009 115.534699 25.8173069 19.4209018 29.5746936 21.5196616
  1 N       FOOD       16.0000000 16.0000000 16.0000000 15.0000000 16.0000000 16.0000000
  1 N       RENT       16.0000000 16.0000000 16.0000000 15.0000000 16.0000000 16.0000000
  1 N       PUBTRANS   16.0000000 16.0000000 16.0000000 15.0000000 16.0000000 16.0000000
  1 N       TEACHER    15.0000000 15.0000000 15.0000000 15.0000000 15.0000000 15.0000000
  1 N       COOK       16.0000000 16.0000000 16.0000000 15.0000000 16.0000000 16.0000000
  1 N       ENGINEER   16.0000000 16.0000000 16.0000000 15.0000000 16.0000000 16.0000000
  1 CORR    FOOD        1.0000000   .3658643   .5372333   .1733358   .1378010   .3778351
  1 CORR    RENT         .3658643  1.0000000   .1045105  -.0735708   .2026299   .1237062
  1 CORR    PUBTRANS     .5372333   .1045105  1.0000000   .6097397   .3877995   .6413121
  1 CORR    TEACHER      .1733358  -.0735708   .6097397  1.0000000   .4314755   .7312415
  1 CORR    COOK         .1378010   .2026299   .3877995   .4314755  1.0000000   .7807327
  1 CORR    ENGINEER     .3778351   .1237062   .6413121   .7312415   .7807327  1.0000000

NUMBER OF CASES READ =        14    NUMBER OF CASES LISTED =        14


FILE:      MATRIX FILE
SEX:   2   MALE

SEX ROWTYPE_ VARNAME_        FOOD       RENT   PUBTRANS    TEACHER       COOK   ENGINEER

  2 MEAN               68.8620690 112.137931 45.1379310 33.9310345 60.2142857 60.1785714
  2 STDDEV             20.4148478 81.3430672 24.1819356 26.9588722 30.2952840 28.8752792
  2 N       FOOD       29.0000000 29.0000000 29.0000000 29.0000000 28.0000000 28.0000000
  2 N       RENT       29.0000000 29.0000000 29.0000000 29.0000000 28.0000000 28.0000000
  2 N       PUBTRANS   29.0000000 29.0000000 29.0000000 29.0000000 28.0000000 28.0000000
  2 N       TEACHER    29.0000000 29.0000000 29.0000000 29.0000000 28.0000000 28.0000000
  2 N       COOK       28.0000000 28.0000000 28.0000000 28.0000000 28.0000000 28.0000000
  2 N       ENGINEER   28.0000000 28.0000000 28.0000000 28.0000000 28.0000000 28.0000000
  2 CORR    FOOD        1.0000000   .2012077   .5977491   .6417034   .4898941   .5190702
  2 CORR    RENT         .2012077  1.0000000  -.1405952  -.0540657   .0727153   .3508598
  2 CORR    PUBTRANS     .5977491  -.1405952  1.0000000   .7172945   .7170419   .6580408
  2 CORR    TEACHER      .6417034  -.0540657   .7172945  1.0000000   .6711871   .6650047
  2 CORR    COOK         .4898941   .0727153   .7170419   .6711871  1.0000000   .7688210
  2 CORR    ENGINEER     .5190702   .3508598   .6580408   .6650047   .7688210  1.0000000

NUMBER OF CASES READ =        14    NUMBER OF CASES LISTED =        14
```

Split Files. When split-file processing is in effect, a full set of matrix materials is written for each split-file group defined by the split variables.

- A split variable cannot have the same variable name as any other variable written to the matrix data file. Not all procedures allow split-file variables in their matrices.
- If split-file processing is in effect when a matrix is written, the same split file must be in effect when that matrix is read by any procedure.

Additional Statistics. Some procedures include statistics with their matrix materials. For example, CORRELATION matrices always include the mean, standard deviation, and number of cases used to compute each coefficient, as shown in Figure 5. Other procedures, for example PROXIMITIES and FACTOR, include no statistics with their matrices. See Table 2 for a list of the statistics written by each procedure. Refer to the description of each command for its requirements for a matrix input file.

Missing Values. The treatment of missing values in a procedure affects the matrix materials written to the data file. With pairwise treatment of missing values, the matrix of *N*'s used to compute each coefficient is included in the matrix. With any other missing-value treatment, the single *N* used to calculate all coefficients in the matrix is included in the form of a vector. Figure 5 includes the matrix of *N*'s written by CORRELATIONS when missing values are excluded pairwise from the analysis. Figure 7 shows the single *N* written by CORRELATIONS when missing values are excluded listwise.

The missing-value treatment that was in effect when the matrix was written must be compatible with the missing-value treatment in effect when the matrix is read. For example, REGRESSION can read a matrix written by CORRELATIONS but only if the missing-value treatment of both procedures is consistent. Either both must refer to a matrix of *N*'s or both must refer to a single *N*. For all procedures, pairwise treatment of missing values generates a matrix of *N*'s; any other treatment of missing values generates a single vector of *N*'s.

Matrix File Dictionaries. As shown in Figure 6, print and write formats of A8 are assigned to the matrix variables that SPSS creates (for example, *ROWTYPE_*, *VARNAME_*, and *FACTOR_*). No labels are assigned to these variables. Print and write formats of F10.7 are assigned to all of the continuous variables in the matrix analysis; the names and variable labels defined for these variables in the original data file are retained, but their original values and value labels are dropped because they do not apply to the matrix data file. When split-file processing is in effect, the variable names, variable and value labels, and print and write formats of the split-file variables are read from the dictionary of the original data file.

Procedures read and write matrices in which each row corresponds to a single case in the matrix data file. For example, the matrix shown in Figure 7 has nine cases. The first three cases with the *ROWTYPE_* values of *MEAN*, *STDDEV*, and *N* have no values for *VARNAME_* but do have values for all the variables from *FOOD* to *ENGINEER*. The fourth case, *CORR*, in the matrix generated for the first split-file group has a value of *FOOD* for *VARNAME_*, a value of 0.3652366 when correlated with variable *RENT*, a value of 0.5371597 when correlated with variable *PUBTRANS*, and so on.

Figure 6 Dictionary of a matrix system file (DISPLAY output)

```
FILE:      MATRIX FILE

             LIST OF VARIABLES ON THE ACTIVE FILE

NAME                                                                POSITION

SEX                                                                        1
                     PRINT FORMAT: F2
                     WRITE FORMAT: F2

           VALUE     LABEL

               1     FEMALE
               2     MALE

ROWTYPE_                                                                   2
                     PRINT FORMAT: A8
                     WRITE FORMAT: A8

VARNAME_                                                                   3
                     PRINT FORMAT: A8
                     WRITE FORMAT: A8

FOOD       AVG FOOD PRICES                                                 4
                     PRINT FORMAT: F10.7
                     WRITE FORMAT: F10.7

RENT       NORMAL RENT                                                     5
                     PRINT FORMAT: F10.7
                     WRITE FORMAT: F10.7

PUBTRANS   PRICE FOR PUBLIC TRANSPORT                                      6
                     PRINT FORMAT: F10.7
                     WRITE FORMAT: F10.7

TEACHER    NET TEACHER'S SALARY                                            7
                     PRINT FORMAT: F10.7
                     WRITE FORMAT: F10.7

COOK       NET COOK'S SALARY                                               8
                     PRINT FORMAT: F10.7
                     WRITE FORMAT: F10.7

ENGINEER   NET ENGINEER'S SALARY                                           9
                     PRINT FORMAT: F10.7
                     WRITE FORMAT: F10.7
```

Figure 7 Single N in the matrix system file

FILE: MATRIX FILE
SEX: 1 FEMALE

SEX	ROWTYPE_	VARNAME_	FOOD	RENT	PUBTRANS	TEACHER	COOK	ENGINEER
1	MEAN		73.4666667	136.800000	54.0000000	46.8000000	73.8666667	60.0000000
1	STDDEV		15.9860058	119.210019	26.6431444	19.4209018	30.0353760	22.2614337
1	N		15.0000000	15.0000000	15.0000000	15.0000000	15.0000000	15.0000000
1	CORR	FOOD	1.0000000	.3652366	.5371597	.1733358	.1358120	.3773434
1	CORR	RENT	.3652366	1.0000000	.0989524	-.0735708	.1914448	.1213899
1	CORR	PUBTRANS	.5371597	.0989524	1.0000000	.6097397	.3811372	.6409265
1	CORR	TEACHER	.1733358	-.0735708	.6097397	1.0000000	.4314755	.7312415
1	CORR	COOK	.1358120	.1914448	.3811372	.4314755	1.0000000	.7893533
1	CORR	ENGINEER	.3773434	.1213899	.6409265	.7312415	.7893533	1.0000000

NUMBER OF CASES READ = 9 NUMBER OF CASES LISTED = 9

2

FILE: MATRIX FILE
SEX: 2 MALE

SEX	ROWTYPE_	VARNAME_	FOOD	RENT	PUBTRANS	TEACHER	COOK	ENGINEER
2	MEAN		69.6428571	114.464286	46.1428571	33.7500000	60.2142857	60.1785714
2	STDDEV		20.3437392	81.8474109	24.0011023	27.4356149	30.2952840	28.8752792
2	N		28.0000000	28.0000000	28.0000000	28.0000000	28.0000000	28.0000000
2	CORR	FOOD	1.0000000	.1752920	.5784136	.6638084	.4898941	.5190702
2	CORR	RENT	.1752920	1.0000000	-.1817862	-.0491139	.0727153	.3508598
2	CORR	PUBTRANS	.5784136	-.1817862	1.0000000	.7447511	.7170419	.6580408
2	CORR	TEACHER	.6638084	-.0491139	.7447511	1.0000000	.6711871	.6650047
2	CORR	COOK	.4898941	.0727153	.7170419	.6711871	1.0000000	.7688210
2	CORR	ENGINEER	.5190702	.3508598	.6580408	.6650047	.7688210	1.0000000

NUMBER OF CASES READ = 9 NUMBER OF CASES LISTED = 9

Variables

To prepare data for processing, you must define variables by assigning variable names and formats. You can also specify variable labels, value labels, and missing values, but they are optional. This section discusses the two essential components of variable definition: variable names and formats.

Variable Names

Each variable must have a unique name. Variable names are stored in the dictionary of an SPSS-format data file or working data file. Observe the following rules when establishing variable names or referring to variables by their names on commands:

- Variable names can contain up to eight characters, the first of which must be a letter or one of the characters @, #, or $.
- A # character in the first position of a variable name defines a scratch variable (see "Scratch Variables" on p. 21).
- A $ sign in the first position indicates that the variable is a system variable (see "System Variables" on p. 20). The $ sign is not allowed as the initial character of a user-defined variable.
- The period, underscore, and the characters $, #, and @ can be used within variable names. For example, *A._$@#1* is a valid variable name.
- Variable names ending with a period should be avoided, since the period may be interpreted as a command terminator.
- Variable names ending in underscores should be avoided, since such names may conflict with names of variables automatically created by a number of commands—for example, *YEAR_* and *DATE_* created by the DATE command.
- Variable names can be established on the DATA LIST, KEYED DATA LIST, MATRIX DATA, NUMERIC, STRING, COMPUTE, RECODE, and COUNT commands. They can be changed with the RENAME VARIABLES command.
- Reserved keywords cannot be used as variable names. Reserved keywords are

ALL	AND	BY	EQ	GE	GT	LE
LT	NE	NOT	OR	TO	WITH	

Keyword TO

You can establish names for a set of variables or to refer to any number of consecutive variables by specifying the beginning and the ending variables joined by the keyword TO.

To establish names for a set of variables with the keyword TO, use a character prefix with a numeric suffix.

- The prefix can be any valid name. Both the beginning and ending variables must use the same prefix.

- The numeric suffix can be any integer, but the first number must be smaller than the second. For example, ITEM1 TO ITEM5 establishes five variables named *ITEM1*, *ITEM2*, *ITEM3*, *ITEM4*, and *ITEM5*.
- Each variable name, including the number, must not exceed eight characters.
- Leading zeros used in numeric suffixes are included in the variable name. For example, V001 TO V100 establishes 100 variables, *V001*, *V002*, *V003*, ..., *V100*. V1 TO V100 establishes 100 variables, *V1*, *V2*, *V3*, ..., *V100*.

The keyword TO can also be used on procedures and other commands to refer to consecutive variables on the working data file. For example, AVAR TO VARB refers to the variables *AVAR* and all subsequent variables up to and including *VARB*.

- In most cases, the TO specification uses the variable order on the working data file. Use the DISPLAY command to see the order of variables on the working data file.
- On some subcommands, the order in which variables are named on a previous subcommand, usually the VARIABLES subcommand, is used to determine which variables are consecutive and therefore are implied by the TO specification. This is noted in the description of individual commands.

Keyword ALL

The keyword ALL can be used in many commands to specify all the variables in the working data file. For example:

```
FREQUENCIES /VARIABLES = ALL.
```

or

```
OLAP CUBES income by ALL.
```

In the second example, a separate table will be created for every variable in the data file, including a table of *income* by *income*.

System Variables

System variables are special variables created during a working session to keep system-required information, such as the number of cases read by the system, the system-missing value, and the current date. System variables can be used in data transformations.

- The names of system variables begin with a dollar sign ($).
- You cannot modify a system variable or alter its print or write format. Except for these restrictions, you can use system variables anywhere a normal variable is used in the transformation language.
- System variables are not available for procedures.

$CASENUM *Permanent case sequence number.* For each case, *$CASENUM* is the number of permanent cases read up to and including that case. The format is F8.0.The value of *$CASENUM* is not necessarily the row number in a Data Editor window (available in windowed environments).

$SYSMIS *System-missing value.* The system-missing value displays as a period (.) or whatever is used as the decimal point.

$JDATE *Current date in number of days from October 14, 1582* (day 1 of the Gregorian calendar). The format is F6.0.

$DATE *Current date in international date format with two-digit year.* The format is A9 in the form dd-mmm-yy.

$DATE11 *Current date in international date format with four-digit year.* The format is A11 in the form dd-mmm-yyyy.

$TIME *Current date and time. $TIME* represents the number of seconds from midnight, October 14, 1582, to the date and time when the transformation command is executed. The format is F20.

$LENGTH *The current page length.* The format is F11.0. For more information, see SET.

$WIDTH *The current page width.* The format is F3.0. For more information, see SET.

Scratch Variables

Scratch variables are variables created for the sole purpose of facilitating operations during a session.

- To create a scratch variable, specify a variable name that begins with the # character—for example, *#ID*. Scratch variables can be either numeric or string.
- Scratch variables are initialized to 0 for numeric variables or blank for string variables.
- SPSS does not reinitialize scratch variables when reading a new case. Their values are always carried across cases. Therefore, a scratch variable is a good choice for a looping index.
- Do not use LEAVE with a scratch variable.
- Scratch variables cannot be used in procedures and cannot be saved in a data file.
- Scratch variables cannot be assigned missing values, variable labels, or value labels.
- Scratch variables can be created between procedures but are always discarded as the next procedure begins.
- Scratch variables are discarded once a TEMPORARY command is specified.
- The keyword TO cannot refer to scratch variables and permanent variables at the same time.
- Scratch variables cannot be named on a WEIGHT command.

Variable Formats

SPSS accepts two variable types: numeric and string (also referred to as alphanumeric). Numeric values are stored internally as double-precision floating-point numbers and string values as codes listed in the SPSS character set (see Appendix B). Variable formats determine how SPSS reads raw data into storage and how it displays and writes values out.

Input and Output Formats

Values are read according to their *input* format and displayed on your terminal or written to a file according to their *output* format. The input and output formats differ in several ways.

- The input format is either specified or implied on the DATA LIST, KEYED DATA LIST, or other data definition commands. It is in effect only when SPSS builds cases in a working data file. Figure 8 shows the command printback for DATA LIST, which includes input format specifications.

Figure 8 Output showing input formats

```
    1  0  DATA LIST  /ID 1-4 SCORE 6-9 (F,2).

This command will read 1 records from the command file

Variable    Rec   Start     End        Format

ID            1       1       4        F4.0
SCORE         1       6       9        F4.2
```

- DATA LIST or any other data definition command automatically generates an output format from the input format and expands the output format to include punctuation characters such as decimal points, commas, dollar signs, and percent signs. To see the current output formats of variables in the working data file, use DISPLAY VARIABLES. The variables defined by the above DATA LIST command are displayed in Figure 9. Note that the output format for *SCORE* has been expanded one space to allow the display of the decimal point (the F4.2 input format indicates a four-character variable with two implied decimal places; the F5.2 output format includes one space for the decimal point).

Figure 9 Output showing output formats

```
List of variables on the active file

Name         Pos  Print Fmt     Write Fmt     Missing Values

ID             1  F4            F4
SCORE          2  F5.2          F5.2
```

- The formats (specified or default) on NUMERIC, COMPUTE, or other commands that create new variables are output formats. You must specify adequate widths to accommodate all punctuation characters.
- The output format is in effect during the entire working session (unless explicitly changed) and is saved in the dictionary of an SPSS-format data file.
- Output formats for numeric variables can be changed with the FORMATS, PRINT FORMATS, or WRITE FORMATS command.
- Output formats (widths) for string variables cannot be changed with command syntax. However, you can use STRING to declare a new variable with the desired format and then use COMPUTE to copy values from the existing string variable into the new variable.
- The format type cannot be changed from string to numeric, or vice versa, with command syntax. However, you can use RECODE to recode values from one variable into another variable of a different type.

See DATA LIST for information on specifying input data formats. See FORMATS, PRINT FORMATS, and WRITE FORMATS for information on specifying output data formats. See STRING for information on declaring new string variables.

Numeric Variable Formats

- The formats used in this manual use FORTRAN-like syntax—for example, Fw.d, where F denotes the format type (numeric), w represents the variable width, and d represents the number of decimal places.
- By default, the DATA LIST and KEYED DATA LIST commands assume that variables are numeric with an F format type. The default width depends on whether the data are in fixed or freefield format. For discussion of fixed data and freefield data, see DATA LIST.
- Numeric variables created by COMPUTE, COUNT, or other commands that create numeric variables are assigned a format type F8.2 (or the default format defined on SET FORMAT).
- If a data value exceeds its width specification, SPSS makes an attempt to display some value nevertheless. It first rounds the decimals, then takes out punctuation characters, then tries scientific notation, and if there is still not enough space, produces asterisks (***), indicating that a value is present but cannot be displayed in the assigned width.
- The output format does not affect the value stored in the file. A numeric value is always stored in double precision.

F, N, and E Formats

Table 3 lists the formats most commonly used to read in and write out numeric data.

Table 3 Common numeric formats

Format type	Description	Sample format	Sample input	Output for fixed input		Output for freefield input	
				Format	Value	Format	Value
Fw.d	Standard numeric	F5.0	1234	F5.0	1234	F5.0	1234
			1.234		1		1*
		F5.2	1234	F6.2	12.34	F6.2	1234.0
			1.234		1.23		1.23
Nw.d	Restricted numeric	N5.0	00123	F5.0	123	F5.0	123
			1.234		. †		1
		N5.2	12345	F6.2	123.45	F6.2	12345
			12.34		.		12.34
Ew.d	Scientific notation	E8.0	1234E3	E10.3	1.234E+06	E10.3	1.234E+06**
			1234		1.234E+03		1.234E+03

* Only the display is truncated. The value is stored in full precision.
† System-missing value. In this case, the value entered contains an illegal decimal point.
** Scientific notation is accepted in input data with F, COMMA, DOLLAR, DOT, and PCT formats. The same rules apply as specified below.

For fixed data:

- If a value has no coded decimal point but the input format specifies decimal positions, the rightmost positions are interpreted as implied decimal digits. For example, if the input F format specifies two decimal digits, the value 1234 is interpreted as 12.34; however, the value 123.4 is still interpreted as 123.4.
- With the N format, decimal places are always implied. Only unsigned integers are allowed. Values not padded with leading zeros to the specified width or those containing decimal points are assigned the system-missing value. This format is useful for reading and checking values that should be integers containing leading zeros.
- The E format reads all forms of scientific notation. If the sign is omitted, + is assumed. If the sign (+ or –) is specified before the exponent, the *E* or *D* can be omitted. A single space is permitted after the *E* or *D* and/or after the sign. If both the sign and the letter *E* or *D* are omitted, implied decimal places are assumed. For example, 1.234E3, 1.234+3, 1.234E+3, 1.234D3, 1.234D+3, 1.234E 3, and 1234 are all legitimate values. Only the last value can imply decimal places.
- E format input values can be up to 40 characters wide and include up to 15 decimal positions.
- The default output width (*w*) for the E format is either the specified input width or the number of specified decimal positions plus 7 (*d*+7), whichever is greater. The minimum width is 10 and the minimum decimal places are 3.

For freefield data:

- F format *w* and *d* specifications do not affect how data are read. They only determine the output formats (expanded, if necessary). 1234 is always read as 1234 in freefield data, but a specified F5.2 format will be expanded to F6.2 and the value will be displayed as 1234.0 (the last decimal place is rounded because of lack of space).
- The N format, when used for freefield data, is treated as the F format.
- The E format for freefield data follows the same rules as for fixed data except that no blank space is permitted in the value. Thus, 1.234E3 and 1.234+3 are allowed, but the value 1.234 3 will cause mistakes when the data are read.
- The default output E format and the width and decimal place limitations are the same as with fixed data.

COMMA, DOT, DOLLAR, and PCT Formats

Table 4 lists the formats that read and write data with embedded punctuation characters and symbols, such as commas, dots, and dollar and percent signs. The input data may or may not contain such characters. The data values read in are stored as numbers but displayed using the appropriate formats. Other formats that use punctuation characters and symbols are date and time formats and currency formats. Date and time are discussed in "Date and Time" on p. 51. Currency formats are output formats only. (See SET and FORMATS.)

Table 4 Numeric formats with punctuation and symbols

Format type	Description	Sample format	Sample input	Default output format	Displayed value
COMMAw.d	Commas in numbers	COMMA6.0	12345	COMMA7.0	12,345
			12,345		12,345
			123,45		12,345
		COMMA6.3	12345	COMMA7.3	12.345
			123,45		12.345
			1.2345		1.234
			1234.5		1234.50*
DOTw.d	Dots in numbers	DOT6.0	12345	DOT7.0	12.345
			123.45		12.345
			123.45		12.345
		DOT6.3	12345	DOT7.3	12,345
			123.45		12,345
			1,2345		1,234
			1234,5		1234,50*
DOLLARw.d	Dollar sign and comma in numbers	DOLLAR7.0	1234	DOLLAR10.0	$1,234
			1,234		$1,234
			$1234		$1,234
			$1,234		$1,234
		DOLLAR7.3	1234	DOLLAR10.3	$1.234
			1,234		$1.234
			$1,23.4		$123.400
			12345.6		$12345.60 0*
PCTw.d	Percent sign after numbers	PCT7.0	1234	PCT8.0	1234%
			12.34		12%
		PCT7.2	1234	PCT9.3	1.234%
			12.3		12.340%
			1234		12.34%

* When the decimal point is coded in input, SPSS displays all specified decimal places whether recorded in the data or not. When the width is inadequate, thousands separators are dropped before decimal places.

- Formats listed in Table 4 cannot be used to read freefield data.
- Data values can appear anywhere within the column specification. Both leading and trailing blanks are allowed.
- The sign (for example, "$" for DOLLAR format) or punctuation mark (for example, "." for DOT format) is ignored in the input data. Its position does not affect the value read into storage.
- The default output format expands the width of the input format by the number of the required signs or punctuation marks plus the decimal point if *d* is not 0. For example, COMMA9.2 is expanded to COMMA12.2 to accommodate two possible commas and one decimal point.
- DOT format is similar to COMMA format but reverses the symbols used for the thousands separator and the decimal point. For example, in DOT format, 1.234 has the value of one thousand, two hundred and thirty-four.

Binary and Hexadecimal Formats

SPSS is capable of reading and writing data in formats used by a number of programming languages such as PL/I, COBOL, FORTRAN, and Assembler. The data can be binary, hexadecimal, or zoned decimal. Formats described in this section can be used both as input formats and output formats, but with fixed data only. The described formats are not available on all systems. Consult the *SPSS Base User's Guide* for your version of SPSS for details.

The default output format for all formats described in this section is an equivalent F format, allowing the maximum number of columns for values with symbols and punctuation. To change the default, use FORMATS or WRITE FORMATS.

IBw.d (integer binary):

The IB format reads fields that contain fixed-point binary (integer) data. The data might be generated by COBOL using COMPUTATIONAL data items, by FORTRAN using INTEGER*2 or INTEGER*4, or by Assembler using fullword and halfword items. The general format is a signed binary number that is 16 or 32 bits in length.

The general syntax for the IB format is IBw.d, where w is the field width in bytes (omitted for column-style specifications) and d is the number of digits to the right of the decimal point. Since the width is expressed in bytes and the number of decimal positions is expressed in digits, *d* can be greater than *w*. For example, both of the following commands are valid:

```
DATA LIST FIXED /VAR1 (IB4.8).

DATA LIST FIXED /VAR1 1-4 (IB,8).
```

Widths of 2 and 4 represent standard 16-bit and 32-bit integers, respectively. Fields read with the IB format are treated as signed. For example, the one-byte binary value 11111111 would be read as –1.

PIBw.d (positive integer binary):

The PIB format is essentially the same as IB except that negative numbers are not allowed. This restriction allows one additional bit of magnitude. The same one-byte value 11111111 would be read as 255.

PIBHEXw (hexadecimal of PIB):

The PIBHEX format reads hexadecimal numbers as unsigned integers and writes positive integers as hexadecimal numbers. The general syntax for the PIBHEX format is PIBHEXw, where w indicates the total number of hexadecimal characters. The w specification must be an even number, with a maximum of 16.

For input data, each hexadecimal number must consist of the exact number of characters. No signs, decimal points, or leading and trailing blanks are allowed. For some operating systems (such as IBM CMS), hexadecimal characters must be upper case. The following example illustrates the kind of data the PIBHEX format can read:

```
DATA LIST FIXED
 /VAR1 1-4 (PIBHEX) VAR2 6-9 (PIBHEX) VAR3 11-14 (PIBHEX).
BEGIN DATA
0001 0002 0003
0004 0005 0006
0007 0008 0009
000A 000B 000C
000D 000E 000F
00F0 0B2C FFFF
END DATA.
LIST.
```

The values for *VAR1*, *VAR2*, and *VAR3* are listed in Figure 10. The PIBHEX format can also be used to write decimal values as hexadecimal numbers, which may be useful for programmers.

Figure 10 Output displaying values read in PIBHEX format

```
VAR1   VAR2   VAR3

   1      2      3
   4      5      6
   7      8      9
  10     11     12
  13     14     15
 240   2860  65535
```

Zw.d (zoned decimal):

The Z format reads data values that contain zoned decimal data. Such numbers may be generated by COBOL systems using DISPLAY data items, by PL/I systems using PICTURE data items, or by Assembler using zoned decimal data items.

In zoned decimal format, one digit is represented by one byte, generally hexadecimal F1 representing 1, F2 representing 2, and so on. The last byte, however, combines the sign for the number with the last digit. In the last byte, hexadecimal A, F, or C assigns +, and B, D, or E assigns –. For example, hexadecimal D1 represents 1 for the last digit and assigns the minus sign (–) to the number.

The general syntax of the Z format is Zw.d, where w is the total number of bytes (which is the same as columns) and d is the number of decimals. For input data, values can appear anywhere within the column specifications. Both leading and trailing blanks are allowed. Decimals can be implied by the input format specification or explicitly coded in the data. Explicitly coded decimals override the input format specifications.

The following example illustrates how the Z format reads zoned decimals in their printed forms on IBM mainframe and PC systems. The printed form for the sign zone (A to I for +1 to +9, and so on) may vary from system to system.

```
DATA LIST FIXED /VAR1 1-5 (Z) VAR2 7-11 (Z,2) VAR3 13-17 (Z)
 VAR4 19-23 (Z,2) VAR5 25-29 (Z) VAR6 31-35 (Z,2).
BEGIN DATA
1234A 1234A 1234B 1234B 1234C 1234C
1234D 1234D 1234E 1234E 1234F 1234F
1234G 1234G 1234H 1234H 1234I 1234I
1234J 1234J 1234K 1234K 1234L 1234L
1234M 1234M 1234N 1234N 1234O 1234O
1234P 1234P 1234Q 1234Q 1234R 1234R
1234{ 1234{ 1234} 1234} 1.23M 1.23M
END DATA.
LIST.
```

The values for *VAR1* to *VAR6* are listed in Figure 11.

Figure 11 Output displaying values read in Z format

```
VAR1     VAR2    VAR3     VAR4    VAR5     VAR6

 12341   123.41   12342   123.42   12343   123.43
 12344   123.44   12345   123.45   12346   123.46
 12347   123.47   12348   123.48   12349   123.49
-12341  -123.41  -12342  -123.42  -12343  -123.43
-12344  -123.44  -12345  -123.45  -12346  -123.46
-12347  -123.47  -12348  -123.48  -12349  -123.49
 12340   123.40  -12340  -123.40      -1    -1.23
```

The default output format for the Z format is the equivalent F format, as shown in Figure 11. The default output width is based on the input width specification plus one column for the sign and one column for the implied decimal point (if specified). For example, an input format of Z4.0 generates an output format of F5.0 and an input format of Z4.2 generates an output format of F6.2.

Pw.d (packed decimal):

The P format is used to read fields with packed decimal numbers. Such numbers are generated by COBOL using COMPUTATIONAL–3 data items and by Assembler using packed decimal data items. The general format of a packed decimal field is two four-bit digits in each byte of the field except the last. The last byte contains a single digit in its four leftmost bits and a four-bit sign in its rightmost bits. If the last four bits are 1111 (hexadecimal F), the value is positive; if they are 1101 (hexadecimal D), the value is negative. One byte under the P format can represent numbers from –9 to 9.

The general syntax of the P format is Pw.d, where w is the number of bytes (not digits) and d is the number of digits to the right of the implied decimal point. The number of digits in a field is (2*w–1).

PKw.d (unsigned packed decimal):

The PK format is essentially the same as P except that there is no sign. That is, even the rightmost byte contains two digits, and negative data cannot be represented. One byte under the PK format can represent numbers from 0 to 99. The number of digits in a field is 2*w.

RBw (real binary):

The RB format is used to read data values that contain internal format floating-point numbers. Such numbers are generated by COBOL using COMPUTATIONAL–1 or COMPUTATIONAL–2 data items, by PL/I using FLOATING DECIMAL data items, by FORTRAN using REAL or REAL*8 data items, or by Assembler using floating-point data items.

The general syntax of the RB format is RBw, where w is the total number of bytes. The width specification must be an even number between 2 and 8. Normally, a width specification of 8 is used to read double-precision values, and a width of 4 is used to read single-precision values.

RBHEXw (hexadecimal of RB):

The RBHEX format interprets a series of hexadecimal characters as a number that represents a floating-point number. This representation is system-specific. If the field width is less than twice the width of a floating-point number, the value is right-padded with binary zeros. For some operating systems (for example, IBM CMS), letters in hexadecimal values must be upper case.

The general syntax of the RBHEX format is RBHEXw, where w indicates the total number of columns. The width must be an even number. The values are real (floating-point) numbers. Leading and trailing blanks are not allowed. Any data values shorter than the specified input width must be padded with leading zeros.

String Variable Formats

- The values of string variables can contain numbers, letters, and special characters and can be up to 255 characters long.
- SPSS differentiates between long strings and short strings. Long strings can be displayed by some procedures and by the PRINT command, and they can be used as break variables to define subgroups in REPORT. They cannot, however, be tabulated in procedures such as CROSSTABS, and they cannot have user-missing values. Short strings, on the other hand, can be tabulated and can have user-missing values. The maximum length of a short string depends on the computer and operating system; it is typically 8 characters.
- System-missing values cannot be generated for string variables, since any character is a legal string value.
- When a transformation command that creates or modifies a string variable yields a missing or undefined result, a null string is assigned. The variable displays as blanks and is not treated as missing.
- String formats are used to read and write string variables. The input values can be alphanumeric characters (A format) or the hexadecimal representation of alphanumeric characters (AHEX format).
- For fixed data, the width can be explicitly specified on DATA LIST or KEYED DATA LIST or implied if column-style specifications are used. For freefield data, the default width is 1; if the input string may be longer, *w* must be explicitly specified. Input strings shorter than the specified width are right-padded with blanks.

- The output format for a string variable is always A. The width is determined by the input format or the format assigned on the STRING command. String formats can be displayed with DISPLAY VARIABLES but cannot be changed.

Aw (Standard Characters)

The A format is used to read standard characters. Characters can include letters, numbers, punctuation marks, blanks, and most other characters on your keyboard. Numbers entered as values for string variables cannot be used in calculations unless you convert them to numeric format with the NUMBER function (see "String Functions" on p. 41).

Fixed data:

With fixed-format input data, any punctuation—including leading, trailing, and embedded blanks—within the column specifications is included in the string value. For example, a string value of "Mr. Ed" (with one embedded blank) is distinguished from a value of "Mr. Ed" (with two embedded blanks). It is also distinguished from a string value of "MR. ED" (all upper case), and all three are treated as separate values. These can be important considerations for any procedures, transformations, or data selection commands involving string variables. Consider the following example:

```
DATA LIST FIXED /ALPHAVAR 1-10 (A).
BEGIN DATA
Mr. Ed
Mr. Ed
MR. ED
Mr.  Ed
 Mr. Ed
END DATA.
AUTORECODE ALPHAVAR /INTO NUMVAR.
LIST.
```

AUTORECODE recodes the values into consecutive integers. Figure 12 shows the recoded values.

Figure 12 Different string values illustrated

```
ALPHAVAR    NUMVAR

Mr. Ed         4
Mr. Ed         4
MR. ED         2
Mr.  Ed        3
 Mr. Ed        1
```

Freefield data:

With freefield data, blanks and commas are treated as delimiters for A format variables unless the value is enclosed in apostrophes or quotation marks. For example,

```
Ed, Mr.
```

is read as two separate values (Ed and Mr.). To include blanks and/or commas in a string value, enclose the value in apostrophes or quotation marks. For example, the following command file will generate a list of values as shown in Figure 13:

```
DATA LIST FREE /ALPHAVAR (A10).
BEGIN DATA
Mr.  Ed
Ed,Mr.
'Mr.  Ed'
'Ed, Mr.'
END DATA.
LIST.
```

Figure 13 Blanks and commas in freefield string input

```
ALPHAVAR

Mr.
Ed
Ed
Mr.
Mr.  Ed
Ed, Mr.
```

AHEXw (Hexadecimal Characters)

The AHEX format is used to read the hexadecimal representation of standard characters. Each set of two hexadecimal characters represents one standard character. For codes used on different operating systems, see Appendix B.

- The w specification refers to columns of the hexadecimal representation and must be an even number. Leading, trailing, and embedded blanks are not allowed, and only valid hexadecimal characters can be used in input values.
- For some operating systems (for example, IBM CMS), letters in hexadecimal values must be upper case.
- The default output format for variables read with the AHEX input format is the A format. The default width is half the specified input width. For example, an input format of AHEX14 generates an output format of A7.
- Used as an output format, the AHEX format displays the printable characters in the hexadecimal characters specific to your system. The following commands run on a UNIX system (where A=41 (decimal 65), a=61 (decimal 97), and so on) produce the output shown in Figure 14:

```
DATA LIST FIXED
   /A,B,C,D,E,F,G,H,I,J,K,L,M,N,O,P,Q,R,S,T,U,V,W,X,Y,Z 1-26 (A).
FORMATS ALL (AHEX2).
BEGIN DATA
ABCDEFGHIJKLMNOPQRSTUVWXYZ
abcdefghijklmnopqrstuvwxyz
END DATA.
LIST.
```

Figure 14 Display of hexadecimal representation of the character set with AHEX format

```
A  B  C  D  E  F  G  H  I  J  K  L  M  N  O  P  Q  R  S  T  U  V  W  X  Y  Z

41 42 43 44 45 46 47 48 49 4A 4B 4C 4D 4E 4F 50 51 52 53 54 55 56 57 58 59 5A
61 62 63 64 65 66 67 68 69 6A 6B 6C 6D 6E 6F 70 71 72 73 74 75 76 77 78 79 7A
```

FORTRAN-like Format Specifications

You can use FORTRAN-like format specifications to define formats for a set of variables, as in the following example:

```
DATA LIST FILE=HUBDATA RECORDS=3
      /MOHIRED, YRHIRED, DEPT1 TO DEPT4 (T12, 2F2.0, 4(1X,F1.0)).
```

- The specification T12 in parentheses tabs to the 12th column. The first variable (*MOHIRED*) will be read beginning from column 12.
- The specification 2F2.0 assigns the format F2.0 to two adjacent variables (*MOHIRED* and *YRHIRED*).
- The next four variables (*DEPT1* to *DEPT4*) are each assigned the format F1.0. The 4 in 4(1X,F1.0) distributes the same format to four consecutive variables. 1X skips one column before each variable. (The column-skipping specification placed within the parentheses is distributed to each variable.)

Transformation Expressions

Transformation expressions are used in commands like COMPUTE, IF, DO IF, LOOP IF, and SELECT IF. This section describes the three types of expressions: numeric, string, and logical, as well as available operators. For date and time functions, see "Date and Time" on p. 51.

Numeric Expressions

Numeric expressions can be used with the COMPUTE and IF command and as part of a logical expression for commands such as IF, DO IF, LOOP IF, and SELECT IF. Arithmetic expressions can also appear in the index portion of a LOOP command, on the REPEATING DATA command, and on the PRINT SPACES command.

Arithmetic Operations

The following arithmetic operators are available:

+ *Addition.*

– *Subtraction.*

* *Multiplication.*

/ *Division.*

** *Exponentiation.*

- No two operators can appear consecutively.
- Arithmetic operators cannot be implied. For example, (VAR1)(VAR2) is not a legal specification; you must specify VAR1*VAR2.
- Arithmetic operators and parentheses serve as delimiters. To improve readability, blanks (not commas) can be inserted before and after an operator.
- To form complex expressions, you can use variables, constants, and functions with arithmetic operators.
- The order of execution is functions first, then exponentiation, then multiplication, division, and unary –, and then addition and subtraction.
- Operators at the same level are executed from left to right.
- To override the order of operation, use parentheses. Execution begins with the innermost set of parentheses and progresses out.

Numeric Constants

- Constants used in numeric expressions or as arguments to functions can be integer or non-integer, depending on the application or function.

- You can specify as many digits in a constant as needed, as long as you understand the precision restrictions of your computer.
- Numeric constants can be signed (+ or –) but cannot contain any other special characters such as the comma or dollar sign.
- Numeric constants can be expressed with scientific notation. Thus, the exponent for a constant in scientific notation is limited to two digits. The range of values allowed for exponents in scientific notation is from –99 to +99.

Complex Numeric Arguments

- Except where explicitly restricted, complex expressions can be formed by nesting functions and arithmetic operators as arguments to functions.
- The order of execution for complex numeric arguments is functions first, then exponentiation, then multiplication, division, and unary –, and then addition and subtraction.
- To control the order of execution in complex numeric arguments, use parentheses.

Numeric Functions

Numeric functions can be used in any numeric expression on IF, SELECT IF, DO IF, ELSE IF, LOOP IF, END LOOP IF, and COMPUTE commands. Numeric functions always return numbers (or the system-missing value whenever the result is indeterminate). The expression to be transformed by a function is called the *argument*. Most functions have a variable or a list of variables as arguments.

- In numeric functions with two or more arguments, each argument must be separated by a comma. Blanks alone cannot be used to separate variable names, expressions, or constants in transformation expressions.
- Arguments should be enclosed in parentheses, as in TRUNC(INCOME), where the TRUNC function returns the integer portion of the variable *INCOME*.
- Multiple arguments should be separated by commas, as in MEAN(Q1,Q2,Q3), where the MEAN function returns the mean of variables *Q1*, *Q2*, and *Q3*.

Arithmetic Functions

- All arithmetic functions except MOD have single arguments; MOD has two. The arguments to MOD must be separated by a comma.
- Arguments can be numeric expressions, as in RND(A**2/B).

ABS(arg) *Absolute value.* ABS(SCALE) is 4.7 when *SCALE* equals 4.7 or –4.7.

RND(arg) *Round the absolute value to an integer and reaffix the sign.* RND(SCALE) is –5 when *SCALE* equals –4.7.

TRUNC(arg) *Truncate to an integer.* TRUNC(SCALE) is –4 when *SCALE* equals –4.7.

MOD(arg,arg) *Remainder (modulo) of the first argument divided by the second.* When *YEAR* equals 1983, MOD(YEAR,100) is 83.

SQRT(arg) *Square root.* SQRT(SIBS) is 1.41 when *SIBS* equals 2.

EXP(arg) *Exponential. e* is raised to the power of the argument. EXP(VARA) is 7.39 when *VARA* equals 2.

LG10(arg) *Base 10 logarithm.* LG10(VARB) is 0.48 when *VARB* equals 3.

LN(arg) *Natural or Naperian logarithm (base* e*).* LN(VARC) is 2.30 when *VARC* equals 10.

LNGAMMA(arg) *Logarithm (base* e*) of complete Gamma function.*

ARSIN(arg) *Arcsine.* (Alias ASIN.) The result is given in radians. ARSIN(ANG) is 1.57 when *ANG* equals 1.

ARTAN(arg) *Arctangent.* (Alias ATAN.) The result is given in radians. ARTAN(ANG2) is 0.79 when *ANG2* equals 1.

SIN(arg) *Sine.* The argument must be specified in radians. SIN(VARD) is 0.84 when *VARD* equals 1.

COS(arg) *Cosine.* The argument must be specified in radians. COS(VARE) is 0.54 when *VARE* equals 1.

Statistical Functions

- Each argument to a statistical function (expression, variable name, or constant) must be separated by a comma.
- The *.n* suffix can be used with all statistical functions to specify the number of valid arguments. For example, MEAN.2(A,B,C,D) returns the mean of the valid values for variables *A*, *B*, *C*, and *D* only if at least two of the variables have valid values. The default for *n* is 2 for SD, VARIANCE, and CFVAR, and 1 for other statistical functions.
- The keyword TO can be used to refer to a set of variables in the argument list.

SUM(arg list) *Sum of the nonmissing values across the argument list.*

MEAN(arg list) *Mean of the nonmissing values across the argument list.*

SD(arg list) *Standard deviation of the nonmissing values across the argument list.*

VARIANCE(arg list) *Variance of the nonmissing values across the argument list.*

CFVAR(arg list) *Coefficient of variation of the nonmissing values across the argument list.* The coefficient of variation is the standard deviation divided by the mean.

MIN(arg list) *Minimum nonmissing value across the argument list.*

MAX(arg list) *Maximum nonmissing value across the argument list.*

Random Variable and Distribution Functions

Random variable and distribution function keywords are all of form prefix.suffix, where the prefix specifies the function to be applied to the distribution and the suffix specifies the distribution.

- Random variable and distribution functions take both constants and variables for arguments.
- A function argument, if required, must come first and is denoted by *q* (quantile) for cumulative distribution and probability density functions and *p* (probability) for inverse distribution functions.
- All random variable and distribution functions must specify distribution parameters, denoted by *a*, *b*, and/or *c*, according to the number required.
- All arguments are real numbers.
- Restrictions to distribution parameters *a*, *b*, and *c* apply to all functions for that distribution. Restrictions for the function parameter *p* or *q* apply to that particular distribution function. The program issues a warning and returns system-missing when it encounters an out-of-range value for an argument.

The following are possible prefixes:

CDF *Cumulative distribution function.* A cumulative distribution function CDF.d_spec(q,a,...) returns a probability *p* that a variate with the specified distribution (d_spec) falls below *q* for continuous functions and at or below *q* for discrete functions.

IDF *Inverse distribution function.* Inverse distribution functions are not available for discrete distributions. An inverse distribution function IDF.d_spec(p,a,...) returns a value *q* such that CDF.d_spec(q,a,...)=*p* with the specified distribution (d_spec).

PDF *Probability density function.* A probability density function PDF.d_spec(q,a,...) returns the density of the specified distribution (d_spec) at *q* for continuous functions and the probability that a random variable with the specified distribution equals *q* for discrete functions.

RV *Random number generation function.* A random number generation function RV.d_spec(a,...) generates an independent observation with the specified distribution (d_spec).

NCDF *Noncentral cumulative distribution function.* A noncentral distribution function NCDF.d_spec(q,a,b,...) returns a probability *p* that a variate with the specified noncentral distribution falls below *q*. It is available only for beta, chi-square, *F*, and Student's *t*.

NPDF *Noncentral probability density function.* A noncentral probability density function NCDF.d_spec(q,a,b,...) returns the density of the specified distribution (d_spec) at *q*. It is available only for beta, chi-square, *F*, and Student's *t*.

SIG *Tail probability function.* A tail probability function SIG.d_spec(q,a,...) returns a probability *p* that a variate with the specified distribution (d_spec) is larger than *q*.

The following are suffixes for continuous distributions:

BETA *Beta distribution.* The beta distribution takes two shape parameters, *a* and *b*; both must be positive. The noncentral beta distribution takes an extra noncentrality parameter, *c*, which must be greater than or equal to 0. The CDF, IDF, PDF, RV, NCDF, and NPDF functions are available for this distribution, where both *q* and *p* must be between 0 and 1, inclusive. The beta distribution is used in Bayesian analyses as a conjugate to the binomial distribution.

BVNOR *Bivariate normal distribution.* The bivariate normal distribution takes one correlation parameter, *r*, which must be between –1 and 1, inclusive. The CDF and PDF functions are available for this distribution and require two quantiles, *q1* and *q2*. Two variables with correlation *r* and marginal normal distributions with a mean of 0 and a standard deviation of 1 have a bivariate normal distribution.

CAUCHY *Cauchy distribution.* The Cauchy distribution takes one location parameter, *a,* and one scale parameter, *b*; *b* must be positive. The CDF, IDF, PDF, and RV functions are available for this distribution, where $0<p<1$. The Cauchy distribution is symmetric about the location parameter, *a,* and has such slowly decaying tails that the expectation does not exist. The harmonic mean of variates that have positive density at 0 is typically distributed as Cauchy.

CHISQ *Chi-square distribution.* The chi-square distribution takes one shape parameter, *a*, which is the degrees of freedom and must be positive. The noncentral chi-square distribution takes an extra noncentrality parameter, *c*, which must be greater than or equal to 0. The CDF, IDF, PDF, RV, NCDF, NPDF, and SIG functions are available for this distribution, where $q \geq 0$ and $0 \leq p<1$. Chi-square is a special case of the gamma distribution and is commonly used to test quadratic forms under the Gaussian assumption.

EXP *Exponential distribution.* The exponential distribution takes one scale parameter, *a*, which can represent the rate of decay and must be positive. The CDF, IDF, PDF, and RV functions are available, where $q \geq 0$ and $0 \leq p<1$. The exponential distribution is a special case of the gamma distribution. A major use of this distribution is life testing.

F F *distribution.* The *F* distribution takes two shape parameters, *a* and *b*, which are the degrees of freedom and must be positive. The noncentral *F* distribution takes an extra noncentrality parameter, *c*, which must be greater than or equal to 0. The CDF, IDF, IDF, RV.F(a,b), NCDF, NPDF, and SIG functions are available, where $q \geq 0$ and $0 \leq p<1$. The *F* distribution is commonly used to test hypotheses under the Gaussian assumption.

GAMMA *Gamma distribution.* The gamma distribution takes one shape parameter, *a* and one scale parameter, *b*. Both parameters must be positive. The CDF, IDF, PDF, and RV functions are available, where $q \geq 0$ and $0 \leq p<1$. The gamma distribution is commonly used in queuing theory, inventory control, and precipitation processes. If *a* is an integer and $b=1$, it is the Erlang distribution.

HALFNRM *Half-normal distribution.* The half-normal distribution takes one location parameter, *a* and one scale parameter, *b*. Parameter *b* must be positive. The CDF, IDF, PDF, and RV functions are available, where $0<p<1$.

IGAUSS *Inverse Gaussian distribution.* The inverse Gaussian, or Wald, distribution takes two parameters, *a* and *b*, both of which must be positive. The CDF, IDF, PDF, and RV functions are available, where $q>0$ and $0\leq p<1$. The inverse Gaussian distribution is commonly used to test hypotheses for model parameter estimates.

LAPLACE *Laplace or double exponential distribution.* The Laplace distribution takes one location parameter, *a,* and one scale parameter, *b*. Parameter *b* must be positive. The CDF, IDF, PDF, and RV functions are available, where $0<p<1$. The Laplace distribution is symmetric about 0 and has exponentially decaying tails on both ends.

LOGISTIC *Logistic distribution.* The logistic distribution takes one location parameter, *a,* and one scale parameter, *b*. Parameter *b* must be positive. The CDF, IDF, PDF, and RV functions are available, where $0<p<1$. The logistic distribution is a unimodal, symmetric distribution with tails that are longer than the Gaussian distribution. It is used to model growth curves.

LNORMAL *Lognormal distribution.* This distribution takes two parameters, *a* and *b*. Both parameters must be positive. The CDF, IDF, PDF, and RV functions are available, where $q\geq 0$ and $0\leq p<1$. Lognormal is used in the distribution of particle sizes in aggregates, flood flows, concentrations of air contaminants, and failure time.

NORMAL *Normal distribution.* The normal, or Gaussian, distribution takes one location parameter, *a*, and one scale parameter, *b*. Parameter *b* must be positive. The CDF, IDF, PDF, and RV functions are available, where $0<p<1$. Three functions in SPSS releases earlier than 6.0 are special cases of the normal distribution functions:

CDFNORM(arg)=CDF.NORMAL(q,0,1)

where arg is *q;*

PROBIT(srg)=IDF.NORMAL(p,0,1)

where arg is *p*; and

NORMAL(arg)=RV.NORMAL(0,b)

where arg is *b*. The normal distribution is symmetric about the mean and is the most widely used in statistics.

PARETO *Pareto distribution.* The Pareto distribution takes a threshold parameter, *a,* and a shape parameter, *b*. Both parameters must be positive. The CDF, IDF, PDF, and RV functions are available, where $q\geq a$ and $0\leq p<1$. Pareto is commonly used in economics as a model for a density function with a slowly decaying tail.

SMOD *Studentized maximum modulus distribution.* The studentized maximum modulus distribution takes parameters *a* and *b*, both of which must be greater than or equal to 1. The CDF and IDF functions are available, where $q>0$ and

$0 \le p < 1$. The studentized maximum modulus is commonly used in post hoc multiple comparisons for GLM and ANOVA.

SRANGE *Studentized range distribution.* The studentized range distribution takes parameters *a* and *b*, both of which must be greater than or equal to 1. The CDF and IDF functions are available, where $q > 0$ and $0 \le p < 1$. The studentized range is commonly used in post hoc multiple comparisons for GLM and ANOVA.

T *Student* t *distribution.* The Student *t* distribution takes one shape parameter, *a*, which is the degrees of freedom and must be positive. The noncentral Student *t* distribution takes an extra noncentrality parameter, *b*. The CDF, IDF, PDF, RV, NCDF, NPDF functions are available, where $0 < p < 1$. The Student *t* distribution is symmetric about 0 and approaches the Gaussian distribution as *a* approaches infinity. The major uses of the Student *t* distribution are to test hypotheses and construct confidence intervals for means of data.

UNIFORM *Uniform distribution.* The uniform distribution takes two parameters, *a* and *b*. The first parameter, *a,* must be less than or equal to the second parameter, *b*. The CDF, IDF, PDF, and RV functions are available, where $a \le q \le b$ and $0 \le p \le 1$. The uniform random number function in SPSS releases earlier than 6.0 is a special case:

```
UNIFORM(arg)=RV.UNIFORM(0,b)
```

where arg is parameter *b*. Among other uses, the uniform distribution commonly models the round-off error.

WEIBULL *Weibull distribution.* The Weibull distribution takes two parameters *a* and *b*, both of which must be positive. The CDF, IDF, PDF, and RV functions are available, where $q \ge 0$ and $0 \le p < 1$. The Weibull distribution is commonly used in survival analysis.

The following are suffixes for discrete distributions:

BERNOULLI *Bernoulli distribution.* The Bernoulli distribution takes one success probability parameter, *a*, which must be between 0 and 1, inclusive. The CDF, PDF, and RV functions are available, where *q* equals 0 or 1. The Bernoulli distribution is a special case of the binomial distribution and is used in simple success-failure experiments.

BINOM *Binomial distribution.* The binomial distribution takes one number of trials parameter, *a*, and one success probability parameter, *b*. Parameter *a* must be a positive integer and parameter *b* must be between 0 and 1, inclusive. The CDF, PDF, and RV functions are available, where *q* is the number of successes in *a* trials. When $a=1$, it is the Bernoulli distribution. The binomial distribution is used in independently replicated success-failure experiments.

GEOM *Geometric distribution.* The geometric distribution takes one success probability parameter, *a*, which must be greater than 0 and less than or equal to 1. The CDF, PDF, and RV functions are available, where *q* is the number of trials needed (including the last trial) before a success is observed.

HYPER

Hypergeometric distribution. The hypergeometric distribution takes three parameters, *a*, *b*, and *c*, where *a* is the total number of objects in an urn model, *b* is the number of objects randomly drawn without replacement from the urn, *c* is the number of objects with distinct characteristics. All three parameters are positive integers, and both *b* and *c* must be less than or equal to *a*. The CDF, PDF, and RV functions are available, where *q* is the number of objects with these distinct characteristics observed out of the withdrawn objects.

NEGBIN

Negative binomial distribution. The negative binomial distribution takes one threshold parameter, *a*, and one success probability parameter, *b*. Parameter *a* must be an integer and parameter *b* must be greater than 0 and less than or equal to 1. The CDF, PDF, and RV functions are available, where *q* is the number of trials needed (including the last trial) before *a* successes are observed. If a=1, it is a geometric distribution.

POISSON

Poisson distribution. The Poisson distribution takes one rate or mean parameter, *a*. Parameter *a* must be positive. The CDF, PDF, and RV functions are available, where *q* is a non-negative integer. The Poisson distribution is used in modeling the distribution of counts, such as traffic counts and insect counts.

Missing Values in Numeric Expressions

- Most numeric expressions receive the system-missing value when any one of the values in the expression is missing.
- Some arithmetic operations involving 0 can be evaluated even when the variables have missing values. These operations are:

Expression	Result
0 * missing	0
0 / missing	0
MOD(0,missing)	0

- The *.n* suffix can be used with the statistical functions SUM, MEAN, MIN, MAX, SD, VARIANCE, and CFVAR to specify the number of valid arguments you consider acceptable. The default of *n* is 2 for SD, VARIANCE, and CFVAR, and 1 for other statistical functions. For example,

```
COMPUTE FACTOR = SUM.2(SCORE1 TO SCORE3).
```

computes the variable *FACTOR* only if a case has valid information for at least two scores. *FACTOR* is assigned the system-missing value if a case has valid values for fewer than two scores.

Domain Errors

Domain errors occur when numeric expressions are mathematically undefined or cannot be represented numerically on the computer for reasons other than missing data. Two common examples are division by 0 and the square root of a negative number. When SPSS detects a domain error, it issues a warning and assigns the system-missing value to the expression. For example, the command COMPUTE TESTVAR = TRUNC(SQRT(X/Y) * .5) returns system-missing if *X/Y* is negative or if *Y* is 0.

The following are domain errors in numeric expressions:

**	*A negative number to a non-integer power.*
/	*A divisor of 0.*
MOD	*A divisor of 0.*
SQRT	*A negative argument.*
EXP	*An argument that produces a result too large to be represented on the computer.*
LG10	*A negative or 0 argument.*
LN	*A negative or 0 argument.*
ARSIN	*An argument whose absolute value exceeds 1.*
NORMAL	*A negative or 0 argument.*
PROBIT	*A negative or 0 argument, or an argument 1 or greater.*

String Expressions

Expressions involving string variables can be used on COMPUTE and IF commands and in logical expressions on commands such as IF, DO IF, LOOP IF, and SELECT IF.

- A string expression can be a constant enclosed in apostrophes (for example, 'IL'), a string function (see "String Functions" below), or a string variable.
- An expression must return a string if the target variable is a string.
- The string returned by a string expression does not have to be the same length as the target variable; no warning messages are issued if the lengths are not the same. If the target variable produced by a COMPUTE command is shorter, the result is right-trimmed. If the target variable is longer, the result is right-padded.

String Functions

- The target variable for each string function must be a string and *must have already been declared* (see STRING).
- Multiple arguments in a list must be separated by commas.

- When two strings are compared, the case in which they are entered is significant. The LOWER and UPCASE functions are useful for making comparisons of strings regardless of case.
- For certain functions (for example, MIN, MAX, ANY, and RANGE), the outcome will be affected by case and by whether the string includes numbers or special characters. The character set in use varies by system. With the ASCII character set, lower case follows upper case in the sort order. Therefore, if *NAME1* is in upper case and *NAME2* is in lower case, MIN(NAME1,NAME2) will return *NAME1* as the minimum. The reverse is true with the EBCDIC character set, which sorts lower case before upper case.

CONCAT(arg list) *Concatenate the arguments into a string.* String variables and strings can be intermixed as arguments. For example, CONCAT(A,'**') creates the string ABCD** for a case with the value *ABCD* for the string variable *A*.

LOWER(arg) *Convert upper case to lower case.* All other characters remain unchanged. The argument can be a string variable or value. For example, LOWER(NAME1) returns charles if the value of *NAME1* is *CHARLES*.

LPAD(a1, a2, a3) *Left-pad.* The variable a1 is left-padded up to the length specified by a2 using the optional single character a3 as the pad character. a2 must be a positive integer from 1 to 255. The default pad character is a blank. For example, LPAD(ALPHA1,10) adds four leading blanks to the target variable if *ALPHA1* has an A6 format. a3 can be any character enclosed in apostrophes or any expression that yields a single character.

LTRIM(a1, a2) *Left-trim.* The character a2 is trimmed from the beginning of a1. For example, LTRIM(ALPHA2,'0') trims leading zeros from the variable *ALPHA2*. a2 can be any character enclosed in apostrophes or any expression that yields a single character. The default for a2 is a blank.

RPAD(a1, a2, a3) *Right-pad.* The variable a1 is right-padded up to the length of a2 using the optional single character a3 as the pad character. a2 must be a positive integer from 1 to 255. The default pad character is a blank. For example, RPAD(ALPHA3,8,'*') adds two trailing asterisks to the target variable if *ALPHA3* has an A6 format. a3 can be any character enclosed in apostrophes or any expression that yields a single character.

RTRIM(a1, a2) *Right-trim.* The character a2 is trimmed from the end of a1. For example, RTRIM(ALPHA4,'*') trims trailing asterisks from variable *ALPHA4*. a2 can be any character enclosed in apostrophes or any expression that yields a single character. The default for a2 is a blank.

SUBSTR(a1, a2, a3) *Substring.* This function returns the substring within a1 beginning with the position specified by a2 and optionally for a length of a3. a2 can be a positive integer from 1 to the length of a1. a3, when added to a2, should not exceed the length of a1. If a3 is not specified, the substring is returned up to the end of a1. For example, if the variable *ALPHA5* has an A6 format, SUBSTR(ALPHA5,3) returns the last four characters of *ALPHA5*. SUBSTR (ALPHA5,3,1) returns the third character of *ALPHA5*.

When used on the left side of an equals sign, the substring is replaced by the string specified on the right side of the equals sign. The rest of the original string remains intact. For example, SUBSTR(ALPHA6,3,1)='*' changes the third character of all values for *ALPHA6* to *. If the replacement string is longer or shorter than the substring, the replacement is truncated or padded with blanks on the right to an equal length.

UPCASE(arg) *Convert lower case to upper case.* The argument can be a string variable or a string. For example, UPCASE(NAME1) returns CHARLES if the value of *NAME1* is *Charles*.

MBLEN.BYTE(arg,a1) *Return the number of bytes in the character at the specified position.* The argument is a string expression and a1 indicates the beginning byte of the character in the specified string.

Search Functions

- The values returned by INDEX and/or RINDEX can be used as arguments to SUBSTR to pull out substrings with the same beginning or ending character but with varying position and length.

INDEX(a1, a2, a3) *Return a number that indicates the position of the first occurrence of a2 in a1.* a1 is the string that is searched. a2 is the string variable or string that is used in the search. If a3 is not specified, all of a2 is used. For example, INDEX(ALPHA8,'**X*') returns 2 for a case with the value *X**X**X** for the variable *ALPHA8*. The optional a3 is the number of characters used to divide a2 into separate strings. Each substring is used for searching and the function returns the first occurrence of any of the substrings. With the same value *X**X**X** for *ALPHA8*, both INDEX(ALPHA8, '**X*', 2) and INDEX(ALPHA8, '**X*', 1) return 1. a3 must be a positive integer and must divide evenly into the length of a2. The target variable must be numeric. If a2 is not found within a1, the value 0 is returned.

LENGTH(arg) *Return the length of the specified string.* The argument can be a string variable or a string. For example, LENGTH(LNAME) always returns 6 if *LNAME* has an A6 format. The target variable must be numeric.

MAX(arg list) *Return the maximum value across the argument list.* For example, MAX(LNAME,FNAME) selects the name that comes last in the sort order, the first or the last name. MAX is also available as a numeric function.

MIN(arg list) *Return the minimum value across the argument list.* For example, MIN(LNAME,FNAME) selects the name that comes first in the sort order, the first or the last name. MIN is also available as a numeric function.

RINDEX(a1,a2,a3) *Return a number indicating the position of the last occurrence of a2 in a1.* a1 is the string that is searched. a2 is the string variable or string that is used in the search. If a3 is not specified, all of a2 is used. For example, RINDEX(ALPHA8,'**X*') returns 5 for a case with the value *X**X**X** for the variable *ALPHA8*. The optional a3 is the number of characters used to divide a2 into separate strings. Each substring is used for searching, and the function returns the last occurrence of any of the substrings. With the same value X**X**X* for *ALPHA8*, RINDEX (ALPHA8, '**X*', 2) returns 7, and RINDEX (ALPHA8, '**X*', 1) returns 8. a3 must be a positive integer and must divide evenly into the length of a2. The target variable must be numeric. If a2 is not found within a1, the value 0 is returned.

Conversion Functions

NUMBER(arg,format) *Convert the argument into a number using the specified format.* The argument is string, the format is a numeric format, and the result is numeric. The string is essentially reread using the format and returned as a number. For example, NUMBER (XALPHA,F3.1) converts all values for *XALPHA* to numbers using the F3.1 format. The function returns the system-missing value if the conversion is invalid.

STRING(arg,format) *Converts the argument into a string using the specified format.* The argument is numeric, the format is a numeric format, and the result is a string. The number is converted from internal representation according to the format and then stored as a string. For example, STRING (INCOME, DOLLAR8) converts the numeric values for *INCOME* to the dollar format and returns it as a string value. If the result is shorter than the string variable that receives the values, it is right-justified. If the result is longer, it is right-trimmed.

Missing Values in String Expressions

- If the numeric argument (which can be an expression) for functions LPAD and RPAD is illegal or missing, the result is a null string. If the padding or trimming is the only operation, the string is then padded to its entire length with blanks. If the operation is nested, the null string is passed to the next nested level.
- If a numeric argument to SUBSTR is illegal or missing, the result is a null string. If SUBSTR is the only operation, the string is blank. If the operation is nested, the null string is passed to the next nested level.
- If a numeric argument to INDEX or RINDEX is illegal or missing, the result is system-missing.

Logical Expressions

Logical expressions can appear on the IF, SELECT IF, DO IF, ELSE IF, LOOP IF, and END LOOP IF commands. SPSS evaluates a logical expression as true or false, or as missing if it is indeterminate. A logical expression returns 1 if the expression is true, 0 if it is false, or system-missing if it is missing. Thus, logical expressions can be any expressions that yield this three-value logic.

- The simplest logical expression is a logical variable. A logical variable is any numeric variable that has values 1, 0, or system-missing. Logical variables cannot be strings.

- Logical expressions can be simple logical variables or relations, or they can be complex logical tests involving variables, constants, functions, relational operators, logical operators, and parentheses to control the order of evaluation.
- On an IF command, a logical expression that is true causes the assignment expression to be executed. A logical expression that returns missing has the same effect as one that is false: the assignment expression is not executed and the value of the target variable is not altered.
- On a DO IF command, a logical expression that is true causes SPSS to execute the commands immediately following the DO IF, up to the next ELSE IF, ELSE, or END IF. If it is false, SPSS looks for the next ELSE IF or ELSE command. If the logical expression returns missing for each of these, the entire structure is skipped.
- On a SELECT IF command, a logical expression that is true causes the case to be selected. A logical expression that returns missing has the same effect as one that is false: the case is not selected.
- On a LOOP IF command, a logical expression that is true causes looping to begin (or continue). A logical expression that returns missing has the same effect as one that is false: the structure is skipped.
- On an END LOOP IF command, a logical expression that is false returns control to the LOOP command for that structure and looping continues. If it is true, looping stops and the structure is terminated. A logical expression that returns a missing value has the same effect as one that is true: the structure is terminated.

String Variables in Logical Expressions

String variables, like numeric variables, can be tested in logical expressions.

- String variables must be declared before they can be used in a string expression.
- String variables cannot be compared to numeric variables.
- If strings of different lengths are compared, the shorter string is right-padded with blanks to equal the length of the longer.
- The magnitude of strings can be compared using LT, GT, and so on, but the outcome depends on the sorting sequence of the computer. Use with caution.

Logical Functions

- Each argument to a logical function (expression, variable name, or constant) must be separated by a comma.
- The target variable for a logical function must be numeric.
- The functions RANGE and ANY can be useful shortcuts to more complicated specifications on the IF, DO IF, and other conditional commands. For example, the command

  ```
  SELECT IF ANY(REGION,'NW','NE','SE').
  ```

  is equivalent to

  ```
  SELECT IF (REGION EQ 'NW' OR REGION EQ 'NE' OR REGION EQ
  'SE').
  ```

RANGE(arg,arg list) *Return 1 or true if the value of the first argument is in the inclusive ranges; return 0 or false if not.* The first argument is usually a variable, and the second argument is a list of one or more pairs of values. The variable can be either numeric or string. For example, RANGE (AGE,1,17,62,99) returns 1 for ages 1 through 17 and 62 through 99, inclusive, and 0 for any other ages. RANGE (LNAME,'A','MZZZZZZ') returns 1 for last names that begin with a letter between A and M, inclusive, and 0 for last names beginning with other letters.

ANY(arg,arg list) *Return 1 or true if the value of the first argument matches one of the arguments in the list; return 0 or false if not.* The first argument is usually a variable, either numeric or string. For example, ANY(PROJECT,3,4,7,9) returns 1 if the value for variable *PROJECT* is 3, 4, 7, or 9, and 0 for other values of *PROJECT*. Similarly, ANY (LNAME,'MARTIN','JONES','EVANS') returns 1 for people whose last names are *MARTIN*, *JONES*, or *EVANS*, and 0 for all other last names.

Relational Operators

A relation is a logical expression that compares two values using a *relational operator*. In the command

```
IF (X EQ 0) Y=1
```

the variable *X* and 0 are expressions that yield the values to be compared by the EQ relational operator. Relational operators are

EQ or = *Equal to.*

NE or ~= ¬ = or <> *Not equal to.*

LT or < *Less than.*

LE or <= *Less than or equal to.*

GT or > *Greater than.*

GE or >= *Greater than or equal to.*

- The symbols representing NE (~= or ¬=) are system dependent (see "NOT Logical Operator" below).
- The expressions in a relation can be variables, constants, or more complicated arithmetic expressions.
- Blanks (not commas) must be used to separate the relational operator from the expressions. To make the command more readable, use extra blanks or parentheses.

NOT Logical Operator

The NOT logical operator reverses the true/false outcome of the expression that immediately follows.

- The NOT operator affects only the expression that immediately follows, unless a more complex logical expression is enclosed in parentheses.
- The valid substitute for NOT varies from operating system to operating system. In general, the tilde (~) is valid for ASCII systems, while ¬ (or the symbol over number 6 on the keyboard) is valid for IBM EBCDIC systems. See the *SPSS Base User's Guide* for your version of SPSS.
- NOT can be used to check whether a numeric variable has the value 0, 1, or any other value. For example, all scratch variables are initialized to 0. Therefore, NOT (#ID) returns false or missing when *#ID* has been assigned a value other than 0.

AND and OR Logical Operators

Two or more relations can be logically joined using the logical operators AND and OR. Logical operators combine relations according to the following rules:

- The ampersand (&) symbol is a valid substitute for the logical operator AND. The vertical bar (|) is a valid substitute for the logical operator OR.
- Only one logical operator can be used to combine two relations. However, multiple relations can be combined into a complex logical expression.
- Regardless of the number of relations and logical operators used to build a logical expression, the result is either true, false, or indeterminate because of missing values.
- Operators or expressions cannot be implied. For example, X EQ 1 OR 2 is illegal; you must specify X EQ 1 OR X EQ 2.
- The ANY and RANGE functions can be used to simplify complex expressions.

AND *Both relations must be true for the complex expression to be true.*

OR *If either relation is true, the complex expression is true.*

Table 5 lists the outcome for AND and OR combinations.

Table 5 Outcome for AND and OR combinations

Expression	Outcome	Expression	Outcome
true AND true	= true	true OR true	= true
true AND false	= false	true OR false	= true
false AND false	= false	false OR false	= false
true AND missing	= missing	true OR missing	= true*
missing AND missing	= missing	missing OR missing	= missing

* Expressions where SPSS can evaluate the outcome with incomplete information. See "Missing Values in Logical Expressions" below.

Order of Evaluation

- When arithmetic operators and functions are used in a logical expression, the order of operations is functions and arithmetic operations first, then relational operators, and then logical operators.
- When more than one logical operator is used, NOT is evaluated first, then AND, and then OR.
- To change the order of evaluation, use parentheses.

Missing Values in Logical Expressions

In a simple relation, the logic is indeterminate if the expression on either side of the relational operator is missing. When two or more relations are joined by logical operators AND and OR, SPSS always returns a missing value if all of the relations in the expression are missing. However, if any one of the relations can be determined, SPSS tries to return true or false according to the logical outcomes shown in Table 5.

- When two relations are joined with the AND operator, the logical expression can never be true if one of the relations is indeterminate. The expression can, however, be false.
- When two relations are joined with the OR operator, the logical expression can never be false if one relation returns missing. The expression, however, can be true.

Other Functions

SPSS also includes a lag function and several missing-value functions.

LAG Function

LAG(arg,n) *The value of the variable* n *cases before*. The first argument is a variable. The second argument, if specified, is a constant and must be a positive integer; the default is 1. For example, PREV4=LAG(GNP,4) returns the value of *GNP* for the fourth case before the current one. The first four cases have system-missing values for *PREV4*.

- The result is of the same type (numeric or string) as the variable specified as the first argument.
- The first *n* cases for string variables are set to blanks. For example, if PREV2=LAG (LNAME,2) is specified, blanks will be assigned to the first two cases for *PREV2*.
- When LAG is used with commands that select cases (for example, SELECT IF and SAMPLE), LAG counts cases *after* case selection, even if specified before these commands (see "Command Order" on p. 6).

Missing-Value Functions

- Each argument to a missing-value function (expression, variable name, or constant) must be separated by a comma.
- Only numeric values can be used as arguments in missing-value functions.
- The keyword TO can be used to refer to a set of variables in the argument list for functions NMISS and NVALID.
- The functions MISSING and SYSMIS are logical functions and can be useful shortcuts to more complicated specifications on the IF, DO IF, and other conditional commands.

VALUE(arg) *Ignore user-defined missing values.* The value is treated as is. The argument must be a variable name.

MISSING(arg) *True or 1 if the value is user-missing or system-missing; false or 0 otherwise.*

SYSMIS(arg) *True or 1 if the value is system-missing; false or 0 otherwise.*

NMISS(arg list) *Number of system-missing values in the argument list.*

NVALID(arg list) *Number of valid values in the argument list.*

Treatment of Missing Values in Arguments

If the logic of an expression is indeterminate because of missing values, the expression returns a missing value, and the command is not executed. Table 6 summarizes how missing values are handled in arguments to various functions.

Table 6 Missing values in arguments

Function	Returns system-missing if
MOD (x1,x2)	x1 is missing, or x2 is missing and x1 is not 0
MAX.n (x1,x2,...xk) MEAN.n (x1,x2,...xk) MIN.n (x1,x2,...x1) SUM.n (x1,x2,...xk)	fewer than *n* arguments are valid; the default *n* is 1

Table 6 Missing values in arguments (Continued)

Function	Returns system-missing if
CFVAR.n (x1,x2,...xk) SD.n (x1,x2,...xk) VARIANCE.n (x1,x2,...xk)	fewer than *n* arguments are valid; the default *n* is 2
LPAD(x1,x2,x3) LTRIM(x1,x2) RTRIM(x1,x2) RPAD(x1,x2,x3)	x1 or x2 is illegal or missing
SUBSTR(x1,x2,x3)	x2 or x3 is illegal or missing
NUMBER(x,format) STRING(x,format)	the conversion is invalid
INDEX(x1,x2,x3) RINDEX(x1,x2,x3)	x3 is invalid or missing
LAG (x,n)	x is missing *n* cases previously (and always for the first *n* cases); the default *n* is 1
ANY (x,x1,x2,...xk) RANGE (x,x1,x2,...xk)	x or all of x1, x2, ..., xk are missing
VALUE (x)	x is system-missing
MISSING (x) NMISS (x1,x2,...xk) NVALID (x1,x2,...xk) SYSMIS (x)	never

- Any function that is not listed in Table 6 returns the system-missing value when the argument is missing.
- The system-missing value is a displayed as a period (.) for numeric variables.
- String variables do not have system-missing values. An invalid string expression nested within a complex transformation yields a null string, which is passed to the next level of operation and treated as missing. However, an invalid string expression that is not nested is displayed as a blank string and is *not* treated as missing.

Date and Time

SPSS reads and writes date and time in many different formats but stores them as floating-point numbers. You can perform arithmetic operations on them, use them in statistical procedures, and display or print them in a format of your choice. This section discusses the input and output formats for date and time, arithmetic operations using date and time variables, and date and time functions.

Date and Time Formats

Date and time formats are both input and output formats. They can be used on DATA LIST and other variable definition commands to read in values representing dates or times or date-time combinations. Like numeric formats, each input format generates a default output format, automatically expanded (if necessary) to accommodate display width. In addition, you can assign or modify output formats using FORMATS, WRITE FORMATS, and PRINT FORMATS commands. The output formats are effective only with LIST, REPORT, and TABLES procedures and the PRINT and WRITE transformation commands. Other procedures use the F format and display the values as numbers.

- All date and time formats have a minimum input width, and some have a different minimum output. Wherever the input minimum width is less than the output minimum, SPSS expands the width automatically when displaying or printing values. However, when you specify output formats, you must allow enough space for displaying the date and time in the format you choose.
- Input data shorter than the specified width are correctly evaluated as long as all the necessary elements are present. For example, with the TIME format, 1:2, 01 2, and 01:02 are all correctly evaluated even though the minimum width is 5. However, if only one element (hours or minutes) is present, you must use a time function to aggregate or convert the data (see "Date and Time Functions" on p. 58).
- If a date or time value cannot be completely displayed in the specified width, values are truncated in the output. For example, an input time value of 1:20:59 (1 hour, 20 minutes, 59 seconds) displayed with a width of 5 will generate an output value of 01:20, not 01:21. The truncation of output does not affect the numeric value stored in the working file.

Table 7 shows all available date and time formats, where *w* indicates the total number of columns and *d* (if present), the number of decimal places for fractional seconds. The example shows the output format with the minimum width and default decimal positions (if applicable). The format allowed in the input data is much less restrictive (see "Input Data Specification" on p. 53).

Table 7 Date and time formats

Format type	Description	Min w		Max w	Max d	General form	Example
		In	Out				
DATEw	International date	8	9	40		dd-mmm-yy	28-OCT-90
		10	11			dd-mmm-yyyy	28-OCT-1990
ADATEw	American date	8	8	40		mm/dd/yy	10/28/90
		10	10			mm/dd/yyyy	10/28/1990
EDATEw	European date	8	8	40		dd.mm.yy	28.10.90
		10	10			dd.mm.yyyy	28.10.1990
JDATEw	Julian date	5	5	40		yyddd	90301
		7	7			yyyyddd	1990301
SDATEw	Sortable date*	8	8	40		yy/mm/dd	90/10/28
		10	10			yyyy/mm/dd	1990/10/28
QYRw	Quarter and year	4	6	40		q Q yy	4 Q 90
		6	8			q Q yyyy	4 Q 1990
MOYRw	Month and year	6	6	40		mmm yy	OCT 90
		8	8			mmm yyyy	OCT 1990
WKYRw	Week and year	6	8	40		ww WK yy	43 WK 90
		8	10			ww WK yyyy	43 WK 1990
WKDAYw	Day of the week	2	2	40		(name of the day)	SU
MONTHw	Month	3	3	40		(name of the month)	JAN
TIMEw	Time	5	5	40		hh:mm	01:02
TIMEw.d		10	10	40	16	hh:mm:ss.s	01:02:34.75
DTIMEw	Days and time	8	8	40		dd hh:mm	20 08:03
DTIMEw.d		13	13	40	16	dd hh:mm:ss.s	20 08:03:00
DATETIMEw	Date and time	17	17	40		dd-mmm-yyyy hh:mm	20-JUN-1990 08:03
DATETIMEw.d		22	22	40	16	dd-mmm-yyyy hh:mm:ss.s	20-JUN-1990 08:03:00

* All date and time formats produce sortable data. SDATE, a date format used in a number of Asian countries, can be sorted in its character form and is used as a sortable format by many programmers.

Input Data Specification

The following general rules apply to date and time input formats:

- Input data must be fixed. Data can appear anywhere within the specified columns. Leading and trailing blanks are allowed. If column-style specifications are used, the width specification can be omitted (see DATA LIST). For example,

  ```
  DATA LIST /BIRTHDAY 1-8 (DATE).
  ```

  is equivalent to

  ```
  DATA LIST /BIRTHDAY (DATE8).
  ```

- You cannot use date and time formats to read freefield data.
- The century value for two-digit years is defined by the *SET EPOCH* value. By default, the century range begins 69 years prior to the current year and end 30 years after the current year. Whether all four digits or only two digits are displayed in output depends on the width specification on the format.
- Dashes, periods, commas, slashes, or blanks can be used as delimiters in the date-month-year input. For example, with the DATE format, the following input forms are all acceptable:

  ```
  28-10-90        28/10/1990        28.OCT.90        October 28, 1990
  ```

  The displayed values, however, will be the same: *28-OCT-90* or *28-OCT-1990*, depending on whether the specified width allows 11 characters in output.
- The JDATE format does not allow internal delimiters and requires leading zeros for day values of less than 100 and two-digit-year values of less than 10. For example, for January 1, 1990, the following two specifications are acceptable:

  ```
  90001                  1990001
  ```

  However, neither of the following is acceptable:

  ```
  90 1                   90/1
  ```

- Months can be represented in digits, Roman numerals, or three-character abbreviations, and they can be fully spelled out. For example, all of the following specifications are acceptable for October:

  ```
  10        X        OCT        October
  ```

- The quarter in QYR format is expressed as 1, 2, 3, or 4. It must be separated from the year by the letter *Q*. Blanks can be used as additional delimiters. For example, for the fourth quarter of 1990, all of the following specifications are acceptable:

  ```
  4Q90        4Q1990        4 Q 90        4 Q 1990
  ```

  On some operating systems, such as IBM CMS, *Q* must be upper case. The displayed output is *4 Q 90* or *4 Q 1990*, depending on whether the width specified allows all four digits of the year.
- The week in the WKYR format is expressed as a number from 1 to 53. Week 1 begins on January 1, week 2 on January 8, and so on. The value may be different from the number of the calendar week. The week and year must be separated by the string WK. Blanks can

be used as additional delimiters. For example, for the 43rd week of 1990, all of the following specifications are acceptable:

```
43WK90      43WK1990      43 WK 90      43 WK 1990
```

On some operating systems, such as IBM CMS, WK must be upper case. The displayed output is *43 WK 90* or *43 WK 1990*, depending on whether the specified width allows enough space for all four digits of the year.

- In time specifications, colons can be used as delimiters between hours, minutes, and seconds. Hours and minutes are required but seconds are optional. A period is required to separate seconds from fractional seconds. Hours can be of unlimited magnitude, but the maximum value for minutes is 59 and for seconds 59.999. . . .
- Data values can contain a sign (+ or –) in TIME and DTIME formats to represent time intervals before or after a point in time.

Example

```
DATA LIST FIXED
 /VAR1 1-17 (DATE) VAR2 21-37 (ADATE) VAR3 41-47 (JDATE).
BEGIN DATA
28-10-90            10/28/90            90301
28.OCT.1990         X 28 1990           1990301
28 October, 2001    Oct.  28, 2001      2001301
END DATA.
LIST.
```

- Internally, all date format variables are stored as the number of seconds from 0 hours, 0 minutes, and 0 seconds of Oct. 14, 1582.

The LIST output from these commands is shown in Figure 15.

Figure 15 Output illustrating DATE, ADATE, and JDATE formats

```
       VAR1              VAR2            VAR3

28-OCT-1990       10/28/1990         1990301
28-OCT-1990       10/28/1990         1990301
28-OCT-2001       10/28/2001         2001301
```

Example

```
DATA LIST FIXED /VAR1 1-10 (QYR) VAR2 12-25 (MOYR) VAR3 28-37 (WKYR).
BEGIN DATA
4Q90        10/90           43WK90
4 Q 90      Oct-1990        43 WK 1990
4 Q 2001    October, 2001   43 WK 2001
END DATA.
LIST.
```

- Internally, the value of a QYR variable is stored as midnight of the first day of the first month of the specified quarter, the value of a MOYR variable is stored as midnight of the first day of the specified month, and the value of a WKYR format variable is stored as midnight of the first day of the specified week. Thus, *4Q90* and *10/90* are both equivalent to October 1, 1990, and *43WK90* is equivalent to October 22, 1990.

The LIST output from these commands is shown in Figure 16.

Figure 16 Output illustrating QYR, MOYR, and WKYR formats

```
    VAR1        VAR2             VAR3

4 Q 1990    OCT 1990       43 WK 1990
4 Q 1990    OCT 1990       43 WK 1990
4 Q 2001    OCT 2001       43 WK 2001
```

Example

```
DATA LIST FIXED
 /VAR1 1-11 (TIME,2) VAR2 13-21 (TIME) VAR3 23-28 (TIME).
BEGIN DATA
1:2:34.75   1:2:34.75 1:2:34
END DATA.
LIST.
```

- TIME reads and writes time of the day or a time interval.
- Internally, the TIME values are stored as the number of seconds from midnight of the day or of the time interval.

The LIST output from these commands is shown in Figure 17.

Figure 17 Output illustrating TIME format

```
      VAR1        VAR2    VAR3

 1:02:34.75   1:02:34    1:02
```

Example

```
DATA LIST FIXED
 /VAR1 1-9 (WKDAY) VAR2 10-18 (WKDAY)
  VAR3 20-29 (MONTH) VAR4 30-32 (MONTH) VAR5 35-37 (MONTH).
BEGIN DATA
Sunday   Sunday    January   1    Jan
Monday   Monday    February  2    Feb
Tues     Tues      March     3    Mar
Wed      Wed       April     4    Apr
Th       Th        Oct       10   Oct
Fr       Fr        Nov       11   Nov
Sa       Sa        Dec       12   Dec
END DATA.
FORMATS VAR2 VAR5 (F2).
LIST.
```

- WKDAY reads and writes the day of the week; MONTH reads and writes the month of the year.
- Values for WKDAY are entered as strings but stored as numbers. They can be used in arithmetic operations but not in string functions.
- Values for MONTH can be entered either as strings or as numbers, but are stored as numbers. They can be used in arithmetic operations but not in string functions.
- To display the values as numbers, assign an F format to the variable, as was done for *VAR2* and *VAR5* in the above example.

The LIST output from these commands is shown in Figure 18.

Figure 18 Output illustrating WKDAY and MONTH formats

```
     VAR1 VAR2          VAR3 VAR4 VAR5

SUNDAY        1  JANUARY      JAN    1
MONDAY        2  FEBRUARY     FEB    2
TUESDAY       3  MARCH        MAR    3
WEDNESDAY     4  APRIL        APR    4
THURSDAY      5  OCTOBER      OCT   10
FRIDAY        6  NOVEMBER     NOV   11
SATURDAY      7  DECEMBER     DEC   12
```

Example

```
DATA LIST FIXED /VAR1 1-14 (DTIME) VAR2 18-42 (DATETIME).
BEGIN DATA
20 8:3            20-6-90 8:3
20:8:03:46        20/JUN/1990 8:03:46
20 08 03 46.75    20 June, 2001 08 03 46.75
END DATA.
LIST.
```

- DTIME and DATETIME read and write time intervals.
- The decimal point explicitly coded in the input data for fractional seconds.
- The DTIME format allows a – or + sign in the data value to indicate a time interval before or after a point in time.
- Internally, values for a DTIME variable are stored as the number of seconds of the time interval while those for a DATETIME variable are stored as the number of seconds from 0 hours, 0 minutes, and 0 seconds of Oct. 14, 1582.

The LIST output from these commands is shown in Figure 19.

Figure 19 Output illustrating DTIME and DATETIME formats

```
        VAR1                       VAR2

20 08:03:00       20-JUN-1990 08:03:00
20 08:03:46       20-JUN-1990 08:03:46
20 08:03:46       20-JUN-2001 08:03:46
```

Arithmetic Operations with Date and Time Variables

Most date and time variables are stored internally as the number of seconds from a particular date or as a time interval and therefore can be used in arithmetic operations:

- A *date* is a floating-point number representing the number of seconds from midnight, October 14, 1582. Dates, which represent a particular point in time, are stored as the number of seconds to that date. For example, November 8, 1957, is stored as 1.2E+10.
- A date includes the time of day, which is the time interval past midnight. When time of day is not given, it is taken as 00:00 and the date is an even multiple of 86,400 (the number of seconds in a day).

- A *time interval* is a floating-point number representing the number of seconds in a time period, for example, an hour, minute, or day. For example, the value representing 5.5 days is 475,200; the value representing the time interval 14:08:17 is 50,897.
- QYR, MOYR, and WKYR variables are stored as midnight of the first day of the respective quarter, month, and week of the year. Therefore, *1 Q 90*, *1/90*, and *1 WK 90* are all equivalents of January 1, 1990 0:0:00. See "Date and Time Functions" on p. 58 for information on how to determine the quarter, month, or week of a year for a certain date.
- WKDAY variables are stored as 1 to 7, and MONTH variables as 1 to 12. For information on how to determine the day of the week or the month of the year for a certain date, see "Date and Time Functions" on p. 58.
- Both dates and time intervals can be used in arithmetic expressions. The results are stored as the number of seconds or days (see Table 8).
- Do not mix time variables (TIME and DTIME) with date variables (DATE, ADATE, EDATE, and so on) in computations. Since date variables have an implicit time value of 00:00:00, calculations involving time values that are not multiples of a whole day (for example, 24 hours, 0 minutes, 0 seconds) will yield unreliable results.
- Mixing a DATETIME variable with a date variable may yield an unreliable result. Operations involving date variables are accurate only to the days. To avoid possible misinterpretation, use the DTIME format and ignore the hours and minutes portion of the resulting value.

You can perform virtually any arithmetic operation with them. Of course, not all of these operations are particularly useful. You can calculate the number of days between two dates by subtracting one date from the other—but adding two dates does not produce a very meaningful result.

By default, any new numeric variables you compute are displayed in F format. In the case of calculations involving time and date variables, this means that the default output is expressed as a number of seconds or days. Use the FORMATS (or PRINT FORMATS) command to specify an appropriate format for the computed variable. Table 8 shows the recommended output formats for some of the calculations possible with date and time variables.

Table 8 Recommended output formats for date and time calculations

Arithmetic operation	Result	Recommended output format
time ± time*	time	TIME, DTIME
date – date †	time	DTIME
DATETIME – DATETIME	time	TIME, DTIME
DATETIME ± time	date	DATETIME

* Including TIME and DTIME formats.
† Including DATE, ADATE, EDATE, JDATE, and SDATE formats.

Example

```
DATA LIST RECORDS=2
 /TIME 1-8 (TIME) DTIME 10-19 (DTIME) DATE 21-29 (DATE)
  ADATE 31-38 (ADATE)
 /DATTIME1 1-18 (DATETIME) DATTIME2 20-37 (DATETIME).
BEGIN DATA
1:10:15  1 0:25:10   13-8-90  10/21/90
28-OCT-90 9:15:17  29/OCT/90 10:30:22
END DATA.
COMPUTE ADDTIME=TIME+DTIME.
COMPUTE DATEDIF1=ADATE-DATE.
COMPUTE DATEDIF2=DATTIME2-DATTIME1.
COMPUTE DATETIME=DATTIME2+DTIME.
LIST VARIABLES=ADDTIME DATEDIF1 DATEDIF2 DATETIME.
FORMATS ADDTIME DATEDIF2 (TIME15) DATEDIF1 (DTIME15)
 DATETIME (DATETIME25).
LIST VARIABLES=ADDTIME DATEDIF1 DATEDIF2 DATETIME.
```

The results of these commands are shown in Figure 20.

Figure 20 Results of arithmetic operations with date and time variables

```
      ADDTIME       DATEDIF1        DATEDIF2                  DATETIME

     25:35:25    69 00:00:00        25:15:05      30-OCT-1990 10:55:32
```

Date and Time Functions

Date and time functions provide aggregation, conversion, and extraction routines for dates and time intervals. Each function transforms an expression consisting of one or more arguments. Arguments can be complex expressions, variable names, or constants. Date and time expressions and variables are legitimate arguments.

All date functions that accept the argument of day—for example, DATE.DMY(d,m,y), DATE.MDY(m,d,y), and DATE.YRDAY(y,d)—check the validity of the argument. The value for day must be an integer between 1 and 31. If an invalid value is encountered, a warning is displayed and the value is set to system-missing. However, if the day value is invalid for a particular month—for example, 31 in September, April, June, and November or 29 through 31 for February in non-leap years—the resulting date is placed in the next month (for example, if you enter 2 for *MONTH*, 31 for *DAY*, and 91 for *YEAR*, the result becomes 03/02/91).

Aggregation Functions

Aggregation functions generate dates and time intervals from values that were not read by date and time input formats.

- All aggregation functions begin with DATE or TIME, depending on whether a date or a time interval is requested. This is followed by a subfunction that corresponds to the type of values found in the data.
- The subfunctions are separated from the function by a period (.) and are followed by an argument list specified in parentheses.
- The arguments to the DATE and TIME functions must be separated by commas and must contain integer values.

DATE.DMY(d,m,y) *Combine day, month, and year.* The value of the argument for day must be expressed as an integer between 1 and 31. The value of the argument for month must be expressed as an integer between 1 and 13 (13 returns January of the following year). Years should be expressed in four digits. For example, the command

```
COMPUTE BIRTHDAY=DATE.DMY(DAY,MONTH,YEAR).
```

stores the value of approximately *1.184E+10* in *BIRTHDAY* when *DAY* is 8, *MONTH* is 11, and *YEAR* is 57. This value can be displayed with a DATE9 format as *08-NOV-57.*

DATE.MDY(m,d,y) *Combine month, day, and year.* This function follows the same rules as DATE.DMY, except for the order of the arguments. For example, the command

```
COMPUTE BIRTHDAY=DATE.MDY(MONTH,DAY,YEAR).
```

stores the same value as the previous example in *BIRTHDAY* for the same values of *MONTH, DAY,* and *YEAR.* The value can be displayed as *11/08/57* with an ADATE8 format.

DATE.YRDAY(y,d) *Combine year and day of the year.* The year can be expressed as either two or four digits. Years should be expressed in four digits. The day can be expressed as any integer between and including 1 and 366. For example, the command

```
COMPUTE BIRTHDAY=DATE.YRDAY(1688,301).
```

when combined with a DATE11 print format produces the date *27-OCT-1688* for *BIRTHDAY.*

DATE.QYR(q,y) *Combine quarter and year.* The quarter must be expressed as a single digit between and including 1 and 4. The year can contain two or four digits. Years should be expressed in four digits. For example, the command

```
COMPUTE QUART=DATE.QYR(QTR,YEAR).
```

with a QDATE6 print format produces a value of *4 Q 57* for *QUART* when *QTR* is 4 and *YEAR* is 57. Since each quarter is assumed to begin on the first day of the first month of the quarter, a DATE9 print format for the same value is displayed as *01-OCT-57*.

DATE.MOYR(m,y) *Combine month and year.* The value of the month must be expressed as an integer between and including 1 and 12. The year can be expressed as two or four digits. For example, the command

```
COMPUTE START=DATE.MOYR(MONTH,YEAR).
```

displays *NOV 57* for *START* when *MONTH* is 11 and *YEAR* is 57 and the print format is MOYR.

DATE.WKYR(w,y) *Combine week and year.* The week must be an integer between and including 1 and 53. The year can be represented by two or four digits. For example, the command

```
COMPUTE WEEK=DATE.WKYR(WK,YEAR).
```

displays *26-NOV-57* for *WEEK* when *WK* is 48 and *YEAR* is 57 and the print format is DATE9. The number of the week in the WKYR format is calculated beginning with the first day of the year. It may be different from the number of the calendar week.

TIME.HMS(h,m,s) *Combine hour, minute, and second into a time interval.* For example, the command

```
COMPUTE PERIOD1= TIME.HMS (HR,MIN,SEC).
```

produces an interval of 45,030 seconds for *PERIOD1* when *HR* equals 12, *MIN* equals 30, and *SEC* equals 30. The value can be displayed as *12:30:30* with a TIME8 print format.

You can supply one, two, or three arguments. Trailing arguments can be omitted and default to 0. The value of the first nonzero argument can spill over into the next higher argument. For example, the command

```
COMPUTE PERIOD2=TIME.HMS(HR,MIN).
```

produces an interval of 5400 seconds for *PERIOD2* when *HR* is 0 and *MIN* is 90. The value can be displayed as 01:30 with a TIME5 print format.

You can have a non-integer value for the last argument. For example, the command

```
COMPUTE PERIOD3=TIME.HMS(HR).
```

produces an interval of 5400 seconds for *PERIOD3* when *HR* equals 1.5 and is displayed as *01:30* with a TIME5 format. When you supply a nonzero argument to a function, each of the lower-level units must be within the range of –60 to +60.

TIME.DAYS(d) *Aggregate days into a time interval.* The argument can be expressed as any numeric value. For example, the command

```
COMPUTE NDAYS=TIME.DAYS(SPELL).
```

with a value of 2.5 for *SPELL* generates a value for *NDAYS* that is displayed as *2 12:00* with a DTIME7 format.

Conversion Functions

The conversion functions convert time intervals from one unit of time to another. Time intervals are stored as the number of seconds in the interval; the conversion functions provide a means for calculating more appropriate units, for example, converting seconds to days.

Each conversion function consists of the CTIME function followed by a period (.), the target time unit, and an argument. The argument can consist of expressions, variable names, or constants. The argument must already be a time interval (see "Aggregation Functions" on p. 59). Time conversions produce non-integer results with a default format of F8.2.

Since time and dates are stored internally as seconds, a function that converts to seconds is not necessary.

CTIME.DAYS(arg) *Convert a time interval to the number of days.* For example, the command

```
COMPUTE NDAYS=CTIME.DAYS(TIME.HMS(HR,MIN,SEC)).
```

with 12 for *HR*, 30 for *MIN*, and 30 for *SEC* yields a value of 0.52 for *NDAYS*. `CTIME.DAYS(45030)` yields the same result.

CTIME.HOURS(arg) *Convert a time interval to the number of hours.* For example, the command

```
COMPUTE NHOURS=CTIME.HOURS(TIME.HMS(HR,MIN,SEC)).
```

using the same values as the previous example produces a value of 12.51 for *NHOURS*.

CTIME.MINUTES(arg) *Convert a time interval to the number of minutes.* Using the same values as the previous example for *HR*, *MIN*, and, *SEC*, the command

```
COMPUTE NMINS=CTIME.MINUTES(TIME.HMS(HR,MIN,SEC)).
```

converts the interval to minutes and produces a value of 750.50 for *NMINS*.

YRMODA Function

YRMODA(arg list) *Convert year, month, and day to a day number.* The number returned is the number of days since October 14, 1582 (day 0 of the Gregorian calendar).

- Arguments for YRMODA can be variables, constants, or any other type of numeric expression but must yield integers.
- Year, month, and day must be specified in that order.
- The first argument can be any year between 0 and 99, or between 1582 to 47516.
- If the first argument yields a number between 00 and 99, 1900 through 1999 is assumed.
- The month can range from 1 through 13. Month 13 with day 0 yields the last day of the year. For example, YRMODA(1990,13,0) produces the day number for December 31, 1990. Month 13 with any other day yields the day of the first month of the coming year, for example, YRMODA(1990,13,1) produces the day number for January 1, 1991.

- The day can range from 0 through 31. Day 0 is the last day of the previous month regardless of whether it is 28, 29, 30, or 31. For example, YRMODA(1990,3,0) yields 148791.00, the day number for February 28, 1990.
- The function returns the system-missing value if any of the three arguments is missing or if the arguments do not form a valid date *after* October 14, 1582.
- Since YRMODA yields the number of days instead of seconds, you can not display it in date format unless you convert it to the number of seconds.

Extraction Functions

The extraction functions extract subfields from dates or time intervals, targeting the day or a time from a date value. This permits you to classify events by day of the week, season, shift, and so forth.

- Each extraction function begins with XDATE, followed by a period, the subfunction name (what you want to extract), and an argument.
- The argument can be an expression, a variable name, or a constant, provided the argument is already in date form.
- In the following examples, the value for the variable *BIRTHDAY* is *05-DEC-1954 5:30:15*, read with a DATE20 input format.

XDATE.MDAY(arg) *Return day number in a month from a date.* The result is an integer between 1 and 31. The date must have occurred after October 14, 1582. For example, you can extract the day number from *BIRTHDAY*, as in

```
COMPUTE DAYNUM=XDATE.MDAY(BIRTHDAY).
```

When the value for *BIRTHDAY* is *05-DEC-1954 5:30:15*, *DAYNUM* is 5.

XDATE.MONTH(arg) *Return month number from a date.* The result is an integer between 1 and 12. The date must have occurred after October 14, 1582. For example, you can extract the month number from *BIRTHDAY*, as in

```
COMPUTE MONTHNUM=XDATE.MONTH(BIRTHDAY).
```

When the value for *BIRTHDAY* is *05-DEC-1954 5:30:15*, this command yields 12 for *MONTHNUM*. If you provide a print format of MONTH12, as in

```
PRINT FORMAT MONTHNUM(MONTH12).
```

the value would be displayed as *DECEMBER*.

XDATE.YEAR(arg) *Return a four-digit year from a date.* The date must have occurred after October 14, 1582. For example, you can extract the year from *BIRTHDAY*, as in

```
COMPUTE YEAR=XDATE.YEAR(BIRTHDAY).
```

When the value for *BIRTHDAY* is *05-DEC-1954 5:30:15*, this command returns 1954 for *YEAR*.

XDATE.HOUR(arg) *Return the hour from a date or time of day.* The result is an integer between 0 and 23. For example, you can extract the hour from *BIRTHDAY*, as in

```
COMPUTE HOUR=XDATE.HOUR(BIRTHDAY).
```

When the value for *BIRTHDAY* is *05-DEC-1954 5:30:15*, this command returns 5 for *HOUR*.

XDATE.MINUTE(arg) *Return the minute of the hour from a date or time of day.* The result is an integer from 0 through 59. For example, you can extract the minute of the hour from *BIRTHDAY*, as in

```
COMPUTE MIN=XDATE.MINUTE(BIRTHDAY).
```

When the value for *BIRTHDAY* is *05-DEC-1954 5:30:15*, this command returns 30 for *MIN*.

XDATE.SECOND(arg) *Return the second of the minute from a date or time of day.* The result is an integer or, if there are fractional seconds, a value with decimals. For example, you can extract the second of the minute from *BIRTHDAY*, as in

```
COMPUTE SEC=XDATE.SECOND(BIRTHDAY).
```

When the value for *BIRTHDAY* is *05-DEC-1954 5:30:15*, this command returns a value of 15.00 for *SEC*.

XDATE.WKDAY(arg) *Return the day within a week from a date.* The result is an integer between and including 1 and 7, with Sunday being 1 and Saturday being 7. The date must have occurred after October 14, 1582. For example, you can extract the day of the week from *BIRTHDAY*, as in

```
COMPUTE DAYNAME=XDATE.WKDAY(BIRTHDAY).
```

When the value for *BIRTHDAY* is *05-DEC-1954 5:30:15*, this command returns the value 1 for *DAYNAME*. If you provide an output format of WKDAY, as in

```
PRINT FORMAT DAYNAME (WKDAY9).
```

the value for *DAYNAME* would display as *SUNDAY*.

XDATE.JDAY(arg) *Return the day of the year from the date.* The result is an integer between 1 and 366 inclusive. The date must have occurred after October 14, 1582. For example, you can extract the day of the year from *BIRTHDAY*, as in

```
COMPUTE DAYNUM=XDATE.JDAY(BIRTHDAY).
```

When the value for *BIRTHDAY* is *05-DEC-1954 5:30:15*, this command returns the value 339 for *DAYNUM*.

XDATE.QUARTER(arg) *Return quarter number within a year for a date.* The result is 1, 2, 3, or 4. The date must have occurred after October 14, 1582. To extract the quarter in which *BIRTHDAY* occurred, use the command

```
COMPUTE Q=XDATE.QUARTER(BIRTHDAY).
```

When *BIRTHDAY* equals *5-DEC-1954 05:30:15*, the value of *Q* is 4.

XDATE.WEEK(arg) *Return the week number of a date.* The result is an integer between 1 and 53. The date must have occurred after October 14, 1582. For example, you can extract the week number from *BIRTHDAY*, as in

```
COMPUTE WEEKNUM=XDATE.WEEK(BIRTHDAY).
```

When the value for *BIRTHDAY* is *5-DEC-1954 05:30:15*, this command returns the value 49 for *WEEKNUM*.

XDATE.TDAY(arg) *Return number of days in a time interval or from October 14, 1582.* The value returned is an integer (the fractional portion of a day is ignored). For example, the command

```
COMPUTE NDAYS=XDATE.TDAY(BIRTHDAY).
```

returns the value 135922 when the value for *BIRTHDAY* is *05-DEC-1954 5:30:15*, indicating the number of days between October 14, 1582 and December 5, 1954. The hours, minutes, and seconds are ignored.

XDATE.TIME(arg) *Return time of day from a date.* The result is expressed as the number of elapsed seconds since midnight of that date. For example, when the value for *BIRTHDAY* is *05-DEC-1954 5:30:15*, the command

```
COMPUTE ELSEC=XDATE.TIME(BIRTHDAY).
```

returns the value 19815 for *ELSEC*. If you provide a TIME print format, as in

```
PRINT FORMAT ELSEC(TIME8).
```

the value is displayed as *5:30:15*.

XDATE.DATE(arg) *Return the date portion of a date.* The result is the integral date portion of a date, which is the number of elapsed seconds between midnight October 14, 1582 and midnight of the date in question. The date must have occurred after October 14, 1582. To extract the date from variable *BIRTHDAY*, use

```
COMPUTE BRTHDATE=XDATE.DATE(BIRTHDAY).
```

The value for *BIRTHDATE* can then be displayed as *12/05/54* using ADATE8 format.

Precautions with Date and Time Variables

Dates and times are represented internally as seconds. The numbers for dates are very large, and arithmetic overflows can result. For example, dates in the 20th century are on the order of 10 to the 10th power (11 digits). For that reason, a few precautions are in order:

- Some machine environments cannot accommodate the computation of higher powers of date and time variables. For example, computations higher than the sixth power may cause overflows on some machines.
- The magnitude of the values may cause inaccuracies in some statistical procedures. It is advisable to subtract a fixed date if you want to keep seconds as the unit, or to convert

days using the XDATE.TDAYS function. REGRESSION, CORRELATIONS, ANOVA, and ONEWAY use an adaptive centering method, so their accuracy will not be affected.

- LIST, REPORT, and TABLES are the only procedures that display values in date and time formats. The PRINT and WRITE transformation commands can also display and write date and time formats. However, some summary variables in REPORT and calculated variables in TABLES display in F format, regardless of the print formats of variables used as arguments.
- All other procedures use F format in all cases. The default width and number of decimal places is taken from the print format, but the format type is ignored. For example, in a frequency table, the date 1/09/57 with a print format of DATE9 will be displayed as *11830147200*, not *01-SEP-57*.
- Changing the print format in no way alters the values that are stored. For example, if you assign a print format of DATE9 for a variable read with DATETIME format, the time of day will not display but continues to be part of the value. This means that seemingly identical values can be displayed as separate entries within procedures.

Commands

ACF

```
ACF [VARIABLES=] series names

 [/DIFF={1}]
        {n}

 [/SDIFF={1}]
         {n}

 [/PERIOD=n]

 [/{NOLOG**}]
   {LN     }

 [/SEASONAL]

 [/MXAUTO={16**}]
          {n   }

 [/SERROR={IND**}]
          {MA   }

 [/PACF]

 [/APPLY [='model name']]
```

**Default if the subcommand is omitted and there is no corresponding specification on the TSET command.

Example

```
ACF TICKETS
  /LN
  /DIFF=1
  /SDIFF=1
  /PER=12
  /MXAUTO=50.
```

Overview

ACF displays and plots the sample autocorrelation function of one or more time series. You can also display and plot the autocorrelations of transformed series by requesting natural log and differencing transformations within the procedure.

Options

Modifying the Series. You can request a natural log transformation of the series using the LN subcommand and seasonal and nonseasonal differencing to any degree using the

SDIFF and DIFF subcommands. With seasonal differencing, you can specify the periodicity on the PERIOD subcommand.

Statistical Output. With the MXAUTO subcommand, you can specify the number of lags for which you want autocorrelations displayed and plotted, overriding the maximum specified on TSET. You can also display and plot values only at periodic lags using the SEASONAL subcommand. In addition to autocorrelations, you can display and plot partial autocorrelations using the PACF subcommand.

Method of Calculating Standard Errors. You can specify one of two methods of calculating the standard errors for the autocorrelations on the SERROR subcommand.

Basic Specification

The basic specification is one or more series names.

- For each series specified, ACF automatically displays the autocorrelation value, standard error, Box-Ljung statistic, and probability for each lag.
- ACF plots the autocorrelations and marks the bounds of two standard errors on the plot. By default, ACF displays and plots autocorrelations for up to 16 lags or the number of lags specified on TSET.
- If a method has not been specified on TSET, the default method of calculating the standard error (IND) assumes the process is white noise.

Subcommand Order

- Subcommands can be specified in any order.

Syntax Rules

- VARIABLES can be specified only once.
- Other subcommands can be specified more than once, but only the last specification of each one is executed.

Operations

- Subcommand specifications apply to all series named on the ACF command.
- If the LN subcommand is specified, any differencing requested on that ACF command is done on the log-transformed series.
- Confidence limits are displayed in the plot, marking the bounds of two standard errors at each lag.

Limitations

- Maximum 1 VARIABLES subcommand. There is no limit on the number of series named on the list.

Example

```
ACF TICKETS
  /LN
  /DIFF=1
  /SDIFF=1
  /PER=12
  /MXAUTO=50.
```

- This example produces a plot of the autocorrelation function for the series *TICKETS* after a natural log transformation, differencing, and seasonal differencing have been applied. Along with the plot, the autocorrelation value, standard error, Box-Ljung statistic, and probability are displayed for each lag.
- LN transforms the data using the natural logarithm (base *e*) of the series.
- DIFF differences the series once.
- SDIFF and PERIOD apply one degree of seasonal differencing with a period of 12.
- MXAUTO specifies that the maximum number of lags for which output is to be produced is 50.

VARIABLES Subcommand

VARIABLES specifies the series names and is the only required subcommand. The actual keyword VARIABLES can be omitted.

DIFF Subcommand

DIFF specifies the degree of differencing used to convert a nonstationary series to a stationary one with a constant mean and variance before the autocorrelations are computed.

- You can specify any positive integer on DIFF.
- If DIFF is specified without a value, the default is 1.
- The number of values used in the calculations decreases by 1 for each degree-1 of differencing.

Example

```
ACF SALES
  /DIFF=1.
```

- In this example, the series *SALES* will be differenced once before the autocorrelations are computed and plotted.

SDIFF Subcommand

If the series exhibits a seasonal or periodic pattern, you can use the SDIFF subcommand to seasonally difference the series before obtaining autocorrelations.

- The specification on SDIFF indicates the degree of seasonal differencing and can be any positive integer.
- If SDIFF is specified without a value, the degree of seasonal differencing defaults to 1.
- The number of seasons used in the calculations decreases by 1 for each degree of seasonal differencing.
- The length of the period used by SDIFF is specified on the PERIOD subcommand. If the PERIOD subcommand is not specified, the periodicity established on the TSET or DATE command is used (see the PERIOD subcommand below).

PERIOD Subcommand

PERIOD indicates the length of the period to be used by the SDIFF or SEASONAL subcommands.

- The specification on PERIOD indicates how many observations are in one period or season and can be any positive integer.
- The PERIOD subcommand is ignored if it is used without the SDIFF or SEASONAL subcommands.
- If PERIOD is not specified, the periodicity established on TSET PERIOD is in effect. If TSET PERIOD is not specified, the periodicity established on the DATE command is used. If periodicity was not established anywhere, the SDIFF and SEASONAL subcommands will not be executed.

Example

```
ACF SALES
  /SDIFF=1M
  /PERIOD=12.
```

- This command applies one degree of seasonal differencing with a periodicity (season) of 12 to the series *SALES* before autocorrelations are computed.

LN and NOLOG Subcommands

LN transforms the data using the natural logarithm (base *e*) of the series and is used to remove varying amplitude over time. NOLOG indicates that the data should not be log transformed. NOLOG is the default.

- If you specify LN on an ACF command, any differencing requested on that command will be done on the log-transformed series.
- There are no additional specifications on LN or NOLOG.
- Only the last LN or NOLOG subcommand on an ACF command is executed.

- If a natural log transformation is requested when there are values in the series that are less than or equal to zero, the ACF will not be produced for that series because nonpositive values cannot be log transformed.
- NOLOG is generally used with an APPLY subcommand to turn off a previous LN specification.

Example

```
ACF SALES
  /LN.
```

- This command transforms the series *SALES* using the natural log transformation and then computes and plots autocorrelations.

SEASONAL Subcommand

Use the SEASONAL subcommand to focus attention on the seasonal component by displaying and plotting autocorrelations only at periodic lags.

- There are no additional specifications on SEASONAL.
- If SEASONAL is specified, values are displayed and plotted at the periodic lags indicated on the PERIOD subcommand. If PERIOD is not specified, the periodicity established on the TSET or DATE command is used (see the PERIOD subcommand on p. 70).
- If SEASONAL is not specified, autocorrelations for all lags up to the maximum are displayed and plotted.

Example

```
ACF SALES
  /SEASONAL
  /PERIOD=12.
```

- In this example, autocorrelations are displayed only at every 12th lag.

MXAUTO Subcommand

MXAUTO specifies the maximum number of lags for a series.

- The specification on MXAUTO must be a positive integer.
- If MXAUTO is not specified, the default number of lags is the value set on TSET MXAUTO. If TSET MXAUTO is not specified, the default is 16.
- The value on MXAUTO overrides the value set on TSET MXAUTO.

Example

```
ACF SALES
  /MXAUTO=14.
```

- This command sets the maximum number of autocorrelations to be displayed for series *SALES* to 14.

SERROR Subcommand

SERROR specifies the method of calculating the standard errors for the autocorrelations.

- You must specify either keyword IND or MA on SERROR.
- The method on SERROR overrides the method specified on the TSET ACFSE command.
- If SERROR is not specified, the method indicated on TSET ACFSE is used. If TSET ACFSE is not specified, the default is IND.

IND *Independence model.* The method of calculating the standard errors assumes the underlying process is white noise.

MA *MA model.* The method of calculating the standard errors is based on Bartlett's approximation. With this method, appropriate where the true MA order of the process is k–1, standard errors grow at increased lags (Pankratz, 1983).

Example

```
ACF SALES
  /SERROR=MA.
```

- In this example, the standard errors of the autocorrelations are computed using the MA method.

PACF Subcommand

Use the PACF subcommand to display and plot sample partial autocorrelations as well as autocorrelations for each series named on the ACF command.

- There are no additional specifications on PACF.
- PACF also displays the standard errors of the partial autocorrelations and indicates the bounds of two standard errors on the plot.
- With the exception of SERROR, all other subcommands specified on that ACF command apply to both the partial autocorrelations and the autocorrelations.

Example

```
ACF SALES
  /DIFFERENCE=1
  /PACF.
```

- This command requests both autocorrelations and partial autocorrelations for the series *SALES* after it has been differenced once.

APPLY Subcommand

APPLY allows you to use a previously defined ACF model without having to repeat the specifications.

- The only specification on APPLY is the name of a previous model in quotes. If a model name is not specified, the model specified on the previous ACF command is used.

- To change one or more model specifications, specify the subcommands of only those portions you want to change after the APPLY subcommand.
- If no series are specified on the ACF command, the series that were originally specified with the model being reapplied are used.
- To change the series used with the model, enter new series names before or after the APPLY subcommand.

Example

```
ACF TICKETS
  /LN
  /DIFF=1
  /SDIFF=1
  /PERIOD=12
  /MXAUTO=50.
ACF ROUNDTRP
  /APPLY.
ACF APPLY
  /NOLOG.
ACF APPLY 'MOD_2'
  /PERIOD=6.
```

- The first command requests a maximum of 50 autocorrelations for the series *TICKETS* after it has been natural log transformed, differenced once, and had one degree of seasonal differencing with a periodicity of 12 applied to it. This model is assigned the default name *MOD_1*.
- The second command displays and plots the autocorrelation function for the series *ROUNDTRP* using the same model that was used for the series *TICKETS*. This model is assigned the name *MOD_2*.
- The third command requests another autocorrelation function of the series *ROUNDTRP* using the same model but without the natural log transformation. Note that when APPLY is the first specification after the ACF command, the slash (/) before it is not necessary. This model is assigned the name *MOD_3*.
- The fourth command reapplies *MOD_2*, autocorrelations for the series *ROUNDTRP* with the natural log and differencing specifications, but this time with a periodicity of 6. This model is assigned the name *MOD_4*. It differs from *MOD_2* only in the periodicity.

References

Box, G. E. P., and G. M. Jenkins. 1976. *Time series analysis: Forecasting and control.* San Francisco: Holden-Day.

Pankratz, A. 1983. *Forecasting with univariate Box-Jenkins models: Concepts and cases.* New York: John Wiley and Sons.

ADD FILES

```
ADD FILES FILE={file}
               {*   }

 [/RENAME=(old varnames=new varnames)...]

 [/IN=varname]

 /FILE=... [/RENAME=...] [/IN=...]

 [/BY varlist]

 [/MAP]

 [/KEEP={ALL**   }] [/DROP=varlist]
        {varlist}

 [/FIRST=varname]   [/LAST=varname]
```

**Default if the subcommand is omitted.

Example

```
ADD FILES FILE=SCHOOL1 /FILE=SCHOOL2.
```

Overview

ADD FILES combines cases from 2 up to 50 SPSS-format data files by concatenating or interleaving cases. When cases are **concatenated,** all cases from one file are added to the end of all cases from another file. When cases are **interleaved,** cases in the resulting file are ordered according to the values of one or more key variables.

The files specified on ADD FILES can be SPSS-format data files created by the SAVE or XSAVE commands or the working data file. The combined file becomes the new working file. Statistical procedures following ADD FILES use this combined file unless you replace it by building another working file. You must use the SAVE or XSAVE commands if you want to save the combined file as an SPSS-format data file.

In general, ADD FILES is used to combine files containing the same variables but different cases. To combine files containing the same cases but different variables, use MATCH FILES. To update existing SPSS-format data files, use UPDATE. ADD FILES cannot concatenate raw data files. To concatenate raw data files, use DATA LIST within an INPUT PROGRAM structure (see p. 252 for an example). Alternatively, convert the raw data files to SPSS-format data files with the SAVE or XSAVE commands and then use ADD FILES to combine them.

Options

Variable Selection. You can specify which variables from each input file are included in the new working file using the DROP and KEEP subcommands.

Variable Names. You can rename variables in each input file before combining the files using the RENAME subcommand. This permits you to combine variables that are the same but whose names differ in different input files, or to separate variables that are different but have the same name.

Variable Flag. You can create a variable that indicates whether a case came from a particular input file using IN. When interleaving cases, you can use the FIRST or LAST subcommands to create a variable that flags the first or last case of a group of cases with the same value for the key variable.

Variable Map. You can request a map showing all variables in the new working file, their order, and the input files from which they came using the MAP subcommand.

Basic Specification

- The basic specification is two or more FILE subcommands, each of which specifies a file to be combined. If cases are to be interleaved, the BY subcommand specifying the key variables is also required.
- All variables from all input files are included in the new working file unless DROP or KEEP is specified.

Subcommand Order

- RENAME and IN must immediately follow the FILE subcommand to which they apply.
- BY, FIRST, and LAST must follow all FILE subcommands and their associated RENAME and IN subcommands.

Syntax Rules

- RENAME can be repeated after each FILE subcommand. RENAME applies only to variables in the file named on the FILE subcommand immediately preceding it.
- BY can be specified only once. However, multiple key variables can be specified on BY. When BY is used, all files must be sorted in ascending order by the key variables (see SORT CASES).
- FIRST and LAST can be used only when files are interleaved (when BY is used).
- MAP can be repeated as often as desired.

Operations

- ADD FILES reads all input files named on FILE and builds a new working data file that replaces any working file created earlier in the session. ADD FILES is executed when the data are read by one of the procedure commands or the EXECUTE, SAVE, or SORT CASES commands.

- The resulting file contains complete dictionary information from the input files, including variable names, labels, print and write formats, and missing-value indicators. It also contains the documents from each input file. See DROP DOCUMENTS for information on deleting documents.
- Variables are copied in order from the first file specified, then from the second file specified, and so on. Variables that are not contained in all files receive the system-missing value for cases that do not have values for those variables.
- If the same variable name exists in more than one file but the format type (numeric or string) does not match, the command is not executed.
- If a numeric variable has the same name but different formats (for example, F8.0 and F8.2) in different input files, the format of the variable in the first-named file is used.
- If a string variable has the same name but different formats (for example, A24 and A16) in different input files, the command is not executed.
- If the working file is named as an input file, any N and SAMPLE commands that have been specified are applied to the working file before files are combined.
- If only one of the files is weighted, the program turns weighting off when combining cases from the two files. To weight the cases, use the WEIGHT command again.

Limitations

- Maximum 50 files can be combined on one ADD FILES command.
- The TEMPORARY command cannot be in effect if the working data file is used as an input file.

Examples

```
ADD FILES FILE=SCHOOL1 /FILE=SCHOOL2.
```

- ADD FILES concatenates cases from the SPSS-format data files *SCHOOL1* and SCHOOL2. All cases from *SCHOOL1* precede all cases from *SCHOOL2* in the resulting file.

```
SORT CASES BY LOCATN DEPT.
ADD FILES  FILE=SOURCE /FILE=* /BY LOCATN DEPT
 /KEEP AVGHOUR AVGRAISE LOCATN DEPT SEX HOURLY RAISE /MAP.
SAVE OUTFILE=PRSNNL.
```

- SORT CASES sorts cases in the working file in ascending order of their values for *LOCATN* and *DEPT*.
- ADD FILES combines two files: the SPSS-format data file *SOURCE* and the sorted working file. The file *SOURCE* must also be sorted by *LOCATN* and *DEPT*.
- BY indicates that the keys for interleaving cases are *LOCATN* and *DEPT*, the same variables used on SORT CASES.
- KEEP specifies the variables to be retained in the resulting file.
- MAP produces a list of variables in the resulting file and the two input files.
- SAVE saves the resulting file as a new SPSS-format data file named *PRSNNL*.

FILE Subcommand

FILE identifies the files to be combined. A separate FILE subcommand must be used for each input file.

- An asterisk may be specified on FILE to indicate the working data file.
- The order in which files are named determines the order of cases in the resulting file.

Raw Data Files

To add cases from a raw data file, you must first define the file as the working data file using the DATA LIST command. ADD FILES can then combine the working file with an SPSS-format data file.

Example

```
DATA LIST FILE=GASDATA/1 OZONE 10-12 CO 20-22 SULFUR 30-32.
ADD FILES  FILE=PARTICLE /FILE=*.
SAVE  OUTFILE=POLLUTE.
```

- The *GASDATA* file is a raw data file and is defined on the DATA LIST command.
- The *PARTICLE* file is a previously saved SPSS-format data file.
- FILE=* on ADD FILES specifies the working data file, which contains the gas data. FILE=PARTICLE specifies the SPSS-format data file *PARTICLE*.
- SAVE saves the resulting file as an SPSS-format data file with the filename *POLLUTE*. Cases from the *GASDATA* file follow cases from the *PARTICLE* file.

RENAME Subcommand

RENAME renames variables in input files *before* they are processed by ADD FILES. RENAME follows the FILE subcommand that specifies the file containing the variables to be renamed.

- RENAME applies only to the FILE subcommand immediately preceding it. To rename variables from more than one input file, enter a RENAME subcommand after each FILE subcommand that specifies a file with variables to be renamed.
- Specifications for RENAME consist of a left parenthesis, a list of old variable names, an equals sign, a list of new variable names, and a right parenthesis. The two variable lists must name or imply the same number of variables. If only one variable is renamed, the parentheses are optional.
- More than one such specification can be entered on a single RENAME subcommand, each enclosed in parentheses.
- The TO keyword can be used to refer to consecutive variables in the file and to generate new variable names (see "Keyword TO" on p. 19).
- RENAME takes effect immediately. KEEP and DROP subcommands entered prior to RENAME must use the old names, while those entered after RENAME must use the new names.
- All specifications within a single set of parentheses take effect simultaneously. For example, the specification RENAME (A,B = B,A) swaps the names of the two variables.
- Variables cannot be renamed to scratch variables.

- Input data files are not changed on disk; only the copy of the file being combined is affected.

Example

```
ADD FILES FILE=CLIENTS /RENAME=(TEL_NO, ID_NO = PHONE, ID)
 /FILE=MASTER /BY ID.
```

- ADD FILES adds new client cases from the file *CLIENTS* to existing client cases in the file *MASTER*.
- Two variables on *CLIENTS* are renamed prior to the match. *TEL_NO* is renamed *PHONE* to match the name used for phone numbers in the master file. *ID_NO* is renamed *ID* so that it will have the same name as the identification variable in the master file and can be used on the BY subcommand.
- The BY subcommand orders the resulting file according to client ID number.

BY Subcommand

BY specifies one or more key variables that determine the order of cases in the resulting file. When BY is specified, cases from the input files are interleaved according to their values for the key variables.

- BY must follow the FILE subcommands and any associated RENAME and IN subcommands.
- The key variables specified on BY must be present and have the same names in all input files.
- Key variables can be long or short string variables or numerics.
- All input files must be sorted in ascending order of the key variables. If necessary, use SORT CASES before ADD FILES.
- Cases in the resulting file are ordered by the values of the key variables. All cases from the first file with the first value for the key variable are first, followed by all cases from the second file with the same value, followed by all cases from the third file with the same value, and so forth. These cases are followed by all cases from the first file with the next value for the key variable, and so on.
- Cases with system-missing values are first in the resulting file. User-missing values are interleaved with other values.

DROP and KEEP Subcommands

DROP and KEEP are used to include only a subset of variables in the resulting file. DROP specifies a set of variables to exclude and KEEP specifies a set of variables to retain.

- DROP and KEEP do not affect the input files on disk.
- DROP and KEEP must follow all FILE and RENAME subcommands.
- DROP and KEEP must specify one or more variables. If RENAME is used to rename variables, specify the new names on DROP and KEEP.
- DROP and KEEP take effect immediately. If a variable specified on DROP or KEEP does not exist in the input files, was dropped by a previous DROP subcommand, or was not retained by a previous KEEP subcommand, the program displays an error message and does not execute the ADD FILES command.

- DROP cannot be used with variables created by the IN, FIRST, or LAST subcommands.
- KEEP can be used to change the order of variables in the resulting file. With KEEP, variables are kept in the order they are listed on the subcommand. If a variable is named more than once on KEEP, only the first mention of the variable is in effect; all subsequent references to that variable name are ignored.
- The keyword ALL can be specified on KEEP. ALL must be the last specification on KEEP, and it refers to all variables not previously named on that subcommand. It is useful when you want to arrange the first few variables in a specific order.

Example

```
ADD FILES FILE=PARTICLE /RENAME=(PARTIC=POLLUTE1)
 /FILE=GAS /RENAME=(OZONE TO SULFUR=POLLUTE2 TO POLLUTE4)
 /KEEP=POLLUTE1 POLLUTE2 POLLUTE3 POLLUTE4.
```

- The renamed variables are retained in the resulting file. KEEP is specified after all the FILE and RENAME subcommands, and it refers to the variables by their new names.

IN Subcommand

IN creates a new variable in the resulting file that indicates whether a case came from the input file named on the preceding FILE subcommand. IN applies only to the file specified on the immediately preceding FILE subcommand.

- IN has only one specification, the name of the flag variable.
- The variable created by IN has value 1 for every case that came from the associated input file and value 0 for every case that came from a different input file.
- Variables created by IN are automatically attached to the end of the resulting file and cannot be dropped. If FIRST or LAST are used, the variable created by IN precedes the variables created by FIRST or LAST.

Example

```
ADD FILES  FILE=WEEK10 /FILE=WEEK11 /IN=INWEEK11 /BY=EMPID.
```

- IN creates the variable *INWEEK11*, which has value 1 for all cases in the resulting file that came from the input file *WEEK11* and value 0 for those cases that were not in the file *WEEK11*.

Example

```
ADD FILES  FILE=WEEK10 /FILE=WEEK11 /IN=INWEEK11 /BY=EMPID.
IF  (NOT INWEEK11) SALARY1=0.
```

- The variable created by IN is used to screen partially missing cases for subsequent analyses.
- Since IN variables have either value 1 or 0, they can be used as logical expressions, where 1=true and 0=false. The IF command sets variable *SALARY1* equal to 0 for all cases that came from the file *INWEEK11*.

FIRST and LAST Subcommands

FIRST and LAST create logical variables that flag the first or last case of a group of cases with the same value on the BY variables. FIRST and LAST must follow all FILE subcommands and their associated RENAME and IN subcommands.

- FIRST and LAST have only one specification, the name of the flag variable.
- FIRST creates a variable with value 1 for the first case of each group and value 0 for all other cases.
- LAST creates a variable with value 1 for the last case of each group and value 0 for all other cases.
- Variables created by FIRST and LAST are automatically attached to the end of the resulting file and cannot be dropped.

Example

```
ADD FILES  FILE=SCHOOL1 /FILE=SCHOOL2
 /BY=GRADE /FIRST=HISCORE.
```

- The variable *HISCORE* contains value 1 for the first case in each grade in the resulting file and value 0 for all other cases.

MAP Subcommand

MAP produces a list of the variables included in the new working file and the file or files from which they came. Variables are listed in the order in which they exist in the resulting file. MAP has no specifications and must follow after all FILE and RENAME subcommands.

- Multiple MAP subcommands can be used. Each MAP subcommand shows the current status of the working file and reflects only the subcommands that precede the MAP subcommand.
- To obtain a map of the working data file in its final state, specify MAP last.
- If a variable is renamed, its original and new names are listed. Variables created by IN, FIRST, and LAST are not included in the map, since they are automatically attached to the end of the file and cannot be dropped.

ADD VALUE LABELS

```
ADD VALUE LABELS varlist value 'label' value 'label'...[/varlist...]
```

Example

```
ADD VALUE LABELS JOBGRADE 'P'  'Parttime Employee'
                          'C'  'Customer Support'.
```

Overview

ADD VALUE LABELS adds or alters value labels without affecting other value labels already defined for that variable. In contrast, VALUE LABELS adds or alters value labels but deletes all existing value labels for that variable when it does so.

Basic Specification

The basic specification is a variable name and individual values with associated labels.

Syntax Rules

- Labels can be assigned to values of any previously defined variable. It is not necessary to enter value labels for all of a variable's values.
- Each value label must be enclosed in apostrophes or quotation marks.
- When an apostrophe occurs as part of a label, enclose the label in quotation marks or enter the internal apostrophe twice with no intervening space.
- Value labels can contain any characters, including blanks.
- The same labels can be assigned to the same values of different variables by specifying a list of variable names. For string variables, the variables on the list must have the same defined width (for example, A8).
- Multiple sets of variable names and value labels can be specified on one ADD VALUE LABELS command as long as each set is separated from the previous one by a slash.
- To continue a label from one command line to the next, specify a plus sign (+) before the continuation of the label and enclose each segment of the label, including the blank between them, in apostrophes or quotes.

Operations

- Unlike most transformations, ADD VALUE LABELS takes effect as soon as it is encountered in the command sequence. Thus, special attention should be paid to its position among commands. See "Command Order" on p. 6 for more information.

- The added value labels are stored in the working file dictionary.
- ADD VALUE LABELS can be used for variables that have no previously assigned value labels.
- Adding labels to some values does not affect labels previously assigned to other values.

Limitations

- Value labels cannot exceed 60 characters. Most procedures display only 20 characters.
- Value labels cannot be assigned to long string variables.

Example

```
ADD VALUE LABELS V1 TO V3 1 'Officials & Managers'
                          6 'Service Workers'
                /V4 'N' 'New Employee'.
```

- Labels are assigned to the values 1 and 6 of the variables between and including *V1* and *V3* in the working data file.
- Following the required slash, a label for value N for variable *V4* is specified. N is a string value and must be enclosed in apostrophes or quotation marks.
- If labels already exist for these values, they are changed in the dictionary. If labels do not exist for these values, new labels are added to the dictionary.
- Existing labels for other values for these variables are not affected.

Example

```
ADD VALUE LABELS OFFICE88 1 "EMPLOYEE'S OFFICE ASSIGNMENT PRIOR"
   + " TO 1988".
```

- The label for value 1 for *OFFICE88* is specified on two command lines. The plus sign concatenates the two string segments and a blank is included at the beginning of the second string in order to maintain correct spacing in the label.

Value Labels for String Variables

- For short string variables, the values and the labels must be enclosed in apostrophes or quotation marks.
- If a specified value is longer than the defined width of the variable, the program displays a warning and truncates the value. The added label will be associated with the truncated value.
- If a specified value is shorter than the defined width of the variable, the program adds blanks to right-pad the value without warning. The added label will be associated with the padded value.
- If a single set of labels is to be assigned to a list of string variables, the variables must have the same defined width (for example, A8).

Example

```
ADD VALUE LABELS   STATE 'TEX' 'TEXAS' 'TEN' 'TENNESSEE'
                         'MIN' 'MINNESOTA'.
```

- ADD VALUE LABELS assigns labels to three values of the variable *STATE*. Each value and each label is specified in apostrophes.
- Assuming that the variable *STATE* is defined as three characters wide, the labels *TEXAS*, *TENNESSEE*, and *MINNESOTA* will be appropriately associated with values TEX, TEN, and MIN. However, if *STATE* were defined as two characters wide, the program would truncate the specified values to two characters and would not be able to associate the labels correctly. Both TEX and TEN would be truncated to TE and would first be assigned the label *TEXAS*, which would then be changed to *TENNESSEE* by the second specification.

Example

```
ADD VALUE LABELS=STATE REGION "U" "UNKNOWN".
```

- The label *UNKNOWN* is assigned to value U for both *STATE* and *REGION*.
- *STATE* and *REGION* must have the same defined width. If they do not, a separate specification must be made for each, as in the following:

```
ADD VALUE LABELS STATE "U" "UNKNOWN" / REGION "U" "UNKNOWN".
```

AGGREGATE

```
AGGREGATE OUTFILE={file} [/MISSING=COLUMNWISE] [/DOCUMENT]
                  {*   }

 [/PRESORTED] /BREAK=varlist[({A})][varlist...]
                              {D}

 /aggvar['label']aggvar['label']...=function(arguments)

 [/aggvar ...]
```

Available functions:

SUM	Sum	MEAN	Mean
SD	Standard deviation	MAX	Maximum
MIN	Minimum	PGT	% of cases greater than value
PLT	% of cases less than value	PIN	% of cases between values
POUT	% of cases not in range	FGT	Fraction greater than value
FLT	Fraction less than value	FIN	Fraction between values
FOUT	Fraction not in range	N	Weighted number of cases
NU	Unweighted number of cases	NMISS	Weighted number of missing cases
NUMISS	Unweighted number of missing cases	FIRST	First nonmissing value
LAST	Last nonmissing value	MEDIAN	Median

Example

```
AGGREGATE OUTFILE=AGGEMP /BREAK=LOCATN DEPT /COUNT=N
  /AVGSAL AVGRAISE = MEAN(SALARY RAISE)
  /SUMSAL SUMRAISE = SUM(SALARY RAISE)
  /BLACKPCT 'Percentage Black' = PIN(RACE,1,1)
  /WHITEPCT 'Percentage White' = PIN(RACE,5,5).
```

Overview

AGGREGATE aggregates groups of cases in the working data file into single cases and creates a new, aggregated file. The values of one or more variables in the working file define the case groups. These variables are called **break variables.** A set of cases with identical values for each break variable is called a **break group.** A series of aggregate functions are applied to **source variables** in the working file to create new, aggregated variables that have one value for each break group.

AGGREGATE is often used with MATCH FILES to add variables with summary measures (sum, mean, etc.) to a file. Transformations performed on the combined file can create composite summary measures. With the REPORT procedure, the composite variables can be used to write reports with nested composite information.

Options

Aggregated File. You can produce either an SPSS-format data file or a new working file.

Documentary Text. You can copy documentary text from the original file into the aggregated file using the DOCUMENT subcommand. By default, documentary text is dropped.

Sorting. By default, cases in the aggregated file are sorted in ascending order of the values of each break variable. Alternatively, you can specify descending order. If the working file is already sorted by the break variables, you can skip this final sorting pass through the file using the PRESORTED subcommand.

Aggregated Variables. You can create aggregated variables using any of 19 aggregate functions. The functions SUM, MEAN, and SD can aggregate only numeric variables. All other functions can use both numeric and string variables.

Labels and Formats. You can specify variable labels for the aggregated variables. Variables created with the functions MAX, MIN, FIRST, and LAST assume the formats and value labels of their source variables. All other variables assume the default formats described under "Aggregate Functions" on p. 88.

Basic Specification

The basic specification is OUTFILE, BREAK, and at least one aggregate function and source variable. OUTFILE specifies a name for the aggregated file. BREAK names the case grouping (break) variables. The aggregate function creates a new aggregated variable.

Subcommand Order

- OUTFILE must be specified first.
- If specified, DOCUMENT and PRESORTED must precede BREAK. No other subcommand can be specified between these two subcommands.
- MISSING, if specified, must immediately follow OUTFILE.
- The aggregate functions must be specified last.

Operations

- When AGGREGATE produces an SPSS-format data file, the working file remains unchanged and is still available for analysis. When AGGREGATE creates a new working file, it replaces the old working file. Only the new working file is available for analysis.
- The aggregated file contains the break variables plus the variables created by the aggregate functions.
- AGGREGATE excludes cases with missing values from all aggregate calculations except those involving functions N, NU, NMISS, and NUMISS.
- Unless otherwise specified, AGGREGATE sorts cases in the aggregated file in ascending order of the values of the grouping variables.

- If PRESORTED is specified, a new aggregate case is created each time a different value or combination of values is encountered on variables named on the BREAK subcommand.
- AGGREGATE ignores split-file processing. To achieve the same effect, name the variable or variables used to split the file as break variables before any other break variables. AGGREGATE produces one file, but the aggregated cases are in the same order as the split files.

Example

```
AGGREGATE OUTFILE=AGGEMP /BREAK=LOCATN DEPT
 /COUNT=N
 /AVGSAL AVGRAISE = MEAN(SALARY RAISE)
 /SUMSAL SUMRAISE = SUM(SALARY RAISE)
 /BLACKPCT 'Percentage Black' = PIN(RACE,1,1)
 /WHITEPCT 'Percentage White' = PIN(RACE,5,5).
```

- AGGREGATE creates a new SPSS-format data file *AGGEMP*. *AGGEMP* contains two break variables (*LOCATN* and *DEPT*) and all the new aggregate variables (*COUNT*, *AVGSAL*, *AVGRAISE*, *SUMSAL*, *SUMRAISE*, *BLACKPCT*, and *WHITEPCT*).
- BREAK specifies *LOCATN* and *DEPT* as the break variables. In the aggregated file, cases are sorted in ascending order of *LOCATN* and in ascending order of *DEPT* within *LOCATN*. The working data file remains unsorted.
- Variable *COUNT* is created as the weighted number of cases in each break group. *AVGSAL* is the mean of *SALARY* and *AVGRAISE* is the mean of *RAISE*. *SUMSAL* is the sum of *SALARY* and *SUMRAISE* is the sum of *RAISE*. *BLACKPCT* is the percentage of cases with value 1 for *RACE*. *WHITEPCT* is the percentage of cases with value 5 for *RACE*.

Example

```
GET FILE=HUBEMPL /KEEP=LOCATN DEPT HOURLY RAISE SEX.
AGGREGATE OUTFILE=AGGFILE /BREAK=LOCATN DEPT
 /AVGHOUR AVGRAISE=MEAN(HOURLY RAISE).
SORT CASES BY LOCATN DEPT.
MATCH FILES  TABLE=AGGFILE /FILE=* /BY LOCATN DEPT
 /KEEP AVGHOUR AVGRAISE LOCATN DEPT SEX HOURLY RAISE /MAP.

COMPUTE HOURDIF=HOURLY/AVGHOUR.
COMPUTE RAISEDIF=RAISE/AVGRAISE.
LIST.
```

- GET reads the SPSS-format data file *HUBEMPL* and keeps a subset of variables.
- AGGREGATE creates a file aggregated by *LOCATN* and *DEPT* with the two new variables *AVGHOUR* and *AVGRAISE*, containing the means by location and department for *HOURLY* and *RAISE*. The aggregated file is saved as an SPSS-format data file named *AGGFILE*. Only the aggregated data file *AGGFILE* is sorted by *LOCATN* and *DEPT*; the working data file remains unchanged.
- SORT CASES sorts the working data file in ascending order of *LOCATN* and *DEPT*, the same variables used as AGGREGATE break variables.

- MATCH FILES specifies a table lookup match with *AGGFILE* as the table file and the sorted working data file as the case file.
- BY indicates that the keys for the match are *LOCATN* and *DEPT*.
- KEEP specifies the subset and order of variables to be retained in the resulting file.
- MAP provides a listing of the variables in the resulting file and the two input files.
- The COMPUTE commands calculate the ratios of each employee's hourly wage and raise to the department averages for wage and raise. The results are stored in the variables *HOURDIF* and *RAISEDIF*.
- LIST displays the resulting file.

OUTFILE Subcommand

OUTFILE specifies a name for the file created by AGGREGATE. If an asterisk is specified on OUTFILE, the aggregated file replaces the working file. OUTFILE must be the first subcommand specified on AGGREGATE.

- If the aggregated file replaces the working file, the file is not automatically saved on disk. To save the file, use the SAVE command.

Example

```
AGGREGATE OUTFILE=AGGEMP
 /BREAK=LOCATN
 /AVGSAL = MEAN(SALARY).
```

- OUTFILE creates an SPSS-format data file named *AGGEMP*. The working file remains unchanged and is available for further analysis.
- The file *AGGEMP* contains two variables, *LOCATN* and *AVGSAL*.

BREAK Subcommand

BREAK lists the grouping variables, also called break variables. Each unique combination of values of the break variables defines one break group.

- The variables named on BREAK can be any combination of variables in the working data file.
- Unless PRESORTED is specified, AGGREGATE sorts cases after aggregating. By default, cases are sorted in ascending order of the values of the break variables. AGGREGATE sorts first on the first break variable, then on the second break variable within the groups created by the first, and so on.
- Sort order can be controlled by specifying an A (for ascending) or D (for descending) in parentheses after any break variables.
- The designations A and D apply to all preceding undesignated variables.
- The subcommand PRESORTED overrides all sorting specifications.

Example

```
AGGREGATE OUTFILE=AGGEMP
 /BREAK=LOCATN DEPT (A) TENURE (D)
 /AVGSAL = MEAN(SALARY).
```

- BREAK names the variables *LOCATN*, *DEPT*, and *TENURE* as the break variables.
- Cases in the aggregated file are sorted in ascending order of *LOCATN*, in ascending order of *DEPT* within *LOCATN*, and in descending order of *TENURE* within *LOCATN* and *DEPT*. For each group defined by these variables, *AVGSAL* is computed as the mean of salary.

DOCUMENT Subcommand

DOCUMENT copies documentation from the original file into the aggregated file. By default, documents are dropped from the aggregated file, whether the file is the working file or an SPSS-format data file. DOCUMENT must appear after OUTFILE but before BREAK.

PRESORTED Subcommand

PRESORTED indicates that cases in the working data file are sorted according to the values of the break variables. This prevents AGGREGATE from sorting cases that have already been sorted and can save a considerable amount of processing time.

- If specified, PRESORTED must precede BREAK. The only specification is the keyword PRESORTED. PRESORTED has no additional specifications.
- When PRESORTED is specified, the program forms an aggregate case out of each group of *adjacent* cases with the same values for the break variables.
- If the working file is not sorted by the break variables in ascending order and PRESORTED is specified, a warning message is generated but the procedure is executed. Each group of adjacent cases with the same values for break variables forms a case in the aggregated file, which may produce multiple cases with the same values for the break variables.

Example

```
AGGREGATE OUTFILE=AGGEMP
 /PRESORTED
 /BREAK=LOCATN DEPT
 /AVGSAL = MEAN(SALARY).
```

- PRESORTED indicates that cases are already sorted by the variables *LOCATN* and *DEPT*.
- AGGREGATE does not make an extra data pass to sort the cases.

Aggregate Functions

An aggregated variable is created by applying an aggregate function to a variable in the working file. The variable in the working file is called the **source** variable, and the new aggregated variable is the **target** variable.

- The aggregate functions must be specified last on AGGREGATE.

- The simplest specification is a target variable list, followed by an equals sign, a function name, and a list of source variables.
- The number of target variables named must match the number of source variables.
- When several aggregate variables are defined at once, the first-named target variable is based on the first-named source variable, the second-named target is based on the second-named source, and so on.
- Only the functions MAX, MIN, FIRST, and LAST copy complete dictionary information from the source variable. For all other functions, new variables do not have labels and are assigned default dictionary print and write formats. The default format for a variable depends on the function used to create it (see the list of available functions below).
- You can provide a variable label for a new variable by specifying the label in apostrophes immediately following the new variable name. Value labels cannot be assigned in AGGREGATE.
- To change formats or add value labels to a working data file created by AGGREGATE, use the PRINT FORMATS, WRITE FORMATS, FORMATS, or VALUE LABELS commands. If the aggregate file is written to disk, first retrieve the file using GET, specify the new labels and formats, and resave the file.

The following is a list of available functions:

SUM(varlist) *Sum across cases.* Default formats are F8.2.

MEAN(varlist) *Mean across cases.* Default formats are F8.2.

MEDIAN(varlist) *Median across cases.* Default formats are F8.2.

SD(varlist) *Standard deviation across cases.* Default formats are F8.2.

MAX(varlist) *Maximum value across cases.* Complete dictionary information is copied from the source variables to the target variables.

MIN(varlist) *Minimum value across cases.* Complete dictionary information is copied from the source variables to the target variables.

PGT(varlist,value) *Percentage of cases greater than the specified value.* Default formats are F5.1.

PLT(varlist,value) *Percentage of cases less than the specified value.* Default formats are F5.1.

PIN(varlist,value1,value2) *Percentage of cases between value1 and value2, inclusive.* Default formats are F5.1.

POUT(varlist,value1,value2) *Percentage of cases not between value1 and value2.* Cases where the source variable equals value1 or value2 are not counted. Default formats are F5.1.

FGT(varlist,value) *Fraction of cases greater than the specified value.* Default formats are F5.3.

FLT(varlist,value) *Fraction of cases less than the specified value.* Default formats are F5.3.

FIN(varlist,value1,value2) *Fraction of cases between value1 and value2, inclusive.* Default formats are F5.3.

FOUT(varlist,value1,value2) *Fraction of cases not between value1 and value2.* Cases where the source variable equals value1 or value2 are not counted. Default formats are F5.3.

N(varlist) *Weighted number of cases in break group.* Default formats are F7.0 for unweighted files and F8.2 for weighted files.

NU(varlist) *Unweighted number of cases in break group.* Default formats are F7.0.

NMISS(varlist) *Weighted number of missing cases.* Default formats are F7.0 for unweighted files and F8.2 for weighted files.

NUMISS(varlist) *Unweighted number of missing cases.* Default formats are F7.0.

FIRST(varlist) *First nonmissing observed value in break group.* Complete dictionary information is copied from the source variables to the target variables.

LAST(varlist) *Last nonmissing observed value in break group.* Complete dictionary information is copied from the source variables to the target variables.

- The functions SUM, MEAN, and SD can be applied only to numeric source variables. All other functions can use short and long string variables as well as numeric ones.
- The N and NU functions do not require arguments. Without arguments, they return the number of weighted and unweighted valid cases in a break group. If you supply a variable list, they return the number of weighted and unweighted valid cases for the variables specified.
- For several functions, the argument includes values as well as a source variable designation. Either blanks or commas can be used to separate the components of an argument list.
- For PIN, POUT, FIN, and FOUT, the first value should be less than or equal to the second. If the first is greater, AGGREGATE automatically reverses them and prints a warning message. If the two values are equal, PIN and FIN calculate the percentages and fractions of values equal to the argument. POUT and FOUT calculate the percentages and fractions of values not equal to the argument.
- String values specified in an argument should be enclosed in apostrophes. They are evaluated in alphabetical order.

Example

```
AGGREGATE OUTFILE=AGGEMP /BREAK=LOCATN
 /AVGSAL 'Average Salary' AVGRAISE = MEAN(SALARY RAISE).
```

- AGGREGATE defines two aggregate variables, *AVGSAL* and *AVGRAISE*.
- *AVGSAL* is the mean of *SALARY* for each break group, and *AVGRAISE* is the mean of *RAISE*.
- The label *Average Salary* is assigned to *AVGSAL*.

Example

```
AGGREGATE OUTFILE=* /BREAK=DEPT
 /LOWVAC,LOWSICK = PLT (VACDAY SICKDAY,10).
```

- AGGREGATE creates two aggregated variables: *LOWVAC* and *LOWSICK*. *LOWVAC* is the percentage of cases with values less than 10 for *VACDAY* and *LOWSICK* is the percentage of cases with values less than 10 for *SICKDAY*.

Example

```
AGGREGATE OUTFILE=GROUPS /BREAK=OCCGROUP
 /COLLEGE = FIN(EDUC,13,16).
```

- AGGREGATE creates the variable *COLLEGE*, which is the fraction of cases with 13 to 16 years of education (variable *EDUC*).

Example

```
AGGREGATE OUTFILE=* /BREAK=CLASS
 /LOCAL = PIN(STATE,'IL','IO').
```

- AGGREGATE creates the variable *LOCAL*, which is the percentage of cases in each break group whose two-letter state code represents Illinois, Indiana, or Iowa. (The abbreviation for Indiana, IN, is between IL and IO in an alphabetical sort sequence.)

MISSING Subcommand

By default, AGGREGATE uses all nonmissing values of the source variable to calculate aggregated variables. An aggregated variable will have a missing value only if the source variable is missing for every case in the break group. You can alter the default missing-value treatment by using the MISSING subcommand. You can also specify the inclusion of user-missing values on any function.

- MISSING must immediately follow OUTFILE.
- COLUMNWISE is the only specification available for MISSING.
- If COLUMNWISE is specified, the value of an aggregated variable is missing for a break group if the source variable is missing for any case in the group.
- COLUMNWISE does not affect the calculation of the N, NU, NMISS, or NUMISS functions.
- COLUMNWISE does not apply to break variables. If a break variable has a missing value, cases in that group are processed and the break variable is saved in the file with the missing value. Use SELECT IF if you want to eliminate cases with missing values for the break variables.

Including Missing Values

You can force a function to include user-missing values in its calculations by specifying a period after the function name.

- AGGREGATE ignores periods used with functions N, NU, NMISS, and NUMISS if these functions have no argument.

- User-missing values are treated as valid when these four functions are followed by a period and have a variable as an argument. NMISS.(AGE) treats user-missing values as valid and thus gives the number of cases for which *AGE* has the system-missing value only.

The effect of specifying a period with N, NU, NMISS, and NUMISS is illustrated by the following:

N = N. = N(AGE) + NMISS(AGE) = N.(AGE) + NMISS.(AGE)

NU = NU. = NU(AGE) + NUMISS(AGE) = NU.(AGE) + NUMISS.(AGE)

- The function N (the same as N. with no argument) yields a value for each break group that equals the number of cases with valid values (N(AGE)) plus the number of cases with user- or system-missing values (NMISS(AGE)).
- This in turn equals the number of cases with either valid or user-missing values (N.(AGE)) plus the number with system-missing values (NMISS.(AGE)).
- The same identities hold for the NU, NMISS, and NUMISS functions.

Example

```
AGGREGATE OUTFILE=AGGEMP /MISSING=COLUMNWISE /BREAK=LOCATN
 /AVGSAL = MEAN(SALARY).
```

- *AVGSAL* is missing for an aggregated case if *SALARY* is missing for any case in the break group.

Example

```
AGGREGATE OUTFILE=* /BREAK=DEPT
 /LOVAC = PLT.(VACDAY,10).
```

- *LOVAC* is the percentage of cases within each break group with values less than 10 for *VACDAY*, even if some of those values are defined as user-missing.

Example

```
AGGREGATE OUTFILE=CLASS /BREAK=GRADE
  /FIRSTAGE = FIRST.(AGE).
```

- The first value of *AGE* in each break group is assigned to the variable *FIRSTAGE*.
- If the first value of *AGE* in a break group is user missing, that value will be assigned to *FIRSTAGE*. However, the value will retain its missing-value status, since variables created with FIRST take dictionary information from their source variables.

Comparing Missing-Value Treatments

Table 1 demonstrates the effects of specifying the MISSING subcommand and a period after the function name. Each entry in the table is the number of cases used to compute the specified function for the variable *EDUC*, which has 10 nonmissing cases, 5 user-missing cases, and 2 system-missing cases for the group. Note that columnwise treatment produces the same results as the default for every function except the MEAN function.

Table 1 Default versus columnwise missing-value treatments

Function	Default	Columnwise
N	17	17
N.	17	17
N(EDUC)	10	10
N.(EDUC)	15	15
MEAN(EDUC)	10	0
MEAN.(EDUC)	15	0
NMISS(EDUC)	7	7
NMISS.(EDUC)	2	2

ALSCAL

```
ALSCAL  VARIABLES=varlist

 [/FILE=file]   [CONFIG   [({INITIAL})]]   [ROWCONF [({INITIAL})]]
                           {FIXED  }                  {FIXED  }

                [COLCONF [({INITIAL})]]   [SUBJWGHT[({INITIAL})]]
                          {FIXED  }                  {FIXED  }

                [STIMWGHT[({INITIAL})]]
                          {FIXED  }

 [/INPUT=ROWS  ({ALL**})]
                { n   }

 [/SHAPE={SYMMETRIC**}]
         {ASYMMETRIC }
         {RECTANGULAR}

 [/LEVEL={ORDINAL**   [([UNTIE]  [SIMILAR])]}]
         {INTERVAL[({1})]                   }
         {          {n}                     }
         {RATIO[({1})]                      }
         {       {n}                        }
         {NOMINAL                           }

 [/CONDITION={MATRIX**       }]
             {ROW            }
             {UNCONDITIONAL  }

 [/{MODEL }={EUCLID**}]
   {METHOD} {INDSCAL }
            {ASCAL   }
            {AINDS   }
            {GEMSCAL }

 [/CRITERIA=[NEGATIVE]  [CUTOFF({0**})]  [CONVERGE({.001})]
                                { n }              {  n }

        [ITER({30})]  [STRESSMIN({.005})]  [NOULB]
              {n }               { n  }

        [DIMENS({2**       })]  [DIRECTIONS(n)]
                {min[,max] }

        [CONSTRAIN]   [TIESTORE(n)]]

 [/PRINT=[DATA]  [HEADER]]      [/PLOT=[DEFAULT]  [ALL]]

 [/OUTFILE=file]

 [/MATRIX=IN({file})]
             { *  }
```

**Default if the subcommand or keyword is omitted.

Example

```
ALSCAL VARIABLES=ATLANTA TO TAMPA.
```

ALSCAL was originally designed and programmed by Forrest W. Young, Yoshio Takane, and Rostyslaw J. Lewyckyj of the Psychometric Laboratory, University of North Carolina.

Overview

ALSCAL uses an alternating least-squares algorithm to perform multidimensional scaling (MDS) and multidimensional unfolding (MDU). You can select one of the five models to obtain stimulus coordinates and/or weights in multidimensional space.

Options

Data Input. You can read inline data matrices, including all types of two- or three-way data, such as a single matrix or a matrix for each of several subjects, using the INPUT subcommand. You can read square (symmetrical or asymmetrical) or rectangular matrices of proximities with the SHAPE subcommand and proximity matrices created by PROXIMITIES and CLUSTER with the MATRIX subcommand. You can also read a file of coordinates and/or weights to provide initial or fixed values for the scaling process with the FILE subcommand.

Methodological Assumptions. You can specify data as matrix-conditional, row-conditional, or unconditional on the CONDITION subcommand. You can treat data as nonmetric (nominal or ordinal) or as metric (interval or ratio) using the LEVEL subcommand. You can also use LEVEL to identify ordinal-level proximity data as measures of similarity or dissimilarity and can specify tied observations as untied (continuous) or leave them tied (discrete).

Model Selection. You can specify most commonly used multidimensional scaling models by selecting the correct combination of ALSCAL subcommands, keywords, and criteria. In addition to the default Euclidean distance model, the MODEL subcommand offers the individual differences (weighted) Euclidean distance model (INDSCAL), the asymmetric Euclidean distance model (ASCAL), the asymmetric individual differences Euclidean distance model (AINDS), and the generalized Euclidean metric individual differences model (GEMSCAL).

Output. You can produce output that includes raw and scaled input data, missing-value patterns, normalized data with means, squared data with additive constants, each subject's scalar product and individual weight space, plots of linear or nonlinear fit, and plots of the data transformations using the PRINT and PLOT subcommands.

Basic Specification

The basic specification is VARIABLES followed by a variable list. By default, ALSCAL produces a two-dimensional nonmetric Euclidean multidimensional scaling solution. Input is assumed to be one or more square symmetric matrices with data elements that are dissimilarities at the ordinal level of measurement. Ties are not untied, and conditionality is by subject. Values less than 0 are treated as missing. The default output includes the improvement in Young's S-stress for successive iterations, two measures of fit for each input matrix (Kruskal's stress and the squared correlation, RSQ), and the derived configurations for each of the dimensions.

Subcommand Order

Subcommands can be named in any order.

Operations

- ALSCAL calculates the number of input matrices by dividing the total number of observations in the data set by the number of rows in each matrix. All matrices must contain the same number of rows. This number is determined by the settings on SHAPE and INPUT (if used). For square matrix data, the number of rows in the matrix equals the number of variables. For rectangular matrix data, it equals the number of rows specified or implied. For additional information, see the INPUT and SHAPE subcommands below.
- ALSCAL ignores user-missing specifications in all variables in the configuration/weights file (see the FILE subcommand on p. 99). The system-missing value is converted to 0.
- With split-file data, ALSCAL reads initial or fixed configurations from the configuration/weights file for each split-file group (see the FILE subcommand on p. 99). If there is only one initial configuration in the file, ALSCAL rereads these initial or fixed values for successive split-file groups.
- By default, ALSCAL estimates upper and lower bounds on missing values in the working data file in order to compute the initial configuration. To prevent this, specify CRITERIA=NOULB. Missing values are always ignored during the iterative process.

Limitations

- Maximum 100 variables on the VARIABLES subcommand.
- Maximum six dimensions can be scaled.
- ALSCAL does not recognize data weights created by the WEIGHT command.
- ALSCAL analyses can include no more than 32,767 values in each of the input matrices. Large analyses may require significant computing time.

Example

```
* Air distances among U.S. cities.
* Data are from Johnson and Wichern (1982), page 563.
DATA LIST
 /ATLANTA BOSTON CINCNATI COLUMBUS DALLAS INDNPLIS
   LITTROCK LOSANGEL MEMPHIS STLOUIS SPOKANE TAMPA 1-60.
BEGIN DATA
   0
1068    0
 461  867    0
 549  769  107    0
 805 1819  943 1050    0
 508  941  108  172  882    0
 505 1494  618  725  325  562    0
2197 3052 2186 2245 1403 2080 1701    0
 366 1355  502  586  464  436  137 1831    0
 558 1178  338  409  645  234  353 1848  294    0
2467 2747 2067 2131 1891 1959 1988 1227 2042 1820    0
 467 1379  928  985 1077  975  912 2480  779 1016 2821    0
END DATA.

ALSCAL VARIABLES=ATLANTA TO TAMPA
 /PLOT.
```

- By default, ALSCAL assumes a symmetric matrix of dissimilarities for ordinal-level variables. Only values below the diagonal are used. The upper triangle can be left blank. The 12 cities form the rows and columns of the matrix.
- The result is a classical MDS analysis that reproduces a map of the United States when the output is rotated to a north-south by east-west orientation.

VARIABLES Subcommand

VARIABLES identifies the columns in the proximity matrix or matrices that ALSCAL reads.

- VARIABLES is required and can name only numeric variables.
- Each matrix must have at least four rows and four columns.

INPUT Subcommand

ALSCAL reads data row by row, with each case in the working data file representing a single row in the data matrix. (VARIABLES specifies the columns.) Use INPUT when reading rectangular data matrices to specify how many rows are in each matrix.

- The specification on INPUT is ROWS. If INPUT is not specified or is specified without ROWS, the default is ROWS(ALL). ALSCAL assumes that each case in the working data file represents one row of a single input matrix, and the result is a square matrix.
- You can specify the number of rows (*n*) in each matrix in parentheses after the keyword ROWS. The number of matrices equals the number of observations divided by the number specified.
- The number specified on ROWS must be at least 4 and must divide evenly into the total number of rows in the data.
- With split-file data, *n* refers to the number of cases in each split-file group. All split-file groups must have the same number of rows.

Example

```
ALSCAL VARIABLES=V1 to V7 /INPUT=ROWS(8).
```

- INPUT indicates that there are eight rows per matrix, with each case in the working data file representing one row.
- The total number of cases must be divisible by 8.

SHAPE Subcommand

Use SHAPE to specify the structure of the input data matrix or matrices.

- You can specify one of the three keywords listed below.
- Both SYMMETRIC and ASYMMETRIC refer to square matrix data.

SYMMETRIC *Symmetric data matrix or matrices.* For a symmetric matrix, ALSCAL looks only at the values below the diagonal. Values on and above the diagonal can be omitted. This is the default.

ASYMMETRIC *Asymmetric data matrix or matrices.* The corresponding values in the upper and lower triangles are not all equal. The diagonal is ignored.

RECTANGULAR *Rectangular data matrix or matrices.* The rows and columns represent different sets of items.

Example

```
ALSCAL VAR=V1 TO V8 /SHAPE=RECTANGULAR.
```

- ALSCAL performs a classical MDU analysis, treating the rows and columns as separate sets of items.

LEVEL Subcommand

LEVEL identifies the level of measurement for the values in the data matrix or matrices. You can specify one of the keywords defined below.

ORDINAL *Ordinal-level data.* This specification is the default. It treats the data as ordinal, using Kruskal's (1964) least-squares monotonic transformation. The analysis is nonmetric. By default, the data are treated as discrete dissimilarities. Ties in the data remain tied throughout the analysis. To change the default, specify UNTIE and/or SIMILAR in parentheses. UNTIE treats the data as continuous and resolves ties in an optimal fashion; SIMILAR treats the data as similarities. UNTIE and SIMILAR cannot be used with the other levels of measurement.

INTERVAL(n) *Interval-level data.* This specification produces a metric analysis of the data using classical regression techniques. You can specify any integer from 1 to 4 in parentheses for the degree of polynomial transformation to be fit to the data. The default is 1.

RATIO(n) *Ratio-level data.* This specification produces a metric analysis. You can specify an integer from 1 to 4 in parentheses for the degree of polynomial transformation. The default is 1.

NOMINAL *Nominal-level data.* This specification treats the data as nominal by using a least-squares categorical transformation (Takane et al., 1977). This option produces a nonmetric analysis of nominal data. It is useful when there are few observed categories, when there are many observations in each category, and when the order of the categories is not known.

Example

```
ALSCAL VAR=ATLANTA TO TAMPA /LEVEL=INTERVAL(2).
```

- This example identifies the distances between U.S. cities as interval-level data. The 2 in parentheses indicates a polynomial transformation with linear and quadratic terms.

CONDITION Subcommand

CONDITION specifies which numbers in a data set are comparable.

MATRIX *Only numbers within each matrix are comparable.* If each matrix represents a different subject, this specification makes comparisons conditional by subject. This is the default.

ROW *Only numbers within the same row are comparable.* This specification is appropriate only for asymmetric or rectangular data. They cannot be used when ASCAL or AINDS is specified on MODEL.

UNCONDITIONAL *All numbers are comparable.* Comparisons can be made among any values in the input matrix or matrices.

Example

```
ALSCAL VAR=V1 TO V8 /SHAPE=RECTANGULAR /CONDITION=ROW.
```

- ALSCAL performs a Euclidean MDU analysis conditional on comparisons within rows.

FILE Subcommand

ALSCAL can read proximity data from the working data file or, with the MATRIX subcommand, from a matrix data file created by PROXIMITIES or CLUSTER. The FILE subcommand reads a file containing additional data: an initial or fixed configuration for the coordinates of the stimuli and/or weights for the matrices being scaled. This file can be created with the OUTFILE subcommand on ALSCAL or with an SPSS input program.

- The minimum specification is the file that contains the configurations and/or weights.
- FILE can include additional specifications that define the structure of the configuration/weights file.
- The variables in the configuration/weights file that correspond to successive ALSCAL dimensions must have the names *DIM1*, *DIM2*,...*DIMr*, where *r* is the maximum number of ALSCAL dimensions. The file must also contain the short string variable *TYPE_* to identify the types of values in all rows.
- Values for the variable *TYPE_* can be CONFIG, ROWCONF, COLCONF, SUBJWGHT, and STIMWGHT, in that order. Each value can be truncated to the first three letters. Stimulus coordinate values are specified as CONFIG; row stimulus coordinates as ROWCONF; column stimulus coordinates as COLCONF; and subject and stimulus weights as SUBJWGHT and STIMWGHT, respectively. ALSCAL accepts CONFIG and ROWCONF interchangeably.
- ALSCAL skips unneeded types as long as they appear in the file in their proper order. Generalized weights (GEM) and flattened subject weights (FLA) cannot be initialized or fixed and will always be skipped. (These weights can be generated by ALSCAL but cannot be used as input.)

The following list summarizes the optional specifications that can be used on FILE to define the structure of the configuration/weights file:

- Each specification can be further identified with option INITIAL or FIXED in parentheses.

- INITIAL is the default. INITIAL indicates that the external configuration or weights are to be used as initial coordinates and are to be modified during each iteration.
- FIXED forces ALSCAL to use the externally defined structure without modification to calculate the best values for all unfixed portions of the structure.

CONFIG *Read stimulus configuration.* The configuration/weights file contains initial stimulus coordinates. Input of this type is appropriate when SHAPE=SYMMETRIC or SHAPE=ASYMMETRIC, or when the number of variables in a matrix equals the number of variables on the ALSCAL command. The value of the *TYPE_* variable must be either CON or ROW for all stimulus coordinates for the configuration.

ROWCONF *Read row stimulus configuration.* The configuration/weights file contains initial row stimulus coordinates. This specification is appropriate if SHAPE=RECTANGULAR and if the number of ROWCONF rows in the matrix equals the number of rows specified on the INPUT subcommand (or, if INPUT is omitted, the number of cases in the working data file). The value of *TYPE_* must be either ROW or CON for the set of coordinates for each row.

COLCONF *Read column stimulus configuration.* The configuration/weights file contains initial column stimulus coordinates. This kind of file can be used only if SHAPE=RECTANGULAR and if the number of COLCONF rows in the matrix equals the number of variables on the ALSCAL command. The value of *TYPE_* must be COL for the set of coordinates for each column.

SUBJWGHT *Read subject (matrix) weights.* The configuration/weights file contains subject weights. The number of observations in a subject-weights matrix must equal the number of matrices in the proximity file. Subject weights can be used only if the model is INDSCAL, AINDS, or GEMSCAL. The value of *TYPE_* for each set of weights must be SUB.

STIMWGHT *Read stimulus weights.* The configuration/weights file contains stimulus weights. The number of observations in the configuration/weights file must equal the number of matrices in the proximity file. Stimulus weights can be used only if the model is AINDS or ASCAL. The value of *TYPE_* for each set of weights must be STI.

If the optional specifications for the configuration/weights file are not specified on FILE, ALSCAL sequentially reads the *TYPE_* values appropriate to the model and shape according to the defaults in Table 1.

Example

```
ALSCAL VAR=V1 TO V8 /FILE=ONE CON(FIXED) STI(INITIAL).
```

- ALSCAL reads the configuration/weights file *ONE*.
- The stimulus coordinates are read as fixed values, and the stimulus weights are read as initial values.

Table 1 Default specifications for the FILE subcommand

Shape	Model	Default specifications
SYMMETRIC	EUCLID	CONFIG (or ROWCONF)
	INDSCAL	CONFIG (or ROWCONF) SUBJWGHT
	GEMSCAL	CONFIG (or ROWCONF) SUBJWGHT
ASYMMETRIC	EUCLID	CONFIG (or ROWCONF)
	INDSCAL	CONFIG (or ROWCONF) SUBJWGHT
	GEMSCAL	CONFIG (or ROWCONF) SUBJWGHT
	ASCAL	CONFIG (or ROWCONF) STIMWGHT
	AINDS	CONFIG (or ROWCONF) SUBJWGHT STIMWGHT
RECTANGULAR	EUCLID	ROWCONF (or CONFIG) COLCONF
	INDSCAL	ROWCONF (or CONFIG) COLCONF SUBJWGHT
	GEMSCAL	ROWCONF (or CONFIG) COLCONF SUBJWGHT

MODEL Subcommand

MODEL (alias METHOD) defines the scaling model for the analysis. The only specification is MODEL (or METHOD) and any one of the five scaling and unfolding model types. EUCLID is the default.

EUCLID *Euclidean distance model.* This model can be used with any type of proximity matrix and is the default.

INDSCAL *Individual differences (weighted) Euclidean distance model.* ALSCAL scales the data using the weighted individual differences Euclidean distance model proposed by Carroll and Chang (1970). This type of analysis can be specified only if the analysis involves more than one data matrix and more than one dimension is specified on CRITERIA.

ASCAL *Asymmetric Euclidean distance model.* This model (Young, 1975) can be used only if SHAPE=ASYMMETRIC and more than one dimension is requested on CRITERIA.

AINDS *Asymmetric individual differences Euclidean distance model.* This option combines Young's (1975) asymmetric Euclidean model with the individual differences model proposed by Carroll and Chang (1970). This model can be used only when SHAPE=ASYMMETRIC, the analysis involves more than one data matrix, and more than one dimension is specified on CRITERIA.

GEMSCAL *Generalized Euclidean metric individual differences model.* The number of directions for this model is set with the DIRECTIONS option on CRITERIA. The number of directions specified can be equal to but cannot exceed the group space dimensionality. By default, the number of directions equals the number of dimensions in the solution.

Example

```
ALSCAL VARIABLES = V1 TO V6
 /SHAPE = ASYMMETRIC
 /CONDITION = ROW
 /MODEL = GEMSCAL
 /CRITERIA = DIM(4) DIRECTIONS(4).
```

- In this example, the number of directions in the GEMSCAL model is set to 4.

CRITERIA Subcommand

Use CRITERIA to control features of the scaling model and to set convergence criteria for the solution. You can specify one or more of the following:

CONVERGE(n) *Stop iterations if the change in S-stress is less than* n. S-stress is a goodness-of-fit index. By default, *n*=0.001. To increase the precision of a solution, specify a smaller value, for example, 0.0001. To obtain a less precise solution (perhaps to reduce computing time), specify a larger value, for example, 0.05. Negative values are not allowed. If *n*=0, the algorithm will iterate 30 times unless a value is specified with the ITER option.

ITER(n) *Set the maximum number of iterations to* n. The default value is 30. A higher value will give a more precise solution but will take longer to compute.

STRESSMIN(n) *Set the minimum stress value to* n. By default, ALSCAL stops iterating when the value of S-stress is 0.005 or less. STRESSMIN can be assigned any value from 0 to 1.

NEGATIVE *Allow negative weights in individual differences models.* By default, ALSCAL does not permit the weights to be negative. Weighted models include INDSCAL, ASCAL, AINDS, and GEMSCAL. The NEGATIVE option is ignored if the model is EUCLID.

CUTOFF(n) *Set the cutoff value for treating distances as missing to* n. By default, ALSCAL treats all negative similarities (or dissimilarities) as missing, and 0 and positive similarities as nonmissing (*n*=0). Changing the CUTOFF value causes ALSCAL to treat similarities greater than or equal to that value as nonmissing. User- and system-missing values are considered missing regardless of the CUTOFF specification.

NOULB *Do not estimate upper and lower bounds on missing values.* By default, ALSCAL estimates the upper and lower bounds on missing values in order to compute the initial configuration. This specification has no effect during the iterative process, when missing values are ignored.

DIMENS(min[,max]) *Set the minimum and maximum number of dimensions in the scaling solution.* By default, ALSCAL calculates a solution with two dimensions. To obtain solutions for more than two dimensions, specify the minimum and the maximum number of dimensions in parentheses after DIMENS. The minimum and maximum can be integers between 2 and 6. A single value represents both the minimum and the maximum. For example, DIMENS(3) is equivalent to DIMENS(3,3). The minimum number of dimensions can be set to 1 only if MODEL=EUCLID.

DIRECTIONS(n) *Set the number of principal directions in the generalized Euclidean model to* n. This option has no effect for models other than GEMSCAL. The number of principal directions can be any positive integer between 1 and the number of dimensions specified on the DIMENS option. By default, the number of directions equals the number of dimensions.

TIESTORE(n) *Set the amount of storage needed for ties to* n. This option estimates the amount of storage needed to deal with ties in ordinal data. By default, the amount of storage is set to 1000 or the number of cells in a matrix, whichever is smaller. Should this be insufficient, ALSCAL terminates and displays a message that more space is needed.

CONSTRAIN *Constrain multidimensional unfolding solution.* This option can be used to keep the initial constraints throughout the analysis.

PRINT Subcommand

PRINT requests output not available by default. You can specify the following:

DATA *Display input data.* The display includes both the initial data and the scaled data for each subject according to the structure specified on SHAPE.

HEADER *Display a header page.* The header includes the model, output, algorithmic, and data options in effect for the analysis.

- Data options listed by PRINT=HEADER include the number of rows and columns, number of matrices, measurement level, shape of the data matrix, type of data (similarity or dissimilarity), whether ties are tied or untied, conditionality, and data cutoff value.
- Model options listed by PRINT=HEADER are the type of model specified (EUCLID, INDSCAL, ASCAL, AINDS, or GEMSCAL), minimum and maximum dimensionality, and whether or not negative weights are permitted.
- Output options listed by PRINT=HEADER indicate whether the output includes the header page and input data, whether ALSCAL plotted configurations and transformations, whether an output data set was created, and whether initial stimulus coordinates, initial column stimulus coordinates, initial subject weights, and initial stimulus weights were computed.

- Algorithmic options listed by PRINT=HEADER include the maximum number of iterations permitted, the convergence criterion, the maximum S-stress value, whether or not missing data are estimated by upper and lower bounds, and the amount of storage allotted for ties in ordinal data.

Example

```
ALSCAL VAR=ATLANTA TO TAMPA /PRINT=DATA.
```

- In addition to scaled data, ALSCAL will display initial data.

PLOT Subcommand

PLOT controls the display of plots. The minimum specification is simply PLOT to produce the defaults.

DEFAULT *Default plots.* Default plots include plots of stimulus coordinates, matrix weights (if the model is INDSCAL, AINDS, or GEMSCAL), and stimulus weights (if the model is AINDS or ASCAL). The default also includes a scatterplot of the linear fit between the data and the model and, for certain types of data, scatterplots of the nonlinear fit and the data transformation.

ALL *Transformation plots in addition to the default plots.* SPSS produces a separate plot for each subject if CONDITION=MATRIX and a separate plot for each row if CONDITION=ROW. For interval and ratio data, PLOT=ALL has the same effect as PLOT=DEFAULT. This option can generate voluminous output, particularly when CONDITION=ROW.

Example

```
ALSCAL VAR=V1 TO V8 /INPUT=ROWS(8) /PLOT=ALL.
```

- This command produces all the default plots. It also produces a separate plot for each subject's data transformation and a plot of *V1* through *V8* in a two-dimensional space for each subject.

OUTFILE Subcommand

OUTFILE saves coordinate and weight matrices to an SPSS data file. The only specification is a name for the output file.

- The output data file has an alphanumeric (short string) variable named *TYPE_* that identifies the kind of values in each row, a numeric variable *DIMENS* that specifies the number of dimensions, a numeric variable *MATNUM* that indicates the subject (matrix) to which each set of coordinates corresponds, and variables *DIM1*, *DIM2,...DIMn* that correspond to the *n* dimensions in the model.
- The values of any split-file variables are also included in the output file.
- The file created by OUTFILE can be used by subsequent ALSCAL commands as initial data.

The following are the types of configurations and weights that can be included in the output file:

CONFIG *Stimulus configuration coordinates.*

ROWCONF *Row stimulus configuration coordinates.*

COLCONF *Column stimulus configuration coordinates.*

SUBJWGHT *Subject (matrix) weights.*

FLATWGHT *Flattened subject (matrix) weights.*

GEMWGHT *Generalized weights.*

STIMWGHT *Stimulus weights.*

Only the first three characters of each identifier are written to variable *TYPE_* in the file. For example, CONFIG becomes CON. The structure of the file is determined by the SHAPE and MODEL subcommands, as shown in Table 2.

Table 2 Types of configurations and/or weights in output files

Shape	Model	TYPE_
SYMMETRIC	EUCLID	CON
	INDSCAL	CON SUB FLA
	GEMSCAL	CON SUB FLA GEM
ASYMMETRIC	EUCLID	CON
	INDSCAL	CON SUB FLA
	GEMSCAL	CON SUB FLA GEM
	ASCAL	CON STI
	AINDS	CON SUB FLA STI
RECTANGULAR	EUCLID	ROW COL
	INDSCAL	ROW COL SUB FLA
	GEMSCAL	ROW COL SUB FLA GEM

Example

```
ALSCAL VAR=ATLANTA TO TAMPA /OUTFILE=ONE.
```

- OUTFILE creates the SPSS configuration/weights file *ONE* from the example of air distances between cities.

MATRIX Subcommand

MATRIX reads SPSS matrix data files. It can read a matrix written by either PROXIMITIES or CLUSTER.

- Generally, data read by ALSCAL are already in matrix form. If the matrix materials are in the working data file, you do not need to use MATRIX to read them. Simply use the VARIABLES subcommand to indicate the variables (or columns) to be used. However, if the matrix materials are not in the working data file, MATRIX must be used to specify the matrix data file that contains the matrix.
- The proximity matrices ALSCAL reads have *ROWTYPE_* values of PROX. No additional statistics should be included with these matrix materials.
- ALSCAL ignores unrecognized *ROWTYPE_* values in the matrix file. In addition, it ignores variables present in the matrix file that are not specified on the VARIABLES subcommand in ALSCAL. The order of rows and columns in the matrix is unimportant.
- Since ALSCAL does not support case labeling, it ignores values for the *ID* variable (if present) in a CLUSTER or PROXIMITIES matrix.
- If split-file processing was in effect when the matrix was written, the same split file must be in effect when ALSCAL reads that matrix.
- The specification on MATRIX is the keyword IN and the matrix file in parentheses.
- MATRIX=IN cannot be used unless a working data file has already been defined. To read an existing matrix data file at the beginning of a session, first use GET to retrieve the matrix file and then specify IN(*) on MATRIX.

IN (filename) *Read a matrix data file.* If the matrix data file is the working data file, specify an asterisk in parentheses (*). If the matrix data file is another file, specify the filename in parentheses. A matrix file read from an external file does not replace the working data file.

Example

```
PROXIMITIES V1 TO V8 /ID=NAMEVAR /MATRIX=OUT(*).
ALSCAL VAR=CASE1 TO CASE10 /MATRIX=IN(*).
```

- PROXIMITIES uses *V1* through *V8* in the working data file to generate a matrix file of Euclidean distances between each pair of cases based on the eight variables. The number of rows and columns in the resulting matrix equals the number of cases. MATRIX=OUT then replaces the working data file with this new matrix data file.
- MATRIX=IN on ALSCAL reads the matrix data file, which is the new working data file. In this instance, MATRIX is optional because the matrix materials are in the working data file.
- If there were 10 cases in the original working data file, ALSCAL performs a multidimensional scaling analysis in two dimensions on *CASE1* through *CASE10*.

Example

```
GET FILE PROXMTX.
ALSCAL VAR=CASE1 TO CASE10 /MATRIX=IN(*).
```

- GET retrieves the matrix data file *PROXMTX*.

- MATRIX=IN specifies an asterisk because the working data file is the matrix. MATRIX is optional, however, since the matrix materials are in the working data file.

Example

```
GET FILE PRSNNL.
FREQUENCIES VARIABLE=AGE.
ALSCAL VAR=CASE1 TO CASE10 /MATRIX=IN(PROXMTX).
```

- This example performs a frequencies analysis on file *PRSNNL* and then uses a different file containing matrix data for ALSCAL. The file is an existing matrix data file.
- MATRIX=IN is required because the matrix data file, *PROXMTX*, is not the working data file. *PROXMTX* does not replace *PRSNNL* as the working data file.

Specification of Analyses

Table 3 summarizes the analyses that can be performed for the major types of proximity matrices you can use with ALSCAL, Table 4 lists the specifications needed to produce these analyses for nonmetric models, and Table 5 lists the specifications for metric models. You can include additional specifications to control the precision of your analysis with CRITERIA.

Table 3 Models for types of matrix input

Matrix mode	Matrix form	Model class	Single matrix	Replications of single matrix	Two or more individual matrices
Object by object	Symmetric	Multi-dimensional scaling	CMDS Classical multi-dimensional scaling	RMDS Replicated multi-dimensional scaling	WMDS(INDSCAL) Weighted multi-dimensional scaling
	Asymmetric single process	Multi-dimensional scaling	CMDS(row conditional) Classical row conditional multi-dimensional scaling	RMDS(row conditional) Replicated row conditional multi-dimensional scaling	WMDS(row conditional) Weighted row conditional multi-dimensional scaling
	Asymmetric multiple process	Internal asymmetric multi-dimensional scaling	CAMDS Classical asymmetric multidimensional scaling	RAMDS Replicated asymmetric multidimensional scaling	WAMDS Weighted asymmetric multidimensional scaling
		External asymmetric multi-dimensional scaling	CAMDS(external) Classical external asymmetric multidimensional scaling	RAMDS(external) Replicated external asymmetric multi-dimensional scaling	WAMDS(external) Weighted external asymmetric multi-dimensional scaling
Object by attribute	Rectangular	Internal unfolding	CMDU Classical internal multidimensional unfolding	RMDU Replicated internal multidimensional unfolding	WMDU Weighted internal multi-dimensional unfolding
		External unfolding	CMDU(external) Classical external multidimensional unfolding	RMDU(external) Replicated external multidimensional unfolding	WMDU(external) Weighted external multi-dimensional unfolding

Table 4 ALSCAL specifications for nonmetric models

Matrix mode	Matrix form	Model class	Single matrix	Replications of single matrix	Two or more individual matrices
Object by object	Symmetric	Multi-dimensional scaling	ALSCAL VAR= varlist.	ALSCAL VAR= varlist.	ALSCAL VAR= varlist /MODEL=INDSCAL.
	Asymmetric single process	Multi-dimensional scaling	ALSCAL VAR= varlist /SHAPE=ASYMMETRIC /CONDITION=ROW.	ALSCAL VAR= varlist /SHAPE=ASYMMETRIC /CONDITION=ROW.	ALSCAL VAR= varlist /SHAPE=ASYMMETRIC /CONDITION=ROW /MODEL=INDSCAL.
	Asymmetric multiple process	Internal asymmetric multi-dimensional scaling	ALSCAL VAR= varlist /SHAPE=ASYMMETRIC /MODEL=ASCAL.	ALSCAL VAR= varlist /SHAPE=ASYMMETRIC /MODEL=ASCAL.	ALSCAL VAR= varlist /SHAPE=ASYMMETRIC /MODEL=AINDS.
		External asymmetric multi-dimensional scaling	ALSCAL VAR= varlist /SHAPE=ASYMMETRIC /MODEL=ASCAL /FILE=file COLCONF(FIX).	ALSCAL VAR= varlist /SHAPE=ASYMMETRIC /MODEL=ASCAL /FILE=file COLCONF(FIX).	ALSCAL VAR= varlist /SHAPE=ASYMMETRIC /MODEL=AINDS /FILE=file COLCONF(FIX).
Object by attribute	Rectangular	Internal unfolding	ALSCAL VAR= varlist /SHAPE=REC /INP=ROWS /CONDITION=ROW.	ALSCAL VAR= varlist /SHAPE=REC /INP=ROWS /CONDITION(ROW).	ALSCAL VAR= varlist /SHAPE=REC /INP=ROWS /CONDITION=ROW /MODEL=INDSCAL.
		External unfolding	ALSCAL VAR= varlist /SHAPE=REC /INP=ROWS /CONDITION=ROW /FILE=file ROWCONF(FIX).	ALSCAL VAR= varlist /SHAPE=REC /INP=ROWS /CONDITION=ROW /FILE=file ROWCONF(FIX).	ALSCAL VAR= varlist /SHAPE=REC /INP=ROWS /CONDITION=ROW /FILE=file ROWCONF(FIX) /MODEL=INDSCAL.

Table 5 ALSCAL specifications for metric models

Matrix mode	Matrix form	Model class	Single matrix	Replications of single matrix	Two or more individual matrices
Object by object	Symmetric	Multidimensional scaling	ALSCAL VAR= varlist /LEVEL=INT.	ALSCAL VAR= varlist /LEVEL=INT.	ALSCAL VAR= varlist /LEVEL=INT /MODEL=INDSCAL.
	Asymmetric single process	Multidimensional scaling	ALSCAL VAR= varlist /SHAPE=ASYMMETRIC /CONDITION=ROW /LEVEL=INT.	ALSCAL VAR= varlist /SHAPE=ASYMMETRIC /CONDITION=ROW /LEVEL=INT.	ALSCAL VAR= varlist /SHAPE=ASYMMETRIC /CONDITION=ROW /LEVEL=INT /MODEL=INDSCAL.
	Asymmetric multiple process	Internal asymmetric multidimensional scaling	ALSCAL VAR= varlist /SHAPE=ASYMMETRIC /LEVEL=INT /MODEL=ASCAL.	ALSCAL VAR= varlist /SHAPE=ASYMMETRIC /LEVEL=INT /MODEL=ASCAL.	ALSCAL VAR= varlist /SHAPE=ASYMMETRIC /LEVEL=INT /MODEL=AINDS.
		External asymmetric multidimensional scaling	ALSCAL VAR= varlist /SHAPE=ASYMMETRIC /LEVEL=INT /MODEL=ASCAL /FILE=file COLCONF(FIX).	ALSCAL VAR= varlist /SHAPE=ASYMMETRIC /LEVEL=INT /MODEL=ASCAL /FILE=file COLCONF(FIX).	ALSCAL VAR= varlist /SHAPE=ASYMMETRIC /LEVEL=INT /MODEL=AINDS /FILE=file COLCONF(FIX).
Object by attribute	Rectangular	Internal unfolding	ALSCAL VAR= varlist /SHAPE=REC /INP=ROWS /CONDITION=ROW /LEVEL=INT.	ALSCAL VAR= varlist /SHAPE=REC /INP=ROWS /CONDITION=ROW /LEVEL=INT.	ALSCAL VAR= varlist /SHAPE=REC /INP=ROWS /CONDITION=ROW /LEVEL=INT /MODEL=INDSCAL.
		External unfolding	ALSCAL VAR= varlist /SHAPE=REC /INP=ROWS /CONDITION=ROW /LEVEL=INT /FILE=file ROWCONF(FIX).	ALSCAL VAR= varlist /SHAPE=REC /INP=ROWS /CONDITION=ROW /LEVEL=INT /FILE=file ROWCONF(FIX).	ALSCAL VAR= varlist /SHAPE=REC /INP=ROWS /CONDITION=ROW /LEVEL=INT /FILE=file ROWCONF(FIX) /MODEL=INDSCAL.

References

Carroll, J. D., and J. J. Chang. 1970. Analysis of individual differences in multidimensional scaling via an *n*-way generalization of "Eckart-Young" decomposition. *Psychometrika*, 35: 238–319.

Johnson, R., and D. W. Wichern. 1982. *Applied multivariate statistical analysis*. Englewood Cliffs, N.J.: Prentice-Hall.

Kruskal, J. B. 1964. Nonmetric multidimensional scaling. *Psychometrika*, 29: 1–27, 115–129.

Takane, Y., F. W. Young, and J. de Leeuw. 1977. Nonmetric individual differences multidimensional scaling: An alternating least squares method with optimal scaling features. *Psychometrika*, 42: 7–67.

Young, F. W. 1975. An asymmetric Euclidean model for multiprocess asymmetric data. In: *Proceedings of US–Japan Seminar on Multidimensional Scaling*.

ANOVA

```
ANOVA [VARIABLES=] varlist BY varlist(min,max)...varlist(min,max)
 [WITH varlist] [/VARIABLES=...]

 [/COVARIATES={FIRST**}]
              {WITH   }
              {AFTER  }

 [/MAXORDERS={ALL** }]
             {n     }
             {NONE  }

 [/METHOD={UNIQUE**    }]
          {EXPERIMENTAL}
          {HIERARCHICAL}

 [/STATISTICS=[MCA] [REG†] [MEAN] [ALL] [NONE]]

 [/MISSING={EXCLUDE**}]
           {INCLUDE  }
```

**Default if the subcommand is omitted.
†REG (table of regression coefficients) is displayed only if the design is relevant.

Example

```
ANOVA VARIABLES=PRESTIGE BY REGION(1,9) SEX,RACE(1,2)
 /MAXORDERS=2
 /STATISTICS=MEAN.
```

Overview

ANOVA performs analysis of variance for factorial designs. The default is the full factorial model if there are five or fewer factors. Analysis of variance tests the hypothesis that the group means of the dependent variable are equal. The dependent variable is interval level, and one or more categorical variables define the groups. These categorical variables are termed **factors**. ANOVA also allows you to include continuous explanatory variables, termed **covariates**. Other procedures that perform analysis of variance are ONEWAY, SUMMARIZE, and GLM. To perform a comparison of two means, use TTEST.

Options

Specifying Covariates. You can introduce covariates into the model using the WITH keyword on the VARIABLES subcommand.

Order of Entry of Covariates. By default, covariates are processed before main effects for factors. You can process covariates with or after main effects for factors using the COVARIATES subcommand.

Suppressing Interaction Effects. You can suppress the effects of various orders of interaction using the MAXORDERS subcommand.

Methods for Decomposing Sums of Squares. By default, the regression approach (keyword UNIQUE) is used. You can request the classic experimental or hierarchical approach using the METHOD subcommand.

Statistical Display. Using the STATISTICS subcommand, you can request means and counts for each dependent variable for groups defined by each factor and each combination of factors up to the fifth level. You also can request unstandardized regression coefficients for covariates and multiple classification analysis (MCA) results, which include the MCA table, the Factor Summary table, and the Model Goodness of Fit table. The MCA table shows **treatment effects** as deviations from the grand mean and includes a listing of unadjusted category effects for each factor, category effects adjusted for other factors, and category effects adjusted for all factors and covariates. The Factor Summary table displays eta and beta values. The Goodness of Fit table shows R and R^2 for each model.

Basic Specification

- The basic specification is a single VARIABLES subcommand with an analysis list. The minimum analysis list specifies a list of dependent variables, the keyword BY, a list of factor variables, and the minimum and maximum integer values of the factors in parentheses.
- By default, the model includes all interaction terms up to five-way interactions. The sums of squares are decomposed using the regression approach, in which all effects are assessed simultaneously, with each effect adjusted for all other effects in the model. A case that has a missing value for any variable in an analysis list is omitted from the analysis.

Subcommand Order

- The analysis list must be first if the keyword VARIABLES is omitted from the specification.
- The remaining subcommands can be named in any order.

Operations

A separate analysis of variance is performed for each dependent variable in an analysis list, using the same factors and covariates.

Limitations

- Maximum 5 analysis lists.
- Maximum 5 dependent variables per analysis list.
- Maximum 10 factor variables per analysis list.
- Maximum 10 covariates per analysis list.
- Maximum 5 interaction levels.
- Maximum 25 value labels per variable displayed in the MCA table.
- The combined number of categories for all factors in an analysis list plus the number of covariates must be less than the sample size.

Example

```
ANOVA VARIABLES=PRESTIGE BY REGION(1,9) SEX, RACE(1,2)
 /MAXORDERS=2
 /STATISTICS=MEAN.
```

- VARIABLES specifies a three-way analysis of variance—*PRESTIGE* by *REGION*, *SEX*, and *RACE*.
- The variables *SEX* and *RACE* each have two categories, with values 1 and 2 included in the analysis. *REGION* has nine categories, valued 1 through 9.
- MAXORDERS examines interaction effects up to and including the second order. All three-way interaction terms are pooled into the error sum of squares.
- STATISTICS requests a table of means of *PRESTIGE* within the combined categories of *REGION*, *SEX*, and *RACE*.

Example

```
ANOVA VARIABLES=PRESTIGE BY REGION(1,9) SEX,RACE(1,2)
  /RINCOME BY SEX,RACE(1,2).
```

- ANOVA specifies a three-way analysis of variance of *PRESTIGE* by *REGION*, *SEX*, and *RACE*, and a two-way analysis of variance of *RINCOME* by *SEX* and *RACE*.

VARIABLES Subcommand

VARIABLES specifies the analysis list. The actual keyword VARIABLES can be omitted.

- More than one design can be specified on the same ANOVA command by separating the analysis lists with a slash.
- Variables named before keyword BY are dependent variables. Value ranges are not specified for dependent variables.
- Variables named after BY are factor (independent) variables.
- Every factor variable must have a value range indicating its minimum and maximum values. The values must be separated by a space or a comma and enclosed in parentheses.
- Factor variables must have integer values. Noninteger values for factors are truncated.
- Cases with values outside the range specified for a factor are excluded from the analysis.
- If two or more factors have the same value range, you can specify the value range once following the last factor to which it applies. You can specify a single range that encompasses the ranges of all factors on the list. For example, if you have two factors, one with values 1 and 2 and the other with values 1 through 4, you can specify the range for both as 1,4. However, this may reduce performance and cause memory problems if the specified range is larger than some of the actual ranges.
- Variables named after the keyword WITH are covariates.
- Each analysis list can include only one BY and one WITH keyword.

COVARIATES Subcommand

COVARIATES specifies the order for assessing blocks of covariates and factor main effects.

- The order of entry is irrelevant when METHOD=UNIQUE.

FIRST *Process covariates before factor main effects.* This is the default.

WITH *Process covariates concurrently with factor main effects.*

AFTER *Process covariates after factor main effects.*

MAXORDERS Subcommand

MAXORDERS suppresses the effects of various orders of interaction.

ALL *Examine all interaction effects up to and including the fifth order.* This is the default.

n *Examine all interaction effects up to and including the* n*th order.* For example, MAXORDERS=3 examines all interaction effects up to and including the third order. All higher-order interaction sums of squares are pooled into the error term.

NONE *Delete all interaction terms from the model.* All interaction sums of squares are pooled into the error sum of squares. Only main and covariate effects appear in the ANOVA table.

METHOD Subcommand

METHOD controls the method for decomposing sums of squares.

UNIQUE *Regression approach.* UNIQUE overrides any keywords on the COVARIATES subcommand. All effects are assessed simultaneously for their partial contribution. The MCA and MEAN specifications on the STATISTICS subcommand are not available with the regression approach. This is the default if METHOD is omitted.

EXPERIMENTAL *Classic experimental approach.* Covariates, main effects, and ascending orders of interaction are assessed separately in that order.

HIERARCHICAL *Hierarchical approach.*

Regression Approach

All effects are assessed simultaneously, with each effect adjusted for all other effects in the model. This is the default when the METHOD subcommand is omitted. Since MCA tables cannot be produced when the regression approach is used, specifying MCA or ALL on STATISTICS with the default method triggers a warning.

Some restrictions apply to the use of the regression approach:

- The lowest specified categories of all the independent variables must have a marginal frequency of at least 1, since the lowest specified category is used as the reference category. If this rule is violated, no ANOVA table is produced and a message identifying the first offending variable is displayed.
- Given an *n*-way crosstabulation of the independent variables, there must be no empty cells defined by the lowest specified category of any of the independent variables. If this restriction is violated, one or more levels of interaction effects are suppressed and a warning message is issued. However, this constraint does not apply to categories defined for an independent variable but not occurring in the data. For example, given two independent variables, each with categories of 1, 2, and 4, the (1,1), (1,2), (1,4), (2,1), and (4,1) cells must not be empty. The (1,3) and (3,1) cells will be empty but the restriction on empty cells will not be violated. The (2,2), (2,4), (4,2), and (4,4) cells may be empty, although the degrees of freedom will be reduced accordingly.

To comply with these restrictions, specify precisely the lowest nonempty category of each independent variable. Specifying a value range of (0,9) for a variable that actually has values of 1 through 9 results in an error, and no ANOVA table is produced.

Classic Experimental Approach

Each type of effect is assessed separately in the following order (unless WITH or AFTER is specified on the COVARIATES subcommand):

- Effects of covariates
- Main effects of factors
- Two-way interaction effects
- Three-way interaction effects
- Four-way interaction effects
- Five-way interaction effects

The effects within each type are adjusted for all other effects of that type and also for the effects of all prior types (see Table 1).

Hierarchical Approach

The hierarchical approach differs from the classic experimental approach only in the way it handles covariate and factor main effects. In the hierarchical approach, factor main effects and covariate effects are assessed hierarchically—factor main effects are adjusted only for the factor main effects already assessed, and covariate effects are adjusted only for the covariates already assessed (see Table 1). The order in which factors are listed on the ANOVA command determines the order in which they are assessed.

Example

The following analysis list specifies three factor variables named *A*, *B*, and *C*:

```
ANOVA VARIABLES=Y BY A,B,C(0,3).
```

Table 1 summarizes the three methods for decomposing sums of squares for this example.

- With the default *regression* approach, each factor or interaction is assessed with all other factors and interactions held constant.
- With the *classic experimental* approach, each main effect is assessed with the two other main effects held constant, and two-way interactions are assessed with all main effects and other two-way interactions held constant. The three-way interaction is assessed with all main effects and two-way interactions held constant.
- With the *hierarchical* approach, the factor main effects A, B, and C are assessed with all prior main effects held constant. The order in which the factors and covariates are listed on the ANOVA command determines the order in which they are assessed in the hierarchical analysis. The interaction effects are assessed the same way as in the experimental approach.

Table 1 Terms adjusted for under each option

Effect	Regression (UNIQUE)	Experimental	Hierarchical
A	All others	B,C	None
B	All others	A,C	A
C	All others	A,B	A,B
AB	All others	A,B,C,AC,BC	A,B,C,AC,BC
AC	All others	A,B,C,AB,BC	A,B,C,AB,BC
BC	All others	A,B,C,AB,AC	A,B,C,AB,AC
ABC	All others	A,B,C,AB,AC,BC	A,B,C,AB,AC,BC

Summary of Analysis Methods

Table 2 describes the results obtained with various combinations of methods for controlling entry of covariates and decomposing the sums of squares.

Table 2 Combinations of COVARIATES and METHOD subcommands

	Assessments between types of effects	**Assessments within the same type of effect**
METHOD=UNIQUE	**Covariates**, **Factors**, and **Interactions** simultaneously	**Covariates**: adjust for factors, interactions, and all other covariates **Factors**: adjust for covariates, interactions, and all other factors **Interactions**: adjust for covariates, factors, and all other interactions
METHOD=EXPERIMENTAL	**Covariates** then **Factors** then **Interactions**	**Covariates:** adjust for all other covariates **Factors:** adjust for covariates and all other factors **Interactions**: adjust for covariates, factors, and all other interactions of the same and lower orders
METHOD=HIERARCHICAL	**Covariates** then **Factors** then **Interactions**	**Covariates**: adjust for covariates that are preceding in the list **Factors**: adjust for covariates and factors preceding in the list **Interactions**: adjust for covariates, factors, and all other interactions of the same and lower orders
COVARIATES=WITH and METHOD=EXPERIMENTAL	**Factors** and **Covariates** concurrently then **Interactions**	**Covariates**: adjust for factors and all other covariates **Factors**: adjust for covariates and all other factors **Interactions**: adjust for covariates, factors, and all other interactions of the same and lower orders
COVARIATES=WITH and METHOD=HIERARCHICAL	**Factors** and **Covariates** concurrently then **Interactions**	**Factors**: adjust only for preceding factors **Covariates**: adjust for factors and preceding covariates **Interactions**: adjust for covariates, factors, and all other interactions of the same and lower orders
COVARIATES=AFTER and METHOD=EXPERIMENTAL	**Factors** then **Covariates** then **Interactions**	**Factors**: adjust for all other factors **Covariates**: adjust for factors and all other covariates **Interactions**: adjust for covariates, factors, and all other interactions of the same and lower orders
COVARIATES=AFTER and METHOD=HIERARCHICAL	**Factors** then **Covariates** then **Interactions**	**Factors**: adjust only for preceding factors **Covariates**: adjust factors and preceding covariates **Interactions**: adjust for covariates, factors, and all other interactions of the same and lower orders

STATISTICS Subcommand

STATISTICS requests additional statistics. STATISTICS can be specified by itself or with one or more keywords.

- If you specify STATISTICS without keywords, ANOVA calculates MEAN and REG (each defined below).
- If you specify a keyword or keywords on the STATISTICS subcommand, ANOVA calculates only the additional statistics you request.

MEAN *Means and counts table.* This statistic is not available when METHOD is omitted or when METHOD=UNIQUE. See "Cell Means" below.

REG *Unstandardized regression coefficients.* Displays unstandardized regression coefficients for the covariates. See "Regression Coefficients for the Covariates" below.

MCA *Multiple classification analysis.* The MCA, the Factor Summary, and the Goodness of Fit tables are not produced when METHOD is omitted or when METHOD=UNIQUE. See "Multiple Classification Analysis" on p. 119.

ALL *Means and counts table, unstandardized regression coefficients, and multiple classification analysis.*

NONE *No additional statistics.* ANOVA calculates only the statistics needed for analysis of variance. This is the default if the STATISTICS subcommand is omitted.

Cell Means

STATISTICS=MEAN displays the Cell Means table.

- This statistic is not available with METHOD=UNIQUE.
- The Cell Means table shows means and counts of each dependent variable for each cell defined by the factors and combinations of factors. Dependent variables and factors appear in their order on the VARIABLES subcommand.
- If MAXORDERS is used to suppress higher-order interactions, cell means corresponding to suppressed interaction terms are not displayed.
- The means displayed are the observed means in each cell, and they are produced only for dependent variables, not for covariates.

Regression Coefficients for the Covariates

STATISTICS=REG requests the unstandardized regression coefficients for the covariates.

- The regression coefficients are computed at the point where the covariates are entered into the equation. Thus, their values depend on the type of design specified by the COVARIATES or METHOD subcommands.
- The coefficients are displayed in the ANOVA table.

Multiple Classification Analysis

STATISTICS=MCA displays the MCA, the Factor Summary, and the Model Goodness of Fit tables.

- The MCA table presents counts, predicted means, and deviations of predicted means from the grand mean for each level of each factor. The predicted and deviation means each appear in up to three forms: unadjusted, adjusted for other factors, and adjusted for other factors and covariates.
- The Factor Summary table displays the correlation ratio (eta) with the unadjusted deviations (the square of eta indicates the proportion of variance explained by all categories of the factor), a partial beta equivalent to the standardized partial regression coefficient that would be obtained by assigning the unadjusted deviations to each factor category and regressing the dependent variable on the resulting variables, and the parallel partial betas from a regression that includes covariates in addition to the factors.
- The Model Goodness of Fit table shows R and R^2 for each model.
- The tables cannot be produced if METHOD is omitted or if METHOD=UNIQUE. When produced, the MCA table does not display values adjusted for factors if COVARIATES is omitted, if COVARIATES=FIRST, or if COVARIATES=WITH and METHOD=EXPERIMENTAL. A full MCA table is produced only if METHOD=HIERARCHICAL or if METHOD=EXPERIMENTAL and COVARIATES=AFTER.

MISSING Subcommand

By default, a case that has a missing value for any variable named in the analysis list is deleted for all analyses specified by that list. Use MISSING to include cases with user-missing data.

EXCLUDE *Exclude cases with missing data.* This is the default.

INCLUDE *Include cases with user-defined missing data.*

References

Andrews, F., J. Morgan, J. Sonquist, and L. Klein. 1973. *Multiple classification analysis.* 2nd ed. Ann Arbor: University of Michigan.

APPLY DICTIONARY

```
APPLY DICTIONARY FROM=file
```

Example

```
APPLY DICTIONARY FROM = 'MASTER.SAV'.
```

Overview

APPLY DICTIONARY applies dictionary information from an external SPSS-format data file to the working data file. The applied dictionary information includes variable and value labels, missing-value flags, print and write formats, and weight. APPLY DICTIONARY does not add or remove variables, and it cannot apply dictionary information selectively to individual variables.

Basic Specification

The basic specification is the FROM subcommand and the name of an SPSS-format data file. The file specification may vary from operating system to operating system, but enclosing the filename in apostrophes generally works.

Syntax Rules

- The equals sign after FROM is optional.
- The file containing the dictionary information to be applied (the **source file**) must be an SPSS-format data file.
- The file to which the dictionary information is applied (the **target file**) must be the working data file. You cannot specify another file.

Operation

- APPLY DICTIONARY adds or replaces dictionary information variable by variable by matching variables that have the same name and the same type (string or numeric) in both files. Variables in the working data file that do not have a match in the source file are not changed.
- APPLY DICTIONARY does not add or remove variables from the working data file.
- If no matched variables are found, the program displays a warning message.
- Variables that have the same name but different types are not considered matching. The program displays a warning message and lists the variables with nonmatching types.

Variable Labels

APPLY DICTIONARY adds labels or replaces old labels with new ones. It cannot be used to remove a defined variable label in the working data file.

- If the variable label in the source file is blank, it will not replace an existing variable label, even if the blanks are in quotes.

Table 1 shows how variable labels are replaced between matched variables.

Table 1 Variable label replacement

Variable	Label in working file (target file)	Label in external file (source file)	Label in resulting file
VAR1	"AGE 86"	"AGE 91"	"AGE 91"
VAR2		"JOBCAT91"	"JOBCAT91"
VAR3	"WORK ID"		"WORK ID"
VAR4	"RACE"	" "	"RACE"

Value Labels

APPLY DICTIONARY treats the value labels of a variable as a set. It adds or replaces the entire set of value labels for a matched variable in the working data file. You cannot remove the defined value label set from a variable or selectively add or replace individual value labels.

- APPLY DICTIONARY does not merge the set of value labels for a variable in the SPSS-format data file with the labels for a matched variable in the working data file. The variable in the resulting file uses the labels from the SPSS-format data file only.
- If the variable in the SPSS-format data file does not have any defined value labels, the matching variable in the working data file keeps its original value labels.
- If the matched variable in the working data file is a long string, value labels are not applied even if the source variable is a short string and has value labels defined. The program displays a message when this occurs.
- If the matched variables are both short strings but the target variable is longer than the source variable, the values for the source variable are right-padded before their labels are applied to the target variable.
- If the matched variables are both short strings but the source variable is longer, the values for the source variable are right-trimmed if there are enough blank spaces on the right. If any one of the values that has labels defined does not have enough blank spaces to be trimmed, the entire set of value labels is not applied and the variable in the working data file maintains its original value label specifications.

Missing Values

APPLY DICTIONARY treats the missing-value specifications of a variable as a set. It adds or replaces the entire set of missing values for a matched variable in the working data file. You can remove the entire set of missing-value specifications from a variable but cannot selectively add or replace individual missing-value specifications.

- APPLY DICTIONARY does not merge the set of missing values for a variable in the SPSS-format data file with the missing-value specifications for a matched variable in the working data file. The variable in the resulting file uses the missing values defined in the SPSS-format data file only.
- If the variable in the SPSS-format data file does not define any missing values, the variable in the working data file keeps its missing-value specifications.
- If the matched variable in the working data file is a long string, missing-value specifications are not applied even if the source variable is a short string and has missing values defined. The program displays a message specifying the missing value and information about the length of the matched variables.
- If the matched variables are both short strings but the target variable is longer than the source variable, the missing values from the source variable are right-padded.
- If the matched variables are both short strings but the source variable is longer, the missing values from the source variable are right-trimmed if there are enough blank spaces on the right. If any one of the defined missing values does not have enough blank spaces to be trimmed, the entire set will not be applied. The variable in the working data file maintains its original missing-value specifications.

Print and Write Formats

APPLY DICTIONARY always replaces the print and write formats of matched numeric variables in the working data file.

- The print and write formats of string variables are not changed. They keep the original length defined on the DATA LIST or STRING command. To change the length of a string variable, define a new variable using STRING and then use the COMPUTE command.

Weight

APPLY DICTIONARY adds or replaces the weighting information in the working data file. Table 2 summarizes how weighting information is applied. In the table, *WTWORK* refers to the weight variable in the working file and *WTSPSS* to the weight variable in the SPSS-format data file.

- A message is displayed when either the weight status or the weight variable is changed.

Table 2 Weight information

Working file		External file		Resulting file	
Status	**Weight**	**Status**	**Weight**	**Status**	**Weight**
Weighted	*WTWORK*	Unweighted	N/A	Weighted	*WTWORK*
		Weighted	*WTSPSS*	Weighted	*WTSPSS** *WTWORK*†
Unweighted	N/A	Weighted	*WTSPSS*	Weighted Unweighted†	*WTSPSS** N/A

*If *WTSPSS* exists in the working file.
†If *WTSPSS* does not exist in the working file.

FROM Subcommand

FROM specifies an SPSS-format data file as the source file whose dictionary information is to be applied to the working file.

- FROM is required.
- Only one SPSS-format data file can be specified on FROM.
- The SPSS-format data file from which the current working file was built can be specified on FROM. This will restore dictionary information from the most recently saved version of the file.

AUTORECODE

```
AUTORECODE VARIABLES=varlist

 /INTO new varlist

 [/DESCENDING]

 [/PRINT]
```

Example

```
AUTORECODE VARIABLES=COMPANY /INTO RCOMPANY.
```

Overview

AUTORECODE recodes the values of string and numeric variables to consecutive integers and puts the recoded values into a new variable called a **target variable**. The value labels or values of the original variable are used as value labels for the target variable. AUTORECODE is useful for creating numeric independent (grouping) variables from string variables for procedures like ONEWAY, ANOVA, MANOVA, and DISCRIMINANT. AUTORECODE can also recode the values of factor variables to consecutive integers, which is required by MANOVA and which reduces the amount of workspace needed by other statistical procedures like ANOVA. AUTORECODE is also useful with the TABLES procedure, where string values are truncated to eight characters but value labels can be displayed in full. (See the *SPSS Tables* manual for more information.)

AUTORECODE is similar to the RECODE command. The main difference is that AUTORECODE automatically generates the values. In RECODE, you must specify the new values.

Options

Displaying Recoded Variables. You can display the values of the original and recoded variables using the PRINT subcommand.

Ordering of Values. By default, values are recoded in ascending order (lowest to highest). You can recode values in descending order (highest to lowest) using the DESCENDING subcommand.

Basic Specification

The basic specification is VARIABLES, and INTO. VARIABLES specifies the variables to be recoded. INTO provides names for the target variables that store the new values. VARIABLES and INTO must name or imply the same number of variables.

Subcommand Order

- VARIABLES must be specified first.
- INTO must immediately follow VARIABLES.

Syntax Rules

A variable cannot be recoded into itself. More generally, target variable names cannot duplicate any variable names already in the working file.

Operations

- The values of each variable to be recoded are sorted and then assigned numeric values. By default, the values are assigned in ascending order: 1 is assigned to the lowest nonmissing value of the original variable, 2 to the second-lowest nonmissing value, and so on for each value of the original variable.
- Values of the original variables are unchanged.
- Missing values are recoded into values higher than any nonmissing values, with their order preserved. For example, if the original variable has 10 nonmissing values, the first missing value is recoded as 11 and retains its user-missing status. System-missing values remain system-missing.
- AUTORECODE does not sort the cases in the working file. As a result, the consecutive numbers assigned to the target variables may not be in order in the file.
- Target variables are assigned the same variable labels as the original source variables. To change the variable labels, use the VARIABLE LABELS command after AUTORECODE.
- Value labels are automatically generated for each value of the target variables. If the original value had a label, that label is used for the corresponding new value. If the original value did not have a label, the old value itself is used as the value label for the new value. The defined print format of the old value is used to create the new value label.
- AUTORECODE ignores SPLIT FILE specifications. However, any SELECT IF specifications are in effect for AUTORECODE.

Example

```
DATA LIST / COMPANY 1-21 (A) SALES 24-28.
BEGIN DATA
CATFOOD JOY            10000
OLD FASHIONED CATFOOD  11200
 . . .
PRIME CATFOOD          10900
CHOICE CATFOOD         14600
END DATA.

AUTORECODE VARIABLES=COMPANY /INTO=RCOMPANY /PRINT.

TABLES TABLE = SALES BY RCOMPANY
  /TTITLE='CATFOOD SALES BY COMPANY'.
```

- Because TABLES truncates string variables to eight characters, AUTORECODE is used to recode the string variable *COMPANY*, which contains the names of various hypothetical cat food companies.
- AUTORECODE recodes *COMPANY* into a numeric variable *RCOMPANY*. Values of *RCOMPANY* are consecutive integers beginning with 1 and ending with the number of different values entered for *COMPANY*. The values of *COMPANY* are used as value labels for *RCOMPANY*'s numeric values. The *PRINT* subcommand displays a table of the original and recoded values.
- The variable *RCOMPANY* is used as the banner variable in the TABLES procedure to produce a table of sales figures for each cat food company. The value labels for *RCOMPANY* are used as column headings. Since TABLES does not truncate value labels, the full company names appear.

Example

```
AUTORECODE VARIABLES=REGION /INTO=RREGION /PRINT.
ANOVA Y BY RREGION (1,5).
```

- In statistical procedures, empty cells can reduce performance and increase memory requirements. In this example, assume that the factor *REGION* has only five nonempty categories, represented by the numeric codes 1, 4, 6, 14, and 20. AUTORECODE recodes those values into 1, 2, 3, 4, and 5 for target variable *RREGION*.
- The variable *RREGION* is used in ANOVA. If the original variable *REGION* were used, the amount of memory required by ANOVA would be 4429 bytes. Using variable *RREGION*, ANOVA requires only 449 bytes of memory.

Example

```
DATA LIST / RELIGION 1-8 (A) Y 10-13.
MISSING VALUES RELIGION (' ').
BEGIN DATA
CATHOLIC 2013
PROTEST  3234
JEWISH   5169
NONE      714
OTHER    2321
  . . .
END DATA.
AUTORECODE VARIABLES=RELIGION /INTO=NRELIG /PRINT /DESCENDING.
MANOVA Y BY NRELIG(1,5).
```

- Because MANOVA requires consecutive integer values for factor levels, the string variable *RELIGION* is recoded into a numeric variable. The five values for *RELIGION* are first sorted in descending order (Z to A) and are then assigned values 1, 2, 3, 4, and 5 in target variable *NRELIG*.
- Since a blank space is specified as a user-missing value, it is assigned the value 6. In the table produced by PRINT, the value 6 is displayed as 6M for the variable *NRELIG* to flag it as a user-missing value.
- The values of *RELIGION* are used as value labels for the corresponding new values in *NRELIG*.
- Target variable *NRELIG* is used as a factor variable in MANOVA.

VARIABLES Subcommand

VARIABLES specifies the variables to be recoded. VARIABLES is required and must be specified first. The actual keyword VARIABLES is optional.

- Values from the specified variables are recoded and stored in the target variables listed on INTO. Values of the original variables are unchanged.

INTO Subcommand

INTO provides names for the target variables that store the new values. INTO is required and must immediately follow VARIABLES.

- The number of target variables named or implied on INTO must equal the number of source variables listed on VARIABLES.

Example

```
AUTORECODE VARIABLES=V1 V2 V3 /INTO=NEWV1 TO NEWV3 /PRINT.
```

- AUTORECODE stores the recoded values of *V1*, *V2*, and *V3* into target variables named *NEWV1*, *NEWV2*, and *NEWV3*.

PRINT Subcommand

PRINT displays a correspondence table of the original values of the source variables and the new values of the target variables. The new value labels are also displayed.

- The only specification is keyword PRINT. There are no additional specifications.

DESCENDING Subcommand

By default, values for the source variable are recoded in ascending order (from lowest to highest). DESCENDING assigns the values to new variables in descending order (from highest to lowest). The largest value is assigned 1, the second-largest, 2, and so on.

- The only specification is keyword DESCENDING. There are no additional specifications.

BEGIN DATA—END DATA

```
BEGIN DATA
data records
END DATA
```

Example

```
BEGIN DATA
1  3424   274 ABU DHABI 2
2 39932    86 AMSTERDAM 4
3  8889   232 ATHENS
4  3424   294 BOGOTA    3
END DATA.
```

Overview

BEGIN DATA and END DATA are used when data are entered within the command sequence (inline data). BEGIN DATA and END DATA are also used for inline matrix data. BEGIN DATA signals the beginning of data lines and END DATA signals the end of data lines.

Basic Specification

The basic specification is BEGIN DATA, the data lines, and END DATA. BEGIN DATA must be specified by itself on the line that immediately precedes the first data line. END DATA is specified by itself on the line that immediately follows the last data line.

Syntax Rules

- BEGIN DATA, the data, and END DATA must precede the first procedure.
- The command terminator after BEGIN DATA is optional. It is best to leave it out so that the program will treat inline data as one continuous specification.
- END DATA must always begin in column 1. It must be spelled out in full and can have only one space between the words END and DATA. Procedures and additional transformations can follow the END DATA command.
- Data lines must *not* have a command terminator. For inline data formats, see DATA LIST.
- Inline data records are limited to a maximum of 80 columns. (On some systems, the maximum may be fewer than 80 columns.) If data records exceed 80 columns, they must be stored in an external file that is specified on the FILE subcommand of the DATA LIST (or similar) command.

Operations

- When the program encounters BEGIN DATA, it begins to read and process data on the next input line. All preceding transformation commands are processed as the working file is built.
- The program continues to evaluate input lines as data until it encounters END DATA, at which point it begins evaluating input lines as commands.
- No other commands are recognized between BEGIN DATA and END DATA.
- The INCLUDE command can specify a file that contains BEGIN DATA, data lines, and END DATA. The data in such a file are treated as inline data. Thus, the FILE subcommand should be omitted from the DATA LIST (or similar) command.
- When running the program from prompts, the prompt DATA> appears immediately after BEGIN DATA is specified. After END DATA is specified, the command line prompt returns.

Example

```
DATA LIST /XVAR 1 YVAR ZVAR 3-12 CVAR 14-22(A) JVAR 24.
BEGIN DATA
1  3424   274 ABU DHABI 2
2 39932    86 AMSTERDAM 4
3  8889   232 ATHENS
4  3424   294 BOGOTA    3
5 11323   332 HONG KONG 3
6   323   232 MANILA    1
7  3234   899 CHICAGO   4
8 78998 2344 VIENNA    3
9  8870   983 ZURICH    5
END DATA.
MEANS XVAR BY JVAR.
```

- DATA LIST defines the names and column locations of the variables. The FILE subcommand is omitted because the data are inline.
- There are nine cases in the inline data. Each line of data completes a case.
- END DATA signals the end of data lines. It begins in column 1 and has only a single space between END and DATA.

BREAK

```
BREAK
```

Overview

BREAK controls looping that cannot be fully controlled with IF clauses. Generally, BREAK is used within a DO IF—END IF structure. The expression on the DO IF command specifies the condition in which BREAK is executed.

Basic Specification

- The only specification is keyword BREAK. There are no additional specifications.
- BREAK must be specified within a loop structure. Otherwise, an error results.

Operations

- A BREAK command inside a loop structure but not inside a DO IF—END IF structure terminates the first iteration of the loop for all cases, since no conditions for BREAK are specified.
- A BREAK command within an inner loop terminates only iterations in that structure, not in any outer loop structures.

Example

```
VECTOR             #X(10).
LOOP               #I = 1 TO #NREC.
+  DATA LIST          NOTABLE/ #X1 TO #X10 1-20.
+  LOOP               #J = 1 TO 10.
+     DO IF              SYSMIS(#X(#J)).
+        BREAK.
+     END IF.
+     COMPUTE            X = #X(#J).
+     END CASE.
+  END LOOP.
END LOOP.
```

- The inner loop terminates when there is a system-missing value for any of the variables *#X1* to *#X10*.
- The outer loop continues until all records are read.

CACHE

```
CACHE.
```

Although the virtual active file can vastly reduce the amount of temporary disk space required, the absence of a temporary copy of the "active" file means that the original data source has to be re-read for each procedure. For data tables read from a database source this means the SQL query that reads the information from the database must be re-executed for any command or procedure that needs to read the data. Since virtually all statistical analysis procedures and charting procedures need to read the data, the SQL query is re-executed for each procedure you run, which can result in a significant increase in processing time if you run a large number of procedures.

If you have sufficient disk space on the computer performing the analysis (either your local computer or a remote server), you can eliminate multiple SQL queries and improve processing time by creating a data cache of the active file with the CACHE command. The CACHE command tells SPSS to copy all the data to a temporary disk file the next time the data are passed to run a procedure. If you want the cache written immediately, use the EXECUTE command after the CACHE command.

- The only specification is the command name CACHE.
- A cache file will not be written during a procedure which uses temporary variables.
- A cache file will not be written if the data are already in a temporary disk file and that file has not been modified since it was written.

Example

```
CACHE.
TEMPORARY.
RECODE alcohol(0 thru .04 = 'sober') (.04 thru .08 = 'tipsy')
  (else = 'drunk') into state.
FREQUENCIES var=state.
GRAPH...
```

No cache file will be written during the FREQUENCIES procedure. It will be written during the GRAPH procedure.

CASEPLOT

```
CASEPLOT [VARIABLES=]varlist

 [/DIFF={1}]
        {n}

 [/SDIFF={1}]
         {n}

 [/PERIOD=n]

 [/{NOLOG**}]
   {LN     }

 [/ID=varname]

 [/MARK={varname           }]
        {date specification}

 [/SPLIT {UNIFORM**}]
         {SCALE    }

 [/APPLY [='model name']]
```

For plots with one variable:

```
 [/FORMAT=[{NOFILL**}]  [{NOREFERENCE**}]
           {LEFT    }    {REFERENCE    }
           {RIGHT   }
```

For plots with multiple variables:

```
 [/FORMAT={NOJOIN**}]
          {JOIN    }
          {HILO    }
```

**Default if the subcommand is omitted.

Example

```
CASEPLOT TICKETS
  /LN
  /DIFF
  /SDIFF
  /PERIOD=12
  /FORMAT=REFERENCE
  /MARK=Y 55 M 6.
```

Overview

CASEPLOT produces a plot of one or more time series or sequence variables. You can request natural log and differencing transformations to produce plots of transformed variables. There are several plot formats available.

Options

Modifying the Variables. You can request a natural log transformation of the variable using the LN subcommand and seasonal and nonseasonal differencing to any degree using the SDIFF and DIFF subcommands. With seasonal differencing, you can also specify the periodicity on the PERIOD subcommand.

Plot Format. With the FORMAT subcommand, you can fill in the area on one side of the plotted values on plots with one variable. You can also plot a reference line indicating the variable mean. For plots with two or more variables, you can specify whether you want to join the values for each case with a horizontal line. With the ID subcommand, you can label the vertical axis with the values of a specified variable. You can mark the onset of an intervention variable on the plot with the MARK subcommand.

Split-File Processing. You can control how to plot data that have been divided into subgroups by a SPLIT FILE command using the SPLIT subcommand.

Basic Specification

The basic specification is one or more variable names.

- If the DATE command has been specified, the vertical axis is labeled with the *DATE_* variable at periodic intervals. Otherwise, sequence numbers are used. The horizontal axis is labeled with the value scale determined by the plotted variables.

Figure 1 shows a default high-resolution plot with DATE=YEAR 1900. Figure 2 shows the same default plot in low resolution.

Figure 1 CASEPLOT=PRICE (in high resolution)

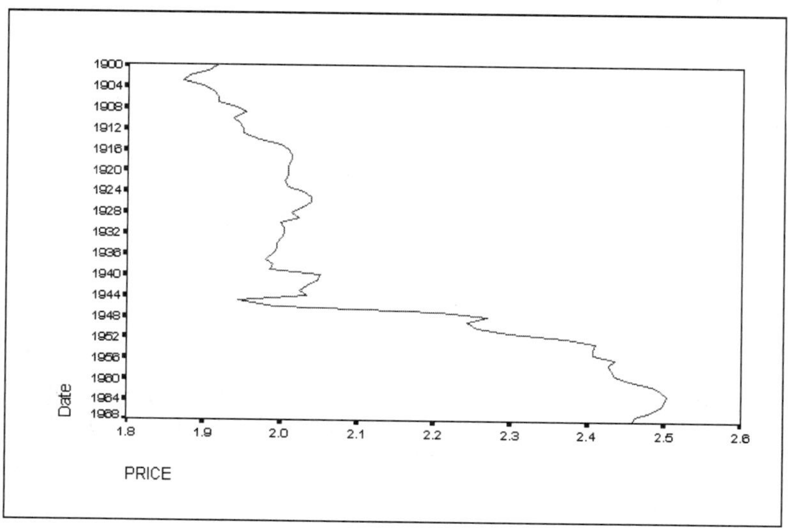

Figure 2 CASEPLOT=PRICE (low resolution)

```
The following plot symbols are used:
    P - Variable PRICE
    M - Missing Data (placed left of the vertical axis)

       1.7       1.9       2.1       2.3       2.5       2.7
YYYY   œ¡fffffffff¡fffffffff¡fffffffff¡fffffffff¡fffffffff¡ø     PRICE
1900   £           P                                       £    1.9176
1901   £          P                                        £    1.9059
1902   £         P                                         £    1.8798
1903   £         P                                         £    1.8727
1904   £          P                                        £    1.8984
1905   £           P                                       £    1.9137
1906   £           P                                       £    1.9176
1907   £           P                                       £    1.9176
1908   £            P                                      £    1.9420
1909  f£             P                                     £f   1.9547
1910   £            P                                      £    1.9379
1911   £            P                                      £    1.9462
1912   £             P                                     £    1.9504
1913   £             P                                     £    1.9504
1914   £              P                                    £    1.9723
1915   £               P                                   £    2.0000
1916   £               P                                   £    2.0097
1917   £                P                                  £    2.0146
1918   £                P                                  £    2.0146
1919  f£               P                                   £f   2.0097
1920   £               P                                   £    2.0097
1921   £               P                                   £    2.0097
1922   £               P                                   £    2.0048
1923   £               P                                   £    2.0097
1924   £                P                                  £    2.0296
1925   £                 P                                 £    2.0399
1926   £                 P                                 £    2.0399
1927   £                P                                  £    2.0296
1928   £                P                                  £    2.0146
1929  f£                P                                  £f   2.0245
1930   £               P                                   £    2.0000
1931   £               P                                   £    2.0048
1932   £               P                                   £    2.0048
1933   £               P                                   £    2.0000
1934   £               P                                   £    1.9952
1935   £               P                                   £    1.9952
1936   £               P                                   £    1.9905
1937   £              P                                    £    1.9813
1938   £               P                                   £    1.9905
1939  f£              P                                    £f   1.9859
1940   £                  P                                £    2.0518
1941   £                 P                                 £    2.0474
1942   £                 P                                 £    2.0341
1943   £                P                                  £    2.0255
1944   £                 P                                 £    2.0341
1945   £            P                                      £    1.9445
1946   £               P                                   £    1.9939
1947   £                         P                         £    2.2082
1948   £                            P                      £    2.2700
1949  f£                           P                       £f   2.2430
1950   £                            P                      £    2.2567
1951   £                              P                    £    2.2988
1952   £                                  P                £    2.3723
1953   £                                    P              £    2.4105
1954   £                                   P               £    2.4081
1955   £                                   P               £    2.4081
1956   £                                     P             £    2.4367
1957   £                                    P              £    2.4284
1958   £                                     P             £    2.4310
1959  f£                                     P             £f   2.4363
1960   £                                      P            £    2.4552
1961   £                                       P           £    2.4838
1962   £                                        P          £    2.4958
1963   £                                        P          £    2.5048
1964   £                                        P          £    2.5017
1965   £                                        P          £    2.4958
1966   £                                       P           £    2.4838
1967   £                                      P            £    2.4636
1968   £                                      P            £    2.4580
YYYY   ¿¶fffffffff¶fffffffff¶fffffffff¶fffffffff¶fffffffff¶Ÿ     PRICE
       1.7       1.9       2.1       2.3       2.5       2.7
```

Subcommand Order

- Subcommands can be specified in any order.

Syntax Rules

- VARIABLES can be specified only once.
- Other subcommands can be specified more than once, but only the last specification of each one is executed.

Operations

- Subcommand specifications apply to all variables named on the CASEPLOT command.
- If the LN subcommand is specified, any differencing requested on that CASEPLOT command is done on the log-transformed variables.
- In high-resolution plots, split-file information is displayed as part of the subtitle and transformation information is displayed as part of the footnote.
- In low-resolution plots, values of plotted variables are displayed along the right axis. A wider page specification on SET allows you to display the values of more variables but does not change the plot frame size.

Limitations

- Maximum 1 VARIABLES subcommand. There is no limit on the number of variables named on the list.

Example

```
CASEPLOT TICKETS
  /LN
  /DIFF
  /SDIFF
  /PERIOD=12
  /FORMAT=REFERENCE
  /MARK=Y 55 M 6.
```

- This example produces a plot of *TICKETS* after a natural log transformation, differencing, and seasonal differencing have been applied.
- LN transforms the data using the natural logarithm (base e) of the variable.
- DIFF differences the variable once.
- SDIFF and PERIOD apply one degree of seasonal differencing with a period of 12.
- FORMAT=REFERENCE adds a reference line at the variable mean. In a low-resolution plot, the area between the plotted values and the mean is filled with the plotting symbol (*T*).

- MARK provides a marker on the plot at June 1955. The marker is displayed as a horizontal reference line in a high-resolution plot.

VARIABLES Subcommand

VARIABLES specifies the names of the variables to be plotted and is the only required subcommand. The actual keyword VARIABLES can be omitted.

DIFF Subcommand

DIFF specifies the degree of differencing used to convert a nonstationary variable to a stationary one with a constant mean and variance before plotting.

- You can specify any positive integer on DIFF.
- If DIFF is specified without a value, the default is 1.
- The number of values displayed decreases by 1 for each degree of differencing.

Example

```
CASEPLOT TICKETS
  /DIFF=2.
```

- In this example, TICKETS is differenced twice before plotting.

SDIFF Subcommand

If the variable exhibits a seasonal or periodic pattern, you can use the SDIFF subcommand to seasonally difference a variable before plotting.

- The specification on SDIFF indicates the degree of seasonal differencing and can be any positive integer.
- If SDIFF is specified without a value, the degree of seasonal differencing defaults to 1.
- The number of seasons displayed decreases by 1 for each degree of seasonal differencing.
- The length of the period used by SDIFF is specified on the PERIOD subcommand. If the PERIOD subcommand is not specified, the periodicity established on the TSET or DATE command is used (see the PERIOD subcommand below).

PERIOD Subcommand

PERIOD indicates the length of the period to be used by the SDIFF subcommand.

- The specification on PERIOD indicates how many observations are in one period or season and can be any positive integer.
- PERIOD is ignored if it is used without the SDIFF subcommand.
- If PERIOD is not specified, the periodicity established on TSET PERIOD is in effect. If TSET PERIOD is not specified either, the periodicity established on the DATE command

is used. If periodicity is not established anywhere, the SDIFF subcommand will not be executed.

Example

```
CASEPLOT TICKETS
  /SDIFF=1
  /PERIOD=12.
```

- This command applies one degree of seasonal differencing with 12 observations per season to *TICKETS* before plotting.

LN and NOLOG Subcommands

LN transforms the data using the natural logarithm (base *e*) of the variable and is used to remove varying amplitude over time. NOLOG indicates that the data should not be log transformed. NOLOG is the default.

- If you specify LN on CASEPLOT, any differencing requested on that command will be done on the log-transformed variable.
- There are no additional specifications on LN or NOLOG.
- Only the last LN or NOLOG subcommand on a CASEPLOT command is executed.
- If a natural log transformation is requested, any value less than or equal to zero is set to system-missing.
- NOLOG is generally used with an APPLY subcommand to turn off a previous LN specification.

Example

```
CASEPLOT TICKETS
  /LN.
```

- In this example, *TICKETS* is transformed using the natural logarithm before plotting.

ID Subcommand

ID names a variable whose values will be used as the left-axis labels.

- The only specification on ID is a variable name. If you have a variable named *ID* in your working data file, the equals sign after the subcommand is required.
- ID overrides the specification on TSET ID.
- If ID or TSET ID is not specified, the left vertical axis is labeled with the *DATE_* variable created by the DATE command. If the *DATE_* variable has not been created, the observation or sequence number is used as the label.

Example

```
CASEPLOT VARA
  /ID=VARB.
```

- In this example, the values of variable *VARB* will be used to label the left axis of the plot of *VARA*.

FORMAT Subcommand

FORMAT controls the plot format.

- The specification on FORMAT is one of the keywords listed below.
- Keywords NOFILL, LEFT, RIGHT, NOREFERENCE, and REFERENCE apply to plots with one variable. NOFILL, LEFT, and RIGHT are alternatives and indicate how the plot is filled. NOREFERENCE and REFERENCE are alternatives and specify whether a reference line is displayed. For low-resolution plots, only one keyword can be specified. One keyword *from each set* can be specified for high-resolution plots. NOFILL and NOREFERENCE are the defaults.
- Keywords JOIN, NOJOIN, and HILO apply to plots with multiple variables and are alternatives. NOJOIN is the default. Only one keyword can be specified on a FORMAT subcommand for plots with two variables.

The following formats are available for plots of one variable:

NOFILL *Plot only the values for the variable with no fill.* NOFILL produces a plot with no fill to the left or right of the plotted values. This is the default format when one variable is specified.

LEFT *Plot the values for the variable and fill in the area to the left.* For high-resolution plots, if the plotted variable has missing or negative values, keyword LEFT is ignored and the default NOFILL is used instead. Figure 3 contains a left-filled high-resolution plot. In low-resolution plots, the area to the left of the plotted curve is filled in with the first character of the variable name.

RIGHT *Plot the values for the variable and fill in the area to the right.* In low-resolution plots, the area to the right of the plotted curve is filled in with the first character of the variable name. For high-resolution plots, RIGHT is ignored; if specified, the default NOFILL is used instead.

Figure 3 FORMAT=LEFT

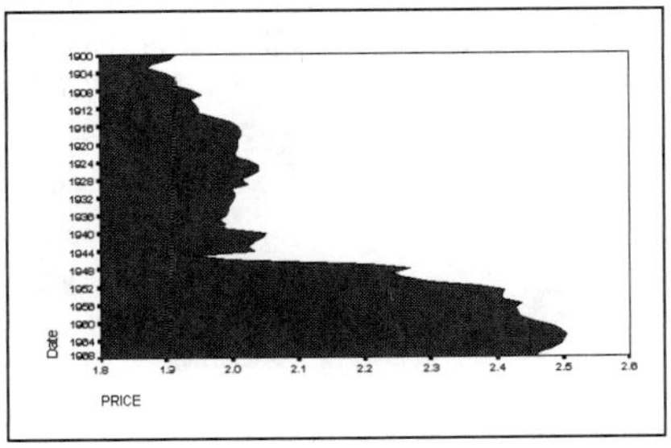

NOREFERENCE *Do not plot a reference line.* This is the default when one variable is specified.

REFERENCE *Plot a reference line indicating the variable mean.* In low resolution, the area between the plotted curve and the reference line is filled in with the plotting character (the first character of the variable name). For low-resolution plots, you cannot specify REFERENCE together with either LEFT or RIGHT. In high resolution, a fill chart is displayed as an area chart with a reference line and a nofill chart is a line chart with a reference line. Figure 4 shows a high-resolution plot with a reference line indicating the mean of the variable.

Figure 4 FORMAT=REFERENCE

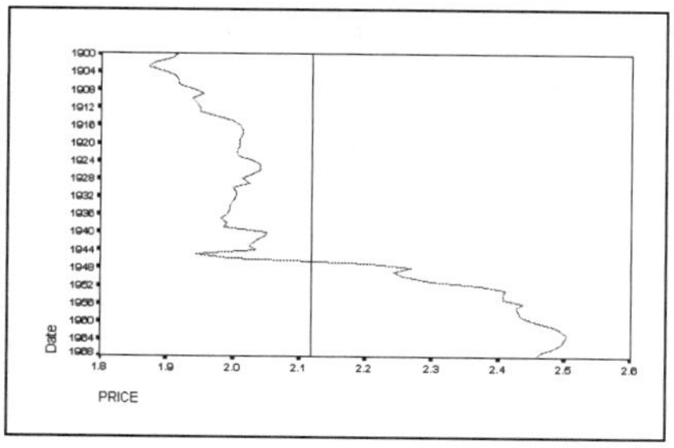

The following formats are available for plots of multiple variables:

NOJOIN *Plot the values of each variable named.* In high-resolution plots, different colors or line patterns are used for multiple variables. In low-resolution plots, the plotting character for each variable is the first character of the variable name. Multiple occurrences of the same value for a single observation are plotted using a dollar sign ($). This is the default format for plots of multiple variables.

JOIN *Plot the values of each variable and join the values for each case.* Values are plotted as described for NOJOIN and the values for each case are joined together by a line. Figure 5 contains a plot in this format with three variables (*PRICE, INCOME,* and *CONSUMP*).

HILO *Plot the highest and lowest values across variables for each case and join the two values together.* The high and low values are plotted as a pair of vertical bars and are joined with a dashed line. For high-resolution plots, HILO is ignored if more than three variables are specified and the default NOJOIN is used instead. Figure 6 contains a plot in this format with three variables (*PRICE, INCOME,* and *CONSUMP*).

Figure 5 FORMAT=JOIN

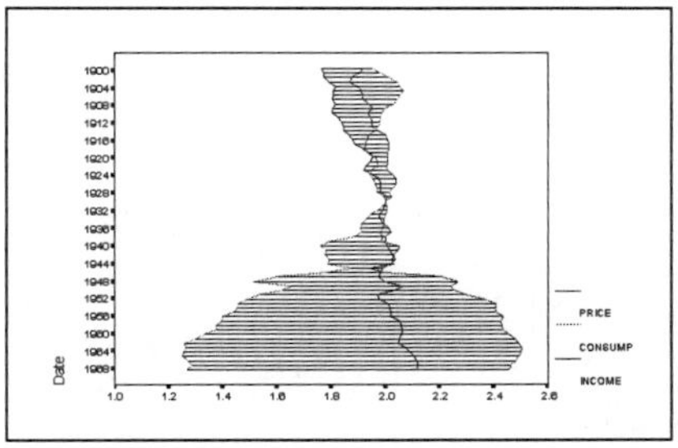

Figure 6 FORMAT=HILO

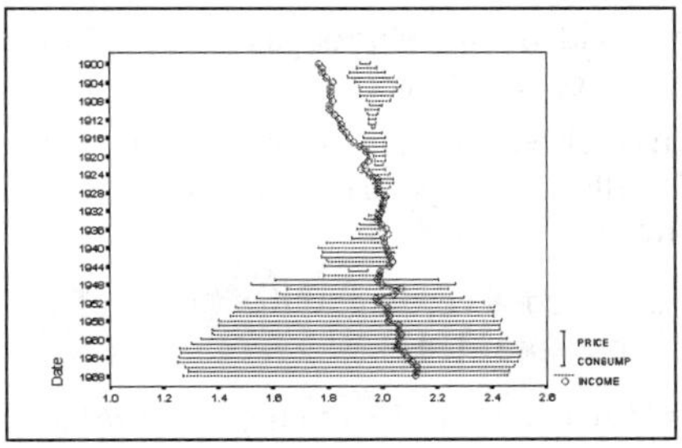

MARK Subcommand

Use MARK to indicate the onset of an intervention variable. Figure 7 shows a high-resolution plot with a reference line indicating the year 1945.

- In high resolution, the onset date is indicated by a horizontal reference line. In low resolution it is indicated by a tick mark on the left axis.
- The specification on MARK can be either a variable name or an onset date if the *DATE_* variable exists.
- If a variable is named, the reference line indicates where the values of that variable change.
- A date specification follows the same format as the DATE command, that is, a keyword followed by a value. For example, the specification for June 1955 is Y 1955 M 6 (or Y 55 M 6 if only the last two digits of the year are used on DATE).

Figure 7 MARK=Y 1945

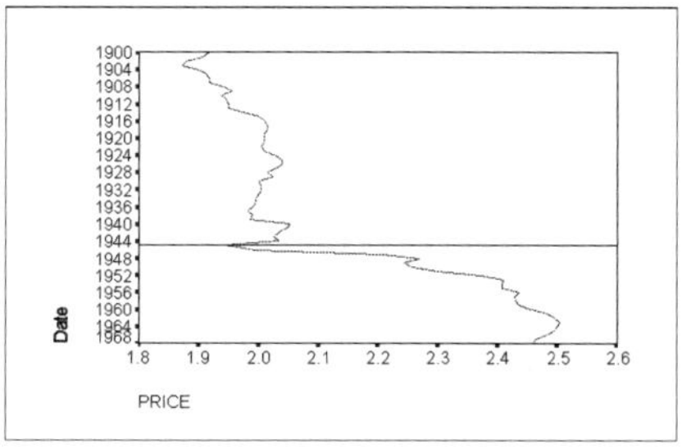

SPLIT Subcommand

SPLIT specifies how to plot data that have been divided into subgroups by a SPLIT FILE command. The specification on SPLIT is either SCALE or UNIFORM.

- If FORMAT=REFERENCE is specified when SPLIT=SCALE, the reference line is placed at the mean of the subgroup. If FORMAT=REFERENCE is specified when SPLIT=UNIFORM, the reference line is placed at the overall mean.

UNIFORM *Uniform scale.* The horizontal axis is scaled according to the values of the entire data set. This is the default if SPLIT is not specified.

SCALE *Individual scale.* The horizontal axis is scaled according to the values of each individual subgroup.

Example

```
SPLIT FILE BY REGION.
CASEPLOT TICKETS / SPLIT=SCALE.
```

- This example produces one plot for each *REGION* subgroup.
- The horizontal axis for each plot is scaled according to the values of *TICKETS* for each particular region.

APPLY Subcommand

APPLY allows you to produce a caseplot using previously defined specifications without having to repeat the CASEPLOT subcommands.

- The only specification on APPLY is the name of a previous model in quotes. If a model name is not specified, the specifications from the previous CASEPLOT command are used.

- If no variables are specified, the variables that were specified for the original plot are used.
- To change one or more plot specifications, specify the subcommands of only those portions you want to change after the APPLY subcommand.
- To plot different variables, enter new variable names before or after the APPLY subcommand.

Example

```
CASEPLOT TICKETS
  /LN
  /DIFF=1
  /SDIFF=1
  /PER=12.
CASEPLOT ROUNDTRP
  /APPLY.
CASEPLOT APPLY
  /NOLOG.
```

- The first command produces a plot of *TICKETS* after a natural log transformation, differencing, and seasonal differencing.
- The second command plots *ROUNDTRP* using the same transformations specified for *TICKETS*.
- The third command produces a plot of *ROUNDTRP*, but this time without any natural log transformation. The variable is still differenced once and seasonally differenced with a periodicity of 12.

CASESTOVARS

```
CASESTOVARS
[/ID = varlist]
[/FIXED = varlist]
[/AUTOFIX = {YES**}]
            {NO   }
[/COUNT = new variable ["label"]]
[/RENAME varname=rootname varname=rootname ...]
[/SEPARATOR = {"."      }]
              {"string" }]
[/INDEX = varlist]
[/GROUPBY = {VARIABLE**}]
            {INDEX     }]
[/DROP = varlist]
```

**Default if the subcommand is omitted.

Example

```
CASESTOVARS /ID idvar /INDEX var1.
```

Overview

A **variable** contains information that you want to analyze, such as a measurement or a test score. A **case** is an observation, such as an individual or an institution. In a simple data structure, each variable is a single **column** in your data. So if you were measuring test scores, for example, all test score values would appear in only one column. In a simple data structure, each case is a single **row** in your data. So if you were measuring scores for all students in a class, there would be a row for each student.

CASESTOVARS restructures **complex** data structures (in which information about a case is stored in more than one row) into a data file in which measurements for that case are organized into separate columns of a single row. It replaces the working data file.

You can use CASESTOVARS to restructure data files in which repeated measurements of a single case were recorded in multiple rows into a new data file in which each case appears in a single row.

Options

Automatic classification of fixed variables. The values of fixed variables do not vary within a row group. You can use the AUTOFIX subcommand to let the procedure determine which variables are fixed and which are to become variable groups in the new data file.

Naming new variables. You can use the RENAME, SEPARATOR, and INDEX subcommands to control the names for the new variables.

Ordering new variables. You can use the GROUPBY subcommand to specify how to order the new variables in the new data file.

Creating a count variable. You can use the COUNT subcommand to create a count variable that contains the number of rows in the original data that were used to create a row in the new data file.

Variable Selection. You can use the DROP subcommand to specify which variables from the original data file are dropped from the new data file.

Basic Specification

The basic specification is simply the command keyword.

- If split file processing is in effect, the basic specification creates a row in the new data file for each combination of values of the SPLIT FILE variables. If split file processing is not in effect, the basic specification results in a new data file with one row.
- Because the basic specification can create quite a few new columns in the new data file, the use of an ID subcommand to identify case groups is recommended.

Subcommand Order

Subcommands can be specified in any order.

Syntax Rules

Each subcommand can be specified only once.

Operations

- **Original row order.** CASESTOVARS assumes that the original data are sorted by SPLIT and ID variables.
- **Identifying row groups in the original file.** A **row group** consists of rows in the original data that share the same values of variables listed on the ID subcommand. Row groups are consolidated into a single row in the new data file. Each time a new combination of ID values is encountered, a new row is created.
- **SPLIT file processing and row groups.** If split file processing is in effect, the split variables are automatically used to identify row groups (they are treated as though they appeared first on the ID subcommand). Split file processing remains in effect in the new data file unless a variable that is used to split the file is named on the DROP subcommand.
- **New variable groups.** A **variable group** is a group of related columns in the new data file that is created from a variable in the original data. Each variable group contains a variable for each index value or combination of index values encountered.

- **Candidate variables.** A variable in the original data is a candidate to become a variable group in the new data file if it is not used on the SPLIT command or the ID, FIXED, or DROP subcommands and its values vary within the row group. Variables named on the SPLIT, ID, and FIXED subcommands are assumed to not vary within the row group and are simply copied into the new data file.
- **New variable names.** The names of the variables in a new group are constructed by the procedure. It uses the rootname specified on the RENAME subcommand and the string named on the SEPARATOR subcommand.
- **New variable formats.** With the exception of names and labels, the dictionary information for all of the new variables in a group (for example, value labels and format) is taken from the variable in the original data.
- **New variable order.** New variables are created in the order specified by the GROUPBY subcommand.
- **Weighted files.** The WEIGHT command does not affect the results of CASESTOVARS. If original data are weighted, the new data file will be weighted unless the variable that is used as the weight is dropped from the new data file.
- **Selected cases.** The FILTER and USE commands do not affect the results of CASESTOVARS. It processes all cases.

Limitations

The TEMPORARY command cannot be in effect when CASESTOVARS is executed.

Example

The following is the LIST output for a data file in which repeated measurements for the same case are stored on separate rows in a single variable:

```
insure    caseid    month    bps    bpd

BCBS         1         1     160    100
BCBS         2         1     120     70
BCBS         2         2     130     86
Prucare      1         1     160     94
Prucare      1         2     200    105
Prucare      1         3     180    105
Prucare      2         1     135     90
```

The commands:

```
SPLIT FILE BY insure.
CASESTOVARS
 /ID=caseid
 /INDEX=month.
```

creates a new variable group for *bps* and a new group for *bpd*. The LIST output for the new working file is as follows:

```
insure    caseid   bps.1    bps.2    bps.3    bpd.1    bpd.2    bpd.3

BCBS      1          160        .        .      100        .        .
BCBS      2          120      130        .       70       86        .
Prucare   1          160      200      180       94      105      105
Prucare   2          135        .        .       90        .        .
```

- The row groups in the original data are identified by *insure* and *caseid*.
- There are four row groups—one for each combination of the values in *insure* and *caseid*.
- The command creates four rows in the new data file, one for each row group.
- The candidate variables from the original file are *bps* and *bpd*. They vary within row group, so they will become variable groups in the new data file.
- The command creates two new variable groups—one for *bps* and one for *bpd*.
- Each variable group contains three new variables—one for each unique value of the index variable *month*.

ID Subcommand

The ID subcommand specifies variables that identify the rows from the original data that should be grouped together in the new data file.

- If the ID subcommand is omitted, only SPLIT FILE variables (if any) will be used to group rows in the original data and to identify rows in the new data file.
- CASESTOVARS expects the data to be sorted by SPLIT FILE variables and then by ID variables. If split file processing is in effect, the original data should be sorted on the split variables, in the order given on the SPLIT FILE command; and then on the ID variables, in the order in which they appear in the ID subcommand.
- A variable may appear on both the SPLIT FILE command and the ID subcommand.
- Variables listed on the SPLIT FILE command and on the ID subcommand are copied into the new data file with their original values and dictionary information unless they are dropped with the DROP subcommand.
- Variables listed on the ID subcommand may not appear on the FIXED or INDEX subcommands.
- Rows in the original data for which any ID variable has the system-missing value or is blank are not included in the new data file, and a warning message is displayed.
- ID variables are not candidates to become a variable group in the new data file.

COUNT Subcommand

CASESTOVARS consolidates row groups in the original data into a single row in the new data file. The COUNT subcommand creates a new variable that contains the number of rows in the original data that were used to generate the row in the new data file.

- One new variable is named on the COUNT subcommand. It must have a unique name.

- The label for the new variable is optional and, if specified, must be delimited by apostrophes or quotation marks.
- The format of the new variable is F4.0.

Example

```
SPLIT FILE BY insure.
CASESTOVARS
 /ID=caseid
 /COUNT=countvar
 /DROP=insure month bpd.

caseid  countvar  bps.1    bpd.2    bps.3

  1         1      160       .        .
  2         2      120      130       .
  1         3      160      200      180
  2         1      135       .        .
```

FIXED Subcommand

The FIXED subcommand names the variables that should be copied from the original data to the new data file.

- CASESTOVARS requires that fixed variables not vary within row group in the original data.
- Fixed variables appear as a single column in the new data file. Their values are simply copied to the new file.
- The AUTOFIX subcommand can automatically determine which variables in the original data are fixed. By default, the AUTOFIX subcommand overrides the FIXED subcommand.

AUTOFIX Subcommand

The AUTOFIX subcommand evaluates candidate variables and classifies them as either fixed or as the source of a variable group.

- A **candidate variable** is a variable in the original data that does not appear on the SPLIT command or on the ID, INDEX, and DROP subcommands.
- An original variable that does not vary within the row group is classified as a **fixed variable** and is copied into a single variable in the new data file.
- An original variable that does vary within the row group is classified as the **source of a variable group**. It becomes a variable group in the new data file.

YES *Evaluate and automatically classify all candidate variables.* The procedure automatically evaluates and classifies all candidate variables. This is the default.
If there is a FIXED subcommand, the procedure displays a warning message for each misclassified variable and automatically corrects the error. Otherwise, no warning messages are displayed.
This option overrides the FIXED subcommand.

NO *Evaluate all candidate variables and terminate if there is an error.* The procedure evaluates all candidate variables. If there is an error—for example, if a variable listed on the FIXED subcommand varies within the row group—an error message is displayed and the command is not executed.

RENAME Subcommand

CASESTOVARS creates variable groups with new variables. The first part of the new variable name is either derived from the name of the original variable or is the rootname specified on the RENAME subcommand.

- The specification is the original variable name followed by a rootname.
- The named variable cannot be a SPLIT FILE variable and cannot appear on the ID, FIXED, INDEX, or DROP subcommands.
- A variable can be renamed only once.
- Only one RENAME subcommand can be used, but it can contain multiple specifications.

SEPARATOR Subcommand

CASESTOVARS creates variable groups that contain new variables. There are two parts to the name of a new variable—a rootname and an index. The parts are separated by a string. The separator string is specified on the SEPARATOR subcommand.

- If a separator is not specified, the default is a period.
- A separator can contain multiple characters. Avoid long strings, since variable names are restricted to eight characters.
- The separator must be delimited by apostrophes or quotation marks.
- You can suppress the separator by specifying /SEPARATOR="".

INDEX Subcommand

In the original data, a variable appears in a single column. In the new data file, that variable will appear in multiple new columns. The INDEX subcommand names the variables in the original data that should be used to create the new columns. INDEX variables are also used to name the new columns and, with the GROUPBY subcommand, can be used to order the new columns.

- String variables can be used as index variables. They cannot contain blank values for rows in the original data that qualify for inclusion in the new data file.
- Numeric variables can be used as index variables. They must contain only non-negative integer values and cannot have system-missing or blank values.
- Within each row group in the original file, each row must have a different combination of values of the index variables.
- If the INDEX subcommand is not used, the index starts with 1 within each row group and increments each time a new value is encountered in the original variable.

- Variables listed on the INDEX subcommand may not appear on the ID, FIXED, or DROP subcommands.
- Index variables are not are not candidates to become a variable group in the new data file.

GROUPBY Subcommand

The GROUPBY subcommand controls the order of the new variables in the new data file.

VARIABLE *Group new variables by original variable.* The procedure groups all variables created from an original variable together. This is the default.

INDEX *Group new variables by index variable.* The procedure groups variables according to the index variables.

Example

If the original variables are:

```
insure    caseid    month    bps    bpd
```

The command:

```
CASESTOVARS
 ID=insure caseid
 INDEX=month
 GROUPBY=INDEX.
```

creates a new file set with the following variable order:

```
insure  caseid  bps.1  bpd.1  bps.2  bpd.2  bps.3  bpd.3
```

- There are two variable groups—one for *bps* and one for *bpd.*
- All variables from an index value appear together.

Example

Using the same original data, the command:

```
CASESTOVARS
 ID=insure caseid
 INDEX=month
 GROUPBY=INDEX.
```

creates a new data file with the following variable order:

```
insure  caseid  bps.1  bpd.1  bps.2  bpd.2  bps.3  bpd.3
```

- Variables are grouped by values of the index variable *month—1*, *2*, and *3*.

DROP Subcommand

The DROP subcommand specifies the subset of variables to exclude from the new data file.

- You can drop variables that appear on the ID list.
- Variables listed on the DROP subcommand may not be appear on the FIXED or INDEX subcommand.
- Dropped variables are not candidates to become a variable group in the new data file.
- You cannot drop all variables. The new data file is required to have at least one variable.

CCF

```
CCF [VARIABLES=] series names [WITH series names]

 [/DIFF={1}]
        {n}

 [/SDIFF={1}]
         {n}

 [/PERIOD=n]

 [/{NOLOG**}]
   {LN     }

 [/SEASONAL]

 [/MXCROSS={7**}]
           {n  }

 [/APPLY[='model name']]
```

**Default if the subcommand is omitted and there is no corresponding specification on the TSET command.

Example

```
CCF VARX VARY
  /LN
  /DIFF=1
  /SDIFF=1
  /PERIOD=12
  /MXCROSS=25.
```

Overview

CCF displays and plots the cross-correlation functions of two or more time series. You can also display and plot the cross-correlations of transformed series by requesting natural log and differencing transformations within the procedure.

Options

Modifying the Series. You can request a natural log transformation of the series using the LN subcommand and seasonal and nonseasonal differencing to any degree using the SDIFF and DIFF subcommands. With seasonal differencing, you can also specify the periodicity on the PERIOD subcommand.

Statistical Display. You can control which series are paired by using the keyword WITH. You can specify the range of lags for which you want values displayed and plotted with the MXCROSS subcommand, overriding the maximum specified on TSET. You can also display and plot values only at periodic lags using the SEASONAL subcommand.

Basic Specification

The basic specification is two or more series names. By default, CCF automatically displays the cross-correlation coefficient and standard error for the negative lags (second series leading), the positive lags (first series leading), and the 0 lag for all possible pair combinations in the series list. It also plots the cross-correlations and marks the bounds of two standard errors on the plot. By default, CCF displays and plots values up to 7 lags (lags –7 to +7), or the range specified on TSET.

Subcommand Order

- Subcommands can be specified in any order.

Syntax Rules

- The VARIABLES subcommand can be specified only once.
- Other subcommands can be specified more than once, but only the last specification of each one is executed.

Operations

- Subcommand specifications apply to all series named on the CCF command.
- If the LN subcommand is specified, any differencing requested on that CCF command is done on the log transformed series.
- Confidence limits are displayed in the plot, marking the bounds of two standard errors at each lag.

Limitations

- Maximum 1 VARIABLES subcommand. There is no limit on the number of series named on the list.

Example

```
CCF VARX VARY
  /LN
  /DIFF=1
  /SDIFF=1
  /PERIOD=12
  /MXCROSS=25.
```

- This example produces a plot of the cross-correlation function for *VARX* and *VARY* after a natural log transformation, differencing, and seasonal differencing have been applied to both series. Along with the plot, the cross-correlation coefficients and standard errors are displayed for each lag.

- LN transforms the data using the natural logarithm (base *e*) of each series.
- DIFF differences each series once.
- SDIFF and PERIOD apply one degree of seasonal differencing with a period of 12.
- MXCROSS specifies 25 for the maximum range of positive and negative lags for which output is to be produced (lags –25 to +25).

VARIABLES Subcommand

VARIABLES specifies the series to be plotted and is the only required subcommand. The actual keyword VARIABLES can be omitted.

- The minimum VARIABLES specification is a pair of series names.
- If you do not use keyword WITH, each series is paired with every other series in the list.
- If you specify keyword WITH, every series named before WITH is paired with every series named after WITH.

Example

```
CCF VARIABLES=VARA VARB WITH VARC VARD.
```

- This example displays and plots the cross-correlation functions for the following pairs of series: *VARA* with *VARC*, *VARA* with *VARD*, *VARB* with *VARC*, and *VARB* with *VARD*.
- *VARA* is not paired with *VARB*, and *VARC* is not paired with *VARD*.

DIFF Subcommand

DIFF specifies the degree of differencing used to convert a nonstationary series to a stationary one with a constant mean and variance before obtaining cross-correlations.

- You can specify any positive integer on DIFF.
- If DIFF is specified without a value, the default is 1.
- The number of values used in the calculations decreases by 1 for each degree of differencing.

Example

```
CCF VARX VARY
  /DIFF=1.
```

- This command differences series *VARX* and *VARY* before calculating and plotting the cross-correlation function.

SDIFF Subcommand

If the series exhibits seasonal or periodic patterns, you can use SDIFF to seasonally difference the series before obtaining cross-correlations.

- The specification on SDIFF indicates the degree of seasonal differencing and can be any positive integer.
- If SDIFF is specified without a value, the degree of seasonal differencing defaults to 1.
- The number of seasons used in the calculations decreases by 1 for each degree of seasonal differencing.
- The length of the period used by SDIFF is specified on the PERIOD subcommand. If the PERIOD subcommand is not specified, the periodicity established on the TSET or DATE command is used (see the PERIOD subcommand below).

Example

```
CCF VAR01 WITH VAR02 VAR03
  /SDIFF=1.
```

- In this example, one degree of seasonal differencing using the periodicity established on the TSET or DATE command is applied to the three series.
- Two cross-correlation functions are then plotted, one for the pair *VAR01* and *VAR02*, and one for the pair *VAR01* and *VAR03*.

PERIOD Subcommand

PERIOD indicates the length of the period to be used by the SDIFF or SEASONAL subcommands.

- The specification on PERIOD indicates how many observations are in one period or season and can be any positive integer.
- PERIOD is ignored if it is used without the SDIFF or SEASONAL subcommands.
- If PERIOD is not specified, the periodicity established on TSET PERIOD is in effect. If TSET PERIOD is not specified, the periodicity established on the DATE command is used. If periodicity was not established anywhere, the SDIFF and SEASONAL subcommands will not be executed.

Example

```
CCF VARX WITH VARY
  /SDIFF=1
  /PERIOD=6.
```

- This command applies one degree of seasonal differencing with a periodicity of 6 to both series and computes and plots the cross-correlation function.

LN and NOLOG Subcommands

LN transforms the data using the natural logarithm (base *e*) of each series and is used to remove varying amplitude over time. NOLOG indicates that the data should not be log transformed. NOLOG is the default.

- There are no additional specifications on LN or NOLOG.
- Only the last LN or NOLOG subcommand on a CCF command is executed.
- LN and NOLOG apply to all series named on the CCF command.

- If a natural log transformation is requested and any values in either series in a pair are less than or equal to 0, the CCF for that pair will not be produced because nonpositive values cannot be log transformed.
- NOLOG is generally used with an APPLY subcommand to turn off a previous LN specification.

Example

```
CCF VAR01 VAR02
  /LN.
```

- This command transforms the series *VAR01* and *VAR02* using the natural log before computing cross-correlations.

SEASONAL Subcommand

Use SEASONAL to focus attention on the seasonal component by displaying and plotting cross-correlations only at periodic lags.

- There are no additional specifications on SEASONAL.
- If SEASONAL is specified, values are displayed and plotted at the periodic lags indicated on the PERIOD subcommand. If no PERIOD subcommand is specified, the periodicity first defaults to the TSET PERIOD specification and then to the DATE command periodicity. If periodicity is not established anywhere, SEASONAL is ignored (see the PERIOD subcommand on p. 154).
- If SEASONAL is not used, cross-correlations for all lags up to the maximum are displayed and plotted.

Example

```
CCF VAR01 VAR02 VAR03
  /SEASONAL.
```

- This command plots and displays cross-correlations at periodic lags.
- By default, the periodicity established on TSET PERIOD (or the DATE command) is used. If no periodicity is established, cross-correlations for all lags are displayed and plotted.

MXCROSS Subcommand

MXCROSS specifies the maximum range of lags for a series.

- The specification on MXCROSS must be a positive integer.
- If MXCROSS is not specified, the default range is the value set on TSET MXCROSS. If TSET MXCROSS is not specified, the default is 7 (lags –7 to +7).
- The value specified on the MXCROSS subcommand overrides the value set on TSET MXCROSS.

Example

```
CCF VARX VARY
  /MXCROSS=5.
```

- The maximum number of cross-correlations can range from lag –5 to lag +5.

APPLY Subcommand

APPLY allows you to use a previously defined CCF model without having to repeat the specifications.

- The only specification on APPLY is the name of a previous model enclosed in apostrophes. If a model name is not specified, the model specified on the previous CCF command is used.
- To change one or more model specifications, specify the subcommands of only those portions you want to change after the APPLY subcommand.
- If no series are specified on the command, the series that were originally specified with the model being applied are used.
- To change the series used with the model, enter new series names before or after the APPLY subcommand.

Example

```
CCF VARX VARY
  /LN
  /DIFF=1
  /MXCROSS=25.
CCF VARX VARY
  /LN
  /DIFF=1
  /SDIFF=1
  /PERIOD=12
  /MXCROSS=25.
CCF VARX VAR01
  /APPLY.
CCF VARX VAR01
  /APPLY='MOD_1'.
```

- The first command displays and plots the cross-correlation function for *VARX* and *VARY* after each series is log transformed and differenced. The maximum range is set to 25 lags. This model is assigned the name *MOD_1* as soon as the command is executed.
- The second command displays and plots the cross-correlation function for *VARX* and *VARY* after each series is log transformed, differenced, and seasonally differenced with a periodicity of 12. The maximum range is again set to 25 lags. This model is assigned the name *MOD_2*.
- The third command requests the cross-correlation function for the series *VARX* and *VAR01* using the same model and the same range of lags as used for *MOD_2*.
- The fourth command applies *MOD_1* (from the first command) to the series *VARX* and *VAR01*.

References

Box, G. E. P., and G. M. Jenkins. 1976. *Time series analysis: Forecasting and control.* San Francisco: Holden-Day.

CLEAR TRANSFORMATIONS

```
CLEAR TRANSFORMATIONS
```

Overview

CLEAR TRANSFORMATIONS discards previous data transformation commands.

Basic Specification

The only specification is the command itself. CLEAR TRANSFORMATIONS has no additional specifications.

Operations

- CLEAR TRANSFORMATIONS discards all data transformation commands that have accumulated since the last procedure.
- CLEAR TRANSFORMATIONS has no effect if a command file is submitted to your operating system for execution. It generates a warning when a command file is present.
- Be sure to delete CLEAR TRANSFORMATIONS and any unwanted transformation commands from the journal file if you plan to submit the file to the operating system for batch-mode execution. Otherwise, the unwanted transformations will cause problems.

Example

```
GET FILE=QUERY.
FREQUENCIES=ITEM1 ITEM2 ITEM3.
RECODE ITEM1, ITEM2, ITEM3 (0=1) (1=0) (2=-1).
COMPUTE INDEXQ=(ITEM1 + ITEM2 + ITEM3)/3.
VARIABLE LABELS INDEXQ 'SUMMARY INDEX OF QUESTIONS'.
CLEAR TRANSFORMATIONS.
DISPLAY DICTIONARY.
```

- The GET and FREQUENCIES commands are executed.
- The RECODE, COMPUTE, and VARIABLE LABELS commands are transformations. They do not affect the data until the next procedure is executed.
- The CLEAR TRANSFORMATIONS command discards the RECODE, COMPUTE, and VARIABLE LABELS commands.
- The DISPLAY command displays the working file dictionary. Data values and labels are exactly as they were when the FREQUENCIES command was executed. Variable *INDEXQ* does not exist because CLEAR TRANSFORMATIONS discarded the COMPUTE command.

CLUSTER

```
CLUSTER varlist [/MISSING=[EXCLUDE**] [INCLUDE]]

[/MEASURE=[{SEUCLID**            }]
           {EUCLID               }
           {COSINE               }
           {CORRELATION          }
           {BLOCK                }
           {CHEBYCHEV            }
           {POWER(p,r)           }
           {MINKOWSKI(p)         }
           {CHISQ                }
           {PH2                  }
           {RR[(p[,np])]         }
           {SM[(p[,np])]         }
           {JACCARD[(p[,np])]    }
           {DICE[(p[,np])]       }
           {SS1[(p[,np])]        }
           {RT[(p[,np])]         }
           {SS2[(p[,np])]        }
           {K1[(p[,np])]         }
           {SS3[(p[,np])]        }
           {K2[(p[,np])]         }
           {SS4[(p[,np])]        }
           {HAMANN[(p[,np])]     }
           {OCHIAI[(p[,np])]     }
           {SS5[(p[,np])]        }
           {PHI[(p[,np])]        }
           {LAMBDA[(p[,np])]     }
           {D[(p[,np])]          }
           {Y[(p[,np])]          }
           {Q[(p[,np])]          }
           {BEUCLID[(p[,np])]    }
           {SIZE[(p[,np])]       }
           {PATTERN[(p[,np])]    }
           {BSEUCLID[(p[,np])]   }
           {BSHAPE[(p[,np])]     }
           {DISPER[(p[,np])]     }
           {VARIANCE[(p[,np])]   }
           {BLWMN[(p[,np])]      }

[/METHOD={BAVERAGE**}[(rootname)] [...]]
         {WAVERAGE  }
         {SINGLE    }
         {COMPLETE  }
         {CENTROID  }
         {MEDIAN    }
         {WARD      }
         {DEFAULT** }

 [/SAVE=CLUSTER({level   })]   [/ID=varname]
                {min,max}

 [/PRINT=[CLUSTER({level   })]  [DISTANCE]  [SCHEDULE**]  [NONE]]
                  {min,max}

 [/PLOT=[VICICLE**[(min[,max[,inc]])]]  [DENDROGRAM]  [NONE]]
        [HICICLE[(min[,max[,inc]])]]

 [/MATRIX=[IN({file})]  [OUT({file})]]
              {*   }          {*   }
```

** Default if subcommand or keyword is omitted.

Example

```
CLUSTER V1 TO V4
 /PLOT=DENDROGRAM
 /PRINT=CLUSTER (2,4).
```

Overview

CLUSTER produces hierarchical clusters of items based on distance measures of dissimilarity or similarity. The items being clustered are usually cases from the working data file, and the distance measures are computed from their values for one or more variables. You can also cluster variables if you read in a matrix measuring distances between variables. Cluster analysis is discussed in Anderberg (1973).

Options

Cluster Measures and Methods. You can specify one of 37 similarity or distance measures on the MEASURE subcommand and any of the seven methods on the METHOD subcommand.

New Variables. You can save cluster membership for specified solutions as new variables in the working data file using the SAVE subcommand.

Display and Plots. You can display cluster membership, the distance or similarity matrix used to cluster variables or cases, and the agglomeration schedule for the cluster solution with the PRINT subcommand. You can request either a horizontal or vertical icicle plot or a dendrogram of the cluster solution and control the cluster levels displayed in the icicle plot with the PLOT subcommand. You can also specify a variable to be used as a case identifier in the display on the ID subcommand.

Matrix Input and Output. You can write out the distance matrix and use it in subsequent CLUSTER, PROXIMITIES, or ALSCAL analyses or read in matrices produced by other CLUSTER or PROXIMITIES procedures using the MATRIX subcommand.

Basic Specification

The basic specification is a variable list. CLUSTER assumes that the items being clustered are cases and uses the squared Euclidean distances between cases on the variables in the analysis as the measure of distance.

Subcommand Order

- The variable list must be specified first.
- The remaining subcommands can be specified in any order.

Syntax Rules

- The variable list and subcommands can each be specified once.

- More than one clustering method can be specified on the METHOD subcommand.

Operations

The CLUSTER procedure involves four steps:

- First, CLUSTER obtains distance measures of similarities between or distances separating initial clusters (individual cases or individual variables if the input is a matrix measuring distances between variables).
- Second, it combines the two nearest clusters to form a new cluster.
- Third, it recomputes similarities or distances of existing clusters to the new cluster.
- It then returns to the second step until all items are combined in one cluster.

This process yields a hierarchy of cluster solutions, ranging from one overall cluster to as many clusters as there are items being clustered. Clusters at a higher level can contain several lower-level clusters. Within each level, the clusters are disjoint (each item belongs to only one cluster).

- CLUSTER identifies clusters in solutions by sequential integers (1, 2, 3, and so on).

Limitations

- CLUSTER stores cases and a lower-triangular matrix of proximities in memory. Storage requirements increase rapidly with the number of cases. You should be able to cluster 100 cases using a small number of variables in an 80K workspace.
- CLUSTER does not honor weights.

Example

```
CLUSTER V1 TO V4
  /PLOT=DENDROGRAM
  /PRINT=CLUSTER (2 4).
```

- This example clusters cases based on their values for all variables between and including *V1* and *V4* in the working data file.
- The analysis uses the default measure of distance (squared Euclidean) and the default clustering method (average linkage between groups).
- PLOT requests a dendrogram.
- PRINT displays a table of the cluster membership of each case for the two-, three-, and four-cluster solutions.

Variable List

The variable list identifies the variables used to compute similarities or distances between cases.

- The variable list is required except when matrix input is used. It must be specified before the optional subcommands.
- If matrix input is used, the variable list can be omitted. The names for the items in the matrix are used to compute similarities or distances.
- You can specify a variable list to override the names for the items in the matrix. This allows you to read in a subset of cases for analysis. Specifying a variable that does not exist in the matrix results in an error.

MEASURE Subcommand

MEASURE specifies the distance or similarity measure used to cluster cases.

- If the MEASURE subcommand is omitted or included without specifications, squared Euclidean distances are used.
- Only one measure can be specified.

Measures for Interval Data

For interval data, use any one of the following keywords on MEASURE:

SEUCLID *Squared Euclidean distance.* The distance between two items, x and y, is the sum of the squared differences between the values for the items. SEUCLID is the measure commonly used with centroid, median, and Ward's methods of clustering. SEUCLID is the default and can also be requested with keyword DEFAULT.

$$\mathrm{SEUCLID}(x, y) = \Sigma_i (x_i - y_i)^2$$

EUCLID *Euclidean distance.* This is the default specification for MEASURE. The distance between two items, x and y, is the square root of the sum of the squared differences between the values for the items.

$$\mathrm{EUCLID}(x, y) = \sqrt{\Sigma_i (x_i - y_i)^2}$$

CORRELATION *Correlation between vectors of values.* This is a pattern similarity measure.

$$\mathrm{CORRELATION}(x, y) = \frac{\Sigma_i (Z_{xi} Z_{yi})}{N - 1}$$

where Z_{xi} is the Z-score (standardized) value of x for the ith case or variable, and N is the number of cases or variables.

COSINE *Cosine of vectors of values.* This is a pattern similarity measure.

$$\mathrm{COSINE}(x, y) = \frac{\Sigma_i (x_i y_i)}{\sqrt{(\Sigma_i x_i^2)(\Sigma_i y_i^2)}}$$

CHEBYCHEV *Chebychev distance metric.* The distance between two items is the maximum absolute difference between the values for the items.

$$\text{CHEBYCHEV}(x, y) = \max_i |x_i - y_i|$$

BLOCK *City-block or Manhattan distance.* The distance between two items is the sum of the absolute differences between the values for the items.

$$\text{BLOCK}(x, y) = \Sigma_i |x_i - y_i|$$

MINKOWSKI(p) *Distance in an absolute Minkowski power metric.* The distance between two items is the *p*th root of the sum of the absolute differences to the *p*th power between the values for the items. Appropriate selection of the integer parameter *p* yields Euclidean and many other distance metrics.

$$\text{MINKOWSKI}(x, y) = (\Sigma_i |x_i - y_i|^p)^{1/p}$$

POWER(p,r) *Distance in an absolute power metric.* The distance between two items is the *r*th root of the sum of the absolute differences to the *p*th power between the values for the items. Appropriate selection of the integer parameters *p* and *r* yields Euclidean, squared Euclidean, Minkowski, city-block, and many other distance metrics.

$$\text{POWER}(x, y) = (\Sigma_i |x_i - y_i|^p)^{1/r}$$

Measures for Frequency Count Data

For frequency count data, use any one of the following keywords on MEASURE:

CHISQ *Based on the chi-square test of equality for two sets of frequencies.* The magnitude of this dissimilarity measure depends on the total frequencies of the two cases or variables whose dissimilarity is computed. Expected values are from the model of independence of cases or variables *x* and *y*.

$$\text{CHISQ}(x, y) = \sqrt{\frac{\Sigma_i (x_i - E(x_i))^2}{E(x_i)} + \frac{\Sigma_i (y_i - E(y_i))^2}{E(y_i)}}$$

PH2 *Phi-square between sets of frequencies.* This is the CHISQ measure normalized by the square root of the combined frequency. Therefore, its value does not depend on the total frequencies of the two cases or variables whose dissimilarity is computed.

$$\text{PH2}(x, y) = \sqrt{\frac{\frac{\Sigma_i (x_i - E(x_i))^2}{E(x_i)} + \frac{\Sigma_i (y_i - E(y_i))^2}{E(y_i)}}{N}}$$

Measures for Binary Data

Different binary measures emphasize different aspects of the relationship between sets of binary values. However, all the measures are specified in the same way. Each measure has two optional integer-valued parameters, *p* (present) and *np* (not present).

- If both parameters are specified, CLUSTER uses the value of the first as an indicator that a characteristic is present and the value of the second as an indicator that a characteristic is absent. CLUSTER skips all other values.
- If only the first parameter is specified, CLUSTER uses that value to indicate presence and all other values to indicate absence.
- If no parameters are specified, CLUSTER assumes that 1 indicates presence and 0 indicates absence.

Using the indicators for presence and absence within each item (case or variable), CLUSTER constructs a 2×2 contingency table for each pair of items in turn. It uses this table to compute a proximity measure for the pair.

	Item 2 characteristics	
	Present	**Absent**
Item 1 characteristics		
Present	*a*	*b*
Absent	*c*	*d*

CLUSTER computes all binary measures from the values of *a*, *b*, *c*, and *d*. These values are tallied across variables (when the items are cases) or across cases (when the items are variables). For example, if variables *V*, *W*, *X*, *Y*, *Z* have values 0, 1, 1, 0, 1 for case 1 and values 0, 1, 1, 0, 0 for case 2 (where 1 indicates presence and 0 indicates absence), the contingency table is as follows:

	Case 2 characteristics	
	Present	**Absent**
Case 1 characteristics		
Present	2	1
Absent	0	2

The contingency table indicates that both cases are present for two variables (*W* and *X*), both cases are absent for two variables (*V* and *Y*), and case 1 is present and case 2 is absent for one variable (*Z*). There are no variables for which case 1 is absent and case 2 is present.

The available binary measures include matching coefficients, conditional probabilities, predictability measures, and others.

Matching Coefficients. Table 1 shows a classification scheme for matching coefficients. In this scheme, *matches* are joint presences (value *a* in the contingency table) or joint absences (value *d*). *Nonmatches* are equal in number to value *b* plus value *c*. Matches and nonmatches may be weighted equally or not. The three coefficients JACCARD, DICE, and SS2 are related monotonically, as are SM, SS1, and RT. All coefficients in Table 1 are similarity measures, and all except two (K1 and SS3) range from 0 to 1. K1 and SS3 have a minimum value of 0 and no upper limit.

Table 1 Binary matching coefficients in CLUSTER

	Joint absences excluded from numerator	**Joint absences included in numerator**
All matches included in denominator		
Equal weight for matches and nonmatches	RR	SM
Double weight for matches		SS1
Double weight for nonmatches		RT
Joint absences excluded from denominator		
Equal weight for matches and nonmatches	JACCARD	
Double weight for matches	DICE	
Double weight for nonmatches	SS2	
All matches excluded from denominator		
Equal weight for matches and nonmatches	K1	SS3

RR[(p[,np])]

Russell and Rao similarity measure. This is the binary dot product.

$$\mathrm{RR}(x, y) = \frac{a}{a + b + c + d}$$

SM[(p[,np])]

Simple matching similarity measure. This is the ratio of the number of matches to the total number of characteristics.

$$\mathrm{SM}(x, y) = \frac{a + d}{a + b + c + d}$$

JACCARD[(p[,np])]

Jaccard similarity measure. This is also known as the *similarity ratio.*

$$\mathrm{JACCARD}(x, y) = \frac{a}{a + b + c}$$

DICE[(p[,np])] *Dice (or Czekanowski or Sorenson) similarity measure.*

$$\text{DICE}(x, y) = \frac{2a}{2a + b + c}$$

SS1[(p[,np])] *Sokal and Sneath similarity measure 1.*

$$\text{SS1}(x, y) = \frac{2(a + d)}{2(a + d) + b + c}$$

RT[(p[,np])] *Rogers and Tanimoto similarity measure.*

$$\text{RT}(x, y) = \frac{a + d}{a + d + 2(b + c)}$$

SS2[(p[,np])] *Sokal and Sneath similarity measure 2.*

$$\text{SS2}(x, y) = \frac{a}{a + 2(b + c)}$$

K1[(p[,np])] *Kulczynski similarity measure 1.* This measure has a minimum value of 0 and no upper limit. It is undefined when there are no nonmatches (b=0 and c=0).

$$\text{K1}(x, y) = \frac{a}{b + c}$$

SS3[(p[,np])] *Sokal and Sneath similarity measure 3.* This measure has a minimum value of 0 and no upper limit. It is undefined when there are no nonmatches (b=0 and c=0).

$$\text{SS3}(x, y) = \frac{a + d}{b + c}$$

Conditional Probabilities. The following binary measures yield values that can be interpreted in terms of conditional probability. All three are similarity measures.

K2[(p[,np])] *Kulczynski similarity measure 2.* This yields the average conditional probability that a characteristic is present in one item given that the characteristic is present in the other item. The measure is an average over both items acting as predictors. It has a range of 0 to 1.

$$\text{K2}(x, y) = \frac{a/(a + b) + a/(a + c)}{2}$$

SS4[(p[,np])] *Sokal and Sneath similarity measure 4.* This yields the conditional probability that a characteristic of one item is in the same state (presence or absence) as the characteristic of the other item. The measure is an average over both items acting as predictors. It has a range of 0 to 1.

$$\text{SS4}(x, y) = \frac{a/(a+b) + a/(a+c) + d/(b+d) + d/(c+d)}{4}$$

HAMANN[(p[,np])] *Hamann similarity measure.* This measure gives the probability that a characteristic has the same state in both items (present in both or absent from both) minus the probability that a characteristic has different states in the two items (present in one and absent from the other). HAMANN has a range of −1 to +1 and is monotonically related to SM, SS1, and RT.

$$\text{HAMANN}(x, y) = \frac{(a+d) - (b+c)}{a+b+c+d}$$

Predictability Measures. The following four binary measures assess the association between items as the predictability of one given the other. All four measures yield similarities.

LAMBDA[(p[,np])] *Goodman and Kruskal's lambda (similarity).* This coefficient assesses the predictability of the state of a characteristic on one item (present or absent) given the state on the other item. Specifically, LAMBDA measures the proportional reduction in error using one item to predict the other when the directions of prediction are of equal importance. LAMBDA has a range of 0 to 1.

$$\text{LAMBDA}(x, y) = \frac{t_1 - t_2}{2(a+b+c+d) - t_2}$$

where

$t_1 = \max(a,b) + \max(c,d) + \max(a,c) + \max(b,d)$

$t_2 = \max(a + c, b + d) + \max(a + d, c + d)$.

D[(p[,np])] *Anderberg's* D *(similarity).* This coefficient assesses the predictability of the state of a characteristic on one item (present or absent) given the state on the other. D measures the actual reduction in the error probability when one item is used to predict the other. The range of D is 0 to 1.

$$\text{D}(x, y) = \frac{t_1 - t_2}{2(a+b+c+d)}$$

where

$t_1 = \max(a,b) + \max(c,d) + \max(a,c) + \max(b,d)$

$t_2 = \max(a + c, b + d) + \max(a + d, c + d)$

Y[(p[,np])] *Yule's* Y *coefficient of colligation (similarity).* This is a function of the cross ratio for a 2×2 table. It has a range of −1 to +1.

$$Y(x, y) = \frac{\sqrt{ad} - \sqrt{bc}}{\sqrt{ad} + \sqrt{bc}}$$

Q[(p[,np])]

Yule's Q *(similarity).* This is the 2×2 version of Goodman and Kruskal's ordinal measure *gamma.* Like Yule's *Y*, *Q* is a function of the cross ratio for a 2×2 table and has a range of −1 to +1.

$$Q(x, y) = \frac{ad - bc}{ad + bc}$$

Other Binary Measures. The remaining binary measures available in CLUSTER are either binary equivalents of association measures for continuous variables or measures of special properties of the relationship between items.

OCHIAI[(p[,np])]

Ochiai similarity measure. This is the binary form of the cosine. It has a range of 0 to 1.

$$\text{OCHIAI}(x, y) = \sqrt{\frac{a}{a+b} \cdot \frac{a}{a+c}}$$

SS5[(p[,np])]

Sokal and Sneath similarity measure 5. The range is 0 to 1.

$$\text{SS5}(x, y) = \frac{ad}{\sqrt{(a+b)(a+c)(b+d)(c+d)}}$$

PHI[(p[,np])]

Fourfold point correlation (similarity). This is the binary form of the Pearson product-moment correlation coefficient.

$$\text{PHI}(x, y) = \frac{ad - bc}{\sqrt{(a+b)(a+c)(b+d)(c+d)}}$$

BEUCLID[(p[,np])]

Binary Euclidean distance. This is a distance measure. Its minimum value is 0, and it has no upper limit.

$$\text{BEUCLID}(x, y) = \sqrt{b + c}$$

BSEUCLID[(p[,np])]

Binary squared Euclidean distance. This is a distance measure. Its minimum value is 0, and it has no upper limit.

$$\text{BSEUCLID}(x, y) = b + c$$

SIZE[(p[,np])]

Size difference. This is a dissimilarity measure with a minimum value of 0 and no upper limit.

$$\text{SIZE}(x, y) = \frac{(b-c)^2}{(a+b+c+d)^2}$$

PATTERN[(p[,np])] *Pattern difference.* This is a dissimilarity measure. The range is 0 to 1.

$$\text{PATTERN}(x, y) = \frac{bc}{(a+b+c+d)^2}$$

BSHAPE[(p[,np])] *Binary shape difference.* This dissimilarity measure has no upper or lower limit.

$$\text{BSHAPE}(x, y) = \frac{(a+b+c+d)(b+c)-(b-c)^2}{(a+b+c+d)^2}$$

DISPER[(p[,np])] *Dispersion similarity measure.* The range is −1 to +1.

$$\text{DISPER}(x, y) = \frac{ad-bc}{(a+b+c+d)^2}$$

VARIANCE[(p[,np])] *Variance dissimilarity measure.* This measure has a minimum value of 0 and no upper limit.

$$\text{VARIANCE}(x, y) = \frac{b+c}{4(a+b+c+d)}$$

BLWMN[(p[,np])] *Binary Lance-and-Williams nonmetric dissimilarity measure.* This measure is also known as the Bray-Curtis nonmetric coefficient. The range is 0 to 1.

$$\text{BLWMN}(x, y) = \frac{b+c}{2a+b+c}$$

METHOD Subcommand

METHOD specifies one or more clustering methods.

- If the METHOD subcommand is omitted or included without specifications, the method of average linkage between groups is used.
- Only one METHOD subcommand can be used, but more than one method can be specified on it.
- When the number of items is large, CENTROID and MEDIAN require significantly more CPU time than other methods.

BAVERAGE *Average linkage between groups (UPGMA).* BAVERAGE is the default and can also be requested with keyword DEFAULT.

WAVERAGE *Average linkage within groups.*

SINGLE *Single linkage or nearest neighbor.*

COMPLETE *Complete linkage or furthest neighbor.*

CENTROID *Centroid clustering (UPGMC).* Squared Euclidean distances are commonly used with this method.

MEDIAN *Median clustering (WPGMC).* Squared Euclidean distances are commonly used with this method.

WARD *Ward's method.* Squared Euclidean distances are commonly used with this method.

Example

```
CLUSTER V1 V2 V3
 /METHOD=SINGLE COMPLETE WARDS.
```

- This example clusters cases based on their values for variables *V1*, *V2*, and *V3*, and uses three clustering methods: single linkage, complete linkage, and Ward's method.

SAVE Subcommand

SAVE allows you to save cluster membership at specified solution levels as new variables in the working data file.

- The specification on SAVE is the CLUSTER keyword, followed by either a single number indicating the level (number of clusters) of the cluster solution or a range separated by a comma indicating the minimum and maximum numbers of clusters when membership of more than one solution is to be saved. The number or range must be enclosed in parentheses and applies to all methods specified on METHOD.
- You can specify a rootname in parentheses after each method specification on the METHOD subcommand. CLUSTER forms new variable names by appending the number of the cluster solution to the rootname.
- If no rootname is specified, CLUSTER forms variable names using the formula *CLUn_m*, where *m* increments to create a unique rootname for the set of variables saved for one method and *n* is the number of the cluster solution.
- As *n* and *m* increase, the prefix *CLU* is truncated to keep names within eight characters.
- The names and descriptive labels of the new variables are displayed in the procedure information notes.
- You cannot use the SAVE subcommand if you are replacing the working data file with matrix materials (see "Matrix Output" on p. 173).

Example

```
CLUSTER A B C
 /METHOD=BAVERAGE SINGLE (SINMEM) WARD
 /SAVE=CLUSTERS(3,5).
```

- This command creates nine new variables: *CLU5_1*, *CLU4_1*, and *CLU3_1* for BAVERAGE, *SINMEM5*, *SINMEM4*, and *SINMEM3* for SINGLE, and *CLU5_2*, *CLU4_2*, and *CLU3_2* for WARD. The variables contain the cluster membership for each case at the five-, four-, and three-cluster solutions using the three clustering methods. Ward's method is the third specification on METHOD but uses the second set of default names since it is the second method specified without a rootname.

- The order of the new variables in the working data file is the same as listed above, since the solutions are obtained in the order from 5 to 3.
- New variables are listed in the procedure information notes.

ID Subcommand

ID names a string variable to be used as the case identifier in cluster membership tables, icicle plots, and dendrograms. If the ID subcommand is omitted, cases are identified by case numbers alone.

- When used with the MATRIX IN subcommand, the variable specified on the ID subcommand identifies the labeling variable in the matrix file.

PRINT Subcommand

PRINT controls the display of cluster output (except plots, which are controlled by the PLOT subcommand).

- If the PRINT subcommand is omitted or included without specifications, an agglomeration schedule is displayed. If any keywords are specified on PRINT, the agglomeration schedule is displayed only if explicitly requested.
- CLUSTER automatically displays summary information (the method and measure used, the number of cases) for each method named on the METHOD subcommand. This summary is displayed regardless of specifications on PRINT.

You can specify any or all of the following on the PRINT subcommand:

SCHEDULE *Agglomeration schedule.* The agglomeration schedule shows the order and distances at which items and clusters combine to form new clusters. It also shows the cluster level at which an item joins a cluster. SCHEDULE is the default and can also be requested with keyword DEFAULT.

CLUSTER(min,max) *Cluster membership.* For each item, the display includes the value of the case identifier (or the variable name if matrix input is used), the case sequence number, and a value (1, 2, 3, and so on) identifying the cluster to which that case belongs in a given cluster solution. Specify either a single integer value in parentheses indicating the level of a single solution or a minimum value and a maximum value indicating a range of solutions for which display is desired. If the number of clusters specified exceeds the number produced, the largest number of clusters is used (the number of items minus 1). If CLUSTER is specified more than once, the last specification is used.

DISTANCE *Proximities matrix.* The proximities matrix table displays the distances or similarities between items computed by CLUSTER or obtained from an input matrix. DISTANCE produces a large volume of output and uses significant CPU time when the number of cases is large.

NONE *None of the above.* NONE overrides any other keywords specified on PRINT.

Example

```
CLUSTER V1 V2 V3 /PRINT=CLUSTER(3,5).
```

- This example displays cluster membership for each case for the three-, four-, and five-cluster solutions.

PLOT Subcommand

PLOT controls the plots produced for each method specified on the METHOD subcommand. For icicle plots, PLOT allows you to control the cluster solution at which the plot begins and ends and the increment for displaying intermediate cluster solutions.

- If the PLOT subcommand is omitted or included without specifications, a vertical icicle plot is produced.
- If any keywords are specified on PLOT, only those plots requested are produced.
- The icicle plots are generated as pivot tables and the dendrogram is generated as text output.
- If there is not enough memory for a dendrogram or an icicle plot, the plot is skipped and a warning is issued.
- The size of an icicle plot can be controlled by specifying range values or an increment for VICICLE or HICICLE. Smaller plots require significantly less workspace and time.

VICICLE(min,max,inc) *Vertical icicle plot.* This is the default. The range specifications are optional. If used, they must be integer and must be enclosed in parentheses. The specification *min* is the cluster solution at which to start the display (the default is 1), and the specification *max* is the cluster solution at which to end the display (the default is the number of cases minus 1). If *max* is greater than the number of cases minus 1, the default is used. The increment to use between cluster solutions is *inc* (the default is 1). If *max* is specified, *min* must be specified, and if *inc* is specified, both *min* and *max* must be specified. If VICICLE is specified more than once, only the last range specification is used.

HICICLE(min,max,inc) *Horizontal icicle plot.* The range specifications are the same as for VICICLE. If both VICICLE and HICICLE are specified, the last range specified is used for both. If a range is not specified on the last instance of VICICLE or HICICLE, the defaults are used even if a range is specified earlier.

DENDROGRAM *Tree diagram.* The dendrogram is scaled by the joining distances of the clusters.

NONE *No plots.*

Example

```
CLUSTER V1 V2 V3 /PLOT=VICICLE(1,20).
```

- This example produces a vertical icicle plot for the one-cluster through the twenty-cluster solution.

Example

```
CLUSTER V1 V2 V3 /PLOT=VICICLE(1,151,5).
```

- This example produces a vertical icicle plot for every fifth cluster solution starting with 1 and ending with 151 (1 cluster, 6 clusters, 11 clusters, and so on).

MISSING Subcommand

MISSING controls the treatment of cases with missing values. A case that has a missing value for any variable on the variable list is omitted from the analysis. By default, user-missing values are exlcuded from the analysis.

EXCLUDE *Exclude cases with user-missing values.* This is the default.

INCLUDE *Include cases with user-missing values.* Only cases with system-missing values are excluded.

MATRIX Subcommand

MATRIX reads and writes SPSS-format matrix data files.

- Either IN or OUT and a matrix file in parentheses are required. When both IN and OUT are used on the same CLUSTER procedure, they can be specified on separate MATRIX subcommands or on the same subcommand.
- The input or output matrix information is displayed in the procedure information notes.

OUT (filename) *Write a matrix data file.* Specify either a filename or an asterisk in parentheses (*). If you specify a filename, the file is stored on disk and can be retrieved at any time. If you specify an asterisk (*), the matrix data file replaces the working data file but is not stored on disk unless you use SAVE or XSAVE.

IN (filename) *Read a matrix data file.* If the matrix data file is the current working data file, specify an asterisk (*) in parentheses. If the matrix data file is another file, specify the filename in parentheses. A matrix file read from an external file does not replace the working data file.

When an SPSS Matrix is produced using the MATRIX OUT subcommand, it corresponds to a unique data set. All subsequent analyses performed on this matrix would match the corresponding analysis on the original data. However, if the data file is altered in any way, this would no longer be true.

For example, if the original file is edited or rearranged it would in general no longer correspond to the initially produced matrix. You need to make sure that the data match the matrix whenever inferring the results from the matrix analysis. Specifically, when saving the cluster membership into a working data file in the CLUSTER procedure, the proximity matrix in the MATRIX IN statement must match the current working data file.

Matrix Output

- CLUSTER writes proximity-type matrices with *ROWTYPE_* values of PROX. CLUSTER neither reads nor writes additional statistics with its matrix materials. See "Format of the Matrix Data File" on p. 173 for a description of the file.
- The matrices produced by CLUSTER can be used by subsequent CLUSTER procedures or by procedures PROXIMITIES and ALSCAL.
- Any documents contained in the working data file are not transferred to the matrix file.

Matrix Input

- CLUSTER can read matrices written by a previous CLUSTER command or by PROXIMITIES, or created by MATRIX DATA. When the input matrix contains distances between variables, CLUSTER clusters all or a subset of the variables.
- Values for split-file variables should precede values for *ROWTYPE_*. *CASENO_* and the labeling variable (if present) should come after *ROWTYPE_* and before *VARNAME_*.
- If *CASENO_* is of type string rather than numeric, it will be considered unavailable and a warning is issued.
- If *CASENO_* appears on a variable list, a syntax error results.
- CLUSTER ignores unrecognized *ROWTYPE_* values.
- When you are reading a matrix created with MATRIX DATA, you should supply a value label for PROX of either *SIMILARITY* or *DISSIMILARITY* so the matrix is correctly identified. If you do not supply a label, CLUSTER assumes *DISSIMILARITY*. (See "Format of the Matrix Data File" below.)
- The program reads variable names, variable and value labels, and print and write formats from the dictionary of the matrix data file.
- MATRIX=IN cannot be specified unless a working data file has already been defined. To read an existing matrix data file at the beginning of a session, use GET to retrieve the matrix file and then specify IN(*) on MATRIX.
- The variable list on CLUSTER can be omitted when a matrix data file is used as input. By default, all cases or variables in the matrix data file are used in the analysis. Specify a variable list when you want to read in a subset of items for analysis.

Format of the Matrix Data File

- The matrix data file can include three special variables created by the program: *ROWTYPE_*, *ID*, and *VARNAME_*.
- Variable *ROWTYPE_* is a string variable with value PROX (for proximity measure). PROX is assigned value labels containing the distance measure used to create the matrix and either *SIMILARITY* or *DISSIMILARITY* as an identifier. Variable *VARNAME_* is a short

string variable whose values are the names of the new variables. Variable *CASENO_* is a numeric variable with values equal to the original case numbers.

- *ID* is included only when an identifying variable is not specified on the ID subcommand. *ID* is a short string and takes the value CASE *m*, where *m* is the actual number of each case. Note that *m* may not be consecutive if cases have been selected.
- If an identifying variable is specified on the ID subcommand, it takes the place of *ID* between *ROWTYPE_* and *VARNAME_*. Up to 20 characters can be displayed for the identifying variable.
- *VARNAME_* is a string variable that takes the values VAR1, VAR2 ...VAR*n*, to correspond to the names of the distance variables in the matrix (*VAR1, VAR2 ... VARn*, where *n* is the number of cases in the largest split file). The numeric suffix for the variable names is consecutive and may not be the same as the actual case number.
- The remaining variables in the matrix file are the distance variables used to form the matrix. The distance variables are assigned variable labels in the form of CASE *m* to identify the actual number of each case.

Split Files

- When split-file processing is in effect, the first variables in the matrix data file are the split variables, followed by *ROWTYPE_*, the case-identifier variable or *ID*, *VARNAME_*, and the distance variables.
- A full set of matrix materials is written for each split-file group defined by the split variables.
- A split variable cannot have the same name as any other variable written to the matrix data file.
- If split-file processing is in effect when a matrix is written, the same split file must be in effect when that matrix is read by any procedure.

Missing Values

Missing-value treatment affects the values written to a matrix data file. When reading a matrix data file, be sure to specify a missing-value treatment on CLUSTER that is compatible with the treatment that was in effect when the matrix materials were generated.

Example

```
DATA LIST FILE=ALMANAC1 RECORDS=3
  /1 CITY 6-18(A) POP80 53-60
  /2 CHURCHES 10-13 PARKS 14-17 PHONES 18-25 TVS 26-32
     RADIOST 33-35 TVST 36-38 TAXRATE 52-57(2).
N OF CASES 8.

CLUSTER CHURCHES TO TAXRATE
  /ID=CITY
  /MEASURE=EUCLID
  /MATRIX=OUT(CLUSMTX).
```

- CLUSTER reads raw data from file *ALMANAC1* and writes one set of matrix materials to file *CLUSMTX.*
- The working data file is still the *ALMANAC1* file defined on DATA LIST. Subsequent commands are executed on *ALMANAC1.*

Example

```
DATA LIST FILE=ALMANAC1 RECORDS=3
  /1 CITY 6-18(A) POP80 53-60
  /2 CHURCHES 10-13 PARKS 14-17 PHONES 18-25 TVS 26-32
     RADIOST 33-35 TVST 36-38 TAXRATE 52-57(2).
N OF CASES 8.

CLUSTER CHURCHES TO TAXRATE
  /ID=CITY
  /MEASURE=EUCLID
  /MATRIX=OUT(*).
LIST.
```

- CLUSTER writes the same matrix as in the previous example. However, the matrix data file replaces the working data file. The LIST command is executed on the matrix file, not on *ALMANAC1.*

Example

```
GET FILE=CLUSMTX.
CLUSTER
  /ID=CITY
  /MATRIX=IN(*).
```

- This example starts a new session and reads an existing matrix data file. GET retrieves the matrix data file *CLUSMTX.*
- MATRIX=IN specifies an asterisk because the matrix data file is the working data file. If MATRIX=IN(CLUSMTX) is specified, the program issues an error message.
- If the GET command is omitted, the program issues an error message.

Example

```
GET FILE=PRSNNL.
FREQUENCIES VARIABLE=AGE.

CLUSTER
  /ID=CITY
  /MATRIX=IN(CLUSMTX).
```

- This example performs a frequencies analysis on file *PRSNNL* and then uses a different file for CLUSTER. The file is an existing matrix data file.
- The variable list is omitted on the CLUSTER command. By default, all cases in the matrix file are used in the analysis.
- MATRIX=IN specifies the matrix data file *CLUSMTX.*

- *CLUSMTX* does not replace *PRSNNL* as the working data file.

Example

```
GET FILE=CRIME.
PROXIMITIES MURDER TO MOTOR
  /VIEW=VARIABLE
  /MEASURE=PH2
  /MATRIX=OUT(*).
CLUSTER
  /MATRIX=IN(*).
```

- GET retrieves an SPSS-format data file.
- PROXIMITIES uses the data from the *CRIME* file, which is now the working data file. The VIEW subcommand specifies computation of proximity values between variables. The MATRIX subcommand writes the matrix to the working data file.
- MATRIX=IN(*) on the CLUSTER command reads the matrix materials from the working data file. Since the matrix contains distances between variables, CLUSTER clusters variables based on distance measures in the input. The variable list is omitted on the CLUSTER command, so all variables are used in the analysis. The slash preceding the MATRIX subcommand is required because there is an implied variable list. Without the slash, CLUSTER would attempt to interpret MATRIX as a variable name rather than a subcommand name.

COMMENT

```
{COMMENT} text
{   *   }
```

Overview

COMMENT inserts explanatory text within the command sequence. Comments are included among the commands printed back in the output; they do not become part of the information saved in an SPSS-format data file. To include commentary in the dictionary of a data file, use the DOCUMENT command.

Syntax Rules

- The first line of a comment can begin with the keyword COMMENT or with an asterisk (*). Comment text can extend for multiple lines and can contain any characters. A period is required at the end of the last line to terminate the comment.
- Use /* and */ to set off a comment within a command. The comment can be placed wherever a blank is valid (except within strings) and should be preceded by a blank. Comments within a command cannot be continued onto the next line.
- The closing */ is optional when the comment is at the end of the line. The command can continue onto the next line just as if the inserted comment was a blank.
- Comments cannot be inserted within data lines.

Example

```
* Create a new variable as a combination of two old variables;
  the new variable is a scratch variable used later in the
  session;  it will not be saved with the data file.

COMPUTE #XYVAR=0.
IF (XVAR EQ 1 AND YVAR EQ 1) #XYVAR=1.
```

- The three-line comment will be included in the display file but will not be part of the data file if the working data file is saved.

Example

```
IF (RACE EQ 1 AND SEX EQ 1) SEXRACE = 1.   /*White males.
```

- The comment is entered on a command line. The closing */ is not needed because the comment is at the end of the line.

COMPUTE

```
COMPUTE target variable=expression
```

For a complete discussion of functions, see “Transformation Expressions” on p. 33.

Arithmetic operators:

+	Addition	–	Subtraction
*	Multiplication	/	Division
**	Exponentiation		

Arithmetic functions:

ABS(arg)	Absolute value
RND(arg)	Round
TRUNC(arg)	Truncate
MOD(arg)	Modulus
SQRT(arg)	Square root
EXP(arg)	Exponential
LG10(arg)	Base 10 logarithm
LN(arg)	Natural logarithm
LNGAMMA(arg)	Logarithm of complete Gamma function
ARSIN(arg)	Arcsine
ARTAN(arg)	Arctangent
SIN(arg)	Sine
COS(arg)	Cosine

Statistical functions:

SUM[.n](arg list)	Sum of values across argument list
MEAN[.n](arg list)	Mean value across argument list
SD[.n](arg list)	Standard deviation of values across list
VAR[.n](arg list)	Variance of values across list
CFVAR[.n](arg list)	Coefficient of variation of values across list
MIN[.n](arg list)	Minimum value across list
MAX[.n](arg list)	Maximum value across list

Cumulative distribution functions (continuous):

CDF.BETA(q,a,b)	Return probability that the beta random variate falls below q ($0 \leq q \leq 1$; $a>0$; $b>0$).
CDF.BVNOR(q1,q2,r)	Return probability that the standard bivariate normal variates with correlation r are less than $q1$ and $q2$ ($-1<r<1$).
CDF.CAUCHY(q,a,b)	Return probability that the Cauchy random variate falls below q ($q \geq 0$; $b>0$).
CDF.CHISQ (q,a)	Return probability that the chi-square random variate falls below q ($q \geq 0$; $a>0$).
CDF.EXP(q,a)	Return probability that the exponential random variate falls below q ($q \geq 0$; $a>0$).
CDF.F(q,a,b)	Return probability that the F random variate falls below q ($q \geq 0$; $a>0$; $b>0$).
CDF.GAMMA(q,a,b)	Return probability that the gamma random variate falls below q ($q \geq 0$; $a>0$; $b>0$).
CDF.HALFNRM(q,a,b)	Return probability that the half normal variate falls below q ($q \geq a$; $b>0$).
CDF.IGAUSS(q,a,b)	Return probability that an inverse Gaussian random variate falls below q ($a>0$; $b>0$)
CDF.LAPLACE(q,a,b)	Return probability that the Laplace random variate falls below q ($b>0$).
CDF.LOGISTIC(q,a,b)	Return probability that the logistic random variate falls below q ($b>0$).
CDF.LNORMAL(q,a,b)	Return probability that the lognormal random variate falls below q ($q \geq 0$; $a>0$; $b>0$).
CDF.NORMAL(q,a,b)	Return probability that the normal random variate falls below q ($b>0$). When $a=0$, $b=1$, alias CDFNORM(q).
CDF.PARETO(q,a,b)	Return probability that the Pareto random variate falls below q ($q \geq a>0$; $b>0$).
CDF.SMOD(q,a,b)	Return probability that the studentized maximum modulus falls below q ($q>0$; $a \geq 1$; $b \geq 1$).
CDF.SRANGE(q,a,b)	Return probability that the studentized range falls below q ($q>0$; $a \geq 1$; $b \geq 1$).
CDF.T(q,a)	Return probability that the Student t random variate falls below q ($a>0$).
CDF.UNIFORM(q,a,b)	Return probability that the uniform random variate falls below q ($a \leq q \leq b$).
CDF.WEIBULL(q,a,b)	Return probability that the Weibull random variate falls below q ($q \geq 0$; $a>0$; $b>0$).

Inverse distribution functions (continuous):

IDF.BETA(p,a,b)	Return value q such that CDF.BETA(q,a,b)=p ($0 \leq p \leq 1$; $a>0$; $b>0$).
IDF.CAUCHY(p,a,b)	Return value q such that CDF.CAUCHY(q,a,b)=p ($0<p<1$; $b>0$).
IDF.CHISQ(p,a)	Return value q such that CDF.CHISQ(q,a)=p ($0 \leq p<1$; $a>0$).
IDF.EXP(p,a)	Return value q such that CDF.EXP(q,a)=p ($0 \leq p<1$; $a>0$).
IDF.F(p,a,b)	Return value q such that CDF.F(q,a,b)=p ($0 \leq p<1$; $a>0$; $b>0$).
IDF.GAMMA(p,a,b)	Return value q such that CDF.GAMMA(q,a,b)=p ($0 \leq p<1$; $a>0$; $b>0$).
IDF.HALFNRM(p,a,b)	Return value q such that CDF.HALFNRM(q,a,b)=p ($0 \leq p<1$; $q \geq a$; $b>0$).
IDF.IGAUSS(p,a,b)	Return value q such that CDF.IGAUSS(q,a,b)=p ($0 \leq p \leq 1$; $a>0$; $b>0$)

IDF.LAPLACE(p,a,b)	Return value q such that CDF.LAPLACE(q,a,b)=p $(0<p<1; b>0)$.
IDF.LOGISTIC(p,a,b)	Return value q such that CDF.LOGISTIC(q,a,b)=p $(0<p<1; b>0)$.
IDF.LNORMAL(p,a,b)	Return value q such that CDF.LNORMAL(q,a,b)=p $(0\leq p\leq 1; a>0; b>0)$.
IDF.NORMAL(p,a,b)	Return value q such that CDF.NORMAL(q,a,b)=p $(0<p<1; b>0)$. When a=0, b=1, alias PROBIT(p).
IDF.PARETO(p,a,b)	Return value q such that CDF.PARETO(q,a,b)=p $(0\leq p<1; a>0; b>0)$.
IDF.SMOD(p,a,b)	Return value q such that CDF.SMOD(q,a,b)=p $(0\leq p<1; a\geq 1; b\geq 1)$.
IDF.SRANGE(p,a,b)	Return value q such that CDF.SRANGE(q,a,b)=p $(0\leq p<1; a\geq 1; b\geq 1)$.
IDF.T(p,a)	Return value q such that CDF.T(q,a)=p $(0<p<1; a>0)$.
IDF.UNIFORM(p,a,b)	Return value q such that CDF.UNIFORM(q,a,b)=p $(0\leq p\leq 1; a\leq b)$.
IDF.WEIBULL(p,a,b)	Return value q such that CDF.WEIBULL(q,a,b)=p $(0\leq p<1; a>0; b>0)$.

Probability density functions (continuous distributions):

PDF.BETA(q,a,b)	Return density of the beta distribution at q $(0\leq q\leq 1; a>0; b>0)$.
PDF.BVNOR(q1,q2,r)	Return density of standard bivariate normal with correlation r at $(q1, q2)$ $(-1<r<1)$
PDF.CAUCHY(q,a,b)	Return density of the Cauchy distribution at q $(q\geq 0; b>0)$.
PDF.CHISQ(q,a)	Return density of the chi-square distribution at q $(q\geq 0; a>0)$.
PDF.EXP(q,a)	Return density of the exponential distribution at q $(q\geq 0; a>0)$.
PDF.F(q,a,b)	Return density of the F distribution at q $(q\geq 0; a>0; b>0)$.
PDF.GAMMA(q,a,b)	Return density of the gamma distribution at q $(q\geq 0; a>0; b>0)$.
PDF.HALFNRM(q,a,b)	Return density of the half normal distribution at q $(q\geq a; b>0)$.
PDF.IGAUSS(q,a,b)	Return density of the inverse Gaussian distribution at q $(q\geq 0; a>0; b>0)$.
PDF.LAPLACE(q,a,b)	Return density of the Laplace distribution at q $(q\geq 0; b>0)$.
PDF.LNORMAL(q,a,b)	Return density of the lognormal distribution at q $(q\geq 0; a>0; b>0)$.
PDF.LOGISTIC(q,a,b)	Return density of the logistic distribution at q $(b>0)$.
PDF.NORMAL(q,a,b)	Return density of the normal distribution at q $(b>0)$.
PDF.PARETO(q,a,b)	Return density of the Pareto distribution at q $(q\geq a>0; b>0)$.
PDF.T(q,a)	Return density of the Student t distribution at q $(a>0)$.
PDF.UNIFORM(q,a,b)	Return density of the uniform distribution at q $(a\leq q\leq b)$.
PDF.WEIBULL(q,a,b)	Return density of the Weibull distribution at q $(q\geq 0; a>0; b>0)$.

Random variable functions (continuous distributions):

RV.BETA(a,b)	Generate a random variable of the beta distribution $(a>0; b>0)$.
RV.CAUCHY(a,b)	Generate a random variable of the Cauchy distribution $(b>0)$.
RV.CHISQ(a)	Generate a random variable of the chi-square distribution $(a>0)$.
RV.EXP(a)	Generate a random variable of the exponential distribution $(a>0)$.
RV.F(a,b)	Generate a random variable of the F distribution $(a>0; b>0)$.
RV.GAMMA(a,b)	Generate a random variable of the gamma distribution $(a>0; b>0)$.

RV.HALFNRM(a,b)	Generate a random variable of the half normal distribution (*b*>0).
RV.IGAUSS(a,b)	Generate a random variable of the inverse Gaussian distribution (*a*>0; *b*>0).
RV.LAPLACE(a,b)	Generate a random variable of the Laplace distribution (*b*>0).
RV.LOGISTIC(a,b)	Generate a random variable of the logistic distribution (*b*>0).
RV.LNORMAL(a,b)	Generate a random variable of the lognormal distribution (*a*>0; *b*>0).
RV.NORMAL(a,b)	Generate a random variable of the normal distribution (*b*>0). When *a*=0, alias NORMAL(b).
RV.PARETO(a,b)	Generate a random variable of the Pareto distribution (*a*>0; *b*>0).
RV.T(a)	Generate a random variable of the Student *t* distribution (*a*>0).
RV.UNIFORM(a,b)	Generate a random variable of the uniform distribution (*a*≤*b*). When *a*=0, alias UNIFORM(b).
RV.WEIBULL(a,b)	Generate a random variable of the Weibull distribution (*a*>0; *b*>0).

Cumulative distribution functions (discrete):

CDF.BERNOULLI(q,a)	Return probability that the Bernoulli distributed variate is less than or equal to *q* (*q*=0 or 1 only, 0≤*a*≤1).
CDF.BINOM(q,a,b)	Return probability that the binomially distributed variate is less than or equal to *q* (0≤*q*≤*a* integer, 0≤*b*≤1).
CDF.GEOM(q,a)	Return probability that the geometrically distributed variate is less than or equal to *q* (*q*>0 integer; 0<*a*≤1).
CDF.HYPER(q,a,b,c)	Return probability that the hypergeometrically distributed variate is less than or equal to *q* (*a*>0 integer, 0≤*c*≤*a*, 0≤*b*≤*a*; max(0,*b*–*a*+*c*)≤*q*≤min(*c*,*b*)).
CDF.NEGBIN(q,a,b)	Return probability that the negative binomially distributed variate is less than or equal to *q* (*a*>0 integer, 0<*b*≤1; *q*≥*a* integer).
CDF.POISSON(q,a)	Return probability that the Poisson distributed variate is less than or equal to *q* (*a*>0; *q*≥0 integer).

Probability functions (discrete distributions):

PDF.BERNOULLI(q,a)	Return probability that the Bernoulli distributed variate is equal to *q* (*q*=0 or 1 only, 0≤*a*≤1).
PDF.BINOM(q,a,b)	Return probability that the binomially distributed variate is equal to *q* (0≤*q*≤*a* integer, 0≤*b*≤1).
PDF.GEOM(q,a)	Return probability that the geometrically distributed variate is equal to *q* (*q*>0 integer; 0<*a*≤1).
PDF.HYPER(q,a,b,c)	Return probability that the hypergeometrically distributed variate is equal to *q* (*a*>0 integer, 0≤*c*≤*a*, 0≤*b*≤*a*; max(0,*b*–*a*+*c*)≤*q*≤min(*c*,*b*)).
PDF.NEGBIN(q,a,b)	Return probability that the negative binomially distributed variate is equal to *q* (*a*>0 integer, 0<*b*≤1; *q*≥*a* integer).
PDF.POISSON(q,a)	Return probability that the Poisson distributed variate is equal to *q* (*a*>0; *q*≥0 integer).

Random variable functions (discrete distributions):

RV.BERNOULLI(a)	Generate a random variable from the Bernoulli distribution ($0 \le a \le 1$).
RV.BINOM(a,b)	Generate a random variable from the binomial distribution (a positive integer, $0 \le b \le 1$).
RV.GEOM(a)	Generate a random variable from the geometric distribution ($0 < a \le 1$).
RV.HYPER(a,b,c)	Generate a random variable from the hypergeometric distribution ($a>0$ integer, $0 \le c \le a$, $0 \le b \le a$).
RV.NEGBIN(a,b)	Generate a random variable from the negative binomial distribution ($a>0$ integer, $0 < b \le 1$).
RV.POISSON(a)	Generate a random variable from the Poisson distribution ($a>0$).

Noncentral distribution functions:

NCDF.BETA(q,a,b,c)	Return probability that the noncentral beta distributed variate falls below q ($0 \le q \le 1$; $a>0$; $b>0$; $c \ge 0$).
NCDF.CHISQ(q,a,c)	Return probability that the noncentral chi-square distributed variate falls below q ($q \ge 0$; $a>0$; $c \ge 0$).
NCDF.F(q,a,b,c)	Return probability that the noncentral F distributed variate falls below q ($q \ge 0$; $a>0$; $b>0$; $c \ge 0$).
NCDF.T(q,a,c)	Return probability that the noncentral Student t distributed variate falls below q ($a>0$, $c \ge 0$).

Noncentral probability density functions:

NPDF.BETA(q,a,b,c)	Return density of the noncentral beta distribution at q ($0 \le q \le 1$; $a>0$; $b>0$; $c \ge 0$).
NPDF.CHISQ(q,a,c)	Return density of the noncentral chi-square distribution at q ($q \ge 0$; $a>0$; $c \ge 0$).
NPDF.F(q,a,b,c)	Return density of the noncentral F distribution at q ($q \ge 0$; $a>0$; $b>0$; $c \ge 0$).
NPDF.T(q,a,c)	Return density of the noncentral Student t distribution at q ($a>0$, $c \ge 0$).

Tail distribution functions:

SIG.CHISQ(q,a)	Return probability that the chi-square distributed variate falls above q ($q \ge 0$; $a>0$).
SIG.F(q,a,b)	Return probability that the F distributed variate falls above q ($q \ge 0$; $a>0$; $b>0$).

Missing-value functions:

VALUE(varname)	Ignore user-missing.
MISSING(varname)	True if missing.
SYSMIS(varname)	True if system-missing.
NMISS(arg list)	Number of missing values across list.
NVALID(arg list)	Number of valid values across list.

Cross-case function:

LAG(varname,n)	Value of variable n cases before.

Logical functions:

RANGE(varname,range)	True if value of variable is in range.
ANY(arg,arg list)	True if value of first argument is included on argument list.

Other functions:

UNIFORM(arg)	Uniform pseudo-random number between 0 and *arg*.
NORMAL(arg)	Normal pseudo-random number with mean of 0 and standard deviation of *arg*.
CDFNORM(arg)	Probability that random variable falls below *arg*.
PROBIT(arg)	Inverse of CDFNORM.

Date and time aggregation functions:

DATE.DMY(d,m,y)	Read day, month, year, and return date.
DATE.MDY(m,d,y)	Read month, day, year, and return date.
DATE.YRDAY(y,d)	Read year, day, and return date.
DATE.QYR(q,y)	Read quarter, year, and return quarter start date.
DATE.MOYR(m,y)	Read month, year, and return month start date.
DATE.WKYR(w,y)	Read week, year, and return week start date.
TIME.HMS(h,m,s)	Read hour, minutes, seconds, and return time interval.
TIME.DAYS(d)	Read days and return time interval.

Date and time conversion functions:

YRMODA(yr,mo,da)	Convert year, month, day to day number.
CTIME.DAYS(arg)	Convert time interval to days.
CTIME.HOURS(arg)	Convert time interval to hours.
CTIME.MINUTES(arg)	Convert time interval to minutes.

Date and time extraction functions:

XDATE.MDAY(arg)	Return day of the month.
XDATE.MONTH(arg)	Return month of the year.
XDATE.YEAR(arg)	Return four-digit year.

XDATE.HOUR(arg)	Return hour of a day.
XDATE.MINUTE(arg)	Return minute of an hour.
XDATE.SECOND(arg)	Return second of a minute.
XDATE.WKDAY(arg)	Return weekday number.
XDATE.JDAY(arg)	Return day number of day in given year.
XDATE.QUARTER(arg)	Return quarter of date in given year.
XDATE.WEEK(arg)	Return week number of date in given year.
XDATE.TDAY(arg)	Return number of days in time interval.
XDATE.TIME(arg)	Return time portion of given date and time.
XDATE.DATE(arg)	Return integral portion of date.

String functions:

ANY(arg,arg list)	Return 1 if value of argument is included on argument list.
CONCAT(arg list)	Join the arguments into a string.
INDEX(a1,a2,a3)	Return number indicating position of first occurrence of *a2* in *a1*; optionally, *a2* in *a3* evenly divided substrings of *a1*.
LAG(arg,n)	Return value of argument *n* cases before.
LENGTH(arg)	Return length of argument.
LOWER(arg list)	Convert upper case to lower case.
LPAD(a1,a2,a3)	Left-pad beginning of *a1* to length *a2* with character *a3*.
LTRIM(a1,a2)	Trim character *a2* from beginning of *a1*.
MAX(arg list)	Return maximum value of argument list.
MIN(arg list)	Return minimum value of argument list.
NUMBER(arg,format)	Convert argument into number using format.
RANGE(arg,arg list)	Return 1 if value of argument is in inclusive range of argument list.
RINDEX(a1,a2,a3)	Return number indicating rightmost occurrence of *a2* in *a1*; optionally, *a2* in *a3* evenly divided substrings of *a1*.
RPAD(a1,a2,a3)	Right-pad end of *a1* to length *a2* with character *a3*.
RTRIM(a1,a2)	Trim character *a2* from end of *a1*.
STRING(arg,format)	Convert argument into string using format.
SUBSTR(a1,a2,a3)	Return substring of *a1* beginning with position *a2* for length *a3*.
UPCASE(arg list)	Convert lower case to upper case.
MBLEN.BYTE(arg,a1)	Return the number of bytes for the character beginning at position *a1* in the string argument. If *a1* is not specified, it defaults to 1.

Example

```
COMPUTE NEWVAR=RND((V1/V2)*100).
STRING DEPT(A20).
COMPUTE DEPT='PERSONNEL DEPARTMENT'.
```

Overview

COMPUTE creates new numeric variables or modifies the values of existing string or numeric variables. The variable named on the left of the equals sign is the **target variable**. The variables, constants, and functions on the right side of the equals sign form an **assignment expression**. For a complete discussion of functions, see "Transformation Expressions" on p. 33.

Numeric Transformations

Numeric variables can be created or modified with COMPUTE. The assignment expression for numeric transformations can include combinations of constants, variables, numeric operators, and functions.

String Transformations

String variables can be modified but cannot be created with COMPUTE. However, a new string variable can be declared and assigned a width with the STRING command and then assigned values by COMPUTE. The assignment expression can include string constants, string variables, and any of the string functions. All other functions are available for numeric transformations only.

Basic Specification

The basic specification is a target variable, an equals sign (required), and an assignment expression.

Syntax Rules

- The target variable must be named first, and the equals sign is required. Only one target variable is allowed per COMPUTE command.
- Numeric and string variables cannot be mixed in an expression. In addition, if the target variable is numeric, the expression must yield a numeric value; if the target variable is a string, the expression must yield a string value.
- Each function must specify at least one argument enclosed in parentheses. If a function has two or more arguments, the arguments must be separated by commas. For a complete discussion of the functions and their arguments, see "Transformation Expressions" on p. 33.
- You can use the TO keyword to refer to a set of variables where the argument is a list of variables.

Numeric Variables

- Parentheses are used to indicate the order of execution and to set off the arguments to a function.
- Numeric functions use simple or complex expressions as arguments. Expressions must be enclosed in parentheses.

String Variables

- String values and constants must be enclosed in apostrophes or quotation marks.
- When strings of different lengths are compared using the ANY or RANGE functions, the shorter string is right-padded with blanks so that its length equals that of the longer string.

Operations

- If the target variable already exists, its values are replaced.
- If the target variable does not exist and the assignment expression is numeric, the program creates a new variable.
- If the target variable does not exist and the assignment expression is a string, the program displays an error message and does not execute the command.
- COMPUTE is not executed if it contains invalid syntax. New variables are not created and existing target variables remain unchanged.

Numeric Variables

- New numeric variables created with COMPUTE are assigned a dictionary format of F8.2 and are initialized to the system-missing value for each case (unless the LEAVE command is used). Existing numeric variables transformed with COMPUTE retain their original dictionary formats. The format of a numeric variable can be changed with the FORMATS command.
- All expressions are evaluated in the following order: first functions, then exponentiation, and then arithmetic operations. The order of operations can be changed with parentheses.
- COMPUTE returns the system-missing value when it doesn't have enough information to evaluate a function properly. Arithmetic functions that take only one argument cannot be evaluated if that argument is missing. The date and time functions cannot be evaluated if any argument is missing. Statistical functions are evaluated if a sufficient number of arguments is valid. For example, in the command

  ```
  COMPUTE FACTOR = SCORE1 + SCORE2 + SCORE3
  ```

  FACTOR is assigned the system-missing value for a case if any of the three score values is missing. It is assigned a valid value only when all score values are valid. In the command

  ```
  COMPUTE FACTOR = SUM(SCORE1 TO SCORE3).
  ```

FACTOR is assigned a valid value if at least one score value is valid. It is system-missing only when all three score values are missing.

String Variables

- String variables can be modified but not created on COMPUTE. However, a new string variable can be created and assigned a width with the STRING command and then assigned new values with COMPUTE.
- Existing string variables transformed with COMPUTE retain their original dictionary formats. String variables declared on STRING and transformed with COMPUTE retain the formats assigned to them on STRING.
- The format of string variables cannot be changed with FORMATS. Instead, use STRING to create a new variable with the desired width and then use COMPUTE to set the values of the new string equal to the values of the original.
- The string returned by a string expression does not have to be the same width as the target variable. If the target variable is shorter, the result is right-trimmed. If the target variable is longer, the result is right-padded. The program displays no warning messages when trimming or padding.
- To control the width of strings, use the functions that are available for padding (LPAD, RPAD), trimming (LTRIM, RTRIM), and selecting a portion of strings (SUBSTR).
- To determine whether a character in a string is single-byte or double-byte, use the MBLEN.BYTE function. Specify the string and, optionally, its beginning byte position. If the position is not specified, it defaults to 1.

Examples

The following examples illustrate the use of COMPUTE. For a complete discussion of each function, see "Transformation Expressions" on p. 33.

Arithmetic Operations

```
COMPUTE V1=25-V2.
COMPUTE V3=(V2/V4)*100.

DO IF TENURE GT 5.
COMPUTE RAISE=SALARY*.12.
ELSE IF TENURE GT 1.
COMPUTE RAISE=SALARY*.1.
ELSE.
COMPUTE RAISE=0.
END IF.
```

- *V1* is 25 minus *V2* for all cases. *V3* is *V2* expressed as a percentage of *V4*.
- *RAISE* is 12% of *SALARY* if *TENURE* is greater than 5. For remaining cases, *RAISE* is 10% of *SALARY* if *TENURE* is greater than 1. For all other cases, *RAISE* is 0.

Arithmetic Functions

```
COMPUTE WTCHANGE=ABS(WEIGHT1-WEIGHT2).
COMPUTE NEWVAR=RND((V1/V2)*100).
COMPUTE INCOME=TRUNC(INCOME).
COMPUTE MINSQRT=SQRT(MIN(V1,V2,V3,V4)).

COMPUTE TEST = TRUNC(SQRT(X/Y)) * .5.
COMPUTE PARENS = TRUNC(SQRT(X/Y) * .5).
```

- *WTCHANGE* is the absolute value of *WEIGHT1* minus *WEIGHT2*.
- *NEWVAR* is the percentage *V1* is of *V2*, rounded to an integer.
- *INCOME* is truncated to an integer.
- *MINSQRT* is the square root of the minimum value of the four variables *V1* to *V4*. MIN determines the minimum value of the four variables, and SQRT computes the square root.
- The last two examples above illustrate the use of parentheses to control the order of execution. For a case with value 2 for *X* and *Y*, *TEST* equals 0.5, since 2 divided by 2 (*X/Y*) is 1, the square root of 1 is 1, truncating 1 returns 1, and 1 times 0.5 is 0.5. However, *PARENS* equals 0 for the same case, since SQRT(*X/Y*) is 1, 1 times 0.5 is 0.5, and truncating 0.5 returns 0.

Statistical Functions

```
COMPUTE NEWSAL = SUM(SALARY,RAISE).
COMPUTE MINVAL = MIN(V1,V2,V3,V4).
COMPUTE MEANVAL = MEAN(V1,V2,V3,V4).
COMPUTE NEWMEAN = MEAN.3(V1,V2,V3,V4).
```

- *NEWSAL* is the sum of *SALARY* plus *RAISE*.
- *MINVAL* is the minimum of the values for *V1* to *V4*.
- *MEANVAL* is the mean of the values for *V1* to *V4*. Since the mean can be computed for one, two, three, or four values, *MEANVAL* is assigned a valid value as long as any one of the four variables has a valid value for that case.
- In the last example above, the .3 suffix specifies the minimum number of valid arguments required. *NEWMEAN* is the mean of variables *V1* to *V4 only* if at least three of these variables have valid values. Otherwise, *NEWMEAN* is system-missing for that case.

Missing-Value Functions

```
MISSING VALUE V1 V2 V3 (0).
COMPUTE ALLVALID=V1 + V2 + V3.
COMPUTE UM=VALUE(V1) + VALUE(V2) + VALUE(V3).
COMPUTE SM=SYSMIS(V1) + SYSMIS(V2) + SYSMIS(V3).
COMPUTE M=MISSING(V1) + MISSING(V2) + MISSING(V3).
```

- The MISSING VALUE command declares value 0 as missing for *V1*, *V2*, and *V3*.
- *ALLVALID* is the sum of three variables only for cases with valid values for all three variables. *ALLVALID* is assigned the system-missing value for a case if any variable in the assignment expression has a system- or user-missing value.

- The VALUE function overrides user-missing value status. Thus, *UM* is the sum of *V1*, *V2*, and *V3* for each case, including cases with value 0 (the user-missing value) for any of the three variables. Cases with the system-missing value for *V1*, *V2*, and *V3* are system-missing.
- The SYSMIS function on the third COMPUTE returns the value 1 if the variable is system-missing. Thus, *SM* ranges from 0 to 3 for each case, depending on whether variables *V1*, *V2*, and *V3* are system-missing for that case.
- The MISSING function on the fourth COMPUTE returns the value 1 if the variable named is system- or user-missing. Thus, *M* ranges from 0 to 3 for each case, depending on whether variables *V1*, *V2*, and *V3* are user- or system-missing for that case.
- Alternatively, you could use the COUNT command to create variables *SM* and *M*.

```
* Test for listwise deletion of missing values.

DATA LIST /V1 TO V6 1-6.
BEGIN DATA
213 56
123457
123457
9234 6
END DATA.
MISSING VALUES V1 TO V6(6,9).

COMPUTE NOTVALID=NMISS(V1 TO V6).
FREQUENCIES VAR=NOTVALID.
```

- COMPUTE determines the number of missing values for each case. For each case without missing values, the value of *NOTVALID* is 0. For each case with one missing value, the value of *NOTVALID* is 1, and so on. Both system- and user-missing values are counted.
- FREQUENCIES generates a frequency table for *NOTVALID*. The table gives a count of how many cases have all valid values, how many cases have one missing value, how many cases have two missing values, and so on, for variables *V1* to *V6*. This table can be used to determine how many cases would be dropped in an analysis that uses listwise deletion of missing values. See p. 324 and p. 548 for other ways to check listwise deletion.

Cross-Case Operations

```
COMPUTE LV1=LAG(V1).
COMPUTE LV2=LAG(V2,3).
```

- *LV1* is the value of *V1* for the previous case.
- *LV2* is the value of *V2* for three cases previous. The first three cases of *LV2* receive the system-missing value.

Logical Functions

```
COMPUTE WORKERS=RANGE(AGE,18,65).
COMPUTE QSAME=ANY(Q1,Q2).
```

- *WORKERS* is 1 for cases where *AGE* is from 18 through 65, 0 for all other valid values of *AGE*, and system-missing for cases with a missing value for *AGE*.
- *QSAME* is 1 whenever *Q1* equals *Q2* and 0 whenever they are different.

Other Functions

```
COMPUTE V1=UNIFORM(10).
COMPUTE V2=NORMAL(1.5).
```

- *V1* is a pseudo-random number from a distribution with values ranging between 0 and the specified value of 10.
- *V2* is a pseudo-random number from a distribution with a mean of 0 and a standard deviation of the specified value of 1.5.
- You can change the seed value of the pseudo-random-number generator with the SEED specification on SET.

Date and Time Aggregation Functions

```
COMPUTE OCTDAY=DATE.YRDAY(1688,301).
COMPUTE QUART=DATE.QYR(QTR,YEAR).
COMPUTE WEEK=DATE.WKYR(WK,YEAR).
```

- *OCTDAY* is the 301st day of the year 1688. With a DATE format, *OCTDAY* displays as 27-OCT-1688.
- *QUART* reads values for the quarter from the variable *QTR* and values for the year from the variable *YEAR*. If *QTR* is 3 and *YEAR* is 88, *QUART* with a QDATE format displays as 3 Q 88.
- *WEEK* takes the value for the week from the variable *WK* and the value for the year from the variable *YEAR*. If *WK* is 48 and *YEAR* is 57, *WEEK* with a DATE format displays as 26-NOV-57.

Date and Time Conversion Functions

```
COMPUTE NMINS=CTIME.MINUTES(TIME.HMS(HR,MIN,SEC)).
COMPUTE AGER=(YRMODA(1992,10,01)-
                    YRMODA(YRBIRTH,MOBIRTH,DABIRTH))/365.25.
```

- The CTIME.MINUTES function converts a time interval to number of minutes. If *HR* equals 12, *MIN* equals 30, and *SEC* equals 30, the TIME.HMS function returns an interval of 45,030, which CTIME.MINUTES converts to minutes. *NMINS* equals 750.50.
- The YRMODA function converts the current date (in this example, October 1, 1992) and birthdate to a number of days. The birthdate is subtracted from the current date and the remainder is divided by the number of days in a year to yield the age in years.

Date and Time Extraction Functions

```
COMPUTE MONTHNUM=XDATE.MONTH(BIRTHDAY).
COMPUTE DAYNUM=XDATE.JDAY(BIRTHDAY).
```

- The XDATE.MONTH function reads a date and returns the month number expressed as an integer from 1 to 12. If *BIRTHDAY* is formatted as DATETIME20 and contains the value 05-DEC-1954 5:30:15, *MONTHNUM* equals 12.
- The XDATE.JDAY function returns the day of the year, expressed as an integer between 1 and 366. For the value *BIRTHDAY* used by the first COMPUTE, *DAYNUM* equals 339.

Equivalence

```
STRING DEPT(A20).
COMPUTE DEPT='Personnel Department'.
COMPUTE OLDVAR=NEWVAL.
```

- *DEPT* is a new string variable and must be specified on STRING before it can be specified on COMPUTE. STRING assigns *DEPT* a width of 20 characters, and COMPUTE assigns the value *Personnel Department* to *DEPT* for each case.
- *OLDVAR* must already exist; otherwise, it would have to be declared on STRING. The values of *OLDVAR* are modified to equal the values of *NEWVAL*. *NEWVAL* must be an existing string variable. If the dictionary width of *NEWVAL* is longer than the dictionary width of *OLDVAR*, the modified values of *OLDVAR* are truncated.

String Functions

```
STRING NEWSTR(A7) / DATE(A8) / #MO #DA #YR (A2).
COMPUTE NEWSTR=LAG(OLDSTR,2).

COMPUTE #MO=STRING(MONTH,F2.0).
COMPUTE #DA=STRING(DAY,F2.0).
COMPUTE #YR=STRING(YEAR,F2.0).
COMPUTE DATE=CONCAT(#MO,'/',#DA,'/',#YR).

COMPUTE LNAME=UPCASE(LNAME).
```

- STRING declares *NEWSTR* as a new string variable with a width of seven characters, *DATE* with a width of eight characters, and scratch variables *#MO, #DA, and #YR* with a width of two characters each.
- The first COMPUTE sets *NEWSTR* equal to the value of *OLDSTR* for two cases previous. The first two cases receive the system-missing value for *NEWSTR*.
- The next three COMPUTE commands convert the existing numeric variables *MONTH*, *DAY*, and *YEAR* to the temporary string variables *#MO*, *#DA*, and *#YR* so that they can be used with the CONCAT function. The next COMPUTE assigns the concatenated value of *#MO*, *#DA*, and *#YR*, separated by slashes, to *DATE*. If *#MO* is 10, *#DA* is 16, and *#YR* is 49, *DATE* is 10/16/49.
- The final COMPUTE converts lowercase letters for the existing string variable *LNAME* to uppercase letters.

CORRELATIONS

```
CORRELATIONS [VARIABLES=] varlist [WITH varlist] [/varlist...]

 [/MISSING={PAIRWISE**}  [{INCLUDE}]]
           {LISTWISE  }   {EXCLUDE}

 [/PRINT={TWOTAIL**}  {SIG**}]
         {ONETAIL  }  {NOSIG}

 [/MATRIX=OUT({*    })]
              {file}

 [/STATISTICS=[DESCRIPTIVES] [XPROD] [ALL]]
```

**Default if the subcommand is omitted.

Example

```
CORRELATIONS VARIABLES=FOOD RENT PUBTRANS TEACHER COOK ENGINEER
  /MISSING=INCLUDE.
```

Overview

CORRELATIONS (alias PEARSON CORR) produces Pearson product-moment correlations with significance levels and, optionally, univariate statistics, covariances, and cross-product deviations. Other procedures that produce correlation matrices are PARTIAL CORR, REGRESSION, DISCRIMINANT, and FACTOR.

Options

Types of Matrices. A simple variable list on the VARIABLES subcommand produces a square matrix. You can also request a rectangular matrix of correlations between specific pairs of variables or between variable lists using the keyword WITH on VARIABLES.

Significance Levels. By default, CORRELATIONS displays the number of cases and significance levels for each coefficient. Significance levels are based on a two-tailed test. You can request a one-tailed test, and you can display the significance level for each coefficient as an annotation using the PRINT subcommand.

Additional Statistics. You can obtain the mean, standard deviation, and number of nonmissing cases for each variable, and the cross-product deviations and covariance for each pair of variables using the STATISTICS subcommand.

Matrix Output. You can write matrix materials to a data file using the MATRIX subcommand. The matrix materials include the mean, standard deviation, number of cases used to compute each coefficient, and Pearson correlation coefficient for each variable. The matrix data file can be read by several other procedures.

Basic Specification

- The basic specification is the VARIABLES subcommand, which specifies the variables to be analyzed. The actual keyword VARIABLES can be omitted.
- By default, CORRELATIONS produces a matrix of correlation coefficients. The number of cases and the significance level are displayed for each coefficient. The significance level is based on a two-tailed test.

Subcommand Order

- The VARIABLES subcommand must be first.
- The remaining subcommands can be specified in any order.

Operations

- The correlation of a variable with itself is displayed as 1.0000.
- A correlation that cannot be computed is displayed as a period (.).
- CORRELATIONS does not execute if long or short string variables are specified on the variable list.

Limitations

- Maximum 40 variable lists.
- Maximum 500 variables total per command.
- Maximum 250 syntax elements. Each individual occurrence of a variable name, keyword, or special delimiter counts as 1 toward this total. Variables implied by the TO keyword do not count toward this total.

Example

```
CORRELATIONS VARIABLES=FOOD RENT PUBTRANS TEACHER COOK ENGINEER
  /VARIABLES=FOOD RENT WITH COOK TEACHER MANAGER ENGINEER
  /MISSING=INCLUDE.
```

- The first VARIABLES subcommand requests a square matrix of correlation coefficients among variables *FOOD*, *RENT*, *PUBTRANS*, *TEACHER*, *COOK*, and *ENGINEER*.
- The second VARIABLES subcommand requests a rectangular correlation matrix in which *FOOD* and *RENT* are the row variables and *COOK*, *TEACHER*, *MANAGER*, and *ENGINEER* are the column variables.
- MISSING requests that user-missing values be included in the computation of each coefficient.

VARIABLES Subcommand

VARIABLES specifies the variable list. The actual keyword VARIABLES is optional.

- A simple variable list produces a square matrix of correlations of each variable with every other variable.
- Variable lists joined by the keyword WITH produce a rectangular correlation matrix. Variables before WITH define the rows of the matrix and variables after WITH define the columns.
- The keyword ALL can be used on the variable list to refer to all user-defined variables.
- You can specify multiple VARIABLES subcommands on a single CORRELATIONS command. The slash between the subcommands is required; the keyword VARIABLES is not.

PRINT Subcommand

PRINT controls whether the significance level is based on a one- or two-tailed test and whether the number of cases and the significance level for each correlation coefficient are displayed.

TWOTAIL *Two-tailed test of significance.* This test is appropriate when the direction of the relationship cannot be determined in advance, as is often the case in exploratory data analysis. This is the default.

ONETAIL *One-tailed test of significance.* This test is appropriate when the direction of the relationship between a pair of variables can be specified in advance of the analysis.

SIG *Do not flag significant values.* SIG is the default.

NOSIG *Flag significant values.* Values significant at the 0.05 level are flagged with a single asterisk; those that are significant at the 0.01 level are flagged with two asterisks.

STATISTICS Subcommand

The correlation coefficients are automatically displayed in the Correlations table for an analysis specified by a VARIABLES list. STATISTICS requests additional statistics.

DESCRIPTIVES *Display mean, standard deviation, and number of nonmissing cases for each variable on the Variables list in the Descriptive Statistics table.* This table precedes all Correlations tables. Variables specified on more than one VARIABLES lists are displayed only once. Missing values are handled on a variable-by-variable basis regardless of the missing-value option in effect for the correlations.

XPROD *Display cross-product deviations and covariance for each pair of variables in the Correlations table(s).*

ALL *All additional statistics.* This produces the same statistics as DESCRIPTIVES and XPROD together.

MISSING Subcommand

MISSING controls the treatment of missing values.

- The PAIRWISE and LISTWISE keywords are alternatives; however, each can be specified with INCLUDE or EXCLUDE.
- The default is LISTWISE and EXCLUDE.

PAIRWISE *Exclude missing values pairwise.* Cases that have missing values for one or both of a pair of variables for a specific correlation coefficient are excluded from the computation of that coefficient. Since each coefficient is based on all cases that have valid values for that particular pair of variables, this can result in a set of coefficients based on a varying number of cases. The valid number of cases is displayed in the Correlations table. This is the default.

LISTWISE *Exclude missing values listwise.* Cases that have missing values for any variable named on any VARIABLES list are excluded from the computation of all coefficients across lists. The valid number of cases is the same for all analyses and is displayed in a single annotation.

INCLUDE *Include user-missing values.* User-missing values are included in the analysis.

EXCLUDE *Exclude all missing values.* Both user- and system-missing values are excluded from the analysis.

MATRIX Subcommand

MATRIX writes matrix materials to a data file. The matrix materials include the mean and standard deviation for each variable, the number of cases used to compute each coefficient, and the Pearson correlation coefficients. Several procedures can read matrix materials produced by CORRELATIONS, including PARTIAL CORR, REGRESSION, FACTOR, and CLUSTER (see "SPSS Matrix Data Files" on p. 13).

- CORRELATIONS cannot write rectangular matrices (those specified with the keyword WITH) to a file.
- If you specify more than one variable list on CORRELATIONS, only the last list that does not use the keyword WITH is written to the matrix data file.
- The keyword OUT specifies the file to which the matrix is written. The filename must be specified in parentheses.
- Documents from the original file will not be included in the matrix file and will not be present if the matrix file becomes the working data file.

OUT (filename) *Write a matrix data file.* Specify either a file or an asterisk (*), enclosed in parentheses. If you specify a file, the file is stored on disk and can be retrieved at any time. If you specify an asterisk, the matrix data file replaces the working file but is not stored on disk unless you use SAVE or XSAVE.

Format of the Matrix Data File

- The matrix data file has two special variables created by the program: *ROWTYPE_* and *VARNAME_*. The variable *ROWTYPE_* is a short string variable with values *MEAN*, *STDDEV*, *N*, and *CORR* (for Pearson correlation coefficient). The next variable, *VARNAME_*, is a short string variable whose values are the names of the variables used to form the correlation matrix. When *ROWTYPE_* is *CORR*, *VARNAME_* gives the variable associated with that row of the correlation matrix.
- The remaining variables in the file are the variables used to form the correlation matrix.

Split Files

- When split-file processing is in effect, the first variables in the matrix file will be split variables, followed by *ROWTYPE_*, *VARNAME_*, and the variables used to form the correlation matrix.
- A full set of matrix materials is written for each subgroup defined by the split variables.
- A split variable cannot have the same name as any other variable written to the matrix data file.
- If split-file processing is in effect when a matrix is written, the same split-file specifications must be in effect when that matrix is read by another procedure.

Missing Values

- With pairwise treatment of missing values (the default), a matrix of the number of cases used to compute each coefficient is included with the matrix materials.
- With listwise treatment, a single number indicating the number of cases used to calculate all coefficients is included.

Example

```
GET FILE=CITY /KEEP FOOD RENT PUBTRANS TEACHER COOK ENGINEER.
CORRELATIONS VARIABLES=FOOD TO ENGINEER
 /MATRIX OUT(CORRMAT).
```

- CORRELATIONS reads data from the file *CITY* and writes one set of matrix materials to the file *CORRMAT*. The working file is still *CITY*. Subsequent commands are executed on *CITY*.

Example

```
GET FILE=CITY /KEEP FOOD RENT PUBTRANS TEACHER COOK ENGINEER.
CORRELATIONS VARIABLES=FOOD TO ENGINEER
 /MATRIX OUT(*).
LIST.
DISPLAY DICTIONARY.
```

- CORRELATIONS writes the same matrix as in the example above. However, the matrix data file replaces the working file. The LIST and DISPLAY commands are executed on the matrix file, not on the *CITY* file.

Example

```
CORRELATIONS VARIABLES=FOOD RENT COOK TEACHER MANAGER ENGINEER
 /FOOD TO TEACHER /PUBTRANS WITH MECHANIC
 /MATRIX OUT(*).
```

- Only the matrix for *FOOD* TO *TEACHER* is written to the matrix data file because it is the last variable list that does not use the keyword WITH.

COUNT

```
COUNT varname=varlist(value list) [/varname=...]
```

Keywords for numeric value lists:

LOWEST, LO, HIGHEST, HI, THRU, MISSING, SYSMIS

Example

```
COUNT TARGET=V1 V2 V3 (2).
```

Overview

COUNT creates a numeric variable that, for each case, counts the occurrences of the same value (or list of values) across a list of variables. The new variable is called the *target* variable. The variables and values that are counted are the *criterion* variables and values. Criterion variables can be either numeric or string.

Basic Specification

The basic specification is the target variable, an equals sign, the criterion variable(s), and the criterion value(s) enclosed in parentheses.

Syntax Rules

- Use a slash to separate the specifications for each target variable.
- The criterion variables specified for a single target variable must be either all numeric or all string.
- Each value on a list of criterion values must be separated by a comma or space. String values must be enclosed in apostrophes.
- The keywords THRU, LOWEST (LO), HIGHEST (HI), SYSMIS, and MISSING can be used only with numeric criterion variables.
- A variable can be specified on more than one criterion variable list.
- You can use the keyword TO to specify consecutive criterion variables that have the same criterion value or values.
- You can specify multiple variable lists for a single target variable to count different values for different variables.

Operations

- Target variables are always numeric and are initialized to 0 for each case. They are assigned a dictionary format of F8.2.
- If the target variable already exists, its previous values are replaced.
- COUNT ignores the missing-value status of user-missing values. It counts a value even if that value has been previously declared as missing.
- The target variable is never system-missing. To define user-missing values for target variables, use the RECODE or MISSING VALUES command.
- SYSMIS counts system-missing values for numeric variables.
- MISSING counts both user- and system-missing values for numeric variables.

Example

```
COUNT TARGET=V1 V2 V3 (2).
```

- The value of *TARGET* for each case will be either 0, 1, 2, or 3, depending on the number of times the value 2 occurs across the three variables for each case.
- *TARGET* is a numeric variable with an F8.2 format.

Example

```
COUNT QLOW=Q1 TO Q10 (LO THRU 0)
  /QSYSMIS=Q1 TO Q10 (SYSMIS).
```

- Assuming that there are 10 variables between and including *Q1* and *Q10* in the working data file, *QLOW* ranges from 0 to 10, depending on the number of times a case has a negative or 0 value across the variables *Q1* to *Q10*.
- *QSYSMIS* ranges from 0 to 10, depending on how many system-missing values are encountered for *Q1* to *Q10* for each case. User-missing values are not counted.
- Both *QLOW* and *QSYSMIS* are numeric variables and have F8.2 formats.

Example

```
COUNT SVAR=V1 V2 ('male  ') V3 V4 V5 ('female').
```

- *SVAR* ranges from 0 to 5, depending on the number of times a case has a value of male for *V1* and *V2* and a value of female for *V3*, *V4*, and *V5*.
- *SVAR* is a numeric variable with an F8.2 format.

COXREG

COXREG is available in the Advanced Models option.

```
[TIME PROGRAM]*
[commands to compute time dependent covariates]

[CLEAR TIME PROGRAM]

COXREG [VARIABLES =] survival varname [WITH varlist]
    / STATUS = varname [EVENT] (vallist) [LOST (vallist)]
   [/STRATA  = varname]
   [/CATEGORICAL = varname]
   [/CONTRAST (varname) = {DEVIATION (refcat)}]
                          {SIMPLE (refcat)   }
                          {DIFFERENCE        }
                          {HELMERT           }
                          {REPEATED          }
                          {POLYNOMIAL(metric)}
                          {SPECIAL (matrix)  }
                          {INDICATOR (refcat)}

   [/METHOD = {ENTER**          }    [{varlist}]]
              {BSTEP [{COND}]}     {ALL    }
                      {LR  }
                      {WALD}
              {FSTEP [{COND}]}
                      {LR  }
                      {WALD}

   [/MISSING = {EXCLUDE**}]
               {INCLUDE  }

   [/PRINT = [{DEFAULT**}]   [CI ({95})]]
              {SUMMARY  }         {n }
              {BASELINE }
              {CORR     }
              {ALL      }

   [/CRITERIA = [{BCON}({1E-4**})]    [LCON({1E-5**})]
                 {PCON} { n     }          { n     }
                [ITERATE({20**})]
                         { n  }
                [PIN({0.05**})]       [POUT({0.1**})]]
                     { n    }              { n   }

   [/PLOT = [NONE**] [SURVIVAL] [HAZARD] [LML] [OMS]]
   [/PATTERN = [varname(value)...] [BY varname]]
   [/OUTFILE = [COEFF(file)] [TABLE(file)]]
   [/SAVE = tempvar [(newvarname)],tempvar ...]
   [/EXTERNAL]
```

* TIME PROGRAM is required to generate time-dependent covariates.

**Default if subcommand or keyword is omitted.

Temporary variables created by COXREG are:

SURVIVAL
SE
HAZARD
RESID
LML
DFBETA

PRESID
XBETA

Example

```
TIME PROGRAM.
COMPUTE Z=AGE + T_.

COXREG SURVIVAL WITH Z
  /STATUS SURVSTA EVENT(1).
```

Overview

COXREG applies Cox proportional hazards regression to analysis of survival times—that is, the length of time before the occurrence of an event. COXREG supports continuous and categorical independent variables (covariates), which can be time-dependent. Unlike SURVIVAL and KM, which compare only distinct subgroups of cases, COXREG provides an easy way of considering differences in subgroups as well as analyzing effects of a set of covariates.

Options

Processing of Independent Variables. You can specify which of the independent variables are categorical with the CATEGORICAL subcommand and control treatment of these variables with the CONTRAST subcommand. You can select one of seven methods for entering independent variables into the model using the METHOD subcommand. You can also indicate interaction terms using the keyword BY between variable names on either the VARIABLES subcommand or the METHOD subcommand.

Specifying Termination and Model-Building Criteria. You can specify the criteria for termination of iteration and control variable entry and removal with the CRITERIA subcommand.

Adding New Variables to Working Data File. You can use the SAVE subcommand to save the cumulative survival, standard error, cumulative hazard, log-minus-log-of-survival function, residuals, XBeta, and, wherever available, partial residuals and DfBeta.

Output. You can print optional output using the PRINT subcommand, suppress or request plots with the PLOT subcommand, and, with the OUTFILE subcommand, write SPSS data files containing coefficients from the final model or a survival table. When only time-constant covariates are used, you can use the PATTERN subcommand to specify a pattern of covariate values in addition to the covariate means to use for the plots and the survival table.

Basic Specification

- The minimum specification on COXREG is a dependent variable with the STATUS subcommand.
- To analyze the influence of time-constant covariates on the survival times, the minimum specification requires either the WITH keyword followed by at least one covariate (independent variable) on the VARIABLES subcommand or a METHOD subcommand with at least one independent variable.

- To analyze the influence of time-dependent covariates on the survival times, the TIME PROGRAM command and transformation language are required to define the functions for the time-dependent covariate(s).

Subcommand Order

- The VARIABLES subcommand must be specified first; the subcommand keyword is optional.
- Remaining subcommands can be named in any order.

Syntax Rules

- Only one dependent variable can be specified for each COXREG command.
- Any number of covariates (independent variables) can be specified. The dependent variable cannot appear on the covariate list.
- The covariate list is required if any of the METHOD subcommands are used without a variable list or if the METHOD subcommand is not used.
- Only one status variable can be specified on the STATUS subcommand. If multiple STATUS subcommands are specified, only the last specification is in effect.
- You can use the BY keyword to specify interaction between covariates.

Operations

- TIME PROGRAM computes the values for time-dependent covariates.
- COXREG replaces covariates specified on CATEGORICAL with sets of contrast variables. In stepwise analyses, the set of contrast variables associated with one categorical variable is entered or removed from the model as a block.
- Covariates are screened to detect and eliminate redundancies.
- COXREG deletes all cases that have negative values for the dependent variable.

Limitations

- Only one dependent variable is allowed.
- Maximum 100 covariates in a single interaction term.
- Maximum 35 levels for a BY variable on PATTERN.

Example

```
TIME PROGRAM.
COMPUTE Z=AGE + T_.

COXREG SURVIVAL WITH Z
  /STATUS SURVSTA EVENT (1).
```

- TIME PROGRAM defines the time-dependent covariate *Z* as the current age. *Z* is then specified as a covariate.
- The dependent variable *SURVIVAL* contains the length of time to the terminal event or to censoring.
- A value of 1 on the variable *SURVSTA* indicates an event.

TIME PROGRAM Command

TIME PROGRAM is required to define time-dependent covariates. These are covariates whose values change during the course of the study.

- TIME PROGRAM and the transformations that define the time-dependent covariate(s) must precede the COXREG command.
- A time-dependent covariate is a function of the current time, which is represented by the special variable *T_*.
- The working data file must not have a variable named *T_*. If it does, rename the variable before you run the COXREG command. Otherwise, you will trigger an error.
- *T_* cannot be specified as a covariate. Any other variable in the TIME PROGRAM can be specified on the covariate list.
- For every time-dependent covariate, values are generated for each valid case for all uncensored times in the same stratum that occur before the observed time. If no STRATA subcommand is specified, all cases are considered to belong to one stratum.
- If any function defined by the time program results in a missing value for a case that has no missing values for any other variable used in the procedure, COXREG terminates with an error.

CLEAR TIME PROGRAM Command

CLEAR TIME PROGRAM deletes all time-dependent covariates created in the previous time program. It is primarily used in interactive mode to remove temporary variables associated with the time program so that you can redefine time-dependent covariates for the Cox Regression procedure. It is not necessary to use this command if you have already executed COXREG. All temporary variables created by the time program are automatically deleted.

VARIABLES Subcommand

VARIABLES identifies the dependent variable and the covariates to be included in the analysis.

- The minimum specification is the dependent variable. The subcommand keyword is optional.
- You must specify the keyword WITH and a list of all covariates if no METHOD subcommand is specified or if a METHOD subcommand is specified without naming the variables to be used.
- If the covariate list is not specified on VARIABLES but one or more METHOD subcommands are used, the covariate list is assumed to be the union of the sets of variables listed on all the METHOD subcommands.

- You can specify an interaction of two or more covariates using the keyword BY. For example, `A B BY C D` specifies the three terms *A*, *B*C*, and *D*.
- The keyword TO can be used to specify a list of covariates. The implied variable order is the same as in the working data file.

STATUS Subcommand

To determine whether the event has occurred for a particular observation, COXREG checks the value of a status variable. STATUS lists the status variable and the code for the occurrence of the event.

- Only one status variable can be specified. If multiple STATUS subcommands are specified, COXREG uses the last specification and displays a warning.
- The keyword EVENT is optional, but the value list in parentheses must be specified.
- The value list must be enclosed in parentheses. All cases with non-negative times that do not have a code within the range specified after EVENT are classified as **censored cases**—that is, cases for which the event has not yet occurred.
- The value list can be one value, a list of values separated by blanks or commas, a range of values using the keyword THRU, or a combination.
- If missing values occur within the specified ranges, they are ignored if MISSING=EXCLUDE (the default) is specified, but they are treated as valid values for the range if MISSING=INCLUDE is specified.
- The status variable can be either numeric or string. If a string variable is specified, the EVENT values must be enclosed in apostrophes and the keyword THRU cannot be used.

Example

```
COXREG SURVIVAL WITH GROUP
  /STATUS SURVSTA (3 THRU 5, 8 THRU 10).
```

- STATUS specifies that *SURVSTA* is the status variable.
- A value between either 3 and 5, or 8 and 10, inclusive, means that the terminal event occurred.
- Values outside the specified ranges indicate censored cases.

STRATA Subcommand

STRATA identifies a stratification variable. A different baseline survival function is computed for each stratum.

- The only specification is the subcommand keyword with one, and only one, variable name.
- If you have more than one stratification variable, create a new variable that corresponds to the combination of categories of the individual variables before invoking the COXREG command.
- There is no limit to the number of levels for the strata variable.

Example

```
COXREG SURVIVAL WITH GROUP
 /STATUS SURVSTA (1)
 /STRATA=LOCATION.
```

- STRATA specifies *LOCATION* as the strata variable.
- Different baseline survival functions are computed for each value of *LOCATION*.

CATEGORICAL Subcommand

CATEGORICAL identifies covariates that are nominal or ordinal. Variables that are declared to be categorical are automatically transformed to a set of contrast variables (see "CONTRAST Subcommand" below). If a variable coded as $0 - 1$ is declared as categorical, by default, its coding scheme will be changed to deviation contrasts.

- Covariates not specified on CATEGORICAL are assumed to be at least interval, except for strings.
- Variables specified on CATEGORICAL but not on VARIABLES or any METHOD subcommand are ignored.
- Variables specified on CATEGORICAL are replaced by sets of contrast variables. If the categorical variable has *n* distinct values, there will be $n - 1$ contrast variables generated. The set of contrast variables associated with one categorical variable are entered or removed from the model together.
- If any one of the variables in an interaction term is specified on CATEGORICAL, the interaction term is replaced by contrast variables.
- All string variables are categorical. Only the first eight characters of each value of a string variable are used in distinguishing among values. Thus, if two values of a string variable are identical for the first eight characters, the values are treated as though they were the same.

CONTRAST Subcommand

CONTRAST specifies the type of contrast used for categorical covariates. The interpretation of the regression coefficients for categorical covariates depends on the contrasts used. The default is DEVIATION. For illustration of contrast types, see the appendix.

- The categorical covariate is specified in parentheses following CONTRAST.
- If the categorical variable has *n* values, there will be $n - 1$ rows in the contrast matrix. Each contrast matrix is treated as a set of independent variables in the analysis.
- Only one variable can be specified per CONTRAST subcommand, but multiple CONTRAST subcommands can be specified.
- You can specify one of the contrast keywords in the parentheses after the variable specification to request a specific contrast type.

The following contrast types are available:

DEVIATION(refcat) *Deviations from the overall effect.* This is the default. The effect for each category of the independent variable except one is compared to the overall effect. Refcat is the category for which parameter estimates are not displayed (they must be calculated from.the others). By default, refcat is the last category. To omit a category other than the last, specify the sequence number of the omitted category (which is not necessarily the same as its value) in parentheses after the keyword DEVIATION.

SIMPLE(refcat) *Each category of the independent variable except the last is compared to the last category.* To use a category other than the last as the omitted reference category, specify its sequence number (which is not necessarily the same as its value) in parentheses following the keyword SIMPLE.

DIFFERENCE *Difference or reverse Helmert contrasts.* The effects for each category of the covariate except the first are compared to the mean effect of the previous categories.

HELMERT *Helmert contrasts.* The effects for each category of the independent variable except the last are compared to the mean effects of subsequent categories.

POLYNOMIAL(metric) *Polynomial contrasts.* The first degree of freedom contains the linear effect across the categories of the independent variable, the second contains the quadratic effect, and so on. By default, the categories are assumed to be equally spaced; unequal spacing can be specified by entering a metric consisting of one integer for each category of the independent variable in parentheses after the keyword POLYNOMIAL. For example, `CONTRAST (STIMULUS) = POLYNOMIAL(1,2,4)` indicates that the three levels of *STIMULUS* are actually in the proportion 1:2:4. The default metric is always (1,2,...,k), where k categories are involved. Only the relative differences between the terms of the metric matter: (1,2,4) is the same metric as (2,3,5) or (20,30,50) because, in each instance, the difference between the second and third numbers is twice the difference between the first and second.

REPEATED *Comparison of adjacent categories.* Each category of the independent variable except the first is compared to the previous category.

SPECIAL(matrix) *A user-defined contrast.* After this keyword, a matrix is entered in parentheses with $k-1$ rows and k columns, where k is the number of categories of the independent variable. The rows of the contrast matrix contain the special contrasts indicating the desired comparisons between categories. If the special contrasts are linear combinations of each other, COXREG reports the linear dependency and stops processing. If k rows are entered, the first row is discarded and only the last $k-1$ rows are used as the contrast matrix in the analysis.

INDICATOR(refcat) *Indicator variables.* Contrasts indicate the presence or absence of category membership. By default, refcat is the last category (represented in the contrast matrix as a row of zeros). To omit a category other than the last, specify the sequence number of the category (which is not necessarily the same as its value) in parentheses after keyword INDICATOR.

Example

```
COXREG SURVIVAL WITH GROUP
 /STATUS SURVSTA (1)
 /STRATA=LOCATION
 /CATEGORICAL = GROUP
 /CONTRAST(GROUP)=SPECIAL(2 -1 -1
                          0  1 -1).
```

- The specification of *GROUP* on CATEGORICAL replaces the variable with a set of contrast variables.
- *GROUP* identifies whether a case is in one of the three treatment groups.
- A SPECIAL type contrast is requested. A three-column, two-row contrast matrix is entered in parentheses.

METHOD Subcommand

METHOD specifies the order of processing and the manner in which the covariates enter the model. If no METHOD subcommand is specified, the default method is ENTER.

- The subcommand keyword METHOD can be omitted.
- You can list all covariates to be used for the method on a variable list. If no variable list is specified, the default is ALL: all covariates named after WITH on the VARIABLES subcommand are used for the method.
- The keyword BY can be used between two variable names to specify an interaction term.
- Variables specified on CATEGORICAL are replaced by sets of contrast variables. The contrast variables associated with a categorical variable are entered or removed from the model together.

Three keywords are available to specify how the model is to be built:

ENTER *Forced entry.* All variables are entered in a single step. This is the default if the METHOD subcommand is omitted.

FSTEP *Forward stepwise.* The covariates specified on FSTEP are tested for entry into the model one by one based on the significance level of the score statistic. The variable with the smallest significance less than PIN is entered into the model. After each entry, variables that are already in the model are tested for possible removal based on the significance of the Wald statistic, likelihood ratio, or conditional criterion. The variable with the largest probability greater than the specified POUT value is removed and the model is reestimated. Variables in the model are then again evaluated for removal. Once no more variables satisfy the removal criteria, covariates not in the model are evaluated for entry. Model building stops when no more variables meet entry or removal criteria, or when the current model is the same as a previous one.

BSTEP *Backward stepwise.* As a first step, the covariates specified on BSTEP are entered into the model together and are tested for removal one by one. Stepwise removal and entry then follow the same process as described for FSTEP until no more variables meet entry and removal criteria, or when the current model is the same as a previous one.

- Multiple METHOD subcommands are allowed and are processed in the order in which they are specified. Each method starts with the results from the previous method. If BSTEP is used, all eligible variables are entered at the first step. All variables are then eligible for entry and removal unless they have been excluded from the METHOD variable list.

The statistic used in the test for removal can be specified by an additional keyword in parentheses following FSTEP or BSTEP. If FSTEP or BSTEP is specified by itself, the default is COND.

COND *Conditional statistic.* This is the default if FSTEP or BSTEP is specified by itself.

WALD *Wald statistic.* The removal of a covariate from the model is based on the significance of the Wald statistic.

LR *Likelihood ratio.* The removal of a covariate from the model is based on the significance of the change in the log-likelihood. If LR is specified, the model must be reestimated without each of the variables in the model. This can substantially increase computational time. However, the likelihood-ratio statistic is better than the Wald statistic for deciding which variables are to be removed.

Example

```
COXREG SURVIVAL WITH GROUP SMOKE DRINK
 /STATUS SURVSTA (1)
 /CATEGORICAL = GROUP SMOKE DRINK
 /METHOD ENTER GROUP
 /METHOD BSTEP (LR) SMOKE DRINK SMOKE BY DRINK.
```

- *GROUP*, *SMOKE*, and *DRINK* are specified as covariates and as categorical variables.
- The first METHOD subcommand enters GROUP into the model.
- Variables in the model at the termination of the first METHOD subcommand are included in the model at the beginning of the second METHOD subcommand.
- The second METHOD subcommand adds *SMOKE*, *DRINK*, and the interaction of *SMOKE* with *DRINK* to the previous model.
- Backward stepwise regression analysis is then done using the likelihood-ratio statistic as the removal criterion. The variable *GROUP* is not eligible for removal because it was not specified on the BSTEP subcommand.
- The procedure continues until the removal of a variable will result in a decrease in the log-likelihood with a probability smaller than POUT.

MISSING Subcommand

MISSING controls missing value treatments. If MISSING is omitted, the default is EXCLUDE.

- Cases with negative values on the dependent variable are automatically treated as missing and are excluded.
- To be included in the model, a case must have nonmissing values for the dependent, status, strata, and all independent variables specified on the COXREG command.

EXCLUDE *Exclude user-missing values.* User-missing values are treated as missing. This is the default if MISSING is omitted.

INCLUDE *Include user-missing values.* User-missing values are included in the analysis.

PRINT Subcommand

By default, COXREG prints a full regression report for each step. You can use the PRINT subcommand to request specific output. If PRINT is not specified, the default is DEFAULT.

DEFAULT *Full regression output including overall model statistics and statistics for variables in the equation and variables not in the equation.* This is the default when PRINT is omitted.

SUMMARY *Summary information.* The output includes –2 log-likelihood for the initial model, one line of summary for each step, and the final model printed with full detail.

CORR *Correlation/covariance matrix of parameter estimates for the variables in the model.*

BASELINE *Baseline table.* For each stratum, a table is displayed showing the baseline cumulative hazard, as well as survival, standard error, and cumulative hazard evaluated at the covariate means for each observed time point in that stratum.

CI (value) *Confidence intervals for* e^{β}. Specify the confidence level in parentheses. The requested intervals are displayed whenever a variables-in-equation table is printed. The default is 95%.

ALL *All available output.*

- Estimation histories showing the last 10 iterations are printed if the solution fails to converge.

Example

```
COXREG SURVIVAL WITH GROUP
 /STATUS = SURVSTA (1)
 /STRATA = LOCATION
 /CATEGORICAL = GROUP
 /METHOD = ENTER
 /PRINT ALL.
```

- PRINT requests summary information, a correlation matrix for parameter estimates, a baseline survival table for each stratum, and confidence intervals for e^{β} with each variables-in-equation table, in addition to the default output.

CRITERIA Subcommand

CRITERIA controls the statistical criteria used in building the Cox Regression models. The way in which these criteria are used depends on the method specified on the METHOD subcommand. The default criteria are noted in the description of each keyword below. Iterations will stop if any of the criteria for BCON, LCON, or ITERATE are satisfied.

BCON(value) *Change in parameter estimates for terminating iteration.* Alias PCON. Iteration terminates when the parameters change by less than the specified value. BCON defaults to $1E-4$. To eliminate this criteria, specify a value of 0.

ITERATE(value) *Maximum number of iterations.* If a solution fails to converge after the maximum number of iterations has been reached, COXREG displays an iteration history showing the last 10 iterations and terminates the procedure. The default for ITERATE is 20.

LCON(value) *Percentage change in the log-likelihood ratio for terminating iteration.* If the log-likelihood decreases by less than the specified value, iteration terminates. LCON defaults to $1E-5$. To eliminate this criterion, specify a value of 0.

PIN(value) *Probability of score statistic for variable entry.* A variable whose significance level is greater than PIN cannot enter the model. The default for PIN is 0.05.

POUT(value) *Probability of Wald, LR, or conditional LR statistic to remove a variable.* A variable whose significance is less than POUT cannot be removed. The default for POUT is 0.1.

Example

```
COXREG SURVIVAL WITH GROUP AGE BP TMRSZ
 /STATUS = SURVSTA (1)
 /STRATA = LOCATION
 /CATEGORICAL = GROUP
 /METHOD BSTEP
 /CRITERIA BCON(0) ITERATE(10) PIN(0.01) POUT(0.05).
```

- A backward stepwise Cox Regression analysis is performed.
- CRITERIA alters four of the default statistical criteria that control the building of a model.
- Zero specified on BCON indicates that change in parameter estimates is not a criterion for termination. BCON can be set to 0 if only LCON and ITER are to be used.
- ITERATE specifies that the maximum number of iterations is 10. LCON is not changed and the default remains in effect. If either ITERATE or LCON is met, iterations will terminate.
- POUT requires that the probability of the statistic used to test whether a variable should remain in the model be smaller than 0.05. This is more stringent than the default value of 0.1.
- PIN requires that the probability of the score statistic used to test whether a variable should be included be smaller than 0.01. This makes it more difficult for variables to be included in the model than does the default PIN, which has a value of 0.05.

PLOT Subcommand

You can request specific plots to be produced with the PLOT subcommand. Each requested plot is produced once for each pattern specified on the PATTERN subcommand. If PLOT is not specified, the default is NONE (no plots are printed). Requested plots are displayed at the end of the final model.

- The set of plots requested is displayed for the functions at the mean of the covariates and at each combination of covariate values specified on PATTERN.
- If time-dependent covariates are included in the model, no plots are produced.
- Lines on a plot are connected as step functions.

NONE *Do not display plots.*

SURVIVAL *Plot the cumulative survival distribution.*

HAZARD *Plot the cumulative hazard function.*

LML *Plot the log-minus-log-of-survival function.*

OMS *Plot the one-minus-survival function.*

PATTERN Subcommand

PATTERN specifies the pattern of covariate values to be used for the requested plots and coefficient tables.

- A value must be specified for each variable specified on PATTERN.
- Continuous variables that are included in the model but not named on PATTERN are evaluated at their means.
- Categorical variables that are included in the model but not named on PATTERN are evaluated at the means of the set of contrasts generated to replace them.
- You can request separate lines for each category of a variable that is in the model. Specify the name of the categorical variable after the keyword BY. The BY variable must be a categorical covariate. You cannot specify a value for the BY covariate.
- Multiple PATTERN subcommands can be specified. COXREG produces a set of requested plots for each specified pattern.
- PATTERN cannot be used when time-dependent covariates are included in the model.

OUTFILE Subcommand

OUTFILE writes an external SPSS data file. COXREG writes two types of data files. You can specify the file type to be created with one of the two keywords, followed by the file specification in parentheses.

COEFF *Write an SPSS data file containing the coefficients from the final model.*

TABLE *Write the survival table to an SPSS data file.* The file contains cumulative survival, standard error, and cumulative hazard statistics for each uncensored time within each stratum evaluated at the baseline and at the mean of the covariates. Additional covariate patterns can be requested on PATTERN.

- The specified SPSS data file must be an external file. You cannot specify an asterisk (*) to identify the working data file.
- The variables saved in the external file are listed in the output.

SAVE Subcommand

SAVE saves the temporary variables created by COXREG. The temporary variables include:

SURVIVAL *Survival function evaluated at the current case.*

SE *Standard error of the survival function.*

HAZARD *Cumulative hazard function evaluated at the current case.* Alias RESID.

LML *Log-minus-log-of-survival function.*

DFBETA *Change in the coefficient if the current case is removed.* There is one *DFBETA* for each covariate in the final model. If there are time-dependent covariates, only *DFBETA* can be requested. Requests for any other temporary variable are ignored.

PRESID *Partial residuals.* There is one residual variable for each covariate in the final model. If a covariate is not in the final model, the corresponding new variable has the system-missing value.

XBETA *Linear combination of mean corrected covariates times regression coefficients from the final model.*

- To specify variable names for the new variables, assign the new names in parentheses following each temporary variable name.
- Assigned variable names must be unique in the working data file. Scratch or system variable names cannot be used (that is, the variable names cannot begin with # or $).
- If new variable names are not specified, COXREG generates default names. The default name is composed of the first three characters of the name of the temporary variable (two for *SE*), followed by an underscore and a number to make it unique.
- A temporary variable can be saved only once on the same SAVE subcommand.

Example

```
COXREG SURVIVAL WITH GROUP
 /STATUS = SURVSTA (1)
 /STRATA = LOCATION
 /CATEGORICAL = GROUP
 /METHOD = ENTER
 /SAVE SURVIVAL HAZARD.
```

- COXREG saves cumulative survival and hazard in two new variables, *SUR_1* and *HAZ_1*, provided that neither of the two names exists in the working data file. If one does, the numeric suffixes will be incremented to make a distinction.

EXTERNAL Subcommand

EXTERNAL specifies that the data for each split-file group should be held in an external scratch file during processing. This helps conserve working space when running analyses with large data sets.

- The EXTERNAL subcommand takes no other keyword and is specified by itself.
- If time-dependent covariates exist, external data storage is unavailable, and EXTERNAL is ignored.

CREATE

```
CREATE new series={CSUM (series)                       }
                  {DIFF (series, order)                }
                  {FFT (series)                        }
                  {IFFT (series)                       }
                  {LAG (series, order [,order ])       }
                  {LEAD (series, order [,order ])      }
                  {MA (series, span [,minimum span])   }
                  {PMA (series, span)                  }
                  {RMED (series, span [,minimum span]) }
                  {SDIFF (series, order [,periodicity])}
                  {T4253H (series)                     }

[/new series=function (series {,span   {,minimum span}})]
                              {,order  {,order        }}
                                       {,periodicity  }
```

Function keywords:

CSUM	Cumulative sum
DIFF	Difference
FFT	Fast Fourier transform
IFFT	Inverse fast Fourier transform
LAG	Lag
LEAD	Lead
MA	Centered moving averages
PMA	Prior moving averages
RMED	Running medians
SDIFF	Seasonal difference
T4253H	Smoothing

Example

```
CREATE NEWVAR1 NEWVAR2 = CSUM(TICKETS RNDTRP).
```

Overview

CREATE produces new series as a function of existing series. You can also use CREATE to replace the values of existing series. The new or revised series can be used in any procedure and can be saved in an SPSS-format data file.

CREATE displays a list of the new series, the case numbers of the first and last nonmissing cases, the number of valid cases, and the functions used to create the variables.

Basic Specification

The basic specification is a new series name, an equals sign, a function, and the existing series, along with any additional specifications needed.

Syntax Rules

- The existing series together with any additional specifications (order, span, or periodicity) must be enclosed in parentheses.
- The equals sign is required.
- Series names and additional specifications must be separated by commas or spaces.
- You can specify only one function per equation.
- You can create more than one new series per equation by specifying more than one new series name on the left side of the equation and either multiple existing series names or multiple orders on the right.
- The number of new series named on the left side of the equation must equal the number of series created on the right. Note that the FFT function creates two new series for each existing series, and IFFT creates one series from two existing series.
- You can specify more than one equation on a CREATE command. Equations are separated by slashes.
- A newly created series can be specified in subsequent equations on the same CREATE command.

Operations

- Each new series created is added to the working data file.
- If the new series named already exist, their values are replaced.
- If the new series named do not already exist, they are created.
- Series are created in the order in which they are specified on the CREATE command.
- If multiple series are created by a single equation, the first new series named is assigned the values of the first series created, the second series named is assigned the values of the second series created, and so on.
- CREATE automatically generates a variable label for each new series describing the function and series used to create it.
- The format of the new series is based on the function specified and the format of the existing series.
- CREATE honors the TSET MISSING setting that is currently in effect.
- CREATE does not honor the USE command.
- When an even-length span is specified for functions MA and RMED, the centering algorithm uses an average of two spans of the specified length. The first span ranges from span/2 cases before the current observation to the span length. The second span ranges from (span/2)–1 cases before the current observation to the span length.

Limitations

- Maximum 1 function per equation.
- There is no limit on the number of series created by an equation.
- There is no limit on the number of equations.

Example

```
CREATE NEWVAR1 = DIFF(OLDVAR,1).
```

- In this example, the series *NEWVAR1* is created by taking the first-order difference of *OLDVAR*.

CSUM Function

CSUM produces new series based on the cumulative sums of the existing series. Cumulative sums are the inverse of first-order differencing.

- The only specification on CSUM is the name or names of the existing series in parentheses.
- Cases with missing values in the existing series are not used to compute values for the new series. The values of these cases are system-missing in the new series.

Example

```
CREATE NEWVAR1 NEWVAR2 = CSUM(TICKETS RNDTRP).
```

- This example produces a new series called *NEWVAR1*, which is the cumulative sum of the series *TICKETS*, and a new series called *NEWVAR2*, which is the cumulative sum of the series *RNDTRP*.

DIFF Function

DIFF produces new series based on nonseasonal differences of existing series.

- The specification on DIFF is the name or names of the existing series and the degree of differencing, in parentheses.
- The degree of differencing must be specified; there is no default.
- Since one observation is lost for each order of differencing, system-missing values will appear at the beginning of the new series.
- You can specify only one degree of differencing per DIFF function.
- If either of the pair of values involved in a difference computation is missing, the result is set to system-missing in the new series.

Example

```
CREATE ADIF2 = DIFF(VARA,2) /
       YDIF1 ZDIF1 = DIFF(VARY VARZ,1).
```

- The series *ADIF2* is created by differencing *VARA* twice.
- The series *YDIF1* is created by differencing *VARY* once.
- The series *ZDIF1* is created by differencing *VARZ* once.

FFT Function

FFT produces new series based on fast Fourier transformations of existing series (Brigham, 1974).

- The only specification on FFT is the name or names of the existing series in parentheses.
- FFT creates two series, the cosine and sine parts (also called real and imaginary parts), for each existing series named. Thus, you must specify two new series names on the left side of the equation for each existing series specified on the right side.
- The first new series named becomes the real series, and the second new series named becomes the imaginary series.
- The existing series cannot have imbedded missing values.
- The existing series must be of even length. If an odd-length series is specified, FFT pads it with a 0 to make it even. Alternatively, you can make the series even by adding or dropping an observation.
- The new series will be only half as long as the existing series. The remaining cases are assigned the system-missing value.

Example

```
CREATE A B = FFT(C).
```

- Two series, *A* (real) and *B* (imaginary), are created by applying a fast Fourier transformation to series *C*.

IFFT Function

IFFT produces new series based on the inverse Fourier transformation of existing series.

- The only specification on IFFT is the name or names of the existing series in parentheses.
- IFFT needs two existing series to compute each new series. Thus, you must specify two existing series names on the right side of the equation for each new series specified on the left.
- The first existing series specified is the real series and the second series is the imaginary.
- The existing series cannot have imbedded missing values.
- The new series will be twice as long as the existing series. Thus, the last half of each existing series must be system-missing to allow enough room to create the new series.

Example

```
CREATE C = IFFT(A B).
```

- This command creates one new series, *C*, from the series *A* (real) and *B* (imaginary).

LAG Function

LAG creates new series by copying the values of the existing series and moving them forward the specified number of observations. This number is called the **lag order**. Table 1 shows a first-order lag for a hypothetical data set.

- The specification on LAG is the name or names of the existing series and one or two lag orders, in parentheses.
- At least one lag order must be specified; there is no default.
- Two lag orders indicate a range. For example, 2,6 indicates lag orders two through six. A new series is created for each lag order in the range.
- The number of new series specified must equal the number of existing series specified times the number of lag orders in the range.
- The first *n* cases at the beginning of the new series, where *n* is the lag order, are assigned the system-missing value.
- Missing values in the existing series are lagged and are assigned the system-missing value in the new series.
- A first-order lagged series can also be created using COMPUTE. COMPUTE does not cause a data pass (see COMPUTE).

Table 1 First-order lag and lead of series X

X	Lag	Lead
198	.	220
220	198	305
305	220	470
470	305	.

Example

```
CREATE LAGVAR2 TO LAGVAR5 = LAG(VARA,2,5).
```

- Four new variables are created based on lags on *VARA*. *LAGVAR2* is *VARA* lagged two steps, *LAGVAR3* is *VARA* lagged three steps, *LAGVAR4* is *VARA* lagged four steps, and *LAGVAR5* is *VARA* lagged five steps.

LEAD Function

LEAD creates new series by copying the values of the existing series and moving them back the specified number of observations. This number is called the lead order. Table 1 shows a first-order lead for a hypothetical data set.

- The specification on LEAD is the name or names of the existing series and one or two lead orders, in parentheses.
- At least one lead order must be specified; there is no default.

- Two lead orders indicate a range. For example, 1,5 indicates lead orders one through five. A new series is created for each lead order in the range.
- The number of new series must equal the number of existing series specified times the number of lead orders in the range.
- The last *n* cases at the end of the new series, where *n* equals the lead order, are assigned the system-missing value.
- Missing values in the existing series are moved back and are assigned the system-missing value in the new series.

Example

```
CREATE LEAD1 TO LEAD4 = LEAD(VARA,1,4).
```

- Four new series are created based on leads of *VARA*. *LEAD1* is *VARA* led one step, *LEAD2* is *VARA* led two steps, *LEAD3* is *VARA* led three steps, and *LEAD4* is *VARA* led four steps.

MA Function

MA produces new series based on the centered moving averages of existing series.

- The specification on MA is the name or names of the existing series and the span to be used in averaging, in parentheses.
- A span must be specified; there is no default.
- If the specified span is odd, the MA is naturally associated with the middle term. If the specified span is even, the MA is centered by averaging each pair of uncentered means (Velleman and Hoaglin, 1981).
- After the initial span, a second span can be specified to indicate the minimum number of values to use in averaging when the number specified for the initial span is unavailable. This makes it possible to produce nonmissing values at or near the ends of the new series.
- The second span must be greater than or equal to 1 and less than or equal to the first span.
- The second span should be even (or 1) if the first span is even; it should be odd if the first span is odd. Otherwise, the next higher span value will be used.
- If no second span is specified, the minimum span is simply the value of the first span.
- If the number of values specified for the span or the minimum span is not available, the case in the new series is set to system-missing. Thus, unless a minimum span of 1 is specified, the endpoints of the new series will contain system-missing values.
- When MA encounters an imbedded missing value in the existing series, it creates two subsets, one containing cases before the missing value and one containing cases after the missing value. Each subset is treated as a separate series for computational purposes.
- The endpoints of these subset series will have missing values according to the rules described above for the endpoints of the entire series. Thus, if the minimum span is 1, the endpoints of the subsets will be nonmissing; the only cases that will be missing in the new series are cases that were missing in the original series.

Example

```
CREATE TICKMA = MA(TICKETS,4,2).
```

- This example creates the series *TICKMA* based on centered moving average values of the series *TICKETS.*
- A span of 4 is used for computing averages. At the endpoints, where four values are not available, the average is based on the specified minimum of two values.

PMA Function

PMA creates new series based on the prior moving averages of existing series. The prior moving average for each case in the original series is computed by averaging the values of a span of cases preceding it.

- The specification on PMA is the name or names of the existing series and the span to be used, in parentheses.
- Only one span can be specified and it is required. There is no default span.
- If the number of values specified for the span is not available, the case is set to system-missing. Thus, the number of cases with system-missing values at the beginning of the new series equals the number specified for the span.
- When PMA encounters an imbedded missing value in the existing series, it creates two subsets, one containing cases before the missing value and one containing cases after the missing value. Each subset is treated as a separate series for computational purposes. The first *n* cases in the second subset will be system-missing, where *n* is the span.

Example

```
CREATE PRIORA = PMA(VARA,3).
```

- This command creates series *PRIORA* by computing prior moving averages for series *VARA*. Since the span is 3, the first three cases in series *PRIORA* are system-missing. The fourth case equals the average of cases 1, 2, and 3 of *VARA*, the fifth case equals the average of cases 2, 3, and 4 of *VARA*, and so on.

RMED Function

RMED produces new series based on the centered running medians of existing series.

- The specification on RMED is the name or names of the existing series and the span to be used in finding the median, in parentheses.
- A span must be specified; there is no default.
- If the specified span is odd, RMED is naturally the middle term. If the specified span is even, the RMED is centered by averaging each pair of uncentered medians (Velleman and Hoaglin, 1981).
- After the initial span, a second span can be specified to indicate the minimum number of values to use in finding the median when the number specified for the initial span is unavailable. This makes it possible to produce nonmissing values at or near the ends of the new series.

- The second span must be greater than or equal to 1 and less than or equal to the first span.
- The second span should be even (or 1) if the first span is even; it should be odd if the first span is odd. Otherwise, the next higher span value will be used.
- If no second span is specified, the minimum span is simply the value of the first span.
- If the number of values specified for the span or the minimum span is not available, the case in the new series is set to system-missing. Thus, unless a minimum span of 1 is specified, the endpoints of the new series will contain system-missing values.
- When RMED encounters an imbedded missing value in the existing series, it creates two subsets, one containing cases before the missing value and one containing cases after the missing value. Each subset is treated as a separate series for computational purposes.
- The endpoints of these subset series will have missing values according to the rules described above for the endpoints of the entire series. Thus, if the minimum span is 1, the endpoints of the subsets will be nonmissing; the only cases that will be missing in the new series are cases that were missing in the original series.

Example

```
CREATE TICKRMED = RMED(TICKETS,4,2).
```

- This example creates the series *TICKRMED* using centered running median values of the series *TICKETS.*
- A span of 4 is used for computing medians. At the endpoints, where four values are not available, the median is based on the specified minimum of two values.

SDIFF Function

SDIFF produces new series based on seasonal differences of existing series.

- The specification on SDIFF is the name or names of the existing series, the degree of differencing, and, optionally, the periodicity, all in parentheses.
- The degree of differencing must be specified; there is no default.
- Since the number of seasons used in the calculations decreases by 1 for each order of differencing, system-missing values will appear at the beginning of the new series.
- You can specify only one degree of differencing per SDIFF function.
- If no periodicity is specified, the periodicity established on TSET PERIOD is in effect. If TSET PERIOD has not been specified, the periodicity established on the DATE command is used. If periodicity was not established anywhere, the SDIFF function cannot be executed.
- If either of the pair of values involved in a seasonal difference computation is missing, the result is set to system-missing in the new series.

Example

```
CREATE SDVAR = SDIFF(VARA,1,12).
```

- The series *SDVAR* is created by applying one seasonal difference with a periodicity of 12 to the series *VARA.*

T4253H Function

T4253H produces new series by applying a compound data smoother to the original series. The smoother starts with a running median of 4, which is centered by a running median of 2. It then resmooths these values by applying a running median of 5, a running median of 3, and hanning (running weighted averages). Residuals are computed by subtracting the smoothed series from the original series. This whole process is then repeated on the computed residuals. Finally, the smoothed residuals are added to the smoothed values obtained the first time through the process (Velleman and Hoaglin, 1981).

- The only specification on T4253H is the name or names of the existing series in parentheses.
- The existing series cannot contain imbedded missing values.
- Endpoints are smoothed through extrapolation and are not system-missing.

Example

```
CREATE SMOOTHA = T4253H(VARA).
```

- The series *SMOOTHA* is a smoothed version of the series *VARA*.

References

Box, G. E. P., and G. M. Jenkins. 1976. *Time series analysis: Forecasting and control.* San Francisco: Holden-Day.

Brigham, E. O. 1974. *The fast Fourier transform.* Englewood Cliffs, N.J.: Prentice-Hall.

Cryer, J. D. 1986. *Time series analysis.* Boston: Duxbury Press.

Makridakis, S., S. C. Wheelwright, and V. E. McGee. 1983. *Forecasting: Methods and applications.* New York: John Wiley and Sons.

Monro, D. M. 1975. Algorithm AS 83: Complex discrete fast Fourier transform. *Applied Statistics*, 24: 153–160.

Monro, D. M., and J. L. Branch. 1977. Algorithm AS 117: The Chirp discrete Fourier transform of general length. *Applied Statistics,* 26: 351–361.

Velleman, P. F., and D. C. Hoaglin. 1981. *Applications, basics, and computing of exploratory data analysis.* Boston: Duxbury Press.

CROSSTABS

General mode:

```
CROSSTABS [TABLES=]varlist BY varlist [BY...] [/varlist...]

 [/MISSING={TABLE**}]
           {INCLUDE}

 [/WRITE[={NONE**}]]
          {CELLS }
```

Integer mode:

```
CROSSTABS VARIABLES=varlist(min,max) [varlist...]

 /TABLES=varlist BY varlist [BY...] [/varlist...]

 [/MISSING={TABLE**}]
           {INCLUDE}
           {REPORT }

 [/WRITE[={NONE**}]]
          {CELLS }
          {ALL   }
```

Both modes:

```
 [/FORMAT= {AVALUE**}  {TABLES**}]
           {DVALUE  }  {NOTABLES}

 [/CELLS=[{COUNT**}]  [ROW   ]  [EXPECTED]  [SRESID ]]
          {NONE   }   [COLUMN]  [RESID   ]  [ASRESID]
                      [TOTAL ]              [ALL    ]

 [/STATISTICS=[CHISQ]  [LAMBDA]  [BTAU ] [GAMMA  ]  [ETA    ]]
              [PHI  ]  [UC    ]  [CTAU ] [D      ]  [CORR   ]
              [CC   ]  [RISK  ]  [KAPPA] [MCNEMAR]  [CMH(1*)]
              [ALL  ]  [NONE  ]

 [/METHOD={MC  [CIN({99.0 })]  [SAMPLES({10000})]]}]††
                    {value}            {value}
          {EXACT [TIMER({5    })]                 }
                        {value}

 [/BARCHART]
```

**Default if the subcommand is omitted.

†† The METHOD subcommand is available only if the Exact Tests option is installed.

Example

```
CROSSTABS TABLES=FEAR BY SEX
 /CELLS=ROW COLUMN EXPECTED RESIDUALS
 /STATISTICS=CHISQ.
```

Overview

CROSSTABS produces contingency tables showing the joint distribution of two or more variables that have a limited number of distinct values. The frequency distribution of one variable is subdivided according to the values of one or more variables. The unique combination of values for two or more variables defines a cell.

CROSSTABS can operate in two different modes: *general* and *integer*. Integer mode builds some tables more efficiently but requires more specifications than general mode. Some subcommand specifications and statistics are available only in integer mode.

Options

Methods for building tables. To build tables in general mode, use the TABLES subcommand. Integer mode requires the TABLES and VARIABLES subcommands and minimum and maximum values for the variables.

Cell contents. By default, CROSSTABS displays only the number of cases in each cell. You can request row, column, and total percentages, and also expected values and residuals by using the CELLS subcommand.

Statistics. In addition to the tables, you can obtain measures of association and tests of hypotheses for each subtable using the STATISTICS subcommand.

Formatting options. With the FORMAT subcommand, you can control the display order for categories in rows and columns of subtables and suppress crosstabulation.

Writing and reproducing tables. You can write cell frequencies to a file and reproduce the original tables with the WRITE subcommand.

Basic Specification

In general mode, the basic specification is TABLES with a table list. The actual keyword TABLES can be omitted. In integer mode, the minimum specification is the VARIABLES subcommand, specifying the variables to be used and their value ranges, and the TABLES subcommand with a table list.

- The minimum table list specifies a list of row variables, the keyword BY, and a list of column variables.
- In integer mode, all variables must be numeric with integer values. In general mode, variables can be numeric (integer or non-integer) or string.
- The default table shows cell counts.

Subcommand Order

- In general mode, the table list must be first if the keyword TABLES is omitted. If the keyword TABLES is explicitly used, subcommands can be specified in any order.

- In integer mode, VARIABLES must precede TABLES. The keyword TABLES must be explicitly specified.

Operations

- Integer mode builds tables more quickly but requires more workspace if a table has many empty cells.
- If a long string variable is used in general mode, only the short string portion (first eight characters) is tabulated.
- Statistics are calculated separately for each two-way table or two-way subtable. Missing values are reported for the table as a whole.
- In general mode, the keyword TO on the TABLES subcommand refers to the order of variables in the working file. ALL refers to all variables in the working file. In integer mode, TO and ALL refer to the position and subset of variables specified on the VARIABLES subcommand.

Limitations

The following limitations apply to CROSSTABS in *general mode*:

- Maximum 200 variables named or implied on the TABLES subcommand
- Maximum 1000 non-empty rows or columns for each table
- Maximum 20 table lists per CROSSTABS command
- Maximum 10 dimensions (9 BY keywords) per table
- Maximum 400 value labels displayed on any single table

The following limitations apply to CROSSTABS in *integer mode*:

- Maximum 100 variables named or implied on the VARIABLES subcommand
- Maximum 100 variables named or implied on the TABLES subcommand
- Maximum 1000 non-empty rows or columns for each table
- Maximum 20 table lists per CROSSTABS command
- Maximum 8 dimensions (7 BY keywords) per table
- Maximum 20 rows or columns of missing values when REPORT is specified on MISSING
- Minimum value that can be specified is –99,999
- Maximum value that can be specified is 999,999

Example

```
CROSSTABS TABLES=FEAR BY SEX
 /CELLS=ROW COLUMN EXPECTED RESIDUALS
 /STATISTICS=CHISQ.
```

- CROSSTABS generates a Case Processing Summary table, a Crosstabulation table, and a Chi-Square Tests table.

- The variable *FEAR* defines the rows and the variable *SEX* defines the columns of the Crosstabulation table. CELLS requests row and column percentages, expected cell frequencies, and residuals.
- STATISTICS requests the chi-square statistics displayed in the Chi-Square Tests table.

Example

```
CROSSTABS TABLES=JOBCAT BY EDCAT BY SEX BY INCOME3.
```

- This table list produces a subtable of *JOBCAT* by *EDCAT* for each combination of values of *SEX* and *INCOME3*.

VARIABLES Subcommand

The VARIABLES subcommand is required for integer mode. VARIABLES specifies a list of variables to be used in the crosstabulations and the lowest and highest values for each variable. Values are specified in parentheses and must be integers. Non-integer values are truncated.

- Variables can be specified in any order. However, the order in which they are named on VARIABLES determines their implied order on TABLES (see the TABLES subcommand below).
- A range must be specified for each variable. If several variables can have the same range, it can be specified once after the last variable to which it applies.
- CROSSTABS uses the specified ranges to allocate tables. One cell is allocated for each possible combination of values of the row and column variables before the data are read. Thus, if the specified ranges are larger than the actual ranges, workspace will be wasted.
- Cases with values outside the specified range are considered missing and are not used in the computation of the table. This allows you to select a subset of values within CROSSTABS.
- If the table is sparse because the variables do not have values throughout the specified range, consider using general mode or recoding the variables.

Example

```
CROSSTABS VARIABLES=FEAR SEX RACE (1,2) MOBILE16 (1,3)
   /TABLES=FEAR BY SEX MOBILE16 BY RACE.
```

- VARIABLES defines values 1 and 2 for *FEAR*, *SEX*, and *RACE*, and values 1, 2, and 3 for *MOBILE16*.

TABLES Subcommand

TABLES specifies the table lists and is required in both integer mode and general mode. The following rules apply to both modes:

- You can specify multiple TABLES subcommands on a single CROSSTABS command. The slash between the subcommands is required; the keyword TABLES is required only in integer mode.

- Variables named before the first BY on a table list are row variables, and variables named after the first BY on a table list are column variables.
- When the table list specifies two dimensions (one BY keyword), the first variable before BY is crosstabulated with each variable after BY, then the second variable before BY with each variable after BY, and so on.
- Each subsequent use of the keyword BY on a table list adds a new dimension to the tables requested. Variables named after the second (or subsequent) BY are control variables.
- When the table list specifies more than two dimensions, a two-way subtable is produced for each combination of values of control variables. The value of the last specified control variable changes the most slowly in determining the order in which tables are displayed.
- You can name more than one variable in each dimension.

General Mode

- The actual keyword TABLES can be omitted in general mode.
- In general mode, both numeric and string variables can be specified. Long strings are truncated to short strings for defining categories.
- The keywords ALL and TO can be specified in any dimension. In general mode, TO refers to the order of variables in the working data file and ALL refers to all variables defined in the working data file.

Example

```
CROSSTABS  TABLES=FEAR BY SEX BY RACE.
```

- This example crosstabulates *FEAR* by *SEX* controlling for *RACE*. In each subtable, *FEAR* is the row variable and *SEX* is the column variable.
- A subtable is produced for each value of the control variable *RACE*.

Example

```
CROSSTABS  TABLES=CONFINAN TO CONARMY BY SEX TO REGION.
```

- This command produces crosstabulations of all variables in the working data file between and including *CONFINAN* and *CONARMY* by all variables between and including *SEX* and *REGION*.

Integer Mode

- In integer mode, variables specified on TABLES must first be named on VARIABLES.
- The keywords TO and ALL can be specified in any dimension. In integer mode, TO and ALL refer to the position and subset of variables specified on the VARIABLES subcommand, not to the variables in the working data file.

Example

```
CROSSTABS  VARIABLES=FEAR (1,2) MOBILE16 (1,3)
  /TABLES=FEAR BY MOBILE16.
```

- VARIABLES names two variables, *FEAR* and *MOBILE16*. Values 1 and 2 for *FEAR* are used in the tables, and values 1, 2, and 3 are used for the variable *MOBILE16*.
- TABLES specifies a Crosstabulation table with two rows (values 1 and 2 for *FEAR*) and three columns (values 1, 2, and 3 for *MOBILE16*). *FEAR* and *MOBILE16* can be named on TABLES because they were named on the previous VARIABLES subcommand.

Example

```
CROSSTABS  VARIABLES=FEAR SEX RACE DEGREE (1,2)
  /TABLES=FEAR BY SEX BY RACE BY DEGREE.
```

- This command produces four subtables. The first subtable crosstabulates *FEAR* by *SEX*, controlling for the first value of *RACE* and the first value of *DEGREE*; the second subtable controls for the second value of *RACE* and the first value of *DEGREE*; the third subtable controls for the first value of *RACE* and the second value of *DEGREE*; and the fourth subtable controls for the second value of *RACE* and the second value of *DEGREE*.

CELLS Subcommand

By default, CROSSTABS displays only the number of cases in each cell of the Crosstabulation table. Use CELLS to display row, column, or total percentages, expected counts, or residuals. These are calculated separately for each Crosstabulation table or subtable.

- CELLS specified without keywords displays cell counts plus row, column, and total percentages for each cell.
- If CELLS is specified with keywords, CROSSTABS displays only the requested cell information.
- Scientific notation is used for cell contents when necessary.

COUNT *Observed cell counts.* This is the default if CELLS is omitted.

ROW *Row percentages.* The number of cases in each cell in a row is expressed as a percentage of all cases in that row.

COLUMN *Column percentages.* The number of cases in each cell in a column is expressed as a percentage of all cases in that column.

TOTAL *Two-way table total percentages.* The number of cases in each cell of a subtable is expressed as a percentage of all cases in that subtable.

EXPECTED *Expected counts.* Expected counts are the number of cases expected in each cell if the two variables in the subtable are statistically independent.

RESID *Residuals.* Residuals are the difference between the observed and expected cell counts.

SRESID *Standardized residuals* (Haberman, 1978).

ASRESID *Adjusted standardized residuals* (Haberman, 1978).

ALL *All cell information.* This includes cell counts; row, column, and total percentages; expected counts; residuals; standardized residuals; and adjusted standardized residuals.

NONE *No cell information.* Use NONE when you want to write tables to a procedure output file without displaying them (see the WRITE subcommand on p. 231). This is the same as specifying NOTABLES on FORMAT.

STATISTICS Subcommand

STATISTICS requests measures of association and related statistics. By default, CROSSTABS does not display any additional statistics.

- STATISTICS without keywords displays the chi-square test.
- If STATISTICS is specified with keywords, CROSSTABS calculates only the requested statistics.
- In integer mode, values that are not included in the specified range are *not* used in the calculation of the statistics, even if these values exist in the data.
- If user-missing values are included with MISSING, cases with user-missing values are included in the calculation of statistics as well as in the tables.

CHISQ *Display the Chi-Square Test table.* Chi-square statistics include Pearson chi-square, likelihood-ratio chi-square, and Mantel-Haenszel chi-square (linear-by-linear association). Mantel-Haenszel is valid only if both variables are numeric. Fisher's exact test and Yates' corrected chi-square are computed for all 2×2 tables. This is the default if STATISTICS is specified with no keywords.

PHI *Display phi and Cramér's* V *in the Symmetric Measures table.*

CC *Display contingency coefficient in the Symmetric Measures table.*

LAMBDA *Display lambda (symmetric and asymmetric) and Goodman and Kruskal's tau in the Directional Measures table.*

UC *Display uncertainty coefficient (symmetric and asymmetric) in the Directional Measures table.*

BTAU *Display Kendall's tau-*b *in the Symmetric Measures table.*

CTAU *Display Kendall's tau-*c *in the Symmetric Measures table.*

GAMMA *Display gamma in the Symmetric Measures table or Zero-Order and Partial Gammas table.* The Zero-Order and Partial Gammas table is produced only for tables with more than two variable dimensions in integer mode.

D *Display Somers'* d *(symmetric and asymmetric) in the Directional Measures table.*

ETA *Display eta in the Directional Measures table.* Available for numeric data only.

CORR *Display Pearson's* r *and Spearman's correlation coefficient in the Symmetric Measures table.* This is available for numeric data only.

KAPPA *Display kappa coefficient* (Kraemer, 1982) *in the Symmetric Measures table*. Kappa can be computed only for square tables in which the row and column values are identical.

RISK *Display relative risk* (Bishop et al., 1975) *in the Risk Estimate table*. Relative risk can be calculated only for 2×2 tables.

MCNEMAR *Display a Crosstabulation table for each pair of related dichotomous variables and a Test Statistics table for all pairs showing the number of valid cases, chi-square, and probability for each pair.* Useful for detecting changes in responses due to experimental intervention in "before-and-after" designs.

CMH(1*) *Conditional independence and homogeneity tests.* Cochran's and the Mantel-Haenszel statistics are computed for the test for conditional independence. The Breslow-Day and Taron's statistics are computed for the test for homogeneity. For each test, the chi-squared statistic with its degrees of freedom and asymptotic *p* value are computed. *Mantel-Haenszel relative risk (common odds ratio) estimate.* The Mantel-Haenszel relative risk (common odds ratio) estimate, the natural log of the estimate, the standard error of the natural log of the estimate, the asymptotic *p* value, and the asymptotic confidence intervals for common odds ratio and for the natural log of the common odds ratio are computed. The user can specify the null hypothesis for the common odds ratio in parentheses after the keyword. The passive default is 1. (The parameter value must be positive.)

ALL *All statistics available.*

NONE *No summary statistics.* This is the default if STATISTICS is omitted.

METHOD Subcommand

METHOD displays additional results for each statistic requested. If no METHOD subcommand is specified, the standard asymptotic results are displayed. If fractional weights have been specified, results for all methods will be calculated on the weight rounded to the nearest integer.

MC Displays an unbiased point estimate and confidence interval based on the Monte Carlo sampling method, for all statistics. Asymptotic results are also displayed. When exact results can be calculated, they will be provided instead of the Monte Carlo results.

CIN(n) Controls the confidence level for the Monte Carlo estimate. CIN is available only when `/METHOD=MC` is specified. CIN has a default value of 99.0. You can specify a confidence interval between 0.01 and 99.9, inclusive.

SAMPLES Specifies the number of tables sampled from the reference set when calculating the Monte Carlo estimate of the exact *p* value. Larger sample sizes lead to narrower confidence limits but also take longer to calculate. You can specify any integer between 1 and 1,000,000,000 as the sample size. SAMPLES has a default value of 10,000.

EXACT Computes the exact significance level for all statistics in addition to the asymptotic results. If both the EXACT and MC keywords are specified, only exact results are provided. Calculating the exact *p* value can be memory-intensive. If you have specified /METHOD=EXACT and find that you have insufficient memory to calculate results, you should first close any other applications that are currently running in order to make more memory available. You can also enlarge the size of your swap file (see your Windows manual for more information). If you still cannot obtain exact results, specify /METHOD=MC to obtain the Monte Carlo estimate of the exact *p* value. An optional TIMER keyword is available if you choose /METHOD=EXACT.

TIMER(n) Specifies the maximum number of minutes allowed to run the exact analysis for each statistic. If the time limit is reached, the test is terminated, no exact results are provided, and the program begins to calculate the next test in the analysis. TIMER is available only when /METHOD=EXACT is specified. You can specify any integer value for TIMER. Specifying a value of 0 for TIMER turns the timer off completely. TIMER has a default value of 5 minutes. If a test exceeds a time limit of 30 minutes, it is recommended that you use the Monte Carlo, rather than the exact, method.

Example

```
CROSSTABS TABLES=FEAR BY SEX
 /CELLS=ROW COLUMN EXPECTED RESIDUALS
 /STATISTICS=CHISQ
 /METHOD=MC SAMPLES(10000) CIN(95).
```

- This example requests chi-square statistics.
- An unbiased point estimate and confidence interval based on the Monte Carlo sampling method are displayed with the asymptotic results.

MISSING Subcommand

By default, CROSSTABS deletes cases with missing values on a table-by-table basis. Cases with missing values for any variable specified for a table are not used in the table or in the calculation of statistics. Use MISSING to specify alternative missing-value treatments.

- The only specification is a single keyword.
- The number of missing cases is always displayed in the Case Processing Summary table.
- If the missing values are not included in the range specified on VARIABLES, they are excluded from the table regardless of the keyword you specify on MISSING.

TABLE *Delete cases with missing values on a table-by-table basis.* When multiple table lists are specified, missing values are handled separately for each list. This is the default.

INCLUDE *Include user-missing values.* Available in integer mode only.

REPORT *Report missing values in the tables.* This option includes missing values in tables but not in the calculation of percentages or statistics. The missing status is indicated on the categorical label. REPORT is available only in integer mode.

FORMAT Subcommand

By default, CROSSTABS displays tables and subtables. The values for the row and column variables are displayed in order from lowest to highest. Use FORMAT to modify the default table display.

AVALUE *Display row and column variables from lowest to highest value.* This is the default.

DVALUE *Display row and column variables from highest to lowest.*

TABLES *Display tables.* This is the default.

NOTABLES *Suppress Crosstabulation tables.* NOTABLES is useful when you want to write tables to a file without displaying them or when you want only the Statistics table. This is the same as specifying NONE on CELLS.

BARCHART Subcommand

BARCHART produces a clustered bar chart where bars represent categories defined by the first variable in a crosstabulation while clusters represent categories defined by the second variable in a crosstabulation. Any controlling variables in a crosstabulation are collapsed over before the clustered bar chart is created.

- BARCHART takes no further specification.
- If integer mode is in effect and MISSING=REPORT, BARCHART displays valid and user-missing values. Otherwise only valid values are used.

WRITE Subcommand

Use the WRITE subcommand to write cell frequencies to a file for subsequent use by the current program or another program. CROSSTABS can also use these cell frequencies as input to reproduce tables and compute statistics. When WRITE is specified, an Output File Summary table is displayed before all other tables.

- The only specification is a single keyword.
- The name of the file must be specified on the PROCEDURE OUTPUT command preceding CROSSTABS.
- If both CELLS and ALL are specified, CELLS is in effect and only the contents of non-empty cells are written to the file.
- If you include missing values with INCLUDE or REPORT on MISSING, no values are considered missing and all non-empty cells, including those with missing values, are written, even if CELLS is specified.
- If you exclude missing values on a table-by-table basis (the default), no records are written for combinations of values that include a missing value.
- If multiple tables are specified, the tables are written in the same order as they are displayed.

NONE *Do not write cell counts to a file.* This is the default.

CELLS *Write cell counts for non-empty and nonmissing cells to a file.* Combinations of values that include a missing value are not written to the file.

ALL *Write cell counts for all cells to a file.* A record for each combination of values defined by VARIABLES and TABLES is written to the file. ALL is available only in integer mode.

The file contains one record for each cell. Each record contains the following:

Columns	Contents
1–4	*Split-file group number, numbered consecutively from 1.* Note that this is not the value of the variable or variables used to define the splits.
5–8	*Table number.* Tables are defined by the TABLES subcommand.
9–16	*Cell frequency.* The number of times this combination of variable values occurred in the data, or, if case weights are used, the sum of case weights for cases having this combination of values.
17–24	*The value of the row variable* (the one named before the first BY).
25–32	*The value of the column variable* (the one named after the first BY).
33–40	*The value of the first control variable* (the one named after the second BY).
41–48	*The value of the second control variable* (the one named after the third BY).
49–56	*The value of the third control variable* (the one named after the fourth BY).
57–64	*The value of the fourth control variable* (the one named after the fifth BY).
65–72	*The value of the fifth control variable* (the one named after the sixth BY).
73–80	*The value of the sixth control variable* (the one named after the seventh BY).

- The split-file group number, table number, and frequency are written as integers.
- In integer mode, the values of variables are also written as integers. In general mode, the values are written according to the print format specified for each variable. Alphanumeric values are written at the left end of any field in which they occur.
- Within each table, records are written from one column of the table at a time, and the value of the last control variable changes the most slowly.

Example

```
PROCEDURE OUTPUT  OUTFILE=CELLDATA.
CROSSTABS VARIABLES=FEAR SEX (1,2)
 /TABLES=FEAR BY SEX
 /WRITE=ALL.
```

- CROSSTABS writes a record for each cell in the table *FEAR* by *SEX* to the file *CELLDATA*. Figure 1 shows the contents of the *CELLDATA* file.

Figure 1 Cell records

```
 1  1     55        1       1
 1  1    172        2       1
 1  1    180        1       2
 1  1     89        2       2
```

Example

```
PROCEDURE OUTPUT  OUTFILE=XTABDATA.
CROSSTABS  TABLES=V1 TO V3 BY V4 BY V10 TO V15
  /WRITE=CELLS.
```

- CROSSTABS writes a set of records for each table to file *XTABDATA*.
- Records for the table *V1* by *V4* by *V10* are written first, followed by records for *V1* by *V4* by *V11*, and so on. The records for *V3* by *V4* by *V15* are written last.

Reading a CROSSTABS Procedure Output File

You can use the file created by WRITE in a subsequent session to reproduce a table and compute statistics for it. Each record in the file contains all the information used to build the original table. The cell frequency information can be used as a weight variable on the WEIGHT command to replicate the original cases.

Example

```
DATA LIST FILE=CELLDATA
 /WGHT 9-16 FEAR 17-24 SEX 25-32.
VARIABLE LABELS FEAR 'AFRAID TO WALK AT NIGHT IN NEIGHBORHOODS'.
VALUE LABELS  FEAR 1 'YES' 2 'NO'/ SEX 1 'MALE' 2 'FEMALE'.
WEIGHT BY WGHT.
CROSSTABS TABLES=FEAR BY SEX
 /STATISTICS=ALL.
```

- DATA LIST reads the cell frequencies and row and column values from the *CELLDATA* file shown in Figure 1. The cell frequency is read as a weighting factor (variable *WGHT*). The values for the rows are read as *FEAR*, and the values for the columns are read as *SEX*, the two original variables.
- The WEIGHT command recreates the sample size by weighting each of the four cases (cells) by the cell frequency.

If you do not have the original data or the CROSSTABS procedure output file, you can reproduce a crosstabulation and compute statistics simply by entering the values from the table:

```
DATA LIST  /FEAR 1 SEX 3 WGHT 5-7.
VARIABLE LABELS  FEAR 'AFRAID TO WALK AT NIGHT IN NEIGHBORHOOD'.
VALUE LABELS  FEAR 1 'YES' 2 'NO'/ SEX 1 'MALE' 2 'FEMALE'.
 WEIGHT  BY WGHT.
BEGIN DATA
1 1  55
2 1 172
1 2 180
2 2  89
END DATA.
CROSSTABS  TABLES=FEAR BY SEX
/STATISTICS=ALL.
```

References

Bishop, Y. M. M., S. E. Feinberg, and P. W. Holland. 1975. *Discrete multivariate analysis: Theory and practice.* Cambridge, Mass.: MIT Press.

Haberman, S. J. 1978. *Analysis of qualitative data.* Vol. 1. London: Academic Press.

Kraemer, H. C. 1982. Kappa coefficient. In: *Encyclopedia of Statistical Sciences*, S. Katz and N. L. Johnson, eds. New York: John Wiley and Sons.

CURVEFIT

```
CURVEFIT [VARIABLES=] varname [WITH varname]

 [/MODEL= [LINEAR**] [LOGARITHMIC] [INVERSE]

          [QUADRATIC] [CUBIC] [COMPOUND]

          [POWER] [S] [GROWTH] [EXPONENTIAL]

          [LGSTIC] [ALL]]

 [/CIN={95** }]
       {value}

 [/UPPERBOUND={NO**}]
              {n   }

 [/{CONSTANT†  }
   {NOCONSTANT}

 [/PLOT={FIT**}]
        {NONE }

 [/ID = varname]

 [/PRINT=ANOVA]

 [/SAVE=[PRED] [RESID] [CIN]]

 [/APPLY [='model name'] [{SPECIFICATIONS}]]
                          {FIT           }
```

**Default if the subcommand is omitted.
†Default if the subcommand is omitted and there is no corresponding specification on the TSET command.

Example

```
CURVEFIT VARY
  /MODEL=CUBIC.
```

Overview

CURVEFIT fits selected curves to a line plot, allowing you to examine the relationship between one or more dependent variables and one independent variable. CURVEFIT also fits curves to time series and produces forecasts, forecast errors, lower confidence limits, and upper confidence limits. You can choose curves from a variety of regression models.

Options

Model Specification. There are 11 regression models available on the MODEL subcommand. You can fit any or all of these to the data. The keyword ALL is available to fit all 11 models. You can control whether the regression equation includes a constant term using the CONSTANT or NOCONSTANT subcommand.

Upperbound Value. You can specify the upperbound value for the logistic model using the UPPERBOUND subcommand.

Output. You can produce an analysis-of-variance summary table using the PRINT subcommand. You can suppress the display of the curve-fitting plot using the PLOT subcommand.

New Variables. To evaluate the regression statistics without saving predicted and residual variables, specify TSET NEWVAR=NONE prior to CURVEFIT. To save the new variables and replace the variables saved earlier, use TSET NEWVAR=CURRENT (the default). To save the new variables without erasing variables saved earlier, use TSET NEWVAR=ALL or the SAVE subcommand on CURVEFIT.

Forecasting. When used with the PREDICT command, CURVEFIT can produce forecasts and confidence limits beyond the end of the series (see PREDICT).

Basic Specification

The basic specification is one or more dependent variables. If the variables are not time series, you must also specify the keyword WITH and an independent variable.

- By default, the LINEAR model is fit.
- A 95% confidence interval is used unless it is changed by a TSET CIN command prior to the procedure.
- CURVEFIT produces a plot of the curve, a regression summary table displaying the type of curve used, the R^2 coefficient, degrees of freedom, overall *F* test and significance level, and the regression coefficients.
- For each variable and model combination, CURVEFIT creates four variables: fit/forecast values, residuals, lower confidence limits, and upper confidence limits. These variables are automatically labeled and added to the working data file unless TSET NEWVAR=NONE is specified prior to CURVEFIT. For the new variable names, see the SAVE subcommand on p. 240.

Subcommand Order

- Subcommands can be specified in any order.

Syntax Rules

- VARIABLES can be specified only once.
- Other subcommands can be specified more than once, but only the last specification of each one is executed.

Operations

- When CURVEFIT is used with the PREDICT command to forecast values beyond the end of a time series, the original and residual series are assigned the system-missing value after the last case in the original series.
- If a model requiring a log transformation (COMPOUND, POWER, S, GROWTH, EXPONENTIAL, or LGSTIC) is requested and there are values in the dependent variable(s) less than or equal to 0, the model cannot be fit because nonpositive values cannot be log-transformed.
- CURVEFIT uses listwise deletion of missing values. Whenever one dependent variable is missing a value for a particular case or observation, that case or observation will not be included in any computations.
- For models QUADRATIC and CUBIC, a message is issued if the tolerance criterion is not met. (See TSET for information on changing the tolerance criterion.)
- Since CURVEFIT automatically generates four variables for each dependent variable and model combination, the ALL specification after MODEL should be used cautiously to avoid creating and adding to the working data file many more variables than are necessary.
- The residual variable is always reported in the original metric. To compute the logged residual (which should be used for diagnostic checks) for the models COMPOUND, POWER, S, GROWTH, and EXPONENTIAL, specify

  ```
  COMPUTE NEWVAR = LN(VAR) - LN(FIT#n).
  ```

  where *NEWVAR* is the logged residual, *VAR* is the name of the dependent variable or observed series, and *FIT#n* is the name of the fitted variable generated by CURVEFIT.

  For the LGSTIC (logistic) model, the logged residual can be obtained by

  ```
  COMPUTE NEWERR = LN(VAR) - LN(1/FIT#n).
  ```

  or, if upperbound value *u* is specified on the UPPERBOUND subcommand, by

  ```
  COMPUTE NEWVAR = LN(1/VAR - 1/u) - LN(1/FIT#n).
  ```

- CURVEFIT obeys the WEIGHT command when there is an independent variable. The WEIGHT specification is ignored if no independent variable is specified.

Limitations

- Maximum 1 VARIABLES subcommand. There is no limit on the number of dependent variables or series named on the subcommand.
- Maximum 1 independent variable can be specified after the keyword WITH.

Example

```
CURVEFIT VARY
  /MODEL=CUBIC.
```

- This example fits a cubic curve to the series *VARY*.

VARIABLES Subcommand

VARIABLES specifies the variables and is the only required subcommand. The actual keyword VARIABLES can be omitted.

- If the dependent variables specified are not time series, you must also specify the keyword WITH and an independent variable.

MODEL Subcommand

MODEL specifies the model or models to be fit to the data. The default model is LINEAR.

- You can fit any or all of the 11 available models.
- Model name keywords can be abbreviated to the first three characters.
- You can use the keyword ALL to fit all models.
- When the LGSTIC model is specified, the upperbound value is included in the output.

The following table lists the available models and their regression equations. The linear transformations for the last six models are also shown.

Keyword	Equation	Linear equation
LINEAR	$Y = b_0 + b_1 t$	
LOGARITHMIC	$Y = b_0 + b_1 \ln(t)$	
INVERSE	$Y = b_0 + b_1 / t$	
QUADRATIC	$Y = b_0 + b_1 t + b_2 t^2$	
CUBIC	$Y = b_0 + b_1 t + b_2 t^2 + b_3 t^3$	
COMPOUND	$Y = b_0 b_1^t$	$\ln(Y) = \ln(b_0) + t \ln(b_1)$
POWER	$Y = b_0(t^{b_1})$	$\ln(Y) = \ln(b_0) + b_1 \ln(t)$
S	$Y = e^{b_0 + b_1/t}$	$\ln(Y) = b_0 + b_1/t$
GROWTH	$Y = e^{b_0 + b_1 t}$	$\ln(Y) = b_0 + b_1 t$
EXPONENTIAL	$Y = b_0(e^{b_1 t})$	$\ln(Y) = \ln(b_0) + b_1 t$
LGSTIC (logistic)	$Y = (1/u + b_0 b_1^t)^{-1}$	$\ln(1/Y - 1/u) = \ln(b_0) + t \ln(b_1)$

where

b_0 = a constant
b_n = regression coefficient
t = independent variable or time value
ln = the natural log base
e = base e logs
u = upperbound value for LGSTIC

Example

```
CURVEFIT VARX.
```

- This command fits a curve to *VARX* using the linear regression model (the default).

Example

```
CURVEFIT VARY
  /MODEL=GROWTH EXPONENTIAL.
```

- This command fits two curves to *VARY*, one using the growth model and the other using the exponential model.

UPPERBOUND Subcommand

UPPERBOUND is used with the logistic model (keyword LGSTIC) to specify an upper boundary value to be used in the regression equation.

- The specification on UPPERBOUND must be a positive number and must be greater than the largest data value in any of the specified dependent variables.
- The default UPPERBOUND value is infinity, so that $1/u = 0$ and is dropped from the equation.
- You can specify UPPERBOUND NO to reset the value to infinity when applying a previous model.
- If you specify UPPERBOUND without LGSTIC, it is ignored.
- Note that UPPERBOUND is a subcommand and cannot be used within a MODEL subcommand. For example, the following specification is *not* valid:

  ```
  /MODEL=CUBIC LGSTIC   /UPPER=99 LINEAR
  ```

  The correct specification is:

  ```
  /MODEL=CUBIC LGSTIC LINEAR
  /UPPER=99
  ```

CONSTANT and NOCONSTANT Subcommands

CONSTANT and NOCONSTANT indicate whether a constant term should be estimated in the regression equation. The specification overrides the corresponding setting on the TSET command.

- CONSTANT indicates that a constant should be estimated. It is the default unless changed by TSET NOCONSTANT prior to the current procedure.
- NOCONSTANT eliminates the constant term from the model.

Example

```
CURVEFIT Y1
  /MODEL=COMPOUND
  /NOCONSTANT.
```

- In this example, a compound curve is fit to *Y1* with no constant term in the model.

CIN Subcommand

CIN controls the size of the confidence interval.

- The specification on CIN must be greater than 0 and less than 100.
- The default confidence interval is 95.
- The CIN subcommand overrides the TSET CIN setting.

PLOT Subcommand

PLOT specifies whether the curve-fitting plot is displayed. If PLOT is not specified, the default is FIT. The curve-fitting plot is displayed. PLOT=FIT is generally used with an APPLY subcommand to turn off a PLOT=NONE specification in the applied model.

FIT *Display the curve-fitting plot.*

NONE *Do not display the plot.*

ID Subcommand

ID specifies an identification variable. When in point selection mode, you can click on an individual chart point to display the value of the ID variable for the selected case.

SAVE Subcommand

SAVE saves the values of predicted, residual, and/or confidence interval variables generated during the current session in the working data file.

- SAVE saves the specified variables with default names: *PRED_n* for predicted values *RESID_n* for residuals, *LCL_n* for the lower confidence limit, and *UCL_n* for the upper confidence limit, where *n* increments each time any variable is saved for a model.
- SAVE overrides the CURRENT or NONE setting on TSET NEWVARS (see TSET).

PRED *Predicted variable.*

RESID *Residual variable.*

CIN *Confidence interval.*

PRINT Subcommand

PRINT is used to produce an additional analysis-of-variance table for each model and variable.

- The only specification on PRINT is the keyword ANOVA.

APPLY Subcommand

APPLY allows you to use a previously defined CURVEFIT model without having to repeat the specifications.

- The specifications on APPLY can include the name of a previous model in quotes and one of two keywords. All of these specifications are optional.
- If a model name is not specified, the model specified on the previous CURVEFIT command is used.
- To change one or more of the specifications of the model, specify the subcommands of only those portions you want to change after the subcommand APPLY.
- If no variables or series are specified on the CURVEFIT command, the dependent variables that were originally specified with the model being reapplied are used.
- To change the dependent variables used with the model, enter new variable names before or after the APPLY subcommand.

The keywords available for APPLY on CURVEFIT are:

SPECIFICATIONS *Use only the specifications from the original model.* This is the default.

FIT *Use the coefficients estimated for the original model in the equation.*

Example

```
CURVEFIT X1
  /MODEL=QUADRATIC.
CURVEFIT Z1
  /APPLY.
```

- The first command fits a quadratic curve to *X1*.
- The second command fits the same type of curve to *Z1*.

Example

```
CURVEFIT X1 Y1 Z1
  /MODEL=QUADRATIC.
CURVEFIT APPLY
  /MODEL=CUBIC.
```

- The first command fits quadratic curves to *X1*, *Y1*, and *Z1*.
- The second command fits curves to the same three series using the cubic model.

References

Abraham, B., and J. Ledolter. 1983. *Statistical methods of forecasting.* New York: John Wiley and Sons.

Draper, N. R., and H. Smith. 1981. *Applied regression analysis.* New York: John Wiley and Sons.

Montgomery, D. C., and E. A. Peck. 1982. *Introduction to linear regression analysis.* New York: John Wiley and Sons.

DATA LIST

```
DATA LIST [FILE=file] [{FIXED}] [RECORDS={1}] [SKIP={n}] [{TABLE  }]
                                         {n}               {NOTABLE}

                          {FREE}  [{("delimiter", "delimiter,..., TAB)}]
                          {LIST}

 /{1    } varname {col location [(format)]} [varname ...]
  {rec #}         {(FORTRAN-like format)  }

 [/{2    } ...] [/ ...]
   {rec #}
```

Numeric and string input formats:

Type	Column-style format	FORTRAN-like format
Numeric (default)	d or F,d	Fw.d
Restricted numeric	N,d	Nw.d
Scientific notation	E,d	Ew.d
Numeric with commas	COMMA,d	COMMAw.d
Numeric with dots	DOT,d	DOTw.d
Numeric with commas and dollar sign	DOLLAR,d	DOLLARw.d
Numeric with percent sign	PCT,d	PCTw.d
Zoned decimal	Z,d	Zw.d
String	A	Aw

Format elements to skip columns:
Some formats are not available on all implementations of the program.

Type	Column-style format	FORTRAN-like format
Tab to column *n*		Tn
Skip *n* columns		nX

Date and time input formats:

Type	Data input	Format	FORTRAN-like format
International date	dd-mmm-yyyy	DATE	DATEw
American date	mm/dd/yyyy	ADATE	ADATEw
European date	dd/mm/yy	EDATE	EDATEw
Julian date	yyddd	JDATE	JDATEw
Sorted date	yy/mm/dd	SDATE	SDATEw
Quarter and year	qQyyyy	QYR	QYRw

Month and year	mm/yyyy	MOYR	MOYRw
Week and year	wkWKyyyy	WKYR	WKYRw
Date and time	dd-mmm-yyyy hh:mm:ss.ss	DATETIME	DATETIMEw.d
Time	hh:mm:ss.ss	TIME	TIMEw.d
Days and time	ddd hh:mm:ss.ss	DTIME	DTIMEw.d
Day of the week	string	WKDAY	WKDAYw
Month	string	MONTH	MONTHw

Example

```
DATA LIST /ID 1-3 SEX 5 (A) AGE 7-8 OPINION1 TO OPINION5 10-14.
```

Overview

DATA LIST defines a raw data file (a raw data file contains numbers and other alphanumeric characters) by assigning names and formats to each variable in the file. Raw data can be inline (entered with your commands between BEGIN DATA and END DATA) or stored in an external file. They can be in fixed format (values for the same variable are always entered in the same location on the same record for each case) or in freefield format (values for consecutive variables are not in particular columns but are entered one after the other, separated by blanks or commas).

For information on defining matrix materials, see MATRIX DATA. For information on defining complex data files that cannot be defined with DATA LIST, see FILE TYPE and REPEATING DATA. For information on reading SPSS-format data files and SPSS-format portable files, see GET and IMPORT.

The program can also read data files created by other software applications. Commands that read these files include GET CAPTURE and GET TRANSLATE.

Options

Data Source. You can use inline data or data from an external file.

Data Formats. You can define numeric (with or without decimal places) and string variables using an array of input formats (percent, dollar, date and time, and so forth). You can also specify column binary and unaligned positive integer binary formats (available only if used with the MODE=MULTIPUNCH setting on the FILE HANDLE command). For a complete list of available formats, see “Variable Formats” on p. 21.

Data Organization. You can define data that are in fixed format (values in the same location on the same record for each case), in freefield format with multiple cases per record, or in freefield format with one case on each record using the FIXED, FREE, and LIST keywords.

Multiple Records. For fixed-format data, you can indicate the number of records per case on the RECORDS subcommand. You can specify which records to read in the variable definition portion of DATA LIST.

Summary Table. For fixed-format data, you can display a table that summarizes the variable definitions using the TABLE subcommand. You can suppress this table using NOTABLE.

Value Delimiter. For freefield-format data (keywords FREE and LIST), you can specify the character(s) that separate data values, or you can use the keyword TAB to specify the tab character as the delimiter. Any delimiter other than the TAB keyword must be enclosed in quotation marks, and the specification must be enclosed in parentheses, as in DATA LIST FREE(",").

End-of-File Processing. You can specify a logical variable that indicates the end of the data using the END subcommand. This logical variable can be used to invoke special processing after all the cases from the data file have been read.

Basic Specification

- The basic specification is the FIXED, LIST, or FREE keyword, followed by a slash that signals the beginning of variable definition.
- FIXED is the default.
- If the data are in an external file, the FILE subcommand must be used.
- If the data are inline, the FILE subcommand is omitted and the data are specified between the BEGIN DATA and END DATA commands.
- Variable definition for fixed-format data includes a variable name, a column location, and a format (unless the default numeric format is used). The column location is not specified if FORTRAN-like formats are used, since these formats include the variable width.
- Variable definition for freefield data includes a variable name and, optionally, a delimiter specification and a FORTRAN-like format specification. If format specifications include a width and number of decimal positions (for example, F8.2), the width and decimal specifications are not used to read the data but are assigned as print and write formats for the variables.

Subcommand Order

Subcommands can be named in any order. However, all subcommands must precede the first slash, which signals the beginning of variable definition.

Syntax Rules

Subcommands on DATA LIST are separated by spaces or commas, not by slashes.

Operations

- DATA LIST clears the working data file and defines a new working file.
- Variable names are stored in the working file dictionary.
- Formats are stored in the working file dictionary and are used to display and write the values. To change output formats of numeric variables defined on DATA LIST, use the FORMATS command.

Fixed-Format Data

- The order of the variables in the working file dictionary is the order in which they are defined on DATA LIST, not their sequence in the input data file. This order is important if you later use the TO keyword to refer to variables on subsequent commands.
- In numeric format, blanks to the left or right of a number are ignored; imbedded blanks are invalid. When the program encounters a field that contains one or more blanks interspersed among the numbers, it issues a warning message and assigns the system-missing value to that case.
- Alphabetical and special characters, except the decimal point and leading plus and minus signs, are not valid in numeric variables and are set to system-missing if encountered in the data.
- The system-missing value is assigned to a completely blank field for numeric variables. The value assigned to blanks can be changed using the BLANKS specification on the SET command.
- The program ignores data contained in columns and records that are not specified in the variable definition.

Freefield Data

FREE can read freefield data with multiple cases recorded on one record or with one case recorded on more than one record. LIST can read freefield data with one case on each record.

- Line endings are read as delimiters between values.
- If you use FORTRAN-like format specifications (for example, DOLLAR12.2), width and decimal specifications are not used to read the data but are assigned as print and write formats for the variable.

For freefield data *without* explicitly specified value delimiters:

- Commas and blanks are interpreted as delimiters between values.
- Extra blanks are ignored.
- Multiple commas with or without blank space between them can be used to specify missing data.
- If a valid value contains commas or blank spaces, enclose the values in quotation marks or apostrophes.

For data with explicitly specified value delimiters (for example, DATA LIST FREE (",")):

- Multiple delimiters without any intervening space can be used to specify missing data.
- The specified delimiters cannot occur within a data value, even if you enclose the value in quotation marks or apostrophes.

Note: Freefield format with specified value delimiters is typically used to read data in text format written by a computer program, not for data manually entered in a text editor.

Example

```
* Column-style format specifications.

DATA LIST /ID 1-3 SEX 5 (A) AGE 7-8 OPINION1 TO OPINION5 10-14.
BEGIN DATA
001 m 28 12212
002 f 29 21212
003 f 45 32145
 ...
128 m 17 11194
END DATA.
```

- The data are inline between the BEGIN DATA and END DATA commands, so the FILE subcommand is not specified. The data are in fixed format. The keyword FIXED is not specified because it is the default.
- Variable definition begins after the slash. Variable *ID* is in columns 1 through 3. Because no format is specified, numeric format is assumed. Variable *ID* is therefore a numeric variable that is three characters wide.
- Variable *SEX* is a short string variable in column 5. Variable *SEX* is one character wide.
- *AGE* is a two-column numeric variable in columns 7 and 8.
- Variables *OPINION1*, *OPINION2*, *OPINION3*, *OPINION4*, and *OPINION5* are named using the TO keyword (see "Keyword TO" on p. 19). Each is a one-column numeric variable, with *OPINION1* located in column 10 and *OPINION5* located in column 14.
- The BEGIN DATA and END DATA commands enclose the inline data. Note that the values of *SEX* are lowercase letters and must be specified as such on subsequent commands.

FILE Subcommand

FILE specifies the raw data file. FILE is required when data are stored in an external data file. FILE must not be used when the data are stored in a file that is included with the INCLUDE command or when the data are inline (see INCLUDE and BEGIN DATA—END DATA).

- FILE must be separated from other DATA LIST subcommands by at least one blank or comma.
- FILE must precede the first slash, which signals the beginning of variable definition.

FIXED, FREE, and LIST Keywords

FIXED, FREE, or LIST indicates the format of the data. Only one of these keywords can be used on each DATA LIST. The default is FIXED.

FIXED *Fixed-format data.* Each variable is recorded in the same column location on the same record for each case in the data. FIXED is the default.

FREE *Freefield data.* The variables are recorded in the same order for each case but not necessarily in the same column locations. More than one case can be entered on the same record. By default, values are separated by blanks or commas. You can also specify different value delimiters.

LIST *Freefield data with one case on each record.* The variables are recorded in freefield format as described for the keyword FREE except that the variables for each case must be recorded on one record.

- FIXED, FREE, or LIST must be separated from other DATA LIST subcommands by at least one blank or comma.
- FIXED, FREE, or LIST must precede the first slash, which signals the beginning of data definition.
- For fixed-format data, you can use column-style or FORTRAN-like formats, or a combination of both. For freefield data, you can use only FORTRAN-like formats.
- For fixed-format data, the program reads values according to the column locations specified or implied by the FORTRAN-like format. Values in the data do *not* have to be in the same order as the variables named on DATA LIST and do *not* have to be separated by a space or column.
- For freefield data, the program reads values sequentially in the order in which the variables are named on DATA LIST. Values in the data *must* be in the order in which the variables are named on DATA LIST and *must* be separated by at least one valid delimiter.
- For freefield data, multiple blank spaces can be used to indicate missing information only if a blank space is explicitly specified as the delimiter. In general, it is better to use multiple non-blank delimiters (for example, two commas with no intervening space) to specify missing data.
- In freefield format, a value cannot be split across records.

Example

```
* Data in fixed format.

DATA LIST FILE=HUBDATA FIXED RECORDS=3
  /1 YRHIRED 14-15 DEPT 19 SEX 20.
```

- FIXED indicates explicitly that the *HUBDATA* file is in fixed format. Because FIXED is the default, the keyword FIXED could have been omitted.
- Variable definition begins after the slash. Column locations are specified after each variable. Since formats are not specified, the default numeric format is used. Variable widths are determined by the column specifications: *YRHIRED* is two characters wide, and *DEPT* and *SEX* are each one character wide.

Example

```
* Data in freefield format.
DATA LIST FREE / POSTPOS NWINS.
BEGIN DATA
2, 19, 7, 5, 10, 25, 5, 17, 8, 11, 3,, 6, 8, 1, 29
END DATA.
```

- Data are inline, so FILE is omitted. The keyword FREE is used because data are in freefield format with multiple cases on a single record. Two variables, *POSTPOS* and *NWINS*, are defined. Since formats are not specified, both variables receive the default F8.2 format.
- All of the data are recorded on one record. The first two values build the first case in the working data file. For the first case, *POSTPOS* has value 2 and *NWINS* has value 19. For

the second case, *POSTPOS* has value 7 and *NWINS* has value 5, and so on. The working data file will contain eight cases.

- The two commas without intervening space after the data value 3 indicate a missing data value.

Example

```
* Data in list format.

DATA LIST LIST (",")/ POSTPOS NWINS.
BEGIN DATA
2,19
7,5
10,25
5,17
8,11
3,
6,8
1,29
END DATA.
```

- This example defines the same data as the previous example, but LIST is used because each case is recorded on a separate record. FREE could also be used. However, LIST is less prone to errors in data entry. If you leave out a value in the data with FREE format, all values after the missing value are assigned to the wrong variable. Since LIST format reads a case from each record, a missing value will affect only one case.
- A comma is specified as the delimiter between values.
- Since line endings are interpreted as delimiters between values, the second comma after the value 3 (in the sixth line of data) is not necessary to indicate that the value of *NWINS* is missing for that case.

TABLE and NOTABLE Subcommands

TABLE displays a table summarizing the variable definitions supplied on DATA LIST. NOTABLE suppresses the summary table. TABLE is the default.

- TABLE and NOTABLE can be used only for fixed-format data.
- TABLE and NOTABLE must be separated from other DATA LIST subcommands by at least one blank or comma.
- TABLE and NOTABLE must precede the first slash, which signals the beginning of variable definition.

RECORDS Subcommand

RECORDS indicates the number of records per case for fixed-format data. In the variable definition portion of DATA LIST, each record is preceded by a slash. By default, DATA LIST reads one record per case.

- The only specification on RECORDS is a single integer indicating the *total* number of records for each case (even if the DATA LIST command does not define all the records).

- RECORDS can be used only for fixed-format data and must be separated from other DATA LIST subcommands by at least one blank or comma. RECORDS must precede the first slash, which signals the beginning of variable definition.
- Each slash in the variable definition portion of DATA LIST indicates the beginning of a new record. The first slash indicates the first (or only) record. The second and any subsequent slashes tell the program to go to a new record.
- To skip a record, specify a slash without any variables for that record.
- The number of slashes in the variable definition cannot exceed the value of the integer specified on RECORDS.
- The sequence number of the record being defined can be specified after each slash. DATA LIST reads the number to determine which record to read. If the sequence number is used, you *do not* have to use a slash for any skipped records. However, the records to be read must be in their sequential order.
- The slashes for the second and subsequent records can be specified within the variable list, or they can be specified on a format list following the variable list (see the example below).
- All variables to be read from one record should be defined before you proceed to the next record.
- Since RECORDS can be used only with fixed format, it is not necessary to define all the variables on a given record or to follow their order in the input data file.

Example

```
DATA LIST FILE=HUBDATA RECORDS=3
 /2 YRHIRED 14-15 DEPT 19 SEX 20.
```

- DATA LIST defines fixed-format data. RECORDS can be used only for fixed-format data.
- RECORDS indicates that there are three records per case in the data. Only one record per case is defined in the data definition.
- The sequence number (2) before the first variable definition indicates that the variables being defined are on the second record. Because the sequence number is provided, a slash is not required for the first record, which is skipped.
- The variables *YRHIRED*, *DEPT*, and *SEX* are defined and will be included in the working data file. Any other variables on the second record or on the other records are not defined and are not included in the working file.

Example

```
DATA LIST FILE=HUBDATA RECORDS=3
  / /YRHIRED 14-15 DEPT 19 SEX 20.
```

- This command is equivalent to the one in the previous example. Because the record sequence number is omitted, a slash is required to skip the first record.

Example

```
DATA LIST FILE=HUBDATA RECORDS=3
  /YRHIRED (T14,F2.0) /  /NAME (T25,A24).
```

- RECORDS indicates there are three records for each case in the data.
- *YRHIRED* is the only variable defined on the first record. The FORTRAN-like format specification T14 means tab over 14 columns. Thus, *YRHIRED* begins in column 14 and has format F2.0.
- The second record is skipped. Because the record sequence numbers are not specified, a slash must be used to skip the second record.
- *NAME* is the only variable defined for the third record. *NAME* begins in column 25 and is a string variable with a width of 24 characters (format A24).

Example

```
DATA LIST FILE=HUBDATA RECORDS=3
  /YRHIRED NAME (T14,F2.0 /  / T25,A24).
```

- This command is equivalent to the one in the previous example. *YRHIRED* is located on the first record, and *NAME* is located on the third record.
- The slashes that indicate the second and third records are specified within the format specifications. The format specifications follow the complete variable list.

END Subcommand

END provides control of end-of-file processing by specifying a variable that is set to a value of 0 until the end of the data file is encountered, at which point the variable is set to 1. The values of all variables named on DATA LIST are left unchanged. The logical variable created with END can then be used on DO IF and LOOP commands to invoke special processing after all the cases from a particular input file have been built.

- DATA LIST and the entire set of commands used to define the cases must be enclosed within an INPUT PROGRAM—END INPUT PROGRAM structure. The END FILE command must also be used to signal the end of case generation.
- END can be used only with fixed-format data. An error is generated if the END subcommand is used with FREE or LIST.

Example

```
INPUT PROGRAM.
NUMERIC         TINCOME (DOLLAR8.0).                        /* Total income
LEAVE           TINCOME.
DO IF           $CASENUM EQ 1.
+   PRINT       EJECT.
+   PRINT       / 'Name        Income'.
END IF
DATA LIST      FILE=INCOME END=#EOF NOTABLE / NAME 1-10(A)
                                              INCOME 16-20(F).
DO IF           #EOF.
+   PRINT       / 'TOTAL     ', TINCOME.
+   END FILE.
ELSE.
+   PRINT       / NAME, INCOME (A10,COMMA8).
+   COMPUTE     TINCOME = TINCOME+INCOME.  /* Accumulate total income
END IF.
END INPUT PROGRAM.

EXECUTE.
```

- The data definition commands are enclosed within an INPUT PROGRAM—END INPUT PROGRAM structure.
- NUMERIC indicates that a new numeric variable, *TINCOME*, will be created.
- LEAVE tells the program to leave variable *TINCOME* at its value for the previous case as each new case is read, so that it can be used to accumulate totals across cases.
- The first DO IF structure, enclosing the PRINT EJECT and PRINT commands, tells the program to display the headings *Name* and *Income* at the top of the display (when *$CASENUM* equals 1).
- DATA LIST defines variables *NAME* and *INCOME*, and it specifies the scratch variable *#EOF* on the END subcommand.
- The second DO IF prints the values for *NAME* and *INCOME* and accumulates the variable *INCOME* into *TINCOME* by passing control to ELSE as long as *#EOF* is not equal to 1. At the end of the file, *#EOF* equals 1, and the expression on DO IF is true. The label *TOTAL* and the value for *TINCOME* are displayed, and control is passed to END FILE.

Example

```
* Concatenate three raw data files.

INPUT PROGRAM.
NUMERIC #EOF1 TO #EOF3.  /*These will be used as the END variables.

DO IF #EOF1 & #EOF2 & #EOF3.
+   END FILE.
ELSE IF #EOF1 & #EOF2.
+     DATA LIST  FILE=THREE END=#EOF3 NOTABLE / NAME 1-20(A)
              AGE 25-26 SEX 29(A).
+     DO IF NOT #EOF3.
+        END CASE.
+     END IF.
ELSE IF #EOF1.
+     DATA LIST  FILE=TWO END=#EOF2 NOTABLE / NAME 1-20(A)
              AGE 21-22 SEX 24(A).
+     DO IF NOT #EOF2.
+        END CASE.
+     END IF.
ELSE.
+     DATA LIST  FILE=ONE END=#EOF1 NOTABLE /1 NAME 1-20(A)
              AGE 21-22 SEX 24 (A).
+     DO IF NOT #EOF1.
+        END CASE.
+     END IF.
END IF.
END INPUT PROGRAM.

REPORT FORMAT AUTOMATIC LIST /VARS=NAME AGE SEX.
```

- The input program contains a DO IF—ELSE IF—END IF structure.
- Scratch variables are used on each END subcommand so the value will not be reinitialized to the system-missing value after each case is built.
- Three data files are read, two of which contain data in the same format. The third requires a slightly different format for the data items. All three DATA LIST commands are placed within the DO IF structure.
- END CASE builds cases from each record of the three files. END FILE is used to trigger end-of-file processing once all data records have been read.
- This application can also be handled by creating three separate SPSS-format data files and using ADD FILES to put them together. The advantage of using the input program is that additional files are not required to store the separate data files prior to performing ADD FILES.

Variable Definition

The variable definition portion of DATA LIST assigns names and formats to the variables in the data. Depending on the format of the file, you may also need to specify record and column location. The following sections describe variable names, location, and formats.

Variable Names

- Variable names can contain up to eight characters. All variable names must begin with a letter or the @ or # character. A # symbol as the first character of the variable name defines the variable as a scratch variable. System variables (beginning with a $) cannot be defined on DATA LIST. An underscore can be used within a variable name, provided the underscore is not the first character.
- The keyword TO can be used to generate names for consecutive variables in the data. Leading zeros in the number are preserved in the name. *X1* TO *X100* and *X001* TO *X100* both generate 100 variable names, but the first 99 names are not the same in the two lists. *X01* TO *X9* is not a valid specification. For more information on the TO keyword and other variable-naming rules, see "Variable Names" on p. 19.
- The order in which variables are named on DATA LIST determines their order in the working data file. If the working file is saved as an SPSS-format data file, the variables are saved in this order unless they are explicitly reordered on the SAVE or XSAVE command.

Example

```
DATA LIST FREE / ID SALARY #V1 TO #V4.
```

- The FREE keyword indicates that the data are in freefield format. Six variables are defined: *ID*, *SALARY*, *#V1*, *#V2*, *#V3*, and *#V4*. *#V1* to *#V4* are scratch variables that are not stored in the working data file. Their values can be used in transformations but not in procedure commands.

Variable Location

For fixed-format data, variable locations are specified either explicitly using column locations or implicitly using FORTRAN-like formats. For freefield data, variable locations are not specified. Values are read sequentially in the order in which variables are named on the variable list.

Fixed-Format Data

- If column-style formats are used, you must specify the column location of each variable after the variable name. If the variable is one column wide, specify the column number. Otherwise, specify the first column number followed by a dash (–) and the last column number.
- If several adjacent variables on the same record have the same width and format type, you can use one column specification after the last variable name. Specify the beginning column location of the first variable, a dash, and the ending column location of the last variable. the program divides the total number of columns specified equally among the variables. If the number of columns does not divide equally, an error message is issued.
- The same column locations can be used to define multiple variables.

- For FORTRAN-like formats, column locations are implied by the width specified on the formats (see “Variable Formats” on p. 255). To skip columns, use the Tn or nX format specifications.
- With fixed format, column-style and FORTRAN-like specifications can be mixed on the same DATA LIST command.
- Record location is indicated by a slash or a slash and record number before the names of the variables on that record. See the RECORDS subcommand on p. 248 for information on specifying record location.
- The program ignores data in columns and on records that are not specified on DATA LIST.
- In the data, values do not have to be separated by a space or comma.

Example

```
DATA LIST  FILE=HUBDATA RECORDS=3
  /1 YRHIRED 14-15 DEPT 19 SEX 20
  /2 SALARY 21-25.
```

- The data are in fixed format (the default) and are read from the file *HUBDATA*.
- Three variables, *YRHIRED*, *DEPT*, and *SEX*, are defined on the first record of the *HUBDATA* file. One variable, *SALARY*, is read from columns 21 through 25 on the second record. The total number of records per case is specified as 3 even though no variables are defined on the third record. The third record is simply skipped in data definition.

Example

```
DATA LIST  FILE=HUBDATA RECORDS=3
  /1 DEPT 19 SEX 20 YRHIRED 14-15 MOHIRED 12-13 HIRED 12-15
  /2 SALARY 21-25.
```

- The first two defined variables are *DEPT* and *SEX*, located in columns 19 and 20 on record 1. The next three variables, *YRHIRED*, *MOHIRED*, and *HIRED*, are also located on the first record.
- *YRHIRED* is read from columns 14 and 15, *MOHIRED* from columns 12 and 13, and *HIRED* from columns 12 through 15. The variable *HIRED* is a four-column variable with the first two columns representing the month when an employee was hired (the same as *MOHIRED*) and the last two columns representing the year of employment (the same as *YRHIRED*).
- The order of the variables in the dictionary is the order in which they are defined on DATA LIST, not their sequence in the *HUBDATA* file.

Example

```
DATA LIST  FILE=HUBDATA RECORDS=3
  /1 DEPT 19 SEX 20 MOHIRED YRHIRED 12-15
  /2 SALARY 21-25.
```

- A single column specification follows *MOHIRED* and *YRHIRED*. DATA LIST divides the total number of columns specified equally between the two variables. Thus, each variable has a width of two columns.

Example

```
* Mixing column-style and FORTRAN-like format specifications.

DATA LIST FILE=PRSNL / LNAME M_INIT STREET (A20,A1,1X,A10)
    AGE 35-36.
```

- FORTRAN-like format specifications are used for string variables *LNAME*, *M_INIT*, and *STREET*. These variables must be adjacent in the data file. *LNAME* is 20 characters wide and is located in columns 1–20. *M_INIT* is one character wide and is located in column 21. The 1X specification defines a blank column between *M_INIT* and *STREET*. *STREET* is 10 characters wide and is located in columns 23–32.
- A column-style format is used for the variable *AGE*. *AGE* begins in column 35, ends in column 36, and by default has numeric format.

Freefield Data

- In freefield data, column location is irrelevant, since values are not in fixed column positions. Instead, values are simply separated from each other by blanks or by commas or a specified delimiter. Any number of consecutive blanks are interpreted as one delimiter unless a blank space is explicitly specified as the value delimiter. A value cannot be split across records.
- If there are not enough values to complete the last case, a warning is issued and the incomplete case is dropped.
- The specified delimiter can only be used within data values if the value is enclosed in quotations marks or apostrophes.
- To include an apostrophe in a string value, enclose the value in quotation marks. To include quotation marks in a value, enclose the value in apostrophes (see “String Values in Command Specifications” on p. 5).

Variable Formats

Two types of format specifications are available: column-style and FORTRAN-like. With each type, you can specify both numeric and string formats. The difference between the two types is that FORTRAN-like formats include the width of the variable and column-style formats do not.

- Column-style formats are available only for fixed-format data.
- Column-style and FORTRAN-like formats can be mixed on the same DATA LIST to define fixed-format data.
- A value that cannot be read according to the format type specified is assigned the system-missing value and a warning message is issued.

The following sections discuss the rules for specifying column-style and FORTRAN-like formats, followed by additional considerations for numeric and string formats. See p. 242 for a partial list of available formats. For a complete discussion of formats, see “Variable Formats” on p. 21.

Column-Style Format Specifications

The following rules apply to column-style formats:

- Data must be in a fixed format.
- Column locations must be specified after variable names. The width of a variable is determined by the number of specified columns. See "Fixed-Format Data" on p. 253 for information on specifying column location.
- Following the column location, specify the format type in parentheses. The format type applies only to the variable or the list of variables associated with the column location specification immediately before it. If no format type is specified, numeric (F) format is used.
- To include decimal positions in the format, specify the format type followed by a comma and the number of decimal positions. For example, (DOLLAR) specifies only whole dollar amounts; (DOLLAR,2) specifies DOLLAR format with two decimal positions.
- Since column positions are explicitly specified, the variables can be named in any order.

FORTRAN-like Format Specifications

The following rules apply to FORTRAN-like formats:

- Data can be in either fixed or freefield format.
- Column locations cannot be specified. The width of a variable is determined by the width portion (w) of the format specification. The width must specify the number of characters in the widest value.
- One format specification applies to only one variable. The format is specified in parentheses after the variable to which it applies. Alternatively, a variable list can be followed by an equal number of format specifications contained in one set of parentheses. When a number of consecutive variables have the same format, the number can be used as a multiplying factor preceding the format. For example, (3F5.2) assigns the format F5.2 to three consecutive variables.
- For fixed data, the number of formats specified (either explicitly or implied by the multiplication factor) must be the same as the number of variables. Otherwise, the program issues an error message. If no formats are specified, all variables have the default format F8.2.
- For freefield data, variables with no specified formats take the default F8.2 format. However, an asterisk (*) must be used to indicate where the default format stops. Otherwise, the program tries to apply the next specified format to every variable before it and issues an error message if the number of formats specified is less than the number of variables.
- For freefield data, width and decimal specifications are not used to read the data but are assigned as print and write formats for the variable.
- For fixed data, Tn can be used before a format to indicate that the variable begins at the *n*th column, and nX can be used to skip *n* columns before reading the variable. When Tn is specified, variables named do not have to follow the order of the variables in the data.

- For freefield data, variables are located according to the sequence in which they are named on DATA LIST. The order of variables on DATA LIST must correspond to the order of variables in the data.
- To include decimal positions in the format for fixed-format data, specify the total width followed by a decimal point and the number of decimal positions. For example, (DOLLAR5) specifies a five-column DOLLAR format without decimal positions; (DOLLAR5.2) specifies a five-column DOLLAR format, two columns of which are decimal positions.

Numeric Formats

- Format specifications on DATA LIST are input formats. Based on the width specification and format type, the program generates output (print and write) formats for each variable. The program automatically expands the output format to accommodate punctuation characters such as decimal points, commas, dollar signs, or date and time delimiters. (The program does not automatically expand the output formats you assign on the FORMATS, PRINT FORMATS, and WRITE FORMATS commands. For information on assigning output formats, refer to these commands.)
- Scientific notation is accepted in input data with F, COMMA, DOLLAR, DOT, and PCT formats. The same rules apply to these formats as to E format. The values 1.234E3, 1.234+3, and 1.234E 3 are all legitimate. The last value (with a blank space) will cause freefield data to be misread and therefore should be avoided when LIST or FREE is specified.

Implied Decimal Positions

- For fixed-format data, decimal positions can be coded in the data or implied by the format. If decimal positions are implied but are not entered in the data, the program interprets the rightmost digits in each value as the decimal digits. A coded decimal point in a value overrides the number of implied decimal places. For example, (DOLLAR,2) specifies two decimal positions. The value 123 is interpreted as 1.23; however, the value 12.3 is interpreted as 12.3 because the coded decimal position overrides the number of implied decimal positions.
- For freefield data, decimal positions cannot be implied but must be coded in the data. If decimal positions are specified in the format but a data value does not include a decimal point, the program fills the decimal places with zeros. For example, with F3.1 format (three columns with one decimal place), the value 22 is displayed as 22.0. If a value in the data has more decimal digits than are specified in the format, the additional decimals are truncated in displayed output (but not in calculations). For example, with F3.1 format, the value 2.22 is displayed as 2.2 even though in calculations it remains 2.22.

Table 1 compares how values are interpreted for fixed and freefield formats. Values in the table are for a four-column numeric variable.

Table 1 Interpretation of values in fixed and freefield format

	Fixed		Freefield	
Values	Default	Two defined decimal places	Default	Two defined decimal places
2001	2001	20.01	2001.00	2001.00
201	201	2.01	201.00	201.00
–201	–201	–2.01	–201.00	–201.00
2	2	.02	2.00	2.00
20	20	.20	20.00	20.00
2.2	2.2	2.2	2.20	2.20
.201	.201	.201	.201	.201
2 01	Undefined	Undefined	Two values	Two values

Example

```
DATA LIST
  /MODEL 1 RATE 2-6(PCT,2) COST 7-11(DOLLAR) READY 12-21(ADATE).
BEGIN DATA
1935   7878811-07-1988
2 16754654606-08-1989
3 17684783612-09-1989
END DATA.
```

- Data are inline and in fixed format (the default).
- Each variable is followed by its column location. After the column location, a column-style format is specified in parentheses.
- *MODEL* begins in column 1, is one column wide, and receives the default numeric F format.
- *RATE* begins in column 2 and ends in column 6. The PCT format is specified with two decimal places. A comma is used to separate the format type from the number of decimal places. Decimal points are not coded in the data. Thus, the program reads the rightmost digits of each value as decimal digits. The value 935 for the first case in the data is interpreted as 9.35. Note that it does not matter where numbers are entered within the column width.
- *COST* begins in column 7 and ends in column 11. DOLLAR format is specified.
- *READY* begins in column 12 and ends in column 21. ADATE format is specified.

Example

```
DATA LIST FILE=DATA1
  /MODEL (F1) RATE (PCT5.2) COST (DOLLAR5) READY (ADATE10).
```

- In this example, the FILE subcommand is used because the data are in an external file.
- The variable definition is the same as in the preceding example except that FORTRAN-like format specifications are used rather than column-style. Column locations are not specified. Instead, the format specifications include a width for each format type.
- The width (w) portion of each format must specify the total number of characters in the widest value. DOLLAR5 format for *COST* accepts the five-digit value 78788, which dis-

plays as $78,788. Thus, the specified input format DOLLAR5 generates an output format DOLLAR7. The program automatically expands the width of the output format to accommodate the dollar sign and comma in displayed output.

String Formats

String (alphanumeric) variables can contain any numbers, letters, or characters, including special characters and imbedded blanks. Numbers entered as values for string variables cannot be used in calculations unless you convert them to numeric format (see RECODE). On DATA LIST, a string variable is defined with an A format if data are in standard character form or an AHEX format if data are in hexadecimal form. For further discussion of string formats, see "String Variable Formats" on p. 29.

- For fixed-format data, the width of a string variable is either implied by the column location specification or specified by the *w* on the FORTRAN-like format. For freefield data, the width must be specified on the FORTRAN-like format.
- The string formats defined on DATA LIST are both input and output formats. You cannot change the format of a defined string variable in this program. However, you can use the STRING command to define a new string variable and COMPUTE to copy the values from the old variable (see COMPUTE).
- AHEX format is available only for fixed-format data. Since each set of two hexadecimal characters represents one standard character, the width specification must be an even number. The output format for a variable in AHEX format is A format with half the specified width.
- If a string in the data is longer than its specified width, the string is truncated and a warning message is displayed. If the string in the data is shorter, it is right-padded with blanks and no warning message is displayed.
- For fixed-format data, all characters within the specified or implied columns, including leading, trailing, and imbedded blanks and punctuation marks, are read as the value of the string.
- For freefield data without a specified delimiter, string values in the data must be enclosed in apostrophes or quotation marks if the string contains a blank or a comma. Otherwise, the blank or comma is treated as a delimiter between values. Apostrophes can be included in a string by enclosing the string in quotation marks. Quotation marks can be included in a string by enclosing the string in apostrophes.

Example

```
DATA LIST FILE=WINS FREE /POSTPOS NWINS * POSNAME (A24).
```

- *POSNAME* is specified as a 24-character string. The asterisk preceding *POSNAME* indicates that *POSTPOS* and *NWINS* are read with the default format. If the asterisk was not specified, the program would apply the A24 format to *POSNAME* and then issue an error message indicating that there are more variables than specified formats.

Example

```
DATA LIST FILE=WINS FREE /POSTPOS * NWINS (A5) POSWINS.
```

- Both *POSTPOS* and *POSWINS* receive the default numeric format F8.2.
- *NWINS* receives the specified format of A5.

DATE

```
DATE  keyword [starting value [periodicity]]
      [keyword [starting value [periodicity]]]
      [BY increment]
```

Keywords for long time periods:

Keyword	Abbreviation	Default starting value	Default periodicity
YEAR	Y	1	none
QUARTER	Q	1	4
MONTH	M	1	12

Keywords for short time periods:

Keyword	Abbreviation	Default starting value	Default periodicity
WEEK	W	1	none
DAY	D	1	7
HOUR	H	0	24
MINUTE	MI	0	60
SECOND	S	0	60

Keywords for any time periods:

Keyword	Abbreviation	Default starting value	Default periodicity
CYCLE	C	1	none
OBS	O	none	none

Example

```
DATE Y 1960 M.
```

Overview

DATE generates date identification variables. You can use these variables to label plots and other output, establish periodicity, and distinguish between historical, validation, and forecasting periods.

Options

You can specify the starting value and periodicity. You can also specify an increment for the lowest-order keyword specified.

Basic Specification

The basic specification on DATE is a single keyword.

- For each keyword specified, DATE creates a numeric variable whose name is the keyword with an underscore as a suffix. Values for this variable are assigned to observations sequentially, beginning with the specified starting value. DATE also creates a string variable named *DATE_*, which combines the information from the numeric date variables and is used for labeling.
- If no starting value is specified, either the default is used or the value is inferred from the starting value of another DATE keyword.
- All variables created by DATE are automatically assigned variable labels that describe periodicity and associated formats. DATE produces a list of the names of the variables it creates and their variable labels.

Subcommand Order

- Keywords can be specified in any order.

Syntax Rules

- You can specify more than one keyword per command.
- If a keyword is specified more than once, only the last one is executed.
- Keywords that describe long time periods (YEAR, QUARTER, MONTH) cannot be used on the same command with keywords that describe short time periods (WEEK, DAY, HOUR, MINUTE, SECOND).
- Keywords CYCLE and OBS can be used with any other keyword.
- The lowest-order keyword specified should correspond to the level at which observations occur. For example, if observations are daily, the lowest-order keyword should be DAY.
- Keywords (except MINUTE) can be abbreviated down to the first character. MINUTE must have at least two characters (MI) to distinguish it from keyword MONTH.
- Keywords and additional specifications are separated by commas or spaces.

Starting Value and Periodicity

- A starting value and periodicity can be entered for any keyword except CYCLE. CYCLE can have only a starting value.
- Starting value and periodicity *must* be specified for keyword OBS.

- The starting value is specified first, followed by the periodicity, if any.
- You cannot specify a periodicity without first specifying a starting value.
- Starting values for HOUR, MINUTE, and SECOND can range from 0 to the periodicity minus 1 (for example, 0 to 59). For all other keywords, the range is 1 to the periodicity.
- If both MONTH and QUARTER are specified, DATE can infer the starting value of one from the other (see "Example 5" on p. 267).
- Specifying conflicting starting values for MONTH and QUARTER, such as Q 1 M 4, results in an error.
- For keyword YEAR, the starting value can be specified as the last two digits (93) instead of the whole year (1993) when the series and any forecasting are all within the same century. The same format (2 digits or 4 digits) must be used in all other commands that use year values.
- If you specify keywords that describe short time periods and skip over a level of measurement (for example, if you specify HOUR and SECOND but not MINUTE), you must specify the starting value and periodicity of the keyword after the skipped keywords. Otherwise, inappropriate periodicities will be generated (see "Example 7" on p. 268).

BY Keyword

- Keyword BY and a positive integer can be specified after the lowest-order keyword on the command to indicate an increment value. This value indicates how much to increment values of the lowest-order date variable as they are assigned to observations (see "Example 4" on p. 266).
- The increment value must divide evenly into the periodicity of the lowest-order DATE variable specified.

Operations

- DATE creates a numeric variable for every keyword specified, plus a string variable *DATE_*, which combines information from all the specified keywords.
- DATE automatically creates variable labels for each keyword specified indicating the variable name and its periodicity. For the *DATE_* variable, the label indicates the variable name and format.
- If the highest-order DATE variable specified has a periodicity, the *CYCLE_* variable will automatically be created. *CYCLE_* cannot have a periodicity (see "Example 3" on p. 265).
- Default periodicities are not used for the highest-order keyword specified. The exception is QUARTER, which will always have a default periodicity.
- The periodicity of the lowest-order variable is the default periodicity used by the procedures when periodicity is not defined either within the procedure or by the TSET command.
- The keyword name with an underscore is always used as the new variable name, even if keyword abbreviations are used in the specifications.
- Each time the DATE command is used, any DATE variables already in the working data file are deleted.

- The DATE command invalidates any previous USE and PREDICT commands specified. The USE and PREDICT periods must be respecified after DATE.

Limitations

- There is no limit on the number of keywords on the DATE command. However, keywords that describe long time periods (YEAR, QUARTER, MONTH) cannot be used on the same command with keywords that describe short time periods (WEEK, DAY, HOUR, MINUTE, SECOND).
- User-defined variable names must not conflict with DATE variable names.

Example 1

```
DATE Y 1960 M.
```

- This command generates variables *DATE_*, *YEAR_*, and *MONTH_*.
- *YEAR_* has a starting value of 1960. *MONTH_* starts at the default value of 1.
- By default, *YEAR_* has no periodicity, and *MONTH_* has a periodicity of 12.

DATE reports the following:

```
Name        Label

YEAR_       YEAR, not periodic
MONTH_      MONTH, period 12
DATE_       DATE.  FORMAT:  "MMM YYYY"
```

The following is a partial listing of the new variables:

```
YEAR_ MONTH_ DATE_

 1960    1    JAN 1960
 1960    2    FEB 1960
 1960    3    MAR 1960
 1960    4    APR 1960
  ...
 1960   10    OCT 1960
 1960   11    NOV 1960
 1960   12    DEC 1960
 1961    1    JAN 1961
 1961    2    FEB 1961
  ...
 1999    4    APR 1999
 1999    5    MAY 1999
 1999    6    JUN 1999
```

Example 2

```
DATE WEEK DAY 1 5 HOUR 1 8.
```

- This command creates four variables (*DATE_*, *WEEK_*, *DAY_*, and *HOUR_*) in a file where observations occur hourly in a 5-day, 40-hour week.
- For *WEEK_*, the default starting value is 1 and the default periodicity is none.

- For *DAY_*, the starting value has to be specified, even though it is the same as the default, because a periodicity is specified. The periodicity of 5 means that observations are measured in a 5-day week.
- For *HOUR_*, a starting value of 1 is specified. The periodicity of 8 means that observations occur in an 8-hour day.

DATE reports the following:

```
Name         Label

WEEK_        WEEK, not periodic
DAY_         DAY, period 5
HOUR_        HOUR, period 24
DATE_        DATE.  FORMAT:  "WWW D HH"
```

The following is a partial listing of the new variables:

```
WEEK_ DAY_ HOUR_ DATE_

    1    1     1    1 1  1
    1    1     2    1 1  2
    1    1     3    1 1  3
    1    1     4    1 1  4
    1    1     5    1 1  5
   ...
    1    1    22    1 1 22
    1    1    23    1 1 23
    1    2     0    1 2  0
    1    2     1    1 2  1
    1    2     2    1 2  2
   ...
    4    5    16    4 5 16
    4    5    17    4 5 17
    4    5    18    4 5 18
```

Example 3

```
DATE DAY 1 5 HOUR 3 8.
```

- This command creates four variables (*DATE_*, *CYCLE_*, *DAY_*, and *HOUR_*) in a file where observations occur hourly.
- For *HOUR_*, the starting value is 3 and the periodicity is 8.
- For *DAY_*, the starting value is 1 and the periodicity is 5. Since *DAY_* is the highest-order variable and it has a periodicity assigned, variable *CYCLE_* is automatically created.

DATE reports the following:

```
Name         Label

CYCLE_       CYCLE, not periodic
DAY_         DAY, period 5
HOUR_        HOUR, period 8
DATE_        DATE.  FORMAT:  "CCCC D H"
```

The following is a partial listing of the new variables:

```
CYCLE_ DAY_ HOUR_ DATE_

     1    1     3       1 1 3
     1    1     4       1 1 4
     1    1     5       1 1 5
     1    1     6       1 1 6
     1    1     7       1 1 7
     1    2     0       1 2 0
     1    2     1       1 2 1
...
    12    4     6      12 4 6
    12    4     7      12 4 7
    12    5     0      12 5 0
    12    5     1      12 5 1
    12    5     2      12 5 2
    12    5     3      12 5 3
    12    5     4      12 5 4
```

Example 4

```
DATE DAY HOUR 1 24 BY 2.
```

- This command creates three variables (*DATE_*, *DAY_*, and *HOUR_*) in a file where observations occur every two hours in a 24-hour day.
- *DAY_* uses the default starting value of 1. It has no periodicity, since none is specified, and it is the highest-order keyword on the command.
- *HOUR_* starts with a value of 1 and has a periodicity of 24.
- Keyword BY specifies an increment of 2 to use in assigning hour values.

DATE reports the following:

```
Name          Label

DAY_          DAY, not periodic
HOUR_         HOUR, period 24 by 2
DATE_         DATE.  FORMAT:  "DDDD HH"
```

The following is a partial listing of the new variables:

```
DAY_ HOUR_ DATE_

    1     1     1  1
    1     3     1  3
    1     5     1  5
...
   39    17    39 17
   39    19    39 19
   39    21    39 21
   39    23    39 23
   40     1    40  1
   40     3    40  3
   40     5    40  5
   40     7    40  7
   40     9    40  9
   40    11    40 11
```

Example 5

```
DATE Y 1950 Q 2 M.
```

- This example creates four variables (*DATE_*, *YEAR_*, *QUARTER_*, and *MONTH_*) in a file where observations are quarterly, starting with April 1950.
- The starting value for *MONTH_* is inferred from *QUARTER_*.
- This specification is equivalent to DATE Y 1950 Q M 4. Here, the starting value for *QUARTER_* (2) would be inferred from MONTH.

DATE reports the following:

```
Name        Label

YEAR_       YEAR, not periodic
QUARTER_    QUARTER, period 4
MONTH_      MONTH, period 12
DATE_       DATE.  FORMAT:  "MMM YYYY"
```

The following is a partial listing of the new variables:

```
YEAR_ QUARTER_ MONTH_ DATE_

 1950    2        4   APR 1950
 1950    2        5   MAY 1950
 1950    2        6   JUN 1950
 1950    3        7   JUL 1950
 1950    3        8   AUG 1950
  ...
 1988    4       11   NOV 1988
 1988    4       12   DEC 1988
 1989    1        1   JAN 1989
 1989    1        2   FEB 1989
 1989    1        3   MAR 1989
 1989    2        4   APR 1989
 1989    2        5   MAY 1989
 1989    2        6   JUN 1989
 1989    3        7   JUL 1989
 1989    3        8   AUG 1989
 1989    3        9   SEP 1989
```

Example 6

```
DATE OBS 9 17.
```

- This command creates variables *DATE_*, *CYCLE_*, and *OBS_* and assigns values to observations sequentially, starting with value 9. The periodicity is 17.

DATE reports the following:

```
Name        Label

CYCLE_      CYCLE, not periodic
OBS_        OBS, period 17
DATE_       DATE.  FORMAT:  "CCCC OO"
```

The following is a partial listing of the new variables:

```
CYCLE_ OBS_ DATE_

     1    9      1  9
     1   10      1 10
     1   11      1 11
     1   12      1 12
     1   13      1 13
     1   14      1 14
     1   15      1 15
     1   16      1 16
     1   17      1 17
     2    1      2  1
     2    2      2  2
   ...
    28   15     28 15
    28   16     28 16
    28   17     28 17
    29    1     29  1
    29    2     29  2
    29    3     29  3
    29    4     29  4
    29    5     29  5
    29    6     29  6
```

Example 7

```
DATE W H 1 168
```

- This example creates three variables (*DATE_*, *WEEK_*, and *HOUR_*) in a file where observations occur hourly.
- Since the DAY keyword is not specified, a periodicity must be specified for HOUR. The value 168 indicates that there are 168 hours in a week.
- The starting value of HOUR is specified as 1.

DATE reports the following:

```
Name        Label

WEEK_       WEEK, not periodic
HOUR_       HOUR, period 168
DATE_       DATE.  FORMAT:  "WWWW HHH"
```

The following is a partial listing of the new variables:

```
WEEK_  HOUR_  DATE_

     1      1      1   1
     1      2      1   2
     1      3      1   3
     1      4      1   4
     1      5      1   5
     1      6      1   6
   ...
     1    161      1 161
     1    162      1 162
     1    163      1 163
     1    164      1 164
     1    165      1 165
     1    166      1 166
     1    167      1 167
     2      0      2   0
     2      1      2   1
     2      2      2   2
     2      3      2   3
     2      4      2   4
     2      5      2   5
   ...
     3    131      3 131
     3    132      3 132
     3    133      3 133
     3    134      3 134
     3    135      3 135
     3    136      3 136
     3    137      3 137
     3    138      3 138
```

DEFINE—!ENDDEFINE

```
DEFINE macro name

  ([{argument name=} [!DEFAULT (string)] [!NOEXPAND] {!TOKENS  (n)             }]
    {!POSITIONAL=   }                              {!CHAREND ('char')        }
                                                   {!ENCLOSE ('char', 'char')}
                                                   {!CMDEND                  }

  [/{argument name=} ...])
    {!POSITIONAL=   }

macro body

!ENDDEFINE
```

SET command controls:

```
PRESERVE
RESTORE
```

Assignment:

```
!LET var=expression
```

Conditional processing:

```
!IF (expression) !THEN statements
    [!ELSE statements]
!IFEND
```

Looping constructs:

```
!DO !varname=start !TO finish [BY step]
   statements  [!BREAK]
!DOEND

!DO !varname !IN (list)
   statements  [!BREAK]
!DOEND
```

Macro directives:

```
!OFFEXPAND
!ONEXPAND
```

String manipulation functions:

```
!LENGTH (string)
!CONCAT (string1,string2)
!SUBSTR (string,from,[length])
!INDEX (string1,string2)
!HEAD (string)
!TAIL (string)
!QUOTE (string)
!UNQUOTE (string)
!UPCASE (string)
!BLANKS (n)
!NULL
!EVAL (string)
```

Example

```
DEFINE sesvars ()
  age sex educ religion.
!ENDDEFINE.
```

Overview

DEFINE—!ENDDEFINE defines a program macro, which can then be used within a command sequence. A macro can be useful in several different contexts. For example, it can be used to:

- Issue a series of the same or similar commands repeatedly, using looping constructs rather than redundant specifications.
- Specify a set of variables.
- Produce output from several program procedures with a single command.
- Create complex input programs, procedure specifications, or whole sessions that can then be executed.

A macro is defined by specifying any part of a valid command and giving it a macro name. This name is then specified in a macro call within a command sequence. When the program encounters the macro name, it expands the macro.

In the examples of macro definition throughout this reference, the macro name, body, and arguments are shown in lower case for readability. Macro keywords, which are always preceded by an exclamation point (!), are shown in upper case. For additional examples of the macro facility, see Appendix D.

Options

Macro Arguments. You can declare and use arguments in the macro definition and then assign specific values to these arguments in the macro call. You can define defaults for the arguments and indicate whether an argument should be expanded when the macro is called. (See pp. 274–281.)

Macro Directives. You can turn macro expansion on and off (see p. 281).

String Manipulation Functions. You can process one or more character strings and produce either a new character string or a character representation of a numeric result (see pp. 281–283).

Conditional Processing. You can build conditional and looping constructs (see p. 285).

Macro Variables. You can directly assign values to macro variables (see p. 287).

Basic Specification

All macros must start with the DEFINE command and end with the macro command !ENDDEFINE. These commands identify the beginning and end of a macro definition and are used to separate the macro definition from the rest of the command sequence.

- Immediately after DEFINE, specify the **macro name**. All macros must have a name. The name is used in the macro call to refer to the macro. Macro names can begin with an exclamation point (!), but other than this, follow the usual naming conventions. Starting a name with an ! ensures that it will not conflict with the other text or variables in the session.
- Immediately after the macro name, specify an optional **argument** definition in parentheses. This specification indicates the arguments that will be read when the macro is called. If you do not want to include arguments, specify just the parentheses; *the parentheses are required, whether or not they enclose an argument.*
- Next specify the body of the macro. The **macro body** can include commands, parts of commands, or macro statements (macro directives, string manipulation statements, and looping and conditional processing statements).
- At the end of the macro body, specify the !ENDDEFINE command.

To invoke the macro, issue a **macro call** in the command sequence. To call a macro, specify the macro name and any necessary arguments. If there are no arguments, only the macro name is required.

Operations

- When macros are used in a prompted session, the command line prompt changes to DEFINE> between the DEFINE and !ENDDEFINE commands.
- When the program reads the macro definition, it translates into upper case all text (except arguments) not enclosed in quotation marks. Arguments are read in upper and lower case.
- The macro facility does not build and execute commands; rather, it expands strings in a process called **macro expansion**. A macro call initiates macro expansion. After the strings are expanded, the commands (or parts of commands) that contain the expanded strings are executed as part of the command sequence.
- Any elements on the macro call that are not used in the macro expansion are read and combined with the expanded strings.
- The expanded strings and the remaining elements from the macro call, if any, must conform to the syntax rules for the program. If not, the program generates either a warning or an error message, depending on the nature of the syntax problem.

Limitations

- The BEGIN DATA—END DATA commands are not allowed within a macro.
- The DEFINE command is not allowed within a macro.

Example

```
* Macro without arguments: Specify a group of variables.

DEFINE sesvars ()
   age sex educ religion.
!ENDDEFINE.

FREQUENCIES VARIABLES=sesvars.
```

- The macro name is sesvars. Because the parentheses are empty, sesvars has no arguments. The macro body defines four variables: *AGE*, *SEX*, *EDUC*, and *RELIGION*.
- The macro call is specified on FREQUENCIES. When the call is executed, sesvars is expanded into the variables *AGE*, *SEX*, *EDUC*, and *RELIGION*.
- After the macro expansion, FREQUENCIES is executed.

Example

```
* Macro without arguments: Repeat a sequence of commands.

DATA LIST FILE = MAC4D /GROUP 1   REACTIME 3-5 ACCURACY 7-9.
VALUE LABELS GROUP    1'normal'
                      2'learning disabled'.
* Macro definition.
DEFINE check ().
split file by group.
frequencies variables = reactime accuracy
  /histogram.
descriptives reactime accuracy.
list.
split file off.
regression variables = group reactime accuracy
  /dependent = accuracy
  /enter
  /scatterplot (reactime, accuracy).
!ENDDEFINE.

check.                        /* First call of defined macro check

COMPUTE REACTIME = SQRT (REACTIME).
COMPUTE ACCURACY = SQRT (ACCURACY).

check.                        /* Second call of defined macro check

COMPUTE REACTIME = lg10 (REACTIME * REACTIME).
COMPUTE ACCURACY = lg10 (ACCURACY * ACCURACY).

check.                        /* Third call of defined macro check
```

- The name of the macro is *CHECK*. The empty parentheses indicate that there are no arguments to the macro.
- The macro definition (between DEFINE and !ENDDEFINE) contains the command sequence to be repeated: SPLIT FILE, FREQUENCIES, DESCRIPTIVES, LIST, SPLIT FILE, and REGRESSION.

- The macro is called three times. Every time check is encountered, it is replaced with the command sequence SPLIT FILE, FREQUENCIES, DESCRIPTIVES, LIST, SPLIT FILE OFF, and REGRESSION. The command sequence using the macro facility is identical to the command sequence in which the specified commands are explicitly stated three separate times.

Example

```
* Macro with an argument.

DEFINE myfreq (vars = !CHAREND('/')).
frequencies variables = !vars
  /format = notable
  /hbar = normal
  /statistics = default skewness kurtosis.
!ENDDEFINE.

myfreq vars = AGE SEX EDUC RELIGION /.
```

- The macro definition defines vars as the macro argument. In the macro call, four variables are specified as the argument to the macro myfreq. When the program expands the myfreq macro, it substitutes the argument, AGE, SEX, EDUC, and RELIGION, for !vars and executes the resulting commands.

Macro Arguments

The macro definition can include macro arguments, which can be assigned specific values in the macro call. There are two types of arguments: keyword and positional. Keyword arguments are assigned names in the macro definition; in the macro call, they are identified by name. Positional arguments are defined after the keyword !POSITIONAL in the macro definition; in the macro call, they are identified by their relative position within the macro definition.

- There is no limit to the number of arguments that can be specified in a macro.
- All arguments are specified in parentheses and must be separated by slashes.
- If both keyword and positional arguments are defined in the same definition, the positional arguments must be defined, used in the macro body, and invoked in the macro call before the keyword arguments.

Example

```
* A keyword argument.

DEFINE macname (arg1 = !TOKENS(1)).
frequencies variables = !arg1.
!ENDDEFINE.

macname arg1 = V1.
```

- The macro definition defines macname as the macro name and arg1 as the argument. The argument arg1 has one token and can be assigned any value in the macro call.

- The macro call expands the macname macro. The argument is identified by its name, arg1, and is assigned the value V1. V1 is substituted wherever !arg1 appears in the macro body. The macro body in this example is the FREQUENCIES command.

Example

```
* A positional argument.

DEFINE macname (!POSITIONAL !TOKENS(1)
               /!POSITIONAL !TOKENS(2)).
frequencies variables = !1 !2.
!ENDDEFINE.

macname V1 V2 V3.
```

- The macro definition defines macname as the macro name with two positional arguments. The first argument has one token and the second argument has two tokens. The tokens can be assigned any values in the macro call.
- The macro call expands the macname macro. The arguments are identified by their positions. V1 is substituted for !1 wherever !1 appears in the macro body. V2 and V3 are substituted for !2 wherever !2 appears in the macro body. The macro body in this example is the FREQUENCIES command.

Keyword Arguments

Keyword arguments are called with user-defined keywords that can be specified in any order. In the macro body, the argument name is preceded by an exclamation point. On the macro call, the argument is specified without the exclamation point.

- Keyword argument definitions contain the argument name, an equals sign, and the !TOKENS, !ENCLOSE, !CHAREND, or !CMDEND keyword (see "Assigning Tokens to Arguments" on p. 277).
- Argument names are limited to seven characters and cannot match the character portion of a macro keyword, such as DEFINE, TOKENS, CHAREND, and so forth. See the syntax chart on p. 270 for a list of macro keywords for the program.
- The keyword !POSITIONAL cannot be used in keyword argument definitions.
- Keyword arguments do not have to be called in the order they were defined.

Example

```
DATA LIST FILE=MAC / V1 1-2 V2 4-5 V3 7-8.

* Macro definition.
DEFINE macdef2 (arg1 = !TOKENS(1)
               /arg2 = !TOKENS(1)
               /arg3 = !TOKENS(1)).
frequencies  variables = !arg1 !arg2 !arg3.
!ENDDEFINE.

* Macro call.
macdef2 arg1=V1  arg2=V2  arg3=V3.
macdef2 arg3=V3  arg1=V1  arg2=V2.
```

- Three arguments are defined: arg1, arg2, and arg3, each with one token. In the first macro call, arg1 is assigned the value V1, arg2 is assigned the value V2, and arg3 is assigned the value V3. V1, V2, and V3 are then used as the variables in the FREQUENCIES command.
- The second macro call yields the same results as the first one. With keyword arguments, you do not need to call the arguments in the order in which they were defined.

Positional Arguments

Positional arguments must be defined in the order in which they will be specified on the macro call. In the macro body, the first positional argument is referred to by !1, the second positional argument defined is referred to by !2, and so on. Similarly, the value of the first argument in the macro call is assigned to !1, the value of the second argument is assigned to !2, and so on.

- Positional arguments can be collectively referred to in the macro body by specifying !*. The !* specification concatenates arguments, separating individual arguments with a blank.

Example

```
DATA LIST FILE=MAC / V1 1-2 V2 4-5 V3 7-8.

* Macro definition.
DEFINE macdef (!POS !TOKENS(1).
              /!POS !TOKENS(1).
              /!POS !TOKENS(1)).
frequencies variables = !1 !2 !3.
!ENDDEFINE.

* Macro call.
macdef  V1     V2    V3.
macdef  V3     V1    V2.
```

- Three positional arguments with one token each are defined. The first positional argument is referred to by !1 on the FREQUENCIES command, the second by !2, and the third by !3.
- When the first call expands the macro, the first positional argument (!1) is assigned the value V1, the second positional argument (!2) is assigned the value V2, and the third positional argument (!3) is assigned the value V3.
- In the second call, the first positional argument is assigned the value V3, the second positional argument is assigned the value V1, and the third positional argument is assigned the value V2.

Example

```
DEFINE macdef (!POS !TOKENS(3)).
frequencies variables = !1.
!ENDDEFINE.

macdef  V1     V2    V3.
```

- This example is the same as the previous one, except that it assigns three tokens to one argument instead of assigning one token to each of three arguments. The result is the same.

Example

```
DEFINE macdef (!POS !TOKENS(1)
               /!POS !TOKENS(1)
               /!POS !TOKENS(1)).
frequencies variables = !*.
!ENDDEFINE.

macdef  V1    V2   V3.
```

- This is a third alternative for achieving the macro expansion shown in the previous two examples. It specifies three arguments but then joins them all together on one FREQUENCIES command using the symbol !*.

Assigning Tokens to Arguments

A **token** is a character or group of characters that has a predefined function in a specified context. The argument definition must include a keyword that indicates which tokens following the macro name are associated with each argument.

- Any program keyword, variable name, or delimiter (a slash, comma, etc.) is a valid token.
- The arguments for a given macro can use a combination of the token keywords.

!TOKENS (n) *Assign the next* n *tokens to the argument.* The value *n* can be any positive integer and must be enclosed in parentheses. !TOKENS allows you to specify exactly how many tokens are desired.

!CHAREND ('char') *Assign all tokens up to the specified character to the argument.* The character must be a one-character string specified in apostrophes and enclosed in parentheses. !CHAREND specifies the character that ends the argument assignment. This is useful when the number of assigned tokens is arbitrary or not known in advance.

!ENCLOSE ('char','char') *Assign all tokens between the indicated characters to the argument.* The starting and ending characters can be any one-character strings, and they do not need to be the same. The characters are each enclosed in apostrophes and separated by a comma. The entire specification is enclosed in parentheses. !ENCLOSE allows you to group multiple tokens within a specified pair of symbols. This is useful when the number of tokens to be assigned to an argument is indeterminate, or when the use of an ending character is not sufficient.

!CMDEND *Assign to the argument all of the remaining text on the macro call, up to the start of the next command.* !CMDEND is useful for changing the defaults on an existing command. Since !CMDEND reads up to the next command, only the last argument on the argument list can be specified with !CMDEND. If !CMDEND is not the final argument, the arguments following !CMDEND are read as text.

Example

```
* Keyword !TOKENS.

DEFINE macname (!POSITIONAL !TOKENS (3)).
frequencies variables = !1.
!ENDDEFINE.

macname ABC DEFG HI.
```

- The three tokens following macname (ABC, DEFG, and HI) are assigned to the positional argument !1, and FREQUENCIES is then executed.

Example

```
* Keyword !TOKENS.

* Macro definition.
DEFINE earnrep (varrep = !TOKENS (1)).
sort cases by !varrep.
report variables = earnings
  /break = !varrep
  /summary = mean.
!ENDDEFINE.

* Call the macro three times.
earnrep varrep= SALESMAN.  /*First macro call
earnrep varrep = REGION.   /*Second macro call
earnrep varrep = MONTH.    /*Third macro call
```

- This macro runs a REPORT command three times, each time with a different break variable.
- The macro name is earnrep, and there is one keyword argument, varrep, which has one token.
- In the first macro call, the token SALESMAN is substituted for !varrep when the macro is expanded. REGION and MONTH are substituted for !varrep when the macro is expanded in the second and third calls.

Example

```
* Keyword !CHAREND'.

DEFINE macname (!POSITIONAL !CHAREND ('/')
               /!POSITIONAL !TOKENS(2)).
frequencies variables = !1.
correlations variables= !2.
!ENDDEFINE.

macname A B C D / E F.
```

- When the macro is called, all tokens up to the slash (A, B, C, and D) are assigned to the positional argument !1. E and F are assigned to the positional argument !2.

Example

```
* Keyword !CHAREND.

DEFINE macname (!POSITIONAL !CHAREND ('/')).
frequencies variables = !1.
!ENDDEFINE.

macname A B C D / E F.
```

- Although E and F are not part of the positional argument and are not used in the macro expansion, the program still reads them as text and interprets them in relation to where the macro definition ends. In this example, macro definition ends after the expanded variable list (D). E and F are names of variables. Thus, E and F are added to the variable list and FREQUENCIES is executed with six variables: *A*, *B*, *C*, *D*, *E*, and *F*.

Example

```
* Keyword !ENCLOSE.

DEFINE macname (!POSITIONAL !ENCLOSE('(',')')).
frequencies variables = !1
  /statistics = default skewness.
!ENDDEFINE.

macname (A B C) D E.
```

- When the macro is called, the three tokens enclosed in parentheses, A, B, and C, are assigned to the positional argument !1 in the macro body.
- After macro expansion is complete, the program reads the remaining characters on the macro call as text. In this instance, the macro definition ends with keyword SKEWNESS on the STATISTICS subcommand. Adding variable names to the STATISTICS subcommand is not valid syntax. The program generates a warning message but is still able to execute the frequencies command. Frequency tables and the specified statistics are generated for the variables *A*, *B*, and *C*.

Example

```
* Keyword !CMDEND'.

DEFINE macname (!POSITIONAL !TOKENS(2)
               /!POSITIONAL !CMDEND).
frequencies variables = !1.
correlations variables= !2.
!ENDDEFINE.

macname A B C D E.
```

- When the macro is called, the first two tokens following macname (A and B) are assigned to the positional argument !1. C, D, and E are assigned to the positional argument !2. Thus, the variables used for FREQUENCIES are *A* and *B*, and the variables used for CORRELATION are *C*, *D*, and *E*.

Example

```
* Incorrect order for !CMDEND.

DEFINE macname   (!POSITIONAL !CMDEND
                 /!POSITIONAL !tokens(2)).
frequencies variables = !1.
correlations variables= !2.
!ENDDEFINE.

macname  A B C D E.
```

- When the macro is called, all five tokens, A, B, C, D, and E, are assigned to the first positional argument. No variables are included on the variable list for CORRELATIONS, causing the program to generate an error message. The previous example declares the arguments in the correct order.

Example

```
* Using !CMDEND.
SUBTITLE 'CHANGING DEFAULTS ON A COMMAND'.

DEFINE myfreq (!POSITIONAL !CMDEND ).
frequencies !1
  /statistics=default skewness   /* Modify default statistics.
!ENDDEFINE.

myfreq VARIABLES = A B /HIST.
```

- The macro myfreq contains options for the FREQUENCIES command. When the macro is called, myfreq is expanded to perform a FREQUENCIES analysis on the variables *A* and *B*. The analysis produces default statistics and the skewness statistic, plus a histogram, as requested on the macro call.

Example

```
* Keyword arguments: Using a combination of token keywords.

DATA LIST FREE / A B C D E.
DEFINE macdef3 (arg1 = !TOKENS(1)
                /arg2 = !ENCLOSE ('(',')')
                /arg3 = !CHAREND('%')).
frequencies variables = !arg1  !arg2 !arg3.
!ENDDEFINE.
macdef arg1 = A  arg2=(B C)  arg3=DE %.
```

- Because arg1 is defined with the !TOKENS keyword, the value for arg1 is simply specified as A. The value for arg2 is specified in parentheses, as indicated by !ENCLOSE. The value for arg3 is followed by a percent sign, as indicated by !CHAREND.

Defining Defaults

The optional !DEFAULT keyword in the macro definition establishes default settings for arguments.

!DEFAULT *Default argument.* After !DEFAULT, specify the value you want to use as a default for that argument. A default can be specified for each argument.

Example

```
DEFINE macdef (arg1 = !DEFAULT (V1) !TOKENS(1)
              /arg2 = !TOKENS(1)
              /arg3 = !TOKENS(1)).
frequencies variables = !arg1 !arg2 !arg3.
!ENDDEFINE.

macdef arg2=V2  arg3=V3.
```

- V1 is defined as the default value for argument arg1. Since arg1 is not specified on the macro call, it is set to V1.
- If !DEFAULT (V1) were not specified, the value of arg1 would be set to a null string.

Controlling Expansion

!NOEXPAND indicates that an argument should not be expanded when the macro is called.

!NOEXPAND *Do not expand the specified argument.* !NOEXPAND applies to a single argument and is useful only when a macro calls another macro (imbedded macros).

Macro Directives

!ONEXPAND and !OFFEXPAND determine whether macro expansion is on or off. !ONEXPAND activates macro expansion and !OFFEXPAND stops macro expansion. All symbols between !OFFEXPAND and !ONEXPAND in the macro definition will not be expanded when the macro is called.

!ONEXPAND *Turn macro expansion on.*

!OFFEXPAND *Turn macro expansion off.* !OFFEXPAND is effective only when SET MEXPAND is ON (the default).

Macro Expansion in Comments

When macro expansion is on, a macro is expanded when its name is specified in a comment line beginning with *. To use a macro name in a comment, specify the comment within slashes and asterisks (/*...*/) to avoid unwanted macro expansion. (See COMMENT.)

String Manipulation Functions

String manipulation functions process one or more character strings and produce either a new character string or a character representation of a numeric result.

- The result of any string manipulation function is treated as a character string.

- The arguments to string manipulation functions can be strings, variables, or even other macros. A macro argument or another function can be used in place of a string.
- The strings within string manipulation functions must be either single tokens, such as ABC, or delimited by apostrophes or quotation marks, as in 'A B C'. See Table 1 for a set of expressions and their results.

Table 1 Expressions and results

Expression	Result
!UPCASE(abc)	ABC
!UPCASE('abc')	ABC
!UPCASE(a b c)	error
!UPCASE('a b c')	A B C
!UPCASE(a/b/c)	error
!UPCASE('a/b/c')	A/B/C
!UPCASE(!CONCAT(a,b,c))	ABC
!UPCASE(!CONCAT('a','b','c'))	ABC
!UPCASE(!CONCAT(a, b, c))	ABC
!UPCASE(!CONCAT('a ','b ','c '))	A B C
!UPCASE(!CONCAT('a,b,c'))	A,B,C
!QUOTE(abc)	'ABC'
!QUOTE('abc')	abc
!QUOTE('Bill''s')	'Bill''s'
!QUOTE("Bill's")	"Bill's"
!QUOTE(Bill's)	error
!QUOTE(!UNQUOTE('Bill''s'))	'Bill''s'

!LENGTH (str) *Return the length of the specified string.* The result is a character representation of the string length. !LENGTH(abcdef) returns 6. If the string is specified with apostrophes around it, each apostrophe adds 1 to the length. !LENGTH ('abcdef') returns 8. If an argument is used in place of a string and it is set to null, this function will return 0.

!CONCAT(str1,str2 . . .) *Return a string that is the concatenation of the strings.* For example, !CONCAT (abc,def) returns abcdef.

!SUBSTR (str,from,[length]) *Return a substring of the specified string.* The substring starts at the *from* position and continues for the specified *length*. If the length is not specified, the substring ends at the end of the input string. For example, !SUBSTR (abcdef, 3, 2) returns cd.

!INDEX (haystack,needle) *Return the position of the first occurrence of the needle in the haystack.* If the needle is not found in the haystack, the function returns 0. !INDEX (abcdef,def) returns 4.

!HEAD (str) *Return the first token within a string.* The input string is not changed. !HEAD ('a b c') returns a.

!TAIL (str) *Return all tokens except the head token.* The input string is not changed. !TAIL('a b c') returns b c.

!QUOTE (str) *Put apostrophes around the argument.* !QUOTE replicates any imbedded apostrophe. !QUOTE(abc) returns 'abc'. If !1 equals Bill's, !QUOTE(!1) returns 'Bill''s'.

!UNQUOTE (str) *Remove quotation marks and apostrophes from the enclosed string.* If !1 equals 'abc', !UNQUOTE(!1) is abc. Internal paired quotation marks are unpaired; if !1 equals 'Bill''s', !UNQUOTE(!1) is Bill's. The specification !UNQUOTE(!QUOTE(Bill)) returns Bill.

!UPCASE (str) *Convert all lowercase characters in the argument to upper case.* !UPCASE('abc def') returns ABC DEF.

!BLANKS (n) *Generate a string containing the specified number of blanks.* The *n* specification must be a positive integer. !BLANKS(5) returns a string of five blank spaces. Unless the blanks are quoted, they cannot be processed, since the macro facility compresses blanks.

!NULL *Generate a string of length 0.* This can help determine whether an argument was ever assigned a value, as in !IF (!1 !EQ !NULL) !THEN. . . .

!EVAL (str) *Scan the argument for macro calls.* During macro definition, an argument to a function or an operand in an expression is not scanned for possible macro calls unless the !EVAL function is used. It returns a string that is the expansion of its argument. For example, if mac1 is a macro, then !EVAL(mac1) returns the expansion of mac1. If mac1 is not a macro, !EVAL(mac1) returns mac1.

SET Subcommands for Use with Macro

Four subcommands on the SET command were designed for use with the macro facility.

MPRINT *Display a list of commands after macro expansion.* The specification on MPRINT is YES or NO (alias ON or OFF). By default, the output does not include a list of commands after macro expansion (MPRINT NO). The MPRINT subcommand on SET is independent of the PRINTBACK command.

MEXPAND *Macro expansion.* The specification on MEXPAND is YES or NO (alias ON or OFF). By default, MEXPAND is on. SET MEXPAND OFF prevents macro expansion. Specifying SET MEXPAND ON reestablishes macro expansion.

MNEST *Maximum nesting level for macros.* The default number of levels that can be nested is 50. The maximum number of levels depends on storage capacity.

MITERATE *Maximum loop iterations permitted in macro expansions.* The default number of iterations is 1000.

Restoring SET Specifications

The PRESERVE and RESTORE commands bring more flexibility and control over SET. PRESERVE and RESTORE are available generally within the program but are especially useful with macros.

- The settings of all SET subcommands—those set explicitly and those set by default (except MEXPAND)—are saved with PRESERVE. PRESERVE has no further specifications.
- With RESTORE, all SET subcommands are changed to what they were when the PRESERVE command was executed. RESTORE has no further specifications.
- PRESERVE...RESTORE sequences can be nested up to five levels.

PRESERVE *Store the SET specifications that are in effect at this point in the session.*

RESTORE *Restore the SET specifications to what they were when PRESERVE was specified.*

Example

```
* Two nested levels of preserve and restore'.

DEFINE macdef ().
preserve.
set format F5.3.
descriptives v1 v2.
+ preserve.
set format F3.0 blanks=999.
descriptives v3 v4.
+ restore.
descriptives v5 v6.
restore.
!ENDDEFINE.
```

- The first PRESERVE command saves all of the current SET conditions. If none have been specified, the default settings are saved.
- Next, the format is set to F5.3 and descriptive statistics for *V1* and *V2* are obtained.
- The second PRESERVE command saves the F5.3 format setting and all other settings in effect.
- The second SET command changes the format to F3.0 and sets BLANKS to 999 (the default is SYSMIS). Descriptive statistics are then obtained for *V3* and *V4*.
- The first RESTORE command restores the format to F5.3 and BLANKS to the default, the setting in effect at the second PRESERVE. Descriptive statistics are then obtained for *V5* and *V6*.
- The last RESTORE restores the settings in effect when the first PRESERVE was specified.

Conditional Processing

The !IF construct specifies conditions for processing. The syntax is as follows:

```
!IF (expression) !THEN statements
                 [!ELSE statements]
!IFEND
```

- !IF, !THEN, and !IFEND are all required. !ELSE is optional.
- If the result of the expression is true, the statements following !THEN are executed. If the result of the expression is false and !ELSE is specified, the statements following !ELSE are executed. Otherwise, the program continues.
- Valid operators for the expressions include !EQ, !NE, !GT, !LT, !GE, !LE, !OR, !NOT, and !AND, or =, ~= (¬=), >, <, >=, <=, |, ~ (¬), and & (see "Relational Operators" on p. 46).
- When a macro is expanded, conditional processing constructs are interpreted after arguments are substituted and functions are executed.
- !IF statements can be nested whenever necessary. Parentheses can be used to specify the order of evaluation. The default order is the same as for transformations: !NOT has precedence over !AND, which has precedence over !OR.

Looping Constructs

Looping constructs accomplish repetitive tasks. Loops can be nested to whatever depth is required, but loops cannot be crossed. The macro facility has two looping constructs: the index loop (DO loop) and the list-processing loop (DO IN loop).

- When a macro is expanded, looping constructs are interpreted after arguments are substituted and functions are executed.

Index Loop

The syntax of an index loop is as follows:

```
!DO !var = start !TO finish [ !BY step ]
    statements
!BREAK
!DOEND
```

- The indexing variable is *!var* and must begin with an exclamation point.
- The start, finish, and step values must be numbers or expressions that evaluate to numbers.
- The loop begins at the start value and continues until it reaches the finish value (unless a !BREAK statement is encountered). The step value is optional and can be used to specify a subset of iterations. If start is set to 1, finish to 10, and step to 3, the loop will be executed four times with the index variable assigned values 1, 4, 7, and 10.
- The statements can be any valid commands or macro keywords. !DOEND specifies the end of the loop.
- !BREAK is an optional specification. It can be used in conjunction with conditional processing to exit the loop.

Example

```
DEFINE macdef (arg1 = !TOKENS(1)
              /arg2 = !TOKENS(1)).
!DO !i = !arg1 !TO !arg2.
frequencies variables = !CONCAT(var,!i).
!DOEND.
!ENDDEFINE.
macdef arg1 = 1 arg2 = 3.
```

- The variable *!i* is initially assigned the value 1 (arg1) and is incremented until it equals 3 (arg2), at which point the loop ends.
- The first loop concatenates var and the value for *!I*, which is 1 in the first loop. The second loop concatenates var and 2, and the third concatenates var and 3. The result is that FREQUENCIES is executed three times, with variables *VAR1*, *VAR2*, and *VAR3*, respectively.

List-processing Loop

The syntax of a list-processing loop is as follows:

```
!DO !var !IN (list)
    statements
!BREAK
!DOEND
```

- The !DO and !DOEND statements begin and end the loop. !BREAK is used to exit the loop.
- The !IN function requires one argument, which must be a list of items. The number of items on the list determines the number of iterations. At each iteration, the index variable *!var* is set to each item on the list.
- The list can be any expression, although it is usually a string. Only one list can be specified in each list-processing loop.

Example

```
DEFINE macdef (!POS !CHAREND('/') ).
!DO !i !IN ( !1).
frequencies variables = !i.
!DOEND.
!ENDDEFINE.
macdef VAR1 VAR2 VAR3  /.
```

- The macro call assigns three variables, *VAR1*, *VAR2*, and *VAR3*, to the positional argument !1. Thus, the loop completes three iterations.
- In the first iteration, *!i* is set to value *VAR1*. In the second and third iterations, *!I* is set to *VAR2* and *VAR3*, respectively. Thus, FREQUENCIES is executed three times, respectively with *VAR1*, *VAR2*, and *VAR3*.

Example

```
DEFINE macdef (!POS !CHAREND('/') ).
!DO !i !IN ( !1).
sort cases by !i.
report var = earnings
  /break = !i
  /summary = mean.
!DOEND.
!ENDDEFINE.

macdef SALESMAN REGION MONTH /.
```

- The positional argument !1 is assigned the three variables *SALESMAN*, *REGION*, and *MONTH*. The loop is executed three times and the index variable *!i* is set to each of the variables in succession. The macro creates three reports.

Direct Assignment of Macro Variables

The macro command !LET assigns values to macro variables. The syntax is as follows:

```
!LET !var = expression
```

- The expression must be either a single token or enclosed in parentheses.
- The macro variable *!var* cannot be a macro keyword (see the syntax chart on p. 270 for a list of macro keywords), and it cannot be the name of one of the arguments within the macro definition. Thus, !LET cannot be used to change the value of an argument.
- The macro variable *!var* can be a new variable or one previously assigned by a !DO command or another !LET command.

Example

```
!LET !a = 1.
!LET !b = !CONCAT(ABC,!SUBSTR(!1,3,1),DEF).
!LET !c = (!2 ~= !NULL).
```

- The first !LET sets *!a* equal to 1.
- The second !LET sets *!b* equal to ABC followed by 1 character taken from the third position of !1 followed by DEF.
- The last !LET sets *!c* equal to 0 (false) if !2 is a null string or to 1 (true) if !2 is not a null string.

DESCRIPTIVES

```
DESCRIPTIVES [VARIABLES=] varname[(zname)] [varname...]

 [/MISSING={VARIABLE**}  [INCLUDE]]
           {LISTWISE  }

 [/SAVE]

 [/STATISTICS=[DEFAULT**]  [MEAN**]  [MIN**]  [SKEWNESS]]
              [STDDEV** ]  [SEMEAN]  [MAX**]  [KURTOSIS]
              [VARIANCE ]  [SUM   ]  [RANGE]  [ALL]

 [/SORT=[{MEAN     }] [{(A)}]]
         {SMEAN    }   {(D)}
         {STDDEV   }
         {VARIANCE }
         {KURTOSIS }
         {SKEWNESS }
         {RANGE    }
         {MIN      }
         {MAX      }
         {SUM      }
         {NAME     }
```

**Default if the subcommand is omitted.

Example

```
DESCRIPTIVES VARIABLES=FOOD RENT, APPL TO COOK, TELLER, TEACHER
  /STATISTICS=VARIANCE DEFAULT
  /MISSING=LISTWISE.
```

Overview

DESCRIPTIVES computes univariate statistics, including the mean, standard deviation, minimum, and maximum, for numeric variables. Because it does not sort values into a frequency table, DESCRIPTIVES is an efficient means of computing descriptive statistics for continuous variables. Other procedures that display descriptive statistics include FREQUENCIES, MEANS, and EXAMINE.

Options

Z Scores. You can create new variables that contain *z* scores (standardized deviation scores from the mean) and add them to the working data file by specifying *z*-score names on the VARIABLES subcommand or by using the SAVE subcommand.

Statistical Display. Optional statistics available with the STATISTICS subcommand include the standard error of the mean, variance, kurtosis, skewness, range, and sum. DESCRIPTIVES does not compute the median or mode (see FREQUENCIES or EXAMINE).

Display Order. You can list variables in ascending or descending alphabetical order or by the numerical value of any of the available statistics using the SORT subcommand.

Basic Specification

The basic specification is the VARIABLES subcommand with a list of variables. The actual keyword VARIABLES can be omitted. All cases with valid values for a variable are included in the calculation of statistics for that variable. Statistics include the mean, standard deviation, minimum, maximum, and number of cases with valid values.

Subcommand Order

- Subcommands can be used in any order.

Operations

- If a string variable is specified on the variable list, no statistics are displayed for that variable.
- If there is insufficient memory available to calculate statistics for all variables requested, DESCRIPTIVES truncates the variable list.

Example

```
DESCRIPTIVES VARIABLES=FOOD RENT, APPL TO COOK, TELLER, TEACHER
 /STATISTICS=VARIANCE DEFAULT
 /MISSING=LISTWISE.
```

- DESCRIPTIVES requests statistics for the variables *FOOD*, *RENT*, *TELLER*, *TEACHER*, and all of the variables between and including *APPL* and *COOK* in the working data file.
- STATISTICS requests the variance and the default statistics: mean, standard deviation, minimum, and maximum.
- MISSING specifies that cases with missing values for any variable on the variable list will be omitted from the calculation of statistics for all variables.

Example

```
DESCRIPTIVES VARS=ALL.
```

- DESCRIPTIVES requests statistics for all variables in the working file.
- Because no STATISTICS subcommand is included, only the mean, standard deviation, minimum, and maximum are displayed.

VARIABLES Subcommand

VARIABLES names the variables for which you want to compute statistics. The actual keyword VARIABLES can be omitted.

- The keyword ALL can be used to refer to all user-defined variables in the working data file.
- Only one variable list can be specified.

Z Scores

The *z*-score transformation standardizes variables to the same scale, producing new variables with a mean of 0 and a standard deviation of 1. These variables are added to the working data file.

- To obtain *z* scores for all specified variables, use the SAVE subcommand.
- To obtain *z* scores for a subset of variables, name the new variable in parentheses following the source variable on the VARIABLES subcommand and do not use the SAVE subcommand.
- Specify new names individually; a list in parentheses is not recognized.
- The new variable name can be any acceptable eight-character name that is not already part of the working data file.

Example

```
DESCRIPTIVES VARIABLES=NTCSAL NTCPUR (PURCHZ) NTCPRI (PRICEZ).
```

- DESCRIPTIVES creates *z*-score variables named *PURCHZ* and *PRICEZ* for *NTCPUR* and *NTCPRI*, respectively. No *z*-score variable is created for *NTCSAL*.

SAVE Subcommand

SAVE creates a *z*-score variable for each variable specified on the VARIABLES subcommand. The new variables are added to the working data file.

- When DESCRIPTIVES creates new *z*-score variables, it displays the source variable names, the new variable names, and their labels in the Notes table.
- DESCRIPTIVES automatically supplies variable names for the new variables. The new variable name is created by prefixing the letter *Z* to the first seven characters of the source variable name. For example, *ZNTCPRI* is the *z*-score variable for *NTCPRI*.
- If the default naming convention duplicates variable names in the working data file, DESCRIPTIVES uses an alternative naming convention: first *ZSC001* through *ZSC099*, then *STDZ01* through *STDZ09*, then *ZZZZ01* through *ZZZZ09*, and then *ZQZQ01* through *ZQZQ09*.
- Variable labels are created by prefixing *ZSCORE* to the first 31 characters of the source variable label. If the alternative naming convention is used, DESCRIPTIVES prefixes *ZSCORE(varname)* to the first 31 characters of the label. If the source variable does not have a label, DESCRIPTIVES uses *ZSCORE(varname)* for the label.
- If you specify new names on the VARIABLES subcommand *and* use the SAVE subcommand, DESCRIPTIVES creates one new variable for each variable on the VARIABLES subcommand, using default names for variables not assigned names on VARIABLES.
- If at any time you want to change any of the variable names, whether those DESCRIPTIVES created or those you previously assigned, you can do so with the RENAME VARIABLES command.

Example

```
DESCRIPTIVES VARIABLES=ALL
  /SAVE.
```

- SAVE creates a *z*-score variable for all variables in the working file. All *z*-score variables receive the default name.

Example

```
DESCRIPTIVES VARIABLES=NTCSAL NTCPUR (PURCHZ) NTCPRI (PRICEZ)
  /SAVE.
```

- DESCRIPTIVES creates three *z*-score variables named *ZNTCSAL* (the default name), *PURCHZ*, and *PRICEZ*.

Example

```
DESCRIPTIVES VARIABLES=SALARY86 SALARY87 SALARY88
  /SAVE.
```

- In this example, the default naming convention would produce duplicate names. Thus, the names of the three *z*-score variables are *ZSALARY8*, *ZSC001*, and *ZSC002*.

STATISTICS Subcommand

By default, DESCRIPTIVES displays the mean, standard deviation, minimum, and maximum. Use the STATISTICS subcommand to request other statistics.

- When you use STATISTICS, DESCRIPTIVES displays *only* those statistics you request.
- The keyword ALL obtains all statistics.
- You can specify the keyword DEFAULT to obtain the default statistics without having to name MEAN, STDDEV, MIN, and MAX.
- The median and mode, which are available in FREQUENCIES and EXAMINE, are not available in DESCRIPTIVES. These statistics require that values be sorted, and DESCRIPTIVES does not sort values (the SORT subcommand does not sort values, it simply lists variables in the order you request).
- If you request a statistic that is not available, DESCRIPTIVES issues an error message and the command is not executed.

MEAN *Mean.*

SEMEAN *Standard error of the mean.*

STDDEV *Standard deviation.*

VARIANCE *Variance.*

KURTOSIS *Kurtosis and standard error of kurtosis.*

SKEWNESS *Skewness and standard error of skewness.*

RANGE *Range.*

MIN *Minimum observed value.*

MAX *Maximum observed value.*

SUM *Sum.*

DEFAULT *Mean, standard deviation, minimum, and maximum.* These are the default statistics.

ALL *All statistics available in DESCRIPTIVES.*

SORT Subcommand

By default, DESCRIPTIVES lists variables in the order in which they are specified on VARIABLES. Use SORT to list variables in ascending or descending alphabetical order of variable name or in ascending or descending order of numeric value of any of the statistics.

- If you specify SORT without any keywords, variables are sorted in ascending order of the mean.
- SORT can sort variables by the value of any of the statistics available with DESCRIPTIVES, but only those statistics specified on STATISTICS (or the default statistics) are displayed.

Only one of the following keywords can be specified on SORT:

MEAN *Sort by mean.* This is the default when SORT is specified without a keyword.

SEMEAN *Sort by standard error of the mean.*

STDDEV *Sort by standard deviation.*

VARIANCE *Sort by variance.*

KURTOSIS *Sort by kurtosis.*

SKEWNESS *Sort by skewness.*

RANGE *Sort by range.*

MIN *Sort by minimum observed value.*

MAX *Sort by maximum observed value.*

SUM *Sort by sum.*

NAME *Sort by variable name.*

Sort order can be specified in parentheses following the specified keyword:

A *Sort in ascending order.* This is the default when SORT is specified without keywords.

D *Sort in descending order.*

Example

```
DESCRIPTIVES VARIABLES=A B C
 /STATISTICS=DEFAULT RANGE
 /SORT=RANGE (D).
```

- DESCRIPTIVES sorts variables *A*, *B*, and *C* in descending order of range and displays the mean, standard deviation, minimum and maximum values, range, and the number of valid cases.

MISSING Subcommand

MISSING controls missing values.

- By default, DESCRIPTIVES deletes cases with missing values on a variable-by-variable basis. A case with a missing value for a variable will not be included in the summary statistics for that variable, but the case *will* be included for variables where it is not missing.
- The VARIABLE and LISTWISE keywords are alternatives; however, each can be specified with INCLUDE.
- When either the keyword VARIABLE or the default missing-value treatment is used, DESCRIPTIVES reports the number of valid cases for each variable. It always displays the number of cases that would be available if listwise deletion of missing values had been selected.

VARIABLE *Exclude cases with missing values on a variable-by-variable basis.* This is the default.

LISTWISE *Exclude cases with missing values listwise.* Cases with missing values for any variable named are excluded from the computation of statistics for all variables.

INCLUDE *Include user-missing values.*

DISCRIMINANT

```
DISCRIMINANT GROUPS=varname(min,max) /VARIABLES=varlist

 [/SELECT=varname(value)]

 [/ANALYSIS=varlist[(level)] [varlist...]]

 [/METHOD={DIRECT** }] [/TOLERANCE={0.001}]
          {WILKS    }              {  n  }
          {MAHAL    }
          {MAXMINF  }
          {MINRESID }
          {RAO      }

 [/MAXSTEPS={n}]

 [/FIN={3.84**}] [/FOUT={2.71**}] [/PIN={n}]
       {  n   }         {  n   }

 [/POUT={n}] [/VIN={0**}]
                   { n }

 [/FUNCTIONS={g-1,100.0,1.0**}] [/PRIORS={EQUAL**   }]
             {n1 , n2  ,n3   }           {SIZE      }
                                         {value list}
 [/SAVE=[CLASS[=varname]] [PROBS[=rootname]]

        [SCORES[=rootname]]]

 [/ANALYSIS=...]

 [/MISSING={EXCLUDE**}]
           {INCLUDE  }

 [/MATRIX=[OUT({*   })] [IN({*   })]]
               {file}       {file}

 [/HISTORY={STEP**} ]
           {NONE  }

 [/ROTATE={NONE**   }]
          {COEFF    }
          {STRUCTURE}

 [/CLASSIFY={NONMISSING  } {POOLED  }  [MEANSUB]]
            {UNSELECTED  } {SEPARATE}
            {UNCLASSIFIED}

 [/STATISTICS=[MEAN]  [COV  ]  [FPAIR]  [RAW ] [STDDEV]
              [GCOV]  [UNIVF]  [COEFF]  [CORR] [TCOV  ]
              [BOXM]  [TABLE]  [CROSSVALID]
              [ALL]]

 [/PLOT=[MAP]  [SEPARATE]  [COMBINED]  [CASES[(n)]]  [ALL]]

 [/OUTFILE MODEL(filename)]
```

**Default if subcommand or keyword is omitted.

Example

```
DISCRIMINANT GROUPS=OUTCOME (1,4)
  /VARIABLES=V1 TO V7
  /SAVE CLASS=PREDOUT.
```

Overview

DISCRIMINANT performs linear discriminant analysis for two or more groups. The goal of discriminant analysis is to classify cases into one of several mutually exclusive groups based on their values for a set of predictor variables. In the analysis phase, a classification rule is developed using cases for which group membership is known. In the classification phase, the rule is used to classify cases for which group membership is not known. The grouping variable must be categorical, and the independent (predictor) variables must be interval or dichotomous, since they will be used in a regression-type equation.

Options

Variable Selection Method. In addition to the direct-entry method, you can specify any of several stepwise methods for entering variables into the discriminant analysis using the METHOD subcommand. You can set the values for the statistical criteria used to enter variables into the equation using the TOLERANCE, FIN, PIN, FOUT, POUT, and VIN subcommands, and you can specify inclusion levels on the ANALYSIS subcommand. You can also specify the maximum number of steps in a stepwise analysis using the MAXSTEPS subcommand.

Case Selection. You can select a subset of cases for the analysis phase using the SELECT subcommand.

Prior Probabilities. You can specify prior probabilities for membership in a group using the PRIORS subcommand. Prior probabilities are used in classifying cases.

New Variables. You can add new variables to the working data file containing the predicted group membership, the probability of membership in each group, and discriminant function scores using the SAVE subcommand.

Classification Options. With the CLASSIFY subcommand, you can classify only those cases that were not selected for inclusion in the discriminant analysis, or only those cases whose value for the grouping variable was missing or fell outside the range analyzed. In addition, you can classify cases based on the separate-group covariance matrices of the functions instead of the pooled within-groups covariance matrix.

Statistical Display. You can request any of a variety of statistics on the STATISTICS subcommand. You can rotate the pattern or structure matrices using the ROTATE subcommand. You can compare actual with predicted group membership using a classification results table requested with the STATISTICS subcommand or compare any of several types of plots or histograms using the PLOT subcommand.

Basic Specification

The basic specification requires two subcommands:

- GROUPS specifies the variable used to group cases.
- VARIABLES specifies the predictor variables.

By default, DISCRIMINANT enters all variables simultaneously into the discriminant equation (the DIRECT method), provided that they are not so highly correlated that multicollinearity problems arise. Default output includes analysis case processing summary, valid numbers of cases in group statistics, variables failing tolerance test, a summary of canonical discriminant functions, standardized canonical discriminant function coefficients, a structure matrix showing pooled within-groups correlations between the discriminant functions and the predictor variables, and functions at group centroids.

Subcommand Order

- The GROUPS, VARIABLES, and SELECT subcommands must precede all other subcommands and may be entered in any order.
- The analysis block follows, which may include ANALYSIS, METHOD, TOLERANCE, MAXSTEPS, FIN, FOUT, PIN, POUT, VIN, FUNCTIONS, PRIORS, and SAVE. Each analysis block performs a single analysis. To do multiple analyses, specify multiple analysis blocks.
- The keyword ANALYSIS is optional for the first analysis block. Each new analysis block must begin with an ANALYSIS subcommand. Remaining subcommands in the block may be used in any order and apply only to the analysis defined within the same block.
- No analysis block subcommands can be specified after any of the global subcommands, which apply to all analysis blocks. The global subcommands are MISSING, MATRIX, HISTORY, ROTATE, CLASSIFY, STATISTICS, and PLOT. If an analysis block subcommand appears after a global subcommand, the program displays a warning and ignores it.

Syntax Rules

- Only one GROUPS, one SELECT, and one VARIABLES subcommand can be specified per DISCRIMINANT command.

Operations

- DISCRIMINANT first estimates one or more discriminant functions that best distinguish among the groups.
- Using these functions, DISCRIMINANT then classifies cases into groups (if classification output is requested).
- If more than one analysis block is specified, the above steps are repeated for each block.

Limitations

- Pairwise deletion of missing data is not available.

Example

```
DISCRIMINANT GROUPS=OUTCOME (1,4)
  /VARIABLES=V1 TO V7
  /SAVE CLASS=PREDOUT
  /STATISTICS=COV GCOV TCOV.
```

- Only cases with values 1, 2, 3, or 4 for the grouping variable *GROUPS* will be used in computing the discriminant functions.
- The variables in the working data file between and including *V1* and *V7* will be used to compute the discriminant functions and to classify cases.
- Predicted group membership will be saved in the variable *PREDOUT*.
- In addition to the default output, the STATISTICS subcommand requests the pooled within-groups covariance matrix and the group and total covariance matrices.
- Since SAVE is specified, DISCRIMINANT also displays a classification processing summary table and a priori probabilities for groups table.

GROUPS Subcommand

GROUPS specifies the name of the grouping variable, which defines the categories or groups, and a range of categories.

- GROUPS is required and can be specified only once.
- The specification consists of a variable name followed by a range of values in parentheses.
- Only one grouping variable may be specified; its values must be integers. To use a string variable as the grouping variable, first use AUTORECODE to convert the string values to integers and then specify the recoded variable as the grouping variable.
- Empty groups are ignored and do not affect calculations. For example, if there are no cases in group 2, the value range (1, 5) will define only four groups.
- Cases with values outside the value range or missing are ignored during the analysis phase but are classified during the classification phase.

VARIABLES Subcommand

VARIABLES identifies the predictor variables, which are used to classify cases into the groups defined on the GROUPS subcommand. The list of variables follows the usual conventions for variable lists.

- VARIABLES is required and can be specified only once. Use the ANALYSIS subcommand to obtain multiple analyses.
- Only numeric variables can be used.

- Variables should be suitable for use in a regression-type equation, either measured at the interval level or dichotomous.

SELECT Subcommand

SELECT limits cases used in the analysis phase to those with a specified value for any one variable.

- Only one SELECT subcommand is allowed. It can follow the GROUPS and VARIABLES subcommands but must precede all other subcommands.
- The specification is a variable name and a single integer value in parentheses. Multiple variables or values are not permitted.
- The selection variable does not have to be specified on the VARIABLES subcommand.
- Only cases with the specified value for the selection variable are used in the analysis phase.
- All cases, whether selected or not, are classified by default. Use CLASSIFY=UNSELECTED to classify only the unselected cases.
- When SELECT is used, classification statistics are reported separately for selected and unselected cases, unless CLASSIFY=UNSELECTED is used to restrict classification.

Example

```
DISCRIMINANT GROUPS=APPROVAL(1,5)
  /VARS=Q1 TO Q10
  /SELECT=COMPLETE(1)
  /CLASSIFY=UNSELECTED.
```

- Using only cases with the value 1 for the variable *COMPLETE*, DISCRIMINANT estimates a function of *Q1* to *Q10* that discriminates between the categories 1 to 5 of the grouping variable *APPROVAL*.
- Because CLASSIFY=UNSELECTED is specified, the discriminant function will be used to classify only the unselected cases (cases for which *COMPLETE* does not equal 1).

ANALYSIS Subcommand

ANALYSIS is used to request several different discriminant analyses using the same grouping variable, or to control the order in which variables are entered into a stepwise analysis.

- ANALYSIS is optional for the first analysis block. By default, all variables specified on the VARIABLES subcommand are included in the analysis.
- The variables named on ANALYSIS must first be specified on the VARIABLES subcommand.
- The keyword ALL includes all variables on the VARIABLES subcommand.
- If the keyword TO is used to specify a list of variables on an ANALYSIS subcommand, it refers to the order of variables on the VARIABLES subcommand, which is not necessarily the order of variables in the working data file.

Example

```
DISCRIMINANT GROUPS=SUCCESS(0,1)
  /VARIABLES=V10 TO V15, AGE, V5
  /ANALYSIS=V15 TO V5
  /ANALYSIS=ALL.
```

- The first analysis will use the variables *V15*, *AGE*, and *V5* to discriminate between cases where *SUCCESS* equals 0 and *SUCCESS* equals 1.
- The second analysis will use all variables named on the VARIABLES subcommand.

Inclusion Levels

When you specify a stepwise method on the METHOD subcommand (any method other than the default direct-entry method), you can control the order in which variables are considered for entry or removal by specifying inclusion levels on the ANALYSIS subcommand. By default, all variables in the analysis are entered according to the criterion requested on the METHOD subcommand.

- An **inclusion level** is an integer between 0 and 99, specified in parentheses after a variable or list of variables on the ANALYSIS subcommand.
- The default inclusion level is 1.
- Variables with higher inclusion levels are considered for entry before variables with lower inclusion levels.
- Variables with even inclusion levels are entered as a group.
- Variables with odd inclusion levels are entered individually, according to the stepwise method specified on the METHOD subcommand.
- Only variables with an inclusion level of 1 are considered for removal. To make a variable with a higher inclusion level eligible for removal, name it twice on the ANALYSIS subcommand, first specifying the desired inclusion level and then an inclusion level of 1.
- Variables with an inclusion level of 0 are never entered. However, the statistical criterion for entry is computed and displayed.
- Variables that fail the tolerance criterion are not entered regardless of their inclusion level.

The following are some common methods of entering variables and the inclusion levels that could be used to achieve them. These examples assume that one of the stepwise methods is specified on the METHOD subcommand (otherwise, inclusion levels have no effect).

Direct. ANALYSIS=ALL(2) forces all variables into the equation. (This is the default and can be requested with METHOD=DIRECT or simply by omitting the METHOD subcommand.)

Stepwise. ANALYSIS=ALL(1) yields a stepwise solution in which variables are entered and removed in stepwise fashion. (This is the default when anything other than DIRECT is specified on the METHOD subcommand.)

Forward. ANALYSIS=ALL(3) enters variables into the equation stepwise but does not remove variables.

Backward. ANALYSIS=ALL(2) ALL(1) forces all variables into the equation and then allows them to be removed stepwise if they satisfy the criterion for removal.

Example

```
DISCRIMINANT GROUPS=SUCCESS(0,1)
  /VARIABLES=A, B, C, D, E
  /ANALYSIS=A TO C (2) D, E (1)
  /METHOD=WILKS.
```

- *A*, *B*, and *C* are entered into the analysis first, assuming that they pass the tolerance criterion. Since their inclusion level is even, they are entered together.
- *D* and *E* are then entered stepwise. The one that minimizes the overall value of Wilks' lambda is entered first.
- After entering *D* and *E*, the program checks whether the partial *F* for either one justifies removal from the equation (see the FOUT and POUT subcommands on p. 301).

Example

```
DISCRIMINANT GROUPS=SUCCESS(0,1)
  /VARIABLES=A, B, C, D, E
  /ANALYSIS=A TO C (2) D, E (1).
```

- Since no stepwise method is specified, inclusion levels have no effect and all variables are entered into the model at once.

METHOD Subcommand

METHOD is used to select a method for entering variables into an analysis.

- A variable will never be entered into the analysis if it does not pass the tolerance criterion specified on the TOLERANCE subcommand (or the default).
- A METHOD subcommand applies only to the *preceding* ANALYSIS subcommand, or to an analysis using all predictor variables if no ANALYSIS subcommand has been specified before it.
- If more than one METHOD subcommand is specified within one analysis block, the last is used.

Any one of the following methods can be specified on the METHOD subcommand:

DIRECT *All variables passing the tolerance criteria are entered simultaneously.* This is the default method.

WILKS *At each step, the variable that minimizes the overall Wilks' lambda is entered.*

MAHAL *At each step, the variable that maximizes the Mahalanobis distance between the two closest groups is entered.*

MAXMINF *At each step, the variable that maximizes the smallest* F *ratio between pairs of groups is entered.*

MINRESID *At each step, the variable that minimizes the sum of the unexplained variation for all pairs of groups is entered.*

RAO *At each step, the variable that produces the largest increase in Rao's* V *is entered.*

OUTFILE subcommand

OUTFILE writes model information to an XML file. *SmartScore* and future releases of *WhatIf?* will be able to use this file.

- The minimum specification is the keyword MODEL and a file name enclosed in parentheses.
- The OUTFILE subcommand cannot be used if split file processing is on (SPLIT FILE command).

TOLERANCE Subcommand

TOLERANCE specifies the minimum tolerance a variable can have and still be entered into the analysis. The tolerance of a variable that is a candidate for inclusion in the analysis is the proportion of its within-groups variance not accounted for by other variables in the analysis. A variable with very low tolerance is nearly a linear function of the other variables; its inclusion in the analysis would make the calculations unstable.

- The default tolerance is 0.001.
- You can specify any decimal value between 0 and 1 as the minimum tolerance.

PIN and POUT Subcommands

PIN specifies the minimum probability of *F* that a variable can have to enter the analysis and POUT specifies the maximum probability of *F* that a variable can have and not be removed from the model.

- PIN and POUT take precedence over FIN and FOUT. That is, if all are specified, PIN and POUT values are used.
- If PIN and POUT are omitted, FIN and FOUT are used by default.
- You can set PIN and POUT to any decimal value between 0 and 1. However, POUT should be greater than PIN if PIN is also specified.
- PIN and POUT apply only to the stepwise methods and are ignored if the METHOD subcommand is omitted or if DIRECT is specified on METHOD.

FIN and FOUT Subcommands

FIN specifies the minimum partial *F* value that a variable must have to enter the analysis. As additional variables are entered into the analysis, the partial *F* for variables already in the equation changes. FOUT specifies the smallest partial *F* that a variable can have and not be removed from the model.

- PIN and POUT take precedence over FIN and FOUT. That is, if all are specified, PIN and POUT values are used.
- If PIN and POUT are omitted, FIN and FOUT are used by default. If FOUT is specified but FIN is omitted, the default value for FIN is 3.84. If FIN is specified, the default value for FOUT is 2.71.
- You can set FIN and FOUT to any non-negative number. However, FOUT should be less than FIN if FIN is also specified.
- FIN and FOUT apply only to the stepwise methods and are ignored if the METHOD subcommand is omitted or if DIRECT is specified on METHOD.

VIN Subcommand

VIN specifies the minimum Rao's *V* that a variable must have to enter the analysis. When you use METHOD=RAO, variables satisfying one of the other criteria for entering the equation may actually cause a decrease in Rao's *V* for the equation. The default VIN prevents this but does not prevent the addition of variables that provide no additional separation between groups.

- You can specify any value for VIN. The default is 0.
- VIN should be used only when you have specified METHOD=RAO. Otherwise, it is ignored.

MAXSTEPS Subcommand

MAXSTEPS is used to decrease the maximum number of steps allowed. By default, the maximum number of steps allowed in a stepwise analysis is the number of variables with inclusion levels greater than 1 plus twice the number of variables with inclusion levels equal to 1. This is the maximum number of steps possible without producing a loop in which a variable is repeatedly cycled in and out.

- MAXSTEPS applies only to the stepwise methods (all except DIRECT).
- MAXSTEPS applies only to the preceding METHOD subcommand.
- The format is MAX=*n*, where *n* is the maximum number of steps desired.
- If multiple MAXSTEPS subcommands are specified, the last is used.

FUNCTIONS Subcommand

By default, DISCRIMINANT computes all possible functions. This is either the number of groups minus 1 or the number of predictor variables, whichever is less. Use FUNCTIONS to set more restrictive criteria for the extraction of functions.

FUNCTIONS has three parameters:

n_1 *Maximum number of functions.* The default is the number of groups minus 1 or the number of predictor variables, whichever is less.

n_2 *Cumulative percentage of the sum of the eigenvalues.* The default is 100.

n_3 *Significance level of function.* The default is 1.0.

- The parameters must always be specified in sequential order (n_1, n_2, n_3). To specify n_2, you must explicitly specify the default for n_1. Similarly, to specify n_3, you must specify the defaults for n_1 and n_2.
- If more than one restriction is specified, the program stops extracting functions when any one of the restrictions is met.
- When multiple FUNCTIONS subcommands are specified, the program uses the last; however, if n_2 or n_3 are omitted on the last FUNCTIONS subcommand, the corresponding specifications on the previous FUNCTIONS subcommands will remain in effect.

Example

```
DISCRIMINANT  GROUPS=CLASS(1,5)
  /VARIABLES = SCORE1 TO SCORE20
  /FUNCTIONS=4,100,.80.
```

- The first two parameters on the FUNCTIONS subcommand are defaults: the default for n_1 is 4 (the number of groups minus 1), and the default for n_2 is 100.
- The third parameter tells DISCRIMINANT to use fewer than four discriminant functions if the significance level of a function is greater than 0.80.

PRIORS Subcommand

By default, DISCRIMINANT assumes equal prior probabilities for groups when classifying cases. You can provide different prior probabilities with the PRIORS subcommand.

- Prior probabilities are used only during classification.
- If you provide unequal prior probabilities, DISCRIMINANT adjusts the classification coefficients to reflect this.
- If adjacent groups have the same prior probability, you can use the notation $n*c$ on the value list to indicate that n adjacent groups have the same prior probability c.
- You can specify a prior probability of 0. No cases are classified into such a group.
- If the sum of the prior probabilities is not 1, the program rescales the probabilities to sum to 1 and issues a warning.

EQUAL *Equal prior probabilities.* This is the default.

SIZE *Proportion of the cases analyzed that fall into each group.* If 50% of the cases included in the analysis fall into the first group, 25% in the second, and 25% in the third, the prior probabilities are 0.5, 0.25, and 0.25, respectively. Group size is determined after cases with missing values for the predictor variables are deleted.

Value list *User-specified prior probabilities.* The list of probabilities must sum to 1.0. The number of prior probabilities named or implied must equal the number of groups.

Example

```
DISCRIMINANT  GROUPS=TYPE(1,5)
  /VARIABLES=A TO H
  /PRIORS = 4*.15,.4.
```

- The PRIORS subcommand establishes prior probabilities of 0.15 for the first four groups and 0.4 for the fifth group.

SAVE Subcommand

SAVE allows you to save casewise information as new variables in the working data file.

- SAVE applies only to the current analysis block. To save casewise results from more than one analysis, specify a SAVE subcommand in each analysis block.
- You can specify a variable name for CLASS and rootnames for SCORES and PROBS to obtain descriptive names for the new variables.
- If you do not specify a variable name for CLASS, the program forms variable names using the formula *DSC_m*, where *m* increments to distinguish group membership variables saved on different SAVE subcommands for different analysis blocks.
- If you do not specify a rootname for SCORES or PROBS, the program forms new variable names using the formula *DSCn_m*, where *m* increments to create unique rootnames and *n* increments to create unique variable names. For example, the first set of default names assigned to discriminant scores or probabilities are *DSC1_1*, *DSC2_1*, *DSC3_1*, and so on. The next set of default names assigned will be *DSC1_2*, *DSC2_2*, *DSC3_2*, and so on, regardless of whether discriminant scores or probabilities are being saved or whether they are saved by the same SAVE subcommand.
- As *m* and/or *n* increase, the prefix *DSC* is truncated to keep variable names within eight characters. For example, *DS999_12* increases to *D1000_12*. The initial character *D* is required.
- The keywords CLASS, SCORES, and PROBS can be used in any order, but the new variables are always added to the end of the working data file in the following order: first the predicted group, then the discriminant scores, and finally probabilities of group membership.
- Appropriate variable labels are automatically generated. The labels describe whether the variables contain predictor group membership, discriminant scores, or probabilities, and for which analysis they are generated.
- The CLASS variable will use the value labels (if any) from the grouping variable specified for the analysis.
- When SAVE is specified with any keyword, DISCRIMINANT displays a classification processing summary table and a prior probabilities for groups table.
- You cannot use the SAVE subcommand if you are replacing the working data file with matrix materials (see "Matrix Output" on p. 309).

CLASS [(varname)] *Predicted group membership.*

SCORES [(rootname)] *Discriminant scores.* One score is saved for each discriminant function derived. If a rootname is specified, DISCRIMINANT will append a sequential number to the name to form new variable names for the discriminant scores.

PROBS [(rootname)] *For each case, the probabilities of membership in each group.* As many variables are added to each case as there are groups. If a rootname is specified, DISCRIMINANT will append a sequential number to the name to form new variable names.

Example

```
DISCRIMINANT GROUPS=WORLD(1,3)
 /VARIABLES=FOOD TO FSALES
 /SAVE CLASS=PRDCLASS SCORES=SCORE PROBS=PRB
 /ANALYSIS=FOOD SERVICE COOK MANAGER FSALES
 /SAVE CLASS SCORES PROBS.
```

- Two analyses are specified. The first uses all variables named on the VARIABLES subcommand and the second narrows down to five variables. For each analysis, a SAVE subcommand is specified.
- For each analysis, DISCRIMINANT displays a classification processing summary table and a prior probabilities for groups table.
- On the first SAVE subcommand, a variable name and two rootnames are provided. With three groups, the following variables are added to each case:

Name	Variable label	Description
PRDCLASS	Predicted group for analysis 1	Predicted group membership
SCORE1	Function 1 for analysis 1	Discriminant score for function 1
SCORE2	Function 2 for analysis 1	Discriminant score for function 2
PRB1	Probability 1 for analysis 1	Probability of being in group 1
PRB2	Probability 2 for analysis 1	Probability of being in group 2
PRB3	Probability 3 for analysis 1	Probability of being in group 3

- Since no variable name or rootnames are provided on the second SAVE subcommand, DISCRIMINANT uses default names. Note that *m* serves only to distinguish variables saved as a set and does not correspond to the sequential number of an analysis. To find out what information a new variable holds, read the variable label, as shown in the following table:

Name	Variable label	Description
DSC_1	Predicted group for analysis 2	Predicted group membership
DSC1_1	Function 1 for analysis 2	Discriminant score for function 1
DSC2_1	Function 2 for analysis 2	Discriminant score for function 2
DSC1_2	Probability 1 for analysis 2	Probability of being in group 1
DSC2_2	Probability 2 for analysis 2	Probability of being in group 2
DSC3_2	Probability 3 for analysis 2	Probability of being in group 3

STATISTICS Subcommand

By default, DISCRIMINANT produces the following statistics for each analysis: analysis case processing summary, valid numbers of cases in group statistics, variables failing tolerance test, a summary of canonical discriminant functions, standardized canonical discriminant function coefficients, a structure matrix showing pooled within-groups correlations between the discriminant functions and the predictor variables, and functions at group centroids.

- *Group statistics.* Only valid number of cases is reported.
- *Summary of canonical discriminant functions.* Displayed in two tables: an eigenvalues table with percentage of variance, cumulative percentage of variance, and canonical correlations and a Wilks' lambda table with Wilks' lambda, chi-square, degrees of freedom, and significance.
- *Stepwise statistics.* Wilks' lambda, equivalent *F*, degrees of freedom, significance of *F* and number of variables are reported for each step. Tolerance, *F*-to-remove, and the value of the statistic used for variable selection are reported for each variable in the equation. Tolerance, minimum tolerance, *F*-to-enter, and the value of the statistic used for variable selection are reported for each variable not in the equation. (These statistics can be suppressed with HISTORY=NONE.)
- *Final statistics.* Standardized canonical discriminant function coefficients, the structure matrix of discriminant functions and all variables named in the analysis (whether they were entered into the equation or not), and functions evaluated at group means are reported following the last step.

In addition, you can request optional statistics on the STATISTICS subcommand. STATISTICS can be specified by itself or with one or more keywords.

- STATISTICS without keywords displays MEAN, STDDEV, and UNIVF. If you include a keyword or keywords on STATISTICS, only the statistics you request are displayed.

MEAN *Means.* Total and group means for all variables named on the ANALYSIS subcommand are displayed.

STDDEV *Standard deviations.* Total and group standard deviations for all variables named on the ANALYSIS subcommand are displayed.

UNIVF *Univariate* F *ratios.* The analysis-of-variance *F* statistic for equality of group means for each predictor variable is displayed. This is a one-way analysis-of-variance test for equality of group means on a single discriminating variable.

COV *Pooled within-groups covariance matrix.*

CORR *Pooled within-groups correlation matrix.*

FPAIR *Matrix of pairwise* F *ratios.* The *F* ratio for each pair of groups is displayed. This *F* is the significance test for the Mahalanobis distance between groups. This statistic is available only with stepwise methods.

BOXM *Box's* M *test.* This is a test for equality of group covariance matrices.

GCOV *Group covariance matrices.*

TCOV *Total covariance matrix.*

RAW *Unstandardized canonical discriminant functions.*

COEFF *Classification function coefficients.* Although DISCRIMINANT does not directly use these coefficients to classify cases, you can use them to classify other samples (see the CLASSIFY subcommand below).

TABLE *Classification results.* If both selected and unselected cases are classified, the results are reported separately. To obtain cross-validated results for selected cases, specify CROSSVALID.

CROSSVALID *Cross-validated classification results.* The cross-validation is done by treating $n-1$ out of n observations as the training data set to determine the discrimination rule and using the rule to classify the one observation left out. The results are displayed only for selected cases.

ALL *All optional statistics.*

ROTATE Subcommand

The coefficient and correlation matrices can be rotated to facilitate interpretation of results. To control varimax rotation, use the ROTATE subcommand.

- Neither COEFF nor STRUCTURE affects the classification of cases.

COEFF *Rotate pattern matrix.* DISCRIMINANT displays a varimax transformation matrix, a rotated standardized canonical discriminant function coefficients table, and a correlations between variables and rotated functions table.

STRUCTURE *Rotate structure matrix.* DISCRIMINANT displays a varimax transformation matrix, a rotated structure matrix, and a rotated standardized canonical discriminant function coefficients table.

NONE *Do not rotate.* This is the default.

HISTORY Subcommand

HISTORY controls the display of stepwise and summary output.

- By default, HISTORY displays both the step-by-step output and the summary table (keyword STEP, alias END).

STEP *Display step-by-step and summary output.* Alias END. This is the default. See *Stepwise statistics* in "STATISTICS Subcommand" on p. 306.

NONE *Suppress the step-by-step and summary table.* Alias NOSTEP, NOEND.

CLASSIFY Subcommand

CLASSIFY determines how cases are handled during classification.

- By default, all cases with nonmissing values for all predictors are classified, and the pooled within-groups covariance matrix is used to classify cases.

- The default keywords for CLASSIFY are NONMISSING and POOLED.

NONMISSING *Classify all cases that do not have missing values on any predictor variables.* Two sets of classification results are produced, one for selected cases (those specified on the SELECT subcommand) and one for unselected cases. This is the default.

UNSELECTED *Classify only unselected cases.* The classification phase is suppressed for cases selected via the SELECT subcommand. If all cases are selected (when the SELECT subcommand is omitted), the classification phase is suppressed for all cases and no classification results are produced.

UNCLASSIFIED *Classify only unclassified cases.* The classification phase is suppressed for cases that fall within the range specified on the GROUPS subcommand.

POOLED *Use the pooled within-groups covariance matrix to classify cases.* This is the default.

SEPARATE *Use separate-groups covariance matrices of the discriminant functions for classification.* DISCRIMINANT displays the group covariances of canonical discriminant functions and Box's test of equality of covariance matrices of canonical discriminant functions. Since classification is based on the discriminant functions and not the original variables, this option is not necessarily equivalent to quadratic discrimination.

MEANSUB *Substitute means for missing predictor values during classification.* During classification, means are substituted for missing values and cases with missing values are classified. Cases with missing values are not used during analysis.

PLOT Subcommand

PLOT requests additional output to help you examine the effectiveness of the discriminant analysis.

- If PLOT is specified without keywords, the default is COMBINED and CASES.
- If any keywords are requested on PLOT, only the requested plots are displayed.
- If PLOT is specified with any keyword except MAP, DISCRIMINANT displays a classification processing summary table and a prior probabilities for groups table.

COMBINED *All-groups plot.* For each case, the first two function values are plotted.

CASES(n) *Casewise statistics.* For each case, classification information, squared Mahalanobis distance to centroid for the highest and second highest groups, and discriminant scores of all functions are plotted. Validated statistics are displayed for selected cases if CROSSVALID is specified on STATISTICS. If *n* is specified, DISCRIMINANT displays the first *n* cases only.

MAP *Territorial map.* A plot of group centroids and boundaries used for classifying groups.

SEPARATE *Separate-groups plots.* These are the same types of plots produced by the keyword COMBINED, except that a separate plot is produced for each group. If only one function is used, a histogram is displayed.

ALL *All available plots.*

MISSING Subcommand

MISSING controls the treatment of cases with missing values in the analysis phase. By default, cases with missing values for any variable named on the VARIABLES subcommand are not used in the analysis phase but are used in classification.

- The keyword INCLUDE includes cases with user-missing values in the analysis phase.
- Cases with missing or out-of-range values for the grouping variable are always excluded.

EXCLUDE *Exclude all cases with missing values.* Cases with user- or system-missing values are excluded from the analysis. This is the default.

INCLUDE *Include cases with user-missing values.* User-missing values are treated as valid values. Only the system-missing value is treated as missing.

MATRIX Subcommand

MATRIX reads and writes SPSS-format matrix data files.

- Either IN or OUT and the matrix file in parentheses are required. When both IN and OUT are used in the same DISCRIMINANT procedure, they can be specified on separate MATRIX subcommands or on the same subcommand.

OUT (filename) *Write a matrix data file.* Specify either a filename or an asterisk in parentheses (*). If you specify a filename, the file is stored on disk and can be retrieved at any time. If you specify an asterisk (*), the matrix data file replaces the working data file but is not stored on disk unless you use SAVE or XSAVE.

IN (filename) *Read a matrix data file.* If the matrix data file is the working data file, specify an asterisk (*) in parentheses. If the matrix file is another file, specify the filename in parentheses. A matrix file read from an external file does not replace the working data file.

Matrix Output

- In addition to Pearson correlation coefficients, the matrix materials written by DISCRIMINANT include weighted and unweighted numbers of cases, means, and standard deviations. (See "Format of the Matrix Data File" on p. 310 for a description of the file.) These materials can be used in subsequent DISCRIMINANT procedures.
- Any documents contained in the working data file are not transferred to the matrix file.
- If BOXM or GCOV is specified on the STATISTICS subcommand or SEPARATE is specified on the CLASSIFY subcommand when a matrix file is written, the *STDDEV* and *CORR* records in the matrix materials represent within-cell data, and separate covariance

matrices are written to the file. When the matrix file is used as input for a subsequent DISCRIMINANT procedure, at least one of these specifications must be used on that DISCRIMINANT command.

Matrix Input

- DISCRIMINANT can read correlation matrices written by a previous DISCRIMINANT command or by other procedures. Matrix materials read by DISCRIMINANT must contain records with *ROWTYPE_* values *MEAN*, *N* or *COUNT* (or both), *STDDEV*, and *CORR*.
- If the data do not include records with *ROWTYPE_* value *COUNT* (unweighted number of cases), DISCRIMINANT uses information from records with *ROWTYPE_* value *N* (weighted number of cases). Conversely, if the data do not have *N* values, DISCRIMINANT uses the *COUNT* values. These records can appear in any order in the matrix input file with the following exceptions: the order of split-file groups cannot be violated and all *CORR* vectors must appear consecutively within each split-file group.
- If you want to use a covariance-type matrix as input to DISCRIMINANT, you must first use the MCONVERT command to change the covariance matrix to a correlation matrix.
- DISCRIMINANT can use a matrix from a previous data set to classify data in the working data file. The program checks to make sure that the grouping variable (specified on GROUPS) and the predictor variables (specified on VARIABLES) are the same in the working data file as in the matrix file. If they are not, the program displays an error message and the classification will not be executed.
- MATRIX=IN cannot be used unless a working data file has already been defined. To read an existing matrix data file at the beginning of a session, first use GET to retrieve the matrix file and then specify IN(*) on MATRIX.

Format of the Matrix Data File

- The matrix data file has two special variables created by the program: *ROWTYPE_* and *VARNAME_*. Variable *ROWTYPE_* is a short string variable having values *N*, *COUNT*, *MEAN*, *STDDEV*, and *CORR* (for Pearson correlation coefficient). The variable *VARNAME_* is a short string variable whose values are the names of the variables used to form the correlation matrix.
- When *ROWTYPE_* is *CORR*, *VARNAME_* gives the variable associated with that row of the correlation matrix.
- Between *ROWTYPE_* and *VARNAME_* is the grouping variable, which is specified on the GROUPS subcommand of DISCRIMINANT.
- The remaining variables are the variables used to form the correlation matrix.

Split Files

- When split-file processing is in effect, the first variables in the matrix data file will be split variables, followed by *ROWTYPE_*, the grouping variable, *VARNAME_*, and then the variables used to form the correlation matrix.

- A full set of matrix materials is written for each subgroup defined by the split variables.
- A split variable cannot have the same variable name as any other variable written to the matrix data file.
- If split-file processing is in effect when a matrix is written, the same split file must be in effect when that matrix is read by another procedure.

STDDEV and CORR Records

Records written with *ROWTYPE_* values *STDDEV* and *CORR* are influenced by specifications on the STATISTICS and CLASSIFY subcommands.

- If BOXM or GCOV is specified on STATISTICS or SEPARATE is specified on CLASSIFY, the *STDDEV* and *CORR* records represent within-cell data and receive values for the grouping variable.
- If none of the above specifications is in effect, the *STDDEV* and *CORR* records represent pooled values. The *STDDEV* vector contains the square root of the mean square error for each variable, and *STDDEV* and *CORR* records receive the system-missing value for the grouping variable.

Missing Values

Missing-value treatment affects the values written to a matrix data file. When reading a matrix data file, be sure to specify a missing-value treatment on DISCRIMINANT that is compatible with the treatment that was in effect when the matrix materials were generated.

Example

```
GET FILE=UNIONBK /KEEP WORLD FOOD SERVICE BUS MECHANIC
                  CONSTRUC COOK MANAGER FSALES APPL RENT.
DISCRIMINANT  GROUPS=WORLD(1,3)
 /VARIABLES=FOOD SERVICE BUS MECHANIC CONSTRUC COOK MANAGER FSALES
 /METHOD=WILKS
 /PRIORS=SIZE
 /MATRIX=OUT(DISCMTX).
```

- DISCRIMINANT reads data from the SPSS-format data file *UNIONBK* and writes one set of matrix materials to the file *DISCMTX*.
- The working data file is still *UNIONBK*. Subsequent commands are executed on this file.

Example

```
* Use matrix output to classify data in a different file.

GET FILE=UB2 /KEEP WORLD FOOD SERVICE BUS MECHANIC
              CONSTRUC COOK MANAGER FSALES APPL RENT.
DISCRIMINANT  GROUPS=WORLD(1,3)
 /VARIABLES=FOOD SERVICE BUS MECHANIC CONSTRUC COOK MANAGER FSALES
 /METHOD=WILKS
 /PRIORS=SIZE
 /MATRIX=IN(DISCMTX).
```

- The matrix data file created in the previous example is used to classify data from the file *UB2*.

Example

```
GET FILE=UNIONBK /KEEP WORLD FOOD SERVICE BUS MECHANIC
                  CONSTRUC COOK MANAGER FSALES APPL RENT.
DISCRIMINANT  GROUPS=WORLD(1,3)
 /VARIABLES=FOOD SERVICE BUS MECHANIC CONSTRUC COOK MANAGER FSALES
 /METHOD=WILKS
 /PRIORS=SIZE
 /MATRIX=OUT(*).
LIST.
```

- DISCRIMINANT writes the same matrix as in the first example. However, the matrix data file replaces the working data file.
- The LIST command is executed on the matrix file, not on the *UNIONBK* file.

Example

```
GET FILE=DISCMTX.
DISCRIMINANT  GROUPS=WORLD(1,3)
 /VARIABLES=FOOD SERVICE BUS MECHANIC CONSTRUC COOK MANAGER FSALES
 /METHOD=RAO
 /MATRIX=IN(*).
```

- This example assumes that you are starting a new session and want to read an existing matrix data file. GET retrieves the matrix data file *DISCMTX*.
- MATRIX=IN specifies an asterisk because the matrix data file is the working data file. If MATRIX=IN(DISCMTX) is specified, the program issues an error message.
- If the GET command is omitted, the program issues an error message.

Example

```
GET FILE=UNIONBK /KEEP WORLD FOOD SERVICE BUS MECHANIC
                  CONSTRUC COOK MANAGER FSALES APPL RENT.
DISCRIMINANT  GROUPS=WORLD(1,3)
 /VARIABLES=FOOD SERVICE BUS MECHANIC CONSTRUC COOK MANAGER FSALES
 /CLASSIFY=SEPARATE
 /MATRIX=OUT(*).
DISCRIMINANT  GROUPS=WORLD(1,3)
 /VARIABLES=FOOD SERVICE BUS MECHANIC CONSTRUC COOK MANAGER FSALES
 /STATISTICS=BOXM
 /MATRIX=IN(*).
```

- The first DISCRIMINANT command creates a matrix with CLASSIFY=SEPARATE in effect. To read this matrix, the second DISCRIMINANT command must specify either BOXM or GCOV on STATISTICS or SEPARATE on CLASSIFY. STATISTICS=BOXM is used.

DISPLAY

```
DISPLAY [SORTED] [{NAMES**     }] [/VARIABLES=varlist]
                  {INDEX       }
                  {VARIABLES   }
                  {LABELS      }
                  {DICTIONARY  }

         { [SCRATCH]   }
         { [VECTOR]    }
         { [MACROS]    }
         { [DOCUMENTS] }
```

**Default if the subcommand is omitted.

Example

```
DISPLAY SORTED DICTIONARY /VARIABLES=DEPT SALARY SEX TO JOBCAT.
```

Overview

DISPLAY exhibits information from the dictionary of the working data file. The information can be sorted, and it can be limited to selected variables.

Basic Specification

The basic specification is simply the command keyword, which displays an unsorted list of the variables in the working data file.

Syntax Rules

DISPLAY can be specified by itself or with one of the keywords defined below. NAMES is the default. To specify two or more keywords, use multiple DISPLAY commands.

NAMES *Variable names.* A list of the variables in the working data file is displayed. The names are not sorted and display in a compressed format, about eight names across the page. This is the default.

DOCUMENTS *Documentary text.* Documentary text is provided on the DOCUMENT command. No error message is issued if there is no documentary information in the working data file.

DICTIONARY *Complete dictionary information for variables.* Information includes variable names, labels, sequential position of each variable in the file, print and write formats, missing values, and value labels. Up to 60 characters can be displayed for variable and value labels.

INDEX *Variable names and positions.*

VARIABLES *Variable names, positions, print and write formats, and missing values.*

LABELS *Variable names, positions, and variable labels.*

SCRATCH *Scratch variable names.*

VECTOR *Vector names.*

MACROS *Currently defined macros.* The macro names are always sorted.

Operations

- DISPLAY directs information to the output.
- If SORTED is not specified, information is displayed according to the order of variables in the working data file.
- DISPLAY is executed as soon as it is encountered in the command sequence, as long as a dictionary has been defined.

Example

```
GET FILE=HUB.
DISPLAY DOCUMENTS.
DISPLAY DICTIONARY.
```

- Each DISPLAY command specifies only one keyword. The first requests documentary text and the second requests complete dictionary information for the *HUB* file.

SORTED Keyword

SORTED alphabetizes the display by variable name. SORTED can precede the keywords NAMES, DICTIONARY, INDEX, VARIABLES, LABELS, SCRATCH, or VECTOR.

Example

```
DISPLAY SORTED DICTIONARY.
```

- This command displays complete dictionary information for variables in the working data file, sorted alphabetically by variable name.

VARIABLES Subcommand

VARIABLES (alias NAMES) limits the displayed information to a set of specified variables. VARIABLES must be the last specification on DISPLAY and can follow any specification that requests information about variables (all except VECTOR, SCRATCH, DOCUMENTS, and MACROS).

- The only specification is a slash followed by a list of variables. The slash is optional.

- If the keyword SORTED is not specified, information is displayed in the order in which variables are stored in the working data file, regardless of the order in which variables are named on VARIABLES.

Example

```
DISPLAY SORTED DICTIONARY
 /VARIABLES=DEPT, SALARY, SEX TO JOBCAT.
```

- DISPLAY exhibits dictionary information only for the variables named and implied by the keyword TO on the VARIABLES subcommand, sorted alphabetically by variable name.

DOCUMENT

```
DOCUMENT text
```

Example

```
DOCUMENT    This file contains a subset of variables from the
            General Social Survey data.  For each case it records
            only the age, sex, education level, marital status,
            number of children, and type of medical insurance
            coverage.
```

Overview

DOCUMENT saves a block of text of any length in an SPSS-format data file. The documentation can be displayed with the DISPLAY command.

When GET retrieves a data file, or when ADD FILES, MATCH FILES, or UPDATE is used to combine data files, all documents from each specified file are copied into the working file. DROP DOCUMENTS can be used to drop those documents from the working file. Whether or not DROP DOCUMENTS is used, new documents can be added to the working file with the DOCUMENT command.

Basic Specification

The basic specification is DOCUMENT followed by any length of text. The text is stored in the file dictionary when the data are saved in an SPSS-format data file.

Syntax Rules

- The text can be entered on as many lines as needed.
- Blank lines can be used to separate paragraphs.
- A period at the end of a line terminates the command, so you should not place a period at the end of any line but the last.
- Multiple DOCUMENT commands can be used within the command sequence. However, the DISPLAY command cannot be used to exhibit the text from a particular DOCUMENT command. DISPLAY shows all existing documentation.

Operations

- The documentation and the date it was entered are saved in the data file's dictionary. New documentation is saved along with any documentation already in the working data file.

- If a DROP DOCUMENTS command *follows* a DOCUMENT command anywhere in the command sequence, the documentation added by that DOCUMENT command is dropped from the working file along with all other documentation.

Example

```
GET FILE=GENSOC /KEEP=AGE SEX EDUC MARITAL CHILDRN MED_INS.
FILE LABEL  General Social Survey subset.

DOCUMENT    This file contains a subset of variables from the
            General Social Survey data.  For each case it records
            only the age, sex, education level, marital status,
            number of children, and type of medical insurance
            coverage.

SAVE OUTFILE=SUBSOC.
```

- GET keeps only a subset of variables from the file *GENSOC*. All documentation from the file *GENSOC* is copied into the working file.
- FILE LABEL creates a label for the new working file.
- DOCUMENT specifies the new document text. Both existing documents from the file *GENSOC* and the new document text are saved in the file *SUBSOC*.

Example

```
GET FILE=GENSOC /KEEP=AGE SEX EDUC MARITAL CHILDRN MED_INS.

DROP DOCUMENTS.

FILE LABEL  General Social Survey subset.

DOCUMENT    This file contains a subset of variables from the
            General Social Survey data.  For each case it records
            only the age, sex, education level, marital status,
            number of children, and type of medical insurance
            coverage.

SAVE OUTFILE=SUBSOC.
```

- DROP DOCUMENTS drops the documentation from the file *GENSOC* as data are copied into the working file. Only the new documentation specified on DOCUMENT is saved in the file *SUBSOC*.

DO IF

```
DO IF [(]logical expression[)]
transformation commands
[ELSE IF [(]logical expression[)]]
transformation commands
[ELSE IF [(]logical expression[)]]
   .
   .
   .
[ELSE]
transformation commands
END IF
```

The following relational operators can be used in logical expressions:

Symbol	Definition	Symbol	Definition
EQ or =	Equal to	NE or <>*	Not equal to
LT or <	Less than	LE or <=	Less than or equal to
GT or >	Greater than	GE or >=	Greater than or equal to

* On ASCII systems (for example, UNIX, VAX, and all PC's), you can also use ~=; on IBM EBCDIC systems (for example, IBM 360 and IBM 370), you can also use ¬=.

The following logical operators can be used in logical expressions:

Symbol	Definition
AND or &	Both relations must be true
OR or |	Either relation can be true
NOT*	Reverses the outcome of an expression

* On ASCII systems, you can also use ~; on IBM EBCDIC systems, you can also use ¬ (or the symbol above number 6).

Example

```
DO IF (YRHIRED GT 87).
COMPUTE             BONUS = 0.
ELSE IF (DEPT87 EQ 3).
COMPUTE             BONUS = .1*SALARY87.
ELSE IF (DEPT87 EQ 1).
COMPUTE             BONUS = .12*SALARY87.
ELSE IF (DEPT87 EQ 4).
COMPUTE             BONUS = .08*SALARY87.
ELSE IF (DEPT87 EQ 2).
COMPUTE             BONUS = .14*SALARY87.
END IF.
```

Overview

The DO IF—END IF structure conditionally executes one or more transformations on subsets of cases based on one or more logical expressions. The ELSE command can be used within the structure to execute one or more transformations when the logical expression on DO IF is not true. The ELSE IF command within the structure provides further control.

The DO IF—END IF structure is best used for conditionally executing multiple transformation commands, such as COMPUTE, RECODE, and COUNT. IF is more efficient for executing a single conditional COMPUTE-like transformation. DO IF—END IF transforms data for subsets of cases defined by logical expressions. To perform repeated transformations on the same case, use LOOP—END LOOP.

A DO IF—END IF structure can be used within an input program to define complex files that cannot be handled by standard file definition facilities. See "Complex File Structures" on p. 326 for an example.

See END FILE for information on using DO IF—END IF to instruct the program to stop reading data before it encounters the end of the file or to signal the end of the file when creating data. See p. 252 for an example of using DO IF—END IF with END FILE to concatenate raw data files.

Basic Specification

The basic specification is DO IF followed by a logical expression, a transformation command, and the END IF command, which has no specifications.

Syntax Rules

- The ELSE IF command is optional and can be repeated as many times as needed.
- The ELSE command is optional. It can be used only once and must follow any ELSE IF commands.
- The END IF command must follow any ELSE IF and ELSE commands.
- A logical expression must be specified on the DO IF and ELSE IF commands. Logical expressions are not used on the ELSE and END IF commands.
- String values used in expressions must be specified in quotation marks and must include any leading or trailing blanks. Lowercase letters are distinguished from uppercase letters.
- To create a new string variable within a DO IF—END IF structure, you must first declare the variable on the STRING command.
- DO IF—END IF structures can be nested to any level permitted by available memory. They can be nested within LOOP—END LOOP structures, and loop structures can be nested within DO IF structures.

Logical Expressions

- Logical expressions can be simple logical variables or relations, or they can be complex logical tests involving variables, constants, functions, relational operators, and logical operators. Logical expressions can use any of the numeric or string functions allowed in COMPUTE transformations (see COMPUTE).

- Parentheses can be used to enclose the logical expression itself and to specify the order of operations within a logical expression. Extra blanks or parentheses can be used to make the expression easier to read.
- Blanks (*not* commas) are used to separate relational operators from expressions.
- A relation can include variables, constants, or more complicated arithmetic expressions. Relations cannot be abbreviated. For example, the first relation below is valid; the second is not:

  Valid: `(A EQ 2 OR A EQ 5)`
  Not valid: `(A EQ 2 OR 5)`

- A relation cannot compare a string variable to a numeric value or variable, or vice versa. A relation cannot compare the result of a logical function (SYSMIS, MISSING, ANY, or RANGE) to a number.

Operations

- DO IF marks the beginning of the control structure and END IF marks the end. Control for a case is passed out of the structure as soon as a logical condition is met on a DO IF, ELSE IF, or ELSE command.
- A logical expression is evaluated as true, false, or missing. A transformation specified for a logical expression is executed only if the expression is true.
- Logical expressions are evaluated in the following order: functions, exponentiation, arithmetic operations, relations, and finally, logical operators. (For strings, the order is functions, relations, and then logical operators.) When more than one logical operator is used, NOT is evaluated first, followed by AND and then OR. You can change the order of operations using parentheses.
- Numeric variables created within a DO IF structure are initially set to the system-missing value. By default, they are assigned an F8.2 format.
- New string variables created within a DO IF structure are initially set to a blank value and are assigned the format specified on the STRING command that creates them.
- If the transformed value of a string variable exceeds the variable's defined format, the value is truncated. If the value is shorter than the format, the value is right-padded with blanks.
- If WEIGHT is specified within a DO IF structure, it takes effect unconditionally.
- Commands like SET, DISPLAY, SHOW, and so forth specified within a DO IF structure are executed when they are encountered in the command file.
- The DO IF—END IF structure (like LOOP—END LOOP) can include commands such as DATA LIST, END CASE, END FILE, and REREAD, which define complex file structures.

Flow of Control

- If the logical expression on DO IF is true, the commands immediately following DO IF are executed up to the next ELSE IF, ELSE, or END IF command. Control then passes to the first statement following END IF.
- If the expression on DO IF is false, control passes to the following ELSE IF command. Multiple ELSE IF commands are evaluated in the order in which they are specified until the logical expression on one of them is true. Commands following that ELSE IF command are executed up to the ELSE or END IF command, and control passes to the first statement following END IF.
- If none of the expressions are true on the DO IF or any of the ELSE IF commands, the commands following ELSE are executed and control passes out of the structure. If there is no ELSE command, a case goes through the entire structure with no change.
- Missing values returned by the logical expression on DO IF or on any ELSE IF cause control to pass to the END IF command at that point.

Missing Values and Logical Operators

When two or more relations are joined by logical operators AND and OR, the program always returns missing if all of the relations in the expression are missing. However, if any one of the relations can be determined, the program tries to return true or false according to the logical outcomes shown in Table 1. The asterisk indicates situations where the program can evaluate the outcome with incomplete information.

Table 1 Logical outcome

Expression	Outcome	Expression	Outcome
true AND true	= true	true OR true	= true
true AND false	= false	true OR false	= true
false AND false	= false	false OR false	= false
true AND missing	= missing	true OR missing	= true*
missing AND missing	= missing	missing OR missing	= missing
false AND missing	= false*	false OR missing	= missing

Example

```
DO IF (YRHIRED LT 87).
RECODE RACE(1=5)(2=4)(4=2)(5=1).
END IF.
```

- The RECODE command recodes *RACE* for those individuals hired before 1987 (*YRHIRED* is less than 87). The *RACE* variable is not recoded for individuals hired in 1987 or later.
- The RECODE command is skipped for any case with a missing value for *YRHIRED*.

Example

```
DATA LIST      FREE / X(F1).
NUMERIC        #QINIT.
DO IF          NOT #QINIT.
+  PRINT EJECT.
+  COMPUTE        #QINIT = 1.
END IF.
PRINT          / X.

BEGIN DATA
1 2 3 4 5
END DATA.
EXECUTE.
```

- This example shows how to execute a command only once.
- The NUMERIC command creates scratch variable *#QINIT*, which is initialized to 0.
- The NOT logical operator on DO IF reverses the outcome of a logical expression. In this example, the logical expression is a numeric variable that takes only 0 (false) or 1 (true) as its values. The PRINT EJECT command is executed only once, when the value of scratch variable *#QINIT* equals 0. After the COMPUTE command sets *#QINIT* to 1, the DO IF structure is skipped for all subsequent cases. A scratch variable is used because it is initialized to 0 and is not reinitialized after each case.

ELSE Command

ELSE executes one or more transformations when none of the logical expressions on DO IF or any ELSE IF commands is true.

- Only one ELSE command is allowed within a DO IF—END IF structure.
- ELSE must follow all ELSE IF commands (if any) in the structure.
- If the logical expression on DO IF or any ELSE IF command is true, the program ignores the commands following ELSE.

Example

```
DO IF (X EQ 0).
COMPUTE Y=1.
ELSE.
COMPUTE Y=2.
END IF.
```

- *Y* is set to 1 for all cases with value 0 for *X*, and *Y* is 2 for all cases with any other valid value for *X*.
- The value of *Y* is not changed by this structure if *X* is missing.

Example

```
DO IF (YRHIRED GT 87).
COMPUTE             BONUS = 0.
ELSE.
IF (DEPT87 EQ 1) BONUS = .12*SALARY87.
IF (DEPT87 EQ 2) BONUS = .14*SALARY87.
IF (DEPT87 EQ 3) BONUS = .1*SALARY87.
IF (DEPT87 EQ 4) BONUS = .08*SALARY87.
END IF.
```

- If an individual was hired after 1987 (*YRHIRED* is greater than 87), *BONUS* is set to 0 and control passes out of the structure. Otherwise, control passes to the IF commands following ELSE.
- Each IF command evaluates every case. The value of *BONUS* is transformed only when the case meets the criteria specified on IF. Compare this structure with ELSE IF in the second example on p. 325, which performs the same task more efficiently.

Example

```
* Test for listwise deletion of missing values.

DATA LIST / V1 TO V6 1-6.
BEGIN DATA
123456
    56
1 3456
123456
123456
END DATA.

DO IF NMISS(V1 TO V6)=0.
+  COMPUTE SELECT='V'.
ELSE
+  COMPUTE SELECT='M'.
END IF.

FREQUENCIES VAR=SELECT.
```

- If there are no missing values for any of the variables *V1* to *V6*, COMPUTE sets the value of *SELECT* equal to V (for valid). Otherwise, COMPUTE sets the value of *SELECT* equal to M (for missing).
- FREQUENCIES generates a frequency table for *SELECT*. The table gives a count of how many cases have missing values for one or more variables, and how many cases have valid values for all variables. Commands in this example can be used to determine how many cases are dropped from an analysis that uses listwise deletion of missing values. See pp. 189 and 548 for alternative ways to check listwise deletion of missing values.

ELSE IF Command

ELSE IF executes one or more transformations when the logical expression on DO IF is not true.

- Multiple ELSE IF commands are allowed within the DO IF—END IF structure.

- If the logical expression on DO IF is true, the program executes the commands immediately following DO IF up to the first ELSE IF. Then control passes to the command following the END IF command.
- If the result of the logical expression on DO IF is false, control passes to ELSE IF.

Example

```
STRING STOCK(A9).
DO IF (ITEM EQ 0).
COMPUTE STOCK='New'.
ELSE IF (ITEM LE 9).
COMPUTE STOCK='Old'.
ELSE.
COMPUTE STOCK='Cancelled'.
END IF.
```

- STRING declares string variable *STOCK* and assigns it a width of nine characters.
- The first COMPUTE is executed for cases with value 0 for *ITEM*, and then control passes out of the structure. Such cases are not reevaluated by ELSE IF, even though 0 is less than 9.
- When the logical expression on DO IF is false, control passes to the ELSE IF command, where the second COMPUTE is executed only for cases with *ITEM* less than or equal to 9. Then control passes out of the structure.
- If the logical expressions on both the DO IF and ELSE IF commands are false, control passes to ELSE, where the third COMPUTE is executed.
- The DO IF—END IF structure sets *STOCK* equal to New when *ITEM* equals 0, to Old when *ITEM* is less than or equal to 9 but not equal to 0 (including negative numbers if they are valid), and to Cancelled for all valid values of *ITEM* greater than 9. The value of *STOCK* remains blank if *ITEM* is missing.

Example

```
DO IF (YRHIRED GT 87).
COMPUTE                BONUS = 0.
ELSE IF (DEPT87 EQ 3).
COMPUTE                BONUS = .1*SALARY87.
ELSE IF (DEPT87 EQ 1).
COMPUTE                BONUS = .12*SALARY87.
ELSE IF (DEPT87 EQ 4).
COMPUTE                BONUS = .08*SALARY87.
ELSE IF (DEPT87 EQ 2).
COMPUTE                BONUS = .14*SALARY87.
END IF.
```

- For cases hired after 1987, *BONUS* is set to 0 and control passes out of the structure. For a case that was hired before 1987 with value 3 for *DEPT87*, *BONUS* equals 10% of salary. Control then passes out of the structure. The other three ELSE IF commands are not evaluated for that case. This differs from the example on p. 324, where the IF command is evaluated for every case. The DO IF—ELSE IF structure shown here is more efficient.
- If Department 3 is the largest, Department 1 the next largest, and so forth, control passes out of the structure quickly for many cases. For a large number of cases or a command file that will be executed frequently, these efficiency considerations can be important.

Nested DO IF Structures

To perform transformations involving logical tests on two variables, you can use nested DO IF—END IF structures.

- There must be an END IF command for every DO IF command in the structure.

Example

```
DO IF (RACE EQ 5).              /*Do whites
+  DO IF (SEX EQ 2).            /*White female
+  COMPUTE SEXRACE=3.
+  ELSE.                        /*White male
+  COMPUTE SEXRACE=1.
+  END IF.                      /*Whites done
ELSE IF (SEX EQ 2).             /*Nonwhite female
COMPUTE SEXRACE=4.
ELSE.                           /*Nonwhite male
COMPUTE SEXRACE=2.
END IF.                         /*Nonwhites done
```

- This structure creates variable *SEXRACE*, which indicates both the sex and minority status of an individual.
- An optional plus sign, minus sign, or period in the first column allows you to indent commands so you can easily see the nested structures.

Complex File Structures

Some complex file structures may require you to imbed more than one DATA LIST command inside a DO IF—END IF structure. For example, consider a data file that has been collected from various sources. The information from each source is basically the same, but it is in different places on the records:

```
111295100FORD      CHAPMAN AUTO SALES
121199005VW    MIDWEST VOLKSWAGEN SALES
11 395025FORD      BETTER USED CARS
11       CHEVY 195005        HUFFMAN SALES & SERVICE
11       VW    595020        MIDWEST VOLKSWAGEN SALES
11       CHEVY 295015        SAM'S AUTO REPAIR
12       CHEVY 210 20        LONGFELLOW CHEVROLET
 9555032 VW                  HYDE PARK IMPORTS
```

In the above file, an automobile part number always appears in columns 1 and 2, and the automobile manufacturer always appears in columns 10 through 14. The location of other information, such as price and quantity, depends on both the part number and the type of automobile. The DO IF—END IF structure in the following example reads records for part type 11.

Example

```
INPUT PROGRAM.
DATA LIST FILE=CARPARTS /PARTNO 1-2 KIND 10-14 (A).

DO IF (PARTNO EQ 11 AND KIND EQ 'FORD').
+ REREAD.
+ DATA LIST /PRICE 3-6 (2) QUANTITY 7-9 BUYER 20-43 (A).
+ END CASE.

ELSE IF (PARTNO EQ 11 AND (KIND EQ 'CHEVY' OR KIND EQ 'VW')).
+ REREAD.
+ DATA LIST /PRICE 15-18 (2) QUANTITY 19-21 BUYER 30-53 (A).
+ END CASE.
END IF.
END INPUT PROGRAM.

PRINT FORMATS PRICE (DOLLAR6.2).
PRINT /PARTNO TO BUYER.
WEIGHT BY QUANTITY.
DESCRIPTIVES PRICE.
```

- The first DATA LIST extracts the part number and the type of automobile.
- Depending on the information from the first DATA LIST, the records are reread, pulling the price, quantity, and buyer from different places.
- The two END CASE commands limit the working file to only those cases with Part 11 and automobile type Ford, Chevrolet, or Volkswagen. Without the END CASE commands, cases would be created in the working file for other part numbers and automobile types with missing values for price, quantity, and buyer.
- The results of the PRINT command are shown in Figure 1.

Figure 1 Printed information for part 11

```
11 FORD  $12.95 100 CHAPMAN AUTO SALES
11 FORD   $3.95  25 BETTER USED CARS
11 CHEVY  $1.95   5 HUFFMAN SALES & SERVICE
11 VW     $5.95  20 MIDWEST VOLKSWAGEN SALES
11 CHEVY  $2.95  15 SAM'S AUTO REPAIR
```

DO REPEAT—END REPEAT

```
DO REPEAT stand-in var={varlist    } [/stand-in var=...]
                       {value list}

transformation commands

END REPEAT [PRINT]
```

Example

```
DO REPEAT R=REGION1 TO REGION5.
COMPUTE R=0.
END REPEAT.
```

Overview

The DO REPEAT—END REPEAT structure repeats the same transformations on a specified set of variables, reducing the number of commands you must enter to accomplish a task. This utility does not reduce the number of commands the program executes, just the number of commands you enter. To display the expanded set of commands the program generates, specify PRINT on END REPEAT.

DO REPEAT uses a *stand-in variable* to represent a *replacement list* of variables or values. The stand-in variable is specified as a place holder on one or more transformation commands within the structure. When the program repeats the transformation commands, the stand-in variable is replaced, in turn, by each variable or value specified on the replacement list.

The following commands can be used within a DO REPEAT—END REPEAT structure:

- Data transformations: COMPUTE, RECODE, IF, COUNT, and SELECT IF
- Data declarations: VECTOR, STRING, NUMERIC, and LEAVE
- Data definition: DATA LIST, MISSING VALUES (but not VARIABLE LABELS or VALUE LABELS)
- Loop structure commands: LOOP, END LOOP, and BREAK
- Do-if structure commands: DO IF, ELSE IF, ELSE, and END IF
- Print and write commands: PRINT, PRINT EJECT, PRINT SPACE, and WRITE
- Format commands: PRINT FORMATS, WRITE FORMATS, and FORMATS

Basic Specification

The basic specification is DO REPEAT, a stand-in variable followed by a required equals sign and a replacement list of variables or values, and at least one transformation command. The structure must end with the END REPEAT command. On the transformation commands, a single stand-in variable represents every variable or value specified on the replacement list.

Syntax Rules

- Multiple stand-in variables can be specified on a DO REPEAT command. Each stand-in variable must have its own equals sign and associated variable or value list and must be separated from other stand-in variables by a slash. All lists must name or generate the same number of items.
- Stand-in variables can be assigned any valid variable names: permanent, temporary, scratch, system, and so forth. A stand-in variable does not exist outside the DO REPEAT—END REPEAT structure and has no effect on variables with the same name that exist outside the structure. However, two stand-in variables cannot have the same name within the same DO REPEAT structure.
- A replacement variable list can include new or existing variables, and they can be string or numeric. Keyword TO can be used to name consecutive existing variables and to create a set of new variables. New string variables must be declared on the STRING command either before DO REPEAT or within the DO REPEAT structure. All replacement variable and value lists must have the same number of items.
- A replacement value list can be a list of strings or numeric values, or it can be of the form n_1 TO n_2, where n_1 is less than n_2 and both are integers. (Note that the keyword is TO, not THRU.)

Operations

- DO REPEAT marks the beginning of the control structure and END REPEAT marks the end. Once control passes out of the structure, all stand-in variables defined within the structure cease to exist.
- The program repeats the commands between DO REPEAT and END REPEAT once for each variable or value on the replacement list.
- Numeric variables created within the structure are initially set to the system-missing value. By default, they are assigned an F8.2 format.
- New string variables declared within the structure are initially set to a blank value and are assigned the format specified on the STRING command that creates them.
- If DO REPEAT is used to create new variables, the order in which they are created depends on how the transformation commands are specified. Variables created by specifying the TO keyword (for example, *V1* TO *V5*) are not necessarily consecutive in the working data file. See the PRINT subcommand on p. 331 for examples.

Example

```
DO REPEAT R=REGION1 TO REGION5.
COMPUTE R=0.
END REPEAT.
```

- DO REPEAT defines the stand-in variable *R*, which represents five new numeric variables: *REGION1*, *REGION2*, *REGION3*, *REGION4*, and *REGION5*.

- The five variables are initialized to 0 by a single COMPUTE specification that is repeated for each variable on the replacement list. Thus, the program generates five COMPUTE commands from the one specified.
- Stand-in variable *R* ceases to exist once control passes out of the DO REPEAT structure.

Example

```
* This example shows a typical application of INPUT PROGRAM, LOOP,
  and DO REPEAT. A data file containing random numbers is generated.

INPUT PROGRAM.
+  LOOP #I = 1 TO 1000.
+     DO REPEAT RESPONSE = R1 TO R400.
+          COMPUTE RESPONSE = UNIFORM(1) > 0.5.
+     END REPEAT.
+     COMPUTE AVG = MEAN(R1 TO R400).
+     END CASE.
+   END LOOP.
+   END FILE.
END INPUT PROGRAM.

FREQUENCIES VARIABLE=AVG
 /FORMAT=CONDENSE
 /HISTOGRAM
 /STATISTICS=MEAN MEDIAN MODE STDDEV MIN MAX.
```

- The INPUT PROGRAM—END INPUT PROGRAM structure encloses an input program that builds cases from transformation commands.
- The indexing variable (*#I*) on LOOP—END LOOP indicates that the loop should be executed 1000 times.
- The DO REPEAT—END REPEAT structure generates 400 variables, each with a 50% chance of being 0 and a 50% chance of being 1. This is accomplished by specifying a logical expression on COMPUTE that compares the values returned by UNIFORM(1) to the value 0.5. (UNIFORM(1) generates random numbers between 0 and 1.) Logical expressions are evaluated as false (0), true (1), or missing. Thus, each random number returned by UNIFORM that is 0.5 or less is evaluated as false and assigned the value 0, and each random number returned by UNIFORM that is greater than 0.5 is evaluated as true and assigned the value 1.
- The second COMPUTE creates variable *AVG*, which is the mean of *R1* to *R400* for each case.
- END CASE builds a case with the variables created within each loop. Thus, the loop structure creates 1000 cases, each with 401 variables (*R1* to *R400*, and *AVG*).
- END FILE signals the end of the data file generated by the input program. If END FILE were not specified in this example, the input program would go into an infinite loop. No working file would be built, and the program would display an error message for every procedure that follows the input program.
- FREQUENCIES produces a condensed frequency table, histogram, and statistics for *AVG*. The histogram for *AVG* shows a normal distribution.

PRINT Subcommand

The PRINT subcommand on END REPEAT displays the commands generated by the DO REPEAT—END REPEAT structure. PRINT can be used to verify the order in which commands are executed.

Example

```
DO REPEAT Q=Q1 TO Q5/ R=R1 TO R5.
COMPUTE Q=0.
COMPUTE R=1.
END REPEAT PRINT.
```

- The DO REPEAT—END REPEAT structure initializes one set of variables to 0 and another set to 1.
- The output from the PRINT subcommand is shown in Figure 1. The generated commands are preceded by plus signs.
- The COMPUTE commands are generated in such a way that variables are created in alternating order: *Q1*, *R1*, *Q2*, *R2*, and so forth. If you plan to use the TO keyword to refer to *Q1* to *Q5* later, you should use two separate DO REPEAT utilities; otherwise, *Q1* to *Q5* will include four of the five *R* variables. Alternatively, use the NUMERIC command to predetermine the order in which variables are added to the working file, or specify the replacement value lists as shown in the next example.

Figure 1 Output from the PRINT subcommand

```
 2  0      DO REPEAT Q=Q1 TO Q5/ R=R1 TO R5
 3  0      COMPUTE Q=0
 4  0      COMPUTE R=1
 5  0      END REPEAT PRINT

 6  0     +COMPUTE Q1=0
 7  0     +COMPUTE R1=1
 8  0     +COMPUTE Q2=0
 9  0     +COMPUTE R2=1
10  0     +COMPUTE Q3=0
11  0     +COMPUTE R3=1
12  0     +COMPUTE Q4=0
13  0     +COMPUTE R4=1
14  0     +COMPUTE Q5=0
15  0     +COMPUTE R5=1
```

Example

```
DO REPEAT Q=Q1 TO Q5,R1 TO R5/ N=0,0,0,0,0,1,1,1,1,1.
COMPUTE Q=N.
END REPEAT PRINT.
```

- In this example, a series of constants is specified as a stand-in value list for *N*. All the *Q* variables are initialized first, and then all the *R* variables, as shown in Figure 2.

Figure 2 Output from the PRINT subcommand

```
  2  0          DO REPEAT Q=Q1 TO Q5,R1 TO R5/ N=0,0,0,0,0,1,1,1,1,1
  3  0          COMPUTE Q=N
  4  0          END REPEAT PRINT

  5  0         +COMPUTE Q1=0
  6  0         +COMPUTE Q2=0
  7  0         +COMPUTE Q3=0
  8  0         +COMPUTE Q4=0
  9  0         +COMPUTE Q5=0
 10  0         +COMPUTE R1=1
 11  0         +COMPUTE R2=1
 12  0         +COMPUTE R3=1
 13  0         +COMPUTE R4=1
 14  0         +COMPUTE R5=1
```

Example

```
DO REPEAT R=REGION1 TO REGION5/ X=1 TO 5.
COMPUTE R=REGION EQ X.
END REPEAT PRINT.
```

- In this example, stand-in variable *R* represents the variable list *REGION1* to *REGION5*. Stand-in variable *X* represents the value list 1 to 5.
- The DO REPEAT—END REPEAT structure creates dummy variables *REGION1* to *REGION5* that equal 0 or 1 for each of 5 regions, depending on whether variable *REGION* equals the current value of stand-in variable *X*.
- PRINT on END REPEAT causes the program to display the commands generated by the structure, as shown in Figure 3.

Figure 3 Commands generated by DO REPEAT

```
 2  0  DO REPEAT R=REGION1 TO REGION5/ X=1 TO 5
 3  0  COMPUTE R=REGION EQ X
 4  0  END REPEAT PRINT

 5  0 +COMPUTE REGION1=REGION EQ 1
 6  0 +COMPUTE REGION2=REGION EQ 2
 7  0 +COMPUTE REGION3=REGION EQ 3
 8  0 +COMPUTE REGION4=REGION EQ 4
 9  0 +COMPUTE REGION5=REGION EQ 5
```

DROP DOCUMENTS

```
DROP DOCUMENTS
```

Overview

When GET retrieves an SPSS-format data file, or when ADD FILES, MATCH FILES, or UPDATE are used to combine SPSS-format data files, all documents from each specified file are copied into the working file. DROP DOCUMENTS is used to drop these or any documents added with the DOCUMENT command from the working file. Whether or not DROP DOCUMENTS is used, new documents can be added to the working file with the DOCUMENT command.

Basic Specification

The only specification is DROP DOCUMENTS. There are no additional specifications.

Operations

- Documents are dropped from the working data file only. The original data file is unchanged, unless it is resaved.
- DROP DOCUMENTS drops all documentation, including documentation added by any DOCUMENT commands specified prior to the DROP DOCUMENTS command.

Example

```
GET FILE=GENSOC /KEEP=AGE SEX EDUC MARITAL CHILDRN MED_INS.

DROP DOCUMENTS.

FILE LABEL  General Social Survey Subset.
DOCUMENT    This file contains a subset of variables from the
            General Social Survey data.  For each case it records
            only the age, sex, education level, marital status,
            number of children, and type of medical insurance
            coverage.

SAVE OUTFILE=SUBSOC.
```

- DROP DOCUMENTS drops the documentation text from file *GENSOC*. Only the new documentation added with the DOCUMENT command is saved in file *SUBSOC*.
- The original file *GENSOC* is unchanged.

EDIT

This command is not available on all operating systems.

```
EDIT
```

Example

```
EDIT.
GET FILE=QUERY.
RECODE ITEM1, ITEM2, ITEM3 (0=1) (1=0) (2=-1).
COMPUTE INDEXQ=(ITEM1 + ITEM2 + ITEM3)/3.
VARIABLE LABELS INDEXQ 'Summary Index of Questions'.
FREQUENCIES=ITEM1 ITEM2 ITEM3.
```

Overview

EDIT causes the program to evaluate a sequence of commands without actually running the commands. EDIT is available only for batch mode.

Syntax Rules

The minimum specification is simply the command keyword. EDIT has no additional specifications.

- EDIT can be positioned anywhere within the sequence of commands and checks all the commands that follow it.

Operations

- EDIT checks for syntax errors, and it checks to see if all variables used in the commands have been defined. EDIT will look for variable definitions in a specified SPSS-format data file, on a DATA LIST command, and on any commands that create variables.
- EDIT cannot determine whether a DATA LIST command correctly defines the data. It can only determine whether the syntax is correct.
- If the variable definitions are contained in an SPSS-format data file that is not available to the program for checking, you can replicate data definitions in the EDIT session by using the DATA LIST, NUMERIC, or STRING commands. The DATA LIST does not need to correspond exactly with the data, but it must name all the variables to be used in the remainder of the session in the same order and with the same format as the variables in the data file.
- If data are inline, the BEGIN DATA and END DATA commands must be in their appropriate positions within the sequence of commands. However, EDIT does not check the data records.

- EDIT reports when a string variable is used where a numeric variable is required and vice versa.
- Some program procedures create variables such as standard scores and residuals and add them to the working data file. EDIT does not know about these variables and issues error messages when it encounters them in subsequent commands.
- EDIT *does not* detect every possible error. For example, it will not recognize that a computation is impossible.

Example

```
EDIT.
DATA LIST  FILE=HUBDATA RECORDS=3
 /1 EMPLOYID 1-5 MOHIRED YRHIRED 12-15 DEPT79 TO DEPT82 SEX 16-20
 /2 SALARY79 TO SALARY82 6-25 HOURLY81 HOURLY82 40-53(2)
     PROMO81 72 AGE 54-55 RAISE82 66-70
 /3 JOBCAT 6 NAME 25-48 (A).
LIST VARIABLES=MOHIRED YRHIRED DEPT82
     SALARY79 TO SALARY82 NAME /FORMAT=NUMBERED.
```

- EDIT ensures that syntax on DATA LIST and LIST is correct and that all variables specified on LIST have been defined.
- The DATA LIST and LIST commands are not executed and the data are not read.

Example

```
EDIT.
GET FILE=HUBDATA.
COMPUTE  CASESEQ2=CASESEQ+1.
LEAVE CASESEQ2.
PRINT FORMATS CASESEQ2 (F3).

SELECT IF DEPT82 EQ 4.
LIST VARIABLES=CASESEQ2 MOHIRED YRHIRED DEPT82
     SALARY79 TO SALARY82 NAME /FORMAT=NUMBERED.
```

- All commands following EDIT are checked for syntax and variable names.
- The program reads the dictionary of the *HUBDATA* data file (specified on the GET command) so that it can check variables used throughout the session.
- EDIT is able to recognize *CASESEQ2* when it is specified on the LIST command because *CASESEQ2* is defined on the COMPUTE command. However, *CASESEQ2* is not created.
- The commands in this session are not executed and the data are not read.

END CASE

```
END CASE
```

Example

```
* Restructure a data file to make each data item into a single case.

INPUT PROGRAM.
DATA LIST /#X1 TO #X3 (3(F1,1X)).

VECTOR V=#X1 TO #X3.

LOOP #I=1 TO 3.
- COMPUTE X=V(#I).
- END CASE.
END LOOP.
END INPUT PROGRAM.
```

Overview

END CASE is used in an INPUT PROGRAM—END INPUT PROGRAM structure to signal that a case is complete. Control then passes to the commands immediately following the input program. After these commands are executed for the newly created case, the program returns to the input program and continues building cases by processing the commands immediately after the last END CASE command that was executed. For more information about the flow control in an input program, see INPUT PROGRAM—END INPUT PROGRAM.

END CASE is especially useful for restructuring files, either building a single case from several cases or building several cases from a single case. It can also be used to generate data without any data input (see p. 330 for an example).

Basic Specification

The basic specification is simply END CASE. There are no additional specifications.

Syntax Rules

- END CASE is available only within an input program and is generally specified within a loop.
- Multiple END CASE commands can be used within an input program. Each builds a case from the transformation and data definition commands executed since the last END CASE command.
- If no END CASE is explicitly specified, an END CASE command is implied immediately before END INPUT PROGRAM and the input program loops until an end-of-file is encountered or specified (see END FILE).

Operations

- When an END CASE command is encountered, the program suspends execution of the rest of the commands before the END INPUT PROGRAM command and passes control to the commands after the input program. After these commands are executed for the new case, control returns to the input program. The program continues building cases by processing the commands immediately after the most recent END CASE command. Use a loop to build cases from the same set of transformation and data definition commands.
- When multiple END CASE commands are specified, the program follows the flow of the input program and builds a case whenever it encounters an END CASE command, using the set of commands executed since the last END CASE.
- Unless LEAVE is specified, all variables are reinitialized each time the input program is resumed.
- When transformations such as COMPUTE, definitions such as VARIABLE LABELS, and utilities such as PRINT are specified between the last END CASE command and END INPUT PROGRAM, they are executed while a case is being initialized, not when it is complete. This may produce undesirable results (see the example beginning on p. 342).

Example

```
* Restructuring a data file to make each data item a single case.

INPUT PROGRAM.
DATA LIST /#X1 TO #X3 (3(F1,1X)).

VECTOR V=#X1 TO #X3.

LOOP #I=1 TO 3.
- COMPUTE X=V(#I).
- END CASE.
END LOOP.
END INPUT PROGRAM.

BEGIN DATA
2 1 1
3 5 1
END DATA.
FORMAT X(F1.0).
PRINT / X.
EXECUTE.
```

- The input program encloses the commands that build cases from the input file. An input program is required because END CASE is used to create multiple cases from single input records.
- DATA LIST defines three variables. In the format specification, the number 3 is a repetition factor that repeats the format in parentheses three times, once for each variable. The specified format is F1 and the 1X specification skips 1 column.
- VECTOR creates the vector *V* with the original scratch variables as its three elements. The indexing expression on the LOOP command increments the variable *#I* three times to control the number of iterations per input case and to provide the index for the vector *V*.

- COMPUTE sets *X* equal to each of the scratch variables. END CASE tells the program to build a case. Thus, the first loop (for the first case) sets *X* equal to the first element of vector *V*. Since *V(1)* references *#X1*, and *#X1* is 2, the value of *X* is 2. Variable *X* is then formatted and printed before control returns to the command END LOOP. The loop continues, since indexing is not complete. Thus, the program then sets *X* to *#X2*, which is 1, builds the second case, and passes it to the FORMAT and PRINT commands. After the third iteration, which sets *X* equal to 1, the program formats and prints the case and terminates the loop. Since the end of the file has not been encountered, END INPUT PROGRAM passes control to the first command in the input program, DATA LIST, to read the next input case. After the second loop, however, the program encounters END DATA and completes building the working data file.
- The six new cases are shown in Figure 1.

Figure 1 Outcome for multiple cases read from a single case

```
2
1
1
3
5
1
```

Example

```
*Restructuring a data file to create a separate case for
 each book order.

INPUT PROGRAM.
DATA LIST  /ORDER 1-4 #X1 TO #X22 (1X,11(F3.0,F2.0,1X)).

LEAVE ORDER.
VECTOR BOOKS=#X1 TO #X22.

LOOP #I=1 TO 21 BY 2 IF NOT SYSMIS(BOOKS(#I)).
- COMPUTE ISBN=BOOKS(#I).
- COMPUTE QUANTITY=BOOKS(#I+1).
- END CASE.
END LOOP.
END INPUT PROGRAM.
BEGIN DATA
1045 182 2 155 1 134 1 153 5
1046 155 3 153 5 163 1
1047 161 5 182 2 163 4 186 6
1048 186 2
1049 155 2 163 2 153 2 074 1 161 1
END DATA.

SORT CASES ISBN.
DO IF $CASENUM EQ 1.
- PRINT EJECT /'Order ISBN Quantity'.
- PRINT SPACE.
END IF.

FORMATS ISBN (F3)/ QUANTITY (F2).
PRINT /'  ' ORDER '  ' ISBN '   ' QUANTITY.

EXECUTE.
```

- Data are extracted from a file whose records store values for an invoice number and a series of book codes and quantities ordered. For example, invoice 1045 is for four different titles and a total of nine books: two copies of book 182, one copy each of 155 and 134, and five copies of book 153. The task is to break each individual book order into a record, preserving the order number on each new case.
- The input program encloses the commands that build cases from the input file. They are required because the END CASE command is used to create multiple cases from single input records.
- DATA LIST specifies *ORDER* as a permanent variable and defines 22 scratch variables to hold the book numbers and quantities (this is the maximum number of numbers and quantities that will fit in 72 columns). In the format specification, the first element skips one space after the value for the variable *ORDER*. The number 11 repeats the formats that follow it 11 times: once for each book number and quantity pair. The specified format is F3.0 for book numbers and F2.0 for quantities. The 1X specification skips 1 column after each quantity value.
- LEAVE preserves the value of the variable *ORDER* across the new cases to be generated.
- VECTOR sets up the vector *BOOKS* with the 22 scratch variables as its elements. The first element is *#X1*, the second is *#X2*, and so on.
- If the element for the vector *BOOKS* is not system-missing, LOOP initiates the loop structure that moves through the vector *BOOKS*, picking off the book numbers and quantities. The indexing clause initiates the indexing variable *#I* at 1, to be increased by 2 to a maximum of 21.
- The first COMPUTE command sets the variable *ISBN* equal to the element in the vector *BOOKS* indexed by *#I*, which is the current book number. The second COMPUTE sets the variable *QUANTITY* equal to the next element in the vector *BOOKS*, *#I* +1, which is the quantity associated with the book number in *BOOKS(#I)*.
- END CASE tells the program to write out a case with the current values of the three variables: *ORDER*, *ISBN*, and *QUANTITY*.
- END LOOP terminates the loop structure and control is returned to the LOOP command, where *#I* is increased by 2 and looping continues until the entire input case is read or until *#I* exceeds the maximum value of 21.
- SORT CASES sorts the new cases by book number.
- The DO IF structure encloses a PRINT EJECT command and a PRINT SPACE command to set up titles for the output.
- FORMATS establishes dictionary formats for the new variables *ISBN* and *QUANTITY*. PRINT displays the new cases.
- EXECUTE runs the commands. The output is shown in Figure 2.

Figure 2 PRINT output showing new cases

```
Order ISBN Quantity

 1049   74    1
 1045  134    1
 1045  153    5
 1046  153    5
 1049  153    2
 1045  155    1
 1046  155    3
 1049  155    2
 1047  161    5
 1049  161    1
 1046  163    1
 1047  163    4
 1049  163    2
 1045  182    2
 1047  182    2
 1047  186    6
 1048  186    2
```

Example

```
* Create variable that approximates a log-normal distribution.

SET FORMAT=F8.0.

INPUT PROGRAM.
LOOP I=1 TO 1000.
+ COMPUTE SCORE=EXP(NORMAL(1)).
+ END CASE.
END LOOP.
END FILE.
END INPUT PROGRAM.

FREQUENCIES VARIABLES=SCORE /FORMAT=NOTABLE /HISTOGRAM
 /PERCENTILES=1 10 20 30 40 50 60 70 80 90 99
 /STATISTICS=ALL.
```

- The input program creates 1000 cases with a single variable *SCORE*. Values for *SCORE* approximate a log-normal distribution.

Example

```
* Restructure a data file to create a separate case for each
  individual.
INPUT PROGRAM.
DATA LIST  /#RECS 1 HEAD1 HEAD2 3-4(A).     /*Read header info
LEAVE  HEAD1 HEAD2.

LOOP  #I=1 TO #RECS.
DATA LIST  /INDIV 1-2(1).                   /*Read individual info
PRINT  /#RECS HEAD1 HEAD2 INDIV.
END CASE.                                   /*Create combined case
END LOOP.
END INPUT PROGRAM.
```

```
BEGIN DATA
1 AC
91
2 CC
35
43
0 XX
1 BA
34
3 BB
42
96
37
END DATA.
LIST.
```

- Data are in a file with header records that indicate the type of record and the number of individual records that follow. The number of records following each header record varies. For example, the 1 in the first column of the first header record (AC) says that only one individual record (91) follows. The 2 in the first column of the second header record (CC) says that two individual records (35 and 43) follow. The next header record has no individual records, indicated by the 0 in column 1, and so on.
- The first DATA LIST reads the expected number of individual records for each header record into temporary variable *#RECS*. *#RECS* is then used as the terminal value in the indexing variable to read the correct number of individual records using the second DATA LIST.
- The variables *HEAD1* and *HEAD2* contain the information in columns 3 and 4, respectively, in the header records. The LEAVE command retains *HEAD1* and *HEAD2* so that this information can be spread to the individual records.
- The variable *INDIV* is the information from the individual record. *INDIV* is combined with *#RECS*, *HEAD1*, and *HEAD2* to create the new case. Notice in the output from the PRINT command in Figure 3 that no case is created for the header record with 0 for *#RECS*.
- END CASE passes each case out of the input program to the LIST command. Without END CASE, the PRINT command would still display the cases as shown in Figure 3 because it is inside the loop. However, only one (the last) case per header record would pass out of the input program. The outcome for LIST will be quite different (compare Figure 4 with Figure 5).

Figure 3 PRINT output

```
1 A C 9.1
2 C C 3.5
2 C C 4.3
1 B A 3.4
3 B B 4.2
3 B B 9.6
3 B B 3.7
```

Figure 4 LIST output when END CASE is specified

```
HEAD1 HEAD2 INDIV

A     C      9.1
C     C      3.5
C     C      4.3
B     A      3.4
B     B      4.2
B     B      9.6
B     B      3.7
```

Figure 5 LIST output when END CASE is not specified

```
HEAD1 HEAD2 INDIV

A     C      9.1
C     C      4.3
X     X       .
B     A      3.4
B     B      3.7
```

Example

```
* Note: the following is an erroneous program! The COMPUTE and
  PRINT commands that follow END CASE are misplaced. They should
  be specified after the END INPUT PROGRAM command.

INPUT PROGRAM.
DATA LIST  /#X1 TO #X3 (3(F1,1X)).

VECTOR V=#X1 TO #X3.

LOOP #I=1 TO 3.
COMPUTE X=V(#I).
END CASE.
END LOOP.

COMPUTE Y=X**2.    /* This should be specified after the input program
VARIABLE LABELS X 'TEST VARIABLE' Y 'SQUARE OF X'.
PRINT FORMATS X Y (F2).
END INPUT PROGRAM.

BEGIN DATA
2 1 1
3 5 1
END DATA.

FREQUENCIES VARIABLES=X Y.
```

- No error or warning is issued for these commands, but the result is not what was intended. The computed value for *X* is passed out of the input program when the END CASE command is encountered. Thus, *Y* is computed from the initialized value of *X*, which is the system-missing value. As Figure 6 shows, all six cases computed for *Y* within the input program have the system-missing value, represented by a period (.).

- The frequencies table for *X* is as expected, because *X* is computed from inline data and no computation is done between END CASE and END INPUT PROGRM.
- The VARIABLE LABELS and PRINT FORMATS commands have their desired effects even though they are executed with the COMPUTE command, because they do not act on any data read in.
- Moving COMPUTE before END CASE will solve the problem, but the preferred solution is to specify END INPUT PROGRAM before all commands in the transformation program, since they operate on the cases created by the input program.

Figure 6 FREQUENCIES output

```
X          TEST VARIABLE

                                                         VALID      CUM
  VALUE LABEL                  VALUE  FREQUENCY  PERCENT  PERCENT  PERCENT

                                   1          3     50.0     50.0     50.0
                                   2          1     16.7     16.7     66.7
                                   3          1     16.7     16.7     83.3
                                   5          1     16.7     16.7    100.0
                                        -------  -------  -------
                               TOTAL          6    100.0    100.0

VALID CASES        6       MISSING CASES      0
- - - - - - - - - - - - - - - - - - - - - - - - - - - - - - - - - - - -

Y          SQUARE OF X

                                                         VALID      CUM
  VALUE LABEL                  VALUE  FREQUENCY  PERCENT  PERCENT  PERCENT

                                   .          6    100.0  MISSING
                                        -------  -------  -------
                               TOTAL          6    100.0    100.0
```

END FILE

```
END FILE
```

Example

```
INPUT PROGRAM.
DATA LIST FILE=PRICES /YEAR 1-4 QUARTER 6 PRICE 8-12(2).
DO IF (YEAR GE 1881).   /*Stop reading before 1881
END FILE.
END IF.
END INPUT PROGRAM.
```

Overview

END FILE is used in an INPUT PROGRAM—END INPUT PROGRAM structure to tell the program to stop reading data before it actually encounters the end of the file. END FILE can be used with END CASE to concatenate raw data files by causing the program to delay end-of-file processing until it has read multiple data files (see p. 252 for an example). END FILE can also be used with LOOP and END CASE to generate data without any data input (see p. 330 for an example).

Basic Specification

The basic specification is simply END FILE. There are no additional specifications. The end of file is defined according to the conditions specified for END FILE in the input program.

Syntax Rules

- END FILE is available only within an INPUT PROGRAM structure.
- Only one END FILE command can be executed per input program. However, multiple END FILE commands can be specified within a conditional structure in the input program.

Operations

- When END FILE is encountered, the program stops reading data and puts an end of file in the working data file it was building. The case that causes the execution of END FILE is not read. To include this case, use the END CASE command before END FILE (see the examples below).
- END FILE has the same effect as the end of the input data file. It terminates the input program (see INPUT PROGRAM—END INPUT PROGRAM).

Example

```
*Select cases.

INPUT PROGRAM.
DATA LIST FILE=PRICES /YEAR 1-4 QUARTER 6 PRICE 8-12(2).

DO IF (YEAR GE 1881).   /*Stop reading before 1881
END FILE.
END IF.

END INPUT PROGRAM.

LIST.
```

- This example assumes that data records are entered chronologically by year. The DO IF—END IF structure specifies an end of file when the first case with a value of 1881 or later for *YEAR* is reached.
- LIST executes the input program and lists cases in the working data file. The case that causes the end of the file is not included in the working data file.
- As an alternative to an input program with END FILE, you can use N OF CASES to select cases if you know the exact number of cases. Another alternative is to use SELECT IF to select cases before 1881, but then the program would unnecessarily read the entire input file.

Example

```
Select cases but retain the case that causes end-of-file processing.

INPUT PROGRAM.
DATA LIST FILE=PRICES /YEAR 1-4 QUARTER 6 PRICE 8-12(2).

DO IF (YEAR GE 1881).   /*Stop reading before 1881 (or at end of file)
END CASE.               /*Create case 1881
END FILE.

ELSE.
END CASE.               /*Create all other cases
END IF.
END INPUT PROGRAM.

LIST.
```

- The first END CASE command forces the program to retain the case that causes end-of-file processing.
- The second END CASE indicates the end of case for all other cases and passes them out of the input program one at a time. It is required because the first END CASE command causes the program to abandon default end-of-case processing (see END CASE).

ERASE

```
ERASE FILE='file'
```

Example

```
ERASE FILE='PRSNL.DAT'.
```

Overview

ERASE removes a file from a disk.

Basic Specification

The basic specification is the keyword FILE followed by a file specification. The specified file is erased from the disk. The file specification may vary from operating system to operating system, but enclosing the filename in apostrophes generally works.

Syntax Rules

- The keyword FILE is required but the equals sign is optional.
- ERASE allows one file specification only and does not accept wildcard characters. To erase more than one file, specify multiple ERASE commands.
- The file to be erased must be specified in full. ERASE does not recognize any default file extension.

Operations

ERASE deletes the specified file regardless of its type. No message is displayed unless the command cannot be executed. Use ERASE with caution.

Example

```
ERASE FILE 'PRSNL.DAT'.
```

- The file *PRSNL.SAV* is deleted from the current directory. Whether it is an SPSS-format data file or a file of any other type makes no difference.

EXAMINE

```
EXAMINE VARIABLES=varlist [[BY varlist] [varname BY varname]]

 [/COMPARE={GROUPS**  }]
           {VARIABLES}

 [/{TOTAL**}]
   {NOTOTAL}

 [/ID={case number**}]
      {varname      }

 [/PERCENTILES [[({5,10,25,50,75,90,95})=[{HAVERAGE  }] [NONE]]
                  {value list          }   {WAVERAGE  }
                                           {ROUND     }
                                           {AEMPIRICAL}
                                           {EMPIRICAL }

 [/PLOT=[STEMLEAF**] [BOXPLOT**] [NPPLOT] [SPREADLEVEL(n)] [HISTOGRAM]]

        [{ALL  }]
         {NONE}

 [/STATISTICS=[DESCRIPTIVES**] [EXTREME({5})]]
                                        {n}
              [{ALL  }]
               {NONE}

 [/CINTERVAL {95**}]
             {n   }

 [/MESTIMATOR=[{NONE**}]]
               {ALL   }

              [HUBER({1.339})] [ANDREW({1.34}]
                     {c    }           {c   }

              [HAMPEL({1.7,3.4,8.5})]
                      {a  ,b  ,c  }

              [TUKEY({4.685})]
                     {c    }

[/MISSING=[{LISTWISE**}] [{EXCLUDE**}] [{NOREPORT**}]]
           {PAIRWISE  }    {INCLUDE  }    {REPORT    }
```

**Default if the subcommand is omitted.

Examples

```
EXAMINE VARIABLES=ENGSIZE,COST.

EXAMINE VARIABLES=MIPERGAL BY MODEL,MODEL BY CYLINDERS.
```

Overview

EXAMINE provides stem-and-leaf plots, histograms, boxplots, normal plots, robust estimates of location, tests of normality, and other descriptive statistics. Separate analyses can be obtained for subgroups of cases.

Options

Cells. You can subdivide cases into cells based on their values for grouping (factor) variables using the BY keyword on the VARIABLES subcommand.

Output. You can control the display of output using the COMPARE subcommand. You can specify the computational method and break points for percentiles with the PERCENTILES subcommand, and you can assign a variable to be used for labeling outliers on the ID subcommand.

Plots. You can request stem-and-leaf plots, histograms, vertical boxplots, spread-versus-level plots with Levene tests for homogeneity of variance, and normal and detrended probability plots with tests for normality. These plots are available through the PLOT subcommand.

Statistics. You can request univariate statistical output with the STATISTICS subcommand and maximum-likelihood estimators with the MESTIMATORS subcommand.

Basic Specification

- The basic specification is VARIABLES and at least one dependent variable.
- The default output includes a Descriptives table displaying univariate statistics (mean, median, standard deviation, standard error, variance, kurtosis, kurtosis standard error, skewness, skewness standard error, sum, interquartile range (IQR), range, minimum, maximum, and 5% trimmed mean), a vertical boxplot and a stem-and-leaf plot. Outliers are labeled on the boxplot with the system variable *$CASENUM*.

Subcommand Order

Subcommands can be named in any order.

Limitations

- When string variables are used as factors, only the first eight characters are used to form cells. String variables cannot be specified as dependent variables.
- When more than eight crossed factors (for example, `A, B, ...` in the specification `Y by A by B by ...`) are specified, the command is not executed.

Example

```
EXAMINE VARIABLES=ENGSIZE,COST.
```

- *ENGSIZE* and *COST* are the dependent variables.
- EXAMINE produces univariate statistics for *ENGSIZE* and *COST* in the Descriptives table and a vertical boxplot and a stem-and-leaf plot for each variable.

Example

```
EXAMINE VARIABLES=MIPERGAL BY MODEL,MODEL BY CYLINDERS.
```

- *MIPERGAL* is the dependent variable. The cell specification follows the first BY keyword. Cases are subdivided based on values of *MODEL* and also based on the combination of values of *MODEL* and *CYLINDERS*.
- Assuming that there are three values for *MODEL* and two values for *CYLINDERS*, this example produces a Descriptives table, a stem-and-leaf plot, and a boxplot for the total sample, a Descriptives table and a boxplot for each factor defined by the first BY (*MIPERGAL* by *MODEL* and *MIPERGAL* by *MODEL* by *CYLINDERS*), and a stem-and-leaf plot for each of the nine cells (three defined by *MODEL* and six defined by *MODEL* and *CYLINDERS* together).

VARIABLES Subcommand

VARIABLES specifies the dependent variables and the cells. The dependent variables are specified first, followed by the keyword BY and the variables that define the cells. Repeated models on the same EXAMINE are discarded.

- To create cells defined by the combination of values of two or more factors, specify the factor names separated by the keyword BY.

Caution. Large amounts of output can be produced if many cells are specified. If there are many factors or if the factors have many values, EXAMINE will produce a large number of separate analyses.

Example

```
EXAMINE VARIABLES=SALARY,YRSEDUC BY RACE,SEX,DEPT,RACE BY SEX.
```

- *SALARY* and *YRSEDUC* are dependent variables.
- Cells are formed first for the values of *SALARY* and *YRSEDUC* individually, and then each by values for *RACE*, *SEX*, *DEPT*, and the combination of *RACE* and *SEX*.
- By default, EXAMINE produces Descriptives tables, stem-and-leaf plots, and boxplots.

COMPARE Subcommand

COMPARE controls how boxplots are displayed. This subcommand is most useful if there is more than one dependent variable and at least one factor in the design.

GROUPS *For each dependent variable, boxplots for all cells are displayed together.* With this display, comparisons across cells for a single dependent variable are easily made. This is the default.

VARIABLES *For each cell, boxplots for all dependent variables are displayed together.* With this display, comparisons of several dependent variables are easily made. This is useful in situations where the dependent variables are repeated measures of the same variable (see the following example) or have similar scales, or when the dependent variable has very different values for different cells, and plotting all cells on the same scale would cause information to be lost.

Example

```
EXAMINE VARIABLES=GPA1 GPA2 GPA3 GPA4 BY MAJOR   /COMPARE=VARIABLES.
```

- The four GPA variables are summarized for each value of *MAJOR*.
- COMPARE=VARIABLES groups the boxplots for the four GPA variables together for each value of *MAJOR*.

Example

```
EXAMINE VARIABLES=GPA1 GPA2 GPA3 GPA4 BY MAJOR /COMPARE=GROUPS.
```

- COMPARE=GROUPS groups the boxplots for *GPA1* for all majors together, followed by boxplots for *GPA2* for all majors, and so on.

TOTAL and NOTOTAL Subcommands

TOTAL and NOTOTAL control the amount of output produced by EXAMINE when factor variables are specified.

- TOTAL is the default. By default, or when TOTAL is specified, EXAMINE produces statistics and plots for each dependent variable overall and for each cell specified by the factor variables.
- NOTOTAL suppresses overall statistics and plots.
- TOTAL and NOTOTAL are alternatives.
- NOTOTAL is ignored when the VARIABLES subcommand does not specify factor variables.

ID Subcommand

ID assigns a variable from the working data file to identify the cases in the output. By default the case number is used for labeling outliers and extreme cases in boxplots.

- The identification variable can be either string or numeric. If it is numeric, value labels are used to label cases. If no value labels exist, the values are used.
- Only one identification variable can be specified.

Example

```
EXAMINE VARIABLES=SALARY BY RACE BY SEX /ID=LASTNAME.
```

- ID displays the value of *LASTNAME* for outliers and extreme cases in the boxplots.

PERCENTILES Subcommand

PERCENTILES displays the Percentiles table. If PERCENTILES is omitted, no percentiles are produced. If PERCENTILES is specified without keywords, HAVERAGE is used with default break points of 5, 10, 25, 50, 75, 90, and 95.

- Values for break points are specified in parentheses following the subcommand. EXAMINE displays up to six decimal places for user-specified percentile values.

- The method keywords follow the specifications for break points.

For each of the following methods of percentile calculation, w is the sum of the weights for all nonmissing cases, p is the specified percentile divided by 100, and X_i is the value of the ith case (cases are assumed to be ranked in ascending order). For details on the specific formulas used, see the *SPSS Statistical Algorithms* chapter for EXAMINE.

HAVERAGE *Weighted average at* $X_{(w+1)p}$. The percentile value is the weighted average of X_i and X_{i+1}, where i is the integer part of $(w+1)p$. This is the default if PERCENTILES is specified without a keyword.

WAVERAGE *Weighted average at* X_{wp}. The percentile value is the weighted average of X_i and $X_{(i+1)}$, where i is the integer part of wp.

ROUND *Observation closest to* wp. The percentile value is X_i or X_{i+1}, depending upon whether i or $i+1$ is "closer" to wp.

EMPIRICAL *Empirical distribution function.* The percentile value is X_i, where i is equal to wp rounded up to the next integer.

AEMPIRICAL *Empirical distribution with averaging.* This is equivalent to EMPIRICAL, except when i=wp, in which case the percentile value is the average of X_i and X_{i+1}.

NONE *Suppress percentile output.* This is the default if PERCENTILES is omitted.

Example

```
EXAMINE VARIABLE=SALARY /PERCENTILES(10,50,90)=EMPIRICAL.
```

- PERCENTILES produces the 10th, 50th, and 90th percentiles for the dependent variable *SALARY* using the EMPIRICAL distribution function.

PLOT Subcommand

PLOT controls plot output. The default is a vertical boxplot and a stem-and-leaf plot for each dependent variable for each cell in the model.

- Spread-versus-level plots can be produced only if there is at least one factor variable on the VARIABLES subcommand. If you request a spread-versus-level plot and there are no factor variables, the program issues a warning and no spread-versus-level plot is produced.
- If you specify the PLOT subcommand, only those plots explicitly requested are produced.

BOXPLOT *Vertical boxplot.* The boundaries of the box are Tukey's hinges. The median is identified by an asterisk. The length of the box is the interquartile range (IQR) computed from Tukey's hinges. Values more than three IQR's from the end of a box are labeled as extreme (E). Values more than 1.5 IQR's but less than 3 IQR's from the end of the box are labeled as outliers (O).

STEMLEAF *Stem-and-leaf plot.* In a stem-and-leaf plot, each observed value is divided into two components—leading digits (stem) and trailing digits (leaf).

HISTOGRAM *Histogram.*

SPREADLEVEL(n) *Spread-versus-level plot with the Test of Homogeneity of Variance table.* If the keyword appears alone, the natural logs of the interquartile ranges are plotted against the natural logs of the medians for all cells. If a power for transforming the data (*n*) is given, the IQR and median of the transformed data are plotted. If 0 is specified for *n*, a natural log transformation of the data is done. The slope of the regression line and Levene tests for homogeneity of variance are also displayed. The Levene tests are based on the original data if no transformation is specified and on the transformed data if a transformation is requested.

NPPLOT *Normal and detrended Q-Q plots with the Tests of Normality table presenting Shapiro-Wilk's statistic and a Kolmogorov-Smirnov statistic with a Lilliefors significance level for testing normality.* If non-integer weights are specified, the Shapiro-Wilk's statistic is calculated when the weighted sample size lies between 3 and 50. For no weights or integer weights, the statistic is calculated when the weighted sample size lies between 3 and 5000.

ALL *All available plots.*

NONE *No plots.*

Example

```
EXAMINE VARIABLES=CYCLE BY TREATMNT /PLOT=NPPLOT.
```

- PLOT produces normal and detrended Q-Q plots for each value of *TREATMNT* and a Tests of Normality table.

Example

```
EXAMINE VARIABLES=CYCLE BY TREATMNT /PLOT=SPREADLEVEL(.5).
```

- PLOT produces a spread-versus-level plot of the medians and interquartile ranges of the square root of *CYCLE*. Each point on the plot represents one of the *TREATMNT* groups.
- A Test of Homogeneity of Variance table displays Levene statistics.

Example

```
EXAMINE VARIABLES=CYCLE BY TREATMNT /PLOT=SPREADLEVEL(0).
```

- PLOT generates a spread-versus-level plot of the medians and interquartile ranges of the natural logs of *CYCLE* for each *TREATMENT* group.
- A Test of Homogeneity of Variance table displays Levene statistics.

Example

```
EXAMINE VARIABLES=CYCLE BY TREATMNT /PLOT=SPREADLEVEL.
```

- PLOT generates a spread-versus-level plot of the natural logs of the medians and interquartile ranges of *CYCLE* for each *TREATMNT* group.
- A Test of Homogeneity of Variance table displays Levene statistics.

STATISTICS Subcommand

STATISTICS requests univariate statistics and determines how many extreme values are displayed. DESCRIPTIVES is the default. If you specify keywords on STATISTICS, only the requested statistics are displayed.

DESCRIPTIVES *Display the Descriptives table showing univariate statistics (the mean, median, 5% trimmed mean, standard error, variance, standard deviation, minimum, maximum, range, interquartile range, skewness, skewness standard error, kurtosis, and kurtosis standard error).* This is the default.

EXTREME(n) *Display the Extreme Values table presenting cases with the* n *largest and* n *smallest values.* If *n* is omitted, the five largest and five smallest values are displayed. Extreme cases are labeled with their values for the identification variable if the ID subcommand is used or with their values for the system variable *$CASENUM* if ID is not specified.

ALL *Display the Descriptives and Extreme Values tables.*

NONE *Display neither the Descriptives nor the Extreme Values tables.*

Example

```
EXAMINE VARIABLE=FAILTIME /ID=BRAND
  /STATISTICS=EXTREME(10) /PLOT=NONE.
```

- STATISTICS identifies the cases with the 10 lowest and 10 highest values for *FAILTIME*. These cases are labeled with the first characters of their values for the variable *BRAND*. The Descriptives table is not displayed.

CINTERVAL Subcommand

CINTERVAL controls the confidence level when the default DESCRIPTIVES statistics is displayed. CINTERVAL has a default value of 95.

- You can specify a CINTERVAL value *(n)* between 50 and 99.99 inclusive. If the value you specify is out of range, the program issues a warning and uses the default 95% intervals.
- If you specify a keyword on STATISTICS subcommand that turns off the default DESCRIPTIVES, the CINTERVAL subcommand is ignored.
- The confidence interval appears in the output with the label *n% CI for Mean*, followed by the confidence interval in parentheses. For example,

  ```
  95% CI for Mean (.0001,.00013)
  ```

  The *n* in the label shows up to six decimal places. That is, input `/CINTERVAL 95` displays as *95% CI* while input `/CINTERVAL 95.975` displays as *95.975% CI.*

MESTIMATORS Subcommand

M-estimators are robust maximum-likelihood estimators of location. Four M-estimators are available for display in the M-Estimators table. They differ in the weights they apply to the cases. MESTIMATORS with no keywords produces Huber's M-estimator with c=1.339; Andrews' wave with c=1.34π; Hampel's M-estimator with a=1.7, b=3.4, and c=8.5; and Tukey's biweight with c=4.685.

HUBER(c) *Huber's M-estimator.* The value of weighting constant c can be specified in parentheses following the keyword. The default is c=1.339.

ANDREW(c) *Andrews' wave estimator.* The value of weighting constant c can be specified in parentheses following the keyword. Constants are multiplied by π. The default is 1.34π.

HAMPEL(a,b,c) *Hampel's M-estimator.* The values of weighting constants a, b, and c can be specified in order in parentheses following the keyword. The default values are a=1.7, b=3.4, and c=8.5.

TUKEY(c) *Tukey's biweight estimator.* The value of weighting constant c can be specified in parentheses following the keyword. The default is c=4.685.

ALL *All four above M-estimators.* This is the default when MESTIMATORS is specified with no keyword. The default values for weighting constants are used.

NONE *No M-estimators.* This is the default if MESTIMATORS is omitted.

Example

```
EXAMINE VARIABLE=CASTTEST /MESTIMATORS.
```

- MESTIMATORS generates all four M-estimators computed with the default constants.

Example

```
EXAMINE VARIABLE=CASTTEST /MESTIMATORS=HAMPELS(2,4,8).
```

- MESTIMATOR produces Hampel's M-estimator with weighting constants a=2, b=4, and c=8.

MISSING Subcommand

MISSING controls the processing of missing values in the analysis. The default is LISTWISE, EXCLUDE, and NOREPORT.

- LISTWISE and PAIRWISE are alternatives and apply to all variables. They are modified for dependent variables by INCLUDE/EXCLUDE and for factor variables by REPORT/NOREPORT.
- INCLUDE and EXCLUDE are alternatives; they apply only to dependent variables.
- REPORT and NOREPORT are alternatives; they determine if missing values for factor variables are treated as valid categories.

LISTWISE *Delete cases with missing values listwise.* A case with missing values for any dependent variable or any factor in the model specification is excluded from statistics and plots unless modified by INCLUDE or REPORT. This is the default.

PAIRWISE *Delete cases with missing values pairwise.* A case is deleted from the analysis only if it has a missing value for the dependent variable or factor being analyzed.

EXCLUDE *Exclude user-missing values.* User-missing values and system-missing values for dependent variables are excluded. This is the default.

INCLUDE *Include user-missing values.* Only system-missing values for dependent variables are excluded from the analysis.

NOREPORT *Exclude user- and system-missing values for factor variables.* This is the default.

REPORT *Include user- and system-missing values for factor variables.* User- and system-missing values for factors are treated as valid categories and are labeled as missing.

Example

```
EXAMINE VARIABLES=RAINFALL MEANTEMP BY REGION.
```

- MISSING is not specified and the default is used. Any case with a user- or system-missing value for *RAINFALL*, *MEANTEMP*, or *REGION* is excluded from the analysis and display.

Example

```
EXAMINE VARIABLES=RAINFALL MEANTEMP BY REGION
  /MISSING=PAIRWISE.
```

- Only cases with missing values for *RAINFALL* are excluded from the analysis of *RAINFALL*, and only cases with missing values for *MEANTEMP* are excluded from the analysis of *MEANTEMP*. Missing values for *REGION* are not used.

Example

```
EXAMINE VARIABLES=RAINFALL MEANTEMP BY REGION
  /MISSING=REPORT.
```

- Missing values for *REGION* are considered valid categories and are labeled as missing.

References

Frigge, M., D. C. Hoaglin, and B. Iglewicz. 1987. Some implementations of the boxplot. In: *Computer Science and Statistics Proceedings of the 19th Symposium on the Interface,* R. M. Heiberger and M. Martin, eds. Alexandria, Virginia: American Statistical Association.

Hoaglin, D. C., F. Mosteller, and J. W. Tukey. 1983. *Understanding robust and exploratory data analysis.* New York: John Wiley and Sons.

_____. 1985. *Exploring data tables, trends, and shapes.* New York: John Wiley and Sons.

Tukey, J. W. 1977. *Exploratory data analysis.* Reading, Mass.: Addison-Wesley.

Velleman, P. F., and D. C. Hoaglin. 1981. *Applications, basics, and computing of exploratory data analysis.* Boston: Duxbury Press.

EXECUTE

```
EXECUTE
```

Overview

EXECUTE forces the data to be read and executes the transformations that precede it in the command sequence.

Basic Specification

The basic specification is simply the command keyword. EXECUTE has no additional specifications.

Operations

- EXECUTE causes the data to be read but has no other influence on the session.
- EXECUTE is designed for use with transformation commands and facilities such as ADD FILES, MATCH FILES, UPDATE, PRINT, and WRITE, which do not read data and are not executed unless followed by a data-reading procedure.

Example

```
DATA LIST  FILE=RAWDATA / 1 LNAME 1-13 (A) FNAME 15-24 (A)
  MMAIDENL 40-55.
VAR LABELS  MMAIDENL 'MOTHER''S MAIDEN NAME'.
DO IF (MMAIDENL EQ 'Smith').
WRITE OUTFILE=SMITHS/LNAME FNAME.
END IF.
EXECUTE.
```

- This example writes the last and first names of all people whose mother's maiden name was Smith to the data file *SMITHS*.
- DO IF—END IF and WRITE do not read data and are executed only when data are read for a procedure. Because there is no procedure in this session, EXECUTE is used to read the data and execute all of the preceding transformation commands. Otherwise, the commands would not be executed.

EXPORT

```
EXPORT OUTFILE=file

 [/TYPE={COMM**}]
        {TAPE  }

 [/UNSELECTED=[{RETAIN}]
               {DELETE}

 [/KEEP={ALL**   }] [/DROP=varlist]
        {varlist}

 [/RENAME=(old varnames=new varnames)...]

 [/MAP]

 [/DIGITS=n]
```

**Default if the subcommand is omitted.

Example

```
EXPORT OUTFILE=NEWDATA /RENAME=(V1 TO V3=ID, SEX, AGE) /MAP.
```

Overview

EXPORT produces a portable data file. A portable data file is a data file created used to transport data between different types of computers and operating systems (such as between IBM CMS and Digital VAX/VMS) or between SPSS, SPSS/PC+, or other software using the same portable file format. Like an SPSS-format data file, a portable file contains all of the data and dictionary information stored in the working data file from which it was created. (To send data to a computer and operating system the same as your own, send an SPSS-format data file, which is easier and faster to process than a portable file.)

EXPORT is similar to the SAVE command. It can occur in the same position in the command sequence as the SAVE command and saves the working data file. The file includes the results of all permanent transformations and any temporary transformations made just prior to the EXPORT command. The working data file is unchanged after the EXPORT command.

Options

Format. You can control the format of the portable file using the TYPE subcommand.

Variables. You can save a subset of variables from the working file and rename the variables using the DROP, KEEP, and RENAME subcommands. You can also produce a record of all variables and their names on the exported file with the MAP subcommand.

Precision. You can specify the number of decimal digits of precision for the values of all numeric variables on the DIGITS subcommand.

Basic Specification

The basic specification is the OUTFILE subcommand with a file specification. All variables from the working data file are written to the portable file, with variable names, variable and value labels, missing-value flags, and print and write formats.

Subcommand Order

Subcommands can be named in any order.

Operations

- Portable files are written with 80-character record lengths.
- Portable files may contain some unprintable characters.
- The working data file is still available for transformations and procedures after the portable file is created.
- The system variables *$CASENUM* and *$DATE* are assigned when the file is read by IMPORT.
- If the WEIGHT command is used before EXPORT, the weighting variable is included in the portable file.

Example

```
EXPORT OUTFILE=NEWDATA /RENAME=(V1 TO V3=ID,SEX,AGE) /MAP.
```

- The portable file is written to *NEWDATA*.
- The variables *V1*, *V2*, and *V3* are renamed *ID*, *SEX*, and *AGE* in the portable file. Their names remain *V1*, *V2*, and *V3* in the working file. None of the other variables written to the portable file are renamed.
- MAP requests a display of the variables in the portable file.

Methods of Transporting Portable Files

Portable files can be transported on magnetic tape or by a communications program.

Magnetic Tape

Before transporting files on a magnetic tape, make sure the receiving computer can read the tape being sent. The following tape specifications must be known before you write the portable file on the tape:

- Number of tracks—either 7 or 9.
- Tape density—200, 556, 800, 1600, or 6250 bits per inch (BPI).
- Parity—even or odd. This must be known only when writing a 7-track tape.

- Tape labeling—labeled or unlabeled. Check whether the site can use tape labels. Also make sure that the site has the ability to read multivolume tape files if the file being written uses more than one tape.
- Blocksize—the maximum blocksize the receiving computer can accept.

A tape written with the following characteristics can be read by most computers: 9 track, 1600 BPI, unlabeled, and a blocksize of 3200 characters. However, there is no guarantee that a tape written with these characteristics can be read successfully. The best policy is to know the requirements of the receiving computer ahead of time.

The following advice may help ensure successful file transfers by magnetic tape:

- Unless you are certain that the receiving computer can read labels, prepare an unlabeled tape.
- Make sure the record length of 80 is not changed.
- Do not use a separate character translation program, especially ASCII/EBCDIC translations. EXPORT/IMPORT takes care of this for you.
- Make sure the same blocking factor is used when writing and reading the tape. A blocksize of 3200 is frequently a good choice.
- If possible, write the portable file directly to tape to avoid possible interference from copy programs. Read the file directly from the tape for the same reason.
- Use the INFO LOCAL command to find out about using the program on your particular computer and operating system. INFO LOCAL generally includes additional information about reading and writing portable files.

Communications Programs

Transmission of a portable file by a communications program may not be possible if the program misinterprets any characters in the file as control characters (for example, as a line feed, carriage return, or end of transmission). This can be prevented by specifying TYPE=COMM on EXPORT. This specification replaces each control character with the character 0. The affected control characters are in positions 0–60 of the IMPORT/EXPORT character set (see Appendix B).

The line length that the communications program uses must be set to 80 to match the 80-character record length of portable files. A transmitted file must be checked for blank lines or special characters inserted by the communications program. These must be edited out prior to reading the file with the IMPORT command.

Character Translation

Portable files are character files, not binary files, and they have 80-character records so they can be transmitted over data links. A receiving computer may not use the same character set as the computer where the portable file was written. When it imports a portable file, the program translates characters in the file to the character set used by the receiving computer. Depending on the character set in use, some characters in labels and in string data may be lost in the translation. For example, if a file is transported from a computer using a seven-bit ASCII character set to a computer using a six-bit ASCII character set, some characters in the file may have no matching characters in six-bit ASCII. For a character that has no match, the program generates an appropriate nonprintable character (the null character in most cases).

For a table of the character-set translations available with IMPORT and EXPORT, refer to Appendix B. A blank in a column of the table means that there is no matching character for that character set and an appropriate nonprintable character will be generated when you import a file.

OUTFILE Subcommand

OUTFILE specifies the portable file. OUTFILE is the only required subcommand on EXPORT.

TYPE Subcommand

TYPE indicates whether the portable file should be formatted for magnetic tape or for a communications program. You can specify either COMM or TAPE. See “Methods of Transporting Portable Files” on p. 358 for more information on magnetic tapes and communications programs.

COMM *Transport portable files by a communications program.* When COMM is specified on TYPE, the program removes all control characters and replaces them with the character 0. This is the default.

TAPE *Transport portable files on magnetic tape.*

Example

```
EXPORT TYPE=TAPE /OUTFILE=HUBOUT.
```

- File *HUBOUT* is saved as a tape-formatted portable file.

UNSELECTED Subcommand

UNSELECTED determines whether cases excluded on a previous FILTER or USE command are to be retained or deleted in the SPSS-format data file. The default is RETAIN. The UNSELECTED subcommand has no effect when the working data file does not contain unselected cases.

RETAIN *Retain the unselected cases.* All cases in the working data file are saved. This is the default when UNSELECTED is specified by itself.

DELETE *Delete the unselected cases.* Only cases that meet the FILTER or USE criteria are saved in the SPSS-format data file.

DROP and KEEP Subcommands

DROP and KEEP save a subset of variables in the portable file.

- DROP excludes a variable or list of variables from the portable file. All variables not named are included in the portable file.
- KEEP includes a variable or list of variables in the portable file. All variables not named are excluded.
- Variables can be specified on DROP and KEEP in any order. With the DROP subcommand, the order of variables in the portable file is the same as their order in the working file. With the KEEP subcommand, the order of variables in the portable file is the order in which they are named on KEEP. Thus, KEEP can be used to reorder variables in the portable file.
- Both DROP and KEEP can be used on the same EXPORT command; the effect is cumulative. If you specify a variable already named on a previous DROP or one not named on a previous KEEP, the variable is considered nonexistent and the program displays an error message. The command is aborted and no portable file is saved.

Example

```
EXPORT OUTFILE=NEWSUM /DROP=DEPT TO DIVISION.
```

- The portable file is written to file *NEWSUM*. Variables between and including *DEPT* and *DIVISION* in the working file are excluded from the portable file.
- All other variables are saved in the portable file.

RENAME Subcommand

RENAME renames variables being written to the portable file. The renamed variables retain their original variable and value labels, missing-value flags, and print formats. The names of the variables are not changed in the working data file.

- To rename a variable, specify the name of the variable in the working data file, an equals sign, and the new name.
- A variable list can be specified on both sides of the equals sign. The number of variables on both sides must be the same, and the entire specification must be enclosed in parentheses.
- The keyword TO can be used for both variable lists (see "Keyword TO" on p. 19).
- If you specify a renamed variable on a subsequent DROP or KEEP subcommand, the new variable name must be used.

Example

```
EXPORT OUTFILE=NEWSUM /DROP=DEPT TO DIVISION
  /RENAME=(NAME,WAGE=LNAME,SALARY).
```

- RENAME renames *NAME* and *WAGE* to *LNAME* and *SALARY*.
- *LNAME* and *SALARY* retain the variable and value labels, missing-value flags, and print formats assigned to *NAME* and *WAGE*.

MAP Subcommand

MAP displays any changes that have been specified by the RENAME, DROP, or KEEP subcommands.

- MAP can be specified as often as desired.
- Each MAP subcommand maps the results of subcommands that precede it; results of subcommands that follow it are not mapped.When MAP is specified last, it also produces a description of the portable file.

Example

```
EXPORT OUTFILE=NEWSUM /DROP=DEPT TO DIVISION /MAP
  /RENAME NAME=LNAME WAGE=SALARY /MAP.
```

- The first MAP subcommand produces a listing of the variables in the file after DROP has dropped the specified variables.
- RENAME renames *NAME* and *WAGE*.
- The second MAP subcommand shows the variables in the file after renaming. Since this is the last subcommand, the listing will show the variables as they are written in the portable file.

DIGITS Subcommand

DIGITS specifies the degree of precision for all noninteger numeric values written to the portable file.

- DIGITS has the general form DIGITS=*n*, where *n* is the number of digits of precision.
- DIGITS applies to all numbers for which rounding is required.
- Different degrees of precision *cannot* be specified for different variables. Thus, DIGITS should be set according to the requirements of the variable that needs the most precision.
- Default precision methods used by EXPORT work perfectly for integers that are not too large and for fractions whose denominators are products of 2, 3, and 5 (all decimals, quarters, eighths, sixteenths, thirds, thirtieths, sixtieths, and so forth.) For other fractions and for integers too large to be represented exactly in the working data file (usually more than 9 digits, often 15 or more), the representation used in the working file contains some error already, so no exact way of sending these numbers is possible. The program sends enough digits to get very close. The number of digits sent in these cases depends on the originating computer: on mainframe IBM versions of the program, it is the equivalent of 13 decimal digits (integer and fractional parts combined). If many numbers on a file require this level of precision, the file can grow quite large. If you do not need the full default precision, you can save some space in the portable file by using the DIGITS subcommand.

Example

```
EXPORT OUTFILE=NEWSUM /DROP=DEPT TO DIVISION /MAP /DIGITS=4.
```

- DIGITS guarantees the accuracy of values to four significant digits. For example, 12.34567890876 will be rounded to 12.35.

FACTOR

```
FACTOR VARIABLES=varlist†  [/MISSING=[{LISTWISE**}] [INCLUDE]]
                                      {PAIRWISE  }
                                      {MEANSUB   }
                                      {DEFAULT** }

 [/MATRIX=[IN({COR=file})]   [OUT({COR=file})]]
              {COR=*   }           {COR=*   }
              {COV=file}           {COV=file}
              {COV=*   }           {COV=*   }
              {FAC=file}           {FAC=file}
              {FAC=*   }           {FAC=*   }
                                   {FSC=file}
                                   {FSC=*   }

 [/METHOD = {CORRELATION**}]
            {COVARIANCE   }

 [/SELECT=varname(value)]

 [/ANALYSIS=varlist...]

 [/PRINT=[DEFAULT**] [INITIAL**] [EXTRACTION**] [ROTATION**]
         [UNIVARIATE] [CORRELATION] [COVARIANCE] [DET] [INV]
         [REPR] [AIC] [KMO] [FSCORE] [SIG] [ALL]]

 [/PLOT=[EIGEN] [ROTATION [(n1,n2)]]]

 [/DIAGONAL={value list}]
            {DEFAULT** }

 [/FORMAT=[SORT] [BLANK(n)] [DEFAULT**]]

 [/CRITERIA=[FACTORS(n)] [MINEIGEN({1.0**})] [ITERATE({25**})]
                                   {n    }            {n   }

          [RCONVERGE({0.0001**})]   [{KAISER**}]
                     {n       }      {NOKAISER}

          [ECONVERGE({0.001**})] [DEFAULT**]]
                     {n      }

 [/EXTRACTION={PC**     }] [/ROTATION={VARIMAX**     }]
              {PA1**    }             {EQUAMAX       }
              {PAF      }             {QUARTIMAX     }
              {ALPHA    }             {OBLIMIN({0}) }
              {IMAGE    }                      {n}
              {ULS      }             {PROMAX({4}    }
              {GLS      }                     {n}
              {ML       }             {NOROTATE      }
              {DEFAULT**}             {DEFAULT**     }

 [/SAVE=[{REG    } ({ALL}[rootname])]]
         {BART   }  {n  }
         {AR     }
         {DEFAULT}
```

† Omit VARIABLES with matrix input.
**Default if subcommand or keyword is omitted.

Example

```
FACTOR VARIABLES=V1 TO V12.
```

Overview

FACTOR performs factor analysis based either on correlations or covariances and using one of the seven extraction methods. FACTOR also accepts matrix input in the form of correlation matrices, covariance matrices, or factor loading matrices and can write the matrix materials to a matrix data file.

Options

Analysis Phase Options. You can choose to analyze a correlation or covariance matrix using the METHOD subcommand. You can select a subset of cases for the analysis phase using the SELECT subcommand. You can tailor the statistical display for an analysis using the PRINT subcommand. You can sort the output in the factor pattern and structure matrices with the FORMAT subcommand. You can also request scree plots and plots of the variables in factor space on the PLOT subcommand.

Extraction Phase Options. With the EXTRACTION subcommand you can specify one of six extraction methods in addition to the default principal components extraction: principal axis factoring, alpha factoring, image factoring, unweighted least squares, generalized least squares, and maximum likelihood. You can supply initial diagonal values for principal axis factoring on the DIAGONAL subcommand. On the CRITERIA subcommand, you can alter the default statistical criteria used in the extraction.

Rotation Phase Options. You can control the criteria for factor rotation with the CRITERIA subcommand. On the ROTATION subcommand you can choose among four rotation methods (equamax, quartimax, promax, and oblimin) in addition to the default varimax rotation, or you can specify no rotation.

Factor Scores. You can save factor scores as new variables in the working data file using any of the three methods available on the SAVE subcommand.

Matrix Input and Output. With the MATRIX subcommand, you can write a correlation matrix, a covariance matrix, or a factor loading matrix. You can also read matrix materials written either by a previous FACTOR procedure or by a procedure that writes correlation or covariance matrices.

Basic Specification

The basic specification is the VARIABLES subcommand with a variable list. FACTOR performs principal components analysis with a varimax rotation on all variables in the analysis using default criteria.

- When matrix materials are used as input, do not specify VARIABLES. Use the ANALYSIS subcommand to specify a subset of the variables in the matrix.

Subcommand Order

- METHOD and SELECT can be specified anywhere. VARIABLES must be specified before any other subcommands, unless an input matrix is specified. MISSING must be specified before ANALYSIS.
- The ANALYSIS, EXTRACTION, ROTATION, and SAVE subcommands must be specified in the order they are listed here. If you specify these subcommands out of order, you may get unpracticed results. For example, if you specify EXTRACTION before ANALYSIS and SAVE before ROTATION, EXTRACTION and SAVE are ignored. If no EXTRACTION and SAVE subcommands are specified in proper order, the default will be used, that is, PC for EXTRACTION and no SAVE.
- The FORMAT subcommand can be specified anywhere after the VARIABLES subcommand.
- If an ANALYSIS subcommand is present, the statistical display options on PRINT, PLOT, or DIAGONAL must be specified after it. PRINT, PLOT, and DIAGONAL subcommands specified before the ANALYSIS subcommand are ignored. If no such commands are specified after the ANALYSIS subcommand, the default is used.
- The CRITERIA subcommand can be specified anywhere, but applies only to the subcommands that follow. If no CRITERIA subcommand is specified before EXTRACTION or ROTATION, the default criteria for the respective subcommand are used.

Example

```
FACTOR VAR=V1 TO V12
  /ANALYSIS=V1 TO V8
  /CRITERIA=FACTORS(3)
  /EXTRACTION=PAF
  /ROTATION=QUARTIMAX.
```

- The default CORRELATION method is used. FACTOR performs a factor analysis of the correlation matrix based on the first eight variables in the working data file (*V1* to *V8*).
- The procedure extracts three factors using the principal axis method and quartimax rotation.
- LISTWISE (the default for MISSING) is in effect. Cases with missing values for any one of the variables from *V1* to *V12* are omitted from the analysis. As a result, if you ask for the factor analysis using VAR=V1 TO V8 and ANALYSIS=ALL, the results may be different even though the variables used in the analysis are the same.

Syntax Rules

- Each FACTOR procedure performs only one analysis with one extraction and one rotation. Use multiple FACTOR commands to perform multiple analyses.
- VARIABLES or MATRIX=IN can be specified only once. Any other subcommands can be specified multiple times but only the last in proper order takes effect.

Operations

- VARIABLES calculates a correlation and a covariance matrix. If SELECT is specified, only the selected cases are used.
- The correlation or covariance matrix (either calculated from the data or read in) is the basis for the factor analysis.
- Factor scores are calculated for all cases (selected and unselected).

Example

```
FACTOR VARIABLES=V1 TO V12.
```

- This example uses the default CORRELATION method.
- It produces the default principal components analysis of 12 variables. Those with eigenvalues greater than 1 (the default criterion for extraction) are rotated using varimax rotation (the default).

VARIABLES Subcommand

VARIABLES names all the variables to be used in the FACTOR procedure.

- VARIABLES is required except when matrix input is used. When FACTOR reads a matrix data file, the VARIABLES subcommand cannot be used.
- The specification on VARIABLES is a list of numeric variables.
- Keyword ALL on VARIABLES refers to all variables in the working data file.
- Only one VARIABLES subcommand can be specified, and it must be specified first.

MISSING Subcommand

MISSING controls the treatment of cases with missing values.

- If MISSING is omitted or included without specifications, listwise deletion is in effect.
- MISSING must precede the ANALYSIS subcommand.
- The LISTWISE, PAIRWISE, and MEANSUB keywords are alternatives, but any one of them can be used with INCLUDE.

LISTWISE *Delete cases with missing values listwise.* Only cases with nonmissing values for all variables named on the VARIABLES subcommand are used. Cases are deleted even if they have missing values only for variables listed on VARIABLES and have valid values for all variables listed on ANALYSIS. Alias DEFAULT.

PAIRWISE *Delete cases with missing values pairwise.* All cases with nonmissing values for each pair of variables correlated are used to compute that correlation, regardless of whether the cases have missing values for any other variable.

MEANSUB *Replace missing values with the variable mean.* All cases are used after the substitution is made. If INCLUDE is also specified, user-missing values are included in the computation of the means, and means are substituted only for the system-missing value. If SELECT is in effect, only the values of selected cases are used in calculating the means used to replace missing values for selected cases in analysis and for all cases in computing factor scores.

INCLUDE *Include user-missing values.* Cases with user-missing values are treated as valid.

METHOD Subcommand

METHOD specifies whether the factor analysis is performed on a correlation matrix or a covariance matrix.

- Only one METHOD subcommand is allowed. If more than one is specified, the last is in effect.

CORRELATION *Perform a correlation matrix analysis.* This is the default.

COVARIANCE *Perform a covariance matrix analysis.* Valid only with principal components, principal axis factoring, or image factoring methods of extraction. The program issues an error if this keyword is specified when the input is a factor loading matrix or a correlation matrix that does not contain standard deviations (STDDEV or SD).

SELECT Subcommand

SELECT limits cases used in the analysis phase to those with a specified value for any one variable.

- Only one SELECT subcommand is allowed. If more than one is specified, the last is in effect.
- The specification is a variable name and a valid value in parentheses. A string value must be specified within quotes. Multiple variables or values are not permitted.
- The selection variable does not have to be specified on the VARIABLES subcommand.
- Only cases with the specified value for the selection variable are used in computing the correlation or covariance matrix. You can compute and save factor scores for the unselected cases as well as the selected cases.
- SELECT is not valid if MATRIX = IN is specified.

Example

```
FACTOR VARIABLES = V1 TO V10
  /SELECT=COMPLETE(1)
  /SAVE (4).
```

- FACTOR analyzes all ten variables named on VARIABLES, using only cases with a value of 1 for the variable *COMPLETE*.

- By default, FACTOR uses the CORRELATION method and performs the principal components analysis of the selected cases. Those with eigenvalues greater than 1 are rotated using varimax rotation.
- Four factor scores, for both selected and unselected cases, are computed using the default regression method and four new variables are saved in the working data file.

ANALYSIS Subcommand

The ANALYSIS subcommand specifies a subset of the variables named on VARIABLES for use in an analysis.

- The specification on ANALYSIS is a list of variables, all of which must have been named on the VARIABLES subcommand. For matrix input, ANALYSIS can specify a subset of the variables in a correlation or covariance matrix.
- Only one ANALYSIS subcommand is allowed. When multiple ANALYSIS subcommands are specified, the last is in effect.
- If no ANALYSIS is specified, all variables named on the VARIABLES subcommand (or included in the matrix input file) are used.
- Keyword TO in a variable list on ANALYSIS refers to the order in which variables are named on the VARIABLES subcommand, not to their order in the working data file.
- Keyword ALL refers to all variables named on the VARIABLES subcommand.

Example

```
FACTOR VARIABLES=V1 V2 V3 V4 V5 V6
  /ANALYSIS=V4 TO V6.
```

- This example requests a factor analysis of *V4*, *V5*, and *V6*. Keyword TO on ANALYSIS refers to the order of variables on VARIABLES, not the order in the working data file.
- Cases with missing values for all variables specified on VARIABLES are omitted from the analysis. (The default setting for MISSING.)
- By default, the CORRELATION method is used and a principal components analysis with a varimax rotation is performed.

FORMAT Subcommand

FORMAT modifies the format of factor pattern and structure matrices.

- FORMAT can be specified anywhere after VARIABLES and MISSING. If more than one FORMAT is specified, the last is in effect.
- If FORMAT is omitted or included without specifications, variables appear in the order in which they are named on ANALYSIS and all matrix entries are displayed.

SORT *Order the factor loadings in descending order.*

BLANK(n) *Suppress coefficients lower than* n *in absolute value.*

DEFAULT *Turn off keywords SORT and BLANK.*

Example

```
FACTOR VARIABLES=V1 TO V12
  /MISSING=MEANSUB
  /FORMAT=SORT BLANK(.3)
  /EXTRACTION=ULS
  /ROTATION=NOROTATE.
```

- This example specifies an analysis of all variables between and including *V1* and *V12* in the working data file.
- The default CORRELATION method is used.
- The MISSING subcommand substitutes variable means for missing values.
- The FORMAT subcommand orders variables in factor pattern matrices by descending value of loadings. Factor loadings with an absolute value less than 0.3 are omitted.
- Factors are extracted using unweighted least squares and are not rotated.

PRINT Subcommand

PRINT controls the statistical display in the output.

- Keywords INITIAL, EXTRACTION, and ROTATION are the defaults if PRINT is omitted or specified without keywords.
- If any keywords are specified, only the output specifically requested is produced.
- The requested statistics are displayed only for variables specified on the last ANALYSIS subcommand.
- If more than one PRINT subcommand is specified, the last is in effect.
- If any ANALYSIS subcommand is explicitly specified, all PRINT subcommands specified before the last ANALYSIS subcommand are ignored. If no PRINT subcommand is specified after the last ANALYSIS subcommand, the default takes effect.

INITIAL *Initial communalities for each variable, eigenvalues of the unreduced correlation matrix, and percentage of variance for each factor.*

EXTRACTION *Factor pattern matrix, revised communalities, the eigenvalue of each factor retained, and the percentage of variance each eigenvalue represents.*

ROTATION *Rotated factor pattern matrix, factor transformation matrix, factor correlation matrix, and the post-rotation sums of squared loadings.*

UNIVARIATE *Valid number of cases, means, and standard deviations.* (Not available with matrix input.) If MISSING=MEANSUB or PAIRWISE, the output also includes the number of missing cases.

CORRELATION *Correlation matrix.* Ignored if the input is a factor loading matrix.

COVARIANCE *Covariance matrix.* Ignored if the input is a factor loading matrix or a correlation matrix that does not contain standard deviations (STDDEV or SD).

SIG *Matrix of significance levels of correlations.*

DET *Determinant of the correlation or covariance matrix, depending on the specification on* METHOD.

INV *Inverse of the correlation or covariance matrix, depending on the specification on* METHOD.

AIC *Anti-image covariance and correlation matrices* (Kaiser, 1970). The measure of sampling adequacy for the individual variable is displayed on the diagonal of the anti-image correlation matrix.

KMO *Kaiser-Meyer-Olkin measure of sampling adequacy and Bartlett's test of sphericity.* Always based on the correlation matrix. Not computed for an input matrix when it does not contain *N* values.

REPR *Reproduced correlations and residuals or reproduced covariance and residuals, depending on the specification on* METHOD.

FSCORE *Factor score coefficient matrix.* Factor score coefficients are calculated using the method requested on the SAVE subcommand. The default is the regression method.

ALL *All available statistics.*

DEFAULT INITIAL, EXTRACTION, *and* ROTATION.

Example

```
FACTOR VARS=V1 TO V12
  /SELECT=COMPLETE ('yes')
  /MISS=MEANSUB
  /PRINT=DEF AIC KMO REPR
  /EXTRACT=ULS
  /ROTATE=VARIMAX.
```

- This example specifies a factor analysis that includes all variables between and including *V1* and *V12* in the working data file.
- Only cases with the value "yes" on *COMPLETE* are used.
- Variable means are substituted for missing values. Only values for the selected cases are used in computing the mean. This mean is used to substitute missing values in analyzing the selected cases and in computing factor scores for all cases.
- The output includes the anti-image correlation and covariance matrices, the Kaiser-Meyer-Olkin measure of sampling adequacy, the reproduced correlation and residual matrix, as well as the default statistics.
- Factors are extracted using unweighted least squares.
- The factor pattern matrix is rotated using the varimax rotation.

PLOT Subcommand

Use PLOT to request scree plots or plots of variables in rotated factor space.

- If PLOT is omitted, no plots are produced. If PLOT is used without specifications, it is ignored.

- If more than one PLOT subcommand is specified, only the last one is in effect.
- If any ANALYSIS subcommand is explicitly specified, all PLOT subcommands specified before the last ANALYSIS subcommand are ignored. If no PLOT subcommand is specified after the last ANALYSIS subcommand, no plot is produced.

EIGEN *Scree plot* (Cattell, 1966). The eigenvalues from each extraction are plotted in descending order.

ROTATION *Plots of variables in factor space.* When used without any additional specifications, ROTATION can produce only high-resolution graphics. If three or more factors are extracted, a 3-D plot is produced with the factor space defined by the first three factors. You can request two-dimensional plots by specifying pairs of factor numbers in parentheses; for example, PLOT ROTATION(1,2)(1,3)(2,3) requests three plots, each defined by two factors. The ROTATION subcommand must be explicitly specified when you enter the keyword ROTATION on the PLOT subcommand.

DIAGONAL Subcommand

DIAGONAL specifies values for the diagonal in conjunction with principal axis factoring.

- If DIAGONAL is omitted or included without specifications, FACTOR uses the default method for specifying the diagonal.
- DIAGONAL is ignored with extraction methods other than PAF. The values are automatically adjusted by corresponding variances if METHOD=COVARIANCE.
- If more than one DIAGONAL subcommand is specified, only the last one is in effect.
- If any ANALYSIS subcommand is explicitly specified, DIAGONAL subcommands specified before the last ANALYSIS subcommand are ignored. If no DIAGONAL is specified after the last ANALYSIS subcommand, the default is used.
- Default communality estimates for PAF are squared multiple correlations. If these cannot be computed, the maximum absolute correlation between the variable and any other variable in the analysis is used.

valuelist *Diagonal values.* The number of values supplied must equal the number of variables in the analysis block. Use the notation n* before a value to indicate that the value is repeated *n* times.

DEFAULT *Initial communality estimates.*

Example

```
FACTOR VARIABLES=V1 TO V12
  /DIAGONAL=.56 .55 .74 2*.56 .70 3*.65 .76 .64 .63
  /EXTRACTION=PAF
  /ROTATION=VARIMAX.
```

- The factor analysis includes all variables between and including *V1* and *V12* in the working data file.
- DIAGONAL specifies 12 values to use as initial estimates of communalities in principal axis factoring.

- The factor pattern matrix is rotated using varimax rotation.

CRITERIA Subcommand

CRITERIA controls extraction and rotation criteria.

- CRITERIA can be specified anywhere after VARIABLES and MISSING.
- Only explicitly specified criteria are changed. Unspecified criteria keep their defaults.
- Multiple CRITERIA subcommands are allowed. Changes made by a previous CRITERIA subcommand are overwritten by a later CRITERIA subcommand.
- Any CRITERIA subcommands specified after the last EXTRACTION subcommand have no effect on extraction.
- Any CRITERIA subcommands specified after the last ROTATION subcommand have no effect on rotation.

The following keywords on CRITERIA apply to extractions:

FACTORS(n) *Number of factors extracted.* The default is the number of eigenvalues greater than MINEIGEN. When specified, FACTORS overrides MINEIGEN.

MINEIGEN(n) *Minimum eigenvalue used to control the number of factors extracted.* If METHOD=CORRELATION, the default is 1. If METHOD=COVARIANCE, the default is computed as *(Total Variance/Number of Variables)*n*, where *Total Variance* is the total weighted variance principal components or principal axis factoring extraction and the total image variance for image factoring extraction.

ECONVERGE(n) *Convergence criterion for extraction.* The default is 0.001.

The following keywords on CRITERIA apply to rotations:

RCONVERGE(n) *Convergence criterion for rotation.* The default is 0.0001.

KAISER *Kaiser normalization in the rotation phase.* This is the default. The alternative is NOKAISER.

NOKAISER *No Kaiser normalization.*

The following keywords on CRITERIA apply to both extractions and rotations:

ITERATE(n) *Maximum number of iterations for solutions in the extraction or rotation phases.* The default is 25.

DEFAULT *Reestablish default values for all criteria.*

Example

```
FACTOR VARIABLES=V1 TO V12
  /CRITERIA=FACTORS(6)
  /EXTRACTION=PC
  /ROTATION=NOROTATE
  /PLOT=ROTATION.
```

- This example analyzes all variables between and including *V1* and *V12* in the working data file.
- Six factors are extracted using the default principal components method, and the factor pattern matrix is not rotated.
- PLOT sends all extracted factors to the graphics editor and shows a 3-D plot of the first three factors.

EXTRACTION Subcommand

EXTRACTION specifies the factor extraction technique.

- Only one EXTRACTION subcommand is allowed. If multiple EXTRACTION subcommands are specified, only the last is performed.
- If any ANALYSIS subcommand is explicitly specified, all EXTRACTION subcommands before the last ANALYSIS subcommand are ignored. If no EXTRACTION subcommand is specified after the last ANALYSIS subcommand, the default extraction is performed.
- If EXTRACTION is not specified or is included without specifications, principal components extraction is used.
- If you specify criteria for EXTRACTION, the CRITERIA subcommand must precede the EXTRACTION subcommand.
- When you specify EXTRACTION, you should always explicitly specify the ROTATION subcommand. If ROTATION is not specified, the factors are not rotated.

PC *Principal components analysis* (Harman, 1967). This is the default. PC can also be requested with keyword PA1 or DEFAULT.

PAF *Principal axis factoring*. PAF can also be requested with keyword PA2.

ALPHA *Alpha factoring* (Kaiser & Caffry, 1965). Invalid if METHOD=COVARIANCE.

IMAGE *Image factoring* (Kaiser, 1963).

ULS *Unweighted least squares* (Jöreskog, 1977). Invalid if METHOD=COVARIANCE.

GLS *Generalized least squares*. Invalid if METHOD=COVARIANCE.

ML *Maximum likelihood* (Jöreskog & Lawley, 1968). Invalid if METHOD=VARIANCE.

Example

```
FACTOR VARIABLES=V1 TO V12
  /ANALYSIS=V1 TO V6
  /EXTRACTION=ULS
  /ROTATE=NOROTATE.
```

- This example analyzes variables *V1* through *V6* with an unweighted least-squares extraction. No rotation is performed.

ROTATION Subcommand

ROTATION specifies the factor rotation method. It can also be used to suppress the rotation phase entirely.

- Only one ROTATION subcommand is allowed. If multiple ROTATION subcommands are specified, only the last is performed.
- If any ANALYSIS subcommand is explicitly specified, all ROTATION subcommands before the last ANALYSIS subcommand are ignored. If any EXTRACTION subcommand is explicitly specified, all ROTATION subcommands before the last EXTRACTION subcommand are ignored.
- If ROTATION is omitted together with EXTRACTION, varimax rotation is used.
- If ROTATION is omitted but EXTRACTION is not, factors are not rotated.
- Keyword NOROTATE on the ROTATION subcommand produces a plot of variables in unrotated factor space if the PLOT subcommand is also included for the analysis.

VARIMAX *Varimax rotation.* This is the default if ROTATION is entered without specifications or if EXTRACTION and ROTATION are both omitted. Varimax rotation can also be requested with keyword DEFAULT.

EQUAMAX *Equamax rotation.*

QUARTIMAX *Quartimax rotation.*

OBLIMIN(n) *Direct oblimin rotation.* This is a nonorthogonal rotation; thus, a factor correlation matrix will also be displayed. You can specify a delta ($n \leq 0.8$) in parentheses. The value must be less than or equal to 0.8. The default is 0.

PROMAX(n) *Promax rotation.* This is a nonorthogonal rotation; thus, a factor correlation matrix will also be displayed. For this method, you can specify a real-number value greater than 1. The default is 4.

NOROTATE *No rotation.*

Example

```
FACTOR VARIABLES=V1 TO V12
  /EXTRACTION=ULS
  /ROTATION
  /ROTATION=OBLIMIN.
```

- The first ROTATION subcommand specifies the default varimax rotation.
- The second ROTATION subcommand specifies an oblimin rotation based on the same extraction of factors.

SAVE Subcommand

SAVE allows you to save factor scores from any rotated or unrotated extraction as new variables in the working data file. You can use any of the three methods for computing the factor scores.

- Only one SAVE subcommand is executed. If you specify multiple SAVE subcommands, only the last is executed.
- SAVE must follow the last ROTATION subcommand.
- If no ROTATION subcommand is specified after the last EXTRACTION subcommand, SAVE must follow the last EXTRACTION subcommand and no rotation is used.
- If neither ROTATION nor EXTRACTION is specified, SAVE must follow the last ANALYSIS subcommand and the default extraction and rotation are used to compute the factor scores.
- SAVE subcommands before any explicitly specified ANALYSIS, EXTRACTION, or ROTATION subcommands are ignored.
- You cannot use the SAVE subcommand if you are replacing the working data file with matrix materials (see "Matrix Output" on p. 376).
- The new variables are added to the end of the working data file.

Keywords to specify the method of computing factor scores are:

REG *Regression method.* This is the default.

BART *Bartlett method.*

AR *Anderson-Rubin method.*

DEFAULT *The same as REG.*

- After one of the above keywords, specify in parentheses the number of scores to save and a rootname to use in naming the variables.
- You can specify either an integer or the keyword ALL. The maximum number of scores you can specify is the number of factors in the solution.
- FACTOR forms variable names by appending sequential numbers to the rootname you specify. The rootname must begin with a letter and conform to the rules for variable names. It must be short enough that the variable names formed will not exceed eight characters.
- If you do not specify a rootname, FACTOR forms unique variable names using the formula *FACn_m,* where *m* increments to create a new rootname and *n* increments to create a unique variable name. For example, *FAC1_1, FAC2_1, FAC3_1,* and so on will be generated for the first set of saved scores and *FAC1_2, FAC2_2, FAC3_2,* and so on for the second set. As *m* and *n* increase, the prefix *FAC* is truncated to keep the variable names within eight characters. For example, *FAC999_12* is increased to *F1000_12.* The initial *F* is required.
- FACTOR automatically generates variable labels for the new variables. Each label contains information about the method of computing the factor score, its sequential number, and the sequential number of the analysis.

Example

```
FACTOR VARIABLES=V1 TO V12
  /CRITERIA FACTORS(4)
  /ROTATION
  /SAVE REG (4,PCOMP).
```

- Since there is no EXTRACTION subcommand before the ROTATION subcommand, the default principal components extraction is performed.

- The CRITERIA subcommand specifies that four principal components should be extracted.
- The ROTATION subcommand requests the default varimax rotation for the principal components.
- The SAVE subcommand calculates scores using the regression method. Four scores will be added to the file: *PCOMP1*, *PCOMP2*, *PCOMP3*, and *PCOMP4*.

MATRIX Subcommand

MATRIX reads and writes SPSS-format matrix data files.

- MATRIX must always be specified first.
- Only one IN and one OUT keyword can be specified on the MATRIX subcommand. If either IN or OUT is specified more than once, the FACTOR procedure is not executed.
- The matrix type must be indicated on IN or OUT. The types are COR for a correlation matrix, COV for a covariance matrix, and FAC for a factor loading matrix. Indicate the matrix type within parentheses immediately before you identify the matrix file.
- If you use both IN and OUT on MATRIX, you can specify them in either order. You cannot write a covariance matrix if the input matrix is a factor loading matrix or a correlation matrix that does not contain standard deviations (STDDEV or SD).
- If you read in a covariance matrix and write out a factor loading matrix, the output factor loadings are rescaled.

OUT (filename) *Write a matrix data file.* Specify the matrix type (COR, COV, FAC, or FSC) and the matrix file in parentheses. For the matrix data file, specify a filename to store the matrix materials on disk or an asterisk to replace the working data file. If you specify an asterisk, the matrix data file is not stored on disk unless you use SAVE or XSAVE.

IN (filename) *Read a matrix data file.* Specify the matrix type (COR, COV, or FAC) and the matrix file in parentheses. For the matrix data file, specify an asterisk if the matrix data file is the working data file. If the matrix file is another file, specify the filename in parentheses. A matrix file read from an external file does not replace the working data file.

Matrix Output

FACTOR can write matrix materials in the form of a correlation matrix, a covariance matrix, a factor loading matrix, or a factor score coefficients matrix.

- The correlation and covariance matrix materials include counts, means, and standard deviations in addition to correlations or covariances.
- The factor loading matrix materials contain only factor values and no additional statistics.
- The factor score coefficients materials include means and standard deviations, in addition to factor score coefficients.
- See "Format of the Matrix Data File" below for a description of the file.
- FACTOR generates one matrix per split file.

- Any documents contained in the working data file are not transferred to the matrix file.

Matrix Input

- FACTOR can read matrix materials written either by a previous FACTOR procedure or by a procedure that writes correlation or covariance matrices. For more information, see Universals on p. 1.
- MATRIX=IN cannot be used unless a working data file has already been defined. To read an existing matrix data file at the beginning of a session, first use GET to retrieve the matrix file and then specify IN(COR=*), IN(COV=*) or IN(FAC=*) on MATRIX.
- The VARIABLES subcommand cannot be used with matrix input.
- For correlation and covariance matrix input, the ANALYSIS subcommand can specify a subset of the variables in the matrix. You cannot specify a subset of variables for factor loading matrix input. By default, the ANALYSIS subcommand uses all variables in the matrix.

Format of the Matrix Data File

- For correlation or covariance matrices, the matrix data file has two special variables created by the program: *ROWTYPE_* and *VARNAME_*. Variable *ROWTYPE_* is a short string variable with the value CORR (for Pearson correlation coefficient) or COV (for covariance) for each matrix row. Variable *VARNAME_* is a short string variable whose values are the names of the variables used to form the correlation matrix.
- For factor loading matrices, the program generates two special variables named *ROWTYPE_* and *FACTOR_*. The value for *ROWTYPE_* is always FACTOR. The values for *FACTOR_* are the ordinal numbers of the factors.
- For factor score coefficient matrices, the matrix data file has two special variables created: *ROWTYPE_* and *VARNAME_*. If split-file processing is in effect, the split variables appear first in the matrix output file, followed by *ROWTYPE_*, *VARNAME_*, and the variables in the analysis. *ROWTYPE_* is a short string with three possible values: MEAN, STDDEV, and FSCOEF. There is always one occurrence of the value MEAN. If /METHOD = CORRELATION then there is one occurrence of the value STDDEV. Otherwise, this value does not appear. There are as many occurrences of FSCOEF as the number of extracted factors. *VARNAME_* is a short string who values are FAC*n* where *n* is the sequence of the saved factor when *ROWTYPE_* equals FSCOEF. Otherwise the value is empty.
- The remaining variables are the variables used to form the matrix.

Split Files

- FACTOR can read or write split-file matrices.
- When split-file processing is in effect, the first variables in the matrix data file are the split variables, followed by *ROWTYPE_*, *VARNAME_* (or *FACTOR_*), and then the variables used to form the matrix.
- A full set of matrix materials is written for each split-file group defined by the split variables.

- A split variable cannot have the same variable name as any other variable written to the matrix data file.
- If split-file processing is in effect when a matrix is written, the same split file must be in effect when that matrix is read by any other procedure.

Example

```
GET FILE=GSS80 /KEEP ABDEFECT TO ABSINGLE.
FACTOR VARIABLES=ABDEFECT TO ABSINGLE
  /MATRIX OUT(COR=CORMTX).
```

- FACTOR retrieves the *GSS80* file and writes a factor correlation matrix to the file *CORMTX*.
- The working data file is still *GSS80*. Subsequent commands will be executed on this file.

Example

```
GET FILE=GSS80 /KEEP ABDEFECT TO ABSINGLE.
FACTOR VARIABLES=ABDEFECT TO ABSINGLE
  /MATRIX OUT(COR=*).
LIST.
```

- FACTOR writes the same matrix as in the previous example.
- The working data file is replaced with the correlation matrix. The LIST command is executed on the matrix file, not on *GSS80*.

Example

```
GET FILE=GSS80 /KEEP ABDEFECT TO ABSINGLE.
FACTOR VARIABLES=ABDEFECT TO ABSINGLE
  /MATRIX OUT(FAC=*).
```

- FACTOR generates a factor loading matrix that replaces the working data file.

Example

```
GET FILE=COUNTRY /KEEP SAVINGS POP15 POP75 INCOME GROWTH.
REGRESSION MATRIX OUT(*)
  /VARS=SAVINGS TO GROWTH
  /MISS=PAIRWISE
  /DEP=SAVINGS /ENTER.
FACTOR MATRIX IN(COR=*) /MISSING=PAIRWISE.
```

- The GET command retrieves the *COUNTRY* file and selects the variables needed for the analysis.
- The REGRESSION command computes correlations among five variables with pairwise deletion. MATRIX=OUT writes a matrix data file, which replaces the working data file.
- MATRIX IN(COR=*) on FACTOR reads the matrix materials REGRESSION has written to the working data file. An asterisk is specified because the matrix materials are in the working

data file. FACTOR uses pairwise deletion, since this is what was in effect when the matrix was built.

Example

```
GET FILE=COUNTRY /KEEP SAVINGS POP15 POP75 INCOME GROWTH.
REGRESSION
  /VARS=SAVINGS TO GROWTH
  /MISS=PAIRWISE
  /DEP=SAVINGS /ENTER.
FACTOR MATRIX IN(COR=CORMTX).
```

- This example performs a regression analysis on file *COUNTRY* and then uses a different file for FACTOR. The file is an existing matrix data file.
- MATRIX=IN specifies the matrix data file *CORMTX*.
- *CORMTX* does not replace *COUNTRY* as the working data file.

Example

```
GET FILE=CORMTX.
FACTOR MATRIX IN(COR=*).
```

- This example starts a new session and reads an existing matrix data file. GET retrieves the matrix data file *CORMTX*.
- MATRIX=IN specifies an asterisk because the matrix data file is the working data file. If MATRIX=IN(CORMTX) is specified, the program issues an error message.
- If the GET command is omitted, the program issues an error message.

Example

```
MATRIX.
GET A /FILE="fsc.sav".
GET B /FILE="ext_data.sav" /VAR=varlist.
COMPUTE SCORES=A*B.
SAVE SCORES /OUTFILE="scored.sav".
END MATRIX.
```

- This example scores an external file using the factor score coefficients from a previous analysis.
- Factor score coefficients are read from *fsc.sav* into *A*.
- The data are read from *ext_data.sav* into *B*. The variable values in the external file should be standardized. If there are missing values, add /MISSING=OMIT or /MISSING=0 to the second GET statement to remove cases with missing values or impute the mean (0, since the variables are standardized).
- The scores are saved to *scored.sav*.

References

Cattell, R. B. 1966. The scree test for the number of factors. *Journal of Multivariate Behavioral. Research.* 1: 245-276.

Harman, H. H. 1967. *Modern factor analysis*. 2nd ed. Chicago: University of Chicago Press.

Jöreskog, K. G. 1977. Factor analysis by least-square and maximum-likelihood method. In: *Statistical Methods for Digital Computers*, volume 3, K. Enslein, A. Ralston, and R.S. Wilf, eds. New York: John Wiley & Sons, Inc.

Jöreskog, K. G., and Lawley, D.N. 1968. New methods in maximum likelihood factor analysis. *British Journal of Mathematical and Statistical Psychology*, 21: 85-96.

Kaiser, H. F. 1963. Image analysis. In: *Problems in Measuring Change*, C. W. Harris, ed. Madison: University of Wisconsin Press.

Kaiser, H. F. 1970. A second-generation Little Jiffy. *Psychometrika*, 35: 401–415.

Kaiser, H. F., and Caffry, J. 1865. Alpha factor analysis. *Psychometrika*, 30: 1-14.

FILE HANDLE

```
FILE HANDLE handle /NAME=file specifications
                   [/MODE={CHARACTER }] [/RECFORM \={FIXED   } [/LRECL=n]
                          {BINARY    }              {VARIABLE}
                          {MULTIPUNCH}              {SPANNED }
                          {IMAGE     }
                          {360       }
```

Overview

FILE HANDLE assigns a unique *file handle* to a file and supplies operating system specifications for the file. A defined file handle can be specified on any subsequent FILE, OUTFILE, MATRIX, or WRITE subcommands of various procedures.

Syntax Rules

- A file handle cannot exceed eight characters and must begin with an alphabetical character (A–Z) or a $, #, or @. It can contain numeric digits (0–9) but not imbedded blanks.
- FILE HANDLE is required for reading IBM VSAM data sets, EBCDIC data files, binary data files, and character data files that are not delimited by ASCII line feeds.
- If you specify 360 on the MODE subcommand, you must specify RECFORM.
- If you specify IMAGE on the MODE subcommand, you must specify LRECL.

Operations

A file handle is used only during the current work session. The handle is never saved as part of an SPSS-format data file.

NAME Subcommand

NAME specifies the file you want to refer to by the file handle. The file specifications must conform to the file naming convention for the type of computer and operating system on which the program is run. See the documentation for your system for specific information about the file naming convention.

MODE Subcommand

MODE specifies the type of file you want to refer to by the file handle.

CHARACTER *Character file whose logical records are delimited by ASCII line feeds.*

BINARY *Unformatted binary file generated by Microsoft FORTRAN.*

MULTIPUNCH *Column binary file.*

IMAGE *Binary file consisting of fixed-length records.*

360 *EBCDIC data file.*

Example

```
FILE HANDLE ELE48 /NAME='OSPS:[SPSSUSER]ELE48.DAT' /MODE=MULTIPUNCH.
DATA LIST FILE=ELE48.
```

- FILE HANDLE defines *ELE48* as the handle for the file.
- The MODE subcommand indicates that the file contains multipunch data.
- The file specification on NAME conforms to VMS convention: the file *ELE48.DAT* is located in the directory *OSPS:[SPSSUSER]*.
- The FILE subcommand on DATA LIST refers to the handle defined on the FILE HANDLE command.

RECFORM Subcommand

RECFORM specifies the record format and is necessary when you specify 360 on MODE. RECFORM has no effect with other specifications on MODE.

FIXED *Fixed-length record.* All records have the same length. Alias F. When FIXED is specified, the record length must be specified on the LRECL subcommand.

VARIABLE *Variable-length record.* No logical record is larger than one physical block. Alias V.

SPANNED *Spanned record.* Records may be larger than fixed-length physical blocks. Alias VS.

LRECL Subcommand

LRECL specifies the length of each record in the file. When you specify IMAGE under UNIX, OS/2, or Microsoft Windows, or 360 for IBM360 EBCDIC data files, you must specify LRECL. You can specify a record length greater than the default (8192) for an image file, a character file, or a binary file. Do not use LRECL with MULTIPUNCH.

Example

```
FILE HANDLE TRGT1 /NAME='OSPS:RGT.DAT'
                  /MODE=IMAGE LRECL=16.
DATA LIST FILE=TRGT1.
```

- IMAGE is specified on the MODE subcommand. Subcommand LRECL must be specified.
- The file handle is used on the DATA LIST command.

FILE LABEL

```
FILE LABEL label
```

Overview

FILE LABEL provides a descriptive label for a data file.

Syntax Rules

The only specification is a label up to 60 characters long.

Operations

- The file label is printed on the first line of each page of output displayed by the program.
- If the specified label is longer than 60 characters, the program truncates the label to 60 characters without warning.
- If the file is saved, the label is included in the dictionary of the SPSS-format data file.

Example

```
FILE LABEL  Hubbard Industrial Consultants Inc. employee data.
SAVE OUTFILE=HUBEMPL
  /RENAME=(AGE JOBCAT=AGE80 JOBCAT82) /MAP.
```

- FILE LABEL assigns a file label to the Hubbard Consultants Inc. employee data.
- The SAVE command saves the file as an SPSS-format data file, renaming two variables and mapping the results to check the renamed variables.

FILE TYPE—END FILE TYPE

For mixed file types:

```
FILE TYPE MIXED [FILE=file] RECORD=[varname] column location [(format)]

                [WILD={NOWARN}]
                      {WARN  }
```

For grouped file types:

```
FILE TYPE GROUPED [FILE=file] RECORD=[varname] column location [(format)]

 CASE=[varname] column location [(format)]

 [WILD={WARN  }] [DUPLICATE={WARN  }]
       {NOWARN}             {NOWARN}

 [MISSING={WARN  }] [ORDERED={YES}]
          {NOWARN}           {NO }
```

For nested file types:

```
FILE TYPE NESTED [FILE=file] RECORD=[varname] column location [(format)]

 [CASE=[varname] column location [(format)]]

 [WILD={NOWARN}] [DUPLICATE={NOWARN}]
       {WARN  }             {WARN  }
                            {CASE  }

 [MISSING={NOWARN}]
          {WARN  }

END FILE TYPE
```

Example

```
FILE TYPE  MIXED RECORD=RECID 1-2.
RECORD TYPE 23.
DATA LIST   /SEX 5 AGE 6-7 DOSAGE 8-10 RESULT 12.
END FILE TYPE.

BEGIN DATA
21  145010 1
22  257200 2
25  235  250  2
35  167         300    3
24  125150 1
23  272075 1
21  149050 2
25  134  035  3
30  138         300    3
32  229         500    3
END DATA.
```

Overview

The FILE TYPE—END FILE TYPE structure defines data for any one of the three types of complex raw data files: *mixed files,* which contain several types of records that define different types of cases; *hierarchical* or *nested files,* which contain several types of records with a defined relationship among the record types; or *grouped files,* which contain several records for each case with some records missing or duplicated. A fourth type of complex file, files with *repeating groups* of information, can be defined with the REPEATING DATA command.

FILE TYPE must be followed by at least one RECORD TYPE command and one DATA LIST command. Each pair of RECORD TYPE and DATA LIST commands defines one type of record in the data. END FILE TYPE signals the end of file definition.

Within the FILE TYPE structure, the lowest-level record in a nested file can be read with a REPEATING DATA command rather than a DATA LIST command. In addition, any record in a mixed file can be read with REPEATING DATA.

Basic Specification

The basic specification on FILE TYPE is one of the three file type keywords (MIXED, GROUPED, or NESTED) and the RECORD subcommand. RECORD names the record identification variable and specifies its column location. If keyword GROUPED is specified, the CASE subcommand is also required. CASE names the case identification variable and specifies its column location.

The FILE TYPE—END FILE TYPE structure must enclose at least one RECORD TYPE and one DATA LIST command. END FILE TYPE is required to signal the end of file definition.

- RECORD TYPE specifies the values of the record type identifier (see RECORD TYPE).
- DATA LIST defines variables for the record type specified on the preceding RECORD TYPE command (see DATA LIST).
- Separate pairs of RECORD TYPE and DATA LIST commands must be used to define each different record type.

The resulting working data file is always a rectangular file, regardless of the structure of the original data file.

Specification Order

- FILE TYPE must be the first command in the FILE TYPE—END FILE TYPE structure. FILE TYPE subcommands can be named in any order.
- Each RECORD TYPE command must precede its corresponding DATA LIST command.
- END FILE TYPE must be the last command in the structure.

Syntax Rules

- For mixed files, if the record types have different variables or if they have the same variables recorded in different locations, separate RECORD TYPE and DATA LIST commands are required for each record type.
- For mixed files, the same variable name can be used on different DATA LIST commands, since each record type defines a separate case.
- For mixed files, if the same variable is defined for more than one record type, the format type and length of the variable should be the same on all DATA LIST commands. The program refers to the *first* DATA LIST command that defines a variable for the print and write formats to include in the dictionary of the working data file.
- For grouped and nested files, the variable names on each DATA LIST must be unique, since a case is built by combining all record types together into a single record.
- For nested files, the order of the RECORD TYPE commands defines the hierarchical structure of the file. The first RECORD TYPE defines the highest-level record type, the next RECORD TYPE defines the next highest-level record, and so forth. The last RECORD TYPE command defines a case in the working data file. By default, variables from higher-level records are spread to the lowest-level record.
- For nested files, the SPREAD subcommand on RECORD TYPE can be used to spread the values in a record type only to the *first* case built from each record of that type. All other cases associated with that record are assigned the system-missing value for the variables defined on that type. See RECORD TYPE for more information.
- String values specified on the RECORD TYPE command must be enclosed in apostrophes or quotation marks.

Operations

- For mixed file types, the program skips all records that are not specified on one of the RECORD TYPE commands.
- If different variables are defined for different record types in mixed files, the variables are assigned the system-missing value for those record types on which they are not defined.
- For nested files, the first record in the file should be the type specified on the first RECORD TYPE command—the highest level of the hierarchy. If the first record in the file is not the highest-level type, the program skips all records until it encounters a record of the highest-level type. If MISSING or DUPLICATE has been specified, these records may produce warning messages but will not be used to build a case in the working file.
- When defining complex files, you are effectively building an input program and can use only commands that are allowed in the input state. See Appendix A for information on program states.

Example

```
* Reading multiple record types from a mixed file.

FILE TYPE  MIXED FILE=TREATMNT RECORD=RECID 1-2.
+ RECORD TYPE 21,22,23,24.
+ DATA LIST   /SEX 5 AGE 6-7 DOSAGE 8-10 RESULT 12.
+ RECORD TYPE 25.
+ DATA LIST   /SEX 5 AGE 6-7 DOSAGE 10-12 RESULT 15.
END FILE TYPE.
```

- Variable *DOSAGE* is read from columns 8–10 for record types 21, 22, 23, and 24 and from columns 10–12 for record type 25. *RESULT* is read from column 12 for record types 21, 22, 23, and 24, and from column 15 for record type 25.
- The working data file contains values for all variables defined on the DATA LIST commands for record types 21 through 25. All other record types are skipped.

Example

```
* Reading only one record type from a mixed file.

FILE TYPE  MIXED RECORD=RECID 1-2.
RECORD TYPE 23.
DATA LIST   /SEX 5 AGE 6-7 DOSAGE 8-10 RESULT 12.
END FILE TYPE.

BEGIN DATA
21  145010 1
22  257200 2
25  235  250  2
35  167             300     3
24  125150 1
23  272075 1
21  149050 2
25  134  035  3
30  138             300     3
32  229             500     3
END DATA.
```

- FILE TYPE begins the file definition and END FILE TYPE indicates the end of file definition. FILE TYPE specifies a mixed file type. Since the data are included between BEGIN DATA—END DATA, the FILE subcommand is omitted. The record identification variable *RECID* is located in columns 1 and 2.
- RECORD TYPE indicates that records with value 23 for variable *RECID* will be copied into the working data file. All other records are skipped. the program does not issue a warning when it skips records in mixed files.
- DATA LIST defines variables on records with the value 23 for variable *RECID*.

Example

```
* A grouped file of student test scores.

FILE TYPE GROUPED RECORD=#TEST 6 CASE=STUDENT 1-4.
RECORD TYPE 1.
DATA LIST  /ENGLISH 8-9 (A).
RECORD TYPE 2.
DATA LIST /READING 8-10.
RECORD TYPE 3.
DATA LIST /MATH 8-10.
END FILE TYPE.

BEGIN DATA
0001 1 B+
0001 2  74
0001 3  83
0002 1 A
0002 2 100
0002 3  71
0003 1 B-
0003 2  88
0003 3  81
0004 1 C
0004 2  94
0004 3  91
END DATA.
```

- FILE TYPE identifies the file as a grouped file. As required for grouped files, all records for a single case are together in the data. The record identification variable *#TEST* is located in column 6. A scratch variable is specified so it won't be saved in the working data file. The case identification variable *STUDENT* is located in columns 1–4.
- Because there are three record types, there are three RECORD TYPE commands. For each RECORD TYPE, there is a DATA LIST to define variables on that record type.
- END FILE TYPE signals the end of file definition.
- The program builds four cases—one for each student. Each case includes the case identification variable plus the variables defined for each record type (the test scores). The values for *#TEST* are not saved in the working data file. Thus, each case in the working file has four variables: *STUDENT*, *ENGLISH*, *READING*, and *MATH*.

Example

```
* A nested file of accident records.

FILE TYPE NESTED RECORD=6 CASE=ACCID 1-4.
RECORD TYPE 1.
DATA LIST /ACC_ID 9-11 WEATHER 12-13 STATE 15-16 (A) DATE 18-24 (A).
RECORD TYPE 2.
DATA LIST /STYLE 11 MAKE 13 OLD 14 LICENSE 15-16(A) INSURNCE 18-21 (A).
RECORD TYPE 3.
DATA LIST /PSNGR_NO 11 AGE 13-14 SEX 16 (A) INJURY 18 SEAT 20-21 (A)
           COST 23-24.
END FILE TYPE.

BEGIN DATA
0001 1  322 1 IL 3/13/88    /* Type 1:  accident record
0001 2    1 44MI 134M       /* Type 2:    vehicle record
0001 3    1 34 M 1 FR  3    /* Type 3:      person record
0001 2    2 16IL 322F       /*            vehicle record
0001 3    1 22 F 1 FR 11    /*              person record
0001 3    2 35 M 1 FR  5    /*              person record
0001 3    3 59 M 1 BK  7    /*              person record
0001 2    3 21IN 146M       /*            vehicle record
0001 3    1 46 M 0 FR  0    /*              person record
END DATA.
```

- FILE TYPE specifies a nested file type. The record identifier, located in column 6, is not assigned a variable name, so the default scratch variable name *####RECD* is used. The case identification variable *ACCID* is located in columns 1–4.
- Because there are three record types, there are three RECORD TYPE commands. For each RECORD TYPE, there is a DATA LIST command to define variables on that record type. The order of the RECORD TYPE commands defines the hierarchical structure of the file.
- END FILE TYPE signals the end of file definition.
- The program builds a case for each lowest-level (type 3) record, representing each person in the file. There can be only one type 1 record for each type 2 record, and one type 2 record for each type 3 record. Each vehicle can be in only one accident, and each person can be in only one vehicle. The variables from the type 1 and type 2 records are spread to their corresponding type 3 records.

Types of Files

The first specification on FILE TYPE is a file type keyword, which defines the structure of the data file. There are three file type keywords: MIXED, GROUPED, and NESTED. Only one of the three types can be specified on FILE TYPE.

MIXED *Mixed file type.* MIXED specifies a file in which each record type named on a RECORD TYPE command defines a case. You do not need to define all types of records in the file. In fact, FILE TYPE MIXED is useful for reading only one type of record because the program can decide whether to execute the DATA LIST for a record by simply reading the variable that identifies the record type.

GROUPED *Grouped file type.* GROUPED defines a file in which cases are defined by grouping together record types with the same identification number. Each case usually has one record of each type. All records for a single case must be together in the file. By default, the program assumes that the records are in the same sequence within each case.

NESTED *Nested file type.* NESTED defines a file in which the record types are related to each other hierarchically. The record types are grouped together by a case identification number that identifies the highest level—the first record type—of the hierarchy. Usually, the last record type specified—the lowest level of the hierarchy—defines a case. For example, in a file containing household records and records for each person living in the household, each person record defines a case. Information from higher record types may be *spread* to each case. For example, the value for a variable on the household record, such as *CITY*, can be spread to the records for each person in the household.

Subcommands and Their Defaults for Each File Type

The specifications on the FILE TYPE differ for each type of file. Table 1 shows whether each subcommand is required or optional and, where applicable, what the default specification is for each file type. N/A indicates that the subcommand is not applicable to that type of file.

Table 1 Summary of FILE TYPE subcommands for different file types

Subcommand	Mixed	Grouped	Nested
FILE	Conditional	Conditional	Conditional
RECORD	Required	Required	Required
CASE	Not Applicable	Required	Optional
WILD	NOWARN	WARN	NOWARN
DUPLICATE	N/A	WARN	NOWARN
MISSING	N/A	WARN	NOWARN
ORDERED	N/A	YES	N/A

- FILE is required unless data are inline (included between BEGIN DATA—END DATA).
- RECORD is always required.
- CASE is required for grouped files.
- The subcommands CASE, DUPLICATE, and MISSING can also be specified on the associated RECORD TYPE commands for grouped files. However, `DUPLICATE=CASE` is invalid.
- For nested files, CASE and MISSING can be specified on the associated RECORD TYPE commands.
- If the subcommands CASE, DUPLICATE, or MISSING are specified on a RECORD TYPE command, the specification on the FILE TYPE command (or the default) is overridden only for the record types listed on that RECORD TYPE command. The FILE TYPE specification or default applies to all other record types.

FILE Subcommand

FILE specifies a text file containing the data. FILE is not used when the data are inline.

Example

```
FILE TYPE  MIXED FILE=TREATMNT RECORD=RECID 1-2.
```

- Data are in file *TREATMNT*. The file type is mixed. The record identification variable *RECID* is located in columns 1 and 2 of each record.

RECORD Subcommand

RECORD specifies the name and column location of the record identification variable.

- The column location of the record identifier is required. The variable name is optional.
- If you do not want to save the record type variable, you can assign a scratch variable name by using the # character as the first character of the name. If a variable name is not specified on RECORD, the record identifier is defined as the scratch variable *####RECD*.
- The value of the identifier for each record type must be unique and must be in the same location on all records. However, records do not have to be sorted according to type.
- A column-style format can be specified for the record identifier. For example, the following two specifications are valid:

  ```
  RECORD=V1 1-2(N)
  RECORD=V1 1-2(F,1)
  ```

  FORTRAN-like formats cannot be used because the column location must be specified explicitly.
- Specify A in parentheses after the column location to define the record type variable as a string variable.

Example

```
FILE TYPE  MIXED FILE=TREATMNT RECORD=RECID 1-2.
```

- The record identifier is variable *RECID*, located in columns 1 and 2 of the hospital treatment data file.

CASE Subcommand

CASE specifies a name and column location for the case identification variable. CASE is required for grouped files and optional for nested files. It cannot be used with mixed files.

- For grouped files, each unique value for the case identification variable defines a case in the working data file.
- For nested files, the case identification variable identifies the highest-level record of the hierarchy. The program issues a warning message for each record with a case identification number not equal to the case identification number on the last highest-level record. However, the record with the invalid case number is used to build the case.

- The column location of the case identifier is required. The variable name is optional.
- If you do not want to save the case identification variable, you can assign a scratch variable name by using the # character as the first character of the name. If a variable name is not specified on CASE, the case identifier is defined as the scratch variable *####CASE*.
- A column-style format can be specified for the case identifier. For example, the following two specifications are valid:

  ```
  CASE=V1 1-2(N)
  CASE=V1 1-2(F,1)
  ```

  FORTRAN-like formats cannot be used because the column location must be specified explicitly.
- Specify A in parentheses after the column location to define the case identification variable as a string variable.
- If the case identification number is not in the same columns on all record types, use the CASE subcommand on the RECORD TYPE commands as well as on the FILE TYPE command (see RECORD TYPE).

Example

```
* A grouped file of student test scores.

FILE TYPE GROUPED RECORD=#TEST 6 CASE=STUDENT 1-4.
RECORD TYPE 1.
DATA LIST  /ENGLISH 8-9 (A).
RECORD TYPE 2.
DATA LIST /READING 8-10.
RECORD TYPE 3.
DATA LIST /MATH 8-10.
END FILE TYPE.

BEGIN DATA
0001 1 B+
0001 2  74
0001 3  83
0002 1 A
0002 2 100
0002 3  71
0003 1 B-
0003 2  88
0003 3  81
0004 1 C
0004 2  94
0004 3  91
END DATA.
```

- CASE is required for grouped files. CASE specifies variable *STUDENT*, located in columns 1–4, as the case identification variable.
- The data contain four different values for *STUDENT*. The working data file therefore has four cases, one for each value of *STUDENT*. In a grouped file, each unique value for the case identification variable defines a case in the working file.
- Each case includes the case identification variable plus the variables defined for each record type. The values for *#TEST* are not saved in the working data file. Thus, each case in the working file has four variables: *STUDENT, ENGLISH, READING*, and *MATH*.

Example

```
* A nested file of accident records.

FILE TYPE NESTED RECORD=6 CASE=ACCID 1-4.
RECORD TYPE 1.
DATA LIST   /ACC_ID 9-11 WEATHER 12-13 STATE 15-16 (A) DATE 18-24 (A).
RECORD TYPE 2.
DATA LIST /STYLE 11 MAKE 13 OLD 14 LICENSE 15-16 (A) INSURNCE 18-21 (A).
RECORD TYPE 3.
DATA LIST /PSNGR_NO 11 AGE 13-14 SEX 16 (A) INJURY 18 SEAT 20-21 (A)
          COST 23-24.
END FILE TYPE.

BEGIN DATA
0001 1  322 1 IL 3/13/88    /* Type 1:  accident record
0001 2    1 44MI 134M       /* Type 2:    vehicle record
0001 3    1 34 M 1 FR  3    /* Type 3:       person record
0001 2    2 16IL 322F       /*            vehicle record
0001 3    1 22 F 1 FR 11    /*               person record
0001 3    2 35 M 1 FR  5    /*               person record
0001 3    3 59 M 1 BK  7    /*               person record
0001 2    3 21IN 146M       /*            vehicle record
0001 3    1 46 M 0 FR  0    /*               person record
END DATA.
```

- CASE specifies variable *ACCID*, located in columns 1–4, as the case identification variable. *ACCID* identifies the highest level of the hierarchy: the level for the accident records.
- As each case is built, the value of the variable *ACCID* is checked against the value of *ACCID* on the last highest-level record (record type 1). If the values do not match, a warning message is issued. However, the record is used to build the case.
- The data in this example contain only one value for *ACCID*, which is spread across all cases. In a nested file, the lowest-level record type determines the number of cases in the working data file. In this example, the working file has five cases because there are five person records.

Example

```
* Specifying case on the RECORD TYPE command.

FILE TYPE GROUPED FILE=HUBDATA RECORD=#RECID 80 CASE=ID 1-5.
RECORD TYPE 1.
DATA LIST   /MOHIRED YRHIRED 12-15 DEPT79 TO DEPT82 SEX 16-20.
RECORD TYPE 2.
DATA LIST   /SALARY79 TO SALARY82 6-25 HOURLY81 HOURLY82 40-53 (2)
             PROMO81 72  AGE 54-55 RAISE82 66-70.
RECORD TYPE 3  CASE=75-79.
DATA LIST   /JOBCAT 6 NAME 25-48 (A).
END FILE TYPE.
```

- The CASE subcommand on FILE TYPE indicates that the case identification number is located in columns 1–5. However, for type 3 records, the case identification number is located in columns 75–79. The CASE subcommand is therefore specified on the third RECORD TYPE command to override the case setting for type 3 records.

- The format of the case identification variable must be the same on all records. If the case identification variable is defined as a string on the FILE TYPE command, it cannot be defined as a numeric variable on the RECORD TYPE command, and vice versa.

WILD Subcommand

WILD determines whether the program issues a warning when it encounters undefined record types in the data file. Regardless of whether the warning is issued, undefined records are not included in the working data file.

- The only specification on WILD is keyword WARN or NOWARN.
- WARN cannot be specified if keyword OTHER is specified on the last RECORD TYPE command to indicate all other record types (see RECORD TYPE).

WARN *Issue warning messages.* The program displays a warning message and the first 80 characters of the record for each record type that is not mentioned on a RECORD TYPE command. This is the default for grouped file types.

NOWARN *Suppress warning messages.* The program simply skips all record types not mentioned on a RECORD TYPE command and does not display warning messages. This is the default for mixed and nested file types.

Example

```
FILE TYPE  MIXED FILE=TREATMNT RECORD=RECID 1-2 WILD=WARN.
```

- WARN is specified on the WILD subcommand. The program displays a warning message and the first 80 characters of the record for each record type that is not mentioned on a RECORD TYPE command.

DUPLICATE Subcommand

DUPLICATE determines how the program responds when it encounters more than one record of each type for a single case. DUPLICATE is optional for grouped and nested files. DUPLICATE cannot be used with mixed files.

- The only specification on DUPLICATE is keyword WARN, NOWARN, or CASE.

WARN *Issue warning messages.* The program displays a warning message and the first 80 characters of the last record of the duplicate set of record types. Only the *last* record from a set of duplicates is included in the working data file. This is the default for grouped files.

NOWARN *Suppress warning messages.* The program does not display warning messages when it encounters duplicate record types. Only the *last* record from a set of duplicates is included in the working data file. This is the default for nested files.

CASE *Build a case in the working data file for each duplicate record.* The program builds one case in the working file for each duplicate record, spreading information from any higher-level records and assigning system-missing values to the variables defined on lower-level records. This option is available only for nested files.

Example

```
* A nested file of accident records.
* Issue a warning for duplicate record types.

FILE TYPE NESTED RECORD=6 CASE=ACCID 1-4 DUPLICATE=WARN.
RECORD TYPE 1.
DATA LIST   /ACC_ID 9-11 WEATHER 12-13 STATE 15-16 (A) DATE 18-24 (A).
RECORD TYPE 2.
DATA LIST /STYLE 11 MAKE 13 OLD 14 LICENSE 15-16 (A) INSURNCE 18-21 (A).
RECORD TYPE 3.
DATA LIST /PSNGR_NO 11 AGE 13-14 SEX 16 (A) INJURY 18 SEAT 20-21 (A)
          COST 23-24.
END FILE TYPE.

BEGIN DATA
0001 1  322 1 IL 3/13/88    /*          accident record
0001 2    1 44MI 134M       /*            vehicle record
0001 3    1 34 M 1 FR   3   /*               person record
0001 2    1 31IL 134M       /*  duplicate vehicle record
0001 2    2 16IL 322F       /*            vehicle record
0001 3    1 22 F 1 FR 11    /*               person record
0001 3    2 35 M 1 FR   5   /*               person record
0001 3    3 59 M 1 BK   7   /*               person record
0001 2    3 21IN 146M       /*            vehicle record
0001 3    1 46 M 0 FR   0   /*               person record
END DATA.
```

- In the data, there are two vehicle (type 2) records above the second set of person (type 3) records. This implies that an empty (for example, parked) vehicle was involved, or that each of the three persons was in two vehicles, which is impossible.
- DUPLICATE specifies keyword WARN. The program displays a warning message and the first 80 characters of the second of the duplicate set of type 2 records. The first duplicate record is skipped, and only the second is included in the working data file. This assumes that no empty vehicles were involved in the accident.
- If the duplicate record represents an empty vehicle, it can be included in the working data file by specifying keyword CASE on DUPLICATE. The program builds one case in the working data file for the first duplicate record, spreading information to that case from the previous type 1 record and assigning system-missing values to the variables defined for type 3 records. The second record from the duplicate set is used to build the three cases for the associated type 3 records.

MISSING Subcommand

MISSING determines whether the program issues a warning when it encounters a missing record type for a case. Regardless of whether the program issues the warning, it builds the case in the working file with system-missing values for the variables defined on the missing record. MISSING is optional for grouped and nested files.

- MISSING cannot be used with mixed files and is optional for grouped and nested files.
- For grouped and nested files, the program verifies that each defined case includes one record of each type.
- The only specification is keyword WARN or NOWARN.

WARN *Issue a warning message when a record type is missing for a case.* This is the default for grouped files.

NOWARN *Suppress the warning message when a record type is missing for a case.* This is the default for nested files.

Example

```
* A grouped file with missing records.

FILE TYPE GROUPED RECORD=#TEST 6 CASE=STUDENT 1-4 MISSING=NOWARN.
RECORD TYPE 1.
DATA LIST  /ENGLISH 8-9 (A).
RECORD TYPE 2.
DATA LIST /READING 8-10.
RECORD TYPE 3.
DATA LIST /MATH 8-10.
END FILE TYPE.

BEGIN DATA
0001 1 B+
0001 2  74
0002 1 A
0002 2 100
0002 3  71
0003 3  81
0004 1 C
0004 2  94
0004 3  91
END DATA.
```

- The data contain records for three tests administered to four students. However, not all students took all tests. The first student took only the English and reading tests. The third student took only the math test.
- One case in the working data file is built for each of the four students. If a student did not take a test, the system-missing value is assigned in the working file to the variable for the missing test. Thus, the first student has the system-missing value for the math test, and the third student has missing values for the English and reading tests.
- Keyword NOWARN is specified on MISSING. Therefore, no warning messages are issued for the missing records.

Example

```
* A nested file with missing records.

FILE TYPE NESTED RECORD=6 CASE=ACCID 1-4 MISSING=WARN.
RECORD TYPE 1.
DATA LIST  /ACC_ID 9-11 WEATHER 12-13 STATE 15-16 (A) DATE 18-24 (A).
RECORD TYPE 2.
DATA LIST /STYLE 11 MAKE 13 OLD 14 LICENSE 15-16 (A) INSURNCE 18-21 (A).
RECORD TYPE 3.
DATA LIST /PSNGR_NO 11 AGE 13-14 SEX 16 (A) INJURY 18 SEAT 20-21 (A)
          COST 23-24.
END FILE TYPE.
```

```
BEGIN DATA
0001 1   322 1 IL 3/13/88    /*          accident record
0001 3     1 34 M 1 FR   3   /*              person record
0001 2     2 16IL 322F       /*            vehicle record
0001 3     1 22 F 1 FR 11    /*              person record
0001 3     2 35 M 1 FR   5   /*              person record
0001 3     3 59 M 1 BK   7   /*              person record
0001 2     3 21IN 146M       /*            vehicle record
0001 3     1 46 M 0 FR   0   /*              person record
END DATA.
```

- The data contain records for one accident. The first record is a type 1 (accident) record, and the second record is a type 3 (person) record. However, there is no type 2 record, and therefore no vehicle associated with the first person. The person may have been a pedestrian, but it is also possible that the vehicle record is missing.
- One case is built for each person record. The first case has missing values for the variables specified on the vehicle record.
- Keyword WARN is specified on MISSING. A warning message is issued for the missing record.

ORDERED Subcommand

ORDERED indicates whether the records are in the same order as they are defined on the RECORD TYPE commands. Regardless of the order of the records in the data file and the specification on ORDERED, the program builds cases in the working data file with records in the order defined on the RECORD TYPE commands.

- ORDERED can be used only for grouped files.
- The only specification is keyword YES or NO.
- If YES is in effect but the records are not in the order defined on the RECORD TYPE commands, the program issues a warning for each record that is out of order. The program still uses these records to build cases.

YES *Records for each case are in the same order as they are defined on the RECORD TYPE commands.* This is the default.

NO *Records are not in the same order within each case.*

Example

```
* A grouped file with records out of order.

FILE TYPE GROUPED RECORD=#TEST 6 CASE=STUDENT 1-4  MISSING=NOWARN
  ORDERED=NO.
RECORD TYPE 1.
DATA LIST  /ENGLISH 8-9 (A).
RECORD TYPE 2.
DATA LIST /READING 8-10.
RECORD TYPE 3.
DATA LIST /MATH 8-10.
END FILE TYPE.
```

```
BEGIN DATA
0001 2  74
0001 1 B+
0002 3  71
0002 2 100
0002 1 A
0003 2  81
0004 2  94
0004 1 C
0004 3  91
END DATA.
```

- The first RECORD TYPE command specifies record type 1, the second specifies record type 2, and the third specifies record type 3. However, records for each case are not always ordered type 1, type 2, and type 3.
- NO is specified on ORDERED. The program builds cases without issuing a warning that they are out of order in the data.
- Regardless of whether YES or NO is in effect for ORDERED, the program builds cases in the working data file in the same order specified on the RECORD TYPE commands.

FILTER

```
FILTER  {BY var}
        {OFF   }
```

Example

```
FILTER BY SEX.
FREQUENCIES BONUS.
```

Overview

FILTER is used to exclude cases from program procedures without deleting them from the working data file. When FILTER is in effect, cases with a zero or missing value for the specified variable are not used in program procedures. Those cases are not actually deleted and are available again if the filter is turned off. To see the current filter status, use the SHOW command.

Basic Specification

The basic specification is keyword BY followed by a variable name. Cases that have a zero or missing value for the filter variable are excluded from subsequent procedures.

Syntax Rules

- Only one numeric variable can be specified. The variable can be one of the original variables in the data file or a variable computed with transformation commands.
- Keyword OFF turns off the filter. All cases in the working data file become available to subsequent procedures.
- If FILTER is specified without a keyword, FILTER OFF is assumed but the program displays a warning message.
- FILTER can be specified anywhere in the command sequence. Unlike SELECT IF, FILTER has the same effect within an input program as it does outside an input program. Attention must be paid to the placement of any transformation command used to compute values for the filter variable (see INPUT PROGRAM).

Operations

- FILTER performs case selection without changing the working data file. Cases that have a zero or missing value are excluded from subsequent procedures but are not deleted from the file.

- Both system-missing and user-missing values are treated as missing. The FILTER command does not offer options for changing selection criteria. To set up different criteria for exclusion, create a numeric variable and conditionally compute its values before specifying it on FILTER.
- If FILTER is specified after TEMPORARY, FILTER affects the next procedure only. After that procedure, the filter status reverts to whatever it was before the TEMPORARY command.
- The filter status does not change until another FILTER command is specified or the working data file is replaced.
- If the specified filter variable is renamed, it is still in effect. The SHOW command will display the new name of the filter variable. However, the filter is turned off if the filter variable is recoded into a string variable or is deleted from the file.
- If the working data file is replaced after a MATCH FILES, ADD FILES, or UPDATE command and the working file is one of the input files, the filter remains in effect if the new working file has a numeric variable with the name of the filter variable. If the working data file does not have a numeric variable with that name (for example, if the filter variable was dropped or renamed), the filter is turned off.
- If the working data file is replaced by an entirely new data file (for example, by a DATA LIST, GET, and IMPORT command), the filter is turned off.
- The FILTER command changes the filter status and takes effect when a procedure is executed or an EXECUTE command is encountered.

Example

```
FILTER BY SEX.
FREQUENCIES BONUS.
```

- This example assumes that *SEX* is a numeric variable, with male and female coded as 0 and 1, respectively. The FILTER command excludes males and cases with missing values for *SEX* from the subsequent procedures. The FREQUENCIES command generates a frequency table of *BONUS* for females only.

Example

```
RECODE SEX (1=0)(0=1).
FILTER BY SEX.
FREQUENCIES BONUS.
```

- This example assumes the same coding scheme for *SEX* as the previous example. Before FILTER is specified, variable *SEX* is recoded. The FILTER command then excludes females and cases with missing values for *SEX*. The FREQUENCIES command generates a frequency table of *BONUS* for males only.

FINISH

```
FINISH
```

Overview

FINISH causes the program to stop reading commands.

Basic Specification

The basic specification is keyword FINISH. There are no additional specifications.

Command Files

- FINISH is optional in a command file and is used to mark the end of a session.
- FINISH causes the program to stop reading commands. Anything following FINISH in the command file is ignored. Any commands following FINISH in an INCLUDE file are ignored.
- FINISH cannot be used within a DO IF structure to end a session conditionally. FINISH within a DO IF structure will end the session unconditionally.

Prompted Sessions

- FINISH is required in a prompted session to terminate the session.
- Because FINISH is a program command, it can be used only after the command line prompt for the program, which expects a procedure name. FINISH cannot be used to end a prompted session from a DATA>, CONTINUE>, HELP>, or DEFINE> prompt.

Operations

- FINISH immediately causes the program to stop reading commands.
- The appearance of FINISH on the printback of commands in the display file indicates that the session has been completed.
- When issued within the SPSS Manager (not available on all systems), FINISH terminates command processing and causes the program to query whether you want to continue working. If you answer *yes*, you can continue creating and editing files in both the input window and the output window; however, you can no longer run commands.

Example

```
* A command file.

DATA LIST FILE=RAWDATA /NAME 1-15(A) V1 TO V15 16-30.
LIST.
FINISH.
REPORT FORMAT=AUTO LIST /VARS=NAME V1 TO V10.
```

- FINISH causes the program to stop reading commands after LIST is executed. The REPORT command is not executed.

Example

```
SPSS> * A prompted session.

SPSS> DATA LIST FILE=RAWDATA /NAME 1-15(A) V1 TO V15 16-30.
SPSS> LIST.
SPSS> FINISH.
```

- FINISH terminates the prompted session.

FIT

```
FIT [[ERRORS=] residual series names]

    [/OBS=observed series names]

    [/{DFE=error degrees of freedom      }]
      {DFH=hypothesis degrees of freedom}
```

Example

```
FIT ERR_4  ERR_8.
```

Overview

FIT displays a variety of descriptive statistics computed from the residual series as an aid in evaluating the goodness of fit of one or more models.

Options

Statistical Output. You can produce statistics for a particular residual series by specifying the names of the series after FIT. You can also obtain percent error statistics for specified residual series by specifying observed series on the OBS subcommand.

Degrees of Freedom. You can specify the degrees of freedom for the residual series using the DFE or DFH subcommands.

Basic Specification

The basic specification is simply the command keyword FIT. All other specifications are optional.

- By default, FIT calculates the mean error, mean percent error, mean absolute error, mean absolute percent error, sum of squared errors, mean square error, root mean square error, and the Durbin-Watson statistic for the last *ERR_n* (residual) series generated and the corresponding observed series in the working data file.
- If neither residual nor observed series are specified, percent error statistics for the default residual and observed series are included.

Syntax Rules

- If OBS is specified, the ERRORS subcommand naming the residual series is required.

Operations

- Observed series and degrees of freedom are matched with residual series according to the order in which they are specified.
- If residual series are explicitly specified but observed series are not, percent error statistics are not included in the output. If neither residual nor observed series are specified, percent error statistics for the default residual and observed series are included.
- If subcommand DFH is specified, FIT calculates the DFE (error degrees of freedom) by subtracting the DFH (hypothesis degrees of freedom) from the number of valid cases in the series.
- If a PREDICT period (validation period) starts before the end of the observed series, statistics are reported separately for the USE period (historical period) and the PREDICT period.

Limitations

- There is no limit on the number of residual series specified. However, the number of observed series must equal the number of residual series.

Example

```
FIT ERR_4 ERR_5 ERR_6.
```

- This command requests goodness-of-fit statistics for the residual series *ERR_4*, *ERR_5*, and *ERR_6*, which were generated by previous procedures. Percent error statistics are not included in the output, since only residual series are named.

ERRORS Subcommand

ERRORS specifies the residual (error) series.

- The actual keyword ERRORS can be omitted. VARIABLES is an alias for ERRORS.
- The minimum specification on ERRORS is a residual series name.
- The ERRORS subcommand is required if the OBS subcommand is specified.

OBS Subcommand

OBS specifies the observed series to use for calculating the mean percentage error and mean absolute percentage error.

- OBS can be used only when the residual series are explicitly specified.
- The number and order of observed series must be the same as that of the residual series.

- If more than one residual series was calculated from a single observed series, the observed series is specified once for each residual series that is based on it.

Example

```
FIT ERRORS=ERR#1 ERR#2
  /OBS=VAR1 VAR1.
```

- This command requests FIT statistics for two residual series, *ERR#1* and *ERR#2*, which were computed from the same observed series, *VAR1*.

DFE and DFH Subcommands

DFE and DFH specify the degrees of freedom for each residual series. With DFE, error degrees of freedom are entered directly. DFH specifies hypothesis degrees of freedom so FIT can compute the DFE.

- Only one DFE or DFH subcommand should be specified. If both are specified, only the last one is in effect.
- The specification on DFE or DFH is a list of numeric values. The order of these values should correspond to the order of the residual series list.
- The error degrees of freedom specified on DFE are used to compute the mean square error (MSE) and root mean square (RMS).
- The value specified for DFH should equal the number of parameters in the model (including the constant if it is present). Differencing is not considered in calculating DFH, since any observations lost due to differencing are system-missing.
- If neither DFE or DFH are specified, FIT sets DFE equal to the number of observations.

Example

```
FIT ERR#1 ERR#2
  /OBS=VAR1 VAR2
  /DFE=47 46.
```

- In this example, the error degrees of freedom for the first residual series, *ERR#1*, is 47. The error degrees of freedom for the second residual series, *ERR#2*, is 46.

Output Considerations for SSE

The sum of squared errors (SSE) reported by FIT may not be the same as the SSE reported by the estimation procedure. The SSE from the procedure is an estimate of sigma squared for that model. The SSE from FIT is simply the sum of the squared residuals.

References

Makridakis, S., S. C. Wheelwright, and V. E. McGee. 1983. *Forecasting: Methods and applications.* New York: John Wiley and Sons.

McLaughlin, R. L. 1984. *Forecasting techniques for decision making.* Rockville, Md.: Control Data Management Institute.

FLIP

```
FLIP [[VARIABLES=] {ALL    }]
                   {varlist}

     [/NEWNAMES=variable]
```

Example

```
FLIP VARIABLES=WEEK1 TO WEEK52 /NEWNAMES=DEPT.
```

Overview

The program requires a file structure in which the variables are the columns and observations (cases) are the rows. If a file is organized such that variables are in rows and observations are in columns, you need to use FLIP to reorganize it. FLIP transposes the rows and columns of the data in the working data file so that, for example, row 1, column 2 becomes row 2, column 1, and so forth.

Options

Variable Subsets. You can transpose specific variables (columns) from the original file using the VARIABLES subcommand.

Variable Names. You can use the values of one of the variables from the original file as the variable names in the new file, using the NEWNAMES subcommand.

Basic Specification

The basic specification is the command keyword FLIP, which transposes all rows and columns.

- By default, FLIP assigns variable names *VAR001* to *VARn* to the variables in the new file. It also creates the new variable *CASE_LBL*, whose values are the variable names that existed before transposition.

Subcommand Order

VARIABLES must precede NEWNAMES.

Operations

- FLIP replaces the working data file with the transposed file and displays a list of variable names in the transposed file.

- FLIP discards any previous VARIABLE LABELS, VALUE LABELS, and WEIGHT settings. Values defined as user-missing in the original file are translated to system-missing in the transposed file.
- FLIP obeys any SELECT IF, N, and SAMPLE commands in effect.
- FLIP does not obey the TEMPORARY command. Any transformations become permanent when followed by FLIP.
- String variables in the original file are assigned system-missing values after transposition.
- Numeric variables are assigned a default format of F8.2 after transposition (with the exceptions of *CASE_LBL* and the variable specified on NEWNAMES).
- The variable *CASE_LBL* is created and added to the working data file each time FLIP is executed.
- If *CASE_LBL* already exists as the result of a previous FLIP, its current values are used as the names of variables in the new file (if NEWNAMES is not specified).

Example

The following is the LIST output for a data file arranged in a typical spreadsheet format, with variables in rows and observations in columns:

```
A                B          C          D

Income       22.00      31.00      43.00
Price        34.00      29.00      50.00
Year       1970.00    1971.00    1972.00
```

The command

```
FLIP.
```

transposes all variables in the file. The LIST output for the transposed file is as follows:

```
CASE_LBL    VAR001     VAR002     VAR003

A                .          .          .
B            22.00      34.00    1970.00
C            31.00      29.00    1971.00
D            43.00      50.00    1972.00
```

- The values for the new variable *CASE_LBL* are the variable names from the original file.
- Case A has system-missing values, since variable *A* had the string values Income, Price, and Year.
- The names of the variables in the new file are *CASE_LBL, VAR001, VAR002,* and *VAR003.*

VARIABLES Subcommand

VARIABLES names one or more variables (columns) to be transposed. The specified variables become observations (rows) in the new working file.

- The VARIABLES subcommand is optional. If it is not used, all variables are transposed.
- The actual keyword VARIABLES can be omitted.
- If the VARIABLES subcommand is specified, variables that are not named are discarded.

Example

Using the untransposed file from the previous example, the command

```
FLIP VARIABLES=A TO C.
```

transposes only variables *A* through *C*. Variable *D* is not transposed and is discarded from the working data file. The LIST output for the transposed file is as follows:

```
CASE_LBL     VAR001     VAR002     VAR003

A               .          .          .
B             22.00      34.00    1970.00
C             31.00      29.00    1971.00
```

NEWNAMES Subcommand

NEWNAMES specifies a variable whose values are used as the new variable names.

- The NEWNAMES subcommand is optional. If it is not used, the new variable names are either *VAR001* to *VARn*, or the values of *CASE_LBL* if it exists.
- Only one variable can be specified on NEWNAMES.
- The variable specified on NEWNAMES does not become an observation (case) in the new working data file, regardless of whether it is specified on the VARIABLES subcommand.
- If the variable specified is numeric, its values become a character string beginning with the letter *V*.
- If the variable specified is a long string, only the first eight characters are used.
- Lowercase character values of a string variable are converted to upper case, and any bad character values, such as blank spaces, are replaced with underscore (_) characters.
- If the variable's values are not unique, a numeric extension *n* is added to the end of a value after its first occurrence, with *n* increasing by 1 at each subsequent occurrence.

Example

Using the untransposed file from the first example, the command

```
FLIP NEWNAMES=A.
```

uses the values for variable *A* as variable names in the new file. The LIST output for the transposed file is as follows:

```
CASE_LBL     INCOME      PRICE       YEAR

B             22.00      34.00    1970.00
C             31.00      29.00    1971.00
D             43.00      50.00    1972.00
```

- Variable *A* does not become an observation in the new file. The string values for *A* are converted to upper case.

The following command transposes this file back to a form resembling its original structure:

```
FLIP.
```

The LIST output for the transposed file is as follows:

```
CASE_LBL         B          C          D

INCOME       22.00      31.00      43.00
PRICE        34.00      29.00      50.00
YEAR       1970.00    1971.00    1972.00
```

- Since the NEWNAMES subcommand is not used, the values of *CASE_LBL* from the previous FLIP (*B, C,* and *D*) are used as variable names in the new file.
- The values of *CASE_LBL* are now INCOME, PRICE, and YEAR.

FORMATS

```
FORMATS varlist(format) [varlist...]
```

Example

```
FORMATS SALARY (DOLLAR8) / HOURLY (DOLLAR7.2) / RAISE BONUS (PCT2).
```

Overview

FORMATS changes variable print and write formats. In this program, print and write formats are *output* formats. Print formats, also called display formats, control the form in which values are displayed by a procedure or by the PRINT command; write formats control the form in which values are written by the WRITE command.

FORMATS changes both print and write formats. To change only print formats, use PRINT FORMATS. To change only write formats, use WRITE FORMATS. For information on assigning input formats during data definition, see DATA LIST.

Table 1 shows the output formats that can be assigned with the FORMATS, PRINT FORMATS, and WRITE FORMATS commands. For additional information on formats, see "Variable Formats" on p. 21.

Basic Specification

The basic specification is a variable list followed by a format specification in parentheses. All variables on the list receive the new format.

Syntax Rules

- You can specify more than one variable or variable list, followed by a format in parentheses. Only one format can be specified after each variable list. For clarity, each set of specifications can be separated by a slash.
- You can use keyword TO to refer to consecutive variables in the working data file.
- The specified width of a format must include enough positions to accommodate any punctuation characters such as decimal points, commas, dollar signs, or date and time delimiters. (This differs from assigning an *input* format on DATA LIST, where the program automatically expands the input format to accommodate punctuation characters in output.)
- Custom currency formats (CCw, CCw.d) must first be defined on the SET command before they can be used on FORMATS.
- FORMATS cannot be used with string variables. To change the length of a string variable, declare a new variable of the desired length with the STRING command and then use COMPUTE to copy values from the existing string into the new variable.
- To save the new print and write formats, you must save the working data file as an SPSS-format data file with the SAVE or XSAVE command.

Table 1 shows the formats that can be assigned by FORMATS, PRINT FORMATS, or WRITE FORMATS. The first column of the table lists the FORTRAN-like specification. The column labeled *PRINT* indicates whether the format can be used to display values. The columns labeled *Min w* and *Max w* refer to the minimum and maximum widths allowed for the format type. The column labeled *Max d* refers to the maximum decimal places.

Table 1 Output data formats

Type	PRINT	Min w	Max w	Max d	
Numeric					
Fw, Fw.d	yes	1*	40	16	
COMMAw, COMMAw.d	yes	1*	40	16	
DOTw, DOTw.d	yes	1*	40	16	
DOLLARw, DOLLARw.d	yes	2*	40	16	
CCw, CCw.d	yes	2*	40	16	
PCTw, PCTw.d	yes	1*	40	16	
PIBHEXw	yes	2†	16†		
RBHEXw	yes	4†	16†		
Zw, Zw.d	yes	1	40	16	
IBw, IBw.d	no	1	8	16	
PIBw, PIBw.d	no	1	8	16	
Nw.d	yes	1	40	16	
Pw, Pw.d	no	1	16	16	
Ew, Ew.d	yes	6	40		
PKw, PKw.d	no	1	16	16	
RBw	no	2	8		
String					
Aw	yes	1	254		
AHEXw	yes	2†	510		
Date and time					Resulting form
DATEw	yes	9	40		dd-mmm-yy
		11			dd-mmm-yyyy
ADATEw	yes	8	40		mm/dd/yy
		10			mm/dd/yyyy
EDATEw	yes	8	40		dd/mm/yy
		10			dd/mm/yyyy
JDATEw	yes	5	40		yyddd
		7			yyyyddd
SDATEw	yes	8	40		yy/mm/dd
		10			yyyy/mm/dd
QYRw	yes	6	40		q Q yy

Table 1 Output data formats (Continued)

Type	PRINT	Min w	Max w	Max d	
		8			q Q yyyy
MOYRw	yes	6	40		mmm yy
		8			mmm yyyy
WKYRw	yes	8	40		ww WK yy
		10			ww WK yyyy
WKDAYw	yes	2**	40		
MONTHw	yes	3**	40		
TIMEw	yes	5††	40		hh:mm
TIMEw.d	yes	10	40	16	hh:mm:ss.s
DTIMEw	yes	8††	40		dd hh:mm
DTIMEw.d	yes	13	40	16	dd hh:mm:ss.s
DATETIMEw	yes	17††	40		dd-mmm-yyyy hh:mm
DATETIMEw.d	yes	22	40	16	dd-mmm-yyyy hh:mm:ss.s

*Add number of decimals plus 1 if number of decimals is more than 0. Total width cannot exceed 40 characters.
†Must be a multiple of 2.
**As the field width is expanded, the output string is expanded until the entire name of the day or month is produced.
††Add 3 to display seconds.

Operations

- Unlike most transformations, FORMATS takes effect as soon as it is encountered in the command sequence. Special attention should be paid to its position among commands. For more information, see "Command Order" on p. 6.
- Variables not specified on FORMATS retain their current print and write formats in the working file. To see the current formats, use the DISPLAY command.
- The new formats are changed only in the working file and are in effect for the duration of the current session or until changed again with a FORMATS, PRINT FORMATS, or WRITE FORMATS command. Formats in the original data file (if one exists) are not changed unless the file is resaved with the SAVE or XSAVE command.
- New numeric variables created with transformation commands are assigned default print and write formats of F8.2 (or the format specified on the FORMAT subcommand of SET). The FORMATS command can be used to change the new variable's print and write formats.
- New string variables created with transformation commands are assigned the format specified on the STRING command that declares the variable. FORMATS cannot be used to change the format of a new string variable.
- If a numeric data value exceeds its width specification, the program attempts to display some value nevertheless. The program first rounds decimal values, then removes punctuation characters, then tries scientific notation, and finally, if there is still not enough space, produces asterisks indicating that a value is present but cannot be displayed in the assigned width.

Example

```
FORMATS SALARY (DOLLAR8) /HOURLY (DOLLAR7.2)
        /RAISE BONUS (PCT2).
```

- The print and write formats for *SALARY* are changed to DOLLAR format with eight positions, including the dollar sign and comma when appropriate. The value 11550 is displayed as $11,550. An eight-digit number would require a DOLLAR11 format: eight characters for the digits, two characters for commas, and one character for the dollar sign.
- The print and write formats for *HOURLY* are changed to DOLLAR format with seven positions, including the dollar sign, decimal point, and two decimal places. The value 115 is displayed as $115.00. If DOLLAR6.2 had been specified, the value 115 would be displayed as $115.0. The program would truncate the last 0 because a width of 6 is not enough to display the full value.
- The print and write formats for both *RAISE* and *BONUS* are changed to PCT with two positions: one position for the percentage and one position for the percent sign. The value 9 is displayed as 9%. Since the width allows for only two positions, the value 10 is displayed as 10, since the percent sign is truncated.

Example

```
COMPUTE V3=V1 + V2.
FORMATS V3 (F3.1).
```

- COMPUTE creates the new numeric variable *V3*. By default, *V3* is assigned an F8.2 format (or the default format specified on SET).
- FORMATS changes both the print and write formats for *V3* to F3.1.

Example

```
SET CCA='-/-.Dfl ..-'.
FORMATS COST (CCA14.2).
```

- SET defines a European currency format for the custom currency format type CCA.
- FORMATS assigns format CCA to variable *COST*. With the format defined for CCA on SET, the value 37419 is displayed as Dfl 37.419,00. See the SET command for more information on custom currency formats.

FREQUENCIES

```
FREQUENCIES [VARIABLES=]varlist [varlist...]

 [/FORMAT= [{NOTABLE }] [{AVALUE**}]
            {LIMIT(n)}    {DVALUE  }
                          {AFREQ   }
                          {DFREQ   }

 [/MISSING=INCLUDE]

 [/BARCHART=[MINIMUM(n)] [MAXIMUM(n)] [{FREQ(n)    }]]
                                       {PERCENT(n) }

 [/PIECHART=[MINIMUM(n)] [MAXIMUM(n)] [{FREQ    }] [{MISSING  }]]
                                       {PERCENT }    {NOMISSING}

 [/HISTOGRAM=[MINIMUM(n)] [MAXIMUM(n)] [{FREQ(n)    }] [{NONORMAL}] ]
                                                         {NORMAL  }

 [/GROUPED=varlist [{(width)         }]]
                    {(boundary list) }

 [/NTILES=n]

 [/PERCENTILES=value list]

 [/STATISTICS=[DEFAULT] [MEAN] [STDDEV] [MINIMUM] [MAXIMUM]
              [SEMEAN] [VARIANCE] [SKEWNESS] [SESKEW] [RANGE]
              [MODE] [KURTOSIS] [SEKURT] [MEDIAN] [SUM] [ALL]
                [NONE]]

 [/ORDER=[{ANALYSIS}] [{VARIABLE}]
```

** Default if subcommand is omitted or specified without keyword.

Example

```
FREQUENCIES VAR=RACE /STATISTICS=ALL.
```

Overview

FREQUENCIES produces Frequency tables showing frequency counts and percentages of the values of individual variables. You can also use FREQUENCIES to obtain Statistics tables for categorical variables and to obtain Statistics tables and graphical displays for continuous variables.

Options

Display Format. You can suppress tables and alter the order of values within tables using the FORMAT subcommand.

Statistical Display. Percentiles and ntiles are available for numeric variables with the PERCENTILES and NTILES subcommands. The following statistics are available with the

STATISTICS subcommand: mean, median, mode, standard deviation, variance, skewness, kurtosis, and sum.

Plots. Histograms can be specified for numeric variables on the HISTOGRAM subcommand. Bar charts can be specified for numeric or string variables on the BARCHART subcommand.

Input Data. On the GROUPED subcommand, you can indicate whether the input data are grouped (or collapsed) so that a better estimate can be made of percentiles.

Basic Specification

The basic specification is the VARIABLES subcommand and the name of at least one variable. By default, FREQUENCIES produces a Frequency table.

Subcommand Order

Subcommands can be named in any order.

Syntax Rules

- You can specify multiple NTILES subcommands.
- BARCHART and HISTOGRAM are mutually exclusive.
- You can specify numeric variables (with or without decimal values) or string variables. Only the short-string portion of long string variables are tabulated.
- Keyword ALL can be used on VARIABLES to refer to all user-defined variables in the working data file.

Operations

- Variables are tabulated in the order they are mentioned on the VARIABLES subcommand.
- If a requested ntile or percentile cannot be calculated, a period (.) is displayed.
- FREQUENCIES dynamically builds the table, setting up one cell for each unique value encountered in the data.

Limitations

- Maximum 500 variables total per FREQUENCIES command.
- Maximum of 32,767 observed values over all variables.

Example

```
FREQUENCIES VAR=RACE /STATISTICS=ALL.
```

- FREQUENCIES requests a Frequency table and a Statistics table showing all statistics for the categorical variable *RACE*.

Example

```
FREQUENCIES STATISTICS=ALL /HISTOGRAM
 /VARIABLES=SEX TVHOURS SCALE1 TO SCALE5
 /FORMAT=NOTABLE.
```

- FREQUENCIES requests statistics and histograms for *SEX, TVHOURS,* and all variables between and including *SCALE1* and *SCALE5* in the working data file.
- FORMAT suppresses the Frequency tables, which are not useful for continuous variables.

VARIABLES Subcommand

VARIABLES names the variables to be tabulated and is the only required subcommand. The actual keyword VARIABLES can be omitted.

FORMAT Subcommand

FORMAT controls various features of the output, including order of categories and suppression of tables.

- The minimum specification is a single keyword.
- By default, FREQUENCIES displays the Frequency table and sort categories in ascending order of values for numeric variables and in alphabetical order for string variables.

Table Order

AVALUE *Sort categories in ascending order of values (numeric variables) or in alphabetical order (string variables).* This is the default.

DVALUE *Sort categories in descending order of values (numeric variables) or in reverse alphabetical order (string variables).* This is ignored when HISTOGRAM, NTILES, or PERCENTILES is requested.

AFREQ *Sort categories in ascending order of frequency.* This is ignored when HISTOGRAM, NTILES, or PERCENTILES is requested.

DFREQ *Sort categories in descending order of frequency.* This is ignored when HISTOGRAM, NTILES, or PERCENTILES is requested.

Table Suppression

LIMIT(n) *Suppress frequency tables with more than* n *categories.* The number of missing and valid cases and requested statistics are displayed for suppressed tables.

NOTABLE *Suppress all frequency tables.* The number of missing and valid cases are displayed for suppressed tables. NOTABLE overrides LIMIT.

BARCHART Subcommand

BARCHART produces a bar chart for each variable named on the VARIABLES subcommand. By default, the horizontal axis for each bar chart is scaled in frequencies, and the interval width is determined by the largest frequency count for the variable being plotted. Bar charts are labeled with value labels or with the value if no label is defined.

- The minimum specification is the BARCHART keyword, which generates default bar charts.
- BARCHART cannot be used with HISTOGRAM.

MIN(n) *Lower bound below which values are not plotted.*

MAX(n) *Upper bound above which values are not plotted.*

FREQ(n) *Vertical axis scaled in frequencies, where optional* n *is the maximum.* If *n* is not specified or if it is too small, FREQUENCIES chooses 5, 10, 20, 50, 100, 200, 500, 1000, 2000, and so forth, depending on the largest category. This is the default.

PERCENT(n) *Vertical axis scaled in percentages, where optional* n *is the maximum.* If *n* is not specified or if it is too small, FREQUENCIES chooses 5, 10, 25, 50, or 100, depending on the frequency count for the largest category.

Example

```
FREQUENCIES VAR=RACE /BARCHART.
```

- FREQUENCIES produces a frequency table and the default bar chart for variable *RACE*.

Example

```
FREQUENCIES VAR=V1 V2 /BAR=MAX(10).
```

- FREQUENCIES produces a frequency table and bar chart with values through 10 for each of variables *V1* and *V2*.

PIECHART Subcommand

PIECHART produces a pie chart for each variable named on the VARIABLES subcommand. By default, one slice corresponds to each category defined by the variable with one slice representing all missing values. Pie charts are labeled with value labels or with the value if no label is defined.

- The minimum specification is the PIECHART keyword, which generates default pie charts.
- PIECHART can be requested together with either BARCHART or HISTOGRAM.
- FREQ and PERCENT are mutually exclusive. If both are specified, only the first specification is in effect.

- MISSING and NOMISSING are mutually exclusive. If both are specified, only the first specification is in effect.

MIN(n) *Lower bound below which values are not plotted.*

MAX(n) *Upper bound above which values are not plotted.*

FREQ *The pie charts are based on frequencies.* Frequencies are displayed when you request values in the Chart Editor. This is the default.

PERCENT *The pie charts are based on percentage.* Percentage is displayed when you request values in the Chart Editor.

MISSING *User-missing and system-missing values are treated as one category.* This is the default. Specify INCLUDE on the MISSING subcommand to display system-missing and user-missing values as separate slices.

NOMISSING *Missing values are excluded from the chart.* If you specify INCLUDE on the MISSING subcommand, each user-missing value is represented by one slice.

Example

```
FREQUENCIES VAR=RACE /PIECHART.
```

- FREQUENCIES produces a frequency table and the default pie chart for variable *RACE*.

Example

```
FREQUENCIES VAR=V1 V2 /PIE=MAX(10).
```

- For each variable *V1* and *V2*, FREQUENCIES produces a frequency table and a pie chart with values through 10.

HISTOGRAM Subcommand

HISTOGRAM displays a plot for each numeric variable named on the VARIABLES subcommand. By default, the horizontal axis of each histogram is scaled in frequencies and the interval width is determined by the largest frequency count of the variable being plotted.

- The minimum specification is the HISTOGRAM keyword, which generates default histograms.
- HISTOGRAM cannot be used with BARCHART.

MIN(n) *Lower bound below which values are not plotted.*

MAX(n) *Upper bound above which values are not plotted.*

FREQ(n) *Vertical axis scaled in frequencies, where optional* n *is the scale.* If *n* is not specified or if it is too small, FREQUENCIES chooses 5, 10, 20, 50, 100, 200, 500, 1000, 2000, and so forth, depending on the largest category. This is the default.

NORMAL *Superimpose a normal curve.* The curve is based on all valid values for the variable, including values excluded by MIN and MAX.

NONORMAL *Suppress the normal curve.* This is the default.

Example

```
FREQUENCIES VAR=V1 /HIST=NORMAL.
```

- FREQUENCIES requests a histogram with a superimposed normal curve.

GROUPED Subcommand

When the values of a variable represent grouped or collapsed data, it is possible to estimate percentiles for the original, ungrouped data from the grouped data. The GROUPED subcommand specifies which variables have been grouped. It affects only the output from the PERCENTILES and NTILES subcommands and the MEDIAN statistic from the STATISTICS subcommand.

- Multiple GROUPED subcommands can be used on a single FREQUENCIES command. Multiple variable lists, separated by slashes, can appear on a single GROUPED subcommand.
- The variables named on GROUPED must have been named on the VARIABLES subcommand.
- The value or value list in the parentheses is optional. When it is omitted, the program treats the values of the variables listed on GROUPED as midpoints. If the values are not midpoints, they must first be recoded with the RECODE command.
- A single value in parentheses specifies the width of each grouped interval. The data values must be group midpoints, but there can be empty categories. For example, if you have data values of 10, 20, and 30 and specify an interval width of 5, the categories are 10 ± 2.5, 20 ± 2.5, and 30 ± 2.5. The categories 15 ± 2.5 and 25 ± 2.5 are empty.
- A value list in the parentheses specifies interval boundaries. The data values do not have to represent midpoints, but the lowest boundary must be lower than any value in the data. If any data values exceed the highest boundary specified (the last value within the parentheses), they will be assigned to an open-ended interval. In this case, some percentiles cannot be calculated.

Example

```
RECODE AGE (1=15) (2=25) (3=35) (4=45) (5=55)
           (6=65) (7=75) (8=85) (9=95)
  /INCOME  (1=5)  (2=15) (3=25) (4=35) (5=45)
           (6=55) (7=65) (8=75) (9=100).

FREQUENCIES VARIABLES=AGE, SEX, RACE, INCOME
  /GROUPED=AGE, INCOME
  /PERCENTILES=5,25,50,75,95.
```

- The *AGE* and *INCOME* categories of 1, 2, 3, and so forth are recoded to category midpoints. Note that data can be recoded to category midpoints on any scale; here *AGE* is recoded in years, but *INCOME* is recoded in thousands of dollars.
- The GROUPED subcommand on FREQUENCIES allows more accurate estimates of the requested percentiles.

Example

```
FREQUENCIES VARIABLES=TEMP
  /GROUPED=TEMP (0.5)
  /NTILES=10.
```

- The values of *TEMP* (temperature) in this example were recorded using an inexpensive thermometer whose readings are precise only to the nearest half degree.
- The observed values of 97.5, 98, 98.5, 99, and so on, are treated as group midpoints, smoothing out the discrete distribution. This yields more accurate estimates of the deciles.

Example

```
FREQUENCIES VARIABLES=AGE
  /GROUPED=AGE (17.5, 22.5, 27.5, 32.5, 37.5, 42.5, 47.5
                52.5, 57.5, 62.5, 67.5, 72.5, 77.5, 82.5)
  /PERCENTILES=5, 10, 25, 50, 75, 90, 95.
```

- The values of *AGE* in this example have been estimated to the nearest five years. The first category is 17.5 to 22.5, the second is 22.5 to 27.5, and so forth. The artificial clustering of age estimates at multiples of five years is smoothed out by treating *AGE* as grouped data.
- It is not necessary to recode the ages to category midpoints, since the interval boundaries are explicitly given.

PERCENTILES Subcommand

PERCENTILES displays the value below which the specified percentage of cases falls. The desired percentiles must be explicitly requested. There are no defaults.

Example

```
FREQUENCIES VAR=V1 /PERCENTILES=10 25 33.3 66.7 75.
```

- FREQUENCIES requests the values for percentiles 10, 25, 33.3, 66.7, and 75 for *V1*.

NTILES Subcommand

NTILES calculates the percentages that divide the distribution into the specified number of categories and displays the values below which the requested percentages of cases fall. There are no default ntiles.

- Multiple NTILES subcommands are allowed. Each NTILES subcommand generates separate percentiles. Any duplicate percentiles generated by different NTILES subcommands are consolidated in the output.

Example

```
FREQUENCIES VARIABLE=V1 /NTILES=4.
```

- FREQUENCIES requests quartiles (percentiles 25, 50, and 75) for *V1*.

Example

```
FREQUENCIES VARIABLE=V1 /NTILES=4 /NTILES=10.
```

- The first NTILES subcommand requests percentiles 25, 50, and 75.
- The second NTILES subcommand requests percentiles 10 through 90 in increments of 10.
- The 50th percentile is produced by both specifications but is displayed only once in the output.

STATISTICS Subcommand

STATISTICS controls the display of statistics. By default, cases with missing values are excluded from the calculation of statistics.

- The minimum specification is the keyword STATISTICS, which generates the mean, standard deviation, minimum, and maximum (these statistics are also produced by keyword DEFAULT).

MEAN *Mean.*

SEMEAN *Standard error of the mean.*

MEDIAN *Median.* Ignored when AFREQ or DFREQ are specified on the FORMAT subcommand.

MODE *Mode.* If there is more than one mode, only the first mode is displayed.

STDDEV *Standard deviation.*

VARIANCE *Variance.*

SKEWNESS *Skewness.*

SESKEW *Standard error of the skewness statistic.*

KURTOSIS *Kurtosis.*

SEKURT *Standard error of the kurtosis statistic.*

RANGE *Range.*

MINIMUM *Minimum.*

MAXIMUM *Maximum.*

SUM *Sum.*

DEFAULT *Mean, standard deviation, minimum, and maximum.*

ALL *All available statistics.*

NONE *No statistics.*

Example

```
FREQUENCIES VAR=AGE /STATS=MODE.
```

- STATISTICS requests the mode of *AGE*.

Example

```
FREQUENCIES VAR=AGE /STATS=DEF MODE.
```

- STATISTICS requests the default statistics (mean, standard deviation, minimum, and maximum) plus the mode of *AGE*.

MISSING Subcommand

By default, both user-missing and system-missing values are labeled as missing in the table but are not included in the valid and cumulative percentages, in the calculation of descriptive statistics, or in charts and histograms.

INCLUDE *Include cases with user-missing values.* Cases with user-missing values are included in statistics and plots.

ORDER Subcommand

You can organize your output by variable or by analysis. Frequencies output that is organized by analysis has a single statistics table for all variables. Output organized by variable has a statistics table and a frequency table for each variable.

ANALYSIS *Organize output by analysis.* Displays a single statistics table for all variables. This is the default.

VARIABLE *Organize output by variable.* Displays a statistics table and a frequency table for each variable.

GENLOG

GENLOG is available in the Advanced Models option.

```
GENLOG varlist[BY] varlist [WITH covariate varlist]

 [/CSTRUCTURE=varname]

 [/GRESID=varlist]

 [/GLOR=varlist]

 [/MODEL={POISSON**   }]
         {MULTINOMIAL}

 [/CRITERIA=[CONVERGE({0.001**})] [ITERATE({20**})] [DELTA({0.5**})]
                      {n      }             {n   }          {n    }

            [CIN({95**})] [EPS({1E-8**})]
                 {n   }        {n      }

            [DEFAULT]

 [/PRINT=[FREQ**] [RESID**] [ADJRESID**] [DEV**]
         [ZRESID] [ITERATE] [COV] [DESIGN] [ESTIM] [COR]
         [ALL] [NONE]
         [DEFAULT]]

 [/PLOT={DEFAULT**                       }]
        {RESID([ADJRESID] [DEV])         }
        {NORMPROB([ADJRESID] [DEV])      }
        {NONE                            }

 [/SAVE=tempvar (newvar)[tempvar (newvar)...]]

 [/MISSING=[{EXCLUDE**}]]
            {INCLUDE  }

 [/DESIGN=effect[(n)] effect[(n)]... effect {BY} effect...]
                                            {* }
```

**Default if subcommand or keyword is omitted.

Overview

GENLOG is a general procedure for model fitting, hypothesis testing, and parameter estimation for any model that has categorical variables as its major components. As such, GENLOG subsumes a variety of related techniques, including general models of multiway contingency tables, logit models, logistic regression on categorical variables, and quasi-independence models.

GENLOG, following the regression approach, uses dummy coding to construct a design matrix for estimation and produces maximum likelihood estimates of parameters by means of the Newton-Raphson algorithm. Since the regression approach uses the original parameter spaces, the parameter estimates correspond to the original levels of the categories and are therefore easier to interpret.

HILOGLINEAR, which uses an iterative proportional-fitting algorithm, is more efficient for hierarchical models and useful in model building, but it cannot produce parameter estimates for unsaturated models, does not permit specification of contrasts for parameters, and does not display a correlation matrix of the parameter estimates.

The General Loglinear Analysis and Logit Loglinear Analysis dialog boxes are both associated with the GENLOG command. In previous releases of SPSS, these dialog boxes were associated with the LOGLINEAR command. The LOGLINEAR command is now available only as a syntax command. The differences are described in the discussion of the LOGLINEAR command.

Options

Cell Weights. You can specify cell weights (such as structural zero indicators) for the model with the CSTRUCTURE subcommand.

Linear Combinations. You can compute linear combinations of observed cell frequencies, expected cell frequencies, and adjusted residuals using the GRESID subcommand.

Generalized Log-Odds Ratios. You can specify contrast variables on the GLOR subcommand and test whether the generalized log-odds ratio equals 0.

Model Assumption. You can specify POISSON or MULTINOMIAL on the MODEL subcommand to request the Poisson loglinear model or the product multinomial loglinear model.

Tuning the Algorithm. You can control the values of algorithm-tuning parameters with the CRITERIA subcommand.

Output Display. You can control the output display with the PRINT subcommand.

Optional Plots. You can request plots of adjusted or deviance residuals against observed and expected counts, or normal plots and detrended normal plots of adjusted or deviance residuals using the PLOT subcommand.

Basic Specification

The basic specification is one or more factor variables that define the tabulation. By default, GENLOG assumes a Poisson distribution and estimates the saturated model. Default output includes the factors or effects, their levels, and any labels; observed and expected frequencies and percentages for each factor and code; and residuals, adjusted residuals, and deviance residuals.

Limitations

- Maximum 10 factor variables (dependent *and* independent).
- Maximum 200 covariates.

Subcommand Order

- The variable specification must come first.
- Subcommands can be specified in any order.
- When multiple subcommands are specified, only the last specification takes effect.

Example

```
GENLOG DPREF RACE CAMP.
```

- *DPREF*, *RACE*, and *CAMP* are categorical variables.
- This is a general loglinear model because no BY keyword appears.
- The design defaults to a saturated model that includes all main effects and two-way and three-way interaction effects.

Example

```
GENLOG GSLEVEL EDUC SEX
  /DESIGN=GSLEVEL EDUC SEX.
```

- *GSLEVEL*, *EDUC*, and *SEX* are categorical variables.
- DESIGN specifies a model with main effects only.

Variable List

The variable list specifies the variables to be included in the model. GENLOG analyzes two classes of variables—categorical and continuous. Categorical variables are used to define the cells of the table. Continuous variables are used as cell covariates.

- The list of categorical variables must be specified first. Categorical variables must be numeric.
- Continuous variables can be specified only after the WITH keyword following the list of categorical variables.
- To specify a logit model, use the keyword BY (see "Logit Model" below). A variable list without the keyword BY generates a general loglinear model.
- A variable can be specified only once in the variable list—as a dependent variable immediately following GENLOG, as an independent variable following the keyword BY, or as a covariate following the keyword WITH.
- No range needs to be specified for categorical variables.

Logit Model

The logit model examines the relationships between dependent and independent factor variables.

- To separate the independent variables from the dependent variables in a logit model, use the keyword BY. The categorical variables preceding BY are the dependent variables; the categorical variables following BY are the independent variables.
- Up to 10 variables can be specified, including both dependent and independent variables.
- For the logit model, you must specify MULTINOMIAL on the MODEL subcommand.
- GENLOG displays an analysis of dispersion and two measures of association—entropy and concentration. These measures are discussed in Haberman (1982) and can be used to quantify the magnitude of association among the variables. Both are proportional-reduction-in-error measures. The entropy statistic is analogous to Theil's entropy measure, while the concentration statistic is analogous to Goodman and Kruskal's tau-*b*. Both statistics measure the strength of association between the dependent variable and the independent variable set.

Example

```
GENLOG  GSLEVEL BY EDUC SEX
  /MODEL=MULTINOMIAL
  /DESIGN=GSLEVEL, GSLEVEL BY EDUC, GSLEVEL BY SEX.
```

- The keyword BY on the variable list specifies a logit model in which *GSLEVEL* is the dependent variable and *EDUC* and *SEX* are the independent variables.
- A logit model is multinomial.
- DESIGN specifies a model that can test for the absence of the joint effect of *SEX* and *EDUC* on *GSLEVEL*.

Cell Covariates

- Continuous variables can be used as covariates. When used, the covariates must be specified after the WITH keyword following the list of categorical variables.
- A variable cannot be named as both a categorical variable and a cell covariate.
- To enter cell covariates into a model, the covariates must be specified on the DESIGN subcommand.
- Cell covariates are not applied on a case-by-case basis. The weighted covariate mean for a cell is applied to that cell.

Example

```
GENLOG DPREF RACE CAMP WITH X
  /DESIGN=DPREF RACE CAMP X.
```

- The variable *X* is a continuous variable specified as a cell covariate. Cell covariates must be specified after the keyword WITH following the variable list. No range is defined for cell covariates.
- To include the cell covariate in the model, the variable *X* is specified on DESIGN.

CSTRUCTURE Subcommand

CSTRUCTURE specifies the variable that contains values for computing cell weights, such as structural zero indicators. By default, cell weights are equal to 1.

- The specification must be a numeric variable.
- Variables specified as dependent or independent variables in the variable list cannot be specified on CSTRUCTURE.
- Cell weights are not applied on a case-by-case basis. The weighted mean for a cell is applied to that cell.
- CSTRUCTURE can be used to impose structural, or *a priori*, zeros on the model. This feature is useful in specifying a quasi-symmetry model and in excluding cells from entering into estimation.
- If multiple CSTRUCTURE subcommands are specified, the last specification takes effect.

Example

```
COMPUTE  CWT=(HUSED NE WIFED).
GENLOG HUSED WIFED WITH DISTANCE
  /CSTRUCTURE=CWT
  /DESIGN=HUSED WIFED DISTANCE.
```

- The Boolean expression assigns *CWT* the value of 1 when *HUSED* is not equal to *WIFED*, and the value of 0 otherwise.
- CSTRUCTURE imposes structural zeros on the diagonal of the symmetric crosstabulation.

GRESID Subcommand

GRESID (Generalized Residual) calculates linear combinations of observed and expected cell frequencies as well as simple, standardized, and adjusted residuals.

- The variables specified must be numeric, and they must contain coefficients of the desired linear combinations.
- Variables specified as dependent or independent variables in the variable list cannot be specified on GRESID.
- The generalized residual coefficient is not applied on a case-by-case basis. The weighted coefficient mean of the value for all cases in a cell is applied to that cell.
- Each variable specified on the GRESID subcommand contains a single linear combination.
- If multiple GRESID subcommands are specified, the last specification takes effect.

Example

```
COMPUTE GR_1=(MONTH LE 6).
COMPUTE GR_2=(MONTH GE 7).
GENLOG  MONTH WITH Z
 /GRESID=GR_1 GR_2
 /DESIGN=Z.
```

- The first variable, *GR_1*, combines the first six months into a single effect; the second variable, *GR_2*, combines the rest of the months.

- For each effect, GENLOG displays the observed and expected counts as well as the simple, standardized, and adjusted residuals.

GLOR Subcommand

GLOR (Generalized Log-Odds Ratio) specifies the population contrast variable(s). For each variable specified, GENLOG tests the null hypothesis that the generalized log-odds ratio equals 0 and displays the Wald statistic and the confidence interval. You can specify the level of the confidence interval using the CIN significance level keyword on CRITERIA. By default, the confidence level is 95%.

- The variable sum is 0 for the loglinear model and for each combined level of independent variables for the logit model.
- Variables specified as dependent or independent variables in the variable list cannot be specified on GLOR.
- The coefficient is not applied on a case-by-case basis. The weighted mean for a cell is applied to that cell.
- If multiple GLOR subcommands are specified, the last specification takes effect.

Example

```
GENLOG A B
 /GLOR=COEFF
 /DESIGN=A B.
```

- Variable *COEFF* contains the coefficients of two dichotomous factors *A* and *B*.
- If the weighted cell mean for *COEFF* is 1 when *A* equals *B* and –1 otherwise, this example tests whether the log-odds ratio equals 0, or in this case, whether variables *A* and *B* are independent.

MODEL Subcommand

MODEL specifies the assumed distribution of your data.

- You can specify only one keyword on MODEL. The default is POISSON.
- If more than one MODEL subcommand is specified, the last specification takes effect.

POISSON *The Poisson distribution.* This is the default.

MULTINOMIAL *The multinomial distribution.* For the logit model, you must specify MULTINOMIAL.

CRITERIA Subcommand

CRITERIA specifies the values used in tuning the parameters for the Newton-Raphson algorithm.

- If multiple CRITERIA subcommands are specified, the last specification takes effect.

CONVERGE(n) *Convergence criterion.* Specify a positive value for the convergence criterion. The default is 0.001.

ITERATE(n) *Maximum number of iterations.* Specify an integer. The default number is 20.

DELTA(n) *Cell delta value.* Specify a non-negative value to add to each cell frequency for the first iteration. (For the saturated model, the delta value is added for all iterations.) The default is 0.5. The delta value is used to solve mathematical problems created by 0 observations; if all of your observations are greater than 0, we recommend that you set DELTA to 0.

CIN(n) *Level of confidence interval.* Specify the percentage interval used in the test of generalized log-odds ratios and parameter estimates. The value must be between 50 and 99.99, inclusive. The default is 95.

EPS(n) *Epsilon value used for redundancy checking in design matrix.* Specify a positive value. The default is 0.00000001.

DEFAULT *Default values are used.* DEFAULT can be used to reset all criteria to default values.

Example

```
GENLOG  DPREF BY RACE ORIGIN CAMP
 /MODEL=MULTINOMIAL
 /CRITERIA=ITERATION(50) CONVERGE(.0001).
```

- ITERATION increases the maximum number of iterations to 50.
- CONVERGE lowers the convergence criterion to 0.0001.

PRINT Subcommand

PRINT controls the display of statistics.

- By default, GENLOG displays the frequency table and simple, adjusted, and deviance residuals.
- When PRINT is specified with one or more keywords, only the statistics requested by these keywords are displayed.
- When multiple PRINT subcommands are specified, the last specification takes effect.

The following keywords can be used on PRINT:

FREQ *Observed and expected cell frequencies and percentages.* This is displayed by default.

RESID *Simple residuals.* This is displayed by default.

ZRESID *Standardized residuals.*

ADJRESID *Adjusted residuals.* This is displayed by default.

DEV *Deviance residuals.* This is displayed by default.

DESIGN *The design matrix of the model.* The design matrix corresponding to the specified model is displayed.

ESTIM *The parameter estimates of the model.* The parameter estimates refer to the original categories.

COR *The correlation matrix of the parameter estimates.*

COV *The covariance matrix of the parameter estimates.*

ALL *All available output.*

DEFAULT *FREQ, RESID, ADJRESID, and DEV.* This keyword can be used to reset PRINT to its default setting.

NONE *The design and model information with goodness-of-fit statistics only.* This option overrides all other specifications on the PRINT subcommand.

Example

```
GENLOG A B
 /PRINT=ALL
 /DESIGN=A B.
```

- The DESIGN subcommand specifies a main-effects model, which tests the hypothesis of no interaction. The PRINT subcommand displays all available output for this model.

PLOT Subcommand

PLOT specifies what plots you want displayed. Plots of adjusted residuals against observed and expected counts, and normal and detrended normal plots of the adjusted residuals are displayed if PLOT is not specified or is specified without a keyword. When multiple PLOT subcommands are specified, only the last specification is executed.

DEFAULT *RESID (ADJRESID) and NORMPROB (ADJRESID).* This is the default if PLOT is not specified or is specified with no keyword.

RESID (type) *Plots of residuals against observed and expected counts.* You can specify the type of residuals to plot. ADJRESID plots adjusted residuals; DEV plots deviance residuals. ADJRESID is the default if you do not specify a type.

NORMPROB (type) *Normal and detrended normal plots of the residuals.* You can specify the type of residuals to plot. ADJRESID plots adjusted residuals; DEV plots deviance residuals. ADJRESID is the default if you do not specify a type.

NONE *No plots.*

Example

```
GENLOG  RESPONSE BY SEASON
  /MODEL=MULTINOMIAL
  /PLOT=RESID(ADJRESID,DEV)
  /DESIGN=RESPONSE SEASON(1) BY RESPONSE.
```

- This example requests plots of adjusted and deviance residuals against observed and expected counts.
- Note that if you specify `/PLOT=RESID(ADJRESID) RESID(DEV)`, only the deviance residuals are plotted. The first keyword specification, `RESID(ADJRESID)`, is ignored.

MISSING Subcommand

MISSING controls missing values. By default, GENLOG excludes all cases with system- or user-missing values for any variable. You can specify INCLUDE to include user-missing values.

EXCLUDE *Delete cases with user-missing values.* This is the default if the subcommand is omitted. You can also specify the keyword DEFAULT.

INCLUDE *Include cases with user-missing values.* Only cases with system-missing values are deleted.

Example

```
MISSING VALUES A(0).
GENLOG A B
 /MISSING=INCLUDE
 /DESIGN=B.
```

- Even though 0 was specified as missing, it is treated as a nonmissing category of *A* in this analysis.

SAVE Subcommand

SAVE saves specified temporary variables into the working data file. You can assign a new name to each temporary variable saved.

- The temporary variables you can save include *RESID* (raw residual), *ZRESID* (standardized residual), *ADJRESID* (adjusted residual), *DEV* (deviance residual), and *PRED* (predicted cell frequency). An explanatory label is assigned to each saved variable.
- A temporary variable can be saved only once on a SAVE subcommand.
- To assign a name to a saved temporary variable, specify the new name in parentheses following that temporary variable. The new name must conform to SPSS naming conventions and must be unique in the working data file. The names cannot begin with # or $.
- If you do not specify a variable name in parentheses, GENLOG assigns default names to the saved temporary variables. A default name starts with the first three characters of the name of the saved temporary variable, followed by an underscore and a unique number. For example, *RESID* will be saved as *RES_n*, where *n* is a number incremented each time a default name is assigned to a saved *RESID*.

- The saved variables are pertinent to cells in the contingency table, *not* to individual observations. In the Data Editor, all cases that define one cell receive the same value. To make sense of these values, you need to aggregate the data to obtain cell counts.

Example

```
GENLOG A B
 /SAVE PRED (PREDA_B)
 /DESIGN = A, B.
```

- SAVE saves the predicted values for two independent variables *A* and *B*.
- The saved variable is renamed *PREDA_B* and added to the working data file.

DESIGN Subcommand

DESIGN specifies the model to be fit. If DESIGN is omitted or used with no specifications, the saturated model is produced. The saturated model fits all main effects and all interaction effects.

- Only one design can be specified on the subcommand.
- To obtain main-effects models, name all of the variables listed on the variables specification.
- To obtain interactions, use the keyword BY or an asterisk (*) to specify each interaction, for example, `A BY B` or `C*D`. To obtain the single-degree-of-freedom partition of a specified factor, specify the partition in parentheses following the factor (see the example below).
- To include cell covariates in the model, first identify them on the variable list by naming them after the keyword WITH, and then specify the variable names on DESIGN.
- Effects that involve only independent variables result in redundancy. GENLOG removes these effects from the model.
- If your variable list includes a cell covariate (identified by the keyword WITH), you cannot imply the saturated model by omitting DESIGN or specifying it alone. You need to request the model explicitly by specifying all main effects and interactions on DESIGN.

Example

```
COMPUTE X=MONTH.
GENLOG MONTH WITH X
  /DESIGN X.
```

- This example tests the linear effect of the dependent variable.
- The variable specification identifies *MONTH* as a categorical variable. The keyword WITH identifies *X* as a covariate.
- DESIGN tests the linear effect of *MONTH*.

Example

```
GENLOG A B
  /DESIGN=A.

GENLOG A B
  /DESIGN=A,B.
```

- Both designs specify main-effects models.
- The first design tests the homogeneity of category probabilities for *B*; it fits the marginal frequencies on *A* but assumes that membership in any of the categories of *B* is equiprobable.
- The second design tests the independence of *A* and *B*. It fits the marginals on both *A* and *B*.

Example

```
GENLOG A  B  C
  /DESIGN=A,B,C, A BY B.
```

- This design consists of the *A* main effect, the *B* main effect, the *C* main effect, and the interaction of *A* and *B*.

Example

```
GENLOG A BY B
 /MODEL=MULTINOMIAL
 /DESIGN=A,A BY B(1).
```

- This example specifies single-degree-of-freedom partitions.
- The value 1 following *B* refers to the first category of *B*.

Example

```
GENLOG HUSED WIFED WITH DISTANCE
  /DESIGN=HUSED WIFED DISTANCE.
```

- The continuous variable *DISTANCE* is identified as a cell covariate by the keyword WITH. The cell covariate is then included in the model by naming it on DESIGN.

Example

```
COMPUTE  X=1.
GENLOG  MONTH WITH X
  /DESIGN=X.
```

- This example specifies an equiprobability model.
- The design tests whether the frequencies in the table are equal by using a constant of 1 as a cell covariate.

References

Haberman, S.J. 1982. Analysis of despersion of multinomial responses. *Journal of the American Statistical Association*, 77: 568-580.

GET

```
GET FILE=file

 [/KEEP={ALL**  }] [/DROP=varlist]
        {varlist}

 [/RENAME=(old varnames=new varnames)...]

 [/MAP]
```

**Default if the subcommand is omitted.

Example

```
GET FILE=EMPL.
```

Overview

GET reads an SPSS-format data file that was created by the SAVE or XSAVE command. An SPSS-format data file contains data plus a dictionary. The dictionary contains a name for each variable in the data file, plus any assigned variable and value labels, missing-value flags, and variable print and write formats. The dictionary also contains document text created with the DOCUMENTS command.

GET is used only for reading SPSS-format data files. See DATA LIST for information on reading and defining data in a text data file. See MATRIX DATA for information on defining matrix materials in a text data file. For information on defining complex data files that cannot be defined with DATA LIST alone, see FILE TYPE and REPEATING DATA.

The program can also read data files created for other software applications. See IMPORT for information on reading *portable files* created with EXPORT. See commands such as GET TRANSLATE and GET SAS for information on reading files created by other software programs.

Options

Variable Subsets and Order. You can read a subset of variables and reorder the variables that are copied into the working data file using the DROP and KEEP subcommands.

Variable Names. You can rename variables as they are copied into the working data file with the RENAME subcommand.

Variable Map. To confirm the names and order of variables in the working data file, use the MAP subcommand. MAP displays the variables in the working file next to their corresponding names in the SPSS-format data file.

Basic Specification

- The basic specification is the FILE subcommand, which specifies the SPSS-format data file to be read.
- By default, GET copies all variables from the SPSS-format data file into the working data file. Variables in the working file are in the same order and have the same names as variables in the SPSS-format data file. Documentary text from the SPSS-format data file is copied into the dictionary of the working file.

Subcommand Order

- FILE must be specified first.
- The remaining subcommands can be specified in any order.

Syntax Rules

- FILE is required and can be specified only once.
- KEEP, DROP, RENAME, and MAP can be used as many times as needed.
- Documentary text copied from the SPSS-format data file can be dropped from the working data file with the DROP DOCUMENTS command.
- GET cannot be used inside a DO IF—END IF or LOOP—END LOOP structure.

Operations

- GET reads the dictionary of the SPSS-format data file.
- If KEEP is not specified, variables in the working data file are in the same order as variables in the SPSS-format data file.
- A file saved with weighting in effect maintains the values of the variable *$WEIGHT*. For a discussion of turning off weights, see WEIGHT.
- The order of cases in the working data file is the same as their order in the SPSS-format data file. The values of *$CASENUM* are those from the original text data file before any selecting (see SELECT IF) or sorting (see SORT). The value of *$CASENUM* may differ from the actual number of a case after selecting or sorting.

FILE Subcommand

FILE specifies the SPSS-format data file to be read. FILE is required and can be specified only once. It must be the first specification on GET.

DROP and KEEP Subcommands

DROP and KEEP are used to copy a subset of variables into the working data file. DROP specifies variables that should not be copied into the working file. KEEP specifies variables that should be copied. Variables not specified on KEEP are dropped.

- Variables can be specified in any order. The order of variables on KEEP determines the order of variables in the working file. The order of variables on DROP does not affect the order of variables in the working file.
- The keyword ALL on KEEP refers to all remaining variables not previously specified on KEEP. ALL must be the last specification on KEEP.
- If a variable is specified twice on the same subcommand, only the first mention is recognized.
- Multiple DROP and KEEP subcommands are allowed. However, specifying a variable named on a previous DROP or not named on a previous KEEP results in an error, and the GET command is not executed.
- The keyword TO can be used to specify a group of consecutive variables in the SPSS-format data file.

Example

```
GET FILE=HUBTEMP /DROP=DEPT79 TO DEPT84 SALARY79.
```

- The working data file is copied from SPSS-format data file *HUBTEMP*. All variables between and including *DEPT79* and *DEPT84*, as well as *SALARY79*, are excluded from the working file. All other variables are copied into the working file.
- Variables in the working data file are in the same order as the variables in the *HUBTEMP* file.

Example

```
GET FILE=PRSNL /DROP=GRADE STORE
               /KEEP=LNAME NAME TENURE JTENURE ALL.
```

- The variables *GRADE* and *STORE* are dropped when the file *PRSNL* is copied into the working data file.
- KEEP specifies that *LNAME*, *NAME*, *TENURE*, and *JTENURE* are the first four variables in the working file, followed by all remaining variables (except those dropped by the previous DROP). These remaining variables are copied into the working file in the same sequence in which they appear in the *PRSNL* file.

RENAME Subcommand

RENAME changes the names of variables as they are copied into the working data file.

- The specification on RENAME is a list of old variable names followed by an equals sign and a list of new variable names. The same number of variables must be specified on both lists. The keyword TO can be used on the first list to refer to consecutive variables in the SPSS-format data file and on the second list to generate new variable names (see "Keyword TO" on p. 19). The entire specification must be enclosed in parentheses.

- Alternatively, you can specify each old variable name individually, followed by an equals sign and the new variable name. Multiple sets of variable specifications are allowed. The parentheses around each set of specifications are optional.
- Old variable names do not need to be specified according to their order in the SPSS-format data file.
- Name changes take place in one operation. Therefore, variable names can be exchanged between two variables.
- Variables cannot be renamed to scratch variables.
- Multiple RENAME subcommands are allowed.
- On a subsequent DROP or KEEP subcommand, variables are referred to by their new names.

Example

```
GET FILE=EMPL88 /RENAME  AGE=AGE88 JOBCAT=JOBCAT88.
```

- RENAME specifies two name changes for the working data file. *AGE* is renamed to *AGE88* and *JOBCAT* is renamed to *JOBCAT88*.

Example

```
GET FILE=EMPL88 /RENAME (AGE JOBCAT=AGE88 JOBCAT88).
```

- The name changes are identical to those in the previous example. *AGE* is renamed to *AGE88* and *JOBCAT* is renamed to *JOBCAT88*. The parentheses are required with this method.

MAP Subcommand

MAP displays a list of the variables in the working data file and their corresponding names in the SPSS-format data file.

- The only specification is the keyword MAP. There are no additional specifications.
- Multiple MAP subcommands are allowed. Each MAP subcommand maps the results of subcommands that precede it; results of subcommands that follow it are not mapped.

Example

```
GET FILE=EMPL88 /RENAME=(AGE=AGE88) (JOBCAT=JOBCAT88)
 /KEEP=LNAME NAME JOBCAT88 ALL /MAP.
```

- MAP is specified to confirm the new names for the variables *AGE* and *JOBCAT* and the order of variables in the working data file (*LNAME*, *NAME*, and *JOBCAT88*, followed by all remaining variables in the SPSS-format data file).

GET CAPTURE

```
GET CAPTURE {ODBC     }*

 [/CONNECT='connection string']
 [/LOGIN=login] [/PASSWORD=password]
 [/SERVER=host] [/DATABASE=database name]†

 /SQL 'select statement'
      ['continuation of select statement']
```

* You can import data from any database for which you have an ODBC driver installed.

† Optional subcommands are database-specific. See "Syntax Rules" below for the subcommand(s) required by a database type.

Example

```
GET CAPTURE ODBC
  /CONNECT='DSN=sales.mdb;DBQ=C:\spss10\saledata.mdb;DriverId=281;FIL=MS'+
  ' Access;MaxBufferSize=2048;PageTimeout=5;'
  /SQL = 'SELECT  T0.ID AS ID`,  T0.JOBCAT AS JOBCAT,  '
  '`T0`.`REGION` AS `REGION`,  `T0`.`DIVISION` AS `DIVISION`,`T0`.`TRAVEL`'
  ' AS `TRAVEL`,  `T0`.`SALES` AS `SALES`,  `T0`.`VOLUME96` AS `VOLUME96`,  '
  '`T1`.`REGION` AS `REGION1`,  `T1`.`AVGINC` AS `AVGINC`,`T1`.`AVGAGE` AS'
  ' `AVGAGE`,  `T1`.`POPULAT` AS `POPULAT` FROM { oj `Regions` `T1` LEFT '
  'OUTER JOIN `EmployeeSales` `T0` ON `T1`.`REGION` = `T0`.`REGION` } '.
```

Overview

GET CAPTURE retrieves data from a database and converts them to a format that can be used by program procedures. GET CAPTURE retrieves data and data information and builds a working data file for the current session.

Basic Specification

The basic specification is one of the subcommands specifying the database type followed by the SQL subcommand and any select statement in quotation marks or apostrophes. Each line of the select statement should be enclosed in quotation marks or apostrophes, and no quoted string should exceed 255 characters.

Subcommand Order

The subcommand specifying the type of database must be the first specification. The SQL subcommand must be the last.

Syntax Rules

- Only one subcommand specifying the database type can be used.

- The CONNECT subcommand must be specified if you use the Microsoft ODBC (Open Database Connectivity) driver.

Operations

- GET CAPTURE retrieves the data specified on SQL.
- The variables are in the same order in which they are specified on the SQL subcommand.
- The data definition information captured from the database is stored in the working data file dictionary.

Limitations

- Maximum 3800 characters (approximately) can be specified on the SQL subcommand. This translates to 76 lines of 50 characters. Characters beyond the limit are ignored.

CONNECT Subcommand

CONNECT is required to access any database that has an installed Microsoft ODBC driver.

- You cannot specify the connection string directly in the syntax window, but you can paste it with the rest of the command from the Results dialog box, which is the last of the series of dialog boxes opened with the Database Wizard.

SQL Subcommand

SQL specifies any SQL select statement accepted by the database you access. With ODBC, you can now select columns from more than one related table in an ODBC data source using either the inner join or the outer join.

Data Conversion

GET CAPTURE converts variable names, labels, missing values, and data types, wherever necessary, to a format that conforms to SPSS-format conventions.

Variable Names and Labels

Database columns are read as variables.

- A column name is converted to a variable name if it conforms to SPSS-format naming conventions and is different from all other names created for the working data file. If not, GET CAPTURE gives the column a name formed from the first few letters of the column and its column number. If this is not possible, the letters COL followed by the column number are used. For example, the seventh column specified in the select statement could be *COL7*.
- GET CAPTURE labels each variable with its full column name specified in the original database.

- You can display a table of variable names with their original database column names using the DISPLAY LABELS command.

Missing Values

Null values in the database are transformed into the system-missing value in numeric variables or into blanks in string variables.

GET DATA

```
GET DATA
  /TYPE = {ODBC}
          {XLS }
          {TXT }

  /FILE = 'filename'

Subcommands for TYPE = ODBC
  /CONNECT='connection string'
  /SQL 'select statement'
      ['select statement continued']

Subcommands for TYPE = XLS*
  [/SHEET = {INDEX**} {sheet number}]
            {NAME   } {'sheet name'}
  [/CELLRANGE = {RANGE }  {'start point:end point' }]
                {FULL**}
  [/READNAMES = {on** }]
                {off  }

Subcommands for TYPE = TXT
  [/ARRANGEMENT = {FIXED        }]
                  {DELIMITED**  }
  [/FIRSTCASE = {n}]
  [/DELCASE = {LINE**     }]¹
              {VARIABLES n}

  [/FIXCASE = n]²
  [/IMPORTCASE = {ALL**     }]
                 {FIRST n   }
                 {PERCENT n }
  [/DELIMITERS = {"delimiters"}]
  [/QUALIFIER = "qualifier"]

VARIABLES subcommand for ARRANGEMENT = DELIMITED
  /VARIABLES = varname  {format}

VARIABLES subcommand for ARRANGEMENT = FIXED
  /VARIABLES varname {startcol - endcol} {format}
     {/rec#} varname {startcol - endcol} {format}
```

*Valid only for Excel 5 or later. For earlier Excel files, use GET TRANSLATE.

**Default if subcommand omitted

[1]Valid only with ARRANGEMENT = DELIMTED

[2] Valid only with ARRANGEMENT = FIXED

Example

```
GET DATA
   /TYPE=XLS
   /FILE='c:\PlanningDocs\files10.xls'
   /SHEET=name 'First Quarter'
   /CELLRANGE=full
   /READNAMES=on.
```

Overview

GET DATA reads data from ODBC data sources (databases), Excel files (release 5 or later), and text data files. It contains functionality and syntax similar to GET CAPTURE, GET TRANSLATE, and DATA LIST.

- GET DATA /TYPE=ODBC is almost identical to GET CAPTURE ODBC in both syntax and functionality.
- GET DATA /TYPE=XLS reads Excel 5 or later files, whereas GET TRANSLATE reads Excel 4 or earlier, Lotus, and dBASE files.
- GET DATA /TYPE=TXT is similar to DATA LIST but does not create a temporary copy of the data file, significantly reducing temporary file space requirements for large data files.

TYPE Subcommand

The TYPE subcommand is required and must be the first subcommand specified.

ODBC *Data sources accessed with ODBC drivers.*

XLS *Excel 5 or later files.* For earlier versions of Excel files, Lotus 1-2-3 files, and dBASE files, see the GET TRANSLATE command.

TXT *Simple (ASCII) text data files.*

FILE Subcommand

The FILE subcommand is required for TYPE=XLS and TYPE=TXT and must immediately follow the TYPE subcommand. It specifies the file to read.

- File specifications should be enclosed in quotes or apostrophes.
- UNC file specifications are recommended for distributed analysis mode (available with the server version of SPSS).

Subcommands for TYPE=ODBC

The CONNECT and SQL subcommands are both required, and SQL must be the last subcommand.

CONNECT Subcommand

The recommended method for generating a valid CONNECT specification is to initially use the Database Wizard and paste the resulting syntax to a syntax window in the last step of the wizard.

SQL Subcommand

SQL specifies any SQL select statement accepted by the database you access. You can select columns from more than one related table in an ODBC data source using either the inner join or the outer join. Each line of the SQL select statement should be enclosed in quotation marks or apostrophes, and no quoted string should exceed 255 characters.

Example

```
GET DATA /TYPE=ODBC
  /CONNECT='DSN=saledata.mdb;DBQ=saledata.mdb;DriverId=281;FIL=MS'+
 ' Access;MaxBufferSize=2048;PageTimeout=5;'
  /SQL='SELECT  'T0'.'DIV' AS 'DIV',   'T0'.'REGION' AS 'REGION',   '
 ''T1'.'AVGAGE' AS 'AVGAGE',   'T1'.'REGION' AS 'REGION1' FROM   '
 ''saledata'.'EmployeeSales' 'T0', ''.'Regions''
 '  'T1' WHERE 'T1'.'REGION' = 'T0'.'REGION' '.
```

Subcommands for TYPE=XLS

For Excel files, you can specify a spreadsheet within the workbook, a range of cells to read, and the contents of the first row of the spreadsheet (variable names or data).

SHEET Subcommand

The SHEET subcommand indicates the worksheet in the Excel file that will be read. Only one sheet can be specified. If no sheet is specified, the first sheet will be read.

INDEX n *Read the specified sheet number.* The number represents the sequential order of the sheet within the workbook.

NAME 'name' *Read the specified sheet name.* If the name contains spaces, it must be enclosed in quotes or apostrophes.

CELLRANGE Subcommand

The CELLRANGE subcommand specifies a range of cells to read within the specified worksheet. By default, the entire worksheet is read.

FULL *Read the entire worksheet.* This is the default.

RANGE 'start:end' *Read the specified range of cells.* Specify the beginning column letter and row number, a colon, and the ending column letter and row number, as in A1:K14. The cell range must be enclosed in quotes or apostrophes.

READNAMES Subcommand

ON *Read the first row of the sheet or specified range as variable names.* This is the default. Values longer than eight characters are truncated. Values that contain invalid characters for variable names are converted to valid variable names.

OFF *Read the first row of the sheet or specified range as data.* SPSS assigns default variable names and reads all rows as data.

Example

```
GET DATA /TYPE=XLS
   /FILE='\\hqdev01\public\sales.xls'
   /SHEET=name 'June Sales'
   /CELLRANGE=range 'A1:C3'
   /READNAMES=on.
```

Subcommands for TYPE=TXT

The VARIABLES subcommand is required and must be the last GET DATA subcommand.

ARRANGEMENT Subcommand

The ARRANGEMENT subcommand specifies the data format.

DELIMITED *Spaces, commas, tabs, or other characters are used to separate variables.* The variables are recorded in the same order for each case but not necessarily in the same column locations. This is the default.

FIXED *Each variable is recorded in the same column location for every case.*

FIRSTCASE Subcommand

FIRSTCASE specifies the first line (row) to read for the first case of data. This allows you to bypass information in the first *n* lines of the file that either don't contain data or contain data you don't want to read. This subcommand applies to both fixed and delimited file formats.

The only specification for this subcommand is an integer greater than zero that indicates the number of lines to skip. The default is 1.

DELCASE Subcommand

The DELCASE subcommand applies to delimited data (ARRANGEMENT=DELIMITED) only.

LINE *Each case is contained on a single line (row).* This is the default.

VARIABLES *n* *Each case contains n variables.* Multiple cases can be contained on the same line, and data for one case can span more than one line. A case is defined by the number of variables.

FIXCASE Subcommand

The FIXCASE subcommand applies to fixed data (ARRANGEMENT=FIXED) only. It specifies the number of lines (records) to read for each case.

The only specification for this subcommand is an integer greater than zero that indicates the number of lines (records) per case. The default is 1.

IMPORTCASES Subcommand

The IMPORTCASES subcommand allows you to specify the number of cases to read.

ALL *Read all cases in the file.* This is the default.

FIRST *n* *Read the first n cases.* The value of *n* must be a positive integer.

PERCENT *n* *Read approximately the first n percent of cases.* The value of *n* must be a positive integer less than 100. The percentage of cases actually selected only approximates the specified percentage. The more cases there are in the data file, the closer the percentage of cases selected is to the specified percentage.

DELIMITERS Subcommand

The DELIMITERS subcommand applies to delimited data (ARRANGEMENT=DELIMITED) only. It specifies the characters to read as delimiters between data values.

- Each delimiter can only be a single character, except for the specification of a tab or a backslash as a delimiter (see below).
- The list of delimiters must be enclosed in quotes or apostrophes.
- There should be no spaces or other delimiters between delimiter specifications, except for a space that indicates a space as a delimiter.
- To specify a tab as a delimiter use "\t". This must be the first delimiter specified.
- To specify a backslash as a delimiter, use two backslashes ("\\"). This must be the first delimiter specified unless you also specify a tab as a delimiter, in which case the backslash specification should come second—immediately after the tab specification.

Missing data with delimited data. Multiple consecutive spaces in a data file are treated as a single space and cannot be used to indicate missing data. For any other delimiter, multiple delimiters without any intervening data indicate missing data.

Example

```
DELIMITERS "\t\\ ,;"
```

In this example, tabs, backslashes, spaces, commas, and semicolons will be read as delimiters between data values.

QUALIFIER Subcommand

The QUALIFIERS subcommand applies to delimited data (ARRANGEMENT=DELIMITED) only. It specifies the character used to enclose values that contain delimiter characters. For example, if a comma is the delimiter, values that contain commas will be read incorrectly unless there is a text qualifier enclosing the value, preventing the commas in the value from being interpreted as delimiters between values. CSV-format data files exported from Excel use a double quote (")as a text qualifier.

- The text qualifier appears at both the beginning and end of the value, enclosing the entire value.
- The qualifier value must be enclosed in single or double quotes. If the qualifier is a single quote, the value should be enclosed in double quotes. If the qualifier value is a double quote, the value should be enclosed in single quotes.

Example

```
/QUALIFIER = '"'
```

VARIABLES Subcommand for ARRANGEMENT = DELIMITED

For delimited files, the VARIABLES subcommand specifies the variable names and variable formats.

- Variable names must begin with a letter and cannot exceed eight characters (see "Variables" on p. 19).
- Each variable name must be followed by a format specification (see "Variable Format Specifications for TYPE = TXT" below).

VARIABLES Subcommand for ARRANGEMENT = FIXED

For fixed-format files, the VARIABLES subcommand specifies variable names, start and end column locations, and variable formats.

- Variable names must begin with a letter and cannot exceed eight characters.
- Each variable name must be followed by column specifications. Start and end columns must be separated by a dash, as in: `0-10`.
- Each column specification must be followed by a format specification.
- Column numbering starts with 0, not 1 (in contrast to DATA LIST).

Multiple records. If each case spans more than one record (as specified with the FIXCASE subcommand), delimit variable specifications for each record with a slash (/) followed by the record number, as in:

```
VARIABLES = /1 var1 0-10 F var2 11-20 DATE
/2 var3 0-5 A var4 6-10 F
/3 var5 0-20 A var6 21-30 DOLLAR
```

Variable Format Specifications for TYPE = TXT

For both fixed and delimited files, available formats include:

F*n.d* *Numeric.* Specification of the total number of characters (*n*) and decimals (*d*) are optional.

A*n* *String (alphanumeric).* Specification of the maximum string length (*n*) is optional.

DATE*n* *Dates of the general format dd-mmm-yyyy.* Specification of the maximum length (*n*) is optional but must be eight or greater if specified.

ADATE*n* *Dates of the general format mm/dd/yyyy.* Specification of the maximum length (*n*) is optional but must be eight or greater if specified.

DOLLAR*n.d* *Currency with or without a leading dollar sign ($).* Input values can include a leading dollar sign, but it is not required. Specification of the total number of characters (*n*) and decimals (*d*) are optional.

For comprehensive lists of available formats, see “Variables” on p. 19 and “Date and Time” on p. 51.

Example

```
GET DATA  /TYPE = TXT
  /FILE = 'D:\Program Files\SPSS\textdata.dat'
  /DELCASE = LINE
  /DELIMITERS = "\t ,"
  /ARRANGEMENT = DELIMITED
  /FIRSTCASE = 2
  /IMPORTCASE = FIRST 200
  /VARIABLES = id F3.2 gender A1 bdate DATE10 educ F2.2
   jobcat F1.2 salary DOLLAR8 salbegin DOLLAR8
   jobtime F2.2 prevexp F3.2 minority F1.2.
```

GET SAS

```
GET SAS DATA=file [DSET(data set)]
 [/FORMATS=file]
```

Example

```
GET SAS DATA='ELECT'.
```

Overview

GET SAS builds an SPSS-format working data file from a SAS data set or a SAS transport file. A SAS transport file is a sequential file written in SAS transport format and can be created by the SAS export engine available in SAS Release 6.06 or higher or by the EXPORT option on the COPY or XCOPY procedure in earlier versions. GET SAS reads SAS files up to version 6.12.

Options

Retrieving User-defined value labels. For native SAS data sets, you can specify a file on the FORMATS subcommand to retrieve user-defined value labels associated with the data being read. This file must be created by the SAS PROC FORMAT statement, and can only be used for native SAS data sets. For SAS transport files, the FORMATS subcommand is ignored.

Specifying the Data Set. You can name a data set contained in a specified SAS file, using DSET on the DATA subcommand. GET SAS reads the specified data set from the SAS file.

Basic Specification

The basic specification is the DATA subcommand followed by the name of the SAS file to read. By default, the first SAS data set is copied into the working data file and any necessary data conversions are made.

Syntax Rules

- The subcommand DATA and the SAS file name are required and must be specified first.
- The subcommand FORMATS is optional. This subcommand is ignored for SAS transport files.
- GET SAS does not allow KEEP, DROP, RENAME, and MAP subcommands. To use a subset of the variables, rename them, or display the file content, you can specify the appropriate commands after the SPSS working data file is created.

Operations

- GET SAS reads data from the specified or default data set contained in the SAS file named on the DATA subcommand.
- Value labels retrieved from a SAS user-defined format are used for variables associated with that format, becoming part of the SPSS dictionary.
- All variables from the SAS data set are included in the working data file, and they are in the same order as in the SAS data set.

DATA Subcommand

DATA specifies the file that contains the SAS data set to be read.

- DATA is required and must be the first specification on GET SAS.
- The file specification varies from operating system to operating system. Enclosing the filename within apostrophes always works.
- The optional DSET keyword on DATA determines which data set within the specified SAS file is to be read. The default is the first data set.

DSET (data set) *Data set to be read.* Specify the name of the data set in parentheses. If the specified data set does not exist in the SAS file, GET SAS displays a message informing you that the data set was not found.

Example

```
GET SAS DATA='ELECT' DSET(Y1948).
```

- The SAS file *ELECT* is opened and the data set named *Y1948* is used to build the working file for the SPSS session.

FORMATS Subcommand

FORMATS specifies the file containing user-defined value labels to be applied to the retrieved data.

- The file specification varies from operating system to operating system. Enclosing the filename within apostrophes always works.
- If FORMATS is omitted, no value labels are available.
- Value labels are only applied to numeric integer values. They are not applied to non-integer numeric values or string variables.
- The file specified on the FORMATS subcommand must be created with the SAS PROC FORMAT statement.
- For SAS transport files, the FORMATS subcommand is ignored.

Example

```
GET SAS /DATA='ELECT' DSET(Y1948)
 /FORMATS='ELECTFM'.
```

- Value labels read from the SAS file *ELECTFM* are converted to conform to SPSS conventions.

Creating a Formats File with PROC FORMAT

To create a file containing SAS value labels, run the following program in SAS:

```
libname mylib 'path';
proc format library = mylib
cntlout = mylib.sas_fmts;
run;
```

where 'path' is the directory that contains your input data file.

This procedure creates a SAS file in the directory 'path' that has the format information for each SAS data file. In this case, the file will have the name *SAS_FMTS.SD2* and be found in the same directory as the input SAS data file.

SAS to SPSS Data Conversion

Although SAS and SPSS data files have similar attributes, they are not identical. SPSS makes the following conversions to force SAS data sets to comply with SPSS conventions.

Variable Names

SAS variable names that do not conform to SPSS variable name rules are converted to valid 8-character SPSS variable names.

Variable Labels

SAS variable labels specified on the LABEL statement in the DATA step are used as variable labels in SPSS.

Value Labels

SAS value formats that assign value labels are read from the data set specified on the FORMATS subcommand. The SAS value labels are then converted to SPSS value labels in the following manner:

- Labels assigned to single values are retained.
- Labels assigned to a range of values are ignored.
- Labels assigned to SAS keywords LOW, HIGH, and OTHER are ignored.
- Labels assigned to string variables and non-integer numeric values are ignored.
- Labels over 60 characters long are truncated.

Missing Values

Since SAS has no user-defined missing values, all SAS missing codes are converted to SPSS system-missing values.

Variable Types

- Both SAS and SPSS allow two basic types of variables: numeric and character string. During conversion, SAS numeric variables become SPSS numeric variables, and SAS string variables become SPSS string variables of the same length.
- Date, time, and datetime SAS variables are converted to equivalent SPSS date, time and datetime variables. All other numeric formats are converted to the default SPSS numeric format.

GET TRANSLATE

```
GET TRANSLATE FILE=file

 [/TYPE={WK }]
        {WK1}
        {WKS}
        {WR1}
        {WRK}
        {SLK}
        {XLS}1
        {DBF}
        {TAB}
        {SYS}

  [/FIELDNAMES]*

  [/RANGE={range name }]*
          {start..stop}
          {start:stop }

  [/KEEP={ALL**   }] [/DROP=varlist]
         {varlist}

[/MAP]
```

[1]Excel 4 or earlier. For Excel 5 or later, use the GET DATA command.

*Available only for spreadsheet and tab-delimited ASCII files.

**Default if the subcommand is omitted.

Keyword	**Type of file**
WK	Any Lotus 1-2-3 or Symphony file
WK1	1-2-3 Release 2.0
WKS	1-2-3 Release 1A
WR1	Symphony Release 2.0
WRK	Symphony Release 1.0
SLK	Microsoft Excel and Multiplan in SYLK (symbolic link) format
XLS	Microsoft Excel
DBF	All dBASE files
TAB	Tab-delimited ASCII file
SYS	Systat data file

Example

```
GET TRANSLATE FILE='PROJECT.WKS'
 /FIELDNAMES
 /RANGE=D3..J279.
```

Overview

GET TRANSLATE creates a working data file from files produced by other software applications. Supported formats are 1-2-3, Symphony, Multiplan, Excel, dBASE II, dBASE III, dBASE IV, and tab-delimited ASCII files.

Options

Variable Subsets. You can use the DROP and KEEP subcommands to specify variables to omit or retain in the resulting working data file.

Variable Names. You can rename variables as they are translated using the RENAME subcommand.

Variable Map. To confirm the names and order of the variables in the working data file, use the MAP subcommand. MAP displays the variables in the working data file and their corresponding names in the other application.

Spreadsheet Files. You can use the RANGE subcommand to translate a subset of cells from a spreadsheet file. You can use the FIELDNAMES subcommand to translate field names in the spreadsheet file to variable names.

Basic Specification

- The basic specification is FILE with a file specification enclosed in apostrophes.
- If the file's extension is not the default for the type of file you are reading, TYPE must also be specified.

Subcommand Order

Subcommands can be named in any order.

Operations

GET TRANSLATE replaces an existing working data file.

Spreadsheets

A spreadsheet file suitable for this program should be arranged so that each row represents a case and each column a variable.

- By default, the new working data file contains all rows and up to 256 columns from Lotus 1-2-3, Symphony, or Excel, or up to 255 columns from Multiplan.
- By default, GET TRANSLATE uses the column letters as variable names in the working data file.

- The first row of a spreadsheet or specified range may contain field labels immediately followed by rows of data. These names can be transferred as SPSS variable names (see the FIELDNAMES subcommand on p. 457).
- The current value of a formula is translated to the working data file.
- Blank, ERR, and NA values in 1-2-3 and Symphony and error values such as #N/A in Excel are translated as system-missing values in the working data file.
- Hidden columns and cells in 1-2-3 Release 2 and Symphony files are translated and copied into the working data file.
- Column width and format type are transferred to the dictionary of the working data file.
- The format type is assigned from values in the first data row. By default, the first data row is row 1. If RANGE is specified, the first data row is the first row in the range. If FIELDNAMES is specified, the first data row follows immediately after the single row containing field names.
- If a cell in the first data row is empty, the variable is assigned the global default format from the spreadsheet.

The formats from 1-2-3, Symphony, Excel, and Multiplan are translated as follows:

1-2-3/Symphony	**Excel**	**SYLK**	**SPSS**
Fixed	0.00; #,##0.00	Fixed	F
	0; #,##0	Integer	F
Scientific	0.00E+00	Exponent	E
Currency	$#,##0_);...	$ (dollar)	DOLLAR
, (comma)			COMMA
General	General	General	F
+/ -		* (bargraph)	F
Percent	0%; 0.00%	Percent	PCT
Date	m/d/yy;d-mmm-yy...		DATE
Time	h:mm; h:mm:ss...		TIME
Text/Literal			F
Label		Alpha	String

- If a string is encountered in a column with numeric format, it is converted to the system-missing value in the working data file.
- If a numeric value is encountered in a column with string format, it is converted to a blank in the working data file.
- Blank lines are translated as cases containing the system-missing value for numeric variables and blanks for string variables.
- 1-2-3 and Symphony date and time indicators (shown at the bottom of the screen) are not transferred from *WKS*, *WK1*, *WRK*, or *WR1* files.

Databases

Database files are logically very similar to SPSS-format data files.

- By default, all fields and records from dBASE II, dBASE III, or dBASE IV files are included in the working data file.
- Field names are automatically translated into variable names. If the FIELDNAMES subcommand is used with database files, it is ignored.
- Field names to be translated should comply with SPSS-format variable naming conventions. Names longer than eight characters are truncated. If a field name is not unique in the first eight characters, the field will be dropped.
- Colons used in dBASE II field names are translated to underscores.
- Records in dBASE II, dBASE III, or dBASE IV that have been marked for deletion but that have not actually been purged are included in the working data file. To differentiate these cases, GET TRANSLATE creates a new string variable *D_R*, which contains an asterisk for cases marked for deletion. Other cases contain a blank for *D_R*.
- Character, floating, and numeric fields are transferred directly to variables. Logical fields are converted into string variables. Memo fields are ignored.

dBASE formats are translated as follows:

dBASE	SPSS
Character	String
Logical	String
Date	Date
Numeric	Number
Floating	Number
Memo	Ignored

Tab-delimited ASCII Files

Tab-delimited ASCII files are simple spreadsheets produced by a text editor, with the columns delimited by tabs and rows by carriage returns. The first row is usually occupied by column headings.

- By default all columns of all rows are treated as data. Default variable names *VAR1*, *VAR2*, and so on are assigned to each column. The data type (numeric or string) for each variable is determined by the first data value in the column.
- If FIELDNAMES is specified, the program reads in the first row as variable names and determines data type by the values in from the second row.
- Any value that contains non-numeric characters is considered a string value. Dollar and date formats are not recognized and are treated as strings. When string values are encountered for a numeric variable, they are converted to the system-missing value.
- For numeric variables, the assigned format is F8.2 or the format of the first data value in the column, whichever is wider. Values that exceed the defined width are rounded for display, but the entire value is stored internally.

- For string variables, the assigned format is A8 or the format of the first data value in the column, whichever is wider. Values that exceed the defined width are truncated.
- ASCII data files delimited by space (instead of tabs) or in fixed format should be read by DATA LIST.

Limitations

The maximum number of variables that can be translated into the working data file depends on the maximum number of variables the other software application can handle:

Application	Maximum variables
1-2-3	256
Symphony	256
Multiplan	255
Excel	256
dBASE IV	255
dBASE III	128
dBASE II	32

FILE Subcommand

FILE names the file to read. The only specification is the name of the file.

- On some systems, file specifications should be enclosed in quotation marks or apostrophes.

Example

```
GET TRANSLATE FILE='PROJECT.WKS'.
```

- GET TRANSLATE creates a working data file from the 1-2-3 Release 1.0 spreadsheet with the name *PROJECT.WKS*.
- The working file contains all rows and columns and uses the column letters as variable names.
- The format for each variable is determined by the format of the value in the first row of each column.

TYPE Subcommand

TYPE indicates the format of the file.

- TYPE can be omitted if the file extension named on FILE is the default for the type of file you are reading.
- The TYPE subcommand takes precedence over the file extension.

- You can create a Lotus format file in Multiplan and translate it to an working data file by specifying WKS on TYPE.

WK *Any Lotus 1-2-3 or Symphony file.*

WK1 *1-2-3 Release 2.0.*

WKS *1-2-3 Release 1A.*

WR1 *Symphony Release 2.0.*

WRK *Symphony Release 1.0.*

SLK *Microsoft Excel and Multiplan saved in SYLK (symbolic link) format.*

XLS *Microsoft Excel, Release 4.0 or earlier. (For Excel 5 or later, use* GET CAPTURE.*)*

DBF *All dBASE files.*

TAB *Tab-delimited ASCII data file.*

Example

```
GET TRANSLATE FILE='PROJECT.OCT' /TYPE=SLK.
```

- GET TRANSLATE creates a working data file from the Multiplan file *PROJECT.OCT*.

FIELDNAMES Subcommand

FIELDNAMES translates spreadsheet field names into variable names.

- FIELDNAMES can be used with spreadsheet and tab-delimited ASCII files only. FIELDNAMES is ignored when used with database files.
- Each cell in the first row of the spreadsheet file (or the specified range) must contain a field name. If a column does not contain a name, the column is dropped.
- Field names to be translated should conform to SPSS-format naming conventions. They must be unique in the first eight characters and cannot have leading blanks.
- Field names that exceed eight characters are truncated.
- If two or more columns in the spreadsheet have the same field name, digits are appended to all field names after the first, making them unique.
- Illegal characters in field names are changed to underscores in this program.
- If the spreadsheet file uses reserved words (ALL, AND, BY, EQ, GE, GT, LE, LT, NE, NOT, OR, TO, or WITH) as field names, GET TRANSLATE appends a dollar sign ($) to the variable name. For example, columns named *GE*, *GT*, *EQ*, and *BY* will be renamed *GE$*, *GT$*, *EQ$*, and *BY$* in the working data file.

Example

```
GET TRANSLATE FILE='MONTHLY.WRK' /FIELDNAMES.
```

- GET TRANSLATE creates a working data file from a Symphony 1.0 spreadsheet. The first row in the spreadsheet contains field names that are used as variable names in the working file.

RANGE Subcommand

RANGE translates a specified set of cells from a spreadsheet file.

- RANGE cannot be used for translating database files.
- For 1-2-3 or Symphony, specify the beginning of the range with a column letter and row number followed by two periods and the end of the range with a column letter and row number, as in A1..K14.
- For Multiplan spreadsheets, specify the beginning and ending cells of the range separated by a colon, as in R1C1:R14C11.
- For Excel files, specify the beginning column letter and row number, a colon, and the ending column letter and row number, as in A1:K14.
- You can also specify the range using range names supplied in Symphony, 1-2-3, or Multiplan.
- If you specify FIELDNAMES with RANGE, the first row of the range must contain field names.

Example

```
GET TRANSLATE FILE='PROJECT.WKS' /FIELDNAMES /RANGE=D3..J279.
```

- GET TRANSLATE creates an SPSS working data file from the 1-2-3 Release 1A file *PROJECT.WKS.*
- The field names in the first row of the range (row 3) are used as variable names.
- Data from cells D4 through J279 are transferred to the working data file.

DROP and KEEP Subcommands

DROP and KEEP are used to copy a subset of variables into the working data file. DROP specifies the variables not to copy into the working file. KEEP specifies variables to copy. Variables not specified on KEEP are dropped.

- DROP and KEEP cannot precede the FILE or TYPE subcommands.
- DROP and KEEP specifications use variable names. By default, this program uses the column letters from spreadsheets and the field names from databases as variable names.
- If FIELDNAMES is specified when translating from a spreadsheet, the DROP and KEEP subcommands must refer to the field names, not the default column letters.
- Variables can be specified in any order. Neither DROP nor KEEP affects the order of variables in the resulting file. Variables are kept in their original order.
- If a variable is referred to twice on the same subcommand, only the first mention of the variable is recognized.
- Multiple DROP and KEEP subcommands are allowed; the effect is cumulative. Specifying a variable named on a previous DROP or not named on a previous KEEP results in an error and the command is not executed.
- If you specify both RANGE and KEEP, the resulting file contains only variables that are both within the range and specified on KEEP.
- If you specify both RANGE and DROP, the resulting file contains only variables within the range and excludes those mentioned on DROP, even if they are within the range.

Example

```
GET TRANSLATE FILE='ADDRESS.DBF' /DROP=PHONENO, ENTRY.
```

- GET TRANSLATE creates an SPSS working data file from the dBASE file *ADDRESS.DBF*, omitting the fields named *PHONENO* and *ENTRY*.

Example

```
GET TRANSLATE FILE='PROJECT.OCT' /TYPE=WK1 /FIELDNAMES
 /KEEP=NETINC, REP, QUANTITY, REGION, MONTH, DAY, YEAR.
```

- GET TRANSLATE creates a working data file from the 1-2-3 Release 2.0 file called *PROJECT.OCT*.
- The subcommand FIELDNAMES indicates that the first row of the spreadsheet contains field names, which will be translated into variable names in the working file.
- The subcommand KEEP translates columns with the field names *NETINC*, *REP*, *QUANTITY*, *REGION*, *MONTH*, *DAY*, and *YEAR* to the working file.

MAP Subcommand

MAP displays a list of the variables in the working data file and their corresponding names in the other application.

- The only specification is the keyword MAP. There are no additional specifications.
- Multiple MAP subcommands are allowed. Each MAP subcommand maps the results of subcommands that precede it; results of subcommands that follow it are not mapped.

Example

```
GET TRANSLATE FILE='ADDRESS.DBF' /DROP=PHONENO, ENTRY /MAP.
```

- MAP is specified to confirm that variables *PHONENO* and *ENTRY* have been dropped.

GLM: Overview

GLM is available in the Advanced Models option.

```
GLM dependent varlist [BY factor list [WITH covariate list]]

[/WSFACTOR=name levels [{DEVIATION [(refcat)]        }] name...
                        {SIMPLE [(refcat)]           }
                        {DIFFERENCE                  }
                        {HELMERT                     }
                        {REPEATED                    }
                        {POLYNOMIAL [({1,2,3...})]** }
                        {             {metric   }    }
                        {SPECIAL (matrix)            }

[/MEASURE=newname newname...]

[/WSDESIGN=effect effect...] †

[/RANDOM=factor factor...]

[/REGWGT=varname]

[/METHOD=SSTYPE({1  })]
                {2  }
                {3**}
                {4  }

[/INTERCEPT=[INCLUDE**] [EXCLUDE]]

[/MISSING=[INCLUDE] [EXCLUDE**]]

[/CRITERIA=[EPS({1E-8**})] [ALPHA({0.05**})]
                {a     }          {a     }

[/PRINT  = [DESCRIPTIVE] [HOMOGENEITY] [PARAMETER] [ETASQ] [RSSCP]
           [GEF] [LOF] [OPOWER] [TEST [([SSCP] [LMATRIX] [MMATRIX])]]

[/PLOT=[SPREADLEVEL] [RESIDUALS]
       [PROFILE (factor factor*factor factor*factor*factor ...)]

[/TEST=effect VS {linear combination [DF(df)]}]
                 {value DF (df)              }

[/LMATRIX={["label"] effect list effect list ...;...}]
          {["label"] effect list effect list ...    }
          {["label"] ALL list; ALL...               }
          {["label"] ALL list                       }

[/CONTRAST (factor name)={DEVIATION[(refcat)]** ‡   }]
                         {SIMPLE [(refcat)]         }
                         {DIFFERENCE                }
                         {HELMERT                   }
                         {REPEATED                  }
                         {POLYNOMIAL  [({1,2,3...})]}
                         {              {metric   } }
                         {SPECIAL (matrix)          }

[/MMATRIX= {["label"] depvar value depvar value ...;["label"]...}]
           {["label"] depvar value depvar value ...             }
           {["label"] ALL list; ["label"] ...                   }
           {["label"] ALL list                                  }
```

```
[/KMATRIX= {list of numbers     }]
           {list of numbers;...}

[/POSTHOC = effect [effect...]
           ([SNK]  [TUKEY]  [BTUKEY] [DUNCAN]
            [SCHEFFE]  [DUNNETT(refcat)]  [DUNNETTL(refcat)]
            [DUNNETTR(refcat)]  [BONFERRONI]  [LSD]  [SIDAK]
            [GT2]  [GABRIEL]  [FREGW]  [QREGW]   [T2]  [T3]  [GH] [C]
            [WALLER ({100** })]]
                     {kratio}
            [VS effect]

[/EMMEANS=TABLES({OVERALL              })] [COMPARE ADJ(LSD(none)) (BONFERRONI) (SIDAK)]
                 {factor                }
                 {factor*factor...      }
                 {wsfactor              }
                 {wsfactor*wsfactor ... }
                 {factor*...wsfactor*...}

[/SAVE=[tempvar [(list of names)]] [tempvar [(list of names)]]...]
       [DESIGN]

[/OUTFILE= [{COVB (filename)}] [EFFECT(filename)] [DESIGN(filename)]
            {CORB (filename)}

[/DESIGN={[INTERCEPT...]     }]
         {[effect effect...]}
```

† WSDESIGN uses the same specification as DESIGN, with only within-subjects factors.

‡ DEVIATION is the default for between-subjects factors, while POLYNOMIAL is the default for within-subjects factors.

** Default if subcommand or keyword is omitted.

Temporary variables (tempvar) are:

PRED, WPRED, RESID, WRESID, DRESID, ZRESID, SRESID, SEPRED, COOK, LEVER

Overview

GLM (general linear model) is a general procedure for analysis of variance and covariance, as well as regression. GLM is the most versatile of the analysis-of-variance procedures in SPSS and can be used for both univariate and multivariate designs. GLM allows you to:

- Include interaction and nested effects in your design model. Multiple nesting is allowed; for example, *A* within *B* within *C* is specified as *A*(*B*(*C*)).
- Include covariates in your design model. GLM also allows covariate-by-covariate and covariate-by-factor interactions such as *X* by *X* (or *X***X*), *X* by *A* (or *X***A*), and *X* by *A* within *B* (or *X***A*(*B*)). Thus, polynomial regression or a test of the homogeneity of regressions can be performed.
- Select appropriate sums-of-squares hypothesis tests for effects in balanced design models, unbalanced all-cells-filled design models, and some-cells-empty design models. The estimable functions corresponding to the hypothesis test for each effect in the model can also be displayed.
- Display the general form of estimable functions.

- Display expected mean squares, automatically detecting and using the appropriate error term for testing each effect in mixed- and random-effects models.
- Select commonly used contrasts or specify custom contrasts to perform hypothesis tests.
- Customize hypothesis testing, based on the null hypothesis **LBM** = **K**, where **B** is the parameter vector or matrix.
- Display a variety of post hoc tests for multiple comparisons.
- Display estimates of population marginal cell means for both between-subjects factors and within-subjects factors, adjusted for covariates.
- Perform multivariate analysis of variance and covariance.
- Estimate parameters using the method of weighted least squares and a generalized inverse technique.
- Compare graphically the levels in a model by displaying plots of estimated marginal cell means for each level of a factor, with separate lines for each level of another factor in the model.
- Display a variety of estimates and measures useful for diagnostic checking. All of these estimates and measures can be saved in a data file for use by another SPSS procedure.
- Perform repeated measures analysis of variance.
- Display homogeneity tests for testing underlying assumptions in multivariate and univariate analyses.

General Linear Model (GLM) and MANOVA

MANOVA, the other generalized procedure for analysis of variance and covariance in SPSS, is available only in syntax. The major distinction between GLM and MANOVA in terms of statistical design and functionality is that GLM uses a non-full-rank, or overparameterized, indicator variable approach to parameterization of linear models, instead of the full-rank reparameterization approach used in MANOVA. The generalized inverse approach and the aliasing of redundant parameters to zero employed by GLM allow greater flexibility in handling a variety of messy data situations, particularly those involving empty cells. GLM offers a variety of features unavailable in MANOVA:

- Identification of the general forms of estimable functions.
- Identification of forms of estimable functions specific to four types of sums of squares (Types I–IV).
- Tests using the four types of sums of squares, including Type IV, specifically designed for situations involving empty cells.
- Flexible specification of general comparisons among parameters, using the syntax subcommands LMATRIX, MMATRIX and KMATRIX; sets of contrasts can be specified that involve any number of orthogonal or nonorthogonal linear combinations.
- Nonorthogonal contrasts for within-subjects factors (using the syntax subcommand WSFACTORS).
- Tests against nonzero null hypotheses can be specified using the syntax subcommand KMATRIX.

- Estimated marginal means (EMMEANS) and standard errors adjusted for other factors and covariates are available for all between- and within-subjects factor combinations in the original variable metrics.
- Uncorrected pairwise comparisons among estimated marginal means for any main effect in the model, for both between- and within-subjects factors.
- Post hoc or multiple comparison tests for unadjusted one-way factor means are available for between-subjects factors in ANOVA designs; 20 different types of comparisons are offered.
- Weighted least squares (WLS) estimation, including saving of weighted predicted values and residuals.
- Automatic handling of random effects in random-effects models and mixed models, including generation of expected mean squares and automatic assignment of proper error terms.
- Specification of several types of nested models via dialog boxes with proper use of the interaction operator (*), due to the nonreparameterized approach.
- Univariate homogeneity-of-variance assumption tested using the Levene test.
- Between-subjects factors do not require specification of levels.
- Profile (interaction) plots of estimated marginal means for visual exploration of interactions involving combinations of between- and/or within-subjects factors.
- Saving of casewise temporary variables for model diagnosis:
  - Predicted values—unstandardized (raw), weighted unstandardized.
  - Residuals—unstandardized, weighted unstandardized, standardized, Studentized, deleted.
  - Standard error of prediction.
  - Cook's distance.
  - Leverage.
- Saving of an SPSS file with parameter estimates and their degrees of freedom, significance level.

To simplify the presentation, reference material on GLM is divided into three sections: *univariate* designs with one dependent variable, *multivariate* designs with several interrelated dependent variables, and *repeated measures* designs, in which the dependent variables represent the same types of measurements taken at more than one time.

The full syntax diagram for GLM is presented here. The GLM sections that follow include partial syntax diagrams showing the subcommands and specifications discussed in that section. Individually, those diagrams are incomplete. Subcommands listed for univariate designs are available for any analysis, and subcommands listed for multivariate designs can be used in any multivariate analysis, including repeated measures.

Models

The following are examples of models that can be specified using GLM:

Model 1: Univariate or multivariate simple and multiple regression

```
GLM Y WITH X1 X2.

GLM Y1 Y2 WITH X1 X2 X3.
```

Model 2: Fixed-effects ANOVA and MANOVA

```
GLM Y1 Y2 by B.
```

Model 3: ANCOVA and multivariate ANCOVA (MANCOVA)

```
GLM Y1 Y2 BY B WITH X1 X2 X3.
```

Model 4: Random-effects ANOVA and ANCOVA

```
GLM Y1 BY C WITH X1 X2
 /RANDOM = C.
```

Model 5: Mixed-model ANOVA and ANCOVA

```
GLM Y1 BY B, C WITH X1 X2
 /RANDOM = C.
```

Model 6: Repeated measures analysis using a split-plot design

```
(Univariate mixed models approach with subject as a random effect)
```

If *drug* is a between-subjects factor and *time* is a within-subjects factor,

```
GLM Y BY DRUG SUBJECT TIME
 /RANDOM = SUBJECT
 /DESIGN = DRUG SUBJECT*DRUG TIME DRUG*TIME.
```

Model 7: Repeated measures using the WSFACTOR subcommand

Use this model only when there is no random between-subjects effect in the model. For example, if *Y1*, *Y2*, *Y3*, and *Y4* are the dependent variables measured at times 1 to 4,

```
GLM Y1 Y2 Y3 Y4 BY DRUG
 /WSFACTOR = TIME 4
 /DESIGN.
```

Model 8: Repeated measures doubly multivariate model

Repeated measures fixed-effects MANOVA is also called a doubly multivariate model. Varying or time-dependent covariates are not available. This model can be used only when there is no random between-subjects effect in the model.

```
GLM X11 X12 X13 X21 X22 X23
    Y11 Y12 Y13 Y21 Y22 Y23 BY C D
/MEASURE = X Y
/WSFACTOR = A 2 B 3
/WSDESIGN = A B A*B
/DESIGN = C D.
```

Model 9: Means model for ANOVA and MANOVA

This model takes only fixed-effect factors (no random effects and covariates) and always assumes the highest order of the interactions among the factors. For example, *B*, *D*, and *E* are fixed factors, and *Y1* and *Y2* are two dependent variables. You can specify a means model by suppressing the intercept effect and specifying the highest order of interaction on the DESIGN subcommand.

```
GLM Y1 Y2 BY B, D, E
/INTERCEPT = EXCLUDE
/DESIGN = B*D*E.
```

Custom Hypothesis Specifications

GLM provides a flexible way for you to customize hypothesis testing based on the general linear hypothesis **LBM** = **K**, where **B** is the parameter vector or matrix. You can specify a customized linear hypothesis by using one or a combination of the subcommands LMATRIX, MMATRIX, KMATRIX, and CONTRAST.

LMATRIX, MMATRIX, and KMATRIX Subcommands

- The **L** matrix is called the **contrast coefficients matrix**. This matrix specifies coefficients of contrasts, which can be used for studying the between-subjects effects in the model. One way to define the **L** matrix is by specifying the CONTRAST subcommand, on which you select a type of contrast. Another way is to specify your own **L** matrix directly by using the LMATRIX subcommand. For details, see the syntax rules for these two subcommands in GLM: Univariate.
- The **M** matrix is called the **transformation coefficients matrix**. This matrix provides a transformation for the dependent variables. This transformation can be used to construct contrasts among the dependent variables in the model. The **M** matrix can be specified on the MMATRIX subcommand. For details, see the syntax rule for this subcommand in GLM: Multivariate.
- The **K** matrix is called the **contrast results matrix**. This matrix specifies the results matrix in the general linear hypothesis. To define your own **K** matrix, the KMATRIX subcommand can be used. For details, see the syntax rules for this subcommand in GLM: Univariate.

For univariate and multivariate models, you can specify one, two, or all three of the **L**, **M**, and **K** matrices. If only one or two types are specified, the unspecified matrices use the defaults shown in Table 1 (read across the rows).

Table 1 Default matrices for univariate and multivariate models if one matrix is specified

L matrix	**M matrix**	**K matrix**
If LMATRIX is used to specify the **L** matrix	Default = identity matrix*	Default = zero matrix
Default = intercept matrix†	If MMATRIX is used to specify the **M** matrix	Default = zero matrix
Default = intercept matrix†	Default = identity matrix*	If KMATRIX is used to specify the **K** matrix

* The dimension of the identity matrix is the same as the number of dependent variables being studied.

† The intercept matrix is the matrix corresponding to the estimable function for the intercept term in the model, provided that the intercept term is included in the model. If the intercept term is not included in the model, the **L** matrix is not defined and this custom hypothesis test cannot be performed.

Example

```
GLM Y1 Y2 BY A B
 /LMATRIX = A 1 -1
 /DESIGN A B.
```

Assume that factor *A* has two levels.

- Since there are two dependent variables, this is a multivariate model with two main factor effects, *A* and *B*.
- A custom hypothesis test is requested by the LMATRIX subcommand.
- Since no MMATRIX or KMATRIX is specified. The **M** matrix is the default two-dimensional identity matrix, and the **K** matrix is a zero-row vector (0, 0).

For a repeated measures model, you can specify one, two, or all three of the **L**, **M**, and **K** matrices. If only one or two types are specified, the unspecified matrices use the defaults shown in Table 2 (read across the rows).

Table 2 Default matrices for repeated measures models if only one matrix is specified

L matrix	**M matrix**	**K matrix**
If LMATRIX is used to specify the **L** matrix	Default = average matrix*	Default = zero matrix
Default = intercept matrix†	If MMATRIX is used to specify the **M** matrix	Default = zero matrix
Default = intercept matrix†	Default = average matrix*	If KMATRIX is used to specify the **K** matrix

* The average matrix is the transformation matrix that corresponds to the transformation for the between-subjects test. The dimension is the number of measures.

† The intercept matrix is the matrix corresponding to the estimable function for the intercept term in the model, provided that the intercept term is included in the model. If the intercept term is not included in the model, the **L** matrix is not defined and this custom hypothesis test cannot be performed.

Example

```
GLM Y1 Y2 BY A B
 /WSFACTOR TIME (2)
 /MMATRIX Y1 1 Y2 1; Y1 1 Y2 -1
 /DESIGN A B.
```

- Since WSFACTOR is specified, this is a repeated measures model with two between-subjects factors *A* and *B*, and a within-subjects factor, *TIME*.
- A custom hypothesis is requested by the MMATRIX subcommand. The **M** matrix is a 2×2 matrix:

$$\begin{matrix} 1 & 1 \\ 1 & -1 \end{matrix}$$

- Since the **L** matrix and the **K** matrix are not specified, their defaults are used. The default for the **L** matrix is the matrix corresponding to the estimable function for the intercept term in the between-subjects model, and the default for the **K** matrix is a zero-row vector (0, 0).

CONTRAST Subcommand

When the CONTRAST subcommand is used, an **L** matrix, which is used in custom hypothesis testing, is generated according to the contrast chosen. The **K** matrix is always taken to be the zero matrix. If the model is univariate or multivariate, the **M** matrix is always the identity matrix and its dimension is equal to the number of dependent variables. For a repeated measures model, the **M** matrix is always the average matrix that corresponds to the average transformation for the dependent variable.

GLM: Univariate

GLM is available in the Advanced Models option.

```
GLM dependent var [BY factor list [WITH covariate list]]

[/RANDOM=factor factor...]

[/REGWGT=varname]

[/METHOD=SSTYPE({1  })]
                {2  }
                {3**}
                {4  }

[/INTERCEPT=[INCLUDE**] [EXCLUDE]]

[/MISSING=[INCLUDE] [EXCLUDE**]]

[/CRITERIA=[EPS({1E-8**})] [ALPHA({0.05**})]
                {a     }           {a     }

[/PRINT = [DESCRIPTIVE] [HOMOGENEITY] [PARAMETER][ETASQ]
          [GEF] [LOF] [OPOWER] [TEST(LMATRIX)]]

[/PLOT=[SPREADLEVEL] [RESIDUALS]
       [PROFILE (factor factor*factor factor*factor*factor ...)]

[/TEST=effect VS {linear combination [DF(df)]}]
                 {value DF (df)              }

[/LMATRIX={["label"] effect list effect list ...;...}]
          {["label"] effect list effect list ...    }
          {["label"] ALL list; ALL...               }
          {["label"] ALL list                       }

[/KMATRIX= {number     }]
           {number;... }

[/CONTRAST (factor name)={DEVIATION[(refcat)]**       }]
                         {SIMPLE [(refcat)]           }
                         {DIFFERENCE                  }
                         {HELMERT                     }
                         {REPEATED                    }
                         {POLYNOMIAL  [({1,2,3...})]  }
                         {               {metric   }  }
                         {SPECIAL (matrix)            }

[/POSTHOC =effect [effect...]
          ([SNK] [TUKEY] [BTUKEY][DUNCAN]
           [SCHEFFE] [DUNNETT(refcat)] [DUNNETTL(refcat)]
           [DUNNETTR(refcat)] [BONFERRONI] [LSD] [SIDAK]
           [GT2] [GABRIEL] [FREGW] [QREGW]  [T2] [T3] [GH] [C]
           [WALLER ({100** })])]
                   {kratio}
           [VS effect]

[/EMMEANS=TABLES({OVERALL         })]  [COMPARE ADJ(LSD(none)) (BONFERRONI) (SIDAK)]
                 {factor          }
                 {factor*factor...}

[/SAVE=[tempvar [(name)]] [tempvar [(name)]]...]

[/OUTFILE= [{COVB (filename)}] [EFFECT(filename)] [DESIGN(filename)]
           {CORB (filename)}

[/DESIGN={[INTERCEPT...]     }]
         {[effect effect...] }
```

** Default if subcommand or keyword is omitted.

Temporary variables (tempvar) are:

PRED, WPRED, RESID, WRESID, DRESID, ZRESID, SRESID, SEPRED, COOK, LEVER

Example

```
GLM YIELD BY SEED FERT
  /DESIGN.
```

Overview

This section describes the use of GLM for univariate analyses. However, most of the subcommands described here can be used in any type of analysis with GLM. For additional subcommands used in those types of analysis, see GLM: Multivariate and GLM: Repeated Measures. For basic specification, syntax rules, and limitations of the GLM procedures, see GLM: Overview. For examples, see the *SPSS Base Applications Guide*.

Options

Design Specification. You can specify which terms to include in the design on the DESIGN subcommand. This allows you to estimate a model other than the default full factorial model, incorporate factor-by-covariate interactions or covariate-by-covariate interactions, and indicate nesting of effects.

Contrast Types. You can specify contrasts other than the default deviation contrasts on the CONTRAST subcommand.

Optional Output. You can choose from a wide variety of optional output on the PRINT subcommand. Output appropriate to univariate designs includes descriptive statistics for each cell, parameter estimates, Levene's test for equality of variance across cells, partial eta-squared for each effect and each parameter estimate, the general estimable function matrix, and a contrast coefficients table (**L'** matrix). The OUTFILE subcommand allows you to write out the covariance or correlation matrix, the design matrix, or the statistics from the between-subjects ANOVA table into a separate SPSS data file.

Using the EMMEANS subcommand, you can request tables of estimated marginal means of the dependent variable and their standard deviations. The SAVE subcommand allows you to save predicted values and residuals in weighted or unweighted and standardized or unstandardized forms. You can specify different means comparison tests for comparing all possible pairs of cell means using the POSTHOC subcommand. In addition, you can specify your own hypothesis tests by specifying an **L** matrix and a **K** matrix to test the univariate hypothesis **LB** = **K**.

Basic Specification

- The basic specification is a variable list identifying the dependent variable, the factors (if any), and the covariates (if any).
- By default, GLM uses a model that includes the intercept term, the covariate (if any), and the full factorial model, which includes all main effects and all possible interactions among factors. The intercept term is excluded if it is excluded in the model by specifying the keyword EXCLUDE on the INTERCEPT subcommand. Sums of squares are calculated and hypothesis tests are performed using type-specific estimable functions. Parameters are estimated using the normal equation and a generalized inverse of the SSCP matrix.

Subcommand Order

- The variable list must be specified first.
- Subcommands can be used in any order.

Syntax Rules

- For many analyses, the GLM variable list and the DESIGN subcommand are the only specifications needed.
- If you do not enter a DESIGN subcommand, GLM will use a full factorial model, with main effects of covariates, if any.
- Minimum syntax—at least one dependent variable must be specified, and at least one of the following must be specified: INTERCEPT, a between-subjects factor, or a covariate. The design contains the intercept by default.
- If more than one DESIGN subcommand is specified, only the last one is in effect.
- Dependent variables and covariates must be numeric, but factors can be numeric or string variables.
- If a string variable is specified as a factor, only the first eight characters of each value are used in distinguishing among values.
- If more than one MISSING subcommand is specified, only the last one is in effect.
- The following words are reserved as keywords or internal commands in the GLM procedure:

  INTERCEPT, BY, WITH, ALL, OVERALL, WITHIN

  Variable names that duplicate these words should be changed before you run GLM.

Limitations

- Any number of factors can be specified, but if the number of between-subjects factors plus the number of split variables exceeds 18, the Descriptive Statistics table is not printed even when you request it.

- Memory requirements depend primarily on the number of cells in the design. For the default full factorial model, this equals the product of the number of levels or categories in each factor.

Example

```
GLM YIELD BY SEED FERT WITH RAINFALL
  /PRINT=DESCRIPTIVE PARAMETER
  /DESIGN.
```

- *YIELD* is the dependent variable; *SEED* and *FERT* are factors; *RAINFALL* is a covariate.
- The PRINT subcommand requests the descriptive statistics for the dependent variable for each cell and the parameter estimates, in addition to the default tables Between-Subjects Factors and Univariate Tests.
- The DESIGN subcommand requests the default design, a full factorial model with a covariate. This subcommand could have been omitted or could have been specified in full as

  ```
  /DESIGN = INTERCEPT RAINFALL, SEED, FERT, SEED BY FERT.
  ```

GLM Variable List

The variable list specifies the dependent variable, the factors, and the covariates in the model.

- The dependent variable must be the first specification on GLM.
- The names of the factors follow the dependent variable. Use the keyword BY to separate the factors from the dependent variable.
- Enter the covariates, if any, following the factors. Use the keyword WITH to separate covariates from factors (if any) and the dependent variable.

Example

```
GLM DEPENDNT BY FACTOR1 FACTOR2, FACTOR3.
```

- In this example, three factors are specified.
- A default full factorial model is used for the analysis.

Example

```
GLM Y BY A WITH X
  /DESIGN.
```

- In this example, the DESIGN subcommand requests the default design, which includes the intercept term, the covariate *X* and the factor *A*.

RANDOM Subcommand

RANDOM allows you to specify which effects in your design are random. When the RANDOM subcommand is used, a table of expected mean squares for all effects in the design is displayed, and an appropriate error term for testing each effect is calculated and used automatically.

- Random always implies a univariate mixed-model analysis.

- If you specify an effect on RANDOM, higher-order effects containing the specified effect (excluding any effects containing covariates) are automatically treated as random effects.
- The keyword INTERCEPT and effects containing covariates are not allowed on this subcommand.
- The RANDOM subcommand cannot be used if there is any within-subjects factor in the model (that is, RANDOM cannot be specified if WSFACTOR is specified).
- When the RANDOM subcommand is used, the appropriate error terms for the hypothesis testing of all effects in the model are automatically computed and used.
- More than one RANDOM subcommand is allowed. The specifications are accumulated.

Example

```
GLM DEP BY A B
  /RANDOM = B
  /DESIGN = A,B, A*B.
```

- In the example, effects *B* and *A*B* are considered as random effects. Notice that if only effect *B* is specified in the RANDOM subcommand, *A*B* is automatically considered as a random effect.
- The hypothesis testing for each effect (*A*, *B*, and *A*B*) in the design will be carried out using the appropriate error term, which is calculated automatically.

REGWGT Subcommand

The only specification on REGWGT is the name of the variable containing the weights to be used in estimating a weighted least-squares model.

- Specify a numeric weight variable name following the REGWGT subcommand. Only observations with positive values in the weight variable will be used in the analysis.
- If more than one REGWGT subcommand is specified, only the last one is in effect.

Example

```
GLM OUTCOME BY TREATMNT
  /REGWGT WT.
```

- The procedure performs a weighted least-squares analysis. The variable *WT* is used as the weight variable.

METHOD Subcommand

METHOD controls the computational aspects of the GLM analysis. You can specify one of four different methods for partitioning the sums of squares. If more than one METHOD subcommand is specified, only the last one is in effect.

SSTYPE(1) *Type I sum-of-squares method.* The Type I sum-of-squares method is also known as the hierarchical decomposition of the sum-of-squares method. Each term is adjusted only for the terms that precede it on the DESIGN subcommand. Under a balanced design, it is an orthogonal decomposition, and the sums of squares in the model add up to the total sum of squares.

SSTYPE(2) *Type II sum-of-squares method.* This method calculates the sum of squares of an effect in the model adjusted for all other "appropriate" effects. An appropriate effect is one that corresponds to all effects that do not *contain* the effect being examined.

For any two effects *F1* and *F2* in the model, *F1* is said to be **contained** in *F2* under the following three conditions:
- Both effects *F1* and *F2* have the same covariate, if any.
- *F2* consists of more factors than *F1*.
- All factors in *F1* also appear in *F2*.

The intercept effect is treated as contained in all the pure factor effects. However, it is not contained in any effect involving a covariate. No effect is contained in the intercept effect. Thus, for any one effect *F* of interest, all other effects in the model can be classified as in one of the following two groups: the effects that do not contain *F* or the effects that contain *F*.

If the model is a main-effects design (that is, only main effects are in the model), the Type II sum-of-squares method is equivalent to the regression approach sums of squares. This means that each main effect is adjusted for every other term in the model.

SSTYPE(3) *Type III sum-of-squares method.* This is the default. This method calculates the sum of squares of an effect *F* in the design as the sum of squares adjusted for any other effects that do not contain it, and *orthogonal* to any effects (if any) that contain it. The Type III sums of squares have one major advantage—they are invariant with respect to the cell frequencies as long as the general form of estimability remains constant. Hence, this type of sums of squares is often used for an unbalanced model with no missing cells. In a factorial design with no missing cells, this method is equivalent to the Yates' weighted squares of means technique, and it also coincides with the overparameterized Σ-restricted model.

SSTYPE(4) *Type IV sum-of-squares method.* This method is designed for a situation in which there are missing cells. For any effect *F* in the design, if *F* is not contained in any other effect, then Type IV = Type III = Type II. When *F* is contained in other effects, then Type IV distributes the contrasts being made among the parameters in *F* to all higher-level effects equitably.

Example

```
GLM DEP BY A B C
  /METHOD=SSTYPE(3)
  /DESIGN=A, B, C.
```

- The design is a main-effects model.
- The METHOD subcommand requests that the model be fitted with Type III sums of squares.

INTERCEPT Subcommand

INTERCEPT controls whether an intercept term is included in the model. If more than one INTERCEPT subcommand is specified, only the last one is in effect.

INCLUDE *Include the intercept term.* The intercept (constant) term is included in the model. This is the default.

EXCLUDE *Exclude the intercept term.* The intercept term is excluded from the model. Specification of the keyword INTERCEPT on the DESIGN subcommand overrides INTERCEPT = EXCLUDE.

MISSING Subcommand

By default, cases with missing values for any of the variables on the GLM variable list are excluded from the analysis. The MISSING subcommand allows you to include cases with user-missing values.

- If MISSING is not specified, the default is EXCLUDE.
- Pairwise deletion of missing data is not available in GLM.
- Keywords INCLUDE and EXCLUDE are mutually exclusive.
- If more than one MISSING subcommand is specified, only the last one is in effect.

EXCLUDE *Exclude both user-missing and system-missing values.* This is the default when MISSING is not specified.

INCLUDE *User-missing values are treated as valid.* System-missing values cannot be included in the analysis.

CRITERIA Subcommand

CRITERIA controls the statistical criteria used to build the models.

- More than one CRITERIA subcommand is allowed. The specifications are accumulated. Conflicts across CRITERIA subcommands are resolved using the conflicting specification given on the last CRITERIA subcommand.
- The keyword must be followed by a positive number in parentheses.

EPS(n) *The tolerance level in redundancy detection.* This value is used for redundancy checking in the design matrix. The default value is 1E-8.

ALPHA(n) *The alpha level.* This keyword has two functions. First, it gives the alpha level at which the power is calculated for the F test. Once the noncentrality parameter for the alternative hypothesis is estimated from the data, then the power is the probability that the test statistic is greater than the critical value under the alternative hypothesis. (The observed power is displayed by default for GLM.) The second function of alpha is to specify the level of the confidence interval. If the alpha level specified is n, the value $(1-n) \times 100$ indicates the level of confidence for all individual and simultaneous confidence intervals generated for the specified model. The value of n must be between 0 and 1, exclusive.

The default value of alpha is 0.05. This means that the default power calculation is at the 0.05 level, and the default level of the confidence intervals is 95%, since $(1 - 0.05) \times 100 = 95$.

PRINT Subcommand

PRINT controls the display of optional output.

- Some PRINT output applies to the entire GLM procedure and is displayed only once.
- Additional output can be obtained on the EMMEANS, PLOT, and SAVE subcommands.
- Some optional output may greatly increase the processing time. Request only the output you want to see.
- If no PRINT command is specified, default output for a univariate analysis includes a factor information table and a Univariate Tests table (ANOVA) for all effects in the model.
- If more than one PRINT subcommand is specified, only the last one is in effect.

The following keywords are available for GLM univariate analyses. For information on PRINT specifications appropriate for other GLM models, see GLM: Multivariate and GLM: Repeated Measures.

DESCRIPTIVES *Basic information about each cell in the design.* Observed means, standard deviations, and counts for the dependent variable in all cells. The cells are constructed from the highest-order crossing of the between-subjects factors. For a multivariate model, statistics are given for each dependent variable. If the number of between-subjects factors plus the number of split variables exceeds 18, the Descriptive Statistics table is not printed.

HOMOGENEITY *Tests of homogeneity of variance.* Levene's test for equality of variances for the dependent variable across all level combinations of the between-subjects factors. If there are no between-subjects factors, this keyword is not valid. For a multivariate model, tests are displayed for each dependent variable.

PARAMETER *Parameter estimates.* Parameter estimates, standard errors, *t* tests, and confidence intervals.

ETASQ *Partial eta-squared* (η^2). This value is an overestimate of the actual effect size in an *F* test. It is defined as

$$\text{partial eta-squared} = \frac{dfh \times F}{dfh \times F + dfe}$$

where *F* is the test statistic and *dfh* and *dfe* are its degrees of freedom and degrees of freedom for error. The keyword EFSIZE can be used in place of ETASQ.

GEF *General estimable function table.* This table shows the general form of the estimable functions.

LOF *Perform a lack-of-fit test (which requires at least one cell to have multiple observations).* If the test is rejected, it implies that the current model cannot adequately account for the relationship between the response variable and the predictors. Either a variable is omitted or extra terms are needed in the model.

OPOWER *Observed power for each test.* The observed power gives the probability that the *F* test would detect a population difference between groups equal to that implied by the sample difference.

TEST(LMATRIX) *Set of contrast coefficients (L) matrices.* The transpose of the **L** matrix (**L'**) is displayed. This set always includes one matrix displaying the estimable function for each between-subjects effect appearing or implied in the DESIGN subcommand. Also, any **L** matrices generated by the LMATRIX or CONTRAST subcommands are displayed. TEST(ESTIMABLE) can be used in place of TEST(LMATRIX).

Example

```
GLM DEP BY A B WITH COV
  /PRINT=DESCRIPTIVE, TEST(LMATRIX), PARAMETER
  /DESIGN.
```

- Since the design in the DESIGN subcommand is not specified, the default design is used. In this case, the design includes the intercept term, the covariate *COV*, and the full factorial terms of *A* and *B*, which are *A*, *B*, and *A*B*.
- For each combination of levels of *A* and *B*, SPSS displays the descriptive statistics of *DEP*.
- The set of **L** matrices that generates the sums of squares for testing each effect in the design is displayed.
- The parameter estimates, their standard errors, *t* tests, confidence intervals, and the observed power for each test are displayed.

PLOT Subcommand

PLOT provides a variety of plots useful in checking the assumptions needed in the analysis. The PLOT subcommand can be specified more than once. All of the plots requested on each PLOT subcommand are produced.

Use the following keywords on the PLOT subcommand to request plots:

SPREADLEVEL *Spread-versus-level plots.* Plots of observed cell means versus standard deviations, and versus variances.

RESIDUALS *Observed by predicted by standardized residuals plot.* A plot is produced for each dependent variable. In a univariate analysis, a plot is produced for the single dependent variable.

PROFILE *Line plots of dependent variable means for one-way, two-way, or three-way crossed factors.* The PROFILE keyword must be followed by parentheses containing a list of one or more factor combinations. All factors specified (either individual or crossed) must be made up of only valid factors on the factor list. Factor combinations on the PROFILE keyword may use an asterisk (*) or the keyword BY to specify crossed factors. A factor cannot occur in a single factor combination more than once.

The order of factors in a factor combination is important, and there is no restriction on the order of factors. If a single factor is specified after the PROFILE keyword, a line plot of estimated means at each level of the factor is produced. If a two-way crossed factor combination is specified, the output includes a multiple-line plot of estimated means at each level of the first specified factor, with a separate line drawn for each level of the second specified factor. If a three-way crossed factor combination is specified, the output includes multiple-line plots of estimated means at each level of the first specified factor, with separate lines for each level of the second factor, and separate plots for each level of the third factor.

Example

```
GLM DEP BY A B
  /PLOT = SPREADLEVEL PROFILE(A A*B A*B*C)
  /DESIGN.
```

Assume each of the factors *A*, *B*, and *C* has three levels.

- Spread-versus-level plots are produced showing observed cell means versus standard deviations and observed cell means versus variances.
- Five profile plots are produced. For factor *A*, a line plot of estimated means at each level of *A* is produced (one plot). For the two-way crossed factor combination *A**B*, a multiple-line plot of estimated means at each level of *A*, with a separate line for each level of *B*, is produced (one plot). For the three-way crossed factor combination *A**B**C*, a multiple-line plot of estimated means at each level of *A*, with a separate line for each level of *B*, is produced for each of the three levels of *C* (three plots).

TEST Subcommand

The TEST subcommand allows you to test a hypothesis term against a specified error term.

- TEST is valid only for univariate analyses. Multiple TEST subcommands are allowed, each executed independently.
- You must specify both the hypothesis term and the error term. There is no default.
- The hypothesis term is specified before the keyword VS. It must be a valid effect specified or implied on the DESIGN subcommand.
- The error term is specified after the keyword VS. You can specify either a linear combination or a value. The linear combination of effects takes the general form: `coefficient*effect +/- coefficient*effect ...`
- All effects in the linear combination must be specified or implied on the DESIGN subcommand. Effects specified or implied on DESIGN but not listed after VS are assumed to have a coefficient of 0.
- Duplicate effects are allowed. GLM adds coefficients associated with the same effect before performing the test. For example, the linear combination `5*A–0.9*B–A` will be combined to `4*A–0.9B`.
- A coefficient can be specified as a fraction with a positive denominator—for example, 1/3 or –1/3, but 1/–3 is invalid.

- If you specify a value for the error term, you must specify the degrees of freedom after the keyword DF. The degrees of freedom must be a positive real number. DF and the degrees of freedom are optional for a linear combination.

Example

```
GLM DEP BY A B
  /TEST = A VS B + A*B
  /DESIGN = A, B, A*B.
```

- *A* is tested against the pooled effect of *B + A*B*.

LMATRIX Subcommand

The LMATRIX subcommand allows you to customize your hypotheses tests by specifying the **L** matrix (contrast coefficients matrix) in the general form of the linear hypothesis **LB** = **K**, where **K** = **0** if it is not specified on the KMATRIX subcommand. The vector **B** is the parameter vector in the linear model.

- The basic format for the LMATRIX subcommand is an optional label in quotes, an effect name or the keyword ALL, and a list of real numbers. There can be multiple effect names (or the keyword ALL) and number lists.
- The optional label is a string with a maximum length of 255 characters. Only one label can be specified.
- Only valid effects appearing or implied on the DESIGN subcommand can be specified on the LMATRIX subcommand.
- The length of the list of real numbers must be equal to the number of parameters (including the redundant ones) corresponding to that effect. For example, if the effect *A*B* takes up six columns in the design matrix, then the list after *A*B* must contain exactly six numbers.
- A number can be specified as a fraction with a positive denominator—for example, 1/3 or –1/3, but 1/–3 is invalid.
- A semicolon (;) indicates the end of a row in the **L** matrix.
- When ALL is specified, the length of the list that follows ALL is equal to the total number of parameters (including the redundant ones) in the model.
- Effects appearing or implied on the DESIGN subcommand but not specified here are assumed to have entries of 0 in the corresponding columns of the **L** matrix.
- Multiple LMATRIX subcommands are allowed. Each is treated independently.

Example

```
GLM DEP BY A B
  /LMATRIX = "B1 vs B2 at A1"
              B 1 -1 0 A*B 1 -1
  /LMATRIX = "Effect A"
              A 1 0 -1
              A*B 1/3  1/3  1/3
                    0    0    0
                 -1/3 -1/3 -1/3;
              A 0 1 -1
              A*B  0    0    0
                  1/3  1/3  1/3
                 -1/3 -1/3 -1/3
```

```
/LMATRIX = "B1 vs B2 at A2"
           ALL  0
                0  0  0
                1 -1  0
                0  0  0  1 -1  0 0  0  0
/DESIGN = A, B, A*B.
```

Assume that factors *A* and *B* each have three levels. There are three LMATRIX subcommands; each is treated independently.

- **B1 versus B2 at A1.** In the first LMATRIX subcommand, the difference is tested between levels 1 and 2 of effect *B* when effect *A* is fixed at level 1. Since there are three levels each in effects *A* and *B*, the interaction effect *A*B* should take up nine columns in the design matrix. Notice that only the first two columns of *A*B* are specified with values 1 and –1; the rest are all assumed to be 0. Columns corresponding to effect *B* are all assumed to be 0.
- **Effect A.** In the second LMATRIX subcommand, effect *A* is tested. Since there are three levels in effect *A*, at most two independent contrasts can be formed; thus, there are two rows in the **L** matrix, which are separated by a semicolon (;). The first row tests the difference between levels 1 and 3 of effect *A*, while the second row tests the difference between levels 2 and 3 of effect *A*.
- **B1 versus B2 at A2.** In the last LMATRIX subcommand, the keyword ALL is used. The first 0 corresponds to the intercept effect; the next three zeros correspond to effect *A*.

KMATRIX Subcommand

The KMATRIX subcommand allows you to customize your hypothesis tests by specifying the **K** matrix (contrast results matrix) in the general form of the linear hypothesis **LB** = **K**. The vector **B** is the parameter vector in the linear model.

- The default **K** matrix is a zero matrix; that is, **LB** = 0 is assumed.
- For the KMATRIX subcommand to be valid, at least one of the following subcommands must be specified: the LMATRIX subcommand or the INTERCEPT = INCLUDE subcommand.
- If KMATRIX is specified but LMATRIX is not specified, the LMATRIX is assumed to take the row vector corresponding to the intercept in the estimable function, provided the subcommand INTERCEPT = INCLUDE is specified. In this case, the **K** matrix can be only a scalar matrix.
- If KMATRIX and LMATRIX are specified, then the number of rows in the requested **K** and **L** matrices must be equal. If there are multiple LMATRIX subcommands, then all requested **L** matrices must have the same number of rows, and **K** must have the same number of rows as these **L** matrices.
- A semicolon (;) can be used to indicate the end of a row in the **K** matrix.
- If more than one KMATRIX subcommand is specified, only the last one is in effect.

Example

```
GLM DEP BY A B
  /LMATRIX = "Effect A"
             A 1  0 -1; A 1 -1  0
  /LMATRIX = "Effect B"
             B 1  0 -1; B 1 -1  0
  /KMATRIX = 0; 0
  /DESIGN = A B.
```

In this example, assume that factors *A* and *B* each have three levels.

- There are two LMATRIX subcommands; both have two rows.
- The first LMATRIX subcommand tests whether the effect of *A* is 0, while the second LMATRIX subcommand tests whether the effect of *B* is 0.
- The KMATRIX subcommand specifies that the **K** matrix also has two rows, each with value 0.

CONTRAST Subcommand

CONTRAST specifies the type of contrast desired among the levels of a factor. For a factor with k levels or values, the contrast type determines the meaning of its $k-1$ degrees of freedom.

- Specify the factor name in parentheses following the subcommand CONTRAST.
- You can specify only one factor per CONTRAST subcommand, but you can enter multiple CONTRAST subcommands.
- After closing the parentheses, enter an equals sign followed by one of the contrast keywords.
- This subcommand creates an **L** matrix such that the columns corresponding to the factor match the contrast given. The other columns are adjusted so that the **L** matrix is estimable.

The following contrast types are available:

DEVIATION *Deviations from the grand mean.* This is the default for between-subjects factors. Each level of the factor except one is compared to the grand mean. One category (by default, the last) must be omitted so that the effects will be independent of one another. To omit a category other than the last, specify the number of the omitted category (which is not necessarily the same as its value) in parentheses after the keyword DEVIATION. For example,

```
GLM Y BY B
  /CONTRAST(B)=DEVIATION(1).
```

Suppose factor *B* has three levels, with values 2, 4, and 6. The specified contrast omits the first category, in which *B* has the value 2. Deviation contrasts are not orthogonal.

POLYNOMIAL *Polynomial contrasts.* This is the default for within-subjects factors. The first degree of freedom contains the linear effect across the levels of the factor, the second contains the quadratic effect, and so on. In a balanced design, polynomial contrasts are orthogonal. By default, the levels are assumed to be equally spaced; you can specify unequal spacing by entering a metric consisting of one integer for each level of the factor in parentheses after the keyword POLYNOMIAL. (All metrics specified cannot be equal; thus, (1, 1, . . . 1) is not valid.) For example,

```
GLM RESPONSE BY STIMULUS
  /CONTRAST(STIMULUS) = POLYNOMIAL(1,2,4).
```

Suppose that factor *STIMULUS* has three levels. The specified contrast indicates that the three levels of *STIMULUS* are actually in the proportion 1:2:4. The default metric is always (1, 2, . . . k), where k levels are involved. Only the relative differences between the terms of the metric matter (1, 2, 4) is the same metric as (2, 3, 5) or (20, 30, 50) because, in each instance, the difference between the second and third numbers is twice the difference between the first and second.

DIFFERENCE *Difference or reverse Helmert contrasts.* Each level of the factor except the first is compared to the mean of the previous levels. In a balanced design, difference contrasts are orthogonal.

HELMERT *Helmert contrasts.* Each level of the factor except the last is compared to the mean of subsequent levels. In a balanced design, Helmert contrasts are orthogonal.

SIMPLE *Each level of the factor except the last is compared to the last level.* To use a category other than the last as the omitted reference category, specify its number (which is not necessarily the same as its value) in parentheses following the keyword SIMPLE. For example,

```
GLM Y BY B
    /CONTRAST(B)=SIMPLE(1).
```

Suppose that factor *B* has three levels with values 2, 4, and 6. The specified contrast compares the other levels to the first level of *B*, in which *B* has the value 2. Simple contrasts are not orthogonal.

REPEATED *Comparison of adjacent levels.* Each level of the factor except the first is compared to the previous level. Repeated contrasts are not orthogonal.

SPECIAL *A user-defined contrast.* Values specified after this keyword are stored in a matrix in column major order. For example, if factor *A* has three levels, then CONTRAST(A)= SPECIAL(1 1 1 1 -1 0 0 1 -1) produces the following contrast matrix:

$$\begin{matrix} 1 & 1 & 0 \\ 1 & -1 & 1 \\ 1 & 0 & -1 \end{matrix}$$

Orthogonal contrasts are particularly useful. In a balanced design, contrasts are orthogonal if the sum of the coefficients in each contrast row is 0 and if, for any pair of contrast rows, the products of corresponding coefficients sum to 0. DIFFERENCE, HELMERT, and POLYNOMIAL contrasts always meet these criteria in balanced designs.

Example

```
GLM DEP BY FAC
  /CONTRAST(FAC)=DIFFERENCE
  /DESIGN.
```

- Suppose that the factor *FAC* has five categories and therefore four degrees of freedom.
- CONTRAST requests DIFFERENCE contrasts, which compare each level (except the first) with the mean of the previous levels.

POSTHOC Subcommand

POSTHOC allows you to produce multiple comparisons between means of a factor. These comparisons are usually not planned at the beginning of the study but are suggested by the data in the course of study.

- Post hoc tests are computed for the dependent variable. The alpha value used in the tests can be specified by using the keyword ALPHA on the CRITERIA subcommand. The default alpha value is 0.05. The confidence level for any confidence interval constructed is $(1-\alpha) \times 100$. The default confidence level is 95. For a multivariate model, tests are computed for all dependent variables specified.
- Only between-subjects factors appearing in the factor list are valid in this subcommand. Individual factors can be specified.
- You can specify one or more effects to be tested. Only fixed main effects appearing or implied on the DESIGN subcommand are valid test effects.
- Optionally, you can specify an effect defining the error term following the keyword VS after the test specification. The error effect can be any single effect in the design that is not the intercept or a main effect named on a POSTHOC subcommand.
- A variety of multiple comparison tests are available. Some tests are designed for detecting homogeneity subsets among the groups of means, some are designed for pairwise comparisons among all means, and some can be used for both purposes.
- For tests that are used for detecting homogeneity subsets of means, non-empty group means are sorted in ascending order. Means that are not significantly different are included together to form a homogeneity subset. The significance for each homogeneity subset of means is displayed. In a case where the numbers of valid cases are not equal in all groups, for most post hoc tests, the harmonic mean of the group sizes is used as the sample size in the calculation. For QREGW or FREGW, individual sample sizes are used.
- For tests that are used for pairwise comparisons, the display includes the difference between each pair of compared means, the confidence interval for the difference, and the significance. The sample sizes of the two groups being compared are used in the calculation.
- Output for tests specified on the POSTHOC subcommand are available according to their statistical purposes. The following table illustrates the statistical purpose of the post hoc tests:

Post Hoc Tests	Statistical Purpose	
Keyword	**Homogeneity Subsets Detection**	**Pairwise Comparison and Confidence Interval**
LSD		Yes
SIDAK		Yes
BONFERRONI		Yes
GH		Yes
T2		Yes
T3		Yes
C		Yes
DUNNETT		Yes*
DUNNETTL		Yes*
DUNNETTR		Yes*
SNK	Yes	
BTUKEY	Yes	
DUNCAN	Yes	
QREGW	Yes	
FREGW	Yes	
WALLER	Yes†	
TUKEY	Yes	Yes
SCHEFFE	Yes	Yes
GT2	Yes	Yes
GABRIEL	Yes	Yes

* Only C.I.'s for differences between test group means and control group means are given.

† No significance for Waller test is given.

- Tests that are designed for homogeneity subset detection display the detected homogeneity subsets and their corresponding significances.
- Tests that are designed for both homogeneity subset detection and pairwise comparisons display both kinds of output.
- For the DUNNETT, DUNNETTL, and DUNNETTR keywords, only individual factors can be specified.
- The default reference category for DUNNETT, DUNNETTL, and DUNNETTR is the last category. An integer greater than 0 within parentheses can be used to specify a different reference category. For example, POSTHOC = A (DUNNETT(2)) requests a DUNNETT test for factor *A*, using the second level of *A* as the reference category.
- The keywords DUNCAN, DUNNETT, DUNNETTL, and DUNNETTR must be spelled out in full; using the first three characters alone is not sufficient.
- If the REGWGT subcommand is specified, weighted means are used in performing post hoc tests.

- Multiple POSTHOC subcommands are allowed. Each specification is executed independently so that you can test different effects against different error terms.

SNK *Student-Newman-Keuls procedure based on the Studentized range test.*

TUKEY *Tukey's honestly significant difference.* This test uses the Studentized range statistic to make all pairwise comparisons between groups.

BTUKEY *Tukey's b.* Multiple comparison procedure based on the average of Studentized range tests.

DUNCAN *Duncan's multiple comparison procedure based on the Studentized range test.*

SCHEFFE *Scheffé's multiple comparison* t *test.*

DUNNETT(refcat) *Dunnett's two-tailed* t *test.* Each level of the factor is compared to a reference category. A reference category can be specified in parentheses. The default reference category is the last category. This keyword must be spelled out in full.

DUNNETTL(refcat) *Dunnett's one-tailed* t *test.* This test indicates whether the mean at any level (except the reference category) of the factor is *smaller* than that of the reference category. A reference category can be specified in parentheses. The default reference category is the last category. This keyword must be spelled out in full.

DUNNETTR(refcat) *Dunnett's one-tailed* t *test.* This test indicates whether the mean at any level (except the reference category) of the factor is *larger* than that of the reference category. A reference category can be specified in parentheses. The default reference category is the last category. This keyword must be spelled out in full.

BONFERRONI *Bonferroni* t *test.* This test is based on Student's *t* statistic and adjusts the observed significance level for the fact that multiple comparisons are made.

LSD *Least significant difference* t *test.* Equivalent to multiple *t* tests between all pairs of groups. This test does not control the overall probability of rejecting the hypotheses that some pairs of means are different, while in fact they are equal.

SIDAK *Sidak* t *test.* This test provides tighter bounds than the Bonferroni test.

GT2 *Hochberg's GT2.* Pairwise comparisons test based on the Studentized maximum modulus test. Unless the cell sizes are extremely unbalanced, this test is fairly robust even for unequal variances.

GABRIEL *Gabriel's pairwise comparisons test based on the Studentized maximum modulus test.*

FREGW *Ryan-Einot-Gabriel-Welsch's multiple stepdown procedure based on an* F *test.*

QREGW *Ryan-Einot-Gabriel-Welsch's multiple stepdown procedure based on the Studentized range test.*

T2 *Tamhane's T2.* Tamhane's pairwise comparisons test based on a *t* test. This test can be applied in situations where the variances are unequal.

T3 *Dunnett's T3.* Pairwise comparisons test based on the Studentized maximum modulus. This test is appropriate when the variances are unequal.

GH *Games and Howell's pairwise comparisons test based on the Studentized range test.* This test can be applied in situations where the variances are unequal.

C *Dunnett's C.* Pairwise comparisons based on the weighted average of Studentized ranges. This test can be applied in situations where the variances are unequal.

WALLER(kratio) *Waller-Duncan* t *test.* This test uses a Bayesian approach. It is restricted to cases with equal sample sizes. For cases with unequal sample sizes, the harmonic mean of the sample size is used. The kratio is the Type 1/Type 2 error seriousness ratio. The default value is 100. You can specify an integer greater than 1 within parentheses.

EMMEANS Subcommand

EMMEANS displays estimated marginal means of the dependent variable in the cells (with covariates held at their overall mean value) and their standard errors for the specified factors. Note that these are predicted, not observed, means. The estimated marginal means are calculated using a modified definition by Searle, Speed, and Milliken (1980).

- TABLES, followed by an option in parentheses, is required. COMPARE is optional; if specified, it must follow TABLES.
- Multiple EMMEANS subcommands are allowed. Each is treated independently.
- If redundant EMMEANS subcommands are specified, only the last redundant subcommand is in effect. EMMEANS subcommands are redundant if the option specified on TABLES is the same (including redundant crossed factor combinations—for example, *A*B* and *B*A*).

TABLES(option) *Table specification.* Valid options are the keyword OVERALL, factors appearing on the factor list, and crossed factors constructed of factors on the factor list. Crossed factors can be specified using an asterisk (*) or the keyword BY. All factors in a crossed factor specification must be unique.

If OVERALL is specified, the estimated marginal means of the dependent variable are displayed, collapsing over between-subjects factors.

If a between-subjects factor, or a crossing of between-subjects factors, is specified on the TABLES keyword, GLM collapses over any other between-subjects factors before computing the estimated marginal means for the dependent variable. For a multivariate model, GLM collapses over any other between- or within-subjects factors.

COMPARE(factor) ADJ(method)

Main- or simple-main-effects omnibus tests and pairwise comparisons of the dependent variable. This option gives the mean difference, standard error, significance, and confidence interval for each pair of levels for the effect specified in the TABLES command, as well as an omnibus test for that effect. If only one factor is specified on TABLES, COMPARE can be specified by itself; otherwise, the factor specification is required. In this case, levels of the specified factor are compared with each other for each level of the other factors in the interaction.

The optional ADJ keyword allows you to apply an adjustment to the confidence intervals and significance values to account for multiple comparisons. Methods available are LSD (no adjustment), BONFERRONI, or SIDAK.

Example

```
GLM DEP BY A B
  /EMMEANS = TABLES(A*B)COMPARE(A)
  /DESIGN.
```

- The output of this analysis includes a pairwise comparisons table for the dependent variable *DEP*.
- Assume that *A* has three levels and *B* has two levels. The first level of *A* is compared with the second and third levels, the second level with the first and third levels, and the third level with the first and second levels. The pairwise comparison is repeated for the two levels of *B*.

SAVE Subcommand

Use SAVE to add one or more residual or fit values to the working data file.

- Specify one or more temporary variables, each followed by an optional new name in parentheses. For a multivariate model, you can optionally specify a new name for the temporary variable related to each dependent variable.
- WPRED and WRESID can be saved only if REGWGT has been specified.
- Specifying a temporary variable on this subcommand results in a variable being added to the active data file for each dependent variable.
- You can specify variable names for the temporary variables. These names must be unique, valid variable names. For a multivariate model, there should be as many variable names specified as there are dependent variables, listed in the order of the dependent variables as specified on the GLM command. If you do not specify enough variable names, default variable names are used for any remaining variables.
- If new names are not specified, GLM generates a rootname using a shortened form of the temporary variable name with a suffix. For a multivariate model, the suffix *_n* is added

to the temporary variable name, where *n* is the ordinal number of the dependent variable as specified on the GLM command.

- If more than one SAVE subcommand is specified, only the last one is in effect.

PRED *Unstandardized predicted values.*

WPRED *Weighted unstandardized predicted values.* Available only if REGWGT has been specified.

RESID *Unstandardized residuals.*

WRESID *Weighted unstandardized residuals.* Available only if REGWGT has been specified.

DRESID *Deleted residuals.*

ZRESID *Standardized residuals.*

SRESID *Studentized residuals.*

SEPRED *Standard errors of predicted value.*

COOK *Cook's distances.*

LEVER *Uncentered leverage values.*

OUTFILE Subcommand

The OUTFILE subcommand writes an SPSS data file that can be used in other procedures.

- You must specify a keyword on OUTFILE. There is no default.
- You must specify a filename in parentheses after a keyword. A filename with a path must be enclosed within quotation marks. The asterisk (*) is not allowed.
- If you specify more than one keyword, a different filename is required for each.
- If more than one OUTFILE subcommand is specified, only the last one is in effect.
- For COVB or CORB, the output will contain, in addition to the covariance or correlation matrix, three rows for each dependent variable: a row of parameter estimates, a row of residual degrees of freedom, and a row of significance values for the *t* statistics corresponding to the parameter estimates. All statistics are displayed separately by split.

COVB (filename) *Writes the parameter covariance matrix.*

CORB (filename) *Writes the parameter correlation matrix.*

EFFECT (filename) *Writes the statistics from the between-subjects ANOVA table.* Invalid for repeated measures analyses.

DESIGN (filename) *Writes the design matrix.* The number of rows equals the number of cases, and the number of columns equals the number of parameters. The variable names are *DES_1*, *DES_2*, ..., *DES_p*, where *p* is the number of the parameters.

DESIGN Subcommand

DESIGN specifies the effects included in a specific model. The cells in a design are defined by all of the possible combinations of levels of the factors in that design. The number of cells equals the product of the number of levels of all the factors. A design is *balanced* if each cell contains the same number of cases. GLM can analyze both balanced and unbalanced designs.

- Specify a list of terms to be included in the model, separated by spaces or commas.
- The default design, if the DESIGN subcommand is omitted or is specified by itself, is a design consisting of the following terms in order: the intercept term (if INTERCEPT=INCLUDE is specified), next the covariates given in the covariate list, and then the full factorial model defined by all factors on the factor list and excluding the intercept.
- To include a term for the main effect of a factor, enter the name of the factor on the DESIGN subcommand.
- To include the intercept term in the design, use the keyword INTERCEPT on the DESIGN subcommand. If INTERCEPT is specified on the DESIGN subcommand, the subcommand INTERCEPT=EXCLUDE is overridden.
- To include a term for an interaction between factors, use the keyword BY or the asterisk (*) to join the factors involved in the interaction. For example, *A*B* means a two-way interaction effect of *A* and *B*, where *A* and *B* are factors. *A*A* is not allowed because factors inside an interaction effect must be distinct.
- To include a term for nesting one effect within another, use the keyword WITHIN or a pair of parentheses on the DESIGN subcommand. For example, *A(B)* means that *A* is nested within *B*. The expression *A(B)* is equivalent to the expression *A WITHIN B*. When more than one pair of parentheses is present, each pair of parentheses must be enclosed or nested within another pair of parentheses. Thus, *A(B)(C)* is not valid.
- Multiple nesting is allowed. For example, *A(B(C))* means that *B* is nested within *C*, and *A* is nested within *B(C)*.
- Interactions between nested effects are not valid. For example, neither *A(C)*B(C)* nor *A(C)*B(D)* is valid.
- To include a covariate term in the design, enter the name of the covariate on the DESIGN subcommand.
- Covariates can be connected, but not nested, through the * operator to form another covariate effect. Therefore, interactions among covariates such as *X1*X1* and *X1*X2* are valid, but not *X1(X2)*. Using covariate effects such as *X1*X1*, *X1*X1*X1*, *X1*X2*, and *X1*X1*X2*X2* makes fitting a polynomial regression model easy in GLM.
- Factor and covariate effects can be connected only by the * operator. Suppose *A* and *B* are factors, and *X1* and *X2* are covariates. Examples of valid factor-by-covariate interaction effects are *A*X1*, *A*B*X1*, *X1*A(B)*, *A*X1*X1*, and *B*X1*X2*.
- If more than one DESIGN subcommand is specified, only the last one is in effect.

Example

```
GLM Y BY A B C WITH X
  /DESIGN A B(A) X*A.
```

- In this example, the design consists of a main effect *A*, a nested effect *B* within *A*, and an interaction effect of a covariate *X* with a factor *A*.

GLM: Multivariate

GLM is available in the Advanced Models option.

```
GLM dependent varlist [BY factor list [WITH covariate list]]

[/REGWGT=varname]

[/METHOD=SSTYPE({1   })]
                {2   }
                {3** }
                {4   }

[/INTERCEPT=[INCLUDE**] [EXCLUDE]]

[/MISSING=[INCLUDE] [EXCLUDE**]]

[/CRITERIA=[EPS({1E-8**})] [ALPHA({0.05**})]
                {a      }         {a      }

[/PRINT  = [DESCRIPTIVE] [HOMOGENEITY] [PARAMETER] [ETASQ] [RSSCP]
           [GEF] [LOF] [OPOWER] [TEST [([SSCP] [LMATRIX] [MMATRIX])]]

[/PLOT=[SPREADLEVEL] [RESIDUALS]
       [PROFILE (factor factor*factor factor*factor*factor ...)]

[/LMATRIX={["label"] effect list effect list ...;...}]
          {["label"] effect list effect list ...     }
          {["label"] ALL list; ALL...                }
          {["label"] ALL list                        }

[/MMATRIX= {["label"] depvar value depvar value ...;["label"]...}]
           {["label"] depvar value depvar value ...              }
           {["label"] ALL list; ["label"] ...                    }
           {["label"] ALL list                                   }

[/KMATRIX= {list of numbers     }]
           {list of numbers;...}

[/SAVE=[tempvar [(list of names)]] [tempvar [(list of names)]]...]
       [DESIGN]

[/OUTFILE= [{COVB (filename)}] [EFFECT(filename)] [DESIGN(filename)]
            {CORB (filename)}

[/DESIGN={[INTERCEPT...]     }]
         {[effect effect...]}
```

** Default if subcommand or keyword is omitted.

Temporary variables (tempvar) are:

PRED, WPRED, RESID, WRESID, DRESID, ZRESID, SRESID, SEPRED, COOK, LEVER

Example

```
GLM SCORE1 TO SCORE4 BY METHOD(1,3).
```

Overview

This section discusses the subcommands that are used in multivariate general linear models and covariance designs with several interrelated dependent variables. The discussion focuses on subcommands and keywords that do not apply, or apply in different manners, to univariate analyses. It does not contain information on all of the subcommands you will need to specify the design. For subcommands not covered here, see GLM: Univariate.

Options

Optional Output. In addition to the output described in GLM: Univariate, you can have both multivariate and univariate *F* tests. Using the PRINT subcommand, you can request the hypothesis and error sums-of-squares and cross-product matrices for each effect in the design, the transformation coefficient table (**M** matrix), Box's *M* test for equality of covariance matrices, and Bartlett's test of sphericity.

Basic Specification

- The basic specification is a variable list identifying the dependent variables, with the factors (if any) named after BY and the covariates (if any) named after WITH.
- By default, GLM uses a model that includes the intercept term, the covariates (if any), and the full factorial model, which includes all main effects and all possible interactions among factors. The intercept term is excluded if it is excluded in the model by specifying EXCLUDE on the INTERCEPT subcommand. GLM produces multivariate and univariate *F* tests for each effect in the model. It also calculates the power for each test based on the default alpha value.

Subcommand Order

- The variable list must be specified first.
- Subcommands can be used in any order.

Syntax Rules

- The syntax rules applicable to univariate analysis, in "Syntax Rules" on p. 470 in GLM: Univariate, also apply to multivariate analysis.
- If you enter one of the multivariate specifications in a univariate analysis, GLM ignores it.

Limitations

- Any number of factors can be specified, but if the number of between-subjects factors plus the number of split variables exceeds 18, the Descriptive Statistics table is not printed even when you request it.

- Memory requirements depend primarily on the number of cells in the design. For the default full factorial model, this equals the product of the number of levels or categories in each factor.

GLM Variable List

- Multivariate GLM calculates statistical tests that are valid for analyses of dependent variables that are correlated with one another. The dependent variables must be specified first.
- The factor and covariate lists follow the same rules as in univariate analyses.
- If the dependent variables are uncorrelated, the univariate significance tests have greater statistical power.

PRINT Subcommand

By default, if no PRINT subcommand is specified, multivariate GLM produces multivariate tests (MANOVA) and univariate tests (ANOVA) for all effects in the model. All of the PRINT specifications described in GLM: Univariate are available in multivariate analyses. The following additional output can be requested:

TEST(SSCP) *Sums-of-squares and cross-product matrices.* Hypothesis (HSSCP) and error (ESSCP) sums-of-squares and cross-product matrices for each effect in the design are displayed. Each between-subjects effect has a different HSSCP matrix, but there is a single ESSCP matrix for all between-subjects effects. For a repeated measures design, each within-subjects effect has an HSSCP matrix and an ESSCP matrix. If there are no within-subjects effects, the ESSCP matrix for the between-subjects effects is the same as the RSSCP matrix.

TEST(MMATRIX) *Set of transformation coefficients (M) matrices.* Any **M** matrices generated by the MMATRIX subcommand are displayed. If no **M** matrix is specified on the MMATRIX subcommand, this specification will be skipped, unless you are using a repeated measures design. In a repeated measures design, this set always includes the **M** matrix determined by the WSFACTOR subcommand. The specification TEST(TRANSFORM) is equivalent to TEST(MMATRIX).

HOMOGENEITY *Tests of homogeneity of variance.* In addition to Levene's test for equality of variances for each dependent variable, the display includes Box's *M* test of homogeneity of the covariance matrices of the dependent variables across all level combinations of the between-subjects factors.

RSSCP *Sums-of-squares and cross-products of residuals.* Three matrices are displayed:

Residual SSCP matrix. A square matrix of sums of squares and cross-products of residuals. The dimension of this matrix is the same as the number of dependent variables in the model.

Residual covariance matrix. The residual SSCP matrix divided by the degrees of freedom of the residual.

Residual correlation matrix. The standardized form of the residual covariance matrix.

Example

```
GLM Y1 Y2 Y3 BY A B
 /PRINT = HOMOGENEITY RSSCP
 /DESIGN.
```

- Since there are three dependent variables, this is a multivariate model.
- The keyword RSSCP produces three matrices of sums of squares and cross-products of residuals. The output also contains the result of Bartlett's test of the sphericity of the residual covariance matrix.
- In addition to the Levene test for each dependent variable, the keyword HOMOGENEITY produces the result of Box's *M* test of homogeneity in the multivariate model.

MMATRIX Subcommand

The MMATRIX subcommand allows you to customize your hypothesis tests by specifying the **M** matrix (transformation coefficients matrix) in the general form of the linear hypothesis **LBM** = **K**, where **K** = **0** if it is not specified on the KMATRIX subcommand. The vector **B** is the parameter vector in the linear model.

- Specify an optional label in quotes. Then either list dependent variable names, each followed by a real number, or specify the keyword ALL followed by a list of real numbers. Only variable names that appear on the dependent variable list can be specified on the MMATRIX subcommand.
- You can specify one label for each column in the **M** matrix.
- If you specify ALL, the length of the list that follows ALL should be equal to the number of dependent variables.
- There is no limit on the length of the label.
- For the MMATRIX subcommand to be valid, at least one of the following must be specified: the LMATRIX subcommand or INTERCEPT=INCLUDE. (Either of these specifications defines an **L** matrix.)
- If both LMATRIX and MMATRIX are specified, the **L** matrix is defined by the LMATRIX subcommand.
- If MMATRIX or KMATRIX is specified but LMATRIX is not specified, the **L** matrix is defined by the estimable function for the intercept effect, provided that the intercept effect is included in the model.
- If LMATRIX is specified, but MMATRIX is not specified, the **M** matrix is assumed to be an $r \times r$ identity matrix, where r is the number of dependent variables.
- A semicolon (;) indicates the end of a column in the **M** matrix.
- Dependent variables not appearing on a list of dependent variable names and real numbers are assigned a value of 0.

- Dependent variables not appearing in the MMATRIX subcommand will have a row of zeros in the **M** matrix.
- A number can be specified as a fraction with a positive denominator—for example, 1/3 or –1/3, but 1/–3 is invalid.
- The number of columns must be greater than 0. You can specify as many columns as you need.
- If more than one MMATRIX subcommand is specified, only the last one is in effect.

Example

```
GLM Y1 Y2 Y3 BY A B
 /MMATRIX = "Y1-Y2" Y1 1 Y2 -1; "Y1-Y3" Y1 1 Y3 -1
            "Y2-Y3" Y2 1 Y3 -1
 /DESIGN.
```

- In the above example, *Y1*, *Y2*, and *Y3* are the dependent variables.
- The MMATRIX subcommand requests all pairwise comparisons among the dependent variables.
- Since LMATRIX was not specified, the **L** matrix is defined by the estimable function for the intercept effect.

GLM: Repeated Measures

GLM is available in the Advanced Models option.

```
GLM dependent varlist [BY factor list [WITH covariate list]]

/WSFACTOR=name levels [{DEVIATION [(refcat)]          }] name...
                       {SIMPLE [(refcat)]             }
                       {DIFFERENCE                    }
                       {HELMERT                       }
                       {REPEATED                      }
                       {POLYNOMIAL [({1,2,3...})]**   }
                       {             {metric  }       }
                       {SPECIAL (matrix)              }

[/MEASURE=newname newname...]

[/WSDESIGN=effect effect...]

[/REGWGT=varname]

[/METHOD=SSTYPE({1  })]
                {2  }
                {3**}
                {4  }

[/INTERCEPT=[INCLUDE**] [EXCLUDE]]

[/MISSING=[INCLUDE] [EXCLUDE**]]

[/PRINT  = [DESCRIPTIVE] [HOMOGENEITY] [PARAMETER][ETASQ] [RSSCP]
           [GEF] [LOF] [OPOWER] [TEST [([SSCP] [LMATRIX] [MMATRIX])]]

[/SAVE=[tempvar [(list of names)]] [tempvar [(list of names)]]...]
       [DESIGN]

[/EMMEANS=TABLES({OVERALL               })] [COMPARE ADJ(LSD(none)(BONFERRONI)(SIDAK))]
                 {factor                 }
                 {factor*factor...       }
                 {wsfactor               }
                 {wsfactor*wsfactor...   }
                 {factor*...wsfactor*...]
                 {factor*factor...       }

[/DESIGN={ [INTERCEPT...]     }]*
         { [effect effect...] }
```

* The DESIGN subcommand has the same syntax as is described in GLM: Univariate.

** Default if subcommand or keyword is omitted.

Example

```
GLM Y1 TO Y4 BY GROUP
  /WSFACTOR=YEAR 4.
```

Overview

This section discusses the subcommands that are used in repeated measures designs, in which the dependent variables represent measurements of the same variable (or variables) taken repeatedly. This section does not contain information on all of the subcommands that you will need to specify the design. For some subcommands or keywords not covered here, such as DESIGN, see GLM: Univariate. For information on optional output and the multivariate significance tests available, see GLM: Multivariate.

- In a simple repeated measures analysis, all dependent variables represent different measurements of the same variable for different values (or levels) of a within-subjects factor. Between-subjects factors and covariates can also be included in the model, just as in analyses not involving repeated measures.
- A **within-subjects factor** is simply a factor that distinguishes measurements made on the same subject or case, rather than distinguishing different subjects or cases.
- GLM permits more complex analyses, in which the dependent variables represent levels of two or more within-subjects factors.
- GLM also permits analyses in which the dependent variables represent measurements of several variables for the different levels of the within-subjects factors. These are known as **doubly multivariate designs**.
- A repeated measures analysis includes a within-subjects design describing the model to be tested with the within-subjects factors, as well as the usual between-subjects design describing the effects to be tested with between-subjects factors. The default for the within-subjects factors design is a full factorial model which includes the main within-subjects factor effects and all their interaction effects.
- If a custom hypothesis test is required (defined by the CONTRAST, LMATRIX, or KMATRIX subcommands), the default transformation matrix (**M** matrix) is taken to be the average transformation matrix, which can be displayed by using the keyword TEST(MMATRIX) on the PRINT subcommand. The default contrast result matrix (**K** matrix) is the zero matrix.
- If the contrast coefficient matrix (**L** matrix) is not specified, but a custom hypothesis test is required by the MMATRIX or the KMATRIX subcommand, the contrast coefficient matrix (**L** matrix) is taken to be the **L** matrix which corresponds to the estimable function for the intercept in the between-subjects model. This matrix can be displayed by using the keyword TEST(LMATRIX) on the PRINT subcommand.

Basic Specification

- The basic specification is a variable list followed by the WSFACTOR subcommand.
- Whenever WSFACTOR is specified, GLM performs special repeated measures processing. The multivariate and univariate tests are provided. In addition, for any within-subjects effect involving more than one transformed variable, the Mauchly test of sphericity is displayed to test the assumption that the covariance matrix of the transformed variables is constant on the diagonal and zero off the diagonal. The Greenhouse-Geisser epsilon and the Huynh-Feldt epsilon are also displayed for use in correcting the significance tests in the event that the assumption of sphericity is violated.

Subcommand Order

- The list of dependent variables, factors, and covariates must be first.

Syntax Rules

- The WSFACTOR (within-subjects factors), WSDESIGN (within-subjects design), and MEASURE subcommands are used only in repeated measures analysis.
- WSFACTOR is required for any repeated measures analysis.
- If WSDESIGN is not specified, a full factorial within-subjects design consisting of all main effects and all interactions among within-subjects factors is used by default.
- The MEASURE subcommand is used for doubly multivariate designs, in which the dependent variables represent repeated measurements of more than one variable.

Limitations

- Any number of factors can be specified, but if the number of between-subjects factors plus the number of split variables exceeds 18, the Descriptive Statistics table is not printed even when you request it.
- Maximum 18 within-subjects factors.
- Memory requirements depend primarily on the number of cells in the design. For the default full factorial model, this equals the product of the number of levels or categories in each factor.

Example

```
GLM Y1 TO Y4 BY GROUP
  /WSFACTOR=YEAR 4 POLYNOMIAL
  /WSDESIGN=YEAR
  /PRINT=PARAMETER
  /DESIGN=GROUP.
```

- WSFACTOR specifies a repeated measures analysis in which the four dependent variables represent a single variable measured at four levels of the within-subjects factor. The within-subjects factor is called *YEAR* for the duration of the GLM procedure.
- POLYNOMIAL requests polynomial contrasts for the levels of *YEAR*. Because the four variables, *Y1*, *Y2*, *Y3*, and *Y4*, in the working data file represent the four levels of *YEAR*, the effect is to perform an orthonormal polynomial transformation of these variables.
- PRINT requests that the parameter estimates be displayed.
- WSDESIGN specifies a within-subjects design that includes only the effect of the *YEAR* within-subjects factor. Because *YEAR* is the only within-subjects factor specified, this is the default design, and WSDESIGN could have been omitted.
- DESIGN specifies a between-subjects design that includes only the effect of the *GROUP* between-subjects factor. This subcommand could have been omitted.

GLM Variable List

The list of dependent variables, factors, and covariates must be specified first.

- WSFACTOR determines how the dependent variables on the GLM variable list will be interpreted.
- The number of dependent variables on the GLM variable list must be a multiple of the number of cells in the within-subjects design. If there are six cells in the within-subjects design, each group of six dependent variables represents a single within-subjects variable that has been measured in each of the six cells.
- Normally, the number of dependent variables should equal the number of cells in the within-subjects design multiplied by the number of variables named on the MEASURE subcommand (if one is used). If you have more groups of dependent variables than are accounted for by the MEASURE subcommand, GLM will choose variable names to label the output, which may be difficult to interpret.
- Covariates are specified after keyword WITH. You can specify constant covariates. Constant covariates represent variables whose values remain the same at each within-subjects level.

Example

```
GLM MATH1 TO MATH4 BY METHOD WITH SES
  /WSFACTOR=SEMESTER 4.
```

- The four dependent variables represent a score measured four times (corresponding to the four levels of *SEMESTER*).
- *SES* is a constant covariate. Its value does not change over the time covered by the four levels of *SEMESTER*.
- Default contrast (POLYNOMIAL) is used.

WSFACTOR Subcommand

WSFACTOR names the within-subjects factors, specifies the number of levels for each, and specifies the contrast for each.

- Presence of the WSFACTOR subcommand implies that the repeated measures model is being used.
- Mauchly's test of sphericity is automatically performed when WSFACTOR is specified.
- Names and number levels for the within-subjects factors are specified on the WSFACTOR subcommand. Factor names must not duplicate any of the dependent variables, factors, or covariates named on the GLM variable list. A type of contrast can also be specified for each within-subjects factor in order to perform comparisons among its levels. This contrast amounts to a transformation on the dependent variables.
- If there are more than one within-subjects factors, they must be named in the order corresponding to the order of the dependent variables on the GLM variable list. GLM varies the levels of the last-named within-subjects factor most rapidly when assigning dependent variables to within-subjects cells (see the example below).
- The number of cells in the within-subjects design is the product of the number of levels for all within-subjects factors.

- Levels of the factors must be represented in the data by the dependent variables named on the GLM variable list.
- The number of levels of each factor must be at least two. Enter an integer equal to or greater than 2 after each factor to indicate how many levels the factor has. Optionally, you can enclose the number of levels in parentheses.
- Enter only the *number of levels* for within-subjects factors, not a range of values.
- If more than one WSFACTOR subcommand is specified, only the last one is in effect.

Contrasts for WSFACTOR

The levels of a within-subjects factor are represented by different dependent variables. Therefore, contrasts between levels of such a factor compare these dependent variables. Specifying the type of contrast amounts to specifying a transformation to be performed on the dependent variables.

- In testing the within-subjects effects, an orthonormal transformation is automatically performed on the dependent variables in a repeated measures analysis.
- The contrast for each within-subjects factor is entered after the number of levels. If no contrast keyword is specified, POLYNOMIAL(1,2,3...) is the default. This contrast is used in comparing the levels of the within-subjects factors. Intrinsically orthogonal contrast types are recommended for within-subjects factors if you wish to examine each degree-of-freedom test, provided compound symmetry is assumed within each within-subjects factor. Other orthogonal contrast types are DIFFERENCE and HELMERT.
- If there are more than one within-subjects factors, the transformation matrix (**M** matrix) is computed as the Kronecker product of the matrices generated by the contrasts specified.
- The transformation matrix (**M** matrix) generated by the specified contrasts can be displayed by using the keyword TEST(MMATRIX) on the subcommand PRINT.
- The contrast types available for within-subjects factors are the same as those on the CONTRAST subcommand for between-subjects factors, described in "CONTRAST Subcommand" on p. 480 in GLM: Univariate.

The following contrast types are available:

DEVIATION *Deviations from the grand mean.* This is the default for between-subjects factors. Each level of the factor except one is compared to the grand mean. One category (by default the last) must be omitted so that the effects will be independent of one another. To omit a category other than the last, specify the number of the omitted category in parentheses after the keyword DEVIATION. For example,

```
GLM Y1 Y2 Y3 BY GROUP
 /WSFACTOR = Y 3 DEVIATION (1)
```

Deviation contrasts are not orthogonal.

POLYNOMIAL *Polynomial contrasts.* This is the default for within-subjects factors. The first degree of freedom contains the linear effect across the levels of the factor, the second contains the quadratic effect, and so on. In a balanced design, polynomial contrasts are orthogonal. By default, the levels are assumed to be equally spaced; you can specify unequal spacing by entering a metric consisting of one integer for each level of the factor in parentheses after the keyword POLYNOMIAL. (All metrics specified cannot be equal; thus (1, 1, ..., 1) is not valid.) For example,

```
/WSFACTOR=D 3 POLYNOMIAL(1,2,4).
```

Suppose that factor D has three levels. The specified contrast indicates that the three levels of D are actually in the proportion 1:2:4. The default metric is always (1,2,...,*k*), where *k* levels are involved. Only the relative differences between the terms of the metric matter (1,2,4) is the same metric as (2,3,5) or (20,30,50) because, in each instance, the difference between the second and third numbers is twice the difference between the first and second.

DIFFERENCE *Difference or reverse Helmert contrasts.* Each level of the factor except the first is compared to the mean of the previous levels. In a balanced design, difference contrasts are orthogonal.

HELMERT *Helmert contrasts.* Each level of the factor except the last is compared to the mean of subsequent levels. In a balanced design, Helmert contrasts are orthogonal.

SIMPLE *Each level of the factor except the last is compared to the last level.* To use a category other than the last as the omitted reference category, specify its number in parentheses following keyword SIMPLE. For example,

```
/WSFACTOR=B 3 SIMPLE (1).
```

Simple contrasts are not orthogonal.

REPEATED *Comparison of adjacent levels.* Each level of the factor except the first is compared to the previous level. Repeated contrasts are not orthogonal.

SPECIAL *A user-defined contrast.* Values specified after this keyword are stored in a matrix in column major order. For example, if factor A has three levels, then WSFACTOR(A)= SPECIAL(1 1 1 1 -1 0 0 1 -1) produces the following contrast matrix:

$$\begin{matrix} 1 & 1 & 0 \\ 1 & -1 & 1 \\ 1 & 0 & -1 \end{matrix}$$

Example

```
GLM X1Y1 X1Y2 X2Y1 X2Y2 X3Y1 X3Y2 BY TREATMNT GROUP
  /WSFACTOR=X 3 Y 2
  /DESIGN.
```

- The GLM variable list names six dependent variables and two between-subjects factors, *TREATMNT* and *GROUP*.

- WSFACTOR identifies two within-subjects factors whose levels distinguish the six dependent variables. *X* has three levels and *Y* has two. Thus, there are $3 \times 2 = 6$ cells in the within-subjects design, corresponding to the six dependent variables.
- Variable *X1Y1* corresponds to levels 1,1 of the two within-subjects factors; variable *X1Y2* corresponds to levels 1,2; *X2Y1* to levels 2,1; and so on up to *X3Y2*, which corresponds to levels 3,2. The first within-subjects factor named, *X*, varies most slowly, and the last within-subjects factor named, *Y*, varies most rapidly on the list of dependent variables.
- Because there is no WSDESIGN subcommand, the within-subjects design will include all main effects and interactions: *X*, *Y*, and *X* by *Y*.
- Likewise, the between-subjects design includes all main effects and interactions (*TREATMNT*, *GROUP*, and *TREATMNT* by *GROUP*) plus the intercept.
- In addition, a repeated measures analysis always includes interactions between the within-subjects factors and the between-subjects factors. There are three such interactions for each of the three within-subjects effects.

Example

```
GLM SCORE1 SCORE2 SCORE3 BY GROUP
  /WSFACTOR=ROUND 3 DIFFERENCE
  /CONTRAST(GROUP)=DEVIATION
  /PRINT=PARAMETER TEST(LMATRIX).
```

- This analysis has one between-subjects factor, *GROUP*, and one within-subjects factor, *ROUND*, with three levels that are represented by the three dependent variables.
- The WSFACTOR subcommand also specifies difference contrasts for *ROUND*, the within-subjects factor.
- There is no WSDESIGN subcommand, so a default full factorial within-subjects design is assumed. This could also have been specified as `WSDESIGN=ROUND`, or simply `WSDESIGN`.
- The CONTRAST subcommand specifies deviation contrasts for *GROUP*, the between-subjects factor. This subcommand could have been omitted because deviation contrasts are the default.
- PRINT requests the display of the parameter estimates for the model and the **L** matrix.
- There is no DESIGN subcommand, so a default full factorial between-subjects design is assumed. This could also have been specified as `DESIGN=GROUP`, or simply `DESIGN`.

WSDESIGN Subcommand

WSDESIGN specifies the design for within-subjects factors. Its specifications are like those of the DESIGN subcommand, but it uses the within-subjects factors rather than the between-subjects factors.

- The default WSDESIGN is a full factorial design, which includes all main effects and all interactions for within-subjects factors. The default is in effect whenever a design is processed without a preceding WSDESIGN or when the preceding WSDESIGN subcommand has no specifications.
- A WSDESIGN specification cannot include between-subjects factors or terms based on them, nor does it accept interval-level variables.
- The keyword INTERCEPT is not allowed on WSDESIGN.

- Nested effects are not allowed. Therefore, the symbols ( ) are not allowed here.
- If more than one WSDESIGN subcommand is specified, only the last one is in effect.

Example

```
GLM JANLO,JANHI,FEBLO,FEBHI,MARLO,MARHI BY SEX
  /WSFACTOR MONTH 3 STIMULUS 2
  /WSDESIGN MONTH, STIMULUS
  /DESIGN SEX.
```

- There are six dependent variables, corresponding to three months and two different levels of stimulus.
- The dependent variables are named on the GLM variable list in an order such that the level of stimulus varies more rapidly than the month. Thus, *STIMULUS* is named last on the WSFACTOR subcommand.
- The WSDESIGN subcommand specifies only the main effects for within-subjects factors. There is no *MONTH* by *STIMULUS* interaction term.

MEASURE Subcommand

In a doubly multivariate analysis, the dependent variables represent multiple variables measured under the different levels of the within-subjects factors. Use MEASURE to assign names to the variables that you have measured for the different levels of within-subjects factors.

- Specify a list of one or more variable names to be used in labeling the averaged results. If no within-subjects factor has more than two levels, MEASURE has no effect. You can use up to 255 characters for each name.
- The number of dependent variables in the dependent variables list should equal the product of the number of cells in the within-subjects design and the number of names on MEASURE.
- If you do not enter a MEASURE subcommand and there are more dependent variables than cells in the within-subjects design, GLM assigns names (normally *MEASURE_1*, *MEASURE_2*, etc.) to the different measures.
- All of the dependent variables corresponding to each measure should be listed together and ordered so that the within-subjects factor named last on the WSFACTORS subcommand varies most rapidly.

Example

```
GLM TEMP11 TEMP12 TEMP21 TEMP22 TEMP31 TEMP32,
  WEIGHT11 WEIGHT12 WEIGHT21 WEIGHT22 WEIGHT31 WEIGHT32 BY GROUP
  /WSFACTOR=DAY 3 AMPM 2
  /MEASURE=TEMP WEIGHT
  /WSDESIGN=DAY, AMPM, DAY BY AMPM
  /DESIGN.
```

- There are 12 dependent variables: 6 temperatures and 6 weights, corresponding to morning and afternoon measurements on three days.
- WSFACTOR identifies the two factors (*DAY* and *AMPM*) that distinguish the temperature and weight measurements for each subject. These factors define six within-subjects cells.
- MEASURE indicates that the first group of six dependent variables correspond to *TEMP* and the second group of six dependent variables correspond to *WEIGHT*.

- These labels, *TEMP* and *WEIGHT*, are used on the output as the measure labels.
- WSDESIGN requests a full factorial within-subjects model. Because this is the default, WSDESIGN could have been omitted.

EMMEANS Subcommand

EMMEANS displays estimated marginal means of the dependent variables in the cells, adjusted for the effects of covariates at their overall means, for the specified factors. Note that these are predicted, not observed, means. The standard errors are also displayed. For a detailed description of the EMMEANS subcommand, see "EMMEANS Subcommand" on p. 485 in GLM: Univariate.

- For the TABLES and COMPARE keywords, valid options include the within-subjects factors specified in the WSFACTOR subcommand, crossings among them, and crossings among factors specified in the factor list and factors specified on the WSFACTOR subcommand.
- All factors in a crossed-factors specification must be unique.
- If a between- or within-subjects factor, or a crossing of between- or within-subjects factors, is specified on the TABLES keyword, then GLM will collapse over any other between- or within-subjects factors before computing the estimated marginal means for the dependent variables.

GRAPH

This command is available only on systems with high-resolution graphics capabilities.

```
GRAPH

  [/TITLE='line 1'  ['line 2']]
  [/SUBTITLE='line 1']
  [/FOOTNOTE='line 1'  ['line 2']]

  {/BAR  [{(SIMPLE)        }]=function/variable specification†        }
         {(GROUPED)        }
         {(STACKED)        }
         {(RANGE)          }

  {/LINE  [{(SIMPLE)      }]=function/variable specification†          }
          {(MULTIPLE)     }
          {(DROP)         }
          {(AREA)         }
          {(DIFFERENCE)   }

  {/PIE                                                               }

  {/PARETO[{(CUM)   }] [{(SIMPLE)  }]=function/variable specification†}
          {(NOCUM)}     {(STACKED)}

  {/HILO[{(SIMPLE)  }]=function/variable specification††             }
        {(GROUPED)}

  {/HISTOGRAM  [(NORMAL)]=var                                         }

  {/SCATTERPLOT[{(BIVARIATE)}]=variable specification†††              }
               {(OVERLAY)  }
               {(MATRIX)   }
               {(XYZ)      }

  {/ERRORBAR[{(CI[{95}])       }]={var  [var var ...] [BY var]}       }
                  {n }             {var BY var BY var         }
             {(STERRIR[{12}]))}
                       {n }
             {(STDDEV[{2}])    }
                      {n}

  [/TEMPLATE=file]

  [/MISSING=[{LISTWISE**}] [{NOREPORT**}] [{EXCLUDE**}]]
            {VARIABLE  }]  {REPORT    }    {INCLUDE  }
```

** Default if the subcommand is omitted.

The following table shows all possible function/variable specifications for BAR, LINE, PIE, BLOCK, and PARETO subcommands. For special restrictions, see individual subcommands. In the table, valuef refers to the value function, countf refers to the count functions, and sumf refers to the summary functions.

	Simple Bar, Simple or Area Line, Pie, Simple High-Low, and Simple Pareto Charts	**Grouped or Stacked Bar, Multiple, Drop or Difference Line, and Stacked Pareto Charts**
Categorical Charts	[countf BY] var	[countf BY] var BY var
	sumf(var) BY var	sumf(var) BY var BY var
	sumf(varlist)	sumf(varlist) BY var
	sumf(var) sumf(var)...	sumf(var) sumf(var)... BY var
Noncategorical Charts	valuef(var) [BY var]	valuef(varlist) [BY var]

The following table shows all possible function/variable specifications for the HILO subcommand. Categorical variables for simple high-low-close charts must be dichotomous or trichotomous.

Simple Range Bar and Simple High-Low-Close Charts	**Clustered Range Bar and Clustered High-Low-Close Charts**
[countf BY] var	(sumf(var) sumf(var) [sumf(var)]) (...) ...BY var
sumf(var) sumf(var) sumf(var) BY var	sumf(var) sumf(var) [sumf(var)] BY var BY var
sumf(var) BY var BY var	
valuef(varlist) [BY var]	valuef(varlist) (...) ... [BY var]

Variable specification is required on all types of scatterplots. The following table shows all possible specifications:

BIVARIATE	var WITH var [BY var] [BY var ({NAME })] {IDENTIFY}
OVERLAY	varlist WITH varlist [(PAIR)] [BY var ({NAME })] {IDENTIFY}
MATRIX	varlist [BY var] [BY var ({NAME })] {IDENTIFY}
XYZ	var WITH var WITH var [BY var] [BY var ({NAME })] {IDENTIFY}

Value function:

The VALUE function yields the value of the specified variable for each case. It always produces one bar, point, or slice for each case. The VALUE(X) specification implies the value of *X* by *n*, where *n* is the number of each case. You can specify multiple variables, as in:

```
GRAPH /BAR = VALUE(SALARY BONUS BENEFIT).
```

This command draws a bar chart with the values of *SALARY*, *BONUS*, and *BENEFIT* for each employee (case). A BY variable can be used to supply case labels, but it does not affect the layout of the chart, even if values of the BY variable are the same for multiple cases.

Aggregation functions:

Two groups of aggregation functions are available: count functions and summary functions.

Count functions:

COUNT *Frequency of cases in each category.*

PCT *Frequency of cases in each category expressed as a percentage of the whole.*

CUPCT *Cumulative percentage sorted by category value.*

CUFREQ *Cumulative frequency sorted by category value.*

- Count functions yield the count or percentage of valid cases within categories determined by one or more BY variables, as in

```
GRAPH /BAR (SIMPLE) = PCT BY REGION.
```

- Count functions do not have any arguments.
- You can omit the keyword COUNT and subsequent keyword BY and specify just a variable, as in

```
GRAPH /BAR = DEPT.
```

This command is interpreted as

```
GRAPH /BAR = COUNT BY DEPT.
```

Summary functions:

MINIMUM *Minimum value of the variable.*

MAXIMUM *Maximum value of the variable.*

N *Number of cases for which the variable has a nonmissing value.*

SUM *Sum of the values of the variable.*

CUSUM *Sum of the summary variable accumulated across values of the category variable.*

MEAN *Mean.*

STDDEV *Standard deviation.*

VARIANCE *Variance.*

MEDIAN *Median.*

GMEDIAN *Group median.*

MODE *Mode.*

PTILE(x) X*th percentile value of the variable.* X must be greater than 0 and less than 100.

PLT(x) *Percentage of cases for which the value of the variable is less than* x.

PGT(x) *Percentage of cases for which the value of the variable is greater than* x.

NLT(x) *Number of cases for which the value of the variable is less than* x.

NGT(x) *Number of cases for which the value of the variable is greater than* x.

PIN(x1,x2) *Percentage of cases for which the value of the variable is greater than or equal to* x1 *and less than or equal to* x2. *x1* cannot exceed *x2*.

NIN(x1,x2) *Number of cases for which the value of the variable is greater than or equal to* x1 *and less than or equal to* x2. *x1* cannot exceed *x2*.

- Summary functions are usually used with summary variables (variables that record continuous values, like age or expenses). To use a summary function, specify the name of one or more variables in parentheses after the name of the function, as in

```
GRAPH /BAR = SUM(SALARY) BY DEPT.
```

- You can specify multiple summary functions for more chart types. For example, the same function can be applied to a list of variables, as in

```
GRAPH /BAR = SUM(SALARY BONUS BENEFIT) BY DEPT.
```

This syntax is equivalent to

```
GRAPH /BAR = SUM(SALARY) SUM(BONUS) SUM(BENEFIT) BY DEPT.
```

Different functions can be applied to the same variable, as in

```
GRAPH /BAR = MEAN(SALARY) MEDIAN(SALARY) BY DEPT.
```

Different functions and variables can be combined, as in

```
GRAPH /BAR = MIN(SALARY81) MAX(SALARY81)
                  MIN(SALARY82) MAX(SALARY82) BY JOBCAT.
```

The effect of multiple summary functions on the structure of the charts is illustrated under the discussion of specific chart types.

Overview

GRAPH generates a high-resolution chart by computing statistics from variables in the working data file and constructing the chart according to your specification. The chart can be a bar chart, pie chart, line chart, error bar chart, high-low-close histogram, scatterplot, or Pareto chart. The chart is displayed where high-resolution display is available and can be edited with a chart editor and saved as a chart file.

Options

Titles and Footnotes. You can specify a title, subtitle, and footnote for the chart using the TITLE, SUBTITLE, and FOOTNOTE subcommands.

Chart Type. You can request a specific type of chart using the BAR, LINE, PIE, ERRORBAR, HILO, HISTOGRAM, SCATTERPLOT, or PARETO subcommand.

Chart Content. You can specify an aggregated categorical chart using various aggregation functions or a nonaggregated categorical chart using the VALUE function (see pp. 504–506 for a list of available functions).

Templates. You can specify a template, using the TEMPLATE subcommand, to override the default chart attribute settings on your system.

Basic Specification

The basic specification is a chart type subcommand. By default, the generated chart will have no title, subtitle, or footnote.

Subcommand Order

Subcommands can be specified in any order.

Syntax Rules

- Only one chart type subcommand can be specified.
- The function/variable specification is required for all subtypes of bar, line, error bar, hilo, and Pareto charts; the variable specification is required for histograms and all subtypes of scatterplots.
- The function/variable or variable specifications should match the subtype keywords. If there is a discrepancy, GRAPH produces the default chart for the function/variable or variable specification regardless of the specified keyword.

Operations

- GRAPH computes aggregated functions to obtain the values needed for the requested chart and calculates an optimal scale for charting.
- The chart title, subtitle, and footnote are assigned as they are specified on TITLE, SUBTITLE, and FOOTNOTE subcommands. If you do not use these subcommands, the chart title, subtitle, and footnote are null. The split-file information is displayed as a subtitle if split-file is in effect.
- GRAPH creates labels that provide information on the source of the values being plotted. Labeling conventions vary for different subtypes. Where variable or value labels are defined in the working data file, GRAPH uses the labels; otherwise, variable names or values are used.

Limitations

Categorical charts cannot display fewer than 2 or more than 3000 categories.

Example

```
GRAPH /BAR=SUM (MURDER) BY CITY.
```

- This command generates a simple (default) bar chart showing the number of murders in each city.
- The category axis (x axis) labels are defined by the value labels (or values if no value labels exit) of the variable *CITY*.

- The default span (2) and sigma value (3) are used.
- Since no BY variable is specified, the *x* axis is labeled by sequence numbers.

TITLE, SUBTITLE, and FOOTNOTE Subcommands

TITLE, SUBTITLE, and FOOTNOTE specify lines of text placed at the top or bottom of the chart.

- One or two lines of text can be specified for TITLE or FOOTNOTE, and one line of text can be specified for SUBTITLE.
- Each line of text must be enclosed in apostrophes or quotation marks. The maximum length of any line is 72 characters.
- The default font sizes and types are used for the title, subtitle, and footnote.
- By default, the title, subtitle, and footnote are left-aligned with the *y* axis.
- If you do not specify TITLE, the default title, subtitle, and footnote are null, which leaves more space for the chart. If split-file processing is in effect, the split-file information is provided as a default subtitle.

Example

```
GRAPH TITLE = 'Murder in Major U.S. Cities'
 /SUBTITLE='per 100,000 people'
 /FOOTNOTE='The above data was reported on August 26, 1987'
 /BAR=SUM(MURDER) BY CITY.
```

BAR Subcommand

BAR creates one of five types of bar charts using keywords SIMPLE, COMPOSITIONAL, GROUPED, STACKED, or RANGE.

- Only one keyword can be specified, and it must be specified in the parentheses.
- When no keyword is specified, the default is either SIMPLE or GROUPED, depending on the type of function/variable specification.

SIMPLE *Simple bar chart.* This is the default if no keyword is specified on the BAR subcommand and the variables define a simple bar chart. A simple bar chart can be defined by a single summary or count function and a single BY variable, or by multiple summary functions and no BY variable (see Figure 1 to Figure 4).

GROUPED *Clustered bar chart.* A clustered bar chart is defined by a single function and two BY variables, or by multiple functions and a single BY variable. This is the default if no keyword is specified on the BAR subcommand and the variables define a clustered bar chart (see Figure 5 to Figure 8).

STACKED *Stacked bar chart.* A stacked bar chart displays a series of bars, each divided into segments stacked one on top of the other. The height of each segment represents the value of the category. Like a clustered bar chart, it is defined by a single function and two BY variables or by multiple functions and a single BY variable (see Figure 9 to Figure 11).

RANGE

Range bar chart. A range bar chart displays a series of floating bars. The height of each bar represents the range of the category and its position in the chart indicates the minimum and maximum values. A range bar chart can be defined by a single function and two BY variables or by multiple functions and a single BY variable. If a variable list is used as the argument for a function, the list must be of an even number. If a second BY variable is used to define the range, the variable must be dichotomous (see Figure 12 to Figure 14).

Figure 1 /BAR=COUNT BY JOBCAT

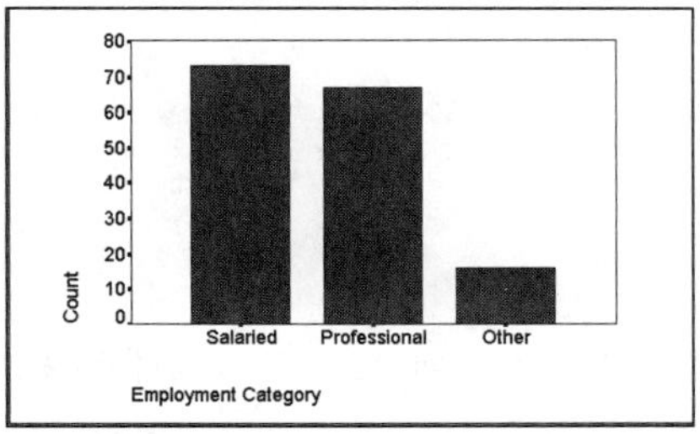

Specification: count_function BY var
or: sum_function(var) BY var

y-axis title:	fn name [+fn var label]
y-axis labels:	fn value scale
x-axis title:	BY var label
x-axis labels:	BY var value labels

Each bar shows the number of cases in the indicated job categories.

Figure 2 /BAR=MEAN(SALBEG, SALNOW)

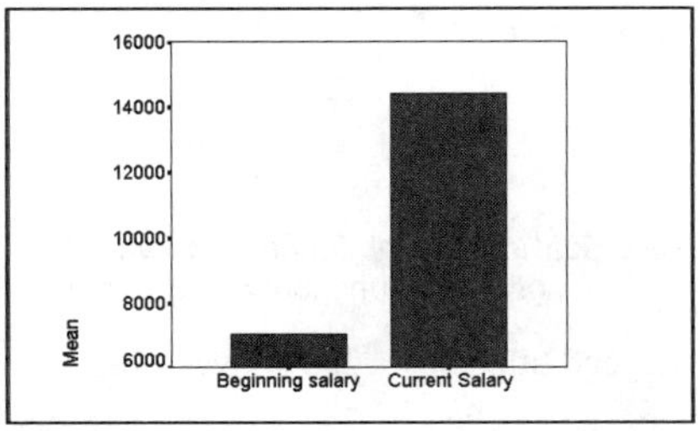

Specification: sum_function (varlist)

y-axis title:	fn name
y-axis labels:	fn value scale
x-axis title:	none
x-axis labels:	fn var labels

One bar is produced for each variable, representing the summary function of that variable across all cases.

Figure 3 /BAR=MEAN(SALBEG) MEDIAN(SALBEG) MEAN(SALNOW) MEDIAN(SALNOW)

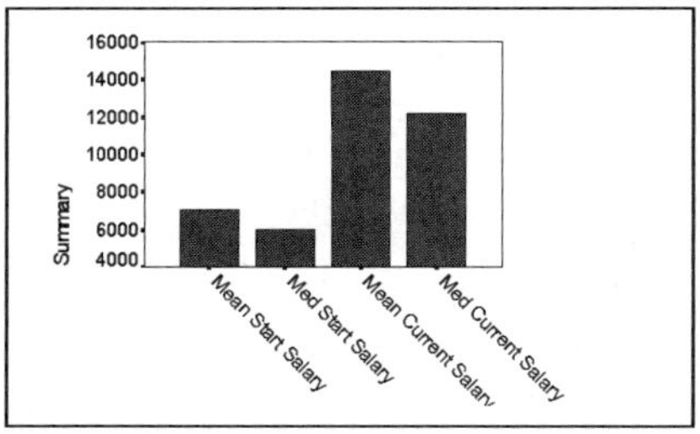

Specification: sum_function list

y-axis title:	Summary
y-axis labels:	fn value scale
x-axis title:	none
x-axis labels:	fn names +var names

One bar is produced for each summary function. The arguments can be the same or different.

Figure 4 /BAR=VALUE(SALNOW) BY ID

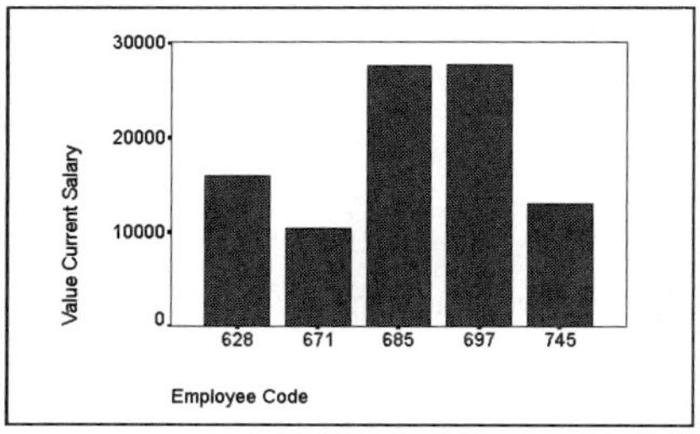

Specification: value_function(var) [BY var]

y-axis title:	value + var label
y-axis labels:	fn value scale
x-axis title:	BY var value labels
x-axis labels:	BY var label

Each bar shows the value of a single case. If no BY variable is specified, the *x*-axis title will be Case Number and the *x*-axis labels will be case numbers.

Figure 5 /BAR=COUNT BY JOBCAT BY SEX

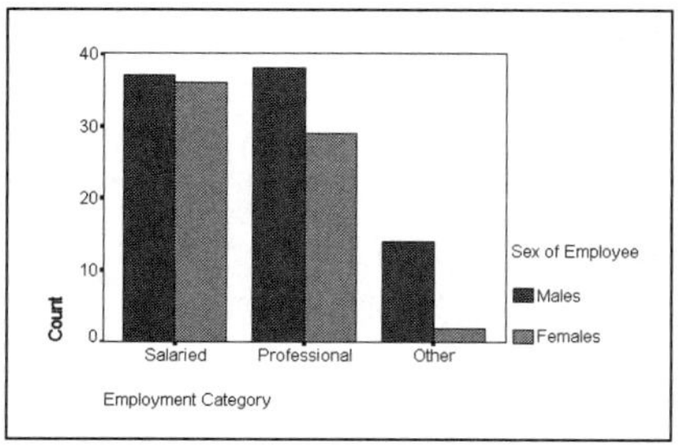

Specification: count_function BY var1 BY var2
or: sum_function(var) BY var1 BY var2

Legend title:	2nd BY var label
Legend labels:	2nd BY var value labels
y-axis title:	fn name [+var label]
y-axis labels:	fn value scale
x-axis title:	1st BY var label
x-axis labels:	1st BY value labels

Cases are broken down into categories by *VAR1* and then by *VAR2*. Each bar shows the valid number of cases or the summary function value within each subcategory.

Figure 6 /BAR=MEAN(SALBEG SALNOW) BY JOBCAT

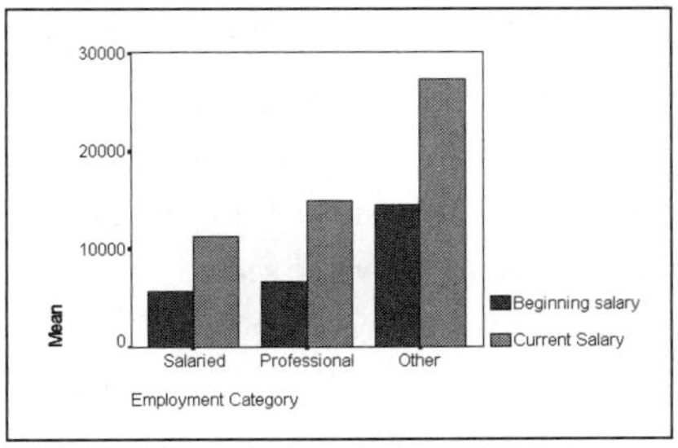

Specification: sum_function (varlist) BY var

Legend title: none
Legend labels: fn var labels
y-axis title: fn name
y-axis labels: fn value scale
x-axis title: var label
x-axis labels: BY value labels

The variables are broken down into categories. Within a category, each bar shows the value of the function for each variable.

Figure 7 /BAR=MEDIAN(SALNOW) MEAN(SALNOW) BY SEX

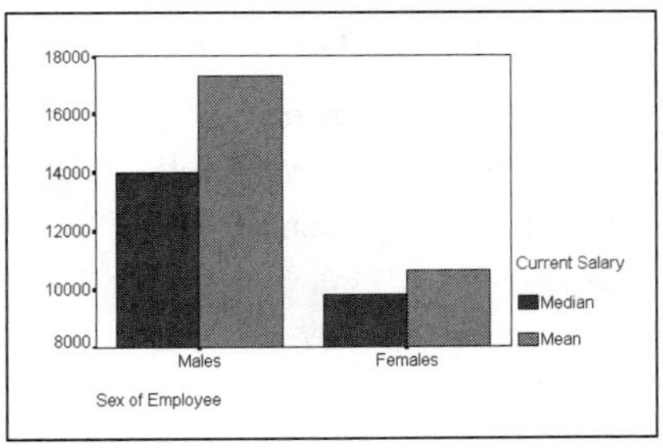

Specification: sum_function list BY var

Legend title: fn var label (if only one fn var)
Legend labels: fn name
y-axis title: none
y-axis labels: fn value scale
x-axis title: BY var label
x-axis labels: BY var value label

The variable is broken down into categories. Within a category, each bar shows a different function of the same variable.

Figure 8 /BAR=VALUE(SALBEG SALNOW) BY ID

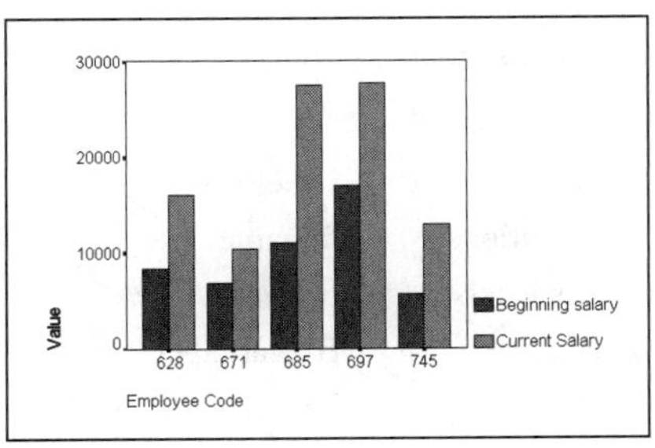

Specification: value_function(varlist) [BY var]

Legend title: none
Legend labels: fn var name
y-axis title: value
y-axis labels: values
x-axis title: BY var label
x-axis labels: BY var value label

Each group shows one case identified by the category variable following BY. Each bar within the case shows the value of one variable for that case.

Figure 9 /BAR(STACKED)=COUNT BY JOBCAT BY SEX

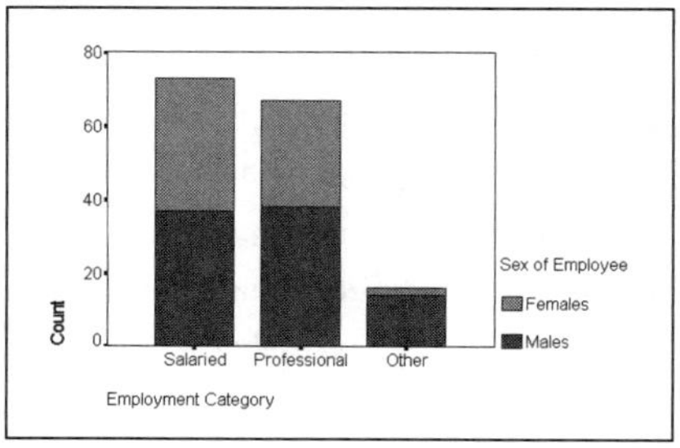

Specification: count_function BY var1 BY var2
or: sum_function(var) BY var1 BY var2

Legend title:	2nd BY var label
Legend labels:	2nd BY var value labels
y-axis title:	fn name [+fn var label]
y-axis labels:	fn value scale
x-axis title:	1st BY var label
x-axis labels:	1st BY var value labels

Each bar represents one subcategory defined by the two category variables. The bars are stacked within each category defined by the first category variable.

Figure 10 /BAR(STACKED)=SUM(THEFT AUTO BURGLARY) BY YEAR

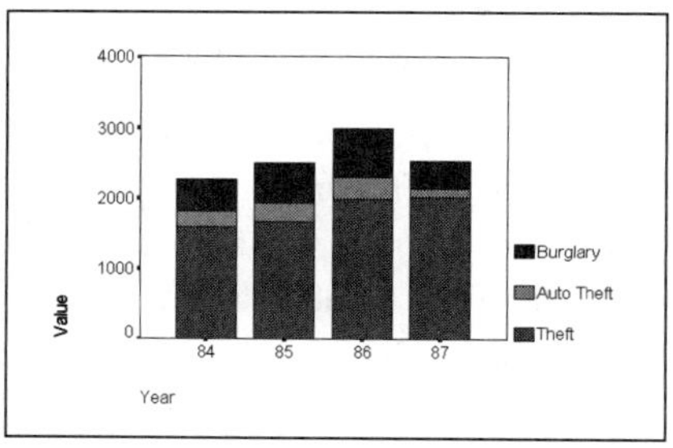

Specification: sum_function (varlist) BY var

Legend title:	none
Legend labels:	fn var labels
y-axis title:	fn name
y-axis labels:	fn value scale
x-axis title:	BY var label
x-axis labels:	BY var value labels

Each bar represents the function value of one variable broken down into categories. Bars within each category are stacked.

Figure 11 /BAR(STACKED)=VALUE(SALNOW FRINGE) BY ID

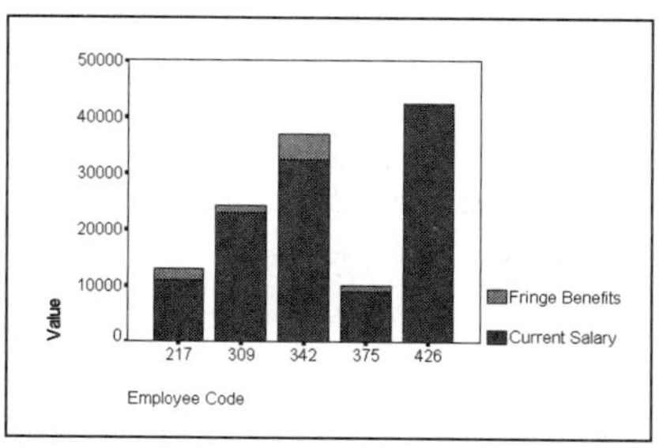

Specification: value_function(varlist)[BY var]

Legend title:	none
Legend labels:	var labels
y-axis title:	fn name
y-axis labels:	fn value scale
x-axis title:	BY var label
x-axis labels:	BY var value labels

Each bar shows the value of each variable for the indicated case. If no BY variable is specified, the *x* axis is labeled by case numbers and its title is Case Number.

Figure 12 /BAR(RANGE)=COUNT BY JOBCAT BY RACE

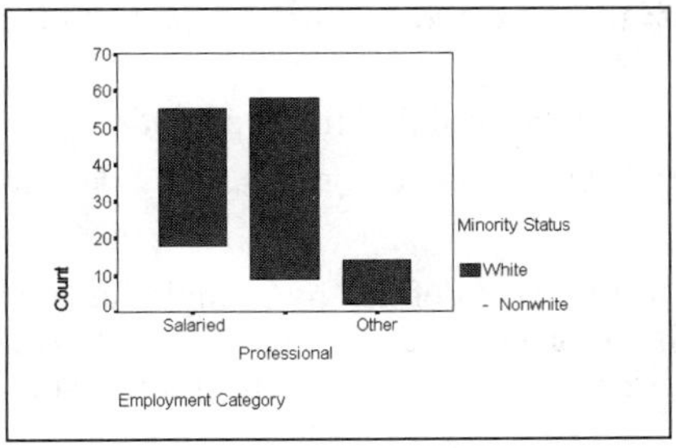

Specification: count_function BY var1 BY var2

Legend title:	var2 label
Legend labels:	var2 value labels
y-axis title:	fn name
y-axis labels:	fn value scale
x-axis title:	var1 label
x-axis labels:	var1 value labels

The height of each bar represents the difference between the two categories defined by *var2*, which must be dichotomous. The direction of difference, that is, whether nonwhite employees in each category defined by *var1* are more or less, is not shown.

Figure 13 /BAR(RANGE)=VALUE(SWI_HI SWI_LO) BY DAY

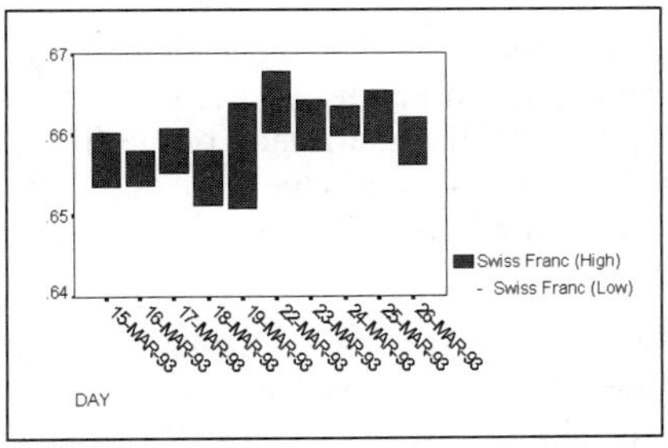

Specification: value_function(var1 var2)[BY var]

Legend title:	none
Legend labels:	var1 label–var2 label
y-axis title:	none
y-axis labels:	fn value scale
x-axis title:	BY var label
x-axis labels:	BY var value labels

The height of each bar represents the difference between the high and the low values of the day. The position of each bar shows the fluctuation over the two-week period.

Figure 14 /BAR(RANGE)=MEAN(SWI_HI SWI_LO GER_HI GER_LO CAN_HI CAN_LO) BY WEEK

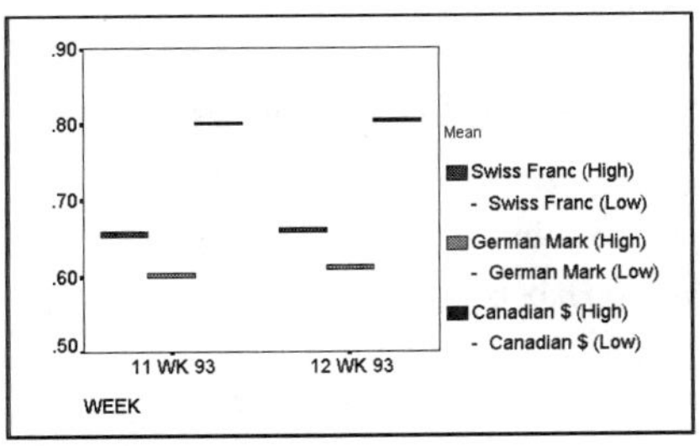

Specification: sum_function (varlist) BY var

Legend title:	fn name
Legend labels:	pairs of var labels
y-axis title:	none
y-axis labels:	fn value scale
x-axis title:	BY var label
x-axis labels:	BY var value labels

The variable list must contain an even number of variables. Each pair of variables is plotted as a separate series.

LINE Subcommand

LINE creates one of five types of line charts using keywords SIMPLE, MULTIPLE, DROP, AREA, or DIFFERENCE.

- Only one keyword can be specified, and it must be specified in the parentheses.
- When no keyword is specified, the default is either SIMPLE or MULTIPLE, depending on the type of function/variable specification.

SIMPLE *Simple line chart.* A simple line chart is defined by a single function and a single BY variable or by multiple functions and no BY keyword. This is the default if no keyword is specified on LINE and the data define a simple line (see Figure 15 to Figure 17).

MULTIPLE *Multiple line chart.* A multiple line chart is defined by a single function and two BY variables or by multiple functions and a single BY variable. This is the default if no keyword is specified on LINE and the data define a multiple line (see Figure 18 to Figure 20).

DROP *Drop-line chart.* A drop-line chart shows the difference between two or more fluctuating variables. It is defined by a single function and two BY variables or by multiple functions and a single BY variable (see Figure 21 to Figure 24).

AREA *Area line chart.* An area line chart fills the area beneath each line with a color or pattern. When multiple lines are specified, the second line is the sum of the first and second variables, the third line is the sum of the first, second, and third variables, and so on. The specification is the same as that for a simple or multiple line chart. Figure 25 to Figure 27 show area line charts with multiple lines.

DIFFERENCE *Difference line chart.* A difference line chart fills the area between a pair of lines. It highlights the difference between two variables or two groups. A difference line chart is defined by a single function and two BY variables or by two summary functions and a single BY variable. If a second BY variable is used to define the two groups, the variable must be dichotomous (see Figure 28 to Figure 31).

Figure 15 /LINE=COUNT BY TIME

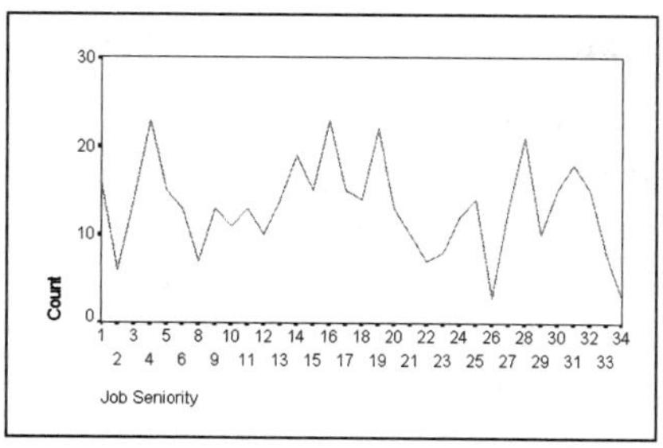

Specification: count_function BY var
or: sum_function(var) BY var

y-axis title:	fn name [+fn var label]
y-axis labels:	fn value scale
x-axis title:	BY var label
x-axis labels:	BY var value labels

Each point on the line represents the number of valid cases for one category.

Figure 16 /LINE=MEAN(SPRING SUMMER FALL WINTER)

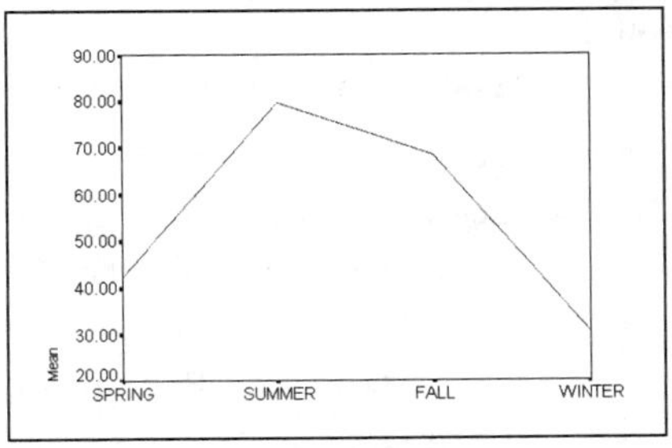

Specification: sum_function (varlist)

y-axis title:	fn name
y-axis labels:	fn value scale
x-axis title:	none
x-axis labels:	fn var labels

Each point on the line shows the function value for one variable across all valid cases.

Figure 17 /LINE=VALUE(POUND) BY DAY

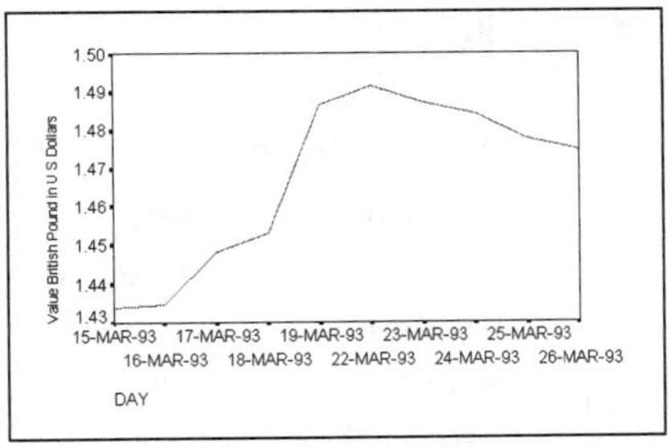

Specification: value_function (var) [BY var]

y-axis title:	value + var name
y-axis labels:	value labels
x-axis title:	BY var label
x-axis label:	BY var value labels

Each point on the line shows the value of a single case. If a BY variable is not specified, the *x*-axis title will be Case Number and the *x*-axis labels will be the number of each case.

Figure 18 /LINE=COUNT BY TIME BY SEX

Specification: count_function BY var1 BY var2
or: sum_function(var) BY var1 BY var2

Legend title:	2nd BY var label
Legend labels:	2nd BY var value labels
y-axis title:	fn name [+fn var label]
y-axis labels:	fn value scale
x-axis title:	1st BY var label
x-axis labels:	1st BY var value labels

Each line represents one category defined by the second BY variable. Each point on the line shows the number of valid cases for one category defined by the first BY variable. Missing values are indicated by unconnected lines.

Figure 19 /LINE=MEAN(THEFT AUTO BURGLARY) BY YEAR

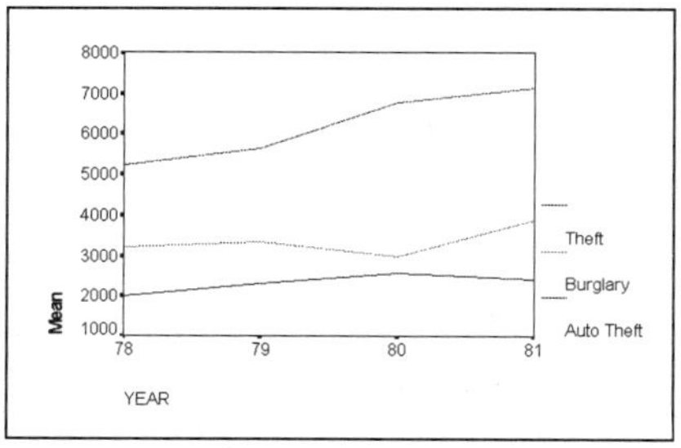

Specification: sum_function (varlist) BY var

Legend title:	none
Legend labels:	fn var labels
y-axis title:	fn name
y-axis labels:	fn value scale
x-axis title:	BY var label
x-axis labels:	BY var value labels

Each line represents one variable. Each point on the line shows the value for one category.

Figure 20 /LINE=VALUE(SALBEG SALNOW) BY ID

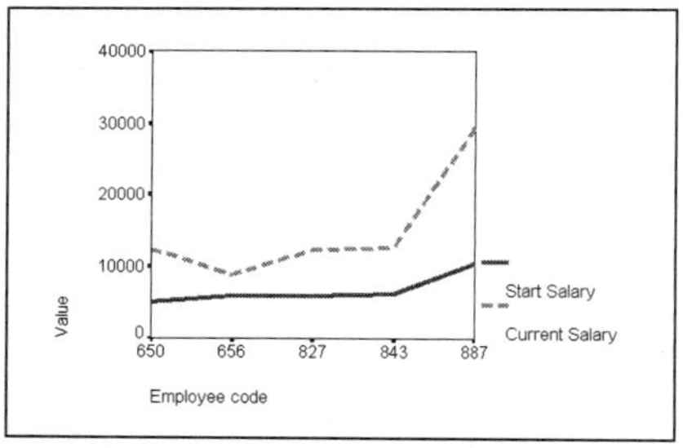

Specification: value_function (varlist) [BY var]

Legend title:	none
Legend labels:	var labels
y-axis title:	value
y-axis labels:	values
x-axis title:	BY var label
x-axis labels:	BY var value labels

Each line represents one variable. Each point shows the value of each case for the variable. If no BY variable is specified, the *x*-axis title will be Case Number and the *x*-axis labels will be the number of each individual case.

Figure 21 LINE(DROP)=NEAN (SALBEG SALNOW) BY SEXRACE

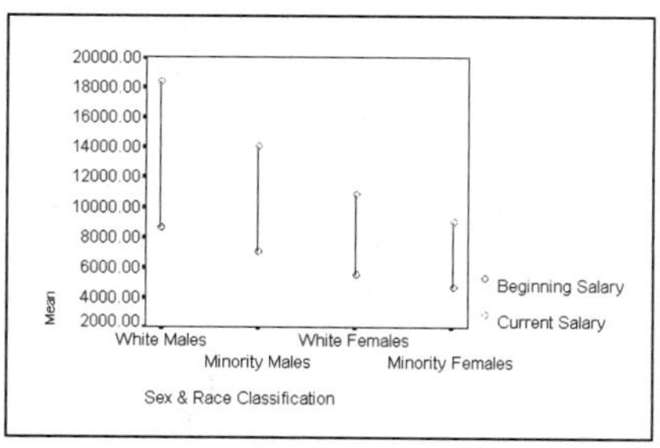

Specification: sum_function (varlist) BY var

Legend title:	none
Legend labels:	var labels
y-axis title:	fn name
y-axis labels:	fn value scale
x-axis title:	BY var label
x-axis labels:	BY var value labels

Each line represents the difference in each sex and race category between summary function values computed from the two variables. If more variables are specified, each will be represented by a symbol on the lines.

Figure 22 LINE(DROP)=MEAN(SALNOW) BY SEXRACE BY JOBCAT

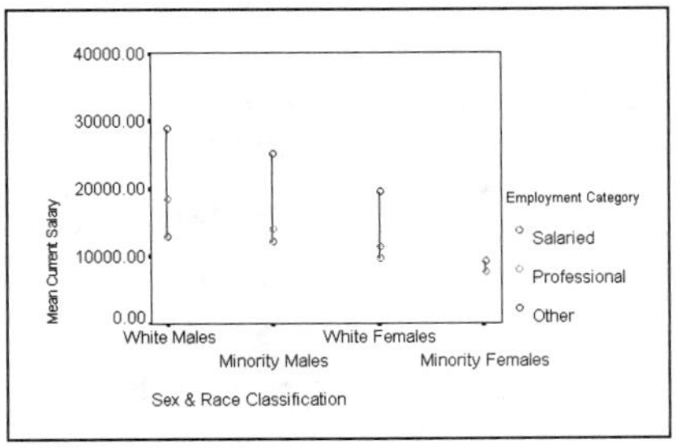

Specification: sum_function BY var BY var

Legend title: 2nd BY var label
Legend labels: 2nd BY var value labels
y-axis title: fn name[+var label]
y-axis labels: fn value scale
x-axis title: 1st BY var label
x-axis labels: 1st BY var value labels

Each line represents the difference in each sex and race category between job categories.

Figure 23 LINE(DROP)=COUNT BY JOBCAT BY SEX

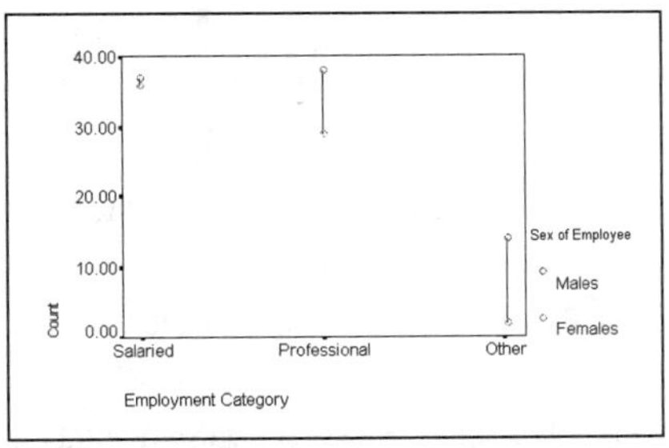

Specification: count_function BY var1 BY var2

Legend title: 2nd BY var label
Legend labels: 2nd BY var value labels
y-axis title: fn name
y-axis labels: fn value scale
x-axis title: 1st BY var label
x-axis labels: 1st BY var value labels

Each line represents the difference in number of valid cases in each job category between male and female.

Figure 24 LINE(DROP)=VALUE(SALBEG SALNOW) BY ID

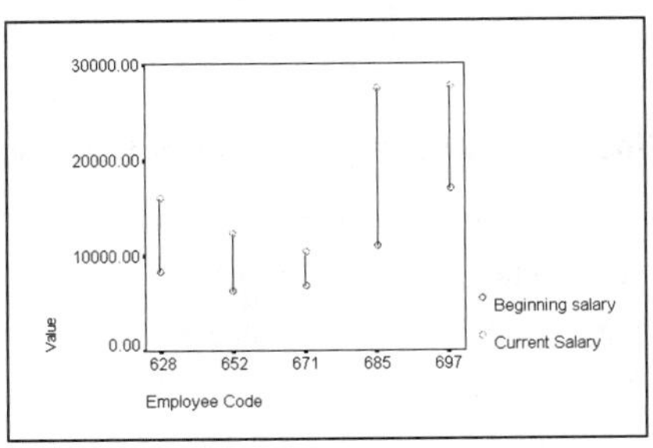

Specification: value_function (varlist) [BY var]

Legend title: none
Legend labels: var labels
y-axis title: fn name
y-axis labels: value scale
x-axis title: BY var label
x-axis labels: BY var value labels

If no BY variable is specified, the *x*-axis title is Case Number and the *x*-axis labels are the numbers of cases.

Figure 25 /LINE(AREA)=COUNT BY TIME

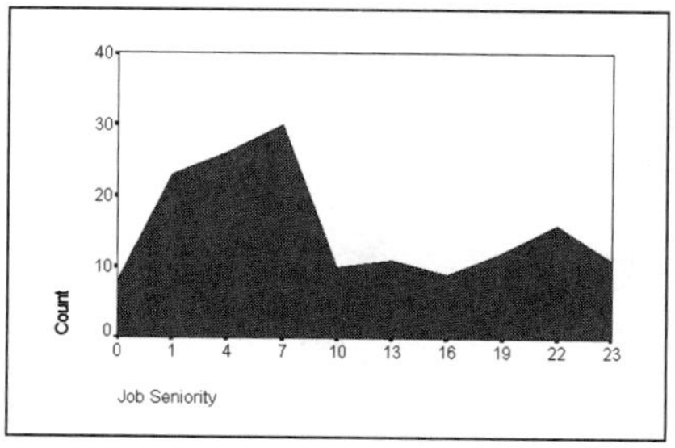

Specification: count_function BY var
or: sum_function(var) BY var

y-axis title:	fn name [+fn var label]
y-axis labels:	fn value scale
x-axis title:	BY var label
x-axis labels:	BY var value labels

The area shows the number of valid cases for categories defined by the BY variable.

Figure 26 /LINE(AREA)=COUNT BY TIME BY SEX

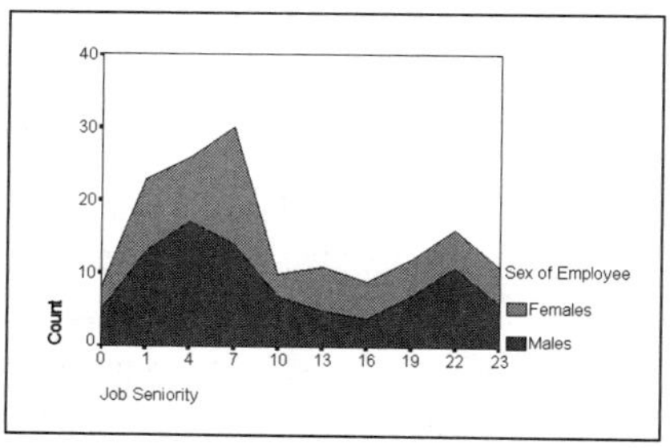

Specification: count_function BY var1 BY var2
or: sum_function(var) BY var1 BY var2

Legend title:	2nd BY var label
Legend labels:	2nd BY var value labels
y-axis title:	fn name [+fn var label]
y-axis labels:	fn value scale
x-axis title:	1st BY var label
x-axis labels:	1st BY var value labels

The two areas respectively represent the categories defined by the second BY variable.

Figure 27 /LINE(AREA)=SUM(VIOLENT PROPERTY) BY YEAR

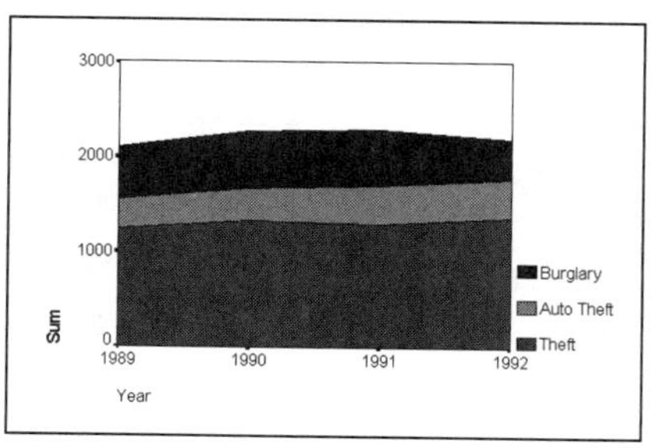

Specification: sum_function (varlist) BY var

Legend title:	none
Legend labels:	fn var labels
y-axis title:	fn name
y-axis labels:	fn value scale
x-axis title:	BY var label
x-axis labels:	BY var value labels

Each area represents one function variable.

Figure 28 LINE(DIFFERENCE)=MEAN(SALBEG SALNOW) BY TIME

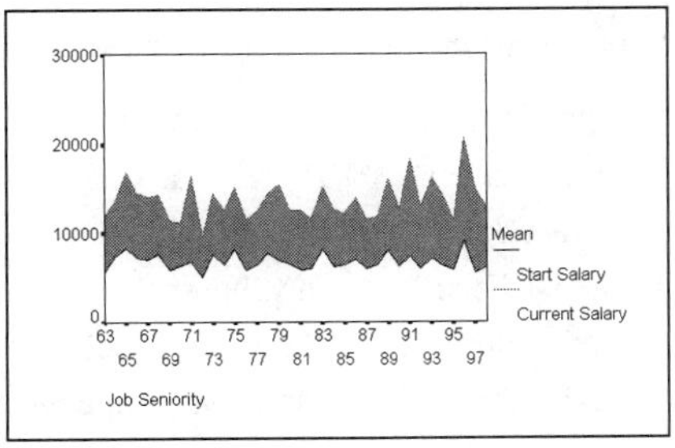

Specification: sum_function (varlist) BY var

Legend title: fn name
Legend labels: fn var labels
y-axis title: none
y-axis labels: fn value scale
x-axis title: BY var label
x-axis labels: BY var value labels

Figure 29 LINE(DIFFERENCE)=MEAN(SALNOW) BY TIME BY SEX

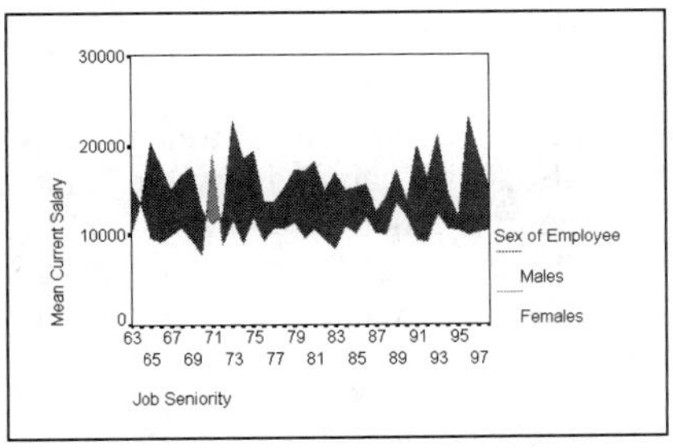

Specification: sum_function(var) BY var BY var

Legend title: 2nd BY var label
Legend labels: 2nd BY var value labels
y-axis title: fn name [+var label]
y-axis labels: fn value scale
x-axis title: 1st BY var label
x-axis labels: 1st BY var value labels

The second BY variable must be dichotomous.

Figure 30 LINE(DIFFERENCE)=COUNT BY TIME BY SEX

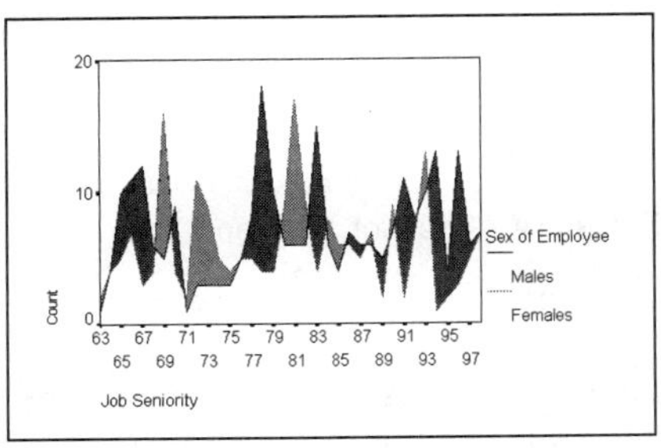

Specification: count_function BY var BY var

Legend title: 2nd BY var label
Legend labels: 2nd BY var value labels
y-axis title: fn name
y-axis labels: fn value scale
x-axis title: 1st BY var label
x-axis labels: 1st BY var value labels

The second BY variable must be dichotomous.

Figure 31 LINE(DIFFERENCE)=VALUE(SALBEG SALNOW) BY TIME

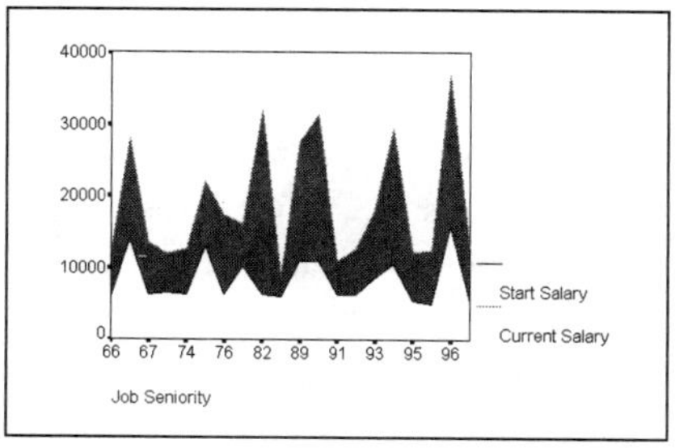

Specification: value_function(var1 var2 [BY var]

Legend title:	2nd BY var label
Legend labels:	2nd BY var value labels
y-axis title:	fn name
y-axis labels:	fn value scale
x-axis title:	1st BY var label
x-axis labels:	1st BY var value labels

If no BY variable is specified, the *x*-axis title is Case Number and *x*-axis labels are the case numbers.

PIE Subcommand

PIE creates pie charts. A pie chart can be defined by a single function and a single BY variable or by multiple summary functions and no BY variable. A pie chart divides a circle into slices. The size of each slice indicates the value of the category relative to the whole (see Figure 32 to Figure 34). Cumulative functions (CUPCT, CUFREQ, and CUSUM) are inappropriate for pie charts but are not prohibited. When specified, all cases except those in the last category are counted more than once in the resulting pie.

Figure 32 /PIE=COUNT BY JOBCAT

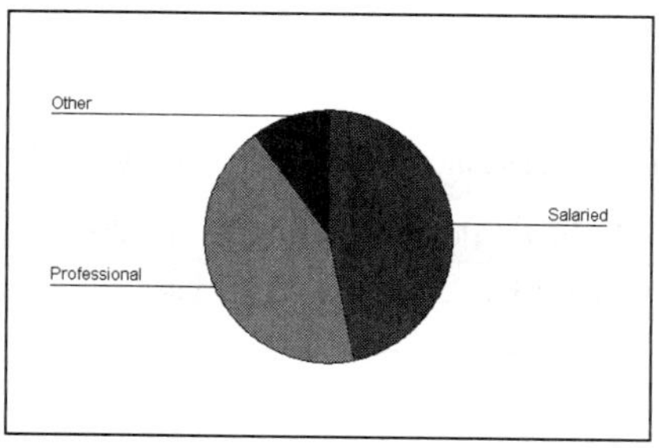

Specification: count_function BY var

Labels:	BY var value labels

Each pie slice shows proportionally the number of cases in each category defined by the BY variable.

Figure 33 /PIE=SUM(THEFT AUTO BURGLARY)

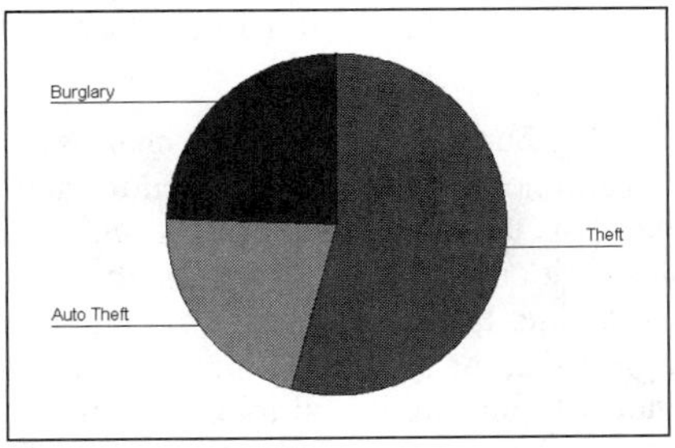

Specification: summary_function(varlist)

Labels: fn var labels

Each pie slice proportionally shows the function value for one variable.

Figure 34 /PIE=VALUE(SALNOW) BY ID

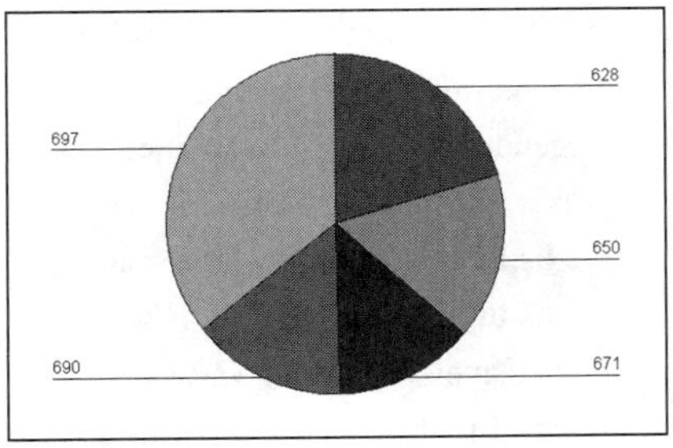

Specification: value_function (var) [BY var]

Labels: BY variable value labels

Each pie slice shows the value of one case. If no BY variable is specified, the number of each case is used as the label.

HILO Subcommand

HILO creates one of two types of high-low-close charts using keywords SIMPLE or GROUPED. High-low-close charts show the range and the closing (or average) value of a series.

- Only one keyword can be specified.
- When a keyword is specified, it must be specified in the parentheses.
- When no keyword is specified, the default is either SIMPLE or GROUPED, depending on the type of function/variable specification.

SIMPLE *Simple high-low-close chart.* A simple high-low-close chart can be defined by a single summary or count function and two BY variables, by three summary functions and one BY variable, or by three values with one or no BY variable. When a second BY variable is used to define a high-low-close chart, the variable must be dichotomous or trichotomous. If dichotomous, the first value defines low and the second value defines high; if trichotomous, the first value defines high, the second defines low and the third defines close (see Figure 35 to Figure 37).

GROUPED *Grouped high-low-close chart.* A grouped high-low-close chart is defined by a single function and two BY variables or by multiple functions and a single BY variable. When a variable list is used for a single function, the list must contain two or three variables. If it contains two variables, the first defines the high value, and the second defines the low value. If it contains three variables, the first defines the high value, the second defines the low value, and the third defines the close value. Likewise, if multiple functions are specified, they must be either in groups of two or in groups of three. The first function defines the high value, the second defines the low value, and the third, if specified, defines the close value (see Figure 38 and Figure 39).

Figure 35 HILO=MEAN(HIGH LOW CLOSE) BY DATE

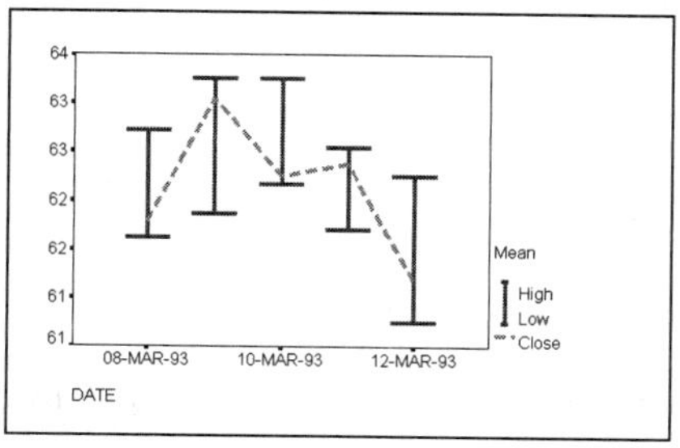

Specification: sum_function(varlist) BY var

Legend title:	fn name
Legend labels:	fn var labels
y-axis title:	none
y-axis labels:	fn value scale
x-axis title:	BY var label
x-axis labels:	BY var value labels

You can specify three variables with one summary function or three summary functions each with one variable. The line represents the close or average series defined by the function. If you specify only two, they are used as high and low values.

Figure 36 HILO=MEAN(VALUE) BY DATE BY HILO

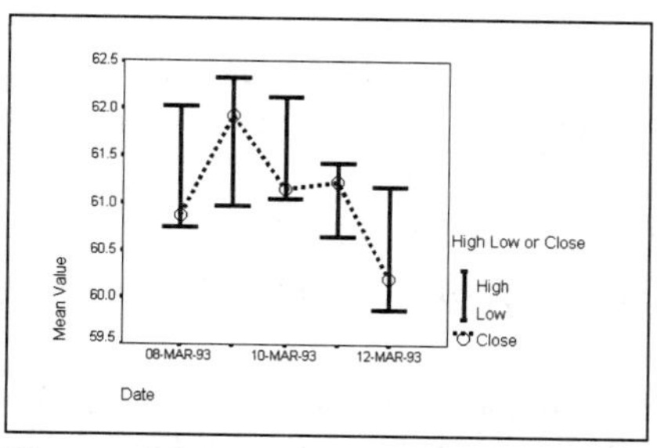

Specification: sum_function(var) BY var BY var

Legend title:	2nd BY var label
Legend labels:	2nd BY var value labels
y-axis title:	fn name+fn var label
y-axis labels:	fn value scale
x-axis title:	1st BY var label
x-axis labels:	1st BY var value labels

The second BY variable must be dichotomous or trichotomous. If dichotomous, the first value defines the high and the second value defines the low value. If trichotomous, the first value defines the high value, the second value defines the low, and the last value defines the close.

Figure 37 HILO=VALUE(HIGH LOW CLOSE) BY TIME

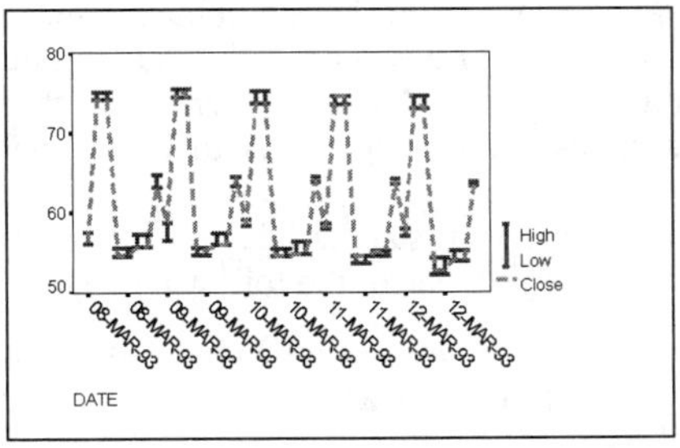

Specification: value_function(varlist) BY var

Legend title:	none
Legend labels:	var labels
y-axis title:	none
y-axis labels:	value scale
x-axis title:	BY var label
x-axis labels:	BY var value labels

The first variable represents the high value, the second, the low value, and the third, the close value.

Figure 38 HILO=MEAN(HIGH) MEAN(LOW) MEAN(CLOSE) BY DATE BY COMPANY

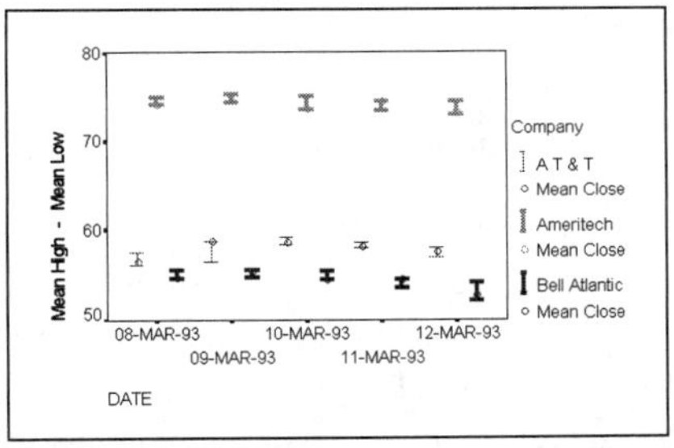

Specification: sum_function list BY var BY var

Legend title:	2nd BY var label
Legend labels:	2nd BY var value labels 3rd fn name + var label
y-axis title:	1st 2 fn names+var labels
y-axis labels:	fn value scale
x-axis title:	1st BY var label
x-axis labels:	1st BY var value labels

The function-variable specification automatically produces a clustered high-low-close chart. The function list must consist of two or three functions. If two functions are specified, they represent the high and the low; if three functions are specified, they represent the high, the low, and the close.

Figure 39 HILO=VALUE(RH RL RA) VALUE(FH HL HA) VALUE(GH GL HA) BY WEEK

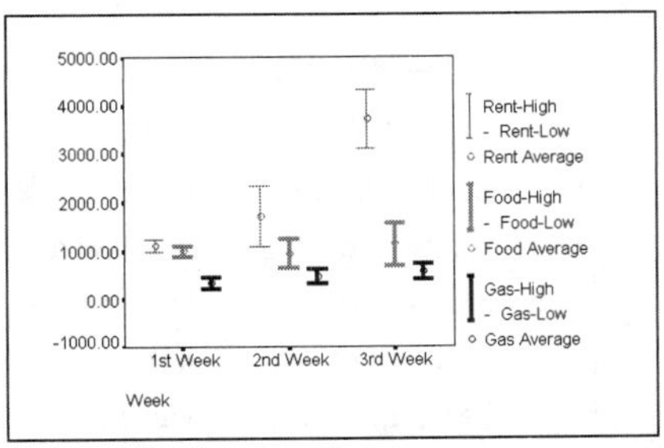

Specification: value_function list BY var

Legend title:	none
Legend labels:	var labels
y-axis title:	none
y-axis labels:	value scale
x-axis title:	BY var label
x-axis labels:	BY var value labels

Each function must have two or three variables to represent high and low values or high, low, and close values. If no BY variable is specified, case numbers are used as *x*-axis labels.

ERRORBAR Subcommand

ERRORBAR creates either a simple or a clustered error bar chart, depending on the variable specification on the subcommand. A simple error bar chart is defined by one numeric variable with or without a BY variable or a variable list. A clustered error bar chart is defined by one numeric variable with two BY variables or a variable list with a BY variable (see Figure 40 to Figure 43).

Error bar charts can display confidence intervals, standard deviations, or standard errors of the mean. To specify the statistics to be displayed, one of the following keywords is required:

CI value *Display confidence intervals for mean.* You can specify a confidence level between 50 and 99.9. The default is 95.

STERROR *n* *Display standard errors of mean.* You can specify any positive number for *n*. The default is 2.

STDDEV *n* *Display standard deviations.* You can specify any positive number for *n*. The default is 2.

Figure 40 ERRORBAR=SALNOW BY SEXRACE

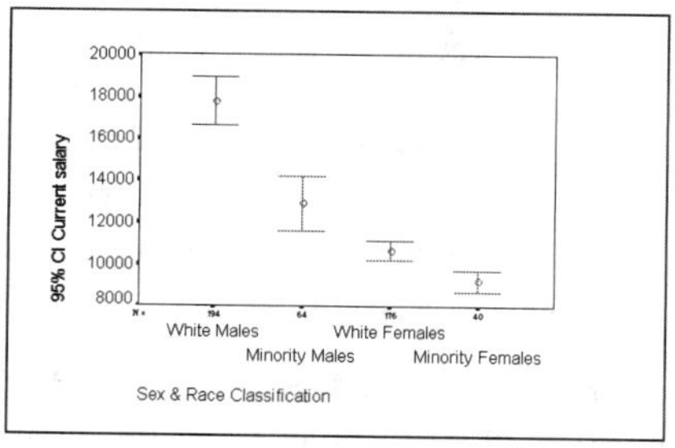

Specification: var by var

Legend title:	none
Legend labels:	none
y-axis title:	display + var label
y-axis labels:	value scale
x-axis title:	BY var label
x-axis labels:	BY var value labels

CI(95) is the default. Error bars can also display standard errors of the mean or standard deviations if you specify the appropriate keyword in the parentheses.

Figure 41 ERRORBAR=FRINGE SALBEG SALNOW

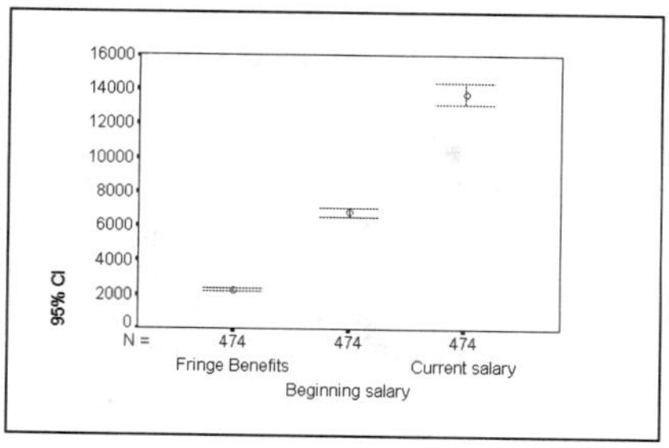

Specification: varlist

Legend title:	none
Legend labels:	none
y-axis title:	displayed statistics
y-axis labels:	value scale
x-axis title:	none
x-axis labels:	var labels

CI(95) is the default. Error bars can also display standard errors of the mean or standard deviations if you specify the appropriate keyword in the parentheses. Numbers of valid cases for each variable are displayed.

Figure 42 ERRORBAR=SALNOW BY JOBCAT BY SEXRACE

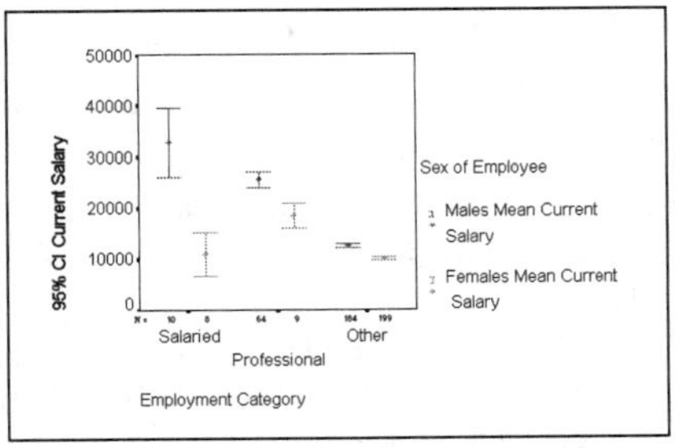

Specification: var1 BY var2 BY var3

Legend title:	var3 label
Legend labels:	var3 value labels+Mean +var1 label
y-axis title:	display+var1 label
y-axis labels:	value scale
x-axis title:	var2 label
x-axis labels:	var2 value labels

Figure 43 ERRORBAR=FRINGE SALBEG SALNOW BY SEX

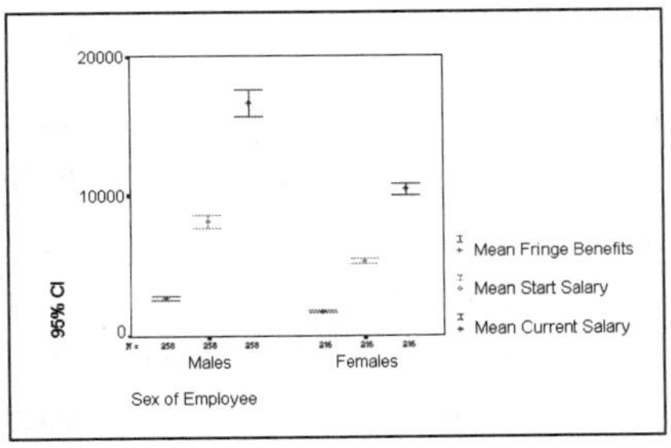

Specification: varlist BY var

Legend title:	none
Legend labels:	Mean+var labels
y-axis title:	displayed statistics
y-axis labels:	values
x-axis title:	BY var label
x-axis labels:	BY var value labels

SCATTERPLOT Subcommand

SCATTERPLOT produces two- or three-dimensional scatterplots. Multiple two-dimensional plots can be plotted within the same frame or as a scatterplot matrix. Only variables can be specified; aggregated functions cannot be plotted. When SCATTERPLOT is specified without keywords, the default is BIVARIATE.

BIVARIATE *One two-dimensional scatterplot.* A basic scatterplot is defined by two variables separated by the keyword WITH (see Figure 44 to Figure 46). This is the default when SCATTERPLOT is specified without keywords.

OVERLAY *Multiple plots drawn within the same frame.* Specify a variable list on both sides of WITH. By default, one scatterplot is drawn for each combination of variables on the left of WITH with variables on the right (see Figure 47). You can specify PAIR in parentheses to indicate that the first variable on the left is paired with the first variable on the right, the second variable on the left with the second variable on the right, and so on. All plots are drawn within the same frame and are differentiated by color or pattern. The axes are scaled to accommodate the minimum and maximum values across all variables.

MATRIX *Scatterplot matrix.* Specify at least two variables. One scatterplot is drawn for each combination of the specified variables above the diagonal and a second below the diagonal in a square matrix (see Figure 48).

XYZ *One three-dimensional plot.* Specify three variables, each separated from the next with the keyword WITH (see Figure 49).

- If you specify a control variable using BY, GRAPH produces a control scatterplot where values of the BY variable are indicated by different colors or patterns. A control variable cannot be specified for overlay plots.
- You can display the value label of an identification variable at the plotting position for each case by adding BY *var* (NAME) or BY *var* (IDENTIFY) to the end of any valid scatterplot specification. When the chart is created, NAME turns the labels on while IDENTIFY turns the labels off. You can use the Point Selection tool to turn individual labels off or on in the scatterplot. Figure 46 shows a simple scatterplot with labels turned on.

Figure 44 /SCATTERPLOT=PROFITS WITH COMPS

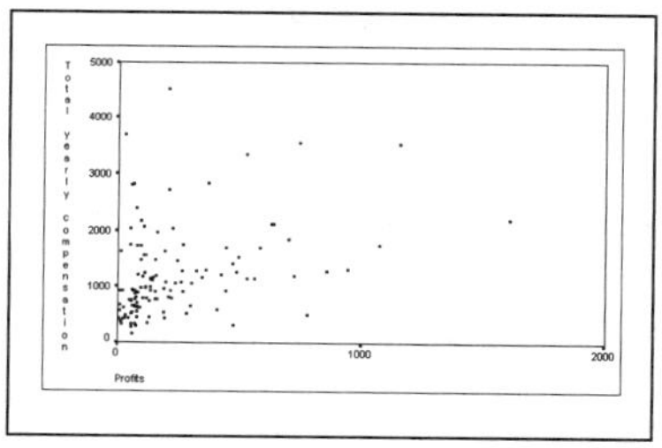

Specification: var1 WITH var2 [BY var] [BY var (NAME)]

y-axis title:	var2 var label
y-axis labels:	scaled values
x-axis title:	var1 var label
x-axis labels:	scaled values

Figure 45 /SCATTERPLOT=SALBEG WITH SALNOW BY SEX

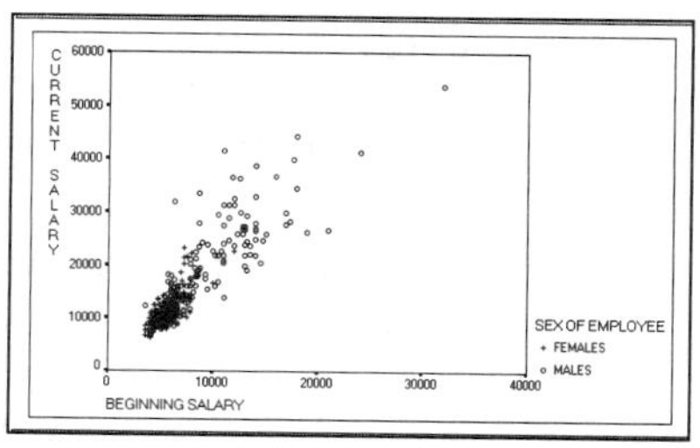

Specification: var1 WITH var2 BY var3*

Legend title	marker var (var3) label
Legend labels:	marker var value [label]
y-axis title:	var2 var label
y-axis labels:	scaled values
x-axis title:	var1 var label
x-axis labels:	scaled values

* *VAR3* is a marker variable. For specification of a label variable, see Figure 46.

Figure 46 /SCATTERPLOT=JOBCAT WITH SALNOW BY ID (NAME)

Specification: var1 WITH var2 BY var3(NAME)*

Point labels:	Label var (*VAR3)* value labels
y-axis title:	var2 var label
y-axis labels:	scaled values
x-axis title:	var1 var label
x-axis labels:	scaled values

*When keyword NAME is specified, *VAR3* serves as a label variable. For the specification of a marker variable, see Figure 45. You can specify both a marker variable and a label variable for a simple scatterplot.

Figure 47 /SCATTERPLOT(OVERLAY)=VERBAL MATH WITH AARATIO)

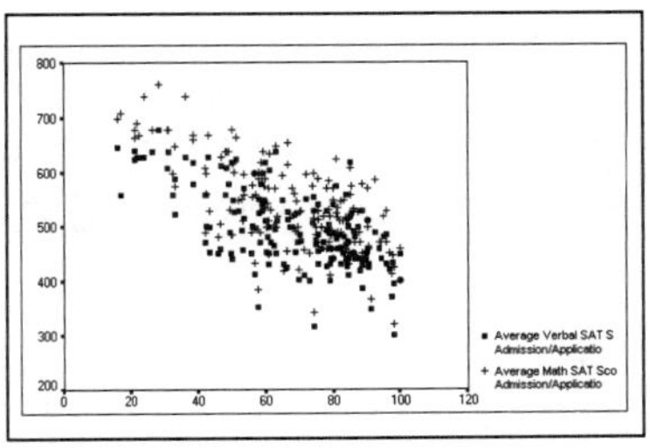

Specification: varlist WITH varlist [BY var(NAME)]*

Legend title:	none
Legend labels:	pairs of var names
y-axis title:	none
y-axis labels:	scaled values**
x-axis title:	none
x-axis labels:	scaled values**

*You can specify only a label variable after BY for an overlay scatterplot. The keyword NAME is required if a BY variable is specified.
**Values are scaled to accommodate the maximum and minimum values of each pair.

Figure 48 /SCATTERPLOT(MATRIX)=SCORE COST SFRATIO

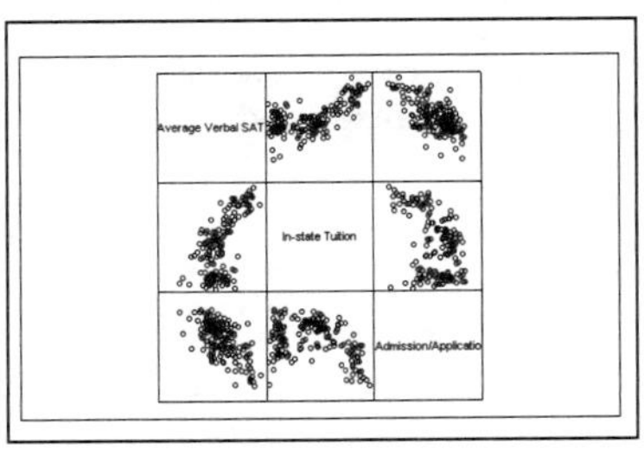

Specification: varlist [BY var] [BY var(NAME)]*

Legend title:	marker var name
Legend labels:	marker var value labels
Point labels:	label value labels
Diagonal titles:	var labels

*Matrix scatterplots can have both marker variable and label variable specifications.

Figure 49 /SCATTERPLOT(XYZ)=JOBCAT WITH SALARY WITH EDLEVEL BY SEX BY ID (NAME)

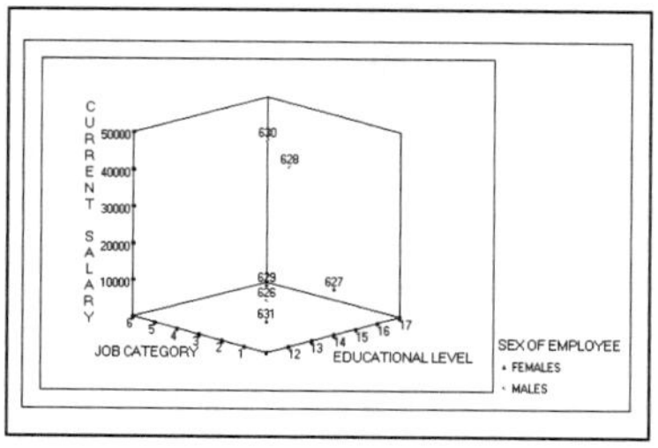

Specification:
xvar WITH yvar WITH zvar [BY var] [BY var(NAME)]

Legend title:	1st BY var label
Legend labels:	1st BY var value labels
Point labels:	2nd BY var value labels
x-axis title:	xvar label
y-axis title:	yvar label
z-axis title:	zvar label

*3-D scatterplots allow both marker variable and label variable specifications.

HISTOGRAM Subcommand

HISTOGRAM creates a histogram (see Figure 50 and Figure 51).

- Only one variable can be specified on this subcommand.
- GRAPH divides the values of the variable into several evenly spaced intervals and produces a bar chart showing the number of times the values for the variable fall within each interval.
- You can request a normal distribution line by specifying the keyword NORMAL in parentheses (see Figure 51).

Figure 50 /HISTOGRAM=RATIO

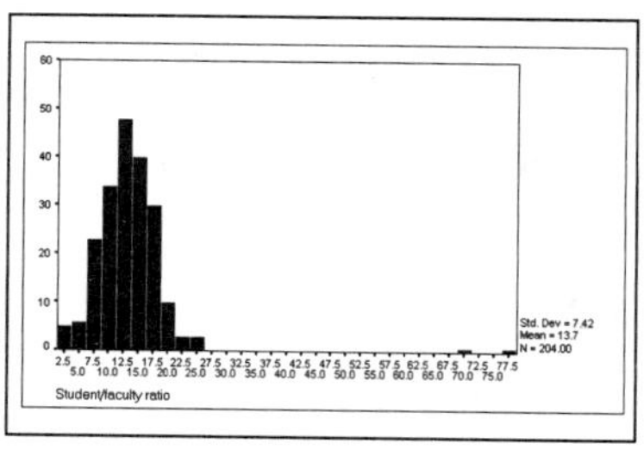

Specification: var

y-axis title:	none
y-axis label:	number of valid cases
x-axis title:	var label
x-axis label:	scaled values

The standard deviation, mean, and number of valid cases are displayed.

Figure 51 /HISTOGRAM(NORMAL)=VERBAL

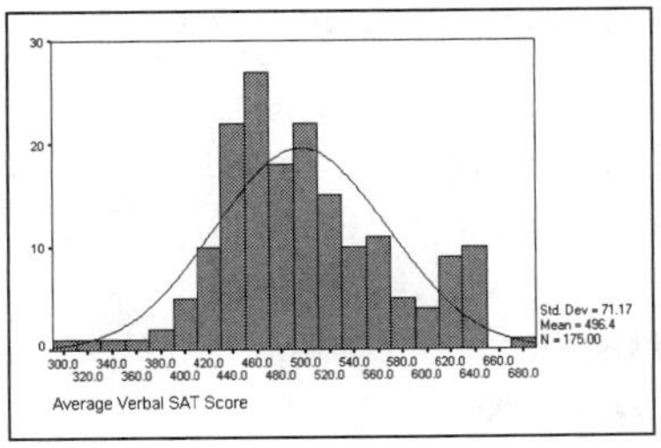

Specification: var

y-axis title:	none
y-axis labels:	number of valid cases
x-axis title:	var label
x-axis labels:	scaled values

The normal distribution line as well as the standard deviation, mean, and number of valid cases are displayed.

PARETO Subcommand

PARETO creates one of two types of Pareto charts. A Pareto chart is used in quality control to identify the few problems that create the majority of nonconformities. Only SUM, VALUE, and COUNT can be used with the PARETO subcommand.

Before plotting, PARETO sorts the plotted values in descending order by category. The right axis is always labeled by the cumulative percentage from 0 to 100. By default, a cumulative line is displayed. You can eliminate the cumulative line or explicitly request it by specifying one of the following keywords:

CUM *Display the cumulative line.* This is the default.

NOCUM *Do not display the cumulative line.*

You can request a simple or a stacked Pareto chart by specifying one of the following keywords and define it with appropriate function/variable specifications:

SIMPLE *Simple Pareto chart.* Each bar represents one type of nonconformity. A simple Pareto chart can be defined by a single variable, a single VALUE function, a single SUM function with a BY variable, or a SUM function with a variable list as an argument with no BY variable (see Figure 52 and Figure 53).

STACKED *Stacked Pareto chart.* Each bar represents one or more types of nonconformity within the category. A stacked Pareto chart can be defined by a single SUM function with two BY variables, a single variable with a BY variable, a VALUE function with a variable list as an argument, or a SUM function with a variable list as an argument and a BY variable (see Figure 54 and Figure 55).

Figure 52 PARETO(CUM SIMPLE)=SUM(DEF1 TO DEF7)

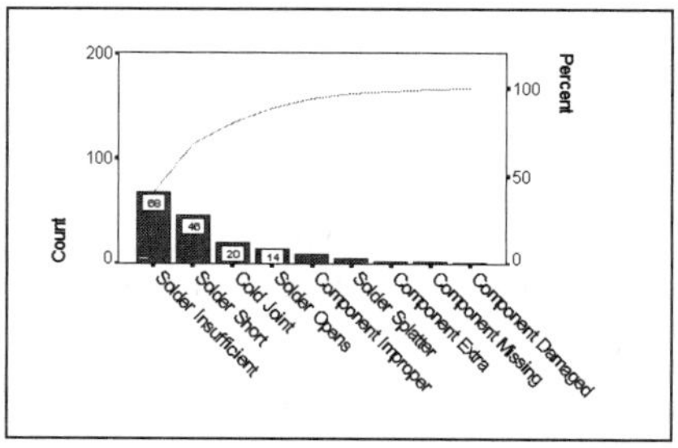

Specification: sum_fun (varlist)

Right axis title:	Percent
Right axis labels:	Cumulative percentage
y-axis title:	Count
y-axis labels:	defect count
x-axis title:	none
x-axis labels:	var labels

The data are sorted in descending order. The cumulative line is displayed. The first two defects account for over 75% of the returned products.

Figure 53 PARETO(CUM SIMPLE)=SUM(DEFECTS) BY SHIFT

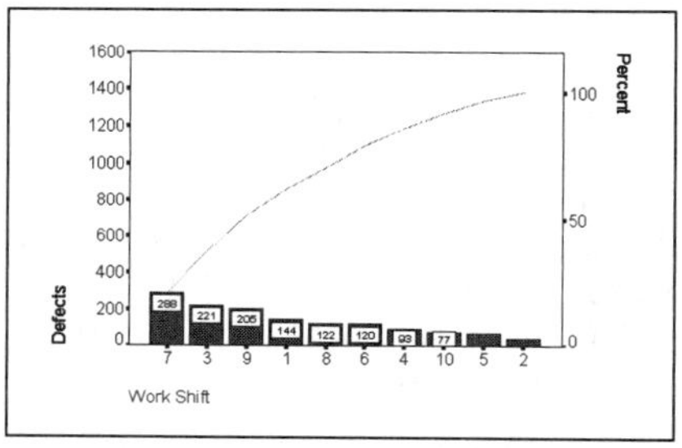

Specification: sum_fun (var) BY var

Right axis title:	Percent
Right axis labels:	Cumulative percentage
y-axis title:	fn var label
y-axis labels:	defect count
x-axis title:	BY var label
x-axis labels:	var labels

The data are sorted in descending order. The cumulative line is displayed. The work shifts 7, 3, and 9 account for 60% of the defective products.

Figure 54 PARETO(CUM STACKED)=SUM(DEF1 TO DEF5) BY SHIFT

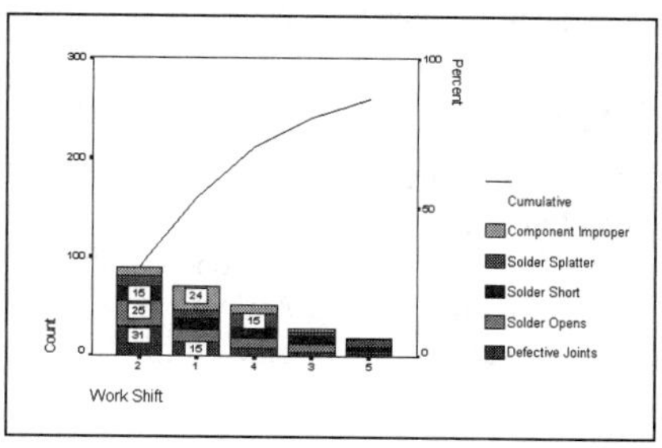

Specification: sum_fn(varlist) BY var

Legend title:	none
Legend labels:	fn variable labels
y-axis title:	Count
y-axis labels:	defect count
x-axis title:	BY var label
x-axis labels:	BY var value labels

The Pareto chart shows the work shifts that are responsible for most of the defects. It also shows the type of defects each work shift produces.

Figure 55 PARETO(CUM STACKED)=SUM(DEFECTS) BY SHIFT BY TYPE

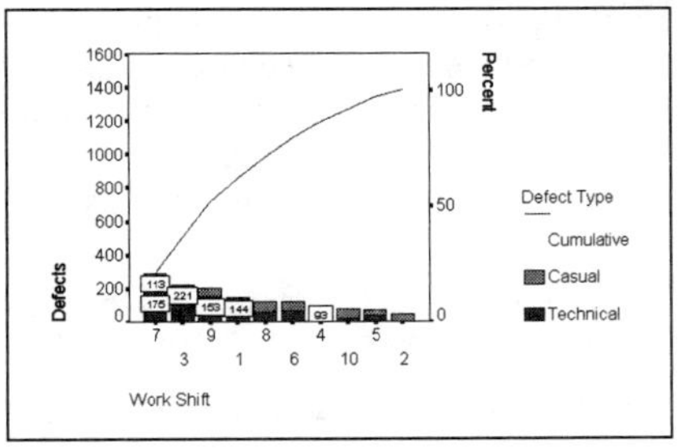

Specification: sum_fn(var1) BY var2 BY var3

Legend title:	var3 label
Legend labels:	var3 value labels
y-axis title:	var1 label
y-axis labels:	defect count
x-axis title:	var2 label
x-axis labels:	var2 value labels

The stacks are defined by the second BY variable (*TYPE*); the categories are defined by the first BY variable (*SHIFT*).

TEMPLATE Subcommand

TEMPLATE uses an existing chart as a template and applies it to the chart requested by the current GRAPH command.

- The specification on TEMPLATE is a chart file saved during a previous session.
- The general rule of application is that the template overrides the default setting, but the specifications on the current GRAPH command override the template. Nonapplicable elements and attributes are ignored.
- Three types of elements and attributes can be applied from a chart template: those dependent on data, those dependent on the chart type, and those dependent on neither.

Elements and Attributes Independent of Chart Types or Data

Elements and attributes common to all chart types are always applied unless overridden by the specifications on the current GRAPH command.

- The title, subtitle, and footnote, including text, color, font type and size, and line alignment are always applied. To give your chart a new title, subtitle, or footnote, specify the text on the TITLE, SUBTITLE, or FOOTNOTE subcommand. You cannot change other attributes.
- The outer frame of the chart, including line style, color, and fill pattern, is always applied. The inner frame is applied except for those charts that do not have an inner frame. The template overrides the system default.
- Label formats are applied wherever applicable. The template overrides the system default. Label text, however, is not applied. GRAPH automatically provides axis labels according to the function/variable specification.
- Legends and the legend title attributes, including color, font type and size, and alignment, are applied provided the current chart requires legends. The legend title text, however, is not applied. GRAPH provides the legend title according to the function/variable specification.

Elements and Attributes Dependent on Chart Type

Elements and attributes dependent on the chart type are those that exist only in a specific chart type. They include bars (in bar charts), lines and areas (in line charts), markers (in scatterplots), boxes (in boxplots), and pie sectors (in pie charts). These elements and their attributes are usually applied only when the template chart and the requested chart are of the same type. Some elements or their attributes may override the default settings across chart type.

- Color and pattern are always applied except for pie charts. The template overrides the system default.
- Scale axis lines are applied across chart types. Scale axis range is never applied.
- Interval axis lines are applied from interval axis to interval axis. Interval axis bins are never applied.
- If the template is a 3-D bar chart and you request a chart with one category axis, attributes of the first axis are applied from the template. If you request a 3-D bar chart and the template is not a 3-D chart, no category axis attributes are applied.

Elements and Attributes Dependent on Data

Data-dependent elements and attributes are applied only when the template and the requested chart are of the same type and the template has at least as many series assigned to the same types of chart elements as the requested chart.

- Category attributes and elements, including fill, border, color, pattern, line style, weight of pie sectors, pie sector explosion, reference lines, projection lines, and annotations, are applied only when category values in the requested chart match those in the template.
- The attributes of data-related elements with on/off states are always applied. For example, the line style, weight, and color of a quadratic fit in a simple bivariate scatterplot are applied if the requested chart is also a simple bivariate scatterplot. The specification on the GRAPH command, for example, HISTOGRAM(NORMAL), overrides the applied on/off status; in this case, a normal curve is displayed regardless of whether the template displays a normal curve.
- In bar, line, and area charts, the assignment of series to bars, lines, and areas is not applied.
- Case weighting status for histograms and scatterplots is not applied. You must turn weighting on or off before specifying the GRAPH command.

MISSING Subcommand

MISSING controls the treatment of missing values in the chart drawn by GRAPH.

- The default is LISTWISE.
- The MISSING subcommand has no effect on variables used with the VALUE function to create nonaggregated charts. User-missing and system-missing values create empty cells.
- LISTWISE and VARIABLE are alternatives and apply to variables used in summary functions for a chart or to variables being plotted in a scatterplot.

- REPORT and NOREPORT are alternatives and apply only to category variables. They control whether categories and series with missing values are created. NOREPORT is the default.
- INCLUDE and EXCLUDE are alternatives and apply to both summary and category variables. EXCLUDE is the default.
- When a case has a missing value for the name variable but contains valid values for the dependent variable in a scatterplot, the case is always included. User-missing values are displayed as point labels; system-missing values are not displayed.
- For an aggregated categorical chart, if every aggregated series is empty in a category, the empty category is excluded.
- A nonaggregated categorical chart created with the VALUE function can contain completely empty categories. There are always as many categories as rows of data. However, at least one nonempty cell must be present; otherwise the chart is not created.

LISTWISE *Listwise deletion of cases with missing values.* A case with a missing value for any dependent variable is excluded from computations and graphs.

VARIABLE *Variable-wise deletion.* A case is deleted from the analysis only if it has a missing value for the dependent variable being analyzed.

NOREPORT *Suppress missing-value categories.* This is the default.

REPORT *Report and graph missing-value categories.*

EXCLUDE *Exclude user-missing values.* Both user- and system-missing values for dependent variables are excluded from computations and graphs. This is the default.

INCLUDE *Include user-missing values.* Only system-missing values for dependent variables are excluded from computations and graphs.

HILOGLINEAR

HILOGLINEAR is available in the Advanced Models option.

```
HILOGLINEAR {varlist} (min,max) [varlist ...]
            {ALL    }

 [/METHOD [= BACKWARD]]

 [/MAXORDER = k]

 [/CRITERIA = [CONVERGE({0.25**})] [ITERATE({20**})] [P({0.05**})]
                        {n     }            {n   }       {prob  }
              [DELTA({0.5**})] [MAXSTEPS({10**})]
                     {d    }             {n   }
              [DEFAULT] ]

 [/CWEIGHT = {varname }]
             {(matrix)}

 [/PRINT = {[FREQ**] [RESID**] [ESTIM**] [ASSOCIATION**]}]
           {DEFAULT**                                   }
           {ALL                                         }
           {NONE                                        }

 [/PLOT = [{NONE**            } ]
           {DEFAULT           }
           {[RESID] [NORMPROB]}
           {ALL               }

 [/MISSING = [{EXCLUDE**}]]
              {INCLUDE  }

 [/DESIGN = effectname effectname*effectname ...]
```

** Default if subcommand or keyword is omitted.

Example

```
HILOGLINEAR V1(1,2) V2(1,2)
  /DESIGN=V1*V2.
```

Overview

HILOGLINEAR fits hierarchical loglinear models to multidimensional contingency tables using an iterative proportional-fitting algorithm. HILOGLINEAR also estimates parameters for saturated models. These techniques are described in Everitt (1977), Bishop et al. (1975), and Goodman (1978). HILOGLINEAR is much more efficient for these models than the LOGLINEAR procedure because HILOGLINEAR uses an iterative proportional-fitting algorithm rather than the Newton-Raphson method used in LOGLINEAR.

Options

Design Specification. You can request automatic model selection using backward elimination with the METHOD subcommand. You can also specify any hierarchical design and request multiple designs using the DESIGN subcommand.

Design Control. You can control the criteria used in the iterative proportional-fitting and model-selection routines with the CRITERIA subcommand. You can also limit the order of effects in the model with the MAXORDER subcommand and specify structural zeros for cells in the tables you analyze with the CWEIGHT subcommand.

Display and Plots. You can select the display for each design with the PRINT subcommand. For saturated models, you can request tests for different orders of effects as well. With the PLOT subcommand, you can request residuals plots or normal probability plots of residuals.

Basic Specification

- The basic specification is a variable list with at least two variables followed by their minimum and maximum values.
- HILOGLINEAR estimates a saturated model for all variables in the analysis.
- By default, HILOGLINEAR displays parameter estimates, measures of partial association, goodness of fit, and frequencies for the saturated model.

Subcommand Order

- The variable list must be specified first.
- Subcommands affecting a given DESIGN must appear before the DESIGN subcommand. Otherwise, subcommands can appear in any order.
- MISSING can be placed anywhere after the variable list.

Syntax Rules

- DESIGN is optional. If DESIGN is omitted or the last specification is not a DESIGN subcommand, a default saturated model is estimated.
- You can specify multiple PRINT, PLOT, CRITERIA, MAXORDER, and CWEIGHT subcommands. The last of each type specified is in effect for subsequent designs.
- PRINT, PLOT, CRITERIA, MAXORDER, and CWEIGHT specifications remain in effect until they are overridden by new specifications on these subcommands.
- You can specify multiple METHOD subcommands, but each one affects only the next design.
- MISSING can be specified only once.

Operations

- HILOGLINEAR builds a contingency table using all variables on the variable list. The table contains a cell for each possible combination of values within the range specified for each variable.
- HILOGLINEAR assumes that there is a category for every integer value in the range of each variable. Empty categories waste space and can cause computational problems. If there are empty categories, use the RECODE command to create consecutive integer values for categories.
- Cases with values outside the range specified for a variable are excluded.
- If the last subcommand is not a DESIGN subcommand, HILOGLINEAR displays a warning and generates the default model. This is the saturated model unless MAXORDER is specified. This model is in addition to any that are explicitly requested.
- If the model is not saturated (for example, when MAXORDER is less than the number of factors), only the goodness of fit and the observed and expected frequencies are given.
- The display uses the WIDTH subcommand defined on the SET command. If the defined width is less than 132, some portions of the display may be deleted.

Limitations

The HILOGLINEAR procedure cannot estimate all possible frequency models, and it produces limited output for unsaturated models.

- It can estimate only hierarchical loglinear models.
- It treats all table variables as nominal. (You can use LOGLINEAR to fit nonhierarchical models to tables involving variables that are ordinal.)
- It can produce parameter estimates for saturated models only (those with all possible main-effect and interaction terms).
- It can estimate partial associations for saturated models only.
- It can handle tables with no more than 10 factors.

Example

```
HILOGLINEAR V1(1,2) V2(1,2) V3(1,3) V4(1,3)
  /DESIGN=V1*V2*V3, V4.
```

- HILOGLINEAR builds a $2 \times 2 \times 3 \times 3$ contingency table for analysis.
- DESIGN specifies the generating class for a hierarchical model. This model consists of main effects for all four variables, two-way interactions among *V1*, *V2*, and *V3*, and the three-way interaction term *V1* by *V2* by *V3*.

Variable List

The required variable list specifies the variables in the analysis. The variable list must precede all other subcommands.

- Variables must be numeric and have integer values. If a variable has a fractional value, the fractional portion is truncated.
- Keyword ALL can be used to refer to all user-defined variables in the working data file.
- A range must be specified for each variable, with the minimum and maximum values separated by a comma and enclosed in parentheses.
- If the same range applies to several variables, the range can be specified once after the last variable to which it applies.
- If ALL is specified, all variables must have the same range.

METHOD Subcommand

By default, HILOGLINEAR tests the model specified on the DESIGN subcommand (or the default model) and does not perform any model selection. All variables are entered and none are removed. Use METHOD to specify automatic model selection using backward elimination for the next design specified.

- You can specify METHOD alone or with the keyword BACKWARD for an explicit specification.
- When the backward-elimination method is requested, a step-by-step output is displayed regardless of the specification on the PRINT subcommand.
- METHOD affects only the next design.

BACKWARD *Backward elimination.* Perform backward elimination of terms in the model. All terms are entered. Those that do not meet the P criterion specified on the CRITERIA subcommand (or the default P) are removed one at a time.

MAXORDER Subcommand

MAXORDER controls the maximum order of terms in the model estimated for subsequent designs. If MAXORDER is specified, HILOGLINEAR tests a model only with terms of that order or less.

- MAXORDER specifies the highest-order term that will be considered for the next design. MAXORDER can thus be used to abbreviate computations for the BACKWARD method.
- If the integer on MAXORDER is less than the number of factors, parameter estimates and measures of partial association are not available. Only the goodness of fit and the observed and expected frequencies are displayed.
- You can use MAXORDER with backward elimination to find the best model with terms of a certain order or less. This is computationally much more efficient than eliminating terms from the saturated model.

Example

```
HILOGLINEAR V1 V2 V3(1,2)
  /MAXORDER=2
  /DESIGN=V1 V2 V3
  /DESIGN=V1*V2*V3.
```

- HILOGLINEAR builds a $2 \times 2 \times 2$ contingency table for *V1*, *V2*, and *V3*.
- MAXORDER has no effect on the first DESIGN subcommand because the design requested considers only main effects.
- MAXORDER restricts the terms in the model specified on the second DESIGN subcommand to two-way interactions and main effects.

CRITERIA Subcommand

Use the CRITERIA subcommand to change the values of constants in the iterative proportional-fitting and model-selection routines for subsequent designs.

- The default criteria are in effect if the CRITERIA subcommand is omitted (see below).
- You cannot specify the CRITERIA subcommand without any keywords.
- Specify each CRITERIA keyword followed by a criterion value in parentheses. Only those criteria specifically altered are changed.
- You can specify more than one keyword on CRITERIA, and they can be in any order.

DEFAULT *Reset parameters to their default values.* If you have specified criteria other than the defaults for a design, use this keyword to restore the defaults for subsequent designs.

CONVERGE(n) *Convergence criterion.* The default is 10^{-3} times the largest cell size, or 0.25, whichever is larger.

ITERATE(n) *Maximum number of iterations.* The default is 20.

P(n) *Probability for change in chi-square if term is removed.* Specify a value between (but not including) 0 and 1 for the significance level. The default is 0.05. P is in effect only when you request BACKWARD on the METHOD subcommand.

MAXSTEPS(n) *Maximum number of steps for model selection.* Specify an integer between 1 and 99, inclusive. The default is 10.

DELTA(d) *Cell delta value.* The value of delta is added to each cell frequency for the first iteration. It is left in the cells for saturated models only. The default value is 0.5. You can specify any decimal value between 0 and 1 for *d*. HILOGLINEAR does not display parameter estimates or the covariance matrix of parameter estimates if any zero cells (either structural or sampling) exist in the expected table after delta is added.

CWEIGHT Subcommand

CWEIGHT specifies cell weights for a model. CWEIGHT is typically used to specify structural zeros in the table. You can also use CWEIGHT to adjust tables to fit new margins.

- You can specify the name of a variable whose values are cell weights, or provide a matrix of cell weights enclosed in parentheses.
- If you use a variable to specify cell weights, you are allowed only one CWEIGHT subcommand.
- If you specify a matrix, you must provide a weight for every cell in the contingency table, where the number of cells equals the product of the number of values of all variables.
- Cell weights are indexed by the values of the variables in the order in which they are specified on the variable list. The index values of the rightmost variable change the most quickly.
- You can use the notation *n*cw* to indicate that cell weight *cw* is repeated *n* times in the matrix.

Example

```
HILOGLINEAR V1(1,2) V2(1,2) V3(1,3)
  /CWEIGHT=CELLWGT
  /DESIGN=V1*V2, V2*V3, V1*V3.
```

- This example uses the variable *CELLWGT* to assign cell weights for the table. Only one CWEIGHT subcommand is allowed.

Example

```
HILOGLINEAR V4(1,3) V5(1,3)
  /CWEIGHT=(0 1 1  1 0 1  1 1 0)
  /DESIGN=V4, V5.
```

- The HILOGLINEAR command sets the diagonal cells in the model to structural zeros. This type of model is known as a **quasi-independence model**.
- Because both *V4* and *V5* have three values, weights must be specified for nine cells.
- The first cell weight is applied to the cell in which *V4* is 1 and *V5* is 1; the second weight is applied to the cell in which *V4* is 1 and *V5* is 2; and so on.

Example

```
HILOGLINEAR V4(1,3) V5(1,3)
  /CWEIGHT=(0 3*1 0 3*1 0)
  /DESIGN=V4,V5.
```

- This example is the same as the previous example except that the *n*cw* notation is used.

Example

```
* An Incomplete Rectangular Table

DATA LIST FREE / LOCULAR RADIAL FREQ.
WEIGHT BY FREQ.
BEGIN DATA
1 1 462
1 2 130
1 3 2
1 4 1
2 1 103
2 2 35
2 3 1
2 4 0
3 5 614
3 6 138
3 7 21
3 8 14
3 9 1
4 5 443
4 6 95
4 7 22
4 8 8
4 9 5
END DATA.
HILOGLINEAR LOCULAR (1,4) RADIAL (1,9)
  /CWEIGHT=(4*1 5*0   4*1 5*0   4*0 5*1   4*0 5*1)
  /DESIGN LOCULAR RADIAL.
```

- This example uses aggregated table data as input.
- The DATA LIST command defines three variables. The values of *LOCULAR* and *RADIAL* index the levels of those variables, so that each case defines a cell in the table. The values of *FREQ* are the cell frequencies.
- The WEIGHT command weights each case by the value of the variable *FREQ*. Because each case represents a cell in this example, the WEIGHT command assigns the frequencies for each cell.
- The BEGIN DATA and END DATA commands enclose the inline data.
- The HILOGLINEAR variable list specifies two variables. *LOCULAR* has values 1, 2, 3, and 4. *RADIAL* has integer values 1 through 9.
- The CWEIGHT subcommand identifies a block rectangular pattern of cells that are logically empty. There is one weight specified for each cell of the 36-cell table.
- In this example, the matrix form needs to be used in CWEIGHT because the structural zeros do not appear in the actual data. (For example, there is no case corresponding to *LOCULAR*=1, *RADIAL*=5.)
- The DESIGN subcommand specifies main effects only for *LOCULAR* and *RADIAL*. Lack of fit for this model indicates an interaction of the two variables.
- Because there is no PRINT or PLOT subcommand, HILOGLINEAR produces the default output for an unsaturated model.

PRINT Subcommand

PRINT controls the display produced for the subsequent designs.

- If PRINT is omitted or included with no specifications, the default display is produced.
- If any keywords are specified on PRINT, only output specifically requested is displayed.
- HILOGLINEAR displays Pearson and likelihood-ratio chi-square goodness-of-fit tests for models. For saturated models, it also provides tests that the *k*-way effects and the *k*-way and higher-order effects are 0.
- Both adjusted and unadjusted degrees of freedom are displayed for tables with sampling or structural zeros. *K*-way and higher-order tests use the unadjusted degrees of freedom.
- The unadjusted degrees of freedom are not adjusted for zero cells, and they estimate the upper bound of the true degrees of freedom. These are the same degrees of freedom you would get if all cells were filled.
- The adjusted degrees of freedom are calculated from the number of non-zero-fitted cells minus the number of parameters that would be estimated if all cells were filled (that is, unadjusted degrees of freedom minus the number of zero-fitted cells). This estimate of degrees of freedom may be too low if some parameters do not exist because of zeros.

DEFAULT *Default displays.* This option includes FREQ and RESID output for nonsaturated models, and FREQ, RESID, ESTIM, and ASSOCIATION output for saturated models. For saturated models, the observed and expected frequencies are equal, and the residuals are zeros.

FREQ *Observed and expected cell frequencies.*

RESID *Raw and standardized residuals.*

ESTIM *Parameter estimates for a saturated model.*

ASSOCIATION *Partial associations.* You can request partial associations of effects only when you specify a saturated model. This option is computationally expensive for tables with many factors.

ALL *All available output.*

NONE *Design information and goodness-of-fit statistics only.* Use of this option overrides all other specifications on PRINT.

PLOT Subcommand

Use PLOT to request residuals plots.

- If PLOT is included without specifications, standardized residuals and normal probability plots are produced.
- No plots are displayed for saturated models.
- If PLOT is omitted, no plots are produced.

RESID *Standardized residuals by observed and expected counts.*

NORMPLOT *Normal probability plots of adjusted residuals.*

NONE *No plots.* Specify NONE to suppress plots requested on a previous PLOT subcommand. This is the default if PLOT is omitted.

DEFAULT *Default plots.* Includes RESID and NORMPLOT. This is the default when PLOT is specified without keywords.

ALL *All available plots.*

MISSING Subcommand

By default, a case with either system-missing or user-missing values for any variable named on the HILOGLINEAR variable list is omitted from the analysis. Use MISSING to change the treatment of cases with user-missing values.

- MISSING can be named only once and can be placed anywhere following the variable list.
- MISSING cannot be used without specifications.
- A case with a system-missing value for any variable named on the variable list is always excluded from the analysis.

EXCLUDE *Delete cases with missing values.* This is the default if the subcommand is omitted. You can also specify keyword DEFAULT.

INCLUDE *Include user-missing values as valid.* Only cases with system-missing values are deleted.

DESIGN Subcommand

By default, HILOGLINEAR uses a saturated model that includes all variables on the variable list. The model contains all main effects and interactions for those variables. Use DESIGN to specify a different generating class for the model.

- If DESIGN is omitted or included without specifications, the default model is estimated. When DESIGN is omitted, SPSS issues a warning message.
- To specify a design, list the highest-order terms, using variable names and asterisks (*) to indicate interaction effects.
- In a hierarchical model, higher-order interaction effects imply lower-order interaction and main effects. `V1*V2*V3` implies the three-way interaction *V1* by *V2* by *V3*, two-way interactions *V1* by *V2*, *V1* by *V3*, and *V2* by *V3*, and main effects for *V1*, *V2*, and *V3*. The highest-order effects to be estimated are the generating class.
- Any PRINT, PLOT, CRITERIA, METHOD, and MAXORDER subcommands that apply to a DESIGN subcommand must appear before it.
- All variables named on DESIGN must be named or implied on the variable list.
- You can specify more than one DESIGN subcommand. One model is estimated for each DESIGN subcommand.
- If the last subcommand on HILOGLINEAR is not DESIGN, the default model will be estimated in addition to models explicitly requested. SPSS issues a warning message for a missing DESIGN subcommand.

References

Bishop, Y.M.M., Fienberg, S.E., and Holland, P.W. 1975. *Discrete multivariate analysis: Theory and practice*. Cambridge, Mass.: MIT Press.
Everitt, B.S. 1977. *The Analysis of Contingency Tables*. Chapman and Hall.
Goodman, L.A. 1978. *Analyzing Qualitative/Categorical Data*. New York: University Press of America.

IF

```
IF [(]logical expression[)] target variable=expression
```

The following relational operators can be used in logical expressions:

Symbol	Definition	Symbol	Definition
EQ or =	Equal to	NE or <>*	Not equal to
LT or <	Less than	LE or <=	Less than or equal to
GT or >	Greater than	GE or >=	Greater than or equal to

* On ASCII systems (for example, UNIX, VAX, and all PC's) you can also use ~=; on IBM EBCDIC systems (for example, IBM 360 and IBM 370) you can also use ¬=.

The following logical operators can be used in logical expressions:

Symbol	Definition
AND or &	Both relations must be true
Or or |	Either relation can be true
Not*	Reverses the outcome of an expression*

* On ASCII systems you can also use ~; on IBM EBCDIC systems you can also use ¬ (or the symbol above number 6).

Example

```
IF (AGE > 20 AND SEX = 1) GROUP=2.
```

Overview

IF conditionally executes a single transformation command based upon logical conditions found in the data. The transformation can create a new variable or modify the values of an existing variable for each case in the working data file. You can create or modify the values of both numeric and string variables. If you create a new string variable, you must first declare it on the STRING command.

IF has three components: a *logical expression* (see "Logical Expressions" on p. 44) that sets up the logical criteria, a *target variable* (the one to be modified or created), and an *assignment expression.* The target variable's values are modified according to the assignment expression.

IF is most efficient when used to execute a single, conditional, COMPUTE-like transformation. If you need multiple IF statements to define the condition, it is usually more efficient to use the RECODE command or a DO IF—END IF structure.

Basic Specification

The basic specification is a logical expression followed by a target variable, a required equals sign, and the assignment expression. The assignment is executed only if the logical expression is true.

Syntax Rules

- Logical expressions can be simple logical variables or relations, or complex logical tests involving variables, constants, functions, relational operators, and logical operators. Both the logical expression and the assignment expression can use any of the numeric or string functions allowed in COMPUTE transformations (see COMPUTE and "Transformation Expressions" on p. 33).
- Parentheses can be used to enclose the logical expression. Parentheses can also be used within the logical expression to specify the order of operations. Extra blanks or parentheses can be used to make the expression easier to read.
- A relation can compare variables, constants, or more complicated arithmetic expressions. Relations cannot be abbreviated. For example, (A EQ 2 OR A EQ 5) is valid, while (A EQ 2 OR 5) is not. Blanks (not commas) must be used to separate relational operators from the expressions being compared.
- A relation cannot compare a string variable to a numeric value or variable, or vice versa. A relation cannot compare the result of the logical functions SYSMIS, MISSING, ANY, or RANGE to a number.
- String values used in expressions must be specified in quotes and must include any leading or trailing blanks. Lowercase letters are considered distinct from uppercase letters.
- String variables that are used as target variables must already exist. To declare a new string variable, first create the variable with the STRING command and then specify the new variable as the target variable on IF.

Operations

- Each IF command evaluates every case in the data. Compare IF with DO IF, which passes control for a case out of the DO IF—END IF structure as soon as a logical condition is met.
- The logical expression is evaluated as true, false, or missing. The assignment is executed only if the logical expression is true. If the logical expression is false or missing, the assignment is not made. Existing target variables remain unchanged; new numeric variables retain their initial (system-missing) values.
- In general, a logical expression is evaluated as missing if any one of the variables used in the logical expression is system- or user-missing. However, when relations are joined by the logical operators AND or OR, the expression can sometimes be evaluated as true or false even when variables have missing values (see "Missing Values and Logical Operators" on p. 546).

Numeric Variables

- Numeric variables created with IF are initially set to the system-missing value. By default, they are assigned an F8.2 format.
- Logical expressions are evaluated in the following order: functions, followed by exponentiation, arithmetic operations, relations, and logical operators. When more than one logical operator is used, NOT is evaluated first, followed by AND and then OR. You can change the order of operations using parentheses.
- Assignment expressions are evaluated in the following order: functions, then exponentiation, and then arithmetic operators.

String Variables

- New string variables declared on IF are initially set to a blank value and are assigned the format specified on the STRING command that creates them.
- Logical expressions are evaluated in the following order: string functions, then relations, and then logical operators. When more than one logical operator is used, NOT is evaluated first, followed by AND and then OR. You can change the order of operations using parentheses.
- If the transformed value of a string variable exceeds the variable's defined width, the transformed value is truncated. If the transformed value is shorter than the defined width, the string is right-padded with blanks.

Missing Values and Logical Operators

When two or more relations are joined by logical operators AND or OR, the program always returns a missing value if all of the relations in the expression are missing. However, if any one of the relations can be determined, the program interprets the expression as true or false according to the logical outcomes shown in Table 1. The asterisk flags expressions where the program can evaluate the outcome with incomplete information.

Table 1 Logical outcome

Expression	Outcome	Expression	Outcome
true AND true	= true	true OR true	= true
true AND false	= false	true OR false	= true
false AND false	= false	false OR false	= false
true AND missing	= missing	true OR missing	= true*
missing AND missing	= missing	missing OR missing	= missing
false AND missing	= false*	false OR missing	= missing

Example

```
IF (AGE > 20 AND SEX = 1) GROUP=2.
```

- The numeric variable *GROUP* is set to 2 for cases where *AGE* is greater than 20 *and SEX* is equal to 1.
- When the expression is false or missing, the value of *GROUP* remains unchanged. If *GROUP* has not been previously defined, it contains the system-missing value.

Example

```
IF (SEX EQ 'F') EEO=QUOTA+GAIN.
```

- The logical expression tests the string variable *SEX* for the value *F*.
- When the expression is true (when *SEX* equals *F*), the value of the numeric variable *EEO* is assigned the value of *QUOTA* plus *GAIN*. Both *QUOTA* and *GAIN* must be previously defined numeric variables.
- When the expression is false or missing (for example, if *SEX* equals *F*), the value of *EEO* remains unchanged. If *EEO* has not been previously defined, it contains the system-missing value.

Example

```
COMPUTE V3=0.
IF ((V1-V2) LE 7) V3=V1**2.
```

- COMPUTE assigns *V3* the value 0.
- The logical expression tests whether *V1* minus *V2* is less than or equal to 7. If it is, the value of *V3* is assigned the value of *V1* squared. Otherwise, the value of *V3* remains at 0.

Example

```
IF (ABS(A-C) LT 100) INT=100.
```

- IF tests whether the absolute value of the variable *A* minus the variable *C* is less than 100. If it is, *INT* is assigned the value 100. Otherwise, the value is unchanged. If *INT* has not been previously defined, it is system-missing.

Example

```
IF (MEAN(V1 TO V5) LE 7) INDEX=1.
```

- If the mean of variables *V1* through *V5* is less than or equal to 7, *INDEX* equals 1.

Example

```
* Test for listwise deletion of missing values.

DATA LIST  /V1 TO V6 1-6.
STRING SELECT(A1).
COMPUTE SELECT='V'.
VECTOR V=V1 TO V6.

LOOP #I=1 TO 6.
IF MISSING(V(#I)) SELECT='M'.
END LOOP.

BEGIN DATA
123456
    56
1 3456
123456
123456
END DATA.

FREQUENCIES VAR=SELECT.
```

- STRING creates the string variable *SELECT* with an A1 format and COMPUTE sets the value of *SELECT* to *V*.
- VECTOR defines the vector *V* as the original variables *V1* to *V6*. Variables on a single vector must be all numeric or all string variables. In this example, because the vector *V* is used as an argument on the MISSING function of IF, the variables must be numeric (MISSING is not available for string variables).
- The loop structure executes six times: once for each VECTOR element. If a value is missing for any element, SELECT is set equal to *M*. In effect, if any case has a missing value for any of the variables *V1* to *V6*, SELECT is set to *M*.
- FREQUENCIES generates a frequency table for SELECT. The table gives a count of how many cases have missing values for at least one variable and how many cases have valid values for all variables. This table can be used to determine how many cases would be dropped from an analysis that uses listwise deletion of missing values. See pp. 189 and 324 for alternative ways to test for listwise deletion of missing values.

Example

```
IF YRHIRED LT 1980 RATE=0.02.
IF DEPT='SALES' DIVISION='TRANSFERRED'.
```

- The logical expression on the first IF command tests whether *YRHIRED* is less than 1980 (hired before 1980). If so, the variable *RATE* is set to 0.02.
- The logical expression on the second IF command tests whether *DEPT* equals *SALES*. When the condition is true, the value for the string variable *DIVISION* is changed to *TRANSFERRED* but is truncated if the format for *DIVISION* is not at least 11 characters wide. For any other value of *DEPT*, the value of *DIVISION* remains unchanged.
- Although there are two IF statements, each defines a separate and independent condition. The IF command is used rather than the DO IF—END IF structure in order to test both con-

ditions on every case. If DO IF—END IF is used, control passes out of the structure as soon as the first logical condition is met.

Example

```
IF (STATE EQ 'IL' AND CITY EQ 13) COST=1.07 * COST.
```

- The logical expression tests whether *STATE* equals *IL* and *CITY* equals 13.
- If the logical expression is true, the numeric variable *COST* is increased by 7%.
- For any other value of *STATE* or *CITY*, the value of *COST* remains unchanged.

Example

```
STRING GROUP (A18).
IF (HIRED GE 1988) GROUP='Hired after merger'.
```

- STRING declares the string variable *GROUP* and assigns it a width of 18 characters.
- When *HIRED* is greater than or equal to 1988, *GROUP* is assigned the value *Hired after merger*. When *HIRED* is less than 1988, *GROUP* remains blank.

Example

```
IF (RECV GT DUE OR (REVNUES GE EXPNS AND BALNCE GT 0))STATUS='SOLVENT.
```

- First, the program tests whether *REVNUES* is greater than or equal to *EXPNS* and whether *BALNCE* is greater than 0.
- Second, the program evaluates if *RECV* is greater than *DUE*.
- If either of these expressions is true, *STATUS* is assigned the value *SOLVENT*.
- If both expressions are false, *STATUS* remains unchanged.
- *STATUS* is an existing string variable in the working data file. Otherwise, it would have to be declared on a preceding STRING command.

IGRAPH

```
IGRAPH

 [/Y=[VAR(varname1)]
     [TYPE={SCALE ([MIN=value] [MAX=value])}]
           {CATEGORICAL                    }
     [TITLE='string']]

 [/X1=[VAR(varname2)]]
     [TYPE={SCALE([MIN=value] [MAX=value])}]
           {CATEGORICAL                   }
     [TITLE='string']]

 [/X2=[VAR(varname3)]]
     [TYPE={SCALE([MIN=value] [MAX=value])}]
           {CATEGORICAL                   }
     [TITLE='string']]

 [/YLENGTH=value]

 [/X1LENGTH=value]

 [/X2LENGTH=value]

 [/CATORDER VAR(varname)
   ({COUNT      }   [{ASCENDING }]  [{SHOWEMPTY])]
    {OCCURRENCE }    {DESCENDING}    {OMITEMPTY}
    {LABEL}
    {VALUE}

 [/COLOR=varname
     [TYPE={SCALE([MIN=value] [MAX=value])}]
           {CATEGORICAL                   }
     [LEGEND={ON|OFF}]
     [TITLE='string']]
     [{CLUSTER}]]
      {STACK  }

 [/REFLINE varname value [LABEL={ON|OFF}]
                         [SPIKE = {ON|OFF}]]
                         [COLOR={ON|OFF}]
                         [STYLE={ON|OFF}]

 [/STYLE=varname
     [LEGEND={ON|OFF}]
     [TITLE='string']]
     [{CLUSTER}]
      {STACK  }

 [/NORMALIZE]

 [/SIZE=varname
     [TYPE={SCALE([MIN=value] [MAX=value])}]
           {CATEGORICAL                   }
     [LEGEND={ON|OFF}]
     [TITLE='string']]

 [/CLUSTER=varname]

 [/SUMMARYVAR=varname]

 [/PANEL varlist]

 [/POINTLABEL=varname]

 [/COORDINATE={HORIZONTAL}]
```

```
              {VERTICAL  }
              {THREE     }

[/EFFECT={NONE }]
         {THREE}

[/TITLE='string']

[/SUBTITLE='string']

[/CAPTION='string']

[/VIEWNAME='line 1']

[/CHARTLOOK='filename']

[/SCATTER
    [COINCIDENT={NONE               }]
                {JITTER[(amount)]   }]

[/BAR [(summary function)]
    [LABEL {INSIDE }[VAL][N]]
           {OUTSIDE}
    [SHAPE={RECTANGLE}]
           {PYRAMID  }
           {OBELISK  }
    [BARBASE={SQUARE}]
             {ROUND }
    [BASELINE (value)]]

[/PIE [(summary function)]
     [START value]
     [{CW|CCW}]
     [SLICE={INSIDE } [LABEL] [PCT] [VAL] [N]]
            {OUTSIDE}
            {TEXTIN }
            {NUMIN  }
     [CLUSTER={URIGHT} [LABEL] [PCT] [VAL] [N]]]
              {LRIGHT}
              {ULEFT }
              {LLEFT }

[/BOX [OUTLIERS={ON|OFF}] [EXTREME={ON|OFF}]
      [MEDIAN={ON|OFF}]
      [LABEL=[N]]
      [BOXBASE={SQUARE}]
               {ROUND }
      [WHISKER={T     }]
               {FANCY}
               {LINE }
      [CAPWIDTH (pct)]]

[/LINE [(summary function)]
    STYLE={DOTLINE}
          {LINE   }
          {DOT    }
          {NONE   }
    [DROPLINE={ON|OFF}]
    [LABEL=[VAL] [N] [PCT]]
    [LINELABEL=[CAT] [N] [PCT]]
    [INTERPOLATE={STRAIGHT}]
                 {LSTEP    }
                 {CSTEP    }
                 {RSTEP    }
                 {LJUMP    }
                 {RJUMP    }
                 {CJUMP    }
                 {SPLINE   }
                 {LAGRANGE3}
                 {LAGRANGE5}
```

```
     [BREAK={MISSING}]]
            {NONE   }

  [/ERRORBAR [{CI(pctvalue) }]
              {SD(sdval)    }
              {SE(seval)    }
     [LABEL [VAL][N]]
     [DIRECTION={BOTH|UP|DOWN|SIGN}
     [CAPWIDTH (pct)]
     [CAPSTYLE {NONE }]
               {T    }
               {FANCY}
     [SYMBOL={ON|OFF}]
     [BASELINE value]]

  [/HISTOGRAM [CUM]
     [SHAPE={HISTOGRAM}]
     [X1INTERVAL={AUTO    }]
                 {NUM=n   }
                 {WIDTH=n }
     [X2INTERVAL={AUTO    }]
                 {NUM=n   }
                 {WIDTH=n }
     [X1START=n]
     [X2START=n]
     [CURVE={OFF|ON}]
     [SURFACE={OFF|ON}]

  [/FITLINE [METHOD={NONE              }]
                    {REGRESSION LINEAR }
                    {ORIGIN LINEAR     }
                    {MEAN              }
                    {LLR [(NORMAL|EPANECHNIKOV|UNIFORM)]
                         [BANDWIDTH={FAST|CONSTRAINED}]
                         [X1MULTIPLIER=multiplier]
                         [X2MULTIPLIER=multiplier]}
     [INTERVAL[(cval)]=[MEAN] [INDIVIDUAL]]
     [LINE=[TOTAL] [MEFFECT]]]

  [/SPIKE {X1                          }]
          {X2                          }
          {Y                           }
          {CORNER                      }
          {ORIGIN                      }
          {FLOOR                       }
          {CENTROID [TOTAL] [MEFFECT]  }

  [/FORMAT [ SPIKE [COLOR={ON|OFF}] [STYLE={ON|OFF}]]
```

Summary function names are found beginning on p. 572.

Example

```
IGRAPH
 /VIEWNAME='Scatterplot'
 /X1=VAR(trial1) TYPE=SCALE
 /Y=VAR(trial3) TYPE=SCALE
 /X2=VAR(trial2) TYPE=SCALE
 /COORDINATE=THREE
 /X1LENGTH=3.0
 /YLENGTH=3.0
 /X2LENGTH=3.0
 /SCATTER COINCIDENT=NONE
 /FITLINE METHOD=REGRESSION LINEAR INTERVAL(90.0)=MEAN  LINE=TOTAL.
```

Overview

The interactive Chart Editor is designed to emulate the experience of drawing a statistical chart with a pencil and paper. The Chart Editor is a highly interactive, direct manipulation environment that automates the data manipulation and drawing tasks required to draw a chart by hand, such as determining data ranges for axes; drawing ticks and labels; aggregating and summarizing data; drawing data representations such as bars, boxes, or clouds; and incorporating data dimensions as legends when the supply of dependent axes is exhausted.

The IGRAPH command creates a chart in an interactive environment. The interactive Chart Editor allows you to make extensive and fundamental changes to this chart instead of creating a new chart. The Chart Editor allows you to replace data, add new data, change dimensionality, create separate chart panels for different groups, or change the way data are represented in a chart (that is, change a bar chart into a boxplot). The Chart Editor is not a "typed" chart system. You can use chart elements in any combination, and you are not limited by "types" that the application recognizes.

To create a chart, you assign data dimensions to the domain (independent) and range (dependent) axes to create a "data region." You also add data representations such as bars or clouds to the data region. Data representations automatically position themselves according to the data dimensions assigned to the data region.

There is no required order for assigning data dimensions or adding data representations; you can add the data dimensions first or add the data representations first. When defining the data region, you can define the range axis first or the domain axis first.

Options

Titles and Captions. You can specify a title, subtitle, and caption for the chart.

Chart Type. You can request a specific type of chart using the BAR, PIE, BOX, LINE, ERRORBAR, HISTOGRAM, and SCATTERPLOT subcommands.

Chart Content. You can combine elements in a single chart. For example, you can add error bars to a bar chart.

Chart Legends. You can specify either scale legends or categorical legends. Moreover, you can define which properties of the chart reflect the legend variables.

Chart Appearance. You can specify a template, using the CHARTLOOK subcommand, to override the default chart attribute settings.

Basic Specification

The minimum syntax to create a graph is simply the IGRAPH command, without any variable assignment. This will create an empty graph. To create an element in a chart, a dependent variable must be assigned and a chart element specified.

Subcommand Order

- Subcommands can be used in any order.

Syntax Rules

- EFFECT=THREE and COORDINATE=THREE cannot be specified together. If they are, the EFFECT keyword will be ignored.

Operations

- The chart title, subtitle, and caption are assigned as they are specified on the TITLE, SUBTITLE, and CAPTION subcommands. In the absence of any of these subcommands, the missing title, subtitle, or caption are null.

General Syntax

Following are the most general-purpose subcommands. Even so, not all plots will use all subcommands. For example, if the only element in a chart is a bar, the SIZE subcommand will not be shown in the graph.

Each general subcommand may be specified only once. If one of these subcommands appears more than once, the last one is used.

X1, Y, and X2 Subcommands

X1, Y, and X2 assign variables to the *X1*, *Y*, and *X2* dimensions of the chart.

- The variable must be enclosed in parentheses after the VAR keyword.
- Each of these subcommands can include the TITLE keyword, specifying a string with which to title the corresponding axis.
- Each variable must be either a scale variable, a categorical variable, or a built-in data dimension. If a type is not specified, a default type is used from the variable's definition.

SCALE A scale dimension is interpreted as a measurement on some continuous scale for each case. Optionally, the minimum (MIN) and maximum (MAX) scale values can be specified. In the absence of MIN and MAX, the entire data range is used.

CATEGORICAL A categorical dimension partitions cases into exclusive groups (each case is a member of exactly one group). The categories are represented by evenly spaced ticks.

A built-in dimension is a user interface object used to create a chart of counts or percentages and to make a casewise chart of elements that usually aggregate data like bars or lines. The built-in dimensions are **count** ($COUNT), **percentage** ($PCT), and **case** ($CASE).

- To create a chart that displays counts or percentages, one of the built-in data dimensions is assigned to the range (*Y*) axis. The VAR keyword is not used for built-in dimensions.
- Built in count and percentage data dimensions cannot be assigned to a domain axis (*X1* or *X2*) or to a legend subcommand.
- The count and percentage data dimensions are all scales and cannot be changed into categorizations.

CATORDER Subcommand

The CATORDER subcommand defines the order in which categories are displayed in a chart and controls the display of empty categories, based on the characteristics of a variable specified in parenthesis after the subcommand name.

- You can display categories in ascending or descending order based on category values, category value labels, counts, or values of a summary variable.
- You can either show or hide empty categories (categories with no cases).

Keywords for the CATORDER subcommand include:

ASCENDING *Display categories in ascending order of the specified order keyword.*

DESCENDING *Display categories in descending order of the specified order keyword.*

SHOWEMPTY *Include empty categories in the chart.*

OMITEMPTY *Do not include empty categories in the chart.*

ASCENDING and DESCENDING are mutually exclusive. SHOWEMPTY and OMITEMPTY are mutually exclusive.

Order keywords include:

COUNT *Sort categories based on the number of observations in each category.*

OCCURRENCE *Sort categories based on the first occurrence of each unique value in the data file.*

LABEL *Sort categories based on defined value labels for each category.* For categories without defined value labels, the category value is used.

VALUE *Sort categories based on the values of the categories or the values of a specified summary function for the specified variable.* Summary functions are defined on p. 572.

Order keywords are mutually exclusive. You can specify only one order keyword on each CATORDER subcommand.

X1LENGTH, YLENGTH, and X2LENGTH Subcommands

X1LENGTH, YLENGTH, and X2LENGTH define the length in inches of the corresponding axis.

Example

```
IGRAPH
 /VIEWNAME='Scatterplot'
 /Y=VAR(sales96) TYPE=SCALE
 /X1=VAR(sales95) TYPE=SCALE
 /X2=VAR(region) TYPE=CATEGORICAL
 /X1LENGTH=2.39
 /YLENGTH=2.42
 /X2LENGTH=2.47
 /SCATTER.
```

- Y assigns *sales96* to the dependent axis, defining it to be continuous.
- X1 assigns *sales95* to the *X1* axis, defining it to be a scale variable (continuous).
- X2 assigns *region* to the *X2* axis, defining it to be categorical.
- X1LENGTH, YLENGTH, and X2LENGTH define the length of each axis in inches.

COLOR, STYLE, and SIZE Subcommands

COLOR, STYLE, and SIZE specify variables used to create a legend. Each value of these variables corresponds to a unique property of the chart. The effect of these variables depends on the type of chart.

- Most charts use color in a similar fashion; casewise elements draw each case representation using the color value for the case, and summary elements draw each group representation in the color that represents a summarized value in the color data dimension.
- For dot-line charts, dot charts, and scatterplots, symbol shape is used for style variables and symbol size is used for size variables.
- For line charts and lines in a scatterplot, dash patterns encode style variables and line thickness encodes size variables.
- For bar charts, pie charts, boxplots, histograms, and error bars, fill pattern encodes style variables. Typically, these charts are not sensitive to size variables.

CATEGORICAL legend variables split the elements in the chart into categories. A categorical legend shows the reader which color, style, or size is associated with which category of the variable. The colors, styles, or sizes are assigned according to the discrete categories of the variable.

SCALE legend variables apply color or size to the elements by the value or a summary value of the legend variable, creating a continuum across the values. COLOR and SIZE can create either scale legends or categorical legends. STYLE can create categorical legends only.

Scale variables have the following keywords:

MIN *Defines the minimum value of the scale.*

MAX *Defines the maximum value of the scale.*

- The keywords MIN and MAX and their assigned values must be enclosed in parentheses.

In addition, the following keywords are available for COLOR, STYLE, and SIZE:

LEGEND *Determines if the legend is displayed or not.* The legend explains how to decode color, size, or style in a chart.

TITLE *Specifies a string used to title the legend.*

The following keywords are available for COLOR and STYLE:

CLUSTER *Creates clustered charts based on color or size variables.*

STACK *Creates stacked charts based on color or size variables.*

CLUSTER and STACK are mutually exclusive. Only one can be specified.

Example

```
IGRAPH
 /VIEWNAME='Scatterplot'
 /Y=VAR(sales96) TYPE=SCALE
 /X1=VAR(sales95) TYPE=SCALE
 /X2=VAR(region) TYPE=CATEGORICAL
 /COLOR=VAR(tenure) TYPE=SCALE
 /STYLE=VAR(vol94)
 /SCATTER.
```

- The chart contains a three-dimensional scatterplot.
- COLOR defines a scale legend corresponding to the variable *TENURE*. Points appear in a continuum of colors, with the point color reflecting the value of *TENURE*.
- STYLE defines a categorical legend. Points appear with different shapes, with the point shape reflecting the value of *VOL94*.

CLUSTER Subcommand

CLUSTER defines the variable used to create clustered pie charts. The variable specified must be categorical. The cluster will contain as many pies as there are categories in the cluster variable.

SUMMARYVAR Subcommand

SUMMARYVAR specifies the variable or function for summarizing a pie element. It can only have the built-in variables $COUNT or $PCT or a user-defined variable name.

Specifying a user-defined variable on SUMMARYVAR requires specifying a summary function on the PIE subcommand. Valid summary functions include SUM, SUMAV, SUMSQ, NLT(x), NLE(x), NEQ(x), NGT(x), and NGE(x). The slices of the pie represent categories defined by the values of the summary function applied to SUMMARYVAR.

PANEL Subcommand

PANEL specifies a categorical variable or variables for which separate charts will be created.

- Specifying a single panel variable results in a separate chart for each level of the panel variable.
- Specifying multiple panel variables results in a separate chart for each combination of levels of the panel variables.

POINTLABEL Subcommand

POINTLABEL specifies a variable used to label points in a boxplot or scatterplot.

- If a label variable is specified without ALL or NONE, no labels are turned on (NONE).
- The keyword NONE turns all labels off.

COORDINATE Subcommand

COORDINATE specifies the orientation of the chart. Three-dimensional charts (THREE) have a default orientation that cannot be altered. Keywords available for two-dimensional charts include:

HORIZONTAL *The* Y *variable appears along the horizontal axis and the* X1 *variable appears along the vertical axis.*

VERTICAL *The* Y *variable appears along the vertical axis and the* X1 *variable appears along the horizontal axis.*

Example

```
IGRAPH
 /VIEWNAME='Scatterplot'
 /Y=VAR(sales96) TYPE=SCALE
 /X1=VAR(region) TYPE=CATEGORICAL
 /COORDINATE=HORIZONTAL
 /BAR (mean).
```

- The COORDINATE subcommand defines the bar chart as horizontal with *region* on the vertical dimension and means of *sales96* on the horizontal dimension.

EFFECT Subcommand

EFFECT displays a two-dimensional chart with additional depth along a third dimension. Two-dimensional objects are displayed as three-dimensional solids.

- EFFECT is unavailable for three-dimensional charts.

TITLE, SUBTITLE, and CAPTION Subcommands

TITLE, SUBTITLE, and CAPTION specify lines of text placed at the top or bottom of a chart.

- Multiple lines of text can be entered using the carriage control character (`\n`).
- Each title, subtitle, or caption must be enclosed in apostrophes or quotation marks.
- The maximum length of a title, subtitle, or caption is 255 characters.
- The font, point size, color, alignment, and orientation of the title, subtitle, and caption text is determined by the ChartLook.

VIEWNAME Subcommand

VIEWNAME assigns a name to the chart, which will appear in the outline pane of the Viewer. The name can have a maximum of 255 characters.

CHARTLOOK Subcommand

CHARTLOOK identifies a file containing specifications concerning the initial visual properties of a chart, such as fill, color, font, style, and symbol. By specifying a ChartLook, you can control cosmetic properties that are not explicitly available as syntax keywords.

Valid ChartLook files have a *.clo* extension. Files designated on CHARTLOOK must either be included with the software or created using the Chart Properties and ChartLooks options on the Format menu.

A ChartLook contains values for the following properties:

- Color sequence for categorical color legends
- Color range for scale color legends
- Line style sequence for categorical style legends
- Symbol style sequence for categorical style legends
- Categorical legend fill styles
- Categorical symbol size sequence for categorical size legends
- Symbol size sequence for scale size sequences
- Categorical line weight sequence for categorical size legends
- Font, size, alignment, bold, and italic properties for text objects
- Fill and border for filled objects
- Style, weight, and color for line objects
- Font, shape, size, and color for symbol objects
- Style, weight, and color for visual connectors
- Axis properties: axis line style, color, weight; major tick shape, location, color, size.

Example

```
IGRAPH
 /VIEWNAME='Slide 1'
 /X1=VAR(sales95) TYPE=SCALE
 /Y=VAR(sales96) TYPE=SCALE
 /X2=VAR(region) TYPE=CATEGORICAL
 /COORDINATE=THREE
 /POINTLABEL=VAR(division) NONE
 /TITLE='Scatterplot Comparing Regions'
 /SUBTITLE='Predicting 1996 Sales\nfrom 1995 Sales'
 /CHARTLOOK='Classic.clo'
 /SCATTER.
```

- VIEWNAME assigns the name *Slide 1* to the chart. The outline pane of the Viewer uses this name for the chart.
- Points in the chart are labeled with the values of *division*. Initially, all labels are off. Labels for individual points can be turned on interactively after creating the chart.
- TITLE and SUBTITLE define text to appear of the plot. The subtitle contains a carriage return between *Sales* and *from*.
- The appearance of the chart is defined in the Classic ChartLook.

REFLINE Subcommand

The REFLINE subcommand inserts a reference line for the specified variable at the specified value. Optional keywords are:

LABEL={ON|OFF} *Display a label for the reference line.* For variables with defined value labels, the value label for the specified value is displayed. If there is no defined value label for the specified value, the specified value is displayed.

SPIKE={ON|OFF} *Display spikes from the reference line to individual data points.*

Example

```
IGRAPH
  /X1 = VAR(gender) TYPE = CATEGORICAL
  /Y = VAR(salary) TYPE = SCALE
  /BAR(MEAN)
  /REFLINE salary 30000 LABEL=ON.
```

SPIKE Subcommand

The SPIKE subcommand inserts spikes from individual data points to the specified location. Keywords for location include:

X1 *Display spikes to the* X1 *axis.*

X2 *Display spikes to the* X2 *axis.*

Y *Display spikes to the* Y *axis.*

CORNER *Display spikes to the corner defined by the lowest displayed values of the* X1, X2, *and* Y *axes.*

ORIGIN *Display spikes to the origin. The origin is the point defined by the 0 values for the* X1, X2, *and* Y *axes.*

FLOOR *Display spikes to the "floor" defined by the* X1 *and* X2 *axes.*

CENTROID *Display spikes to the point defined by the mean values of the* X1, X2, *and* Y *variables.* CENTROID=TOTAL displays spikes to the overall mean. CENTROID=MEFFECT displays spikes to subgroup means defined by color and/or style variables.

Example:

```
IGRAPH
  /X1 = VAR(salbegin) TYPE = SCALE
  /Y = VAR(salary) TYPE = SCALE
  /COLOR = VAR(gender) TYPE = CATEGORICAL
  /SPIKE CENTROID=MEFFECT.
```

FORMAT Subcommand

For charts with color or style variables, the FORMAT subcommand controls the color and style attributes of spikes. The keywords are:

SPIKE *Applies color and style specifications to spikes.* This keyword is required.

COLOR{ON|OFF} *Controls use of color in spikes as defined by color variable.* The default is ON.

STYLE {ON|OFF} *Controls use of line style in spikes as defined by style variable.* The default is ON.

Example

```
IGRAPH
  /X1 = VAR(salbegin) TYPE = SCALE
  /Y = VAR(salary) TYPE = SCALE
  /COLOR = VAR(gender) TYPE = CATEGORICAL
  /SPIKE CENTROID=MEFFECT
  /FORMAT COLOR=OFF.
```

KEY Keyword

All interactive chart types except histograms include a key element that identifies the summary measures displayed in the chart (for example, counts, means, medians). The KEY keyword controls the display of the key in the chart. The default is ON, which displays the key. The OFF specification hides the key. The KEY specification is part of the subcommand that defines the chart type.

Example

```
IGRAPH
  /X1 = VAR(jobcat) TYPE = CATEGORICAL
  /Y = $count
  /BAR KEY=OFF.
```

Element Syntax

The following subcommands add elements to a chart. The same subcommand can be specified more than once. Each subcommand adds another element to the chart.

SCATTER Subcommand

SCATTER produces two- or three-dimensional scatterplots. Scatterplots can use either categorical or scale dimensions to create color or size legends. Categorical dimensions are required to create style legends.

The keyword COINCIDENT controls the placement of markers that have identical values on all axes. COINCIDENT can have one of the following two values:

NONE *Places coincident markers on top of one another.* This is the default value.

JITTER(amount) *Adds a small amount of random noise to all scale axis dimensions.* Amount indicates the percentage of noise added and ranges from 0 to 10.

Example

```
IGRAPH
 /Y=VAR(sales96) TYPE=SCALE
 /X1=VAR(sales95) TYPE=SCALE
 /COORDINATE=VERTICAL
 /SCATTER COINCIDENT=JITTER(5).
```

- COORDINATE defines the chart as two-dimensional with *sales96* on the vertical dimension.
- SCATTER creates a scatterplot of *sales96* and *sales95.*
- The scale axes have 5% random noise added by the JITTER keyword allowing separation of coincident points.

AREA Subcommand

AREA creates area charts. These charts summarize categories of one or more variables. The following keywords are available:

summary function *Defines a function used to summarize the variable defined on the* Y *subcommand.* If the *Y* axis assignment is $COUNT or $PCT, the AREA subcommand cannot have a summary function. If the Y subcommand specifies TYPE=CATEGORICAL, then AREA can only specify MODE as the summary function. Otherwise, all summary functions described on p. 572 are available.

POINTLABEL *Labels points with the actual values corresponding to the dependent axis (*VAL*), the percentage of cases (*PCT*), and the number of cases included in each data point (*N*).* The default is no labels.

AREALABEL *Labels area with category labels (*CAT*), the percentage of cases (*PCT*), and the number of cases included in each line (*N*).* The default is no labels.

BREAK *Indicates whether the lines break at missing values (*MISSING*) or not (*NONE*).*

BASELINE *The baseline value determines the location from which the areas will hang (vertical) or extend (horizontal).* The default value is 0.

The INTERPOLATE keyword determines how the lines connecting the points are drawn. Options include:

STRAIGHT *Straight lines.*

LSTEP *A horizontal line extends from each data point.* A vertical riser connects the line to the next data point.

CSTEP *Each data point is centered on a horizontal line that extends half of the distance between consecutive points.* Vertical risers connect the line to the next horizontal line.

RSTEP *A horizontal line terminates at each data point.* A vertical riser extends from each data point, connecting to the next horizontal line.

BAR Subcommand

BAR creates a bar element in a chart, corresponding to the *X1*, *X2*, and *Y* axis assignments. Bars can by clustered by assigning variables to COLOR or STYLE. Horizontal or vertical orientation is specified by the COORDINATE subcommand.

summary function *Defines a function used to summarize the variable defined on the* Y *subcommand.* If the *Y* axis assignment is $COUNT or $PCT, the BAR subcommand cannot have a summary function. If the Y subcommand specifies TYPE=CATEGORICAL, then BAR can specify only MODE as the summary function. Otherwise, all summary functions described on p. 572 are available.

LABEL *Bars can be labeled with the actual values corresponding to the dependent axis* (VAL) *or with the number of cases included in each bar* (N). The default is no labels. The placement of the labels is inside the bars (INSIDE) or outside the bars (OUTSIDE).

SHAPE *Determines whether the bars are drawn as rectangles* (RECTANGLE)*, pyramids* (PYRAMID)*, or obelisks* (OBELISK). The default is rectangular bars.

BARBASE *For three-dimensional bars, the base can be round* (ROUND) *or square* (SQUARE). The default is square.

BASELINE *The baseline value determines the location from which the bars will hang (vertical) or extend (horizontal).* The default value is 0.

Example

```
IGRAPH
 /X1=VAR(volume96) TYPE=CATEGORICAL
 /Y=$count
 /COORDINATE=VERTICAL
 /EFFECT=THREE
 /BAR LABEL INSIDE N SHAPE=RECTANGLE.
```

- X1 assigns the categorical variable *volume96* to the *X1* axis.
- Y assigns the built-in dimension *$count* to the range axis.
- VERTICAL defines the counts to appear along the vertical dimension.
- BAR adds a bar element to the chart.
- LABEL labels the bars in the chart with the number of cases included in the bars. These labels appear inside the bars.

- SHAPE indicates that the bars are rectangles. However, EFFECT adds a third dimension to the chart, yielding three-dimensional solids.

Example

```
IGRAPH
 /X1=VAR(volume94) TYPE=CATEGORICAL
 /Y=VAR(sales96) TYPE=SCALE
 /COORDINATE=HORIZONTAL
 /EFFECT=NONE
 /BAR (MEAN) LABEL OUTSIDE VAL SHAPE=PYRAMID BASELINE=370.00.
```

- X1 assigns the categorical variable *volume94* to the *X1* axis.
- Y assigns the scale variable *sales96* to the range axis.
- HORIZONTAL defines *sales96* to appear along the horizontal dimension.
- EFFECT defines the chart as two-dimensional.
- BAR adds a bar element to the chart.
- MEAN defines the summary function to apply to *sales96*. Each bar represents the mean *sales96* value for the corresponding category of *volume94*.
- LABEL labels the bars in the chart with the mean *sales96* value. These labels appear outside the bars.
- SHAPE indicates that the bars are pyramids.
- BASELINE indicates that bars should extend from 370. Any bar with a mean value above 370 extends to the right. Any bar with a mean value below 370 extends to the left.

PIE Subcommand

A simple pie chart summarizes categories defined by a single variable or by a group of related variables. A clustered pie chart contains a cluster of simple pies, all of which are stacked into categories by the same variable. The pies are of different sizes and appear to be stacked on top of one another. The cluster contains as many pies as there are categories in the cluster variable. For both simple and clustered pie charts, the size of each slice represents the count, the percentage, or a summary function of a variable.

The following keywords are available:

summary function *Defines a function used to summarize the variable defined on the* SUMMARYVAR *subcommand.* If the SUMMARYVAR assignment is $COUNT or $PCT, the PIE subcommand cannot have a summary function. Otherwise, of the summary functions described on p. 572, SUM, SUMAV, SUMSQ, NGT(x), NLE(x), NEQ(x), NGE(x), NGT(x), and NIN(x1,x2) are available.

START num *Indicates the starting position of the smallest slice of the pie chart.* Any integer can be specified for num. The value is converted to a number between 0 and 360, which represents the degree of rotation of the smallest slice.

CW | CCW *Sets the positive rotation of the pie to either clockwise (*CW*) or counterclockwise (*CCW*).* The default rotation is clockwise.

SLICE *Sets the labeling characteristics for the slices of the pie.* The pie slices can be labeled with the category labels (LABEL), the category percentages (PCT), the number of cases (N), and the category values (VAL). Label position is either all labels inside the pie (INSIDE), all labels outside the pie (OUTSIDE), text labels inside the pie with numeric labels outside (TEXTIN), or numeric labels inside the pie with text labels outside (NUMIN).

CLUSTER *Sets the labeling characteristics for the pies from clusters.* The pies can be labeled with the category labels (LABEL), the category percentages (PCT), the number of cases (N), and the category values (VAL). Label position is either upper left (ULEFT), upper right (URIGHT), lower left (LLEFT), or lower right (LRIGHT) of the figure.

Example

```
IGRAPH
 /SUMMARYVAR=$count
 /COLOR=VAR(volume96) TYPE=CATEGORICAL
 /EFFECT=THREE
 /PIE START 180 CW SLICE=TEXTIN LABEL PCT N.
```

- The pie slices represent the number of cases (SUMMARYVAR=$count) in each category of *volume96* (specified on the COLOR subcommand).
- EFFECT yields a pie chart with an additional third dimension.
- PIE creates a pie chart.
- The first slice begins at 180 degrees and the rotation of the pie is clockwise.
- SLICE labels the slices with category labels, the percentage in each category, and the number of cases in each category. TEXTIN places the text labels (category labels) inside the pie slices and the numeric labels outside.

Example

```
IGRAPH
 /SUMMARYVAR=VAR(sales96)
 /COLOR=VAR(volume95) TYPE=CATEGORICAL
 /X1=VAR(region) TYPE=CATEGORICAL
 /Y=VAR(division) TYPE=CATEGORICAL
 /COORDINATE=VERTICAL
 /PIE (SUM) START 0 CW SLICE=INSIDE VAL.
```

- The pie slices represent the sums of *sales96* values for each category of *volume95* (specified on the COLOR subcommand).
- X1 and Y define two axes representing *region* and *division.* A pie chart is created for each combination of these variables.
- The first slice in each pie begins at 0 degrees and the rotation of the pie is clockwise.
- SUM indicates the summary function applied to the summary variable, *sales96.* The pie slices represent the sum of the *sales96* values.

- SLICE labels the slices with the value of the summary function. INSIDE places the labels inside the pie slices.

BOX Subcommand

BOX creates a boxplot, sometimes called a box-and-whiskers plot, showing the median, quartiles, and outlier and extreme values for a scale variable. The interquartile range (IQR) is the difference between the 75th and 25th percentiles and corresponds to the length of the box.

The following keywords are available:

OUTLIERS *Indicates whether outliers should be displayed.* Outliers are values between 1.5 IQR's and 3 IQR's from the end of a box. By default, the boxplot displays outliers (ON).

EXTREME *Indicates whether extreme values should be displayed.* Values more than 3 IQR's from the end of a box are defined as extreme. By default, the boxplot displays extreme values (ON).

MEDIAN *Indicates whether a line representing the median should be included in the box.* By default, the boxplot displays the median line (ON).

LABEL *Displays the number of cases (N) represented by each box.*

BOXBASE *Controls the shape of the box for three dimensional plots.* SQUARE results in rectangular solids. ROUND yields cylinders.

WHISKER *Controls the appearance of the whiskers.* Whiskers can be straight lines (LINE), end in a *T*-shape (T), or end in a fancy *T*-shape (FANCY). Fancy whiskers are unavailable for three-dimensional boxplots.

CAPWIDTH(pct) *Controls the width of the whisker cap relative to the corresponding box.* Pct equals the percentage of the box width. The default value for pct is 45.

Example

```
IGRAPH
 /X1=VAR(region) TYPE=CATEGORICAL
 /Y=VAR(sales96) TYPE=SCALE
 /COORDINATE=HORIZONTAL
 /BOX OUTLIERS=ON EXTREME=ON MEDIAN=ON WHISKER=FANCY.
```

- X1 assigns the variable *region* to the *X1* axis.
- Y assigns the variable *sales96* to the range axis.
- COORDINATE positions the range axis along the horizontal dimension.
- BOX creates a boxplot. The outliers and extreme vales are shown. In addition, a line representing the median is added to the box.
- WHISKER yields whiskers ending in a fancy *T*.

Example

```
IGRAPH
 /X1=VAR(region) TYPE=CATEGORICAL
 /Y=VAR(sales96) TYPE=SCALE
 /X2=VAR(division) TYPE=CATEGORICAL
 /COORDINATE=THREE
 /BOX OUTLIERS=OFF EXTREME=ON MEDIAN=OFF LABEL=N BOXBASE=ROUND WHISKER=T.
```

- X2 adds a third dimension, corresponding to *division*, to the boxplot in the previous example.
- COORDINATE indicates that the chart displays the third dimension.
- BOX creates a boxplot without outliers or a median line. Extreme values are shown.
- LABEL labels each box with the number of cases represented by each box.
- BOXBASE defines the three-dimensional representation of the boxes to be cylindrical.

LINE Subcommand

LINE creates line charts, dot charts, and ribbon charts. These charts summarize categories of one or more variables. Line charts tend to emphasize flow or movement instead of individual values. They are commonly used to display data over time and therefore can be used to give a good sense of trends. A ribbon chart is similar to a line chart, with the lines displayed as ribbons in a third dimension. Ribbon charts can either have two dimensions displayed with a 3-D effect, or they can have three dimensions.

The following keywords are available:

summary function *Defines a function used to summarize the variable defined on the* Y *subcommand.* If the *Y* axis assignment is $COUNT or $PCT, the LINE subcommand cannot have a summary function. If the Y subcommand specifies TYPE=CATEGORICAL, then LINE can specify only MODE as the summary function. Otherwise, all summary functions described on p. 572 are available.

STYLE *Chart can include dots and lines (*DOTLINE*), lines only (*LINE*), or dots only (*DOT*).* The keyword NONE creates an empty chart.

DROPLINE *Indicates whether drop lines between points having the same value of a variable are included in the chart (*ON*) or not (*OFF*).* To include drop lines, specify a categorical variable on the STYLE, COLOR, or SIZE subcommands.

LABEL *Labels points with the actual values corresponding to the dependent axis (*VAL*), the percentage of cases (*PCT*), and the number of cases included in each data point (*N*).* The default is no labels.

LINELABEL *Labels lines with category labels (*CAT*), the percentage of cases (*PCT*), and the number of cases included in each line (*N*).* The default is no labels.

BREAK *Indicates whether the lines break at missing values (*MISSING*) or not (*NONE*).*

The INTERPOLATE keyword determines how the lines connecting the points are drawn. Options include:

STRAIGHT *Straight lines.*

LSTEP *A horizontal line extends from each data point.* A vertical riser connects the line to the next data point.

CSTEP *Each data point is centered on a horizontal line that extends half of the distance between consecutive points.* Vertical risers connect the line to the next horizontal line.

RSTEP *A horizontal line terminates at each data point.* A vertical riser extends from each data point, connecting to the next horizontal line.

LJUMP *A horizontal line extends from each data point.* No vertical risers connect the lines to the points.

RJUMP *A horizontal line terminates at each data point.* No vertical risers connect the points to the next horizontal line.

CJUMP *A horizontal line is centered at each data point, extending half of the distance between consecutive points.* No vertical risers connect the lines.

SPLINE *Connects data points with a cubic spline.*

LAGRANGE3 *Connects data points with third-order Lagrange interpolations, in which a third-order polynomial is fit to the nearest four points.*

LAGRANGE5 *Connects data points with fifth-order Lagrange interpolations, in which a fifth-order polynomial is fit to the nearest six points.*

Example

```
IGRAPH
 /X1=VAR(volume95) TYPE=CATEGORICAL
 /Y=VAR(sales96) TYPE=SCALE
 /COLOR=VAR(volume94) TYPE=CATEGORICAL
 /COORDINATE=VERTICAL
 /LINE (MEAN) STYLE=LINE DROPLINE=ON LABEL VAL
        INTERPOLATE=STRAIGHT BREAK=MISSING.
```

- LINE creates a line chart. The lines represent the mean value of *sales96* for each category of *volume95*.
- The chart contains a line for each category of *volume94*, with droplines connecting the lines at each category of *volume95*.
- LABEL labels the lines with the mean *sales96* value for each category of *volume95*.
- INTERPOLATE specifies that straight lines connect the mean *sales96* values across the *volume95* categories.
- BREAK indicates that the lines will break at any missing values.

ERRORBAR Subcommand

Error bars help you to visualize distributions and dispersion by indicating the variability of the measure being displayed. The mean of a scale variable is plotted for a set of categories, and the length of an error bar on either side of the mean value indicates a confidence interval or a specified number of standard errors or standard deviations. Error bars can extend in one direction or in both directions from the mean. Error bars are sometimes displayed in the same chart with other chart elements, such as bars.

One of the following three keywords indicating the statistic and percentage/multiplier applied to the error bars must be specified:

CI(Pct) *Error bars represent confidence intervals.* Pct indicates the level of confidence and varies from 0 to 100.

SD(sdval) *Error bars represent standard deviations.* Sdval indicates how many standard deviations above and below the mean the error bars extend. Sdval must between 0 and 6.

SE(seval) *Error bars represent standard errors.* Seval indicates how many standard errors above and below the mean the error bars extend. Seval must between 0 and 6.

In addition, the following keywords can be specified:

LABEL *Labels error bars with means (*VAL*) and the number of cases (*N*).*

DIRECTION *Error bars can extend both above and below the mean values (*BOTH*), only above the mean values (*UP*), only below the mean values (*DOWN*), or above for error bars above the baseline and below for error bars below the baseline (*SIGN*).*

CAPSTYLE *For error bars, the style can be* T*-shaped (*T*), no cap (*NONE*), or a cap with end pieces (*FANCY*).* The default style is *T*-shaped.

SYMBOL *Displays the mean marker (*ON*).* For no symbol, specify OFF.

BASELINE val *Defines the value (*val*) above which the error bars extend above the bars and below which the error bars extend below the bars.*

CAPWIDTH(pct) *Controls the width of the cap relative to the distance between categories.* Pct equals the percent of the distance. The default value for pct is 45.

Example

```
IGRAPH
 /X1=VAR(volume94) TYPE=CATEGORICAL
 /Y=VAR(sales96) TYPE=SCALE
 /BAR (MEAN) LABEL INSIDE VAL SHAPE=RECTANGLE BASELINE=0.00
 /ERRORBAR SE(2.0) DIRECTION=BOTH CAPWIDTH (45) CAPSTYLE=FANCY.
```

- BAR creates a bar chart with rectangular bars. The bars represent the mean *sales96* values for the *volume94* categories.
- ERRORBAR adds error bars to the bar chart. The error bars extend two standard errors above and below the mean.

HISTOGRAM Subcommand

HISTOGRAM creates a histogram element in a chart, corresponding to the *X1*, *X2*, and *Y* axis assignments. Horizontal or vertical orientation is specified by the COORDINATE subcommand. A histogram groups the values of a variable into evenly spaced groups (intervals or bins) and plots a count of the number of cases in each group. The count can be expressed as a percentage. Percentages are useful for comparing data sets of different sizes. The count or percentage can also be accumulated across the groups.

- $COUNT or $PCT must be specified on the Y subcommand.

The following keywords are available:

SHAPE *Defines the shape of the histogram.* Currently, the only value for SHAPE is HISTOGRAM.

CUM *Specifies a cumulative histogram.* Counts or percentages are aggregated across the values of the domain variables.

X1INTERVAL *Intervals on the* X1 *axis can be set automatically, or you can specify the number of intervals (1 to 250) along the axis* (NUM) *or the width of an interval* (WIDTH).

X2INTERVAL *Intervals on the* X2 *axis can be set automatically, or you can specify the number of intervals (1 to 250) along the axis* (NUM) *or the width of an interval* (WIDTH).

CURVE *Superimposes a normal curve on a 2-D histogram.* The normal curve has the same mean and variance as the data.

X1START *The starting point along the* X1 *axis.* Indicates the percentage of an interval width above the minimum value along the *X1* axis at which to begin the histogram. The value can range from 0 to 99.

X2START *The starting point along the* X2 *axis.* Indicates the percentage of an interval width above the minimum value along the *X2* axis at which to begin the histogram. The value can range from 0 to 99.

Example

```
IGRAPH
 /X1=VAR(sales96) TYPE=SCALE
 /Y=$count
 /Histogram SHAPE=HISTOGRAM CURVE=ON X1INTERVAL WIDTH=100.
```

- Histogram creates a histogram of *sales96*. The *sales96* intervals are 100 units wide.
- CURVE superimposes a normal curve on the histogram.

FITLINE Subcommand

FITLINE adds a line or surface to a scatterplot to help you discern the relationship shown in the plot. The following general methods are available:

NONE *No line is fit.*

REGRESSION *Fits a straight line (or surface) using ordinary least squares.* Must be followed by the keyword LINEAR.

ORIGIN *Fits a straight line (or surface) through the origin.* Must be followed by the keyword LINEAR.

MEAN *For a 2-D chart, fits a line at the mean of the dependent (Y) variable.* For a 3-D chart, the *Y* mean is shown as a plane.

LLR *Fits a local linear regression curve or surface.* A normal (NORMAL) kernel is the default. With EPANECHNIKOV, the curve is not as smooth as with a normal kernel and is smoother than with a uniform (UNIFORM) kernel. (For more information, see Simonoff, J. S. 1966. *Smoothing methods in statistics.* New York: Springer-Verlag.)

The keyword LINE indicates the number of fit lines. TOTAL fits the line to all of the cases. MEFFECT fits a separate line to the data for each value of a legend variable.

The REGRESSION, ORIGIN, and MEAN methods offer the option of including prediction intervals with the following keyword:

INTERVAL[(cval)] *The intervals are based on the mean* (MEAN) *or on the individual cases* (INDIVIDUAL). Cval indicates the size of the interval and ranges from 50 to 100.

The local linear regression (LLR) smoother offers the following controls for the smoothing process:

BANDWIDTH *Constrains the bandwidth to be constant across subgroups or panels* (CONSTRAINED). The default is unconstrained (FAST).

X1MULTIPLIER *Specifies the bandwidth multiplier for the* X1 *axis.* The bandwidth multiplier changes the amount of data that is included in each calculation of a small part of the smoother. The multiplier can be adjusted to emphasize specific features of the plot that are of interest. Any positive multiplier (including fractions) is allowed. The larger the multiplier, the smoother the curve. The range between 0 and 10 should suffice in most applications.

X2MULTIPLIER *Specifies the bandwidth multiplier for the* X2 *axis.* The bandwidth multiplier changes the amount of data that is included in each calculation of a small part of the smoother. The multiplier can be adjusted to emphasize specific features of the plot that are of interest. Any positive multiplier (including fractions) is allowed. The larger the multiplier, the smoother the curve. The range between 0 and 10 should suffice in most applications.

Example

```
IGRAPH
 /X1=VAR(sales95) TYPE=SCALE
 /Y=VAR(sales96) TYPE=SCALE
 /COLOR=VAR(region) TYPE=CATEGORICAL
 /SCATTER
 /FITLINE METHOD=LLR EPANECHNIKOV BANDWIDTH=CONSTRAINED
        X1MULTIPLIER=2.00 LINE=MEFFECT.
```

- SCATTER creates a scatterplot of *sales95* and *sales96*.
- FITLINE adds a local linear regression smoother to the scatterplot. The Epanechnikov smoother is used with an *X1* multiplier of 2. A separate line is fit for each category of region and the bandwidth is constrained to be equal across region categories.

Summary Functions

Summary functions apply to scale variables selected for a dependent axis or a slice summary. Percentages are based on the specified percent base. For a slice summary, only summary functions appropriate for the type of chart are available.

The following summary functions are available:

First Values (FIRST). The value found in the first case for each category in the data file at the time the summary was defined.

Kurtosis (KURTOSIS). A measure of the extent to which observations cluster around a central point. For a normal distribution, the value of the kurtosis statistic is 0. Positive kurtosis indicates that the observations cluster more and have longer tails than those in the normal distribution, and negative kurtosis indicates the observations cluster less and have shorter tails.

Last Values (LAST). The value found in the last case for each category in the data file at the time the summary was defined.

Maximum Values (MAXIMUM). The largest value for each category.

Minimum Values (MINIMUM). The smallest value within the category.

Means (MEAN). The arithmetic average for each category.

Medians (MEDIAN). The values below which half of the cases fall in each category.

Modes (MODE). The most frequently occurring value within each category.

Number of Cases Above (NGT(x)). The number of cases having values above the specified value.

Number of Cases Between (NIN(x1,x2)). The number of cases between two specified values.

Number of Cases Equal to (NEQ(x)). The number of cases equal to the specified value.

Number of Cases Greater Than or Equal to (NGE(x)). The number of cases having values above or equal to the specified value.

Number of Cases Less Than (NLT(x)). The number of cases below the specified value.

Number of Cases Less Than or Equal to (NLE(x)). The number of cases below or equal to the specified value.

Percentage of Cases Above (PGT(x)). The percentage of cases having values above the specified value.

Percentage of Cases Between (PIN(x1,x2)). The percentage of cases between two specified values.

Percentage of Cases Equal to (PEQ(x)). The percentage of cases equal to the specified value.

Percentage of Cases Greater Than or Equal to (PGE(x)). The percentage of cases having values above or equal to the specified value.

Percentage of Cases Less Than (PLT(x)). The percentage of cases having values below the specified value.

Percentage of Cases Less Than or Equal to (PLE(x)). The percentage of cases having values below or equal to the specified value.

Percentiles (PTILE(x)). The data value below which the specified percentage of values fall within each category.

Skewness (SKEW). A measure of the asymmetry of a distribution. The normal distribution is symmetric and has a skewness value of 0. A distribution with a significant positive skewness has a long right tail. A distribution with a significant negative skewness has a long left tail.

Standard Deviations (STDDEV). A measure of dispersion around the mean, expressed in the same units of measurement as the observations, equal to the square root of the variance. In a normal distribution, 68% of cases fall within one SD of the mean and 95% of cases fall within two SD's.

Standard Errors of Kurtosis (SEKURT). The ratio of kurtosis to its standard error can be used as a test of normality (that is, you can reject normality if the ratio is less than –2 or greater than +2). A large positive value for kurtosis indicates that the tails of the distribution are longer than those of a normal distribution; a negative value for kurtosis indicates shorter tails (becoming like those of a box-shaped uniform distribution).

Standard Errors of the Mean (SEMEAN). A measure of how much the value of the mean may vary from sample to sample taken from the same distribution. It can be used to roughly compare the observed mean to a hypothesized value (that is, you can conclude the two values are different if the ratio of the difference to the standard error is less than –2 or greater than +2).

Standard Errors of Skewness (SESKEW). The ratio of skewness to its standard error can be used as a test of normality (that is, you can reject normality if the ratio is less than –2 or greater than +2). A large positive value for skewness indicates a long right tail; an extreme negative value, a long left tail.

Sums (SUM). The sums of the values within each category.

Sums of Absolute Values (SUMAV). The sums of the absolute values within each category.

Sums of Squares (SUMSQ). The sums of the squares of the values within each category.

Variances (VARIANCE). A measure of how much observations vary from the mean, expressed in squared units.

IMPORT

```
IMPORT FILE=file

 [/TYPE={COMM}]
        {TAPE}

 [/KEEP={ALL**  }] [/DROP=varlist]
        {varlist}

 [/RENAME=(old varnames=new varnames)...]

 [/MAP]
```

**Default if the subcommand is omitted.

Example

```
IMPORT FILE=NEWDATA /RENAME=(V1 TO V3=ID, SEX, AGE) /MAP.
```

Overview

IMPORT reads SPSS-format portable data files created with the EXPORT command. A portable data file is a data file created by the program and used to transport data between different types of computers and operating systems (such as between IBM CMS and Digital VAX/VMS) or between SPSS, SPSS/PC+, or other software using the same portable file format. Like an SPSS-format data file, a portable file contains all of the data and dictionary information stored in the working data file from which it was created.

The program can also read data files created by other software programs. See GET TRANSLATE for information on reading files created by spreadsheet and database programs such as dBASE, Lotus, and Excel.

Options

Format. You can specify the format of the portable file (magnetic tape or communications program) on the TYPE subcommand. For more information on magnetic tapes and communications programs, see "Methods of Transporting Portable Files" on p. 358.

Variables. You can read a subset of variables from the working data file with the DROP and KEEP subcommands. You can rename variables using RENAME. You can also produce a record of all variables and their names in the working file with the MAP subcommand.

Basic Specification

The basic specification is the FILE subcommand with a file specification. All variables from the portable file are copied into the working data file with their original names, variable and value labels, missing-value flags, and print and write formats.

Subcommand Order

- FILE and TYPE must precede all other subcommands.
- No specific order is required between FILE and TYPE or among other subcommands.

Operations

- The portable data file and dictionary become the working data file and dictionary.
- A file saved with weighting in effect (using the WEIGHT command) automatically uses the case weights when the file is read.

Example

```
IMPORT FILE=NEWDATA /RENAME=(V1 TO V3=ID,SEX,AGE) /MAP.
```

- The working data file is generated from the portable file *NEWDATA*.
- Variables *V1, V2,* and *V3* are renamed *ID, SEX,* and *AGE* in the working file. Their names remain *V1, V2,* and *V3* in the portable file. None of the other variables copied into the working file are renamed.
- MAP requests a display of the variables in the working data file.

FILE Subcommand

FILE specifies the portable file. FILE is the only required subcommand on IMPORT.

TYPE Subcommand

TYPE indicates whether the portable file is formatted for magnetic tape or for a communications program. TYPE can specify either COMM or TAPE. For more information on magnetic tapes and communications programs, see EXPORT.

COMM *Communications-formatted file.* This is the default.

TAPE *Tape-formatted file.*

Example

```
IMPORT TYPE=TAPE /FILE=HUBOUT.
```

- The file *HUBOUT* is read as a tape-formatted portable file.

DROP and KEEP Subcommands

DROP and KEEP are used to read a subset of variables from the portable file.

- DROP excludes a variable or list of variables from the working data file. All variables not named are included in the file.
- KEEP includes a variable or list of variables in the working file. All variables not specified on KEEP are excluded.
- DROP and KEEP cannot precede the FILE or TYPE subcommands.
- Variables can be specified in any order. The order of variables on KEEP determines the order of variables in the working file. The order on DROP does not affect the order of variables in the working file.
- If a variable is referred to twice on the same subcommand, only the first mention is recognized.
- Multiple DROP and KEEP subcommands are allowed; the effect is cumulative. Specifying a variable named on a previous DROP or not named on a previous KEEP results in an error and the command is not executed.
- The keyword TO can be used to specify a group of consecutive variables in the portable file.
- The portable file is not affected by DROP or KEEP.

Example

```
IMPORT FILE=NEWSUM /DROP=DEPT TO DIVISION.
```

- The working data file is generated from the portable file *NEWSUM*. Variables between and including *DEPT* and *DIVISION* in the portable file are excluded from the working file.
- All other variables are copied into the working file.

RENAME Subcommand

RENAME renames variables being read from the portable file. The renamed variables retain the variable and value labels, missing-value flags, and print formats contained in the portable file.

- To rename a variable, specify the name of the variable in the portable file, a required equals sign, and the new name.
- A variable list can be specified on both sides of the equals sign. The number of variables on both sides must be the same, and the entire specification must be enclosed in parentheses.
- The keyword TO can be used for both variable lists (see "Keyword TO" on p. 19).
- Any DROP or KEEP subcommand after RENAME must use the new variable names.

Example

```
IMPORT FILE=NEWSUM /DROP=DEPT TO DIVISION
  /RENAME=(NAME,WAGE=LNAME,SALARY).
```

- RENAME renames *NAME* and *WAGE* to *LNAME* and *SALARY*.
- *LNAME* and *SALARY* retain the variable and value labels, missing-value flags, and print formats assigned to *NAME* and *WAGE*.

MAP Subcommand

MAP displays a list of variables in the working data file, showing all changes that have been specified on the RENAME, DROP, or KEEP subcommands.

- MAP can be specified as often as desired.
- MAP confirms only the changes specified on the subcommands that precede the MAP request.
- Results of subcommands that follow MAP are not mapped. When MAP is specified last, it also produces a description of the file.

Example

```
IMPORT FILE=NEWSUM /DROP=DEPT TO DIVISION /MAP
  /RENAME NAME=LNAME WAGE=SALARY /MAP.
```

- The first MAP subcommand produces a listing of the variables in the file after DROP has dropped the specified variables.
- RENAME renames *NAME* and *WAGE*.
- The second MAP subcommand shows the variables in the file after renaming.

INCLUDE

```
INCLUDE FILE=file
```

Example

```
INCLUDE FILE=GSSLABS.
```

Overview

INCLUDE includes a file of commands in a session. INCLUDE is especially useful for including a long series of data definition statements or transformations. Another use for INCLUDE is to set up a library of commonly used commands and include them in the command sequence as they are needed.

INCLUDE allows you to run multiple commands together during a session and can save time. Complex or repetitive commands can be stored in a command file and included in the session, while simpler commands or commands unique to the current analysis can be entered during the session, before and after the included file.

Basic Specification

The only specification is the FILE subcommand, which specifies the file to include. When INCLUDE is executed, the commands in the specified file are processed.

Syntax Rules

- Commands in an included file must begin in column 1, and continuation lines for each command must be indented at least one column.
- A raw data file can be used as an include file if the first line of the included file contains the BEGIN DATA command and the last line contains the END DATA command. However, because the data are specified between BEGIN DATA and END DATA, they are limited to a maximum of 80 columns (the maximum may be fewer than 80 columns on some systems).
- As many INCLUDE commands as needed can be used in a session.
- INCLUDE commands can be nested so that one set of included commands includes another set of commands. This nesting can go to five levels. However, a file cannot be included that is still open from a previous step.

Operations

- If an included file contains a FINISH command, the session ends and no further commands are processed.

- If a journal file is created for the session, INCLUDE is copied to the journal file. Commands from the included file are also copied to the journal file but are treated like printed messages. Thus, INCLUDE can be executed from the journal file if the journal file is later used as a command file. Commands from the included file are executed only once.

FILE Subcommand

FILE identifies the file containing commands. FILE is the only specification on INCLUDE and is required.

Example

```
INCLUDE FILE=GSSLABS.
```

- INCLUDE includes the file *GSSLABS* in the prompted session. When INCLUDE is executed, the commands in *GSSLABS* are processed.
- Assume that the include file *GSSLABS* contains the following:

```
DATA LIST FILE=DATA52
  /RELIGION 5 OCCUPAT 7 SES 12 ETHNIC 15
   PARTY 19 VOTE48 33 VOTE52 41.
```

The working data file will be defined and ready for analysis after INCLUDE is executed.

INFO

This command is not available on all operating systems.

```
INFO [OUTFILE = file]
     [OVERVIEW]
     [LOCAL]
     [ERRORS]
     [FACILITIES]
     [PROCEDURES]
     [ALL]
     [procedure name] [/procedure name...]
     [SINCE release number]
```

Example

```
INFO LOCAL.
```

Overview

INFO makes available two kinds of online documentation: local and update.

Local Documentation

Local documentation concerns the environment in which the program is run. It includes some or all of the following, depending on the operating system:

- Commands or job control language for running the program.
- Conventions for referring to files. These include instructions on how your computer's operating system accesses or creates a particular file.
- Conventions for handling tapes and other input/output devices.
- Data formats. The formats the program reads and writes may differ from one computer and operating system to another.
- Default values for parameters controlled by the SET command. Many defaults for these parameters are set at the individual installation. The SHOW command displays the values that are currently in effect. Local documentation may contain information on why one setting is preferred over another.
- Information about your computer and operating system or your individual installation.

Update Documentation

Update documentation includes changes to existing procedures and facilities made after publication of this manual, new procedures and facilities, and corrections to this manual. Update documentation can be requested for all available releases, or for releases after a particular release.

Basic Specification

- The minimum specification is the command name. When specified by itself, the program displays an overview of available documents.

Syntax Rules

- Multiple keywords and/or procedure names can be specified on a single INFO command.
- Multiple procedure names must be separated by slashes.
- The order of specifications is unimportant and does not affect the order in which the documentation is printed.
- Three- or four-character truncation does *not* apply to INFO command specifications. Spell all keywords in full. For procedure names, spell the first word in full and subsequent words through at least the first three characters.

Operations

- By default, the INFO command produces update information only for the current release. Documentation for earlier releases may also be available; read the INFO overview to find out whether it is available on your system.
- If overlapping sets of information are requested, only one copy is printed.
- If there is no available documentation for the requested information, only a copyright page is printed.
- If information is requested for an unrecognized topic, the program prints an error message.
- The characteristics of the output produced by the INFO command may vary by computer type. As implemented at SPSS Inc., the output includes carriage control, with the maximum length of a page determined by the LENGTH subcommand on SET. A printer width of 132 characters is assumed for some examples, although the text is generally much narrower.
- The program requires more computer resources than most printing utilities. Your installation may therefore provide an alternative method for printing INFO documentation. In this case, the INFO command may simply provide instructions for using the alternative method.

Example

```
INFO  OVERVIEW FACILITIES FREQUENCIES / CROSSTABS.
```

- INFO produces an overview and documentation for any changes made to system facilities and to the FREQUENCIES and CROSSTABS procedures.
- Because the keyword SINCE is not specified, INFO prints only documentation for the current release.

Types of Information

The following types of information can be requested on INFO:

OVERVIEW *Overview of available documentation.* This includes a table of contents for the documentation available with INFO, along with information about SPSS manuals.

LOCAL *Local documentation.* See "Local Documentation" on p. 580.

ERRORS *List of known unfixed errors.* This lists the known unfixed errors in the current release of the program. Since ERRORS applies only to the current release, the SINCE keyword (described below) has no effect with ERRORS.

FACILITIES *Update information for system facilities.* This covers all differences, except in procedures, between the system as documented in this manual and the system as installed on your computer—whether those differences result from updates to the system, revisions required for conversions to particular operating systems, or errors in this manual. Only updates for the most current release are printed unless keyword SINCE is specified.

PROCEDURES *Update information for procedures.* This includes full documentation for procedures new in the current release and update information for procedures that existed prior to the current release.

PROCEDURE *Documentation for the procedure named.* This is the same information as that printed by the PROCEDURES keyword, but limited to the procedure named. You can specify multiple procedures, separating each from the other with a slash.

ALL *All available documentation.* ALL includes OVERVIEW, LOCAL, ERRORS, FACILITIES, and PROCEDURES.

SINCE Keyword

Releases of SPSS are numbered by integers, with decimal digits indicating maintenance releases between major releases. The release number appears in the default heading for SPSS output. Each SPSS manual is identified in the preface by the number of the release it documents.

The keyword SINCE obtains information for earlier releases or limits the information to maintenance releases since the last major release.

- The minimum specification is the keyword SINCE followed by a release number.
- SINCE is not inclusive. Specifying 3.0 does not include changes made to the system in release 3.0.
- To identify a maintenance release, enter the exact number, with decimal, as in 3.1.
- Information for some earlier releases may not be available. For example, information for release 2.2 and earlier is not available if INFO is run with SPSS release 5.0 or later.

Example

```
INFO  OVERVIEW FACILITIES FREQUENCIES / CROSSTABS SINCE 3.
```

- INFO prints documentation for all changes to system facilities and to procedures FREQUENCIES and CROSSTABS since release 3.0.

OUTFILE Subcommand

By default, the information generated by INFO is part of the output. OUTFILE sends INFO output to a separate file.

Example

```
INFO OUTFILE=SPSSDOC ALL SINCE 3.
```

- INFO creates a text file that includes an overview, local documentation, error, and update information for facilities and procedures since release 3.0.
- The OUTFILE subcommand sends the documentation to the file *SPSSDOC*.

INPUT PROGRAM—END INPUT PROGRAM

```
INPUT PROGRAM

commands to create or define cases

END INPUT PROGRAM
```

Example

```
INPUT PROGRAM.
DATA LIST FILE=PRICES /YEAR 1-4 QUARTER 6 PRICE 8-12(2).

DO IF (YEAR GE 1881).    /*Stop reading before 1881
END FILE.
END IF.
END INPUT PROGRAM.
```

Overview

The INPUT PROGRAM and END INPUT PROGRAM commands enclose data definition and transformation commands that build cases from input records. The input program often encloses one or more DO IF—END IF or LOOP—END LOOP structures, and it must include at least one file definition command, such as DATA LIST. One of the following utility commands is also usually used:

END CASE *Build cases from the commands within the input program and pass the cases to the commands immediately following the input program.*

END FILE *Terminate processing of a data file before the actual end of the file or define the end of the file when the input program is used to read raw data.*

REREAD *Reread the current record using a different* DATA LIST.

REPEATING DATA *Read repeating groups of data from the same input record.*

For more information on the commands used in an input program, see the discussion of each command.

Input programs create a dictionary and data for a working file from raw data files; they cannot be used to read SPSS-format data files. They can be used to process direct-access and keyed data files. For details, see KEYED DATA LIST.

Input Programs

The program builds the working data file dictionary when it encounters commands that create and define variables. At the same time, the program builds an *input program* that constructs cases and an optional *transformation program* that modifies cases prior to analysis or display. By the time the program encounters a procedure command that tells it to read the data, the working file dictionary is ready, and the programs that construct and modify the cases in the working file are built.

The internal input program is usually built from either a single DATA LIST command or from any of the commands that read or combine SPSS-format data files (for example, GET, ADD FILES, MATCH FILES, UPDATE, and so on). The input program can also be built from the FILE TYPE—END FILE TYPE structure used to define nested, mixed, or grouped files. The third type of input program is specified with the INPUT PROGRAM—END INPUT PROGRAM commands.

With INPUT PROGRAM—END INPUT PROGRAM, you can create your own input program to perform many different operations on raw data. You can use transformation commands to build cases. You can read nonrectangular files, concatenate raw data files, and build cases selectively. You can also create a working data file without reading any data at all.

Input State

There are four program states in the program: the *initial state,* in which there is no working file dictionary; the *input state,* in which cases are created from the input file; the *transformation state,* in which cases are transformed; and the *procedure state,* in which procedures are executed. When you specify INPUT PROGRAM—END INPUT PROGRAM, you must pay attention to which commands are allowed within the input state, which commands can appear only within the input state, and which are not allowed within the input state. See Appendix A for a discussion of program states, command order, and a table that describes what happens to each command when it is encountered in each of the four states.

Basic Specification

The basic specification is INPUT PROGRAM, the commands used to create cases and define the working data file, and END INPUT PROGRAM.

- INPUT PROGRAM and END INPUT PROGRAM each must be specified on a separate line and have no additional specifications.
- To define a working data file, the input program must include at least one DATA LIST or END FILE command.

Operations

- The INPUT PROGRAM—END INPUT PROGRAM structure defines a working data file and is not executed until the program encounters a procedure or the EXECUTE command.
- INPUT PROGRAM clears the current working data file.

Example

```
* Select cases with an input program.

INPUT PROGRAM.
DATA LIST FILE=PRICES /YEAR 1-4 QUARTER 6 PRICE 8-12(2).

DO IF (YEAR GE 1881).   /*Stop reading when reaching 1881
END FILE.
END IF.
END INPUT PROGRAM.

LIST.
```

- The input program is defined between the INPUT PROGRAM and END INPUT PROGRAM commands.
- This example assumes that data records are entered chronologically by year. The DO IF—END IF structure specifies an end of file when the first case with a value of 1881 or later for *YEAR* is reached.
- LIST executes the input program and lists cases in the working data file. The case that causes the end of the file is not included in the working file generated by the input program.
- As an alternative to this input program, you can use N OF CASES to select cases if you know the exact number of cases. Another alternative is to use SELECT IF to select cases before 1881, but then the program would unnecessarily read the entire input file.

Example

```
* Skip the first n records in a file.

INPUT PROGRAM.
NUMERIC        #INIT.
DO IF          NOT (#INIT).
+  LOOP           #I = 1 TO 5.
+     DATA LIST      NOTABLE/.    /* No data - just skip record
+  END LOOP.
+  COMPUTE        #INIT = 1.
END IF.
DATA LIST      NOTABLE/ X 1.
END INPUT PROGRAM.

BEGIN DATA
A                            /* The first 5 records are skipped
B
C
D
E
1
2
3
4
5
END DATA.
LIST.
```

- NUMERIC declares the scratch variable *#INIT*, which is initialized to system-missing.
- The DO IF structure is executed as long as *#INIT* does not equal 1.
- LOOP is executed five times. Within the loop, DATA LIST is specified without variable names, causing the program to read records in the data file without copying them into the working file. LOOP is executed five times, so the program reads five records in this manner. END LOOP terminates this loop.
- COMPUTE creates the scratch variable *#INIT* and sets it equal to 1. The DO IF structure is therefore not executed again.
- END IF terminates the DO IF structure.
- The second DATA LIST specifies numeric variable *X*, which is located in column 1 of each record. Because the program has already read five records, the first value for *X* that is copied into the working file is read from record 6.

More Examples

For additional examples of input programs, refer to DATA LIST (p. 252), DO IF (p. 327), DO REPEAT (p. 330), END CASE, END FILE, LOOP, NUMERIC (p. 219), POINT (p. 266), REPEATING DATA, REREAD, and VECTOR (p. 631).

KEYED DATA LIST

```
KEYED DATA LIST KEY=varname IN=varname

 FILE=file [{TABLE   }]
           {NOTABLE}

 /varname {col location [(format)]} [varname ..]
          {(FORTRAN-like format)   }
```

Example

```
FILE HANDLE EMPL/ file specifications.
KEYED DATA LIST FILE=EMPL KEY=#NXTCASE IN=#FOUND
          /YRHIRED 1-2 SEX 3 JOBCLASS 4.
```

Overview

KEYED DATA LIST reads raw data from two types of nonsequential files: direct-access files, which provide direct access by a record number, and keyed files, which provide access by a record key. An example of a direct-access file is a file of 50 records, each corresponding to one of the United States. If you know the relationship between the states and the record numbers, you can retrieve the data for any specific state. An example of a keyed file is a file containing social security numbers and other information about a firm's employees. The social security number can be used to identify the records in the file.

Direct-Access Files

There are various types of direct-access files. This program's concept of a direct-access file, however, is very specific. The file must be one from which individual records can be selected according to their number. The records in a 100-record direct-access file, for example, are numbered from 1 to 100.

Although the concept of record number applies to almost any file, not all files can be treated by this program as direct-access files. In fact, some operating systems provide no direct-access capabilities at all, and others permit only a narrowly defined subset of all files to be treated as direct access.

Very few files turn out to be good candidates for direct-access organization. In the case of an inventory file, for example, the usual large gaps in the part numbering sequence would result in large amounts of wasted file space. Gaps are not a problem, however, if they are predictable. For example, if you recognize that telephone area codes have first digits of 2 through 9, second digits of 0 or 1, and third digits of 0 through 9, you can transform an area code into a record number by using the following COMPUTE statement:

```
COMPUTE RECNUM = 20*(DIGIT1-2) + 10*DIGIT2 + DIGIT3 + 1.
```

where *DIGIT1*, *DIGIT2*, and *DIGIT3* are variables corresponding to the respective digits in the area code, and *RECNUM* is the resulting record number. The record numbers would range from 1, for the non-existent area code 200, through 160, for area code 919. The file would then have a manageable number of unused records.

Keyed Files

Of the many kinds of keyed files, the ones to which the program can provide access are generally known as *indexed sequential files.* A file of this kind is basically a sequential file in which an index is maintained so that the file can be processed either sequentially or selectively. In effect, there is an underlying data file that is accessed through a file of index entries. The file of index entries may, for example, contain the fact that data record 797 is associated with social security number 476-77-1359. Depending on the implementation, the underlying data may or may not be maintained in sequential order.

The key for each record in the file generally comprises one or more pieces of information found within the record. An example of a complex key is a customer's last name and house number, plus the consonants in the street name, plus the zip code, plus a unique digit in case there are duplicates. Regardless of the information contained in the key, the program treats it as a character string.

On some systems, more than one key is associated with each record. That is, the records in a file can be identified according to different types of information. Although the primary key for a file normally must be unique, sometimes the secondary keys need not be. For example, the records in an employee file might be identified by social security number and job classification.

Options

Data Source. You can specify the name of the keyed file on the FILE subcommand. By default, the last file that was specified on an input command, such as DATA LIST or REPEATING DATA, is read.

Summary Table. You can display a table that summarizes the variable definitions.

Basic Specification

- The basic specification requires FILE, KEY, and IN, each of which specifies one variable, followed by a slash and variable definitions.
- FILE specifies the direct-access or keyed file. The file must have a file handle already defined.
- KEY specifies the variable whose value will be used to read a record. For direct-access files, the variable must be numeric; for keyed files, it must be string.
- IN creates a logical variable that flags whether a record was successfully read.
- Variable definitions follow all subcommands; the slash preceding them is required. Variable definitions are similar to those specified on DATA LIST.

Subcommand Order

- Subcommands can be named in any order.
- Variable definitions must follow all specified subcommands.

Syntax Rules

- Specifications for the variable definitions are the same as those described for DATA LIST. The only difference is that only one record can be defined per case.
- The FILE HANDLE command must be used if the FILE subcommand is specified on KEYED DATA LIST.
- KEYED DATA LIST can be specified in an input program, or it can be used as a transformation language to change an existing working data file. This differs from all other input commands, such as GET and DATA LIST, which create new working files.

Operations

- Variable names are stored in the working file dictionary.
- Formats are stored in the working file dictionary and are used to display and write the values. To change output formats of numeric variables, use the FORMATS command.

Example

```
FILE HANDLE EMPL/ file specifications.
KEYED DATA LIST FILE=EMPL KEY=#NXTCASE IN=#FOUND
          /YRHIRED 1-2 SEX 3 JOBCLASS 4.
```

- FILE HANDLE defines the handle for the data file to be read by KEYED DATA LIST. The handle is specified on the FILE subcommand of KEYED DATA LIST.
- KEY on KEYED DATA LIST specifies the variable to be used as the access key. For a direct-access file, the value of the variable must be between 1 and the number of records in the file. For a keyed file, the value must be a string.
- IN creates the logical scratch variable *#FOUND*, whose value will be 1 if the record is successfully read, or 0 if the record is not found.
- The variable definitions are the same as those used for DATA LIST.

Example

```
* Reading a direct-access file: sampling 1 out of every 25 records.

FILE HANDLE     EMPL/ file specifications.
INPUT PROGRAM.
COMPUTE #INTRVL = TRUNC(UNIF(48))+1.  /* Mean interval = 25
COMPUTE #NXTCASE = #NXTCASE+#INTRVL.  /* Next record number
COMPUTE #EOF = #NXTCASE > 1000.       /* End of file check
DO IF   #EOF.
+  END FILE.
ELSE.
+  KEYED DATA LIST  FILE=EMPL, KEY=#NXTCASE, IN=#FOUND, NOTABLE
                   /YRHIRED 1-2 SEX 3 JOBCLASS 4.
+  DO IF       #FOUND.
+     END CASE.                      /* Return a case
+  ELSE.
+     PRINT / 'Oops. #NXTCASE=' #NXTCASE.
+  END IF.
END IF.
END INPUT PROGRAM.
EXECUTE.
```

- FILE HANDLE defines the handle for the data file to be read by the KEYED DATA LIST command. The record numbers for this example are generated by the transformation language; they are not based on data taken from another file.
- The INPUT PROGRAM and END INPUT PROGRAM commands begin and end the block of commands that build cases from the input file. Since the session generates cases, an input program is required.
- The first two COMPUTE statements determine the number of the next record to be selected. This is done in two steps. First, the integer portion is taken from the sum of 1 and a uniform pseudo-random number between 1 and 49. The result is a mean interval of 25. Second, the variable *#NXTCASE* is added to this number to generate the next record number. This record number, *#NXTCASE*, will be used for the key variable on the KEYED DATA LIST command. The third COMPUTE creates a logical scratch variable, *#EOF*, that has a value of 0 if the record number is less than or equal to 1000, or 1 if the value of the record number is greater than 1000.
- The DO IF—END IF structure controls the building of cases. If the record number is greater than 1000, *#EOF* equals 1, and the END FILE command tells the program to stop reading data and end the file.
- If the record number is less than or equal to 1000, the record is read via KEYED DATA LIST using the value of *#NXTCASE*. A case is generated if the record exists (*#FOUND* equals 1). If not, the program displays the record number and continues to the next case. The sample will have about 40 records.
- EXECUTE causes the transformations to be executed.
- This example illustrates the difference between DATA LIST, which always reads the next record in a file, and KEYED DATA LIST, which reads only specified records. The record numbers must be generated by another command or be contained in the working data file.

Example

```
* Reading a keyed file: reading selected records.

GET FILE=STUDENTS/KEEP=AGE,SEX,COURSE.
FILE HANDLE COURSES/ file specifications.
STRING #KEY(A4).
COMPUTE #KEY = STRING(COURSE,N4). /* Create a string key
KEYED DATA LIST FILE=COURSES KEY=#KEY IN=#FOUND NOTABLE
     /PERIOD 13 CREDITS 16.
SELECT IF #FOUND.
LIST.
```

- GET reads the *STUDENTS* file, which contains information on students, including a course identification for each student. The course identification will be used as the key for selecting one record from a file of courses.
- The FILE HANDLE command defines a file handle for the file of courses.
- The STRING and COMPUTE commands transform the course identification from numeric to string for use as a key. For keyed files, the key variable must be a string.
- KEYED DATA LIST uses the value of the newly created string variable *#KEY* as the key to search the course file. If a record that matches the value of *#KEY* is found, *#FOUND* is set to 1; otherwise, it is set to 0. Note that KEYED DATA LIST appears outside an input program in this example.
- If the course file contains the requested record, *#FOUND* equals 1. The variables *PERIOD* and *CREDITS* are added to the case and the case is selected via the SELECT IF command; otherwise, the case is dropped.
- LIST lists the values of the selected cases.
- This example shows how existing cases can be updated on the basis of information read from a keyed file.
- This task could also be accomplished by reading the entire course file with DATA LIST and combining it with the student file via the MATCH FILES command. The technique you should use depends on the percentage of the records in the course file that need to be accessed. If fewer than 10% of the course file records are read, KEYED DATA LIST is probably more efficient. As the percentage of the records that are read increases, reading the entire course file and using MATCH makes more sense.

FILE Subcommand

FILE specifies the handle for the direct-access or keyed data file. The file handle must have been defined on a previous FILE HANDLE command (or, in the case of the IBM OS environment, on a DD statement in the JCL).

KEY Subcommand

KEY specifies the variable whose value will be used as the key. This variable must already exist as the result of a prior DATA LIST, KEYED DATA LIST, GET, or transformation command.

- KEY is required. Its only specification is a single variable. The variable can be a permanent variable or a scratch variable.
- For direct-access files, the key variable must be numeric, and its value must be between 1 and the number of records in the file.
- For keyed files, the key variable must be string. If the keys are numbers, such as social security numbers, the STRING function can be used to convert the numbers to strings. For example, the following might be required to get the value of a numeric key into exactly the same format as used on the keyed file:

```
COMPUTE #KEY=STRING(123,IB4).
```

IN Subcommand

IN creates a numeric variable whose value indicates whether or not the specified record is found.

- IN is required. Its only specification is a single numeric variable. The variable can be a permanent variable or a scratch variable.
- The value of the variable is 1 if the record is successfully read or 0 if the record is not found. The IN variable can be used to select all cases that have been updated by KEYED DATA LIST.

Example

```
FILE HANDLE EMPL/ file specifications.
KEYED DATA LIST FILE=EMPL KEY=#NXTCASE IN=#FOUND
          /YRHIRED 1-2 SEX 3 JOBCLASS 4.
```

- IN creates the logical scratch variable *#FOUND*. The values of *#FOUND* will be 1 if the record indicated by the key value in *#NXTCASE* is found or 0 if the record does not exist.

TABLE and NOTABLE Subcommands

TABLE and NOTABLE determine whether the program displays a table that summarizes the variable definitions. TABLE, the default, displays the table. NOTABLE suppresses the table.

- TABLE and NOTABLE are optional and mutually exclusive.
- The only specification for TABLE or NOTABLE is the subcommand keyword. Neither subcommand has additional specifications.

KM

KM is available in the Advanced Models option.

```
KM varname [BY factor varname]

   /STATUS = varname [EVENT](vallist)  [LOST(vallist)]

   [/STRATA = varname]

   [/PLOT = {NONE**                              }]
            {[SURVIVAL][LOGSURV][HAZARD][OMS]}

   [/ID  = varname]

   [/PRINT = [TABLE**][MEAN**][NONE]]

   [/PERCENTILE = [(]{25, 50, 75 }[)]]
                     {value list }

   [/TEST = [LOGRANK**][BRESLOW][TARONE]]

   [/COMPARE = [{OVERALL**}][{POOLED**}]]
                {PAIRWISE }  {STRATA  }

   [/TREND = [(METRIC)]]

   [/SAVE = tempvar[(newvar)],...]
```

**Default if subcommand or keyword is omitted.

Temporary variables created by Kaplan-Meier are:

SURVIVAL
HAZARD
SE
CUMEVENT

Example

```
KM LENGTH BY SEXRACE
 /STATUS=EMPLOY  EVENT (1) LOST (2)
 /STRATA=LOCATION.
```

Overview

KM (alias K-M) uses the Kaplan-Meier (product-limit) technique to describe and analyze the length of time to the occurrence of an event, often known as **survival time**. KM is similar to SURVIVAL in that it produces nonparametric estimates of the survival functions. However, instead of dividing the period of time under examination into arbitrary intervals, KM evaluates the survival function at the observed event times. For analysis of survival times with covariates, including time-dependent covariates, see the COXREG command.

Options

KM Tables. You can include one factor variable on the KM command. A KM table is produced for each level of the factor variable. You can also suppress the KM tables in the output with the PRINT subcommand.

Survival Status. You can specify the code(s) indicating that an event has occurred as well as code(s) for cases lost to follow-up using the STATUS subcommand.

Plots. You can plot the survival functions on a linear or log scale or plot the hazard function for each combination of factor and stratum with the PLOT subcommand.

Test Statistics. When a factor variable is specified, you can specify one or more tests of equality of survival distributions for the different levels of the factor using the TEST subcommand. You can also specify a trend metric for the requested tests with the TREND subcommand.

Display ID and Percentiles. You can specify an ID variable on the ID subcommand to identify each case. You can also request display of percentiles in the output with the PERCENTILES subcommand.

Comparisons. When a factor variable is specified, you can use the COMPARE subcommand to compare the different levels of the factor, either pairwise or across all levels, and either pooled across all strata or within a stratum.

Add New Variables to Working Data File. You can save new variables appended to the end of the working data file with the SAVE subcommand.

Basic Specification

- The basic specification requires a survival variable and the STATUS subcommand naming a variable that indicates whether the event occurred.
- The basic specification prints one survival table followed by the mean and median survival time with standard errors and 95% confidence intervals.

Subcommand Order

- The survival variable and the factor variable (if there is one) must be specified first.
- Remaining subcommands can be specified in any order.

Syntax Rules

- Only one survival variable can be specified. To analyze multiple survival variables, use multiple KM commands.
- Only one factor variable can be specified following the BY keyword. If you have multiple factors, use the transformation language to create a single factor variable before invoking KM.

- Only one status variable can be listed on the STATUS subcommand. You must specify the value(s) indicating that the event occurred.
- Only one variable can be specified on the STRATA subcommand. If you have more than one stratum, use the transformation language to create a single variable to specify on the STRATA subcommand.

Operations

- KM deletes all cases that have negative values for the survival variable.
- KM estimates the survival function and associated statistics for each combination of factor and stratum.
- Three statistics can be computed to test the equality of survival functions across factor levels within a stratum or across all factor levels while controlling for strata. The statistics are the log rank (Mantel-Cox), the generalized Wilcoxon (Breslow), and the Tarone-Ware tests.
- When the PLOTS subcommand is specified, KM produces one plot of survival functions for each stratum, with all factor levels represented by different symbols or colors.

Limitations

- Maximum 35 factor levels (symbols) can appear in a plot.

Example

```
KM LENGTH BY SEXRACE
 /STATUS=EMPLOY EVENT (1) LOST (2)
 /STRATA=LOCATION.
```

- Survival analysis is used to examine the length of unemployment. The survival variable *LENGTH* contains the number of months a subject is unemployed. The factor variable *SEXRACE* combines sex and race factors.
- A value of 1 on the variable *EMPLOY* indicates the occurrence of the event (employment). All other observed cases are censored. A value of 2 on *EMPLOY* indicates cases lost to follow-up. Cases with other values for *EMPLOY* are known to have remained unemployed during the course of the study. KM separates the two types of censored cases in the KM table if LOST is specified.
- For each combination of *SEXRACE* and *LOCATION*, one KM table is produced, followed by the mean and median survival time with standard errors and confidence intervals.

Survival and Factor Variables

You must identify the survival and factor variables for the analysis.

- The minimum specification is one, and only one, survival variable.
- Only one factor variable can be specified using the BY keyword. If you have more than one factor, create a new variable combining all factors. There is no limit to the factor levels.

Example

```
DO IF SEX = 1.
+ COMPUTE SEXRACE = RACE.
ELSE.
+ COMPUTE SEXRACE = RACE + SEX.
END IF.
KM LENGTH BY SEXRACE
 /STATUS=EMPLOY EVENT (1) LOST (2).
```

- The two control variables, *SEX* and *RACE*, each with two values, 1 and 2, are combined into one factor variable, *SEXRACE*, with four values, 1 to 4.
- KM specifies *LENGTH* as the survival variable and *SEXRACE* as the factor variable.
- One KM table is produced for each factor level.

STATUS Subcommand

To determine whether the terminal event has occurred for a particular observation, KM checks the value of a status variable. STATUS lists the status variable and the code(s) for the occurrence of the event. The code(s) for cases lost to follow-up can also be specified.

- Only one status variable can be specified. If multiple STATUS subcommands are specified, KM uses the last specification and displays a warning.
- The keyword EVENT is optional, but the value list in parentheses must be specified. Use EVENT for clarity's sake, especially when LOST is specified.
- The value list must be enclosed in parentheses. All cases with non-negative times that do not have a code within the range specified after EVENT are classified as **censored cases**—that is, cases for which the event has not yet occurred.
- The keyword LOST and the following value list are optional. LOST cannot be omitted if the value list for lost cases is specified.
- When LOST is specified, all cases with non-negative times that have a code within the specified value range are classified as lost to follow-up. Cases lost to follow-up are treated as censored in the analysis, and the statistics do not change, but the two types of censored cases are listed separately in the KM table.
- The value lists on EVENT or LOST can be one value, a list of values separated by blanks or commas, a range of values using the keyword THRU, or a combination.
- The status variable can be either numeric or string. If a string variable is specified, the EVENT or LOST values must be enclosed in apostrophes, and the keyword THRU cannot be used.

Example

```
KM LENGTH BY SEXRACE
 /STATUS=EMPLOY  EVENT (1) LOST (3,5 THRU 8).
```

- STATUS specifies that *EMPLOY* is the status variable.
- A value of 1 for *EMPLOY* means that the event (employment) occurred for the case.
- Values of 3 and 5 through 8 for *EMPLOY* mean that contact was lost with the case. The different values code different causes for the loss of contact.
- The summary table in the output includes columns for number lost and percentage lost, as well as for number censored and percentage censored.

STRATA Subcommand

STRATA identifies a **stratification variable**—that is, a variable whose values are used to form subgroups (strata) within the categories of the factor variable. Analysis is done within each level of the strata variable for each factor level, and estimates are pooled over strata for an overall comparison of factor levels.

- The minimum specification is the subcommand keyword with one, and only one, variable name.
- If you have more than one strata variable, create a new variable to combine the levels on separate variables before invoking the KM command.
- There is no limit to the number of levels for the strata variable.

Example

```
KM LENGTH BY SEXRACE
 /STATUS=EMPLOY EVENT (1) LOST (3,5 THRU 8)
 /STRATA=LOCATION.
```

- STRATA specifies *LOCATION* as the stratification variable. Analysis of the length of unemployment is done for each location within each sex and race subgroup.

PLOT Subcommand

PLOT plots the cumulative survival distribution on a linear or logarithmic scale or plots the cumulative hazard function. A separate plot with all factor levels is produced for each stratum. Each factor level is represented by a different symbol or color. Censored cases are indicated by markers.

- When PLOT is omitted, no plots are produced. The default is NONE.
- When PLOT is specified without a keyword, the default is SURVIVAL. A plot of survival functions for each stratum is produced.
- To request specific plots, specify, following the PLOT subcommand, any combination of the keywords defined below.
- Multiple keywords can be used on the PLOT subcommand, each requesting a different plot. The effect is cumulative.

NONE *Suppress all plots.* NONE is the default if PLOT is omitted.

SURVIVAL *Plot the cumulative survival distribution on a linear scale.* SURVIVAL is the default when PLOT is specified without a keyword.

LOGSURV *Plot the cumulative survival distribution on a logarithmic scale.*

HAZARD *Plot the cumulative hazard function.*

OMS *Plot the one-minus-survival function.*

Example

```
KM LENGTH BY SEXRACE
 /STATUS=EMPLOY EVENT (1) LOST (3,5 THRU 8)
 /STRATA=LOCATION
 /PLOT = SURVIVAL HAZARD.
```

- PLOT produces one plot of the cumulative survival distribution on a linear scale and one plot of the cumulative hazard rate for each value of *LOCATION*.

ID Subcommand

ID specifies a variable used for labeling cases. If the ID variable is a string, KM uses the string values as case identifiers in the KM table. If the ID variable is numeric, KM uses value labels or numeric values if value labels are not defined.

- ID is the first column of the KM table displayed for each combination of factor and stratum.
- If a string value or a value label exceeds 20 characters in width, KM truncates the case identifier and displays a warning.

PRINT Subcommand

By default, KM prints survival tables and the mean and median survival time with standard errors and confidence intervals if PRINT is omitted. If PRINT is specified, only the specified keyword is in effect. Use PRINT to suppress tables or the mean statistics.

TABLE *Print the KM tables.* If PRINT is not specified, TABLE, together with MEAN, is the default. Specify TABLE on PRINT to suppress the mean statistics.

MEAN *Print the mean statistics.* KM prints the mean and median survival time with standard errors and confidence intervals. If PRINT is not specified, MEAN, together with TABLE, is the default. Specify MEAN on PRINT to suppress the KM tables.

NONE *Suppress both the KM tables and the mean statistics.* Only plots and comparisons are printed.

Example

```
KM LENGTH BY SEXRACE
 /STATUS=EMPLOY EVENT (1) LOST (3,5 THRU 8)
 /STRATA=LOCATION
 /PLOT=SURVIVAL HAZARD
 /PRINT=NONE.
```

- PRINT=NONE suppresses both the KM tables and the mean statistics.

PERCENTILES Subcommand

PERCENTILES displays percentiles for each combination of factor and stratum. Percentiles are not displayed without the PERCENTILES subcommand. If the subcommand is specified without a value list, the default is 25, 50, and 75 for quartile display. You can specify any values between 0 and 100.

TEST Subcommand

TEST specifies the test statistic to use for testing the equality of survival distributions for the different levels of the factor.

- TEST is valid only when a factor variable is specified. If no factor variable is specified, KM issues a warning and TEST is not executed.
- If TEST is specified without a keyword, the default is LOGRANK. If a keyword is specified on TEST, only the specified test is performed.
- Each of the test statistics has a chi-square distribution with one degree of freedom.

LOGRANK *Perform the log rank (Mantel-Cox) test.*

BRESLOW *Perform the Breslow (generalized Wilcoxon) test.*

TARONE *Perform the Tarone-Ware test.*

COMPARE Subcommand

COMPARE compares the survival distributions for the different levels of the factor. Each of the keywords specifies a different method of comparison.

- COMPARE is valid only when a factor variable is specified. If no factor variable is specified, KM issues a warning and COMPARE is not executed.
- COMPARE uses whatever tests are specified on the TEST subcommand. If no TEST subcommand is specified, the log rank test is used.
- If COMPARE is not specified, the default is OVERALL and POOLED. All factor levels are compared across strata in a single test. The test statistics are displayed after the summary table at the end of output.
- Multiple COMPARE subcommands can be specified to request different comparisons.

OVERALL *Compare all factor levels in a single test.* OVERALL, together with POOLED, is the default when COMPARE is not specified.

PAIRWISE *Compare each pair of factor levels.* KM compares all distinct pairs of factor levels.

POOLED *Pool the test statistics across all strata.* The test statistics are displayed after the summary table for all strata. POOLED, together with OVERALL, is the default when COMPARE is not specified.

STRATA *Compare the factor levels for each stratum.* The test statistics are displayed for each stratum separately.

- If a factor variable has different levels across strata, you cannot request a pooled comparison. If you specify POOLED on COMPARE, KM displays a warning and ignores the request.

Example

```
KM LENGTH BY SEXRACE
 /STATUS=EMPLOY EVENT (1) LOST (3,5 THRU 8)
 /STRATA=LOCATION
 /TEST = BRESLOW
 /COMPARE = PAIRWISE.
```

- TEST specifies the Breslow test.
- COMPARE uses the Breslow test statistic to compare all distinct pairs of *SEXRACE* values and pools the test results over all strata defined by *LOCATION.*
- Test statistics are displayed at the end of output for all strata.

TREND Subcommand

TREND specifies that there is a trend across factor levels. This information is used when computing the tests for equality of survival functions specified on the TEST subcommand.

- The minimum specification is the subcommand keyword by itself. The default metric is chosen as follows:

  if g is even,

  $$(-(g-1), \ldots, -3, -1, 1, 3, \ldots, (g-1))$$

  otherwise,

  $$\left(-\frac{(g-1)}{2}, \ldots, -1, 0, 1, \ldots, \frac{(g-1)}{2}\right)$$

  where g is the number of levels for the factor variable.
- If TREND is specified but COMPARE is not, KM performs the default log rank test with the trend metric for an OVERALL POOLED comparison.
- If the metric specified on TREND is longer than required by the factor levels, KM displays a warning and ignores extra values.

Example

```
KM LENGTH BY SEXRACE
 /STATUS=EMPLOY EVENT (1) LOST (3,5 THRU 8)
 /STRATA=LOCATION
 /TREND.
```

- TREND is specified by itself. KM uses the default metric. Since *SEXRACE* has four levels, the default is (–3,–1, 1, 3).
- Even though no TEST or COMPARE subcommand is specified, KM performs the default log rank test with the trend metric and does a default OVERALL POOLED comparison.

SAVE Subcommand

SAVE saves the temporary variables created by KM. The following temporary variables can be saved:

SURVIVAL *Survival function evaluated at current case.*

SE *Standard error of the survival function.*

HAZARD *Cumulative hazard function evaluated at current case.*

CUMEVENT *Cumulative number of events.*

- To specify variable names for the new variables, assign the new names in parentheses following each temporary variable name.
- Assigned variable names must be unique in the working data file. Scratch or system variable names cannot be used (that is, variable names cannot begin with # or $).
- If new variable names are not specified, KM generates default names. The default name is composed of the first three characters of the name of the temporary variable (two for *SE*), followed by an underscore and a number to make it unique.
- A temporary variable can be saved only once on the same SAVE subcommand.

Example

```
KM LENGTH BY SEXRACE
 /STATUS=EMPLOY EVENT (1) LOST (3,5 THRU 8)
 /STRATA=LOCATION
 /SAVE SURVIVAL HAZARD.
```

- KM saves cumulative survival and cumulative hazard rates in two new variables, *SUR_1* and *HAZ_1*, provided that neither name exists in the working data file. If one does, the numeric suffixes will be incremented to make a distinction.

LEAVE

```
LEAVE varlist
```

Example

```
COMPUTE TSALARY=TSALARY+SALARY.
LEAVE TSALARY.
FORMAT TSALARY (DOLLAR8)/ SALARY (DOLLAR7).
EXECUTE.
```

Overview

Normally, the program reinitializes variables each time it prepares to read a new case. LEAVE suppresses reinitialization and retains the current value of the specified variable or variables when the program reads the next case. It also sets the initial value received by a numeric variable to 0 instead of system-missing. LEAVE is frequently used with COMPUTE to create a variable to store an accumulating sum. LEAVE is also used to spread a variable's values across multiple cases when VECTOR is used within an input program to restructure a data file (see p. 338 for an example).

LEAVE cannot be used with scratch variables. For information on using scratch variables, see "Scratch Variables" on p. 21.

Basic Specification

The basic specification is the variable(s) whose values are not to be reinitialized as each new case is read.

Syntax Rules

- Variables named on LEAVE must already exist and cannot be scratch variables.
- Multiple variables can be named. The keyword TO can be used to refer to a list of consecutive variables.
- String and numeric variables can be specified on the same LEAVE command.

Operations

- Unlike most transformations, which do not take effect until the data are read, LEAVE takes effect as soon as it is encountered in the command sequence. Thus, special attention should be paid to its position among commands. For more information, see "Command Order" on p. 6.

- Numeric variables named on LEAVE are initialized to 0 for the first case, and string variables are initialized to blanks. These variables are not reinitialized when new cases are read.

Example

```
COMPUTE TSALARY=TSALARY+SALARY.
LEAVE TSALARY.
FORMAT TSALARY (DOLLAR8)/ SALARY (DOLLAR7).
```

- These commands keep a running total of salaries across all cases. *SALARY* is the variable containing the employee's salary, and *TSALARY* is the new variable containing the cumulative salaries for all previous cases.
- For the first case, *TSALARY* is initialized to 0, and *TSALARY* equals *SALARY*. For the rest of the cases, *TSALARY* stores the cumulative totals for *SALARY*.
- LEAVE follows COMPUTE because *TSALARY* must first be defined before it can be specified on LEAVE.
- If LEAVE were not specified for this computation, *TSALARY* would be initialized to system-missing for all cases. *TSALARY* would remain system-missing because its value would be missing for every computation.

Example

```
SORT CASES DEPT.
IF DEPT NE LAG(DEPT,1) TSALARY=0.    /*Initialize for new dept
COMPUTE TSALARY=TSALARY+SALARY.      /*Sum salaries
LEAVE TSALARY.                      /*Prevent  initialization
each case
FORMAT TSALARY (DOLLAR8)/ SALARY (DOLLAR7).
```

- These commands accumulate a sum across cases for each department.
- SORT first sorts cases by the values of variable *DEPT*.
- IF specifies that if the value of *DEPT* for the current case is not equal to the value of *DEPT* for the previous case, *TSALARY* equals 0. Thus, *TSALARY* is reset to 0 each time the value of *DEPT* changes. (For the first case in the file, the logical expression on IF is missing. However, the desired effect is obtained because LEAVE initializes *TSALARY* to 0 for the first case, independent of the IF statement.)
- LEAVE prevents *TSALARY* from being initialized for cases within the same department.

LIST

```
LIST [[VARIABLES=]{ALL**   }] [/FORMAT=[{WRAP**}] [{UNNUMBERED**}]]
                  {varlist}              {SINGLE}   {NUMBERED    }

 [/CASES=[FROM {1**}] [TO {eof**}] [BY {1**}]]
               {n  }      {n    }      {n  }
```

**Default if the subcommand is omitted.

Example

```
LIST VARIABLES=V1 V2 /CASES=FROM 10 TO 100 BY 2.
```

Overview

LIST displays case values for variables in the working data file. The output is similar to the output produced by the PRINT command. However, LIST is a procedure and reads data, whereas PRINT is a transformation and requires a procedure (or the EXECUTE command) to execute it.

Options

Selecting and Ordering Variables. You can specify a list of variables to be listed using the VARIABLES subcommand.

Format. You can limit each case listing to a single line, and you can display the case number for each listed case with the FORMAT subcommand.

Selecting Cases. You can limit the listing to a particular sequence of cases using the CASES subcommand.

Basic Specification

- The basic specification is simply LIST, which displays the values for all variables in the working data file.
- By default, cases wrap to multiple lines if all the values do not fit within the page width (the page width is determined by the SET WIDTH command). Case numbers are not displayed for the listed cases.

Subcommand Order

All subcommands are optional and can be named in any order.

Operations

- If VARIABLES is not specified, variables are listed in the order in which they appear in the working file.
- LIST does not display values for scratch or system variables.
- LIST uses print formats contained in the dictionary of the working data file. Alternative formats cannot be specified on LIST. See FORMATS or PRINT FORMATS for information on changing print formats.
- LIST output uses the width specified on SET.
- If a numeric value is longer than its defined width, the program first attempts to list the value by removing punctuation characters, then uses scientific notation, and finally prints asterisks.
- If a long string variable cannot be listed within the output width, it is truncated.
- Values of the variables listed for a case are always separated by at least one blank.
- System-missing values are displayed as a period for numeric variables and a blank for string variables.
- If cases fit on one line, the column width for each variable is determined by the length of the variable name or the format, whichever is greater. If the variable names do not fit on one line, they are printed vertically.
- If cases do not fit on one line within the output width specified on SET, they are wrapped. LIST displays a table illustrating the location of the variables in the output and prints the name of the first variable in each line at the beginning of the line.
- Each execution of LIST begins at the top of a new page. If SPLIT FILE is in effect, each split also begins at the top of a new page.

Example

```
LIST.
```

- LIST by itself requests a display of the values for all variables in the working file.

Example

```
LIST VARIABLES=V1 V2 /CASES=FROM 10 TO 100 BY 2.
```

- LIST produces a list of every second case for variables *V1* and *V2*, starting with case 10 and stopping at case 100.

VARIABLES Subcommand

VARIABLES specifies the variables to be listed. The actual keyword VARIABLES can be omitted.

- The variables must already exist, and they cannot be scratch or system variables.
- If VARIABLES is used, only the specified variables are listed.

- Variables are listed in the order in which they are named on VARIABLES.
- If a variable is named more than once, it is listed more than once.
- The keyword ALL (the default) can be used to request all variables. ALL can also be used with a variable list (see example below).

ALL *List all user-defined variables.* Variables are listed in the order in which they appear in the working data file. This is the default if VARIABLES is omitted.

Example

```
LIST VARIABLES=V15 V31 ALL.
```

- VARIABLES is used to list values for *V15* and *V31* before all other variables. The keyword ALL then lists all variables, including *V15* and *V31*, in the order in which they appear in the working data file. Values for *V15* and *V31* are therefore listed twice.

FORMAT Subcommand

FORMAT controls whether cases wrap if they cannot fit on a single line and whether the case number is displayed for each listed case. The default display uses more than one line per case (if necessary) and does not number cases.

- The minimum specification is a single keyword.
- WRAP and SINGLE are alternatives, as are NUMBERED and UNNUMBERED. Only one of each pair can be specified.
- If SPLIT FILE is in effect for NUMBERED, case numbering restarts at each split. To get sequential numbering regardless of splits, create a variable and set it equal to the system variable *$CASENUM* and then name this variable as the first variable on the VARIABLES subcommand. An appropriate format should be specified for the new variable before it is used on LIST.

WRAP *Wrap cases if they do not fit on a single line.* Page width is determined by the SET WIDTH command. This is the default.

SINGLE *Limit each case to one line.* Only variables that fit on a single line are displayed.

UNNUMBERED *Do not include the sequence number of each case.* This is the default.

NUMBERED *Include the sequence number of each case.* The sequence number is displayed to the left of the listed values.

CASES Subcommand

CASES limits the number of cases listed. By default, all cases in the working data file are listed.

- Any or all of the keywords below can be used. Defaults that are not changed remain in effect.
- If LIST is preceded by a SAMPLE or SELECT IF command, case selections specified by CASES are taken from those cases that were selected by SAMPLE or SELECT IF.

- If SPLIT FILE is in effect, case selections specified by CASES are restarted for each split.

FROM n *Number of the first case to be listed.* The default is 1.

TO n *Number of the last case to be listed.* The default is the end of the working file. CASES 100 is interpreted as CASES TO 100.

BY n *Increment used to choose cases for listing.* The default is 1.

Example

```
LIST CASES BY 3 /FORMAT=NUMBERED.
```

- Every third case is listed for all variables in the working data file. The listing begins with the first case and includes every third case up to the end of the file.
- FORMAT displays the case number of each listed case.

Example

```
LIST CASES FROM 10 TO 20.
```

- Cases from case 10 through case 20 are listed for all variables in the working file.

LOGISTIC REGRESSION

LOGISTIC REGRESSION is available in the Regression Models option.

```
LOGISTIC REGRESSION [VARIABLES =] dependent var
        [WITH independent varlist [BY var [BY var] ... ]]

[/CATEGORICAL = var1, var2, ... ]

[/CONTRAST (categorical var) = [{INDICATOR [(refcat)]    }]]
                                {DEVIATION [(refcat)]    }
                                {SIMPLE [(refcat)]       }
                                {DIFFERENCE              }
                                {HELMERT                 }
                                {REPEATED                }
                                {POLYNOMIAL[({1,2,3...})]}
                                             {metric   }
                                {SPECIAL (matrix)        }

 [/METHOD = {ENTER**           }   [{ALL    }]]
            {BSTEP [{COND}]}        {varlist}
                    {LR  }
                    {WALD}
            {FSTEP [{COND}]}
                    {LR  }
                    {WALD}

 [/SELECT = {ALL**                   }]
            {varname relation value}

 [/{NOORIGIN**}]
   {ORIGIN    }

 [/ID = [variable]]

 [/PRINT = [DEFAULT**] [SUMMARY] [CORR] [ALL] [ITER [({1})]] [GOODFIT]]
                                                     {n}
           [CI(level)]

 [/CRITERIA = [BCON ({0.001**})] [ITERATE({20**})] [LCON({0.01**})]
                     {value  }            {n   }         {value }

              [PIN({0.05**})] [POUT({0.10**})] [EPS({.00000001**})]]
                   {value }        {value }         {value      }

              [CUT[{0.5**  }]]
                   [value  }

 [/CLASSPLOT]

 [/MISSING = {EXCLUDE **}]
             {INCLUDE   }

 [/CASEWISE = [tempvarlist]  [OUTLIER({2    })]]
                                      {value}

 [/SAVE = tempvar[(newname)] tempvar[(newname)]...]

 [/EXTERNAL]
```

** Default if the subcommand or keyword is omitted.

Temporary variables created by LOGISTIC REGRESSION are:

PRED	*LEVER*	*COOK*
PGROUP	*LRESID*	*DFBETA*
RESID	*SRESID*	
DEV	*ZRESID*	

Example

```
LOGISTIC REGRESSION PROMOTED WITH AGE, JOBTIME, JOBRATE.
```

Overview

LOGISTIC REGRESSION regresses a dichotomous dependent variable on a set of independent variables (Aldrich and Nelson, 1984; Fox, 1984; Hosmer and Lemeshow, 1989; McCullagh and Nelder, 1989; Agresti, 1990). Categorical independent variables are replaced by sets of contrast variables, each set entering and leaving the model in a single step.

Options

Processing of Independent Variables. You can specify which independent variables are categorical in nature on the CATEGORICAL subcommand. You can control treatment of categorical independent variables by the CONTRAST subcommand. Seven methods are available for entering independent variables into the model. You can specify any one of them on the METHOD subcommand. You can also use the keyword BY between variable names to enter interaction terms.

Selecting Cases. You can use the SELECT subcommand to define subsets of cases to be used in estimating a model.

Regression through the Origin. You can use the ORIGIN subcommand to exclude a constant term from a model.

Specifying Termination and Model-Building Criteria. You can further control computations when building the model by specifying criteria on the CRITERIA subcommand.

Adding New Variables to the Working Data File. You can save the residuals, predicted values, and diagnostics generated by LOGISTIC REGRESSION in the working data file.

Output. You can use the PRINT subcommand to print optional output, use the CASEWISE subcommand to request analysis of residuals, and use the ID subcommand to specify a variable whose values or value labels identify cases in output. You can request plots of the actual and predicted values for each case with the CLASSPLOT subcommand.

Basic Specification

- The minimum specification is the VARIABLES subcommand with one dichotomous dependent variable. You must specify a list of independent variables either following the keyword WITH on the VARIABLES subcommand or on a METHOD subcommand.

- The default output includes goodness-of-fit tests for the model (–2 log-likelihood, goodness-of-fit statistic, Cox and Snell R^2, and NagelKerke R^2) and a classification table for the predicted and observed group memberships. The regression coefficient, standard error of the regression coefficient, Wald statistic and its significance level, and a multiple correlation coefficient adjusted for the number of parameters (Atkinson, 1980) are displayed for each variable in the equation.

Subcommand Order

- Subcommands can be named in any order. If the VARIABLES subcommand is not specified first, a slash (/) must precede it.
- The ordering of METHOD subcommands determines the order in which models are estimated. Different sequences may result in different models.

Syntax Rules

- Only one dependent variable can be specified for each LOGISTIC REGRESSION.
- Any number of independent variables may be listed. The dependent variable may not appear on this list.
- The independent variable list is required if any of the METHOD subcommands are used without a variable list or if the METHOD subcommand is not used. The keyword TO cannot be used on any variable list.
- If you specify the keyword WITH on the VARIABLES subcommand, all independent variables must be listed.
- If the keyword WITH is used on the VARIABLES subcommand, interaction terms do not have to be specified on the variable list, but the individual variables that make up the interactions must be listed.
- Multiple METHOD subcommands are allowed.
- The minimum truncation for this command is LOGI REG.

Operations

- Independent variables specified on the CATEGORICAL subcommand are replaced by sets of contrast variables. In stepwise analyses, the set of contrast variables associated with a categorical variable is entered or removed from the model as a single step.
- Independent variables are screened to detect and eliminate redundancies.
- If the linearly dependent variable is one of a set of contrast variables, the set will be reduced by the redundant variable or variables. A warning will be issued, and the reduced set will be used.
- For the forward stepwise method, redundancy checking is done when a variable is to be entered into the model.
- When backward stepwise or direct-entry methods are requested, all variables for each METHOD subcommand are checked for redundancy before that analysis begins.

Limitations

- The dependent variable must be dichotomous for each split-file group. Specifying a dependent variable with more or less than two nonmissing values per split-file group will result in an error.

Example

```
LOGISTIC REGRESSION PASS WITH GPA, MAT, GRE.
```

- *PASS* is specified as the dependent variable.
- *GPA*, *MAT*, and *GRE* are specified as independent variables.
- LOGISTIC REGRESSION produces the default output for the logistic regression of *PASS* on *GPA*, *MAT*, and *GRE*.

VARIABLES Subcommand

VARIABLES specifies the dependent variable and, optionally, all independent variables in the model. The dependent variable appears first on the list and is separated from the independent variables by the keyword WITH.

- One VARIABLES subcommand is allowed for each Logistic Regression procedure.
- The dependent variable must be dichotomous—that is, it must have exactly two values other than system-missing and user-missing values for each split-file group.
- The dependent variable may be a string variable if its two values can be differentiated by their first eight characters.
- You can indicate an interaction term on the variable list by using the keyword BY to separate the individual variables.
- If all METHOD subcommands are accompanied by independent variable lists, the keyword WITH and the list of independent variables may be omitted.
- If the keyword WITH is used, *all* independent variables must be specified. For interaction terms, only the individual variable names that make up the interaction (for example, `X1, X2`) need to be specified. Specifying the actual interaction term (for example, `X1 BY X2`) on the VARIABLES subcommand is optional if you specify it on a METHOD subcommand.

Example

```
LOGISTIC REGRESSION PROMOTED WITH AGE,JOBTIME,JOBRATE,
    AGE BY JOBTIME.
```

- *PROMOTED* is specified as the dependent variable.
- *AGE*, *JOBTIME*, *JOBRATE*, and the interaction *AGE* by *JOBTIME* are specified as the independent variables.
- Because no METHOD is specified, all three single independent variables and the interaction term are entered into the model.
- LOGISTIC REGRESSION produces the default output.

CATEGORICAL Subcommand

CATEGORICAL identifies independent variables that are nominal or ordinal. Variables that are declared to be categorical are automatically transformed to a set of contrast variables as specified on the CONTRAST subcommand. If a variable coded as $0-1$ is declared as categorical, its coding scheme will be changed to deviation contrasts by default.

- Independent variables not specified on CATEGORICAL are assumed to be at least interval level, except for string variables.
- Any variable specified on CATEGORICAL is ignored if it does not appear either after WITH on the VARIABLES subcommand or on any METHOD subcommand.
- Variables specified on CATEGORICAL are replaced by sets of contrast variables. If the categorical variable has n distinct values, there will be $n-1$ contrast variables generated. The set of contrast variables associated with a categorical variable is entered or removed from the model as a step.
- If any one of the variables in an interaction term is specified on CATEGORICAL, the interaction term is replaced by contrast variables.
- All string variables are categorical. Only the first eight characters of each value of a string variable are used in distinguishing between values. Thus, if two values of a string variable are identical for the first eight characters, the values are treated as though they were the same.

Example

```
LOGISTIC REGRESSION PASS WITH GPA, GRE, MAT, CLASS, TEACHER
 /CATEGORICAL = CLASS,TEACHER.
```

- The dichotomous dependent variable *PASS* is regressed on the interval-level independent variables *GPA*, *GRE*, and *MAT* and the categorical variables *CLASS* and *TEACHER*.

CONTRAST Subcommand

CONTRAST specifies the type of contrast used for categorical independent variables. The interpretation of the regression coefficients for categorical variables depends on the contrasts used. The default is INDICATOR. The categorical independent variable is specified in parentheses following CONTRAST. The closing parenthesis is followed by one of the contrast-type keywords.

- If the categorical variable has n values, there will be $n-1$ rows in the contrast matrix. Each contrast matrix is treated as a set of independent variables in the analysis.
- Only one categorical independent variable can be specified per CONTRAST subcommand, but multiple CONTRAST subcommands can be specified.

The following contrast types are available. See Finn (1974) and Kirk (1982) for further information on a specific type.

INDICATOR(refcat) *Indicator variables.* Contrasts indicate the presence or absence of category membership. By default, refcat is the last category (represented in the contrast matrix as a row of zeros). To omit a category other than the last, specify the sequence number of the omitted category (which is not necessarily the same as its value) in parentheses after the keyword INDICATOR.

DEVIATION(refcat) *Deviations from the overall effect.* This is the default. The effect for each category of the independent variable except one is compared to the overall effect. Refcat is the category for which parameter estimates are not displayed (they must be calculated from the others). By default, refcat is the last category. To omit a category other than the last, specify the sequence number of the omitted category (which is not necessarily the same as its value) in parentheses after the keyword DEVIATION.

SIMPLE(refcat) *Each category of the independent variable except the last is compared to the last category.* To use a category other than the last as the omitted reference category, specify its sequence number (which is not necessarily the same as its value) in parentheses following the keyword SIMPLE.

DIFFERENCE *Difference or reverse Helmert contrasts.* The effects for each category of the independent variable except the first are compared to the mean effects of the previous categories.

HELMERT *Helmert contrasts.* The effects for each category of the independent variable except the last are compared to the mean effects of subsequent categories.

POLYNOMIAL(metric) *Polynomial contrasts.* The first degree of freedom contains the linear effect across the categories of the independent variable, the second contains the quadratic effect, and so on. By default, the categories are assumed to be equally spaced; unequal spacing can be specified by entering a metric consisting of one integer for each category of the independent variable in parentheses after the keyword POLYNOMIAL. For example, `CONTRAST(STIMULUS)=POLYNOMIAL(1,2,4)` indicates that the three levels of STIMULUS are actually in the proportion 1:2:4. The default metric is always (1,2,...,k), where k categories are involved. Only the relative differences between the terms of the metric matter: (1,2,4) is the same metric as (2,3,5) or (20,30,50) because the difference between the second and third numbers is twice the difference between the first and second in each instance.

REPEATED *Comparison of adjacent categories.* Each category of the independent variable except the first is compared to the previous category.

SPECIAL(matrix) *A user-defined contrast.* After this keyword, a matrix is entered in parentheses with $k-1$ rows and k columns (where k is the number of categories of the independent variable). The rows of the contrast matrix contain the special contrasts indicating the desired comparisons between categories. If the special contrasts are linear combinations of each other, LOGISTIC REGRESSION reports the linear dependency and stops processing. If k rows are entered, the first row is discarded and only the last $k-1$ rows are used as the contrast matrix in the analysis.

Example

```
LOGISTIC REGRESSION PASS WITH GRE, CLASS
 /CATEGORICAL = CLASS
 /CONTRAST(CLASS)=HELMERT.
```

- A logistic regression analysis of the dependent variable *PASS* is performed on the interval independent variable *GRE* and the categorical independent variable *CLASS*.
- *PASS* is a dichotomous variable representing course pass/fail status and *CLASS* identifies whether a student is in one of three classrooms. A HELMERT contrast is requested.

Example

```
LOGISTIC REGRESSION PASS WITH GRE, CLASS
 /CATEGORICAL = CLASS
 /CONTRAST(CLASS)=SPECIAL(2 -1 -1
                          0  1 -1).
```

- In this example, the contrasts are specified with the keyword SPECIAL.

METHOD Subcommand

METHOD indicates how the independent variables enter the model. The specification is the METHOD subcommand followed by a single method keyword. The keyword METHOD can be omitted. Optionally, specify the independent variables and interactions for which the method is to be used. Use the keyword BY between variable names of an interaction term.

- If no variable list is specified or if the keyword ALL is used, all of the independent variables following the keyword WITH on the VARIABLES subcommand are eligible for inclusion in the model.
- If no METHOD subcommand is specified, the default method is ENTER.
- Variables specified on CATEGORICAL are replaced by sets of contrast variables. The set of contrast variables associated with a categorical variable is entered or removed from the model as a single step.
- Any number of METHOD subcommands can appear in a Logistic Regression procedure. METHOD subcommands are processed in the order in which they are specified. Each method starts with the results from the previous method. If BSTEP is used, all remaining eligible variables are entered at the first step. All variables are then eligible for entry and removal unless they have been excluded from the METHOD variable list.
- The beginning model for the first METHOD subcommand is either the constant variable (by default or if NOORIGIN is specified) or an empty model (if ORIGIN is specified).

The available METHOD keywords are:

ENTER *Forced entry.* All variables are entered in a single step. This is the default if the METHOD subcommand is omitted.

FSTEP *Forward stepwise.* The variables (or interaction terms) specified on FSTEP are tested for entry into the model one by one, based on the significance level of the score statistic. The variable with the smallest significance less than PIN is entered into the model. After each entry, variables that are already in the model are tested for possible removal, based on the significance of the conditional statistic, the Wald statistic, or the likelihood-ratio criterion. The variable with the largest probability greater than the specified POUT value is removed and the model is reestimated. Variables in the model are then evaluated again for removal. Once no more variables satisfy the removal criterion, covariates not in the model are evaluated for entry. Model building stops when no more variables meet entry or removal criteria, or when the current model is the same as a previous one.

BSTEP *Backward stepwise.* As a first step, the variables (or interaction terms) specified on BSTEP are entered into the model together and are tested for removal one by one. Stepwise removal and entry then follow the same process as described for FSTEP until no more variables meet entry or removal criteria, or when the current model is the same as a previous one.

The statistic used in the test for removal can be specified by an additional keyword in parentheses following FSTEP or BSTEP. If FSTEP or BSTEP is specified by itself, the default is COND.

COND *Conditional statistic.* This is the default if FSTEP or BSTEP is specified by itself.

WALD *Wald statistic.* The removal of a variable from the model is based on the significance of the Wald statistic.

LR *Likelihood ratio.* The removal of a variable from the model is based on the significance of the change in the log-likelihood. If LR is specified, the model must be reestimated without each of the variables in the model. This can substantially increase computational time. However, the likelihood-ratio statistic is the best criterion for deciding which variables are to be removed.

Example

```
LOGISTIC REGRESSION PROMOTED WITH AGE JOBTIME JOBRATE RACE SEX AGENCY
 /CATEGORICAL RACE SEX AGENCY
 /METHOD ENTER AGE  JOBTIME
 /METHOD BSTEP (LR) RACE SEX JOBRATE AGENCY.
```

- *AGE*, *JOBTIME*, *JOBRATE*, *RACE*, *SEX*, and *AGENCY* are specified as independent variables. *RACE*, *SEX*, and *AGENCY* are specified as categorical independent variables.
- The first METHOD subcommand enters *AGE* and *JOBTIME* into the model.
- Variables in the model at the termination of the first METHOD subcommand are included in the model at the beginning of the second METHOD subcommand.
- The second METHOD subcommand adds the variables *RACE*, *SEX*, *JOBRATE*, and *AGENCY* to the previous model.
- Backward stepwise logistic regression analysis is then done with only the variables on the BSTEP variable list tested for removal using the LR statistic.
- The procedure continues until all variables from the BSTEP variable list have been removed or the removal of a variable will not result in a decrease in the log-likelihood with a probability larger than POUT.

SELECT Subcommand

By default, all cases in the working data file are considered for inclusion in LOGISTIC REGRESSION. Use the optional SELECT subcommand to include a subset of cases in the analysis.

- The specification is either a logical expression or keyword ALL. ALL is the default. Variables named on VARIABLES, CATEGORICAL, or METHOD subcommands cannot appear on SELECT.
- In the logical expression on SELECT, the relation can be EQ, NE, LT, LE, GT, or GE. The variable must be numeric and the value can be any number.
- Only cases for which the logical expression on SELECT is true are included in calculations. All other cases, including those with missing values for the variable named on SELECT, are unselected.
- Diagnostic statistics and classification statistics are reported for both selected and unselected cases.
- Cases deleted from the working data file with the SELECT IF or SAMPLE command are not included among either the selected or unselected cases.

Example

```
LOGISTIC REGRESSION VARIABLES=GRADE WITH GPA,TUCE,PSI
 /SELECT SEX EQ 1 /CASEWISE=RESID.
```

- Only cases with the value 1 for *SEX* are included in the logistic regression analysis.
- Residual values generated by CASEWISE are displayed for both selected and unselected cases.

ORIGIN and NOORIGIN Subcommands

ORIGIN and NOORIGIN control whether or not the constant is included. NOORIGIN (the default) includes a constant term (intercept) in all equations. ORIGIN suppresses the constant term and requests regression through the origin. (NOCONST can be used as an alias for ORIGIN.)

- The only specification is either ORIGIN or NOORIGIN.
- ORIGIN or NOORIGIN can be specified only once per Logistic Regression procedure, and it affects all METHOD subcommands.

Example

```
LOGISTIC REGRESSION VARIABLES=PASS WITH GPA,GRE,MAT /ORIGIN.
```

- ORIGIN suppresses the automatic generation of a constant term.

ID Subcommand

ID specifies a variable whose values or value labels identify the casewise listing. By default, cases are labeled by their case number.

- The only specification is the name of a single variable that exists in the working data file.
- Only the first eight characters of the variable's value labels are used to label cases. If the variable has no value labels, the values are used.
- Only the first eight characters of a string variable are used to label cases.

PRINT Subcommand

PRINT controls the display of optional output. If PRINT is omitted, DEFAULT output (defined below) is displayed.

- The minimum specification is PRINT followed by a single keyword.
- If PRINT is used, only the requested output is displayed.

DEFAULT *Goodness-of-fit tests for the model, classification tables, and statistics for the variables in and not in the equation at each step.* Tables and statistics are displayed for each split file and METHOD subcommand.

SUMMARY *Summary information.* Same output as DEFAULT, except that the output for each step is not displayed.

CORR *Correlation matrix of parameter estimates for the variables in the model.*

ITER(value) *Iterations at which parameter estimates are to be displayed.* The value in parentheses controls the spacing of iteration reports. If the value is *n*, the parameter estimates are displayed for every *n*th iteration starting at 0. If a value is not supplied, intermediate estimates are displayed at each iteration.

GOODFIT *Hosmer-Lemeshow goodness-of-fit statistic* (Hosmer and Lemeshow, 1989).

CI(level) *Confidence interval for exp(B).* The value in parentheses must be an integer between 1 and 99.

ALL *All available output.*

Example

```
LOGISTIC REGRESSION VARIABLES=PASS WITH GPA,GRE,MAT
 /METHOD FSTEP
 /PRINT CORR SUMMARY ITER(2).
```

- A forward stepwise logistic regression analysis of *PASS* on *GPA*, *GRE*, and *MAT* is specified.
- The PRINT subcommand requests the display of the correlation matrix of parameter estimates for the variables in the model (CORR), classification tables and statistics for the variables in and not in the equation for the final model (SUMMARY), and parameter estimates at every second iteration (ITER(2)).

CRITERIA Subcommand

CRITERIA controls the statistical criteria used in building the logistic regression models. The way in which these criteria are used depends on the method specified on the METHOD subcommand. The default criteria are noted in the description of each keyword below. Iterations will stop if the criterion for BCON, LCON, or ITERATE is satisfied.

BCON(value) *Change in parameter estimates to terminate iteration.* Iteration terminates when the parameters change by less than the specified value. The default is 0.001. To eliminate this criterion, specify a value of 0.

ITERATE *Maximum number of iterations.* The default is 20.

LCON(value) *Percentage change in the log-likelihood ratio for termination of iterations.* If the log-likelihood decreases by less than the specified value, iteration terminates. The default is 0.01. To eliminate this criterion, specify a value of 0.

PIN(value) *Probability of score statistic for variable entry.* The default is 0.05. The larger the specified probability, the easier it is for a variable to enter the model.

POUT(value) *Probability of conditional, Wald, or LR statistic to remove a variable.* The default is 0.1. The larger the specified probability, the easier it is for a variable to remain in the model.

EPS(value) *Epsilon value used for redundancy checking.* The specified value must be less than or equal to 0.05 and greater than or equal to 10^{-12}. The default is 10^{-8}. Larger values make it harder for variables to pass the redundancy check—that is, they are more likely to be removed from the analysis.

CUT(value) *Cutoff value for classification.* A case is assigned to a group when the predicted event probability is greater than or equal to the cutoff value. The cutoff value affects the value of the dichotomous derived variable in the classification table, the predicted group (PGROUP on CASEWISE), and the classification plot (CLASSPLOT). The default cutoff value is 0.5. You can specify a value between 0 and 1 ($0 < \text{value} < 1$).

Example

```
LOGISTIC REGRESSION PROMOTED WITH AGE JOBTIME RACE
 /CATEGORICAL RACE
 /METHOD BSTEP
 /CRITERIA BCON(0.01) PIN(0.01) POUT(0.05).
```

- A backward stepwise logistic regression analysis is performed for the dependent variable *PROMOTED* and the independent variables *AGE*, *JOBTIME*, and *RACE*.
- CRITERIA alters four of the statistical criteria that control the building of a model.
- BCON specifies that if the change in the absolute value of all of the parameter estimates is less than 0.01, the iterative estimation process should stop. Larger values lower the number of iterations required. Notice that the ITER and LCON criteria remain unchanged and that if either of them is met before BCON, iterations will terminate. (LCON can be set to 0 if only BCON and ITER are to be used.)
- POUT requires that the probability of the statistic used to test whether a variable should remain in the model be smaller than 0.05. This is more stringent than the default value of 0.1.
- PIN requires that the probability of the score statistic used to test whether a variable should be included be smaller than 0.01. This makes it more difficult for variables to be included in the model than the default value of 0.05.

CLASSPLOT Subcommand

CLASSPLOT generates a classification plot of the actual and predicted values of the dichotomous dependent variable at each step.

- Keyword CLASSPLOT is the only specification.
- If CLASSPLOT is not specified, plots are not generated.

Example

```
LOGISTIC REGRESSION PROMOTED WITH JOBTIME RACE
 /CATEGORICAL RACE
 /CLASSPLOT.
```

- A logistic regression model is constructed for the dichotomous dependent variable *PROMOTED* and the independent variables *JOBTIME* and *RACE*.
- CLASSPLOT produces a classification plot for the dependent variable *PROMOTED*. The vertical axis of the plot is the frequency of the variable *PROMOTED*. The horizontal axis is the predicted probability of membership in the second of the two levels of *PROMOTED*.

CASEWISE Subcommand

CASEWISE produces a casewise listing of the values of the temporary variables created by LOGISTIC REGRESSION.

The following keywords are available for specifying temporary variables (see Fox, 1984). When CASEWISE is specified by itself, the default lists *PRED*, *PGROUP*, *RESID*, and *ZRESID*. If a list of variable names is given, only those named temporary variables are displayed.

PRED *Predicted probability.* For each case, the predicted probability of having the second of the two values of the dichotomous dependent variable.

PGROUP *Predicted group.* The group to which a case is assigned based on the predicted probability.

RESID *Difference between observed and predicted probabilities.*

DEV *Deviance values.* For each case, a log-likelihood-ratio statistic, which measures how well the model fits the case, is computed.

LRESID *Logit residual.* Residual divided by the product of *PRED* and 1–šš*PRED*.

SRESID *Studentized residual.*

ZRESID *Normalized residual.* Residual divided by the square root of the product of *PRED* and 1–šš*PRED*.

LEVER *Leverage value.* A measure of the relative influence of each observation on the model's fit.

COOK *Analog of Cook's influence statistic.*

DFBETA *Difference in beta.* The difference in the estimated coefficients for each independent variable if the case is omitted.

The following keyword is available for restricting the cases to be displayed, based on the absolute value of *SRESID*:

OUTLIER (value) *Cases with absolute values of SRESID greater than or equal to the specified value are displayed.* If OUTLIER is specified with no value, the default is 2.

Example

```
LOGISTIC REGRESSION PROMOTED WITH JOBTIME SEX RACE
 /CATEGORICAL SEX RACE
 /METHOD ENTER
 /CASEWISE SRESID LEVER DFBETA.
```

- CASEWISE produces a casewise listing of the temporary variables *SRESID*, *LEVER*, and *DFBETA*.
- There will be one *DFBETA* value for each parameter in the model. The continuous variable *JOBTIME*, the two-level categorical variable *SEX*, and the constant each require one parameter while the four-level categorical variable *RACE* requires three parameters. Thus, six values of *DFBETA* will be produced for each case.

MISSING Subcommand

LOGISTIC REGRESSION excludes all cases with missing values on any of the independent variables. For a case with a missing value on the dependent variable, predicted values are calculated if it has nonmissing values on all independent variables. The MISSING subcommand controls the processing of user-missing values. If the subcommand is not specified, the default is EXCLUDE.

EXCLUDE *Delete cases with user-missing values as well as system-missing values.* This is the default.

INCLUDE *Include user-missing values in the analysis.*

SAVE Subcommand

SAVE saves the temporary variables created by LOGISTIC REGRESSION. To specify variable names for the new variables, assign the new names in parentheses following each temporary variable name. If new variable names are not specified, LOGISTIC REGRESSION generates default names.

- Assigned variable names must be unique in the working data file. Scratch or system variable names (that is, names that begin with # or $) cannot be used.
- A temporary variable can be saved only once on the same SAVE subcommand.

Example

```
LOGISTIC REGRESSION PROMOTED WITH JOBTIME AGE
 /SAVE PRED (PREDPRO) DFBETA (DF).
```

- A logistic regression analysis of *PROMOTED* on the independent variables *JOBTIME* and *AGE* is performed.
- SAVE adds four variables to the working data file: one variable named *PREDPRO*, containing the predicted value from the specified model for each case, and three variables named *DF0*, *DF1*, and *DF2*, containing, respectively, the *DFBETA* values for each case of the constant, the independent variable *JOBTIME*, and the independent variable *AGE*.

EXTERNAL Subcommand

EXTERNAL indicates that the data for each split-file group should be held in an external scratch file during processing. This can help conserve memory resources when running complex analyses or analyses with large data sets.

- The keyword EXTERNAL is the only specification.
- Specifying EXTERNAL may result in slightly longer processing time.
- If EXTERNAL is not specified, all data are held internally and no scratch file is written.

References

Agresti, A. 1990. *Categorical data analysis*. New York: John Wiley and Sons.

Aldrich, J. H., and F. D. Nelson. 1984. *Linear probability, logit, and probit models*. Beverly Hills, Calif.: Sage Publications.

Finn, J. D. 1974. *A general model for multivariate analysis*. New York: Holt, Rinehart and Winston.

Fox, J. 1984. *Linear statistical models and related methods: With applications to social research*. New York: John Wiley and Sons.

Hosmer, D. W., and S. Lemeshow. 1989. *Applied logistic regression*. New York: John Wiley and Sons.

Kirk, R. E. 1982. *Experimental design*. 2nd ed. Monterey, Calif.: Brooks/Cole.

McCullagh, P., and J. A. Nelder. 1989. *Generalized linear models*. 2nd ed. London: Chapman and Hall.

LOGLINEAR

LOGLINEAR is available in the Advanced Models option.

The syntax for LOGLINEAR is available only in a syntax window, not from the dialog box interface. See GENLOG for information on the LOGLINEAR command available from the dialog box interface.

```
LOGLINEAR varlist(min,max)...[BY] varlist(min,max)

          [WITH covariate varlist]

 [/CWEIGHT={varname }] [/CWEIGHT=(matrix)...]
           {(matrix)}

 [/GRESID={varlist }]  [/GRESID=(matrix)...]
          {(matrix)}

 [/CONTRAST (varname)={DEVIATION [(refcat)]        } [/CONTRAST...]]
                      {DIFFERENCE                  }
                      {HELMERT                     }
                      {SIMPLE [(refcat)]           }
                      {REPEATED                    }
                      {POLYNOMIAL [({1,2,3,...})]  }
                      {             {metric    }   }
                      { [BASIS] SPECIAL(matrix)    }

 [/CRITERIA=[CONVERGE({0.001**})] [ITERATE({20**})] [DELTA({0.5**})]
                      {n      }            {n   }          {n    }
           [DEFAULT]]

 [/PRINT={ [FREQ**] [RESID**] [DESIGN] [ESTIM] [COR] }]
         {DEFAULT                                    }
         {ALL                                        }
         {NONE                                       }

 [/PLOT={NONE**   }]
        {DEFAULT  }
        {RESID    }
        {NORMPROB }

 [/MISSING=[{EXCLUDE**}]]
            {INCLUDE  }

 [/DESIGN=effect[(n)] effect[(n)]... effect BY effect...] [/DESIGN...]
```

**Default if subcommand or keyword is omitted.

Example

```
LOGLINEAR JOBSAT (1,2) ZODIAC (1,12) /DESIGN=JOBSAT.
```

Overview

LOGLINEAR is a general procedure for model fitting, hypothesis testing, and parameter estimation for any model that has categorical variables as its major components. As such, LOGLINEAR subsumes a variety of related techniques, including general models of multiway contingency tables, logit models, logistic regression on categorical variables, and quasi-independence models.

LOGLINEAR models cell frequencies using the multinomial response model and produces maximum likelihood estimates of parameters by means of the Newton-Raphson algorithm (Haberman, 1978). HILOGLINEAR, which uses an iterative proportional-fitting algorithm, is more efficient for hierarchical models, but it cannot produce parameter estimates for unsaturated models, does not permit specification of contrasts for parameters, and does not display a correlation matrix of the parameter estimates.

Comparison of the GENLOG and LOGLINEAR Commands

The General Loglinear Analysis and Logit Loglinear Analysis dialog boxes are both associated with the GENLOG command. In previous releases of SPSS, these dialog boxes were associated with the LOGLINEAR command. The LOGLINEAR command is now available only as a syntax command. The differences are described below.

Distribution assumptions

- GENLOG can handle both Poisson and multinomial distribution assumptions for observed cell counts.
- LOGLINEAR assumes only multinomial distribution.

Approach

- GENLOG uses a regression approach to parameterize a categorical variable in a design matrix.
- LOGLINEAR uses contrasts to reparameterize a categorical variable. The major disadvantage of the reparameterization approach is in the interpretation of the results when there is a redundancy in the corresponding design matrix. Also, the reparameterization approach may result in incorrect degrees of freedom for an incomplete table, leading to incorrect analysis results.

Contrasts and generalized log-odds ratios (GLOR)

- GENLOG doesn't provide contrasts to reparameterize the categories of a factor. However, it offers generalized log-odds ratios (GLOR) for cell combinations. Often, comparisons among categories of factors can be derived from GLOR.
- LOGLINEAR offers contrasts to reparameterize the categories of a factor.

Deviance residual

- GENLOG calculates and displays the deviance residual and its normal probability plot, in addition to the other residuals.
- LOGLINEAR does not calculate the deviance residual.

Factor-by-covariate design

- When there is a factor-by-covariate term in the design, GENLOG generates one regression coefficient of the covariate for each combination of factor values. The estimates of these regression coefficients are calculated and displayed.
- LOGLINEAR estimates and displays the contrasts of these regression coefficients.

Partition effect

- In GENLOG, the term *partition effect* refers to the category of a factor.
- In LOGLINEAR, the term *partition effect* refers to a particular contrast.

Options

Model Specification. You can specify the model or models to be fit using the DESIGN subcommand.

Cell Weights. You can specify cell weights, such as structural zeros, for the model with the CWEIGHT subcommand.

Output Display. You can control the output display with the PRINT subcommand.

Optional Plots. You can produce plots of adjusted residuals against observed and expected counts, normal plots, and detrended normal plots with the PLOT subcommand.

Linear Combinations. You can calculate linear combinations of observed cell frequencies, expected cell frequencies, and adjusted residuals using the GRESID subcommand.

Contrasts. You can indicate the type of contrast desired for a factor using the CONTRAST subcommand.

Criteria for Algorithm. You can control the values of algorithm-tuning parameters with the CRITERIA subcommand.

Basic Specification

The basic specification is two or more variables that define the crosstabulation. The minimum and maximum values for each variable must be specified in parentheses after the variable name.

By default, LOGLINEAR estimates the saturated model for a multidimensional table. Output includes the factors or effects, their levels, and any labels; observed and expected frequencies and percentages for each factor and code; residuals, standardized residuals, and adjusted residuals; two goodness-of-fit statistics (the likelihood-ratio chi-square and Pearson's chi-square); and estimates of the parameters with accompanying *z* values and 95% confidence intervals.

Limitations

- Maximum 10 independent (factor) variables.
- Maximum 200 covariates.

Subcommand Order

- The variables specification must come first.
- The subcommands that affect a specific model must be placed before the DESIGN subcommand specifying the model.

- All subcommands can be used more than once and, with the exception of the DESIGN subcommand, are carried from model to model unless explicitly overridden.
- If the last subcommand is not DESIGN, LOGLINEAR generates a saturated model in addition to the explicitly requested model(s).

Example

```
LOGLINEAR JOBSAT (1,2) ZODIAC (1,12) /DESIGN=JOBSAT, ZODIAC.
```

- The variable list specifies two categorical variables, *JOBSAT* and *ZODIAC*. *JOBSAT* has values 1 and 2. *ZODIAC* has values 1 through 12.
- DESIGN specifies a model with main effects only.

Example

```
LOGLINEAR DPREF (2,3) RACE CAMP (1,2).
```

- *DPREF* is a categorical variable with values 2 and 3. *RACE* and *CAMP* are categorical variables with values 1 and 2.
- This is a general loglinear model because no BY keyword appears. The design defaults to a saturated model that includes all main effects and interaction effects.

Example

```
LOGLINEAR GSLEVEL (4,8) EDUC (1,4) SEX (1,2)
  /DESIGN=GSLEVEL EDUC SEX.
```

- *GSLEVEL* is a categorical variable with values 4 through 8. *EDUC* is a categorical variable with values 1 through 4. *SEX* has values 1 and 2.
- DESIGN specifies a model with main effects only.

Example

```
LOGLINEAR GSLEVEL (4,8) BY EDUC (1,4) SEX (1,2)
  /DESIGN=GSLEVEL, GSLEVEL BY EDUC, GSLEVEL BY SEX.
```

- The keyword BY on the variable list specifies a logit model in which *GSLEVEL* is the dependent variable and *EDUC* and *SEX* are the independent variables.
- DESIGN specifies a model that can test for the absence of joint effect of *SEX* and *EDUC* on *GSLEVEL*.

Variable List

The variable list specifies the variables to be included in the model. LOGLINEAR analyzes two classes of variables: categorical and continuous. Categorical variables are used to define the cells of the table. Continuous variables are used as cell covariates. Continuous variables can be specified only after the keyword WITH following the list of categorical variables.

- The list of categorical variables must be specified first. Categorical variables must be numeric and integer.
- A range must be defined for each categorical variable by specifying, in parentheses after each variable name, the minimum and maximum values for that variable. Separate the two values with at least one space or a comma.
- To specify the same range for a list of variables, specify the list of variables followed by a single range. The range applies to all variables on the list.
- To specify a logit model, use the keyword BY (see "Logit Model" below). A variable list without the keyword BY generates a general loglinear model.
- Cases with values outside the specified range are excluded from the analysis. Non-integer values within the range are truncated for the purpose of building the table.

Logit Model

- To segregate the independent (factor) variables from the dependent variables in a logit model, use the keyword BY. The categorical variables preceding BY are the dependent variables; the categorical variables following BY are the independent variables.
- A total of 10 categorical variables can be specified. In most cases, one of them is dependent.
- A DESIGN subcommand should be used to request the desired logit model.
- LOGLINEAR displays an analysis of dispersion and two measures of association: entropy and concentration. These measures are discussed in Haberman (1982) and can be used to quantify the magnitude of association among the variables. Both are proportional reduction in error measures. The entropy statistic is analogous to Theil's entropy measure, while the concentration statistic is analogous to Goodman and Kruskal's tau-*b*. Both statistics measure the strength of association between the dependent variable and the predictor variable set.

Cell Covariates

- Continuous variables can be used as covariates. When used, the covariates must be specified after the keyword WITH following the list of categorical variables. Ranges are not specified for the continuous variables.
- A variable cannot be named as both a categorical variable and a cell covariate.
- To enter cell covariates into a model, the covariates must be specified on the DESIGN subcommand.

- Cell covariates are not applied on a case-by-case basis. The mean covariate value for a cell in the contingency table is applied to that cell.

Example

```
LOGLINEAR DPREF(2,3) RACE CAMP (1,2) WITH CONSTANT
  /DESIGN=DPREF RACE CAMP CONSTANT.
```

- Variable *CONSTANT* is a continuous variable specified as a cell covariate. Cell covariates must be specified after the keyword WITH following the variable list. No range is defined for cell covariates.
- To include the cell covariate in the model, variable *CONSTANT* is specified on DESIGN.

CWEIGHT Subcommand

CWEIGHT specifies cell weights, such as structural zeros, for a model. By default, cell weights are equal to 1.

- The specification is either one numeric variable or a matrix of weights enclosed in parentheses.
- If a matrix of weights is specified, the matrix must contain the same number of elements as the product of the levels of the categorical variables. An asterisk can be used to signify repetitions of the same value.
- If weights are specified for a multiple-factor model, the index value of the rightmost factor increments the most rapidly.
- If a numeric variable is specified, only one CWEIGHT subcommand can be used on LOGLINEAR.
- To use multiple cell weights on the same LOGLINEAR command, specify all weights in matrix format. Each matrix must be specified on a separate CWEIGHT subcommand, and each CWEIGHT specification remains in effect until explicitly overridden by another CWEIGHT subcommand.
- CWEIGHT can be used to impose structural, or *a priori*, zeros on the model. This feature is useful in the analysis of symmetric tables.

Example

```
COMPUTE  CWT=1.
IF (HUSED EQ WIFED) CWT=0.
LOGLINEAR HUSED WIFED(1,4) WITH DISTANCE
  /CWEIGHT=CWT
  /DESIGN=HUSED WIFED DISTANCE.
```

- COMPUTE initially assigns *CWT* the value 1 for all cases.
- IF assigns *CWT* the value 0 when *HUSED* equals *WIFED*.
- CWEIGHT imposes structural zeros on the diagonal of the symmetric crosstabulation. Because a variable name is specified, only one CWEIGHT can be used.

Example

```
LOGLINEAR  HUSED WIFED(1,4) WITH DISTANCE
  /CWEIGHT=(0, 4*1, 0, 4*1, 0, 4*1, 0)
  /DESIGN=HUSED WIFED DISTANCE
  /CWEIGHT=(16*1)
  /DESIGN=HUSED WIFED DISTANCE.
```

- The first CWEIGHT matrix specifies the same values as variable *CWT* provided in the first example. The specified matrix is as follows:

```
0 1 1 1
1 0 1 1
1 1 0 1
1 1 1 0
```

- The same matrix can be specified in full as `(0 1 1 1 1 0 1 1 1 1 0 1 1 1 1 0)`.
- By using the matrix format on CWEIGHT rather than a variable name, a different CWEIGHT subcommand can be used for the second model.

GRESID Subcommand

GRESID (Generalized Residual) calculates linear combinations of observed cell frequencies, expected cell frequencies, and adjusted residuals.

- The specification is either a numeric variable or a matrix whose contents are coefficients of the desired linear combinations.
- If a matrix of coefficients is specified, the matrix must contain the same number of elements as the number of cells implied by the variables specification. An asterisk can be used to signify repetitions of the same value.
- Each GRESID subcommand specifies a single linear combination. Each matrix or variable must be specified on a separate GRESID subcommand. All GRESID subcommands specified are displayed for each design.

Example

```
LOGLINEAR  MONTH(1,18) WITH Z
 /GRESID=(6*1,12*0)
 /GRESID=(6*0,6*1,6*0)
 /GRESID=(12*0,6*1)
 /DESIGN=Z.
```

- The first GRESID subcommand combines the first six months into a single effect. The second GRESID subcommand combines the second six months, and the third GRESID subcommand combines the last six months.
- For each effect, LOGLINEAR displays the observed and expected counts, the residual, and the adjusted residual.

CONTRAST Subcommand

CONTRAST indicates the type of contrast desired for a factor, where a factor is any categorical dependent or independent variable. The default contrast is DEVIATION for each factor.

- The specification is CONTRAST, which is followed by a variable name in parentheses and the contrast-type keyword.
- To specify a contrast for more than one factor, use a separate CONTRAST subcommand for each specified factor. Only one contrast can be in effect for each factor on each DESIGN.
- A contrast specification remains in effect for subsequent designs until explicitly overridden by another CONTRAST subcommand.
- The design matrix used for the contrasts can be displayed by specifying keyword DESIGN on the PRINT subcommand. However, this matrix is the basis matrix that is used to determine contrasts; it is not the contrast matrix itself.
- CONTRAST can be used for a multinomial logit model, in which the dependent variable has more than two categories.
- CONTRAST can be used for fitting linear logit models. The keyword BASIS is not appropriate for such models.
- In a logit model, CONTRAST is used to transform the independent variable into a metric variable. Again, the keyword BASIS is not appropriate.

The following contrast types are available:

DEVIATION(refcat) *Deviations from the overall effect.* DEVIATION is the default contrast if the CONTRAST subcommand is not used. Refcat is the category for which parameter estimates are not displayed (they are the negative of the sum of the others). By default, refcat is the last category of the variable.

DIFFERENCE *Levels of a factor with the average effect of previous levels of a factor.* Also known as reverse Helmert contrasts.

HELMERT *Levels of a factor with the average effect of subsequent levels of a factor.*

SIMPLE(refcat) *Each level of a factor to the reference level.* By default, LOGLINEAR uses the last category of the factor variable as the reference category. Optionally, any level can be specified as the reference category enclosed in parentheses after the keyword SIMPLE. The sequence of the level, not the actual value, must be specified.

REPEATED *Adjacent comparisons across levels of a factor.*

POLYNOMIAL(metric) *Orthogonal polynomial contrasts.* The default is equal spacing. Optionally, the coefficients of the linear polynomial can be specified in parentheses, indicating the spacing between levels of the treatment measured by the given factor.

[BASIS]SPECIAL(matrix) *User-defined contrast.* As many elements as the number of categories squared must be specified. If BASIS is specified before SPECIAL, a basis matrix is generated for the special contrast, which makes the coefficients of the contrast equal to the special matrix. Otherwise, the matrix specified is transposed and then used as the basis matrix to determine coefficients for the contrast matrix.

Example

```
LOGLINEAR  A(1,4) BY B(1,4)
 /CONTRAST(B)=POLYNOMIAL
 /DESIGN=A A BY B(1)
 /CONTRAST(B)=SIMPLE
 /DESIGN=A A BY B(1).
```

- The first CONTRAST subcommand requests polynomial contrasts of *B* for the first design.
- The second CONTRAST subcommand requests the simple contrast of *B*, with the last category (value 4) used as the reference category for the second DESIGN subcommand.

Example

```
* Multinomial logit model

LOGLINEAR  PREF(1,5) BY RACE ORIGIN CAMP(1,2)
  /CONTRAST(PREF)=SPECIAL(5*1, 1 1 1 1 -4, 3 -1 -1 -1 0,
       0 1 1 -2 0, 0 1 -1 0 0).
```

- LOGLINEAR builds special contrasts among the five categories of the dependent variable *PREF*, which measures preference for training camps among Army recruits. For *PREF*, 1=stay, 2=move to north, 3=move to south, 4=move to unnamed camp, and 5=undecided.
- The four contrasts are: (1) move or stay versus undecided, (2) stay versus move, (3) named camp versus unnamed, and (4) northern camp versus southern. Because these contrasts are orthogonal, SPECIAL and BASIS SPECIAL produce equivalent results.

Example

```
* Contrasts for a linear logit model

LOGLINEAR RESPONSE(1,2) BY YEAR(0,20)
 /PRINT=DEFAULT ESTIM
 /CONTRAST(YEAR)=SPECIAL(21*1, -10, -9, -8, -7, -6, -5, -4,
                          -3, -2, -1, 0, 1, 2, 3, 4, 5, 6, 7,
                           8, 9, 10, 399*1)
 /DESIGN=RESPONSE RESPONSE BY YEAR(1).
```

- *YEAR* measures years of education and ranges from 0 through 20. Therefore, allowing for the constant effect, *YEAR* has 20 estimable parameters associated with it.
- The SPECIAL contrast specifies the constant—that is, 21*1—and the linear effect of *YEAR*—that is, –10 to 10. The other 399 1's fill out the 21*21 matrix.

Example

```
* Contrasts for a logistic regression model

LOGLINEAR RESPONSE(1,2) BY TIME(1,4)
  /CONTRAST(TIME) = SPECIAL(4*1, 7 14 27 51, 8*1)
  /PRINT=ALL /PLOT=DEFAULT
  /DESIGN=RESPONSE, TIME(1) BY RESPONSE.
```

- CONTRAST is used to transform the independent variable into a metric variable.
- *TIME* represents elapsed time in days. Therefore, the weights in the contrast represent the metric of the passage of time.

CRITERIA Subcommand

CRITERIA specifies the values of some constants in the Newton-Raphson algorithm. Defaults or specifications remain in effect until overridden with another CRITERIA subcommand.

CONVERGE(n) *Convergence criterion.* Specify a value for the convergence criterion. The default is 0.001.

ITERATE(n) *Maximum number of iterations.* Specify the maximum number of iterations for the algorithm. The default number is 20.

DELTA(n) *Cell delta value.* The value of delta is added to each cell frequency for the first iteration. For saturated models, it remains in the cell. The default value is 0.5. LOGLINEAR does not display parameter estimates or correlation matrices of parameter estimates if any sampling zero cells exist in the expected table after delta is added. Parameter estimates and correlation matrices can be displayed in the presence of structural zeros.

DEFAULT *Default values are used.* DEFAULT can be used to reset the parameters to the default.

Example

```
LOGLINEAR  DPREF(2,3) BY RACE ORIGIN CAMP(1,2)
 /CRITERIA=ITERATION(50) CONVERGE(.0001).
```

- ITERATION increases the maximum number of iterations to 50.
- CONVERGE lowers the convergence criterion to 0.0001.

PRINT Subcommand

PRINT requests statistics that are not produced by default.

- By default, LOGLINEAR displays the frequency table and residuals. The parameter estimates of the model are also displayed if DESIGN is not used.
- Multiple PRINT subcommands are permitted. The specifications are cumulative.

The following keywords can be used on PRINT:

FREQ *Observed and expected cell frequencies and percentages.* This is displayed by default.

RESID *Raw, standardized, and adjusted residuals.* This is displayed by default.

DESIGN *The design matrix of the model, showing the basis matrix corresponding to the contrasts used.*

ESTIM *The parameter estimates of the model.* If you do not specify a design on the DESIGN subcommand, LOGLINEAR generates a saturated model and displays the parameter estimates for the saturated model. LOGLINEAR does not display parameter estimates or correlation matrices of parameter estimates if any sampling zero cells exist in the expected table after delta is added. Parameter estimates and a correlation matrix are displayed when structural zeros are present.

COR *The correlation matrix of the parameter estimates.* Alias COV.

ALL *All available output.*

DEFAULT *FREQ and RESID.* ESTIM is also displayed by default if the DESIGN subcommand is not used.

NONE *The design information and goodness-of-fit statistics only.* This option overrides all other specifications on the PRINT subcommand. The NONE option applies only to the PRINT subcommand.

Example

```
LOGLINEAR A(1,2) B(1,2)
 /PRINT=ESTIM
 /DESIGN=A,B,A BY B
 /PRINT=ALL
 /DESIGN=A,B.
```

- The first design is the saturated model. The parameter estimates are displayed with ESTIM specified on PRINT.
- The second design is the main-effects model, which tests the hypothesis of no interaction. The second PRINT subcommand displays all available display output for this model.

PLOT Subcommand

PLOT produces optional plots. No plots are displayed if PLOT is not specified or is specified without any keyword. Multiple PLOT subcommands can be used. The specifications are cumulative.

RESID *Plots of adjusted residuals against observed and expected counts.*

NORMPROB *Normal and detrended normal plots of the adjusted residuals.*

NONE *No plots.*

DEFAULT *RESID and NORMPROB.* Alias ALL.

Example

```
LOGLINEAR  RESPONSE(1,2) BY TIME(1,4)
  /CONTRAST(TIME)=SPECIAL(4*1, 7 14 27 51, 8*1)
  /PLOT=DEFAULT
  /DESIGN=RESPONSE TIME(1) BY RESPONSE
  /PLOT=NONE
  /DESIGN.
```

- RESID and NORMPROB plots are displayed for the first design.
- No plots are displayed for the second design.

MISSING Subcommand

MISSING controls missing values. By default, LOGLINEAR excludes all cases with system- or user-missing values on any variable. You can specify INCLUDE to include user-missing values. If INCLUDE is specified, user-missing values must also be included in the value range specification.

EXCLUDE *Delete cases with user-missing values.* This is the default if the subcommand is omitted. You can also specify the keyword DEFAULT.

INCLUDE *Include user-missing values.* Only cases with system-missing values are deleted.

Example

```
MISSING VALUES A(0).
LOGLINEAR A(0,2) B(1,2) /MISSING=INCLUDE
 /DESIGN=B.
```

- Even though 0 was specified as missing, it is treated as a nonmissing category of *A* in this analysis.

DESIGN Subcommand

DESIGN specifies the model or models to be fit. If DESIGN is omitted or used with no specifications, the saturated model is produced. The saturated model fits all main effects and all interaction effects.

- To specify more than one model, use more than one DESIGN subcommand. Each DESIGN specifies one model.
- To obtain main-effects models, name all the variables listed on the variables specification.
- To obtain interactions, use the keyword BY to specify each interaction, as in `A BY B` and `C BY D`. To obtain the single-degree-of-freedom partition of a specified contrast, specify the partition in parentheses following the factor (see the example below).
- To include cell covariates in the model, first identify them on the variable list by naming them after the keyword WITH, and then specify the variable names on DESIGN.
- To specify an equiprobability model, name a cell covariate that is actually a constant of 1.

Example

```
* Testing the linear effect of the dependent variable

COMPUTE X=MONTH.
LOGLINEAR MONTH (1,12) WITH X
  /DESIGN X.
```

- The variable specification identifies *MONTH* as a categorical variable with values 1 through 12. The keyword WITH identifies *X* as a covariate.
- DESIGN tests the linear effect of *MONTH*.

Example

```
* Specifying main effects models

LOGLINEAR A(1,4) B(1,5)
  /DESIGN=A
  /DESIGN=A,B.
```

- The first design tests the homogeneity of category probabilities for *B*; it fits the marginal frequencies on *A*, but assumes that membership in any of the categories of *B* is equiprobable.
- The second design tests the independence of *A* and *B*. It fits the marginals on both *A* and *B*.

Example

```
* Specifying interactions

LOGLINEAR A(1,4) B(1,5) C(1,3)
  /DESIGN=A,B,C, A BY B.
```

- This design consists of the *A* main effect, the *B* main effect, the *C* main effect, and the interaction of *A* and *B*.

Example

```
* Single-degree-of-freedom partitions

LOGLINEAR A(1,4) BY B(1,5)
  /CONTRAST(B)=POLYNOMIAL
  /DESIGN=A,A BY B(1).
```

- The value 1 following *B* refers to the first partition of *B*, which is the linear effect of *B*; this follows from the contrast specified on the CONTRAST subcommand.

Example

```
* Specifying cell covariates

LOGLINEAR HUSED WIFED(1,4) WITH DISTANCE
   /DESIGN=HUSED WIFED DISTANCE.
```

- The continuous variable *DISTANCE* is identified as a cell covariate by specifying it after WITH on the variable list. The cell covariate is then included in the model by naming it on DESIGN.

Example

```
* Equiprobability model

COMPUTE  X=1.
LOGLINEAR  MONTH(1,18) WITH X
  /DESIGN=X.
```

- This model tests whether the frequencies in the 18-cell table are equal by using a cell covariate that is a constant of 1.

LOOP—END LOOP

```
LOOP [varname=n TO m [BY {1**}]]  [IF [(]logical expression[)]]
                         {n  }

transformation commands

END LOOP [IF [(]logical expression[)]]
```

**Default if the subcommand is omitted.

Examples

```
SET MXLOOPS=10.        /*Maximum number of loops allowed
LOOP.                  /*Loop with no limit other than MXLOOPS
COMPUTE X=X+1.
END LOOP.

LOOP #I=1 TO 5.        /*Loop five times
COMPUTE X=X+1.
END LOOP.
```

Overview

The LOOP—END LOOP structure performs repeated transformations specified by the commands within the loop until they reach a specified cutoff. The cutoff can be specified by an indexing clause on the LOOP command, an IF clause on the END LOOP command, or a BREAK command within the loop structure (see BREAK). In addition, the maximum number of iterations within a loop can be specified on the MXLOOPS subcommand on SET. The default MXLOOPS is 40.

The IF clause on the LOOP command can be used to perform repeated transformations on a subset of cases. The effect is similar to nesting the LOOP—END LOOP structure within a DO IF—END IF structure, but using IF on LOOP is simpler and more efficient. You have to use the DO IF—END IF structure, however, if you want to perform different transformations on different subsets of cases. You can also use IF on LOOP to specify the cutoff, especially when the cutoff may be reached before the first iteration.

LOOP and END LOOP are usually used within an input program or with the VECTOR command. Since the loop structure repeats transformations on a single case or on a single input record containing information on multiple cases, it allows you to read complex data files or to generate data for a working data file. For more information, see INPUT PROGRAM—END INPUT PROGRAM and VECTOR.

The loop structure repeats transformations on single cases across variables. It is different from the DO REPEAT—END REPEAT structure, which replicates transformations on a specified set of variables. When both can be used to accomplish a task, such as selectively transforming data for some cases on some variables, LOOP and END LOOP are generally more efficient and more flexible, but DO REPEAT allows selection of nonadjacent variables and use of replacement values with different intervals.

Options

Missing Values. You can prevent cases with missing values for any of the variables used in the loop structure from entering the loop (see "Missing Values" on p. 644).

Creating Data. A loop structure within an input program can be used to generate data (see "Creating Data" on p. 645).

Defining Complex File Structures. A loop structure within an input program can be used to define complex files that cannot be handled by standard file definition facilities (see pp. 337, 338, and 340 for examples).

Basic Specification

The basic specification is LOOP followed by at least one transformation command. The structure must end with the END LOOP command. Commands within the loop are executed until the cutoff is reached.

Syntax Rules

- If LOOP and END LOOP are specified before a working data file exists, they must be specified within an input program.
- If both an indexing and an IF clause are used on LOOP, the indexing clause must be first.
- Loop structures can be nested within other loop structures or within DO IF structures, and vice versa.

Operations

- The LOOP command defines the beginning of a loop structure and the END LOOP command defines its end. The END LOOP command returns control to LOOP unless the cutoff has been reached. When the cutoff has been reached, control passes to the command immediately following END LOOP.
- When specified within a loop structure, definition commands (such as MISSING VALUES and VARIABLE LABELS) and utility commands (such as SET and SHOW) are invoked only once, when they are encountered for the first time within the loop.

Example

```
SET MXLOOPS=10.
LOOP.      /*Loop with no limit other than MXLOOPS
COMPUTE X=X+1.
END LOOP.
```

- This and the following examples assume that a working data file and all of the variables mentioned in the loop exist.

- The SET MXLOOPS command limits the number of times the loop is executed to 10. The function of MXLOOPS is to prevent infinite loops when there is no iteration clause.
- Within the loop structure, each iteration increments *X* by 1. After 10 iterations, the value of *X* for all cases is increased by 10, and, as specified on the SET command, the loop is terminated.

IF Keyword

The keyword IF and a logical expression can be specified on LOOP or on END LOOP to control iterations through the loop.

- The specification on IF is a logical expression enclosed in parentheses. For more information, see "Logical Expressions" on p. 44.

Example

```
LOOP.
COMPUTE X=X+1.
END LOOP IF (X EQ 5).         /*Loop until X is 5
```

- Iterations continue until the logical expression on END LOOP is true, which for every case is when *X* equals 5. Each case does not go through the same number of iterations.
- This corresponds to the programming notion of DO UNTIL. The loop is always executed at least once.

Example

```
LOOP IF (X LT 5).             /*Loop while X is less than 5
COMPUTE X=X+1.
END LOOP.
```

- The IF clause is evaluated each trip through the structure, so looping stops once *X* equals 5.
- This corresponds to the programming notion of DO WHILE. The loop may not be executed at all.

Example

```
LOOP IF (Y GT 10).            /*Loop only for cases with Y GT 10
COMPUTE X=X+1.
END LOOP IF (X EQ 5).         /*Loop until X IS 5
```

- The IF clause on LOOP allows transformations to be performed on a subset of cases. *X* is increased by 5 only for cases with values greater than 10 for *Y*. *X* is not changed for all other cases.

Indexing Clause

The indexing clause limits the number of iterations for a loop by specifying the number of times the program should execute commands within the loop structure.The indexing clause is specified on the LOOP command and includes an indexing variable followed by initial and terminal values.

- The program sets the *indexing variable* to the *initial value* and increases it by the specified increment each time the loop is executed for a case. When the indexing variable reaches the specified *terminal value*, the loop is terminated for that case.
- By default, the program increases the indexing variable by 1 for each iteration. The keyword BY overrides this increment.
- The indexing variable can have any valid variable name. Unless you specify a scratch variable, the indexing variable is treated as a permanent variable and is saved on the working data file. If the indexing variable is assigned the same name as an existing variable, the values of the existing variable are altered by the LOOP structure as it is executed, and the original values are lost.
- The indexing clause overrides the maximum number of loops specified by SET MXLOOPS.
- The initial and terminal values of the indexing clause can be numeric expressions. Noninteger and negative expressions are allowed.
- If the expression for the initial value is greater than the terminal value, the loop is not executed. For example, #J=X TO Y is a zero-trip loop if *X* is 0 and *Y* is –1.
- If the expressions for the initial and terminal values are equal, the loop is executed once. #J=0 TO Y is a one-trip loop when *Y* is 0.
- If the loop is exited via BREAK or a conditional clause on the END LOOP statement, the iteration variable is not updated. If the LOOP statement contains both an indexing clause and a conditional clause, the indexing clause is executed first, and the iteration variable is updated regardless of which clause causes the loop to terminate.

Example

```
LOOP #I=1 TO 5.                  /*LOOP FIVE TIMES
COMPUTE X=X+1.
END LOOP.
```

- The scratch variable *#I* (the indexing variable) is set to the initial value of 1 and increased by 1 each time the loop is executed for a case. When *#I* increases beyond the terminal value 5, no further loops are executed. Thus, the value of *X* will be increased by 5 for every case.

Example

```
LOOP #I=1 TO 5 IF (Y GT 10). /*Loop to X=5 only if Y GT 10
COMPUTE X=X+1.
END LOOP.
```

- Both an indexing clause and an IF clause are specified on LOOP. *X* is increased by 5 for all cases where *Y* is greater than 10.

Example

```
LOOP #I=1 TO Y.                  /*Loop to the value of Y
COMPUTE X=X+1.
END LOOP.
```

- The number of iterations for a case depends on the value of the variable *Y* for that case. For a case with value 0 for the variable *Y*, the loop is not executed and *X* is unchanged. For a case with value 1 for the variable *Y*, the loop is executed once and *X* is increased by 1.

Example

```
* Factorial routine.

DATA LIST FREE / X.
BEGIN DATA
1 2 3 4 5 6 7
END DATA.

COMPUTE FACTOR=1.
LOOP #I=1 TO X.
COMPUTE FACTOR=FACTOR * #I.
END LOOP.
LIST.
```

- The loop structure computes *FACTOR* as the factorial value of *X*.

Example

```
* Example of nested loops: compute every possible combination of values
  for each variable.

INPUT PROGRAM.
-LOOP #I=1 TO 4.        /* LOOP TO NUMBER OF VALUES FOR I
+    LOOP #J=1 TO 3.        /* LOOP TO NUMBER OF VALUES FOR J
@        LOOP #K=1 TO 4.        /* LOOP TO NUMBER OF VALUES FOR K

@            COMPUTE I=#I.
@            COMPUTE J=#J.
@            COMPUTE K=#K.
@            END CASE.

@        END LOOP.
+    END LOOP.
-END LOOP.
END FILE.
END INPUT PROGRAM.
LIST.
```

- The first loop iterates four times. The first iteration sets the indexing variable *#I* equal to 1 and then passes control to the second loop. *#I* remains 1 until the second loop has completed all of its iterations.
- The second loop is executed 12 times, three times for each value of *#I*. The first iteration sets the indexing variable *#J* equal to 1 and then passes control to the third loop. *#J* remains 1 until the third loop has completed all of its iterations.
- The third loop results in 48 iterations ($4 \times 3 \times 4$). The first iteration sets *#K* equal to 1. The COMPUTE statements set the variables *I*, *J*, and *K* each to 1, and END CASE creates a case. The third loop iterates a second time, setting *#K* equal to 2. Variables *I*, *J*, and *K* are then computed with values 1, 1, 2, respectively, and a second case is created. The third and fourth iterations of the third loop produce cases with *I*, *J*, and *K*, equal to 1, 1, 3 and 1, 1, 4, respectively. After the fourth iteration within the third loop, control passes back to the second loop.
- The second loop is executed again. *#I* remains 1, while *#J* increases to 2, and control returns to the third loop. The third loop completes its iterations, resulting in four more cases with *I* equal to 1, *J* to 2, and *K* increasing from 1 to 4. The second loop is executed a third

time, resulting in cases with *I*=1, *J*=3, and *K* increasing from 1 to 4. Once the second loop has completed three iterations, control passes back to the first loop, and the entire cycle is repeated for the next increment of *#I*.

- Once the first loop completes four iterations, control passes out of the looping structures to END FILE. END FILE defines the resulting cases as a data file, the input program terminates, and the LIST command is executed.
- This example does not require a LEAVE command because the iteration variables are scratch variables. If the iteration variables were *I, J,* and *K,* LEAVE would be required because the variables would be reinitialized after each END CASE command.

Example

```
* Modifying the loop iteration variable.

INPUT PROGRAM.
PRINT SPACE     2.
LOOP            A = 1 TO 3.                 /*Simple iteration
+  PRINT           /'A WITHIN LOOP: ' A(F1).
+  COMPUTE         A = 0.
END LOOP
PRINT           /'A AFTER LOOP:   ' A(F1).

NUMERIC         #B.
LOOP            B = 1 TO 3.                 /*Iteration + UNTIL
+  PRINT           /'B WITHIN LOOP: ' B(F1).
+  COMPUTE         B = 0.
+  COMPUTE         #B = #B+1.
END LOOP        IF #B = 3.
PRINT           /'B AFTER LOOP:   ' B(F1).

NUMERIC         #C.
LOOP            C = 1 TO 3 IF #C NE 3.      /*Iteration + WHILE
+  PRINT           /'C WITHIN LOOP: ' C(F1).
+  COMPUTE         C = 0.
+  COMPUTE         #C = #C+1.
END LOOP.
PRINT           /'C AFTER LOOP:   ' C(F1).

NUMERIC         #D.
LOOP            D = 1 TO 3.                 /*Iteration + BREAK
+  PRINT           /'D WITHIN LOOP: ' D(F1).
+  COMPUTE         D = 0.
+  COMPUTE         #D = #D+1.
+  DO IF           #D = 3.
+     BREAK.
+  END IF.
END LOOP.
PRINT           /'D AFTER LOOP:   ' D(F1).

LOOP            E = 3 TO 1.                 /*Zero-trip iteration
+  PRINT           /'E WITHIN LOOP: ' E(F1).
+  COMPUTE         E = 0.
END LOOP.
PRINT           /'E AFTER LOOP:   ' E(F1).
END FILE.
END INPUT PROGRAM.
EXECUTE.
```

- If a loop is exited via BREAK or a conditional clause on the END LOOP statement, the iteration variable is not updated.
- If the LOOP statement contains both an iteration clause and a conditional clause, the iteration clause is executed first, and the actual iteration variable will be updated regardless of which clause causes termination of the loop.

Figure 1 shows the output from this example.

Figure 1 Modify the loop iteration variable

```
A WITHIN LOOP: 1
A WITHIN LOOP: 2
A WITHIN LOOP: 3
A AFTER LOOP:  4
B WITHIN LOOP: 1
B WITHIN LOOP: 2
B WITHIN LOOP: 3
B AFTER LOOP:  0
C WITHIN LOOP: 1
C WITHIN LOOP: 2
C WITHIN LOOP: 3
C AFTER LOOP:  4
D WITHIN LOOP: 1
D WITHIN LOOP: 2
D WITHIN LOOP: 3
D AFTER LOOP:  0
E AFTER LOOP:  3
```

BY Keyword

By default, the program increases the indexing variable by 1 for each iteration. The keyword BY overrides this increment.

- The *increment value* can be a numeric expression and can therefore be non-integer or negative. Zero causes a warning and results in a zero-trip loop.
- If the initial value is greater than the terminal value and the increment is positive, the loop is never entered. #I=1 TO 0 BY 2 results in a zero-trip loop.
- If the initial value is less than the terminal value and the increment is negative, the loop is never entered. #I=1 TO 2 BY –1 also results in a zero-trip loop.
- Order is unimportant: 2 BY 2 TO 10 is equivalent to 2 TO 10 BY 2.

Example

```
LOOP #I=2 TO 10 BY 2.          /*Loop five times by 2'S
COMPUTE X=X+1.
END LOOP.
```

- The scratch variable *#I* starts at 2 and increases by 2 for each of five iterations until it equals 10 for the last iteration.

Example

```
LOOP #I=1 TO Y BY Z.           /*Loop to Y incrementing by Z
COMPUTE X=X+1.
END LOOP.
```

- The loop is executed once for a case with *Y* equal to 2 and *Z* equal to 2 but twice for a case with *Y* equal to 3 and *Z* equal to 2.

Example

```
* Repeating data using LOOP.

INPUT PROGRAM.
DATA LIST      NOTABLE/ ORDER 1-4(N) #BKINFO 6-71(A).
LEAVE ORDER.
LOOP           #I = 1 TO 66 BY 6 IF SUBSTR(#BKINFO,#I,6) <> ' '.
+  REREAD         COLUMN = #I+5.
+  DATA LIST      NOTABLE/ ISBN 1-3(N) QUANTITY 4-5.
+  END CASE.
END LOOP.
END INPUT PROGRAM.
SORT CASES     BY ISBN ORDER.
BEGIN DATA
1045 182 2 155 1 134 1 153 5
1046 155 3 153 5 163 1
1047 161 5 182 2 163 4 186 6
1048 186 2
1049 155 2 163 2 153 2 074 1 161 1
END DATA.

DO IF          $CASENUM = 1.
+  PRINT EJECT    /'Order' 1  'ISBN' 7  'Quantity' 13.
END IF.
PRINT          /ORDER 2-5(N) ISBN 8-10(N) QUANTITY 13-17.
EXECUTE.
```

- This example uses LOOP to simulate a REPEATING DATA command.
- DATA LIST specifies the scratch variable *#BKINFO* as a string variable (format A) to allow blanks in the data.
- LOOP is executed if the SUBSTR function returns anything other than a blank or null value. SUBSTR returns a six-character substring of *#BKINFO*, beginning with the character in the position specified by the value of the indexing variable *#I*. As specified on the indexing clause, *#I* begins with a value of 1 and is increased by 6 for each iteration of LOOP, up to a maximum *#I* value of 61 ($1 + 10 \times 6 = 61$). The next iteration would exceed the maximum *#I* value ($1 + 11 \times 6 = 67$).

Missing Values

- If the program encounters a case with a missing value for the initial, terminal, or increment value or expression, or if the conditional expression on the LOOP command returns missing, a zero-trip loop results and control is passed to the first command after the END LOOP command.
- If a case has a missing value for the conditional expression on an END LOOP command, the loop is terminated after the first iteration.
- To prevent cases with missing values for any variable used in the loop structure from entering the loop, use the IF clause on the LOOP command (see third example below).

Example

```
LOOP #I=1 TO Z  IF (Y GT 10). /*Loop to X=Z for cases with Y GT 10
COMPUTE X=X+1.
END LOOP.
```

- The value of *X* remains unchanged for cases with a missing value for *Y* or a missing value for *Z* (or if *Z* is less than 1).

Example

```
MISSING VALUES X(5).
LOOP.
COMPUTE X=X+1.
END LOOP IF (X GE 10). /*Loop until X is at least 10 or missing
```

- Looping is terminated when the value of *X* is 5 because 5 is defined as missing for *X*.

Example

```
LOOP IF NOT MISSING(Y).      /*Loop only when Y isn't missing
COMPUTE X=X+Y.
END LOOP IF (X GE 10).       /*Loop until X is at least 10
```

- The variable *X* is unchanged for cases with a missing value for *Y*, since the loop is never entered.

Creating Data

A loop structure and an END CASE command within an input program can be used to create data without any data input. The END FILE command must be used outside the loop (but within the input program) to terminate processing.

Example

```
INPUT PROGRAM.
LOOP #I=1 TO 20.
COMPUTE AMOUNT=RND(UNIFORM(5000))/100.
END CASE.
END LOOP.
END FILE.
END INPUT PROGRAM.

PRINT FORMATS AMOUNT (DOLLAR6.2).
PRINT /AMOUNT.
EXECUTE.
```

- This example creates 20 cases with a single variable, *AMOUNT*. *AMOUNT* is a uniformly distributed number between 0 and 5000, rounded to an integer and divided by 100 to provide a variable in dollars and cents.
- The END FILE command is required to terminate processing once the loop structure is complete.

See pp. 330 and 340 for other examples of creating data without any data input.

Subject Index

Syntax Index